COUNSELING
AND PSYCHOTHERAPY
A Multicultural Perspective

FOURTH EDITION

Allen E. Ivey
University of Massachusetts, Amherst

Mary Bradford Ivey
Amherst, Massachusetts, Regional Schools
University of Massachusetts, Amherst

Lynn Simek-Morgan
Florida International University

With contributions from
Harold E. Cheatham, Paul B. Pedersen,
Sandra A. Rigazio-DiGilio, Derald Wing Sue

ALLYN AND BACON
Boston • London • Toronto • Sydney • Tokyo • Singapore

Senior Editor: Ray Short
Editorial Assistant: Christine Svitila
Marketing Manager: Kris Farnsworth
Production Administrator: Rob Lawson
Editorial-Production Service: Trinity Publishers Services
Composition Buyer: Linda Cox
Manufacturing Buyer: Megan Cochran
Cover Administrator: Linda Knowles

Library of Congress Cataloging-in-Publication Data

Ivey, Allen E.
    Counseling and psychotherapy : a multicultural perspective / Allen
E. Ivey, Mary Bradford Ivey, Lynn Simek-Morgan ; with contributions
from Harold E. Cheatham . . . [et al.]. — 4th ed.
      p.   cm.
    Includes bibliographical references and indexes.
    ISBN 0-205-19890-2 (hardcover)
    1. Cross-cultural counseling.   2. Psychotherapy—Cross-cultural
studies. I. Ivey, Mary Bradford. II. Simek-Morgan, Lynn.
III. Title.
BF637.C6I93   1996
158'.3—dc20
                                     96-15078
                                     CIP

Printed in the United States of America

10 9 8 7 6 5 4 3 2 1   02 01 00 99 98 97

About the Authors

ALLEN E. IVEY received his doctorate from Harvard University. He is Distinguished University Professor, School and Counseling Psychology Program at the University of Massachusetts, Amherst. During the writing of this book, he served as visiting professor in the Clinical Psychology Program at the University of Hawai'i, Manoa. He is a diplomate of the American Board of Professional Psychology. Dr. Ivey is past president and fellow of the American Psychological Association's Division of Counseling Psychology and a fellow of the Society for the Psychological Study of Ethnic and Minority Issues. A life member of the American Counseling Association, he received their Professional Development Award for his lifetime contributions to counseling. The author or coauthor of twenty-five books and over two hundred chapters and articles, his works have been translated into thirteen languages.

MARY BRADFORD IVEY received her doctorate at the University of Massachusetts, Amherst. She is a nationally certified counselor in the Amherst Regional School System. During the writing of this book, she served as visiting professor in the Counselor Education Program at the University of Hawai'i, Manoa. Dr. Ivey's guidance program at the Fort River School was named one of the ten best in the United States. She has lectured and conducted workshops throughout Australia and New Zealand, Europe, Canada, Mexico, and Japan. She is the author or coauthor of seven books and many articles that have been translated into several languages. She has developed videotapes illustrating the skills of counseling and therapy. Dr. Ivey received the *O'hana* Award from the American Counseling Association for her work in multicultural counseling in the schools.

LYNN SIMEK-MORGAN received her doctorate from the University of Massachusetts, Amherst. She is director of secondary special education at the Bennington-Rutland Supervisory Union, Manchester, Vermont. She also is adjunct associate professor at Goddard College and the School of International Training. She has been a director of counseling services at three universities, most recently at Florida International University, Miami. She has taught at five universities in departments of psychology, education, sociology, health, and communication skills and in family and community medicine at the University of Massachusetts Medical Center. A certified secondary teacher in three states, she serves on the research review committee of three professional journals. She has authored and coauthored several texts and many research articles.

HAROLD E. CHEATHAM received his doctorate from Case Western Reserve University. He serves as professor and head of the Department of Counselor Education, Counseling Psychology, and Rehabilitation Services at The Pennsylvania State University. He has worked as a social studies teacher, director of counseling, and professor of psychology. He has served as senior Fulbright Scholar to India and on numerous editorial boards; he is a Danforth Associate and has presented his ideas widely nationally and internationally. In 1993, the American College Personnel Association honored Dr. Cheatham with the Contribution to Knowledge Award and with induction as a senior scholar. He was elected to serve as ACPA president from 1995 to 1996. He is the coauthor or coeditor of numerous books, chapters, and articles.

PAUL B. PEDERSEN received his doctorate in Asian Studies from Claremont Graduate School and a master's degree in counseling from the University of Minnesota. At the University of Alabama–Birmingham campus, he is professor in the Department of Human Studies, where he teaches courses in counseling and multicultural issues. He has taught in Indonesia, Malaysia, and Taiwan and has lectured throughout the world on multicultural issues and his triad training model. He has also been a faculty member at the University of Minnesota, University of Hawai'i–Manoa, Harvard University, and Syracuse University. He is a fellow of three American Psychological Association divisions (9, 17, 45). The author of twenty-six books and over one hundred chapters, monographs, and articles, Dr. Pedersen was recently honored by the American Psychological Association, which named him a master lecturer at the 1995 convention.

SANDRA A. RIGAZIO-DiGILIO received her doctorate from the University of Massachusetts, Amherst. She is associate professor in Marriage and Family Therapy at the University of Connecticut–Storrs and holds a joint appointment in the university's Department of Psychiatry. She serves on the board of directors of the American Association of Marriage and Family Therapy and received the 1994 AAMFT Divisional Contribution Award. Dr. Rigazio-DiGilio is associate editor of the *Journal of Mental Health Counseling* and of the Teachers College Press Series on Counseling and Development. She is known for her development of systemic cognitive-developmental therapy and a companion supervisory model. She has presented her work nationally and internationally and is the author or coauthor of numerous articles and chapters.

DERALD WING SUE received his doctorate from the University of Oregon. He is professor at the California School of Professional Psychology, Alameda, and at California State University, Hayward. He is a fellow of the American Psychological Association, American Psychological Society, and the American Association of Applied and Preventive Psychology. He was a founder and first president of the Asian Psychological Association. A past editor of the *Personnel and Guidance Journal,* Dr. Sue has published extensively in the field of multicultural psychology, and a Fordham University research team identified him as "without a doubt the most influential multicultural scholar in the United States." He has presented widely throughout the United States and internationally. The author of many articles and books, Dr. Sue's *Counseling the Culturally Different* (1991) has been acclaimed as foundational to the field of counseling and therapy.

Contents

6   Multicultural Counseling and Therapy II: Integrative Practice   170

Harold E. Cheatham, Allen E. Ivey, Mary Bradford Ivey,
Paul B. Pedersen, Sandra A. Rigazio-DiGilio, Lynn Simek-Morgan,
Derald Wing Sue

PART   III   Historical Theories of Counseling and Psychotherapy: The First, Second, and Third Forces   207

7   Psychodynamic Counseling and Therapy I: Conception and Theory   209

Taking Theory into Practice:
Specific Strategies for Mastery and Action in the Interview

===

Counseling and Psychotherapy: A Multicultural Perspective, Fourth Edition, is designed so that the reader can apply theory directly in practice. Key counseling and therapeutic strategies are presented throughout this book in practice exercises. These strategies have been useful to readers of past editions of this book, who often refer to these strategies when working with clients with whom they feel the need for a new or different approach. The following list of practice exercises provides a summary of the counseling strategies you can use now and in following years for your professional development.

Preface

Taking theory into practice is the major aim of this results-oriented book. Our curriculum in counseling and therapy is full of techniques and approaches, but the basic issue remains: How can we make a difference with our students and how can they become effective with their clients? Each chapter of this fourth edition of *Counseling and Psychotherapy: A Multicultural Perspective* contains practice exercises that will make theoretical ideas real and immediately understandable. This book is based on the idea that we can learn theory best by actually testing it in the interview.

Counseling and Psychotherapy: A Multicultural Perspective, Fourth Edition, has been designed for use in undergraduate and graduate courses in psychology, counselor education, human and mental health services, and social work. We have found that students enjoy the opportunity to master the three traditional areas of counseling and therapy (psychodynamic, cognitive-behavioral, and existential-humanistic) and that they appreciate a chance to develop competency in multicultural dimensions.

The foundations of counseling and therapy form the introductory portion of this book. This foundation is provided in the belief that a review of and additional competence in the empathic dimensions, microskills, and developmental theory enable counselors and psychotherapists to understand and master important theories more rapidly and effectively. Moreover, employing such strategies as the community and family genograms, the well-organized interview, solution-based counseling and therapy, and developmental constructs constitutes the basis of a theoretical and practical approach to the field.

Our Mission

Our mission in writing *Counseling and Psychotherapy: A Multicultural Perspective,* Fourth Edition, is to

- provide you with a solid foundation in the theoretical concepts of the major theories of counseling and psychotherapy
- enable you to take these theories into direct counseling and clinical practice
- assist you in examining present-day counseling and therapy from a practical culture-centered perspective while simultaneously respecting traditional individual approaches to the field
- start you on the journey toward skilled counseling and therapy practice

What's New in the Fourth Edition?

Positive feedback from students and professors has led us to maintain the structure of the last edition, but there are some important changes, including the following:

1. There is more extensive use of practice exercises to ensure that theory can be tested in the reality of the interview.

2. An additional chapter on multicultural counseling and therapy has been added to give it co-equal status with psychodynamic, cognitive-behavioral, and existential-humanistic theory.

3. Family therapy theory is integrated throughout the text.

4. The cognitive-behavioral chapters have been expanded to include more specifics of practice, the work of Arnold Lazarus, and Albert Ellis's newly re-labeled rational-emotive behavior therapy. Stress management has been given even more attention in this revision.

5. Solution-oriented therapy has been added to the microskills chapter, and the decisional and microskills chapters have been combined.

6. The community genogram, a new practice strategy, has been added to Chapter 1. This strategy gives students, even during the first week in class, a concrete way to consider how the individual develops in the family and cultural contexts.

7. Spiritual issues are identified for the first time as an important part of the counseling and therapy process. Although this may be controversial, students and clients have continually requested consideration of this area. The authors especially look forward to the readers' feedback on this new material.

The Portfolio Concept Helps Ensure Competence

The authors believe that this is a book that "works"—that students will be able to make practical use of what they learn in *Counseling and Psychotherapy: A Multicultural Perspective.* Students will be able to take pride in their accomplishments and achieve major gains throughout the school term. Students' progress can be enhanced by using the portfolio concept discussed in more detail in the *Instructor's Resource Manual.* By accumulating the completed exercises in this book, students can assemble an impressive portfolio detailing their competencies in the course. Many students take their portfolios to their internship sites and to prospective employers as a way of documenting their work.

A Brief Overview of the Fourth Edition

This edition continues an emphasis on worldview and multiple perspectives and the need for counselors and clinicians to generate their own constructions of the helping process. The authors maintain that each theory presented has value. Our experience has led us from a position of "Which theory is best?" to a belief that each theory has value for some clients. We believe it is important for students to understand and master the basics of sometimes competing ideologies.

The first section of this book focuses on foundational and integrative aspects of helping. Empathy, microskills, decisional counseling, and developmental counseling and therapy (DCT) are presented in the early chapters both as practical skills and as theories in themselves. Students who master these concepts and theories early are better prepared to understand and work with the theoretical and practical material presented in later chapters.

The two chapters on multicultural counseling and therapy (MCT) are based on new theoretical work by Derald Wing Sue. Sue has given us an integrated way to think about a culture-centered approach that builds on and respects person-centered methods and theories. In the last edition, MCT was presented mainly as a theory. In this new edition, MCT has become very explicit, with many suggestions for practical work in the interview.

This book is simultaneously traditional and new. The writings of such giants in the field as Freud, Rogers, Frankl, and Skinner are always impressive in the wisdom and the value of their contributions. At the same time, more modern theorists, such as Aaron Beck, Donald Meichenbaum, Albert Ellis, and the family therapists, have enriched the traditional legacy.

Each of the traditional chapters is balanced by offerings from multicultural theorists committed to psychodynamic, cognitive-behavioral, and existential-humanistic thought. Such theorists as Bruce Taub-Bynum (psychodynamic), Donald Cheek (cognitive-behavioral), and Clemmont Vontress (existential-humanistic) show how to continue the traditional approaches and also add some useful new dimensions to both theory and practice. Multicultural theory and practice enrich and are enriched by the traditional theories in the field.

The importance of research informing counseling and clinical practice cannot be overstressed. Each chapter includes a research exhibit, and the concluding chapter focuses on the importance of including some form of research and evaluation in every counseling and therapeutic encounter. As Kurt Lewin has rightly stated: "No research without action. No action without research."

The Internet and World Wide Web

Allen and Mary Ivey will be developing a web site to support this book. The web site will provide links to many sources for further information and study. As new ideas and exercises present themselves, the authors will make them immediately available. The intention is to keep the fourth edition of *Counseling and Psychotherapy: A Multicultural Perspective* fully up to date. Links to the developing site may be found at http://www-unix.oit.umass.edu/~ivey/ or by e-mailing ivey@educ.umass.edu and/or micro@crocker.com. As www and e-mail addresses can change, write Allen Ivey at Box 9641, North Amherst, MA 01059-0941 for current information on addresses if you cannot reach these addresses.

Acknowledgments

The world of counseling and therapy has become too complex for any one author. Thus, we have assembled a multiculturally diverse group of contributors to share their ideas with you: Harold Cheatham of The Pennsylvania State University; Paul Pedersen of the University of Alabama, Birmingham; Derald Wing Sue of the California School of Professional Psychology, Alameda; and Sandra Rigazio-DiGilio of the University of Connecticut. The participation was important, valuable, and deeply appreciated.

Comments by the following authors and institutions were especially helpful: Sandra Rigazio-DiGilio (Chapters 1 and 2); Leon Mann, William Matthews, and Robert Marx (Chapter 3); Evelyn Brooks, Machiko Fukuhara, Fran Howe, Maurie Howe, and Oscar Gonçalves (Chapter 4); Mary Ballou, Mary Fukuyama, Donald Locke, and Koji Tamase (Chapters 5 and 6); Fran Howe and Bruce Taub-Bynum (Chapters 7 and 8); Donald Cheek, Donald Meichenbaum, and Beth Sulzer-Azaroff (Chapter 9); Aaron Beck, Albert Ellis, and the Institute for Reality Therapy (Chapter 10); Viktor Frankl, Elisabeth Lucas, Alfried Längle, Joseph Fabry, and Inga van Pelt (Chapter 12).

Special appreciation is expressed to Stephen Weinrach, Villanova University, for his incisive criticism of the first draft of this manuscript. He, perhaps more than anyone else, sensed the multicultural spirit of this book and encouraged us to make these ideas even clearer.

Other reviewers of the manuscript provided key insights and suggestions. They were:

Eileen McCabe O'Mara
University of Nevada/Reno

Fred H. Borgen
Iowa State University

We'd also like to thank Editor Ray Short of Allyn & Bacon, who has helped restore our faith in corporate America. His patience and support were endless and are truly appreciated. Again, it is delightful to work with Evelyn and John Ward of Trinity Publishers Services. There could be no better or more helpful editing and production services. Finally, Elizabeth Koss and Bruce Oldershaw were critical in maintaining stability and organization in the midst of the chaos of writing. Without them, it wouldn't have happened.

The Culturally Intentional Counselor or Therapist: Introduction and Overview

CHAPTER GOALS

Humans are natural storytellers, and our clients come to us with tales of their life challenges, their defeats, and, best of all, their triumphs. Our task is to listen and learn with them. If we are effective, their stories become more positive, or they learn new ways to live with them. Clients can take their new knowledge into action in their tasks and relationships.

The complexity of our ever-changing world brings clients to counseling and therapy seeking answers to a wide array of story lines. When working with stories in which personal abuse is an issue, our responsibility is to act quickly and provide safety. Other times, when listening to the narratives of survivors of long-past trauma, sometimes our best action may be to work directly on the societal conditions that allowed the abusive story to occur. With other clients facing existential issues of meaning, sometimes our task is to listen carefully and perhaps to point out that life often gives us more questions than specific answers. With a client dealing with the early phases of depression, our task may focus on some concrete skills of cognitive and behavioral change.

The postmodern world is complex and full of many stories. People experiencing the same event may provide widely varying narratives of what they saw, heard, and felt. This book outlines some important theories—stories told by the counseling and therapy profession. These stories provide some structure for working with the complexity and variety of the clients you will encounter in your daily practice. This book asks you to look at the multiple theories and practices existing within the field and develop your own theoretical integration.

Five key concepts are presented in this chapter to orient you to the major theoretical stories of this book:

1. *Worldview.* You and your clients are constantly making meaning in the world. The way you frame the world and what it means to you is also a story you tell about what you experience and observe throughout your life. Not only do you make meaning of this complex world, but so do counseling and therapy theorists. The stories told by existential-humanistic, cognitive-behavioral, psychodynamic, and multicultural theorists are different and sometimes competing, but they provide rich ways for you and your clients to think, feel, and act differently now and in the future.

2. *Cultural intentionality.* Intentionality is described in this chapter as the ability to communicate thoughts, words, and behaviors with self and others in a cultural context. Although we are all unique humans, we are also influenced by multicultural factors. It is vital that you as a counselor or therapist develop awareness of how issues such as language, gender, ethnicity/race, spirituality, affectional orientation, age, physical or emotional issues, socioeconomic situation, and experience with trauma affect the way you and your clients construct meaning in the world. Our worldviews are deeply influenced by our family history and cultural surround.

3. *The scientist-practitioner.* Therapy and counseling derive from scientific approaches but in practice resemble an art form. This chapter introduces you to the art and science of counseling and therapy.

4. *Ethics.* All of our helping interventions rest on a moral base. An outline of some central issues is presented here. Effective practice is ethical practice. Ethical practice involves respect for and understanding of individuals and their family and cultural backgrounds.

5. *Theory into practice—the community genogram.* We urge you to take theory into practice throughout this book. In each chapter we present practice exercises that will enable you to use theoretical ideas directly in clinical and counseling practice. This chapter presents the community genogram, a specific way to help you and your clients identify the roots of personal worldviews.

Relativity: Our Stories about Reality Depend on Our Perspectives

We are all in the same world, but each of us makes different sense of what we see. Take a moment to reflect on the print entitled "Relativity" (Figure 1.1). Where is your attention drawn? Rotate the print; each new perspective proffers a new meaning. As you focus on the characters, you may find yourself wondering: Where are they going? What relation do these people moving in different directions have to each other? Why does the picture make as much sense when viewed upside down or sideways?

Figure 1.1 "Relativity," by M. C. Escher

SOURCE: Cordon Art (Baarn, Holland). Copyright 1995 M. C. Escher/Cordon Art-Baarn-Holland. Reprinted by permission.

Discussing the meaning, the Dutch artist Escher (1960) focuses on two individuals located on the stairs at the top and center: "Two people are moving side by side and in the same direction, and yet one of them is going downstairs and the other upstairs. Contact between them is out of the question, because they live in different worlds and therefore have no knowledge of each other's existence."

Counseling and therapy operate on the assumption that significant contact between client and counselor is possible. You, as a counselor or psychotherapist, are called on to show creativity and artistry in the way you observe and interact with your clients as they walk down life's path. If you can enter your clients' worlds for a time and join them on their journey, you may find a new understanding and respect for how their worlds are different from your own. Sometimes, simply validating your clients' alternative perceptions of reality may be all that is needed. Other clients may want to change direction, to find new perspectives and new ways of acting. In these cases, your task is more difficult because you will need to see their ways of thinking and being, to share yourself and your knowledge, and to work with them to seek new directions for the future.

Worldview: Examining How You Think about the Client's World

Consider again the Escher print and Escher's comments about the two individuals walking on the same stairs but in different directions. Imagine that a client, walking in a different direction, comes to you for help and says, "My eight-year-old isn't doing well in school. It worries me. I never succeeded either. I hated school. My parents sometimes had to beat me to get me out of the door. But the same approach doesn't seem to work with him. Now I'm told by the school counselor that I'm being abusive and that they are going to file a complaint with youth services. They said that my child might be taken away unless I change. I don't want to be here. What are you going to do to help me?"

How would you respond to this client? What feelings and thoughts are going through your mind as you think about this person? Take a moment to think about yourself, your "gut" feelings about a case of this type, and then on a sheet of paper write down your possible response. After you have written your response, compare and contrast your ideas with those presented in the following section.

We all tell our stories in our own unique fashion. This book is about joining your clients' worlds and learning to respect their ways of thinking, feeling, and behaving that are different than your own. Psychotherapeutic and counseling theory will help you understand and work with clients' uniqueness from varying perspectives. Each theory tells us a different story, and at times one theoretical approach may be more helpful than another. Often, you will want to integrate theories in a unique fashion to meet client needs. Your major challenge in this book is to master several approaches and then develop your own integrated approach that is true to yourself but flexible enough to meet the needs of people who may be very different than you.

Effect of Theoretical Orientation on Therapeutic Response

The first task in a case that involves potential and actual abuse is to protect the client. This is both a legal and ethical issue. No matter what theory or worldview is used, protecting children and adult clients from harm is our first responsibility. Thus, careful assessment of the client's story is essential so that appropriate action may be taken. It is also vital that you consider the accuracy of the story and cultural attitudes toward the maltreatment of others.

Let us assume that your client is a child at risk for physical abuse. You have listened and acted, and the child is now safe. You have been asked to counsel the potential perpetrator of violence. Following are some ways therapists of major theoretical orientations might approach this issue.

The Existential-Humanistic Worldview

The existential-humanistic worldview seeks to understand how the client makes sense of the world. Believing firmly in self-actualization, these therapists often listen to clients carefully in the belief that clients will ultimately find their own positive direction in life. Thus, the response of the existential-humanistic therapist might be:

> It sounds as if you are deeply troubled and angry about being here. At the same time, I hear that you desperately want to straighten things out. Am I hearing you accurately?

The Psychodynamic Worldview

The psychodynamic worldview stresses that the past is often a prelude to the future. Research clearly indicates that those who abuse often suffer from abusive childhoods themselves. A psychodynamic counselor believes that change will not be lasting unless clients have some sense of how their present actions relate to their past experience. A possible response from a psychodynamic professional might be:

> You say you were beaten by your own parents and now you find you are doing the same thing with your own child. It will take some time, but our goal is to find out how your past experiences are being reflected in your present behavior with your child. Let's start by you sharing some of your own thoughts and feelings of what happened to you during childhood.

The Cognitive-Behavioral Worldview

The cognitive-behavioral worldview is more oriented to action and short-term treatment. Relaxation training, parent education, and stress management are some of many techniques and strategies that might be used. The cognitive-behavioral counselor will focus on short-term observable change but will keep an eye to the future and work with the client for long-term maintenance of behavioral change. The counselor's response might be:

> There's a lot happening in your life. We'll be doing a lot of things in our time together. What I find most helpful as a beginning step is dealing with your personal frustration and issues of loss of self-control. We'll be working on some very practical issues of how you think and behave to help you work with your child more effectively and to feel better about yourself. We'll start with some stress management techniques and then move on to look at some specifics of behavior.

The Multicultural Worldview

Multicultural counseling and therapy (MCT) has now become a major theoretical orientation in its own right. This framework is integrative and freely uses other orientations to helping, such as the three described above. In addition, MCT focuses on the individual in a family and cultural context. This means that one part of the therapeutic process is to help clients see how their difficulties may be related to societal and social justice issues concerning race or ethnicity, gender, or socioeconomic status.

The following might be the response of a counselor using language appropriate to the client:

> We'll need to look at this issue from three levels. First, I'd like to hear your story as you make sense of it. Then, I'd like to introduce some stress management techniques that may help you deal with the immediate problem. As part of this process, we'll be looking at how gender, race, and class may play a part in your issues. I'd particularly like to know about what the word *community* means to you and the nature of your present support systems.

The MCT worldview may require more than individual action. The client is seen as part of a larger social system in which past and present communities are important. Counselors adopting an MCT approach may refer the client to consciousness-raising groups or become involved in community action themselves.

Postmodernism, Multiple Realities, and Worldviews in Counseling and Therapy

The four frames of reference presented above are major ways in which clients' problems can be conceptualized. Needless to say, the techniques and methods of each of the theoretical frameworks lead to very different treatment methodologies.

Postmodernism has a multiplicity of points of view at its center. Gergen (1991, 1994) talks of the postmodern "saturated self," a person who feels overwhelmed by the amount of stimulation and number of alternatives life offers. Think about your own situation and the many forces and possibilities that challenge you. Family, friends, media, community, cultural change, conflict, recreation, work influences—all can combine in a massive sense of "overchoice," leaving the individual overstimulated, confused, and often feeling just plain "lost." One response to feeling overwhelmed by our complex postmodern world is to tell stories about our experiences. Telling old stories helps us understand and synthesize the past. Through storytelling we may develop new stories that make possible a more integrated, meaningful future life.

Which is the "correct" worldview and treatment? At one time—not so long ago—counseling and therapy theory operated on the assumption that there existed a "best" therapy. Students and professionals were encouraged to select one theory and then defend that position. Not too surprisingly, we have learned that each of the systems has something to contribute. The importance of listening to the unique human being before you, as stressed by the existential-humanists, has become foundational to all helping approaches. The psychodynamic framework's emphasis that past history affects the present is becoming more widely accepted, although it is still somewhat controversial.

The existential-humanistic, psychodynamic, and cognitive-behavioral traditions have tended in the past to focus solely on the individual, with little or no attention given to family, cultural, or social context issues. These three approaches have been seriously questioned by women and those of non-European background. As a result of such challenges, these traditional theories have increasingly embraced a broader view of counseling and therapy. Multicultural counseling and therapy (MCT) emphasizes social-contextual issues—individuals are seen in relation to their contexts. MCT also has been influenced by traditional theory and considers traditional theory vital for fully developed practice.

The position taken in this book is that effective counselors and therapists need to become familiar with the skills, competencies, and knowledge base of multiple theories. Some clients respond best to individualistic methods, some to family orientations, and some to a multicultural orientation. Many clients profit from a combination of approaches. It is important that you develop expertise in several approaches so that you can meet the needs of your culturally diverse clientele more effectively.

Examining Your Worldview

Theories provide a map for action, but it is important to remember that in implementing a theory, you are applying a worldview that may or may not be fully compatible with your own. Even more important, the worldview of a particular theory may be incompatible with your clients' ways of thinking and behaving. Since you will be the one who applies theory to practice, you are the central ingredient in working with the ideas of this book. What will be your approach to helping? Some will focus on a single theory, whereas others will develop competence in several theories simultaneously. Regardless of which method you choose, you will still be implementing your own worldview.

Each individual has a unique life experience, even within the same family, and this recognition has long been central to individually oriented counseling and therapy. As we grow and develop in a family context, our experience in the family is basic to the ways we view the world. Your family experience has been important in the way you construct and think about reality. It is of great benefit in your development as a helper to think about your own family influences on your worldview. Furthermore, cultural context deeply affects the way you and your family interact with the world. What groups are most important to you and your family? Peer groups and friends, spiritual groups, school and political groups, support groups such as Alcoholics Anonymous, the media, and many other groups can be important influences. The word *community* encompasses these concepts, and our community puts us most closely in touch with culture. As a first step toward developing and clarifying your own worldview, the community genogram can be a useful practice technique.

Spirituality and Religion

Psychotherapy and counseling have tended to give minimal attention to issues of spirituality. Yet, as we encounter the complexity of the postmodern world, more and more clients are seeking the feeling of wholeness and relationship to the transcendent that spirituality and religion make possible. Van Pelt (1993, 1995), a physician and a logotherapy practitioner (see Chapter 12), argues that issues of faith and spirituality arise from the very core of human experience, whether physical or psychological. Human beings are storytellers, and a vital part of the narrative is something beyond the individual. Religious or spiritual awareness is seen by Van Pelt as central to individual, family, and community well-being. Unless we touch on that core, she argues, we are missing the most essential part of our humanity (see Figure 1.2).

From an existential-humanistic perspective (see Chapter 11), Vontress (1995, pp. 1–2) comments:

> People cannot be segmented into parts, as if the pieces are somehow unrelated to the whole. My research in West Africa has convinced me that the spiritual dimension of human beings impacts the physical, psychological, and social aspects of living. . . . Human beings need the respect, direction, love, and affection of parents, elders, departed ones, and spiritual figures.

The authors have found that counseling and psychotherapy students, as well as many of their clients, have meaningful and deep spiritual interests. Surveys of our classes constantly reveal that 60 percent or more of students openly say that these issues are important to them and a source of strength. As individuals get in touch with multicultural experience, they often find that spirituality is closely related. For example, the emphasis on individual decision making in much of Western psychotherapy and

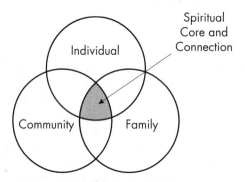

Figure 1.2 The Spiritual Core, or the Intersection among Individual, Family, and Community Spheres

counseling can be related to the Judeo-Christian tradition. Yet many would argue that individuals make decisions best when they consider spiritual foundations. The connection of the individual to community in the Afrocentric orientation is reflected in a spirituality of relationship. This being-in-relationship orientation—as found in Islamic, Buddhist, Mormon, Earth-centered, Native American Indian, and other forms of religion and spirituality—may become a more recognized part of psychotherapy in the next several years.

Narrative and storytelling are important in this book. Eventually, you will tell your own story of counseling and psychotherapy and share it with your clients. As you work through this book, you may want to consider the role that spirituality and religion may play in your practice. Your stories and your clients' stories, images, and metaphors are an important part of a person-centered and culture-centered practice. Some practical exercises in this book (the community genogram in this chapter and developing cultural and spiritual images in Chapter 8) provide an introduction to possible methods.

The Community Genogram: A Practice Strategy

"It takes a village to raise a child." This well-known African proverb underlies the community genogram. Our original community is where we learn the culture that will remain with us through our lifetime. Communities can consist of nuclear families as well as extended families, friends and neighbors, school and work environments, the physical setting of the community, church or spiritual connections, and other factors. Our personal experiences with community are as unique as our fingerprints.

Culture, communities, families, groups, and individuals are all interconnected. Difficulty or trauma in the community—such as a tornado, a mass shooting, or the loss of jobs through the closure of a manufacturing plant—deeply affects not only individual lives but also what occurs in families and various community groups. One major community event can change the individual's total culture. In turn, one individual can affect the total culture as well. Consider the negative impact of a criminal terrorizing a family or the positive impact of a leader such as Martin Luther King. Individual counseling and therapy exist within a social context. If we want to understand any individual, we need to see that person in a complete way.

The community genogram is presented as the first practice exercise, and it provides a way for you and your clients to learn more directly how cultural factors, implicit and explicit in the community, underlie individual and family development. Chapter 2 explores the more formal family chart, or genogram, and discusses family factors in further depth. Together, the family and community genograms provide a solid way to ensure that individual issues are seen in their full contextual background. The community genogram was developed by Ivey (1995) as a way to introduce a positive, strengths-oriented view of self that reflects how we are all selves-in-relation to one another. The community genogram can also help in identifying the important groups (church, school, peer, neighborhood) that influence the individual. In addition, taking a life-span perspective makes us aware that the nature of community changes and expands as we grow. For example, the family is the center for the child, then the peer group for many teens, then the work environment for many adults, and finally, the family, once again, for elders.

Many individual problems and concerns are related to community, especially when we consider family as central to that community. The community genogram, while focusing on personal, family, and group strengths, also provides an opportunity to understand the context of past or current issues. Vosvick (personal communication, Stanford University, October 1995) notes that the community genogram also offers an important alternative or supplement to the family genogram in that this new approach helps clients see the total breadth of their social support systems and histories. Another advantage is that many people, such as single parents, gay or lesbian individuals, and those from cultural backgrounds in which community takes precedent over the nuclear family, are comfortable with this technique.

The specific steps toward developing a community genogram are presented in Practice Exercise 1.1. It is a good idea to first develop your own community genogram and then later use this strategy with your clients. As you work with the strategy, note that the visual approach used in this technique can be changed to match your clients' specific style, whether visual, auditory, or kinesthetic.

To realize the potential of the community genogram, it is essential that you not just read about it but actually do the practice exercise yourself. Additionally, rather than fixing on a single visual framework for a community genogram, Ivey (1995) suggests working with clients to develop their own models. Many clients like to make literal maps of their communities and draw pictures of their families, schools, and other groups. One useful representation is of a star with interacting influences written in around it. Circles and squares, with lines of connection, can also be used. Oetting's (1992) conceptual frame of person-in-community is shown in Figure 1.3.

Case Example

One client began his community genogram by talking about the negative name calling he had experienced in his home community and peer group because he was Jewish. As he talked about this negative recollection, it became apparent that much of his current problem of lack of trust in his partner related to issues of anti-Semitism. He also noted that his way of dealing with prejudice in the past was to withdraw and avoid social contact. He realized that he was doing the same thing in his present job and relationship.

The counselor listened carefully to this discussion and commented that the client's issues were very much tied to ethnic prejudice in the community, thereby reframing the individual problem as a community and systemic issue. Before having the client relate more stories, the counselor suggested a comprehensive community genogram and a search for strengths and positive resources. This approach did not deny the client's problems and concerns, but rather helped remind the client of personal strengths that would help him deal with real issues.

═══ **Practice Exercise 1.1** ═══

 # The Community Genogram: Identifying Strengths

This exercise has three goals: (1) to generate a narrative story of the client in community context; (2) to help the client (or you, in this case) generate an understanding of how we all develop in community; and (3) to use visual, auditory, or kinesthetic images as sources of strength. These images of strengths can be called on later in the counseling and therapy interview as positive resources to help clients cope with life's difficulties.

In addition, this exercise will help you understand the cultural background of your client, for it is through family and community that we learn our cultural framework. Finally, many clients will have had difficult life experiences in their communities. They may be tempted to first focus on the negative as they develop their awareness and present stories of how they have grown and lived in a community setting. Although you will need to attend to negative stories, we urge you to focus first on positive strengths.

Develop a Visual Representation of the Community

1. Consider a large piece of paper as representing your broad culture and community. You should select the community in which you primarily were raised, but any other community, past or present, may be used.
2. Place yourself or the client in that community, either at the center or other appropriate place. Represent yourself or the client by a circle, a star, or other significant symbol.
3. Place your own or the client's family or families on the paper, again represented by the symbol most relevant. The family can be nuclear or extended or both.
4. Place the important and most influential groups on the community genogram, again representing them by circles or other visual symbols. School, family, neighborhood, and spiritual groups are most often selected. For teens, the peer group is often particularly important. For adults, work groups and other special groups tend to become more central.
5. Connect the groups to the focus individual, perhaps drawing heavier lines to indicate the most influential groups.

Search for Images and Narratives of Strengths

Although many individual difficulties and problems arise in a family, community, and cultural context, the community genogram focuses on strengths. Ivey (1995, pp. 1–2) comments:

> The community genogram provides a frame of reference to help the client see self-in-context. The client is asked to generate narratives of key stories from the community where he or she grew up. If relevant, key stories from the present living community may also be important. The

emphasis is on positive stories from the community and positive images. The community genogram is kept and posted on newsprint during the entire counseling series of interviews.

The community genogram in its first stages focuses on positive stories and images. The importance of this point cannot be overstated. If this positive approach has been used first, clients will have a foundation for exploring more difficult and troublesome areas of their lives. In addition, the counselor will have a good foundation that will help in understanding the community, family, and cultural background of the client.

The specific steps of the positive resource search follow:

1. Focus on one single community group or the family. You or the client may want to start with a negative story or image, but do not work with the negative until positive strengths are solidly in mind.

2. Develop a visual, auditory, or kinesthetic image that represents an important positive experience. Allow the image to build in your mind, and note the positive feelings that occur with the image. If you allow yourself or the client to fully experience this positive image, you may experience tears and/or strong bodily feelings. These anchored bodily experiences represent positive strengths that can be drawn on to help you and your clients deal with difficult issues in therapy and in life.

3. Tell the story of the image. If it is your story, you may want to write it down in journal form. If you are drawing out the story from a client, listen sensitively.

4. Develop at least two more positive images from different groups within the community. It is useful to have a positive family image, spiritual image, and cultural image. Again, many will want to focus on negative issues, but maintain the search for positive resources.

5. Summarize the positive images in your own words and reflect on them. Encourage clients to summarize their learning, thoughts, and feelings in their own words. As you or your client thinks back, what occurs? Record the responses, for these can be drawn on in many settings in therapy or in daily life.

Although the word *images* is used here, some clients will find it easier to represent their experiences in terms of auditory (sounds), kinesthetic (tactile sensation), or olfactory (smell and taste) events. Thus, using the community genogram requires you as a counselor or therapist to be sensitive and creative in working with clients' individual cultural, ethnic, and perceptual style differences.

The community genogram can be a very emotional and dramatic strategy. At a minimum, it will help you to understand the special cultural backgrounds of your clients. The community genogram can also serve as a reservoir of positive experiences that can be drawn on to help you and your clients throughout therapy.

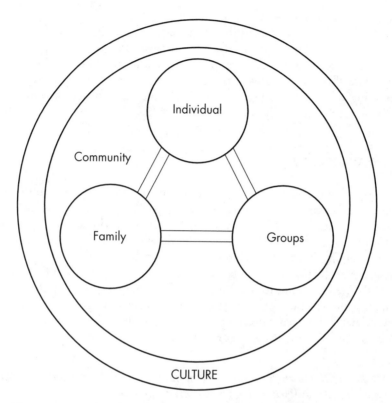

Figure 1.3 Individual Development within a Cultural Framework

SOURCE: Adapted from "Planning Programs for Prevention of Deviant Behavior: A Psychosocial Model" by E. R. Oetting (1992) in C. Bolek and S. Miemcryk (Eds.), *Ethnic and Multicultural Drug Abuse: Perspectives on Current Research.* New York: Haworth. Copyright 1992. Reprinted by permission.

Strengths found in the client's community genogram first focused on the synagogue, and a positive image of the client's relationship with his Sunday school teacher was generated. The positive image focused on a class in which the client had made a successful oral presentation to the group, something he now had difficulty doing. This positive image of strength and the feelings associated with it were helpful later in assertiveness training as the client drew on past history to face the present more effectively. As this example illustrates, spirituality can be an important resource for many clients. It can be a vital part of counseling and therapy and can help access multicultural issues.

Other positive images in the community included the warmth and caring of the neighborhood he had enjoyed on occasional visits to his grandfather, an accepting and supportive teacher, and his sports success in grammar school. Finding a positive experience in his home community was more difficult, but he eventually recalled an older man across the street who seemed to go out of his way to be nice to him. This positive experience helped him look more completely at his problematic home neighborhood, and he was able to identify several other positive dimensions.

The community genogram was posted in the office and became an important part of the therapy. At the conclusion of the sessions, the client was able to be more assertive and to deal more effectively with others on the job. He commented that the community genogram had been particularly important, as he now realized he had overgeneralized his negative experience from the past to the present. Assertiveness training was a key component in this change in cognition, but assertiveness training without community and cultural awareness would have been less effective.

Cultural Intentionality

A common theme underlying most approaches to interviewing, counseling, and psychotherapy, regardless of culture, is expansion of alternatives for living—the development of intentionality or purpose. Intentional individuals, or fully functioning persons, can be described as follows: Those who act with intentionality have a sense of capability. They can generate alternative behaviors in a given situation and "approach" a problem from different vantage points. Intentional, fully functioning individuals are not bound to one course of action but can respond in the moment to changing life situations and look forward to longer-term goals.

Intentional living occurs in a cultural context. Cultural expertise and intentionality imply the following three major abilities:

1. *The ability to generate a maximum number of thoughts, words, and behaviors to communicate with self and others within a given culture.*

Common to people who come for assistance on personal issues is immobility, the inability to act intentionally and resolve problems—the experience of feeling fixed in one place. Immobility is described differently in the several helping theories.[1] For example, Gestalt therapists talk about splits and impasses, Rogerian therapists talk about discrepancies between ideal and real self, and psychodynamic theorists discuss polarities and unconscious conflicts.

A multiculturally oriented therapist might examine the person's historical, cultural, and social contexts, giving special attention to the different modes of being that exist among different cultural groups. A family therapist might work with the entire family in the belief that the "identified patient" somehow is enacting family wishes. These are only a few of a myriad of therapeutic approaches, any one of which can be used effectively to free clients so they can generate new behaviors and be more fully functioning.

This points to an underlying purpose or overall goal of all counseling and therapy, which is to increase response capacity and the ability to generate or create new behaviors and thoughts.

2. *The ability to generate the thoughts, words, and behaviors necessary to communicate with a variety of diverse groups and individuals. Both clients and coun-*

selors need to communicate within their own culture and learn the ability to under-stand other cultures as well.

It has been demonstrated in several research studies that 50 percent of minority individuals do not return for a second counseling interview (see Sue & Sue, 1990). Most counseling theories operating in North America are rooted in European-American middle-class culture. However, what is appropriate behavior for the European-American may be unsuitable for an African-American or Latina/o. For example, the expression of emotions necessary in client-centered and psycho-dynamic therapy may be totally inappropriate and alien for some Asian-Americans and Native Americans (as well as many European-Americans). Thus, not only the goal but also the very process, style, and techniques of traditional helping may be inappropriate for those of minority cultures.

Fortunately, most theories and approaches stress the importance of evaluating whether or not the therapeutic methods are appropriate for the particular client. The counselor must reflect, analyze, and choose appropriate responses and tech-niques. A therapist who is skilled and knowledgeable in many theories thus has a strong basis for cultural intentionality. It is rapidly becoming evident that culture, religious background, socioeconomic status, age, and gender can be as important as the unique personality of the client and the problem itself.

3. *The ability to formulate plans, act on many possibilities existing in a culture, and reflect on these actions.*

"Unfreezing" individuals so that they are able to generate new behaviors is vital, but the simple generation of new ways of responding and acting creatively is not enough. At some point, individuals must become committed to action and decide on an alter-native. Not all counseling theories have a clear commitment to action as a goal.

Behavioral approaches to counseling place a particular emphasis on action. Clear, observable goals are developed, accompanied by follow-up and evaluation. The cognitive-behavioral therapist often assigns specific "homework" so that ideas generated in the interview are taken home and practiced. Most approaches to psy-chotherapy are not this specific, but all therapeutic approaches encourage clients to look at their plans and the results of their actions.

As an example of the difficulty of establishing culturally appropriate goals, con-sider the treatment of eating disorders such as bulimia and anorexia. Generally, these are problems of women in North American culture, although male eating dis-orders are on the increase. Thinness is valued in the North American culture. Thus, in helping clients generate a more positive body image and accept their weight, the counselor often works against cultural imperatives. Therefore, cultural awareness and consciousness raising often need to be included in the treatment of bulimia and anorexia. Such awareness should include the fact that some cultures consider heavi-ness desirable, viewing thinness as less attractive. The therapist must be aware that what is successful adjustment and adaptation in one culture can result in serious problems in another.

For example, middle-class European-Americans are considered adjusted if they have accumulated private wealth. If they distributed their material possessions to friends and family, they would be considered to have serious psychiatric problems. In South Pacific Fiji, the custom is that the individual must give away any material good if a friend or family member requests it—and give it away forever. The Native American potlatch in which wealth is given to others in an elaborate ceremony is another example of how individuals in some cultures gain status and prestige by sharing rather than acquiring. As can be seen, "mental health" depends on cultural perspective.

The Scientist-Practitioner

Counseling and psychotherapy draw heavily on the concept of the scientist-practitioner, a helping professional who draws on research for more effective practice and who uses information from clinical work to generate new research questions and plans. You personally may not be a researcher, but regardless of the therapeutic model you select, you will be affected by the scientific background of the field.

Kurt Lewin summarizes the relationship between practice and research succinctly: "No research without action; no action without research" (quoted in Marrow, 1969, p. 193). Research Exhibit 1.1 provides a summary of research on the effectiveness of therapy.

There are three avenues to major change and growth in the field: (1) new theoretical orientations, such as family therapy, and developmental and multicultural approaches; (2) research; and (3) clinical discoveries made through direct practice. All three methods are critical for effective practice, useful theory, and meaningful research. Currently, the field is moving toward accountability—for example, supporting theory with research and contracting with clients for specific results from therapy. With accountability as a goal, the scientist-practitioner model becomes of central importance. Ideas for case study research will be detailed in this book in the belief that most clients benefit from clear, jointly established objectives for the helping process. It is possible—and desirable—to integrate research on therapeutic action as part of the helping process.

Each chapter in this book includes practice exercises in the belief that each of us can learn by (1) generating hypotheses about a client, (2) testing these hypotheses in the client's world, (3) evaluating the results, and then (4) modifying the hypotheses as a result of clinical and research findings. In many cases, you will want to work with your clients as coinvestigators conducting joint research on the human condition.

Ethics and the Counseling and Psychotherapy Process

Effective practice is not only scientific but is also ethical. Professional helping organizations such as the American Association of Marriage and Family Therapy (AAMFT),

Research Exhibit 1.1

Research Summary on the Effectiveness of Individual Counseling and Psychotherapy: Eysenck and Meta-Analysis

Studying the extensive data on the effectiveness of psychotherapy, Hans J. Eysenck let loose a bombshell on the therapeutic profession in 1952:

> In general, certain conclusions are possible from these data. They fail to prove that psychotherapy, Freudian or otherwise, facilitates the recovery of neurotic patients. They show that roughly two-thirds of a group of neurotic patients will recover or improve to a marked extent within about two years of the onset of their illness, whether they are treated by means of psychotherapy or not. This figure appears to be remarkably stable from one investigation to another, regardless of type of patient treated, standard of recovery employed, or method of therapy used. (cited in Eysenck, 1966, pp. 29–30)

Eysenck's claim has been ably and sharply rebutted in numerous articles, but he was pivotal in forcing the field to look at its work and evaluate its effectiveness more carefully. The claims for the effectiveness of therapy include the following:

- Eysenck considered only 20 of over 400 studies then available (Smith & Glass, 1977).
- Meta-analysis (a complex statistical procedure) of 375 studies of therapy effectiveness found that clients who experienced therapy were indeed better off than untreated control subjects (Smith & Glass, 1977).
- An updated meta-analysis of 475 controlled studies supported the earlier findings of Smith and Glass (1977). However, two years after treatment, the effectiveness of therapy had diminished (Glass & Kliegl, 1983).
- Looking at benefits provides another way to review effectiveness data:

	Less benefit	Greater benefit
Psychotherapy	34%	66%
No therapy	66	34

"We are doing considerably better in our softer, wilder sciences than we may have thought we were doing" (Rosenthal, 1990, p. 776).

- McNeilly and Howard (1991) reexamined Eysenck's original data and found a 50 percent improvement rate among his subjects in about fifteen sessions, as compared to a 2 percent rate among those not treated. They comment that "Eysenck's data reveal that psychotherapy is very effective" (p. 74).
- Lambert and Bergin (1994) have reviewed the extensive literature on psychotherapy effectiveness to date and conclude that research is "not only statistically significant, but also clinically meaningful. Psychotherapy facilitates the remission of symptoms. It not only speeds up the natural healing process but also often provides additional coping strategies and methods for dealing with future problems. . . . The effects of therapy tend to be lasting" (pp. 180–81).

the American Counseling Association (ACA), and the American Psychological Association (APA) stress the importance of ethics in the helping relationship.

The Multicultural Foundation of Ethics

At a major conference on the future of professional psychology, Korman (1973, p. 105) stated:

> The provision of professional services to persons of culturally diverse backgrounds by persons not competent in understanding and providing professional services to such group shall be considered unethical; . . . it shall be equally unethical to deny such persons professional services because the present staff is inadequately prepared; . . . it shall be the obligation of all service agencies to employ competent persons or to provide continuing education for the present staff to meet the service needs of the culturally diverse population it serves.

Despite the clarity of this statement, the field moved slowly to implement these recommendations. Pedersen and Marsella (1982) comment: "A serious moral vacuum exists in the delivery of cross-cultural counseling and therapy because the values of a dominant culture have been imposed on a culturally different consumer" (p. 498).

Finally, in 1987, the American Psychological Association provided the first formal recognition of the importance of multicultural issues in psychology. Its *General Guidelines for Providers of Psychological Services* define good practice for the field, stating as part of the preamble: "These *General Guidelines* have been developed with the understanding that psychological services must be planned and implemented so that they are sensitive to factors related to life in a pluralistic society such as age, gender, affectional orientation, culture, and ethnicity" (p. 1).

Ethical practice, then, requires a multicultural orientation. Most of the theories presented in this book are based on traditional North American and European perspectives. Although traditional theory continues to remain of great value, ethical practice requires us to move beyond present theory to new approaches to the field.

We indeed are facing a paradigm shift. As a counselor or therapist, you will be taking part in the increasing awareness of multicultural issues as they relate to the helping process. Thus, it is imperative that you challenge the theories presented in this text and shape them for more culturally relevant counseling and psychotherapy.

Ethics and Responsibility

The core of ethical responsibility is to *do nothing that will harm the client or society*. The bulk of ethical responsibility lies with you as the helper. A person who comes for help is vulnerable and open to destructive action by the counselor. Knowledge of psychological, counseling, social work, and family therapy guidelines is essential. Following are some simple guidelines for you to consider as you review ethical standards in more detail.

1. *Maintain confidentiality.* Counseling and psychotherapy depend on trust between counselor and client. You as the therapist are in a powerful relationship; the more trust you build, the more power you have. This book asks you to practice many basic strategies of counseling and therapy. It is essential that you maintain the confidence of your clients, but if you are a student, you do not have legal confidentiality, and your clients should be made aware of this. Confidentiality is designed to protect clients (not counselors), and only the courts, in the final analysis, can provide a guarantee of confidentiality.

2. *Recognize your limitations.* It is vital that you maintain an egalitarian atmosphere with your clients, classmates, or coworkers. Share beforehand with them the task you wish to work through. Inform them that they are free to stop the process at any time. Do not use the interview as a place to delve into the life of another person. The interview is for helping others, not examining them.

3. *Seek consultation.* As you practice the exercises presented throughout this text, remain in consultation with your professor, workshop leader, mentor, or coworker. Counseling and psychotherapy are often very private. It is important that you obtain supervision and/or consultation in your work. You may also find it helpful to discuss your own growth as a helper with others. At the same time, be very careful in discussing what you have learned about your clients.

4. *Treat the client as you would like to be treated.* Put yourself in the place of the client. Every person deserves to be treated with respect, dignity, kindness, and honesty.

5. *Be aware of individual and cultural differences.* This point has been stressed throughout this chapter. An emphasis on cultural issues can lead at times to stereotyping an individual. At the same time, an overemphasis on individuality may obscure multicultural issues.

6. *Review ethical standards constantly.* Read and reread professional ethical codes as you encounter new ideas in this text.

Taking Theory into Practice

Your task as a therapist and counselor is multiple. You must not only learn therapeutic theories at a cognitive level, but also you must practice them. Each chapter has a number of practical exercises that will give you an opportunity to take theory into direct practice and learn whether or not the theory "works" for you—that is, if it is applicable to your personal experience and if you wish to consider the issues in more detail.

Reading a text such as this should be considered at best a beginning. You will learn far more about the theories if you do the exercises seriously. We recommend that you develop a portfolio of your experiences with the ideas and theories presented in this book. A portfolio of clinical competencies will stay with you long after you have read this text. You may also find it useful to return to these exercises during practicum and your professional experience. Repeating the exercise will give you not only a firm foundation but also a base on which you can develop new ideas for practice.

NOTE

1. The basic concept of immobility, the inability to act effectively and intentionally, will appear in many forms in this book among many types of clients. Words and phrases such as *stuckness, inability to respond, polarized emotions, frozen behavioral pattern, indecision, rigidity, fixated,* and many others all represent the loss of intentionality and resulting immobility.

REFERENCES

AMERICAN PSYCHOLOGICAL ASSOCIATION. (1987). *General guidelines for providers of psychological services.* Washington, DC: Author.

ESCHER, M. (1960). *The graphic work of M. C. Escher.* New York: Ballantine.

EYSENCK, H. J. (1966). *The effects of psychotherapy.* New York: International Science.

GERGEN, K. (1991). *The saturated self: Dilemmas of identity in contemporary life.* New York: Basic Books.

GERGEN, K. (1994). Warranting voice and the elaboration of the self. In J. Shotter & K. Gergen, *Texts of identity.* Newbury Park, CA: Sage.

GLASS, G., & KLIEGL, R. (1983). An apology for research integration in the study of psychotherapy. *Journal of Consulting and Clinical Psychology, 51,* 28–41.

IVEY, A. (1995). *The community genogram: A strategy to assess culture and community resources.* Paper presented at the American Counseling Association Convention, Denver.

KORMAN, M. (1973). *Levels and patterns of professional training in psychology.* Washington, DC: American Psychological Association.

LAMBERT, M., & BERGIN, A. (1994). The effectiveness of psychotherapy. In A. Bergin & S. Garfield, *Handbook of psychotherapy and behavior change* (4th ed.). New York: Wiley.

MARROW, A. (1969). *The practical theorist.* New York: Basic Books.

MCNEILLY, C., & HOWARD, K. (1991). The effects of psychotherapy: A reevaluation based on dosage. *Psychotherapy Research, 1,* 74–78.

OETTING, E. (1992). Planning programs for prevention of deviant behavior: A psychosocial model. In J. Trimble, C. Bolek, & S. Niemcryk (Eds.), *Ethnic and multicultural drug abuse: Perspectives on current research.* New York: Haworth.

PEDERSEN, P., & MARSELLA, T. (1982). The ethical crisis for cross-cultural counseling and therapy. *Professional Psychology, 13,* 492–500.

ROSENTHAL, R. (1990). How are we doing in soft psychology? *American Psychologist, 45,* 775–76.

SMITH, M., & GLASS, G. (1977). Meta-analysis of psychotherapy outcome studies. *American Psychologist, 32,* 752–60.

SUE, D., & SUE, S. (1990). *Counseling the culturally different* (2nd ed.). New York: Wiley.

VAN PELT, I. (1993). Logotherapy: Mission for the future. *International Forum for Logotherapy, 16,* 105–8.

VAN PELT, I. (1995). Spirituality and logotherapy. Personal communication, Amherst, MA.

VONTRESS, C. (1995). Existentialism: My view. Personal communication, George Washington University.

FOUNDATIONAL THEORIES AND SKILLS FOR EFFECTIVE COUNSELING AND THERAPY

Foundational to counseling and psychotherapy are theories that focus on basic underlying dimensions of the helping process. These theories, discussed in Part I, have the following dimensions in common:

1. *A belief in multiple approaches to the helping process.* Each of the chapters presents a specific theoretical and practical orientation and also stresses the need to incorporate ideas from other theories into counseling and clinical practice.

2. *An emphasis on multicultural issues.* Each theoretical framework gives attention to issues related to client diversity.

3. *An ability to operate as a separate and distinct helping theory.* Each framework discussed emphasizes linkage. In addition, the ideas in each chapter provide a working set of theories and skills within which counseling and therapy can be conducted.

4. *An emphasis on those underlying processes believed important to all approaches to helping.* Empathic dimensions, listening skills, and developmental concepts are crucial to all forms of helping.

The chapters in this part focus on three foundational theoretical and practical frameworks. Chapter 2 presents the basis of empathic theory—namely, that each client is a unique individual who is intimately involved in the family experience. The family, in turn, is the primary place in which culture is learned.

All counselors and therapists, whether they work at the individual, family, or multicultural level, use specific interviewing skills, which are discussed in Chapter 3. However, different cultural groups tend to use the skills differently. Solution-based counseling and therapy is presented as an important strategy.

Individual development can be considered the goal of counseling and psychotherapy. Developmental counseling and therapy (DCT) is presented in Chapter 4 as an integrative model that is helpful in assessing client cognitive and emotional processes, matching interviewing style to client needs, and generating treatment plans.

The concepts presented in these chapters will prepare you to look to the future and integrate the complex precepts of the four major traditional theoretical forces in psychotherapy and counseling: psychodynamic, cognitive-behavioral, existential-humanistic, and multicultural counseling and therapy.

The Empathic Attitude:
Individual, Family, and Culture

CHAPTER GOALS

This chapter seeks to help you:

1. Define individual empathy and its personal meaning to you.

2. Understand and use central empathic concepts, particularly, positive regard, respect and warmth, concreteness, immediacy, and genuineness.

3. Expand the concept of individual empathy to include multicultural issues.

4. Understand the importance of family heritage and the family as the primary transmitter of the culture in your own construction of the meaning of empathy.

5. Define key multicultural competencies and standards basic to individual, family, and cultural empathy.

6. Through practice exercises, direct or engage in
   - generating positive images of past situations in which you or clients feel safe and accepted
   - developing positive assets in your clients as a way of centering them before dealing with difficult issues
   - identifying yourself and your clients as multicultural beings
   - developing a family genogram or chart with an emphasis on cultural issues

Individual, Family, and Cultural Empathy

Empathy is often described as seeing the world through another's eyes, hearing as they might hear, and feeling and experiencing their internal world. Native American Indians called this "walking in another's moccasins." However, empathy does not involve mixing your thoughts and feelings with those of your client. Although the empathic attitude requires that you accept the client's being, as therapist and counselor you need to remain separate, true to yourself and your own beliefs. Empathy is most often considered an individual issue, but it also rests on an understanding and acceptance of the other person's total life experience. Family and culture deeply intertwine in the clients' lives. Really entering the worlds of others requires you to understand not only the concrete individual in front of you, but also how family and culture affect their very being.

This chapter first focuses on traditional concepts of empathic understanding, examines multicultural factors that affect the way individuals construct their worlds, considers family issues, and presents some central multicultural dimensions to be considered in approaching empathic understanding and relationship in the helping interview.

Defining Empathy: The Facilitative Conditions

In 1957 Carl Rogers produced a landmark paper, "The Necessary and Sufficient Conditions of Therapeutic Personality Change," which made a strong case that empathy and related constructs are all that is needed to produce change in a client. To help another person grow, Rogers said, requires an integrated congruent relationship with the client, unconditional positive regard for the client, and the communication of empathy from the counselor to the client—"No other conditions are necessary" (p. 27).

The influence of this article has continually expanded, and its tenets are now articles of faith for those of the existential-humanistic orientation. Moreover, cognitive-behavioral, psychodynamic, and most other orientations to counseling and therapy now accept the importance of empathy. Empathy and the accompanying empathic conditions, such as respect, warmth, and genuineness, are foundational to most helping theories.

Rogers offers the following contemporary definition of empathy:

> This is not laying trips on people. . . . You only listen and say back the other person's thing, step by step, just as that person seems to have it at that moment. You never mix into it any of your own things or ideas, never lay on the other person anything that person didn't express. . . . To show that you understand exactly, making a sentence or two which gets exactly at the personal meaning this person wanted to put across. This might be in your own words, usually, but use that person's own words for the touchy main things. (Gendlin & Hendricks, 1978, p. 120)

This definition takes empathy beyond an attitude. Rogers suggests specific actions and skills of empathic attitude the counselor or therapist can use in the interview to

Research Exhibit 2.1

Research Summary on Empathy

Does empathy exist? Can it be measured? Does it make a difference? The answers to these questions seem to be affirmative. Following are some of the key findings over the years:

- A landmark series of studies by Fiedler (1950a, 1950b, 1951) is often considered foundational in the study of empathy. He discovered that expert therapists of varying theoretical orientations appear to have much in common. For example, psychodynamic, Adlerian, and client-centered experts have more in common with each other than they do with inexperienced therapists of their own theoretical orientation.
- An avalanche of research in the 1960s and 1970s supported Fiedler's conclusions (see Anthony & Carkhuff, 1977; Auerbach & Johnson, 1977).
- Some reviewers criticized the facilitative conditions studies as flawed (Lambert, DeJulio, & Stein, 1978; Rachman & Wilson, 1980). Some of these reviews were written by behavioral researchers who at that time were seeking to prove the superior validity of behavioral methods.
- Pivotal to an integration and acceptance of the facilitative conditions outside the Rogerian and human resource development groups were the Sloane et al. (1975) and Sloane and Staples (1984) studies. These researchers found that behavioral therapists exhibited higher or equal levels of empathic conditions than did other psychotherapists. Successful patients in both therapies rated their personal interaction with the therapist as the single most important part of treatment.
- More reviews related to this area may be found in Bergin and Garfield (1986) and Goldfried, Greenberg, and Marmar (1990). The latter conclude their review by noting that "no orientation has consistently been found superior to any other" (p. 680), although they do indicate that research is beginning to reveal that clients who suffer from different types of problems (such as depression or personality disorder) may benefit from varying the style of relationship in the interview.
- Lambert and Bergin (1994), in an exhaustive and important review of dimensions of effective psychotherapy research over the years, summarize the extensive data by commenting: "Interpersonal, social, and affective factors common across therapies still loom large as stimulators of patient improvement. It should come as no surprise that helping people deal with depression, inadequacy, anxiety, and inner conflicts, as well as helping them form viable relationships and meaningful directions in their lives, can be greatly facilitated in a therapeutic relationship that is characterized by trust, warmth, acceptance, and human wisdom" (p. 181).

It is difficult to dismiss such powerful data, and the field has gradually come to accept the vital importance of counselor-client relationship as central to the helping process. Empathy and the facilitative techniques appear to have been accepted by the field as part of a generic approach to the helping process.

communicate empathy and understanding to the client. A summary of research on the role of empathy in therapy can be found in Research Exhibit 2.1. Practice Exercise 2.1 offers you an opportunity to examine your life experience with empathy.

Positive Regard and the Positive Asset Search

Positive regard is part of the empathic attitude and is aptly demonstrated by Rogers, whose positive attitude and hope for his clients have become legendary. Positive re-

Practice Exercise 2.1

Acceptance as the Foundation of Empathy

Acceptance may be described as the foundation of empathy. How would you define and experience acceptance? The following exercise may be helpful:

> Recall a time when you felt accepted by someone else just as you are or were. Recreate the situation in your mind. What is happening and what are you seeing? What is being said? What are your thoughts and feelings that go with the image? Focus on your body. Can you locate a specific place in your body for your feelings? If you are not as comfortable with visual images, use words, poetry, sounds, scents and odors, or bodily feelings.

Counseling and therapy ask you to accept the client. It is easy to feel acceptance toward a small child suffering from an emotional hurt or toward a survivor of spousal abuse. However, it is far less easy to feel accepting of the bully on the playground or the perpetrator of family violence. The following exercise can help you explore your ability to be accepting:

> How do you imagine yourself if you were to work with a bully or an abuser? Take time to let this image arise. What do you see and hear? Most important, what do you feel? Can you locate that feeling in a specific place in your own body?

The feelings you experience in your own body may be the best indicator of your degree of acceptance and ability to be empathic. Most of us have difficulty when we work with those who hurt others. Yet the bully, the abuser, and the rapist need empathy and acceptance as much as the child, adolescent, or adult who has survived attack. We should not use empathic understanding as a way to excuse the behavior of the perpetrator.

NOTE: This example shows the challenge of empathy. We need not accept the behavior, but at some level we must accept the person.

SOURCE: This exercise was derived from the work of Gladys Lam of Hong Kong Polytechnic.

gard means that you as therapist are able to recognize values and strengths in clients, even when the client holds widely different attitudes from yours. Positive regard is a concept basic to all counseling and therapy theory. If you as therapist cannot believe there is something positive and valuable in the client, there is little hope for client change.

Leona Tyler, in her classic counseling text (1961), presents a concrete explanation of the importance of positive regard:

> The initial stages of . . . therapy include a process that might be called *exploration of resources*. The counselor pays little attention to personality weaknesses. . . . [He or she] is most persistent in trying to locate . . . ways of coping with anxiety and stress, already existing resources that may be enlarged and strengthened once their existence is recognized.

In essence, positive regard asks that you look at clients affirmatively, expecting that they have potential resources. By positively identifying clients' strengths, together you can build a foundation for a working future. Tyler calls this "minimum change therapy," which is based on the assumption that if you can identify a strength or resource in the client and if you support it over time, it will grow and become more central to the client's life.

Positive regard is an attitude that can be fostered through some very specific actions of counselors and therapists. The following areas concerning client strengths are emphasized by different theorists in varying ways: resource development (Carkhuff, 1969); encouragement and strength assessment (Dinkmeyer & Dinkmeyer, 1995); resources, strengths, and the positive asset search (Ivey, 1993); and exceptions to the problem in solution-oriented therapy (O'Hanlon & Weiner-Davis, 1989). The positive asset search is a technique for building positive regard and is explored in Practice Exercise 2.2.

The concept of respectfully entering the other person's world has profound implications for family work and multicultural relationships. Multicultural empathy requires that we respect worldviews different than our own. As we seek to understand those who have different ethnic/racial, religious, or gender experiences from our own, we will find ourselves in a lifelong learning process.

Positive regard asks that we find positives in the worldviews and attitudes of those who are different from us. The Mexican-American counselor working with a European-American client has a responsibility to find positive meanings in the client's life experience. Similarly, the European-American counselor faces the same challenge with a Mexican-American client. The counselor must learn to respect, understand, and be able to work with different clients.

Respect and Warmth

An impassive counselor or therapist can appear professional and competent, but underlying the façade of professionalism may be unconscious hostility toward and dislike of the client. The intentional counselor likes and respects other people and communicates these feelings to them.

Practice Exercise 2.2

The Positive Asset Search: Building Empathy on Strengths

The tendency in counseling and therapy is to focus too much on clients' problems and concerns. If you give some attention early in the interview to positive strengths, clients will feel empowered and better able to cope with the negatives in their lives.

With a volunteer client, work through the following brief exercise.

1. Mention that too often counseling and therapy focus solely on the negative. To counter this tendency, you wish to begin your session with a strength assessment, and you will need the client's help in this process.
2. Discuss with the client possible areas of strengths in present-day life or the past. These positive resources may include many things, but important among them are (a) present and past successes the client has enjoyed, (b) supportive family members or friends, (c) spirituality, (d) love of nature, (e) success in sports, and (f) important cultural or personal hero figures. As part of the client's history, specifically search out times when the client felt stronger and was doing well—that is, times that were exceptions to the current problem. These positives may provide ideas for full or partial solutions to many current client issues.
3. Draw out from the client a personal narrative or story that concretizes the positive strengths. As you listen to the story, note how the client's body may shift to a less tense position. Reinforce that bodily experience by focusing for a moment on how the client feels when discussing a positive resource. Comment that this resource may be drawn on in the future, both in counseling and in daily life.
4. As appropriate during later contacts when the client seems stressed, draw on this positive story and the bodily sensations that go with it.

It is important to think about the client. Clients come in to talk with you about a series of problems and difficulties. All this talk often "decenters" clients from a feeling of competency. To ground clients and "center" them, spend time on positive strengths. Clients grow and develop from strengths that are already present as well as from the new ideas counseling and therapy provide.

Respect is close to positive regard and can be communicated verbally through the language of respect. Virtually all of the comments concerning positive regard and exploration of resources communicate respect for another person. Enhancing statements might include such comments as "You express your opinion well" and "Good insight."

Respect is also communicated nonverbally through individually and culturally appropriate eye contact and body language.

It is important to remember that you do not have to support or respect the behavior to respect the client. It is especially important to sort out negative behaviors. At times, these behaviors must be forcefully stopped. Those individuals traditionally identified as antisocial and borderline offer a particular challenge to your ability to respect. However, most clients so categorized have histories of extremely severe child abuse and/or multiple trauma. Thus, these are the very clients who most need your positive regard and respect.

It is possible to respect another person's point of view but still lack the critical dimension of personal warmth. Together, however, respect and warmth present a powerful combination. Warmth of counselor response has been demonstrated to be an important factor underlying an empathic relationship. But what is warmth? Warmth may be defined as an emotional attitude toward the client expressed through nonverbal means. Vocal tone, posture, gestures, and facial expression are how the counselor's warmth and support are communicated to the client. Smiling has been found to be the best single predictor of warmth ratings in an interview.

Delineating warmth, respect, and positive regard as separate categories is perhaps not really possible. Yet, one can imagine a person expressing positive feedback, respect, and positive regard to a client in a cold, distant fashion. The lack of warmth can negate the positive message. The communication of warmth through smiling, vocal tone, and other nonverbal means adds power and conviction to counselor comments.

Concreteness

The idea of concreteness seems relatively simple, but it is a vital dimension for effective counseling and therapy (Carkhuff, 1969). Counselors and therapists tend to think in an abstract, formal operational manner and thus often fail to work directly with their clients. Piagetian scholars note that children operate primarily in a concrete manner and that approximately 25 percent of the adult U.S. population fails to reach full formal operations (Ivey, 1986). Many clients will give very concrete, linear descriptions of their experiences. If you tend toward abstractness and formal operations, you may lose contact with these clients. They, in turn, may be put off by your emphasis on abstract patterns and representations of experience.

Developmental counseling and therapy (DCT) (discussed in Chapter 4) gives special attention to client styles of making meaning (Ivey, 1986, 1991). DCT stresses the importance of the counselor's willingness to enter clients' concrete worlds and listen in detail to their stories. At a later point, you may be able to help them see patterns and discuss their issues more abstractly, but concreteness and willingness to work with specific situations is a critical counselor skill.

There are two main issues concerning concreteness. The first, as just noted, is your willingness to be concrete with concrete operational clients. Later, after listening to their stories, you can help them see patterns of acting and responding. The second is to help overly abstract clients become more concrete and in touch with what actually happens and the need for specific action to resolve issues. Abstract clients at times may have difficulty taking ideas into practice. The concept of concreteness is particularly helpful in working with these clients.

Some clients come to therapy with vague, ambiguous complaints. A task of the intentional therapist is to clarify and understand vague ideas and problems expressed by the client. Effective interviews tend to move from vague descriptions of global issues to highly concrete discussions of what happened or is happening in the daily life of the client. Through interviewing leads that focus on concrete client experience, the helper can move from generalization to a clear understanding of what actually happened. Becoming empathic and understanding is easier when you understand specific facts. Generally, most clients will welcome concreteness, as "objective facts" are less susceptible to distortion. Furthermore, specificity and concreteness will provide a more solid base for client and therapist problem solving.

The search for concreteness underlies many, perhaps even most, helping interviews. Clients often lack full understanding and label situations incorrectly. Some clients use very abstract language and may talk in generalities. If you ask these clients for an example of a specific situation, they will often become more concrete. Asking clients the open-ended question "Could you give me a specific example?" can help clients organize their thinking and become less abstract.

Sometimes an emotional experience may be too intense for immediate discussion of concrete specifics. In cases of rape and abuse, it may be wise to delay the search for concreteness. North Americans in general tend to prefer discussing concrete specifics of a problem, but this approach can put off many Europeans, Asians, or Native Americans whose cultures may be oriented toward a more subtle approach.

Immediacy

Immediacy means that you move toward a more present-tense helping orientation and focus on the here-and-now experience of the interview by asking clients such questions as "What's going on with you, right now?" or "What are you feeling/experiencing at this moment?"

Egan (1994) describes "self-involving statements" in which you share your own reactions with the client. For example, you might share your own feelings with the client who refuses to return home: "I'm glad you're taking your own direction and having faith in yourself. I'm impressed with your strength." Such statements tell clients where you are in relationship to them. At the same time, the primary focus in such statements is on the client rather than the therapist.

Egan also explores here-and-now immediacy in the counselor-client relationship. In the following example, the client and counselor talk directly about what is happening between them:

Counselor: I'd like to stop a moment and take a look at what's happening right now between you and me.

Agnes: I'm not sure what you mean?

Counselor: Well, our conversation today started out quite lively, and now it seems rather subdued to me. I've noticed that the muscles in my shoulders have become tense and I feel a little flushed. I sense something's up that way when I feel I might have said something wrong. [*Note how the counselor uses awareness of his own body to facilitate communication*]

Agnes: What could that have been?

Counselor: Agnes, is it just me, or do you also feel that things are a bit strained between us right now?

Agnes: Well, a little.

Counselor: Last month you discussed how you control your friends with your emotions. This gets you what you want, but the price you pay can be too high. . . . Now all of a sudden you've gone a bit quiet, and I've been asking myself what I might have done wrong. To be truthful, I'm feeling a bit controlled too. What's your perspective on all this? (pp. 226–27)

This use of here-and-now immediacy in examining the client-counselor relationship can be very powerful and enlightening. At the same time, it obviously can be overdone and thus needs to be used sparingly, with care and a sense of ethics.

Congruence, Genuineness, and Authenticity

Rogers (1957) has stated that the person who conducts a therapy or counseling interview should be authentic and real. His views on genuineness have become central to many in the field. It is important that you be yourself, "freely and deeply . . . the opposite of presenting a facade either knowingly or unknowingly" (p. 97). Rogers asks you to allow yourself to experience yourself as a full, authentic human being. The helping experience at its best is core to the meaning of being a person. Who you are in the session as a person will have a deep impact on the client.

It is difficult to fault such a statement, as it is clear that openness and honesty on your part are central to your effectiveness as a counselor. There are times, however, when complete openness and spontaneity of expression may be damaging to the client. This point was forcefully made in a study of encounter group casualties by Lieberman, Yalom, and Miles (1972). They found that "open, authentic" group leaders produced more emotional casualties than did more conservative counselors, who developed relationships with group members more slowly and naturally.

There are two types of authenticity to consider. The first is authenticity to yourself. Being authentic, truthful, and open may be a laudable stance, but your client may not be ready for such behavior. A more important type of authenticity rests in having a genuine, congruent relationship with your client. This means taking into account where your clients "are at," listening to them, and opening an empathic dialogue.

The following exchange illustrates some issues in regard to genuineness:

Client: Yes, I can't decide what to do about the bab . . . I mean abortion until I know where I stand with Ronnie. He used to treat me nice, especially when we were first dating. He came over and fixed my car and my stereo, he liked to run errands for me. Now if I ask him anything, he makes a big hassle out of it.

Helper: At this moment, I can sense some confusion. Let me check this out with you. When someone is nice to me, I get to trust them and I feel comfortable. But then if they let me down, I get low and lost and really confused. Is my experience at all like yours?

Client: I guess I have felt like that. I know I blame him for getting me pregnant because he wouldn't do anything to prevent it. It makes me damn mad!

Helper: Right now, you really are angry with him.

The counselor shows genuineness in relationship to self through skillful self-disclosure and shares feelings and thoughts in a very real and personal manner. Self-disclosure does not necessarily have to be specific and detailed; it can be relatively vague and nonconcrete.

Suppose the counselor was thinking of a past event concerning his or her parents. If that concrete event had been presented, the counselor would still be genuine in relation to self, but the introduction of an example so different from the client's immediate personal experience could disturb the counseling relationship. Genuine and appropriate self-disclosure, on the other hand, can produce increased genuineness on the part of the client. Intentional counselors tend to produce intentional clients.

The Language of Multicultural Identity

Just as this book attempts to use respectful terms, so should you not label or stereotype your clients with your conception of the most appropriate term or even the "politically correct" term. Rather, you may wish to help your clients define their own identities in a multicultural world. Many clients will be bicultural or multicultural. If their issues are culturally related, you may work more effectively if you use their descriptions rather than labeling them from your frame of reference.

There is no fully satisfactory set of terms describing the vast array of multicultural experience that is our world. For example, Bumpus (1991) argues that designations such as "Black" and "White" are inappropriate: "Describing people by their skin color is patently racist." According to Bumpus, very few are satisfied with the U.S. census categories of "White," "Black," or "Hispanic." He asks: "What is a 'White' student? Is there a 'White' culture? . . . People of European descent are of many cultures . . . (for example, Irish-American, Polish-American). . . . Multiculturalism should reflect more than skin color. . . . We have cultural groups who can't even be defined by traditional anthropological terms . . . [including] lesbians, gays, single parents, and bicultural families" (p. 4).

The very word *multicultural* itself can be controversial. The Association of Multicultural Counseling and Development, for example, has stated that the word *mul-*

ticultural focuses on race, ethnicity, and culture. "Diversity refers to other characteristics by which persons may prefer to self-define. This includes, but is not limited to, an individual's age, gender, sexual identity, religious/spiritual identification, social and economic class background and residential location (i.e. urban, suburban, rural)" (Arredondo & D'Andrea, 1995, p. 28).

Recognizing the difficulties of language, the authors attempt to respect the many possible perspectives on multicultural identity. At times we will use the designations of "White" and "Black" (due to common usage or the context of the discussion), and both will be capitalized, following recognized American Psychological Association standards of usage. However, we will primarily use more specific terminology, such as Asian-American (and preferably Japanese-American and Cambodian-American, etc.), African-American, European-American (and preferably German-American, Italian-American, etc.), Latina/o (and preferably Puerto Rican, Chicana/o, Mexican-American), and Native American (or Native American Indian). In turn, the designation "American" is believed inappropriate by many, as it overlooks Canada, Mexico, and South American lands.

It seems important to recall that the original Americans are Native American Indians. As such, the designation "Native American Indian" will not be hyphenated, as an indication of respect for their hospitality and patience with their many "uninvited guests." They, like African-Americans who were forced to come to the United States through slavery, had very little say in the colonizing and governing of North America. The authors also recognize that the Hopi, Sioux, and Yakima Nations vary among themselves as much as or more so than do French-Canadian and Irish-Canadian cultures. This book also attempts to give some attention to groups that can be considered distinct cultures—for example, the culturally deaf, those with physical issues, lesbians and gay males, Vietnam and Persian Gulf veterans, and others.

The Concept of a "White Culture"

Many in North America refer to the "White culture," and in truth, there is a general set of privileges extended to the White majority. The light-skinned European-American majority tends to discriminate against those with darker skin. Given this reality, the concept of White culture can be useful.

The idea of a single White culture is likely as much a myth as a single Asian-American or African-American culture. Just as Britain (predominantly Anglo) and Ireland (predominantly Celtic) represent widely varying worldviews, so do worldviews from other cultural groups have many facets.

Biculturality

Biculturality is a fact of life. Many of your clients will come from more than one cultural tradition. You may work with a person who first identifies as Hispanic, and then you may find that the mother was Puerto Rican and the father Polish-American. Or you may work with clients who have Mexican-American and African-American parents or who are half Irish-American and half Italian-American or who are part Cherokee and part New England Yankee. Many people in Canada and the United States combine four or more differing cultural backgrounds. Hawaii is perhaps the most multicultural state, having a large population of mixed races and ethnicities. Thus, biculturality is increasingly more common than monocultural experience.

However, many in the United States and, to some extent, Canada tend to define people by relatively narrow categories and to ignore the important issue of biculturality or multiculturality. For many clients, living in two or more cultures is an important strength. But for others, biculturality can bring with it a feeling of being torn between two loyalties. A major issue in counseling may be helping such clients work through these divided loyalty issues as they find their own personal identity. It is important to be sensitive to multicultural difference and to beware of categorizing your clients as one-dimensional human beings. Clients are each unique in their relationship to the culture as well as being unique individuals.

The Multicultural Cube

Regardless of the concern the client presents, it is important to remain aware of specific multicultural issues that apply to clients and their level of awareness of these issues. Many clients who seek counseling and therapy have suffered some personal insult around multicultural issues. For African-American, Asian-American, Latina/o, and Native American clients, cultural oppression will likely play a role in whatever problems they present. Failing to recognize clients' cultural issues can be a serious limitation in therapy. The White male European-American is unlikely to suffer discrimination and personal injury for cultural reasons. This is not the case for White female European-Americans or for White male European-Americans who are of gay or bisexual orientation, for these individuals often encounter some sort of discrimination. As those in the men's movement remind us, European-American males do face many concerns and issues surrounding cultural demands and expectations (Osherton, 1986).

Figure 2.1 presents a cube model illustrating the various types of multicultural concerns clients can present in therapy. All clients present combinations of many multicultural issues, and different issues may be prepotent at different times. A range of multicultural issues affecting the counseling relationship make up one side of the multicultural cube. Along the left side of the cube is the locus of the issue. Although therapists traditionally tend to locate the concern within the individual, an individual issue may actually be derivative of the family, and the family issue may derive from problems in the group, community, state, or country. This points to the need to engage in family therapy, group work, or even community and political action to promote change.

Clients also have differing levels of awareness of how multicultural issues affect their lives. Five levels of awareness, or cultural identity, are presented in the cube model. Chapter 5 explores these levels in more detail, but briefly they are as follows:

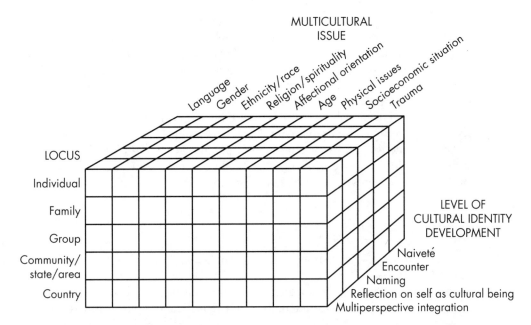

Figure 2.1 The Multicultural Cube

SOURCE: The multicultural cube is reproduced here by permission of Allen E. Ivey, copyright 1992, 1995.

Naiveté. The individual is unaware of the importance and impact of cultural difference on life experiences. A Latina/o may believe that discrimination is not a cultural or societal problem but rather an entirely individual issue.

Encounter. The person encounters a situation or situations in which the original lack of awareness is challenged. For example, an immigrant from Pakistan experiences racism after an initial honeymoon period in the United States, Canada, or England. There may be a period of time of passive or active acceptance of the original status quo.

Naming. Discrimination, oppression, and lack of attention by others to difference is named and identified. For example, a woman identifies the issue of sexism. Often associated with this level is a good deal of anger at those associated with the behavior (men, in this example).

Reflection on self as a cultural being. The person or client focuses on developing a positive sense of self—for example, taking pride in being gay or lesbian or a Vietnam veteran.

Multiperspective integration The individual is able to combine the strengths of the above levels and integrate them into a positive sense of self.

Consider, as an example, the following use of the multicultural cube: A Hawaiian-American may have a keen level 4 or 5 awareness of self as Hawaiian but a limited (stage 1 or 2) gender awareness. As a World War II veteran, this individual's awareness of personal trauma may range from very limited to full awareness. Each of these multicultural dimensions may be important in establishing a working interview and treatment plan. The same procedure applies to a family or group, which could have multiple issues on multiple levels of awareness, thereby requiring a multifaceted treatment approach.

The multicultural cube can also be viewed over linear time. Thus a client, family, group, or even community might change in awareness of issues over the time of counseling and therapy or a group/community intervention. Although most of the multicultural issues listed in Figure 2.1 should be self-evident, further elaboration on some issues is provided in the following subsections.

Language and Translation Issues

Language is one of the most powerful, yet most often ignored, multicultural issues. Good language skills are usually essential for social and economic success. Thus, clients who are not yet fully proficient in English may be seen by some as "disadvantaged." Consider, instead, the alternative view that clients who have English as their second language should be viewed as intellectually advantaged—that is, if you cannot talk to your clients in their natural language, you are the one lacking in skills.

If you must talk to clients in a language with which they are less familiar, it is important that they be encouraged to discuss particularly important issues and feelings in their own language, even though you may not understand them. After they have expressed their ideas, they then may translate for you. Clients come closer to their deeper experiences when expressing themselves in their own language.

Nowhere does language become more of an issue than when counselors and therapists work with translators. Marcos (1979, p. 173) offers the following example, in which interpreter-to-patient and patient responses are translated back into English:

Clinician to Chinese-speaking patient: What kinds of moods have you been in recently?

Interpreter to patient: How have you been feeling?

Patient's response: No, I don't have any more pain, my stomach is fine, and I can eat much better since I take the medication.

Interpreter to clinician: He says that he feels fine, no problem. . . .

Clinician to patient: What about worries, do you have many worries?

Interpreter to patient: Is there anything that bothers you?

Patient's response: I know, I know that God is with me. I'm not afraid, they cannot get me. (pause) I'm wearing these new pants and I feel protected. I feel good. I don't get headaches anymore.

Interpreter to clinician: He says that he is not afraid, he feels good, he doesn't have headaches anymore.

Obviously, effective practice with non-English-speaking clients is greatly enhanced by counselor facility in language issues.

Religion and Spirituality

The Invitational Summit on Spirituality in Counseling developed an inclusive approach to defining spirituality: "Spirituality is innate to all persons and is the animating force in life" (American Counseling Association, 1995, p. 30). This definition, of course, must be adapted to meet the individual beliefs of your clients. The summit also proposed a series of spiritual competencies, which are "influenced by individual, cultural, and universal elements." Among these competencies for the professional counselor are (1) self-exploration of one's own spiritual universe; (2) understanding of and empathy for other religious and spiritual orientations beyond one's own; (3) having available referral sources for spiritual issues; and (4) the ability to use spiritual, transpersonal, and religious beliefs as part of counseling and therapy.

Age

Children are perhaps the most oppressed of all groups. They are treated as property and have limited legal rights. In addition, they frequently suffer emotional and physical abuse and neglect. Although each age group has its special issues and concerns, children and the elderly are separate cultural groupings, each with their own separate issues.

Socioeconomic and Class Differences

These are the least-discussed multicultural issues. Economic deprivation, the absence of adequate health care, and discrimination are only some of the issues faced by those of less advantaged status. Ortiz (1978) quotes Domitila, a woman of the Bolivian mines who attended a conference on women's issues, as she addresses a wealthy woman at the conference:

> Señora, I've known you for a week. Every morning you show up in a different outfit and on the other hand, I don't. Every day you show up all made up and combed like someone who has time to spend in an elegant beauty parlor and who can spend money on that, and yet I don't. . . . I'm sure you live in a really elegant home, in an elegant neighborhood, no? And yet we miners' wives only have a small house on loan to us, and when our husbands die or get sick or are fired from the company, we have ninety days to leave the house and then we're in the street. Now señora, tell me: is your situation at all similar to mine? Is my situation at all similar to yours? . . . We can't, at this moment, be equal, even as women. (pp. 202–3)

Trauma

As a distinct culture, trauma has tended to be ignored. Rape and sexual exploitation traumatize a large number of women each year. Gavey (1991) cites data indicating that 24 percent of San Francisco women and 27.5 percent of U.S. college students have experienced rape. A large number of Vietnam veterans suffer from posttraumatic stress disorder. Those who find themselves HIV infected and face the ordeal of AIDS experience initial and continuing trauma.

Brassard, Germain, and Hart (1987) document that there were over 1.7 million cases of *reported* child maltreatment in 1984, suggesting that actual abuse and neglect may be much more extensive. Many of these children live in alcoholic homes in which spousal abuse is common. In one study, nineteen of twenty diagnosed female borderline clients had been subjected to sexual abuse (Flaherty, 1989). A study of clinically depressed inpatients revealed that seventeen of twenty had clear histories of trauma or abuse (Rigazio-DiGilio, 1989).

Recognizing individuals who experience common traumas as a distinct cultural grouping is of increasing importance. People challenged by cancer, multiple sclerosis, heart attacks, and the aftereffects of serious automobile accidents all demonstrate some aspects of posttraumatic stress disorder. Moreover, caregivers of loved ones suffering serious trauma also need support and treatment. You can expect the family to be traumatized if one member is seriously traumatized.

If all the above groups are accepted as separate cultures, it is clear that every session we have with clients will be a multicultural encounter. However, the warning of both Fukuyama (1990) and Locke (1990) must always remain before us: *If we define culture too broadly, we may miss significant issues.* Cultural expertise demands continuing and expanding awareness, knowledge, and skills for culture-specific counseling and therapy.

Empathy, the Family, and Multicultural Issues

As noted in Chapter 1, the well-known African proverb "It takes a village to raise a child" underlies the community genogram and also provides us with a different way to frame the ideas of empathic understanding and to consider the individual. Ogbonnaya (1994) talks about the "person as community," and his ideas, although focused on the African experience, have profound implications for the way we consider our clients, regardless of their cultural backgrounds. Rather than consider the person as a single entity, Ogbonnaya believes that the person represents a plurality of experience. This suggests that we cannot consider a client without considering the family and community contexts. In many ways, we all are extensions of these past and present experiences. The practice exercise in Chapter 1 on the community genogram is a practical application of this idea and is designed to help counselors and therapists consider the self in relation to others (see also Baker Miller, 1991). Empathy demands more than just attention to the individual. We also need to understand the individual's context.

The community genogram can be a guide to strengths and positive assets, particularly if you as the therapist focus on specific images of strength in the culture. One challenge in multicultural counseling is to understand cultural experiences different than your own. The use of images and stories derived from the community genogram is a way to learn about different cultural frameworks. In addition, the focus on individual strengths in relation to community means that you will not be exploiting culturally different clients by forcing them to "teach" you about their culture. This section focuses on the family of origin, for it is in the family that much of our culture is learned. Furthermore, the family we are born into helps us develop strengths and also, unhappily, is where we often experience important issues that bring us to counseling and therapy.

Think about your own family. How does your family feel about issues such as where children are expected to live after they marry? How much emotional and financial support does your family offer? What is the attitude toward intellectual achievement? What are the expected roles of men and women? What are attitudes toward pain? About drinking? Then examine yourself and your life. How are your constructs similar to and different from those of your family? Practice Exercise 2.3 offers a way to develop your self-awareness based on the multicultural cube model.

Family interactions and values vary across cultures. For instance, you may think it inappropriate that a young Italian couple lives with the parents and has a very close relationship if this is different from your own cultural background. Alternatively, an Italian-American therapist might view a Jewish-, Irish-, or British-Ameri-

---

Practice Exercise 2.3

Identifying Yourself as a Multicultural Being

The nine dimensions of the multicultural cube are listed below. Think about yourself in each area. Are you able to speak more than one language and what does this mean to you? What influence does your gender have on your life? With what ethnicities and races do you identify? Are you monocultural, bicultural, or multicultural? Continue through the following list, examining your cultural uniqueness.

Language(s)
Gender
Ethnicity/race
Religion/spirituality
Affectional orientation
Age
Physical issues
Socioeconomic
    situation
Trauma

Next, consider your level of awareness of each dimension, using the categories of naiveté, encounter, naming, reflection on self, and multiperspective integration (see Figure 2.1).

Finally, how do family attitudes and behaviors affect the way you think about these issues? How do peer groups and other associations in the community and broader aspects of society affect your thinking and feeling about your unique cultural self? Save this exercise, as you may wish to complete it again later in this book.

can family as strange and different if these families are not as closely knit as an Italian family. An African-American, Asian-American, or Latina/o might see the situation differently still. Clients and counselors should beware of grouping together those whose heritage can be traced to Colombia, Cuba, El Salvador, Haiti, Mexico, Puerto Rico, and other South or Latin American countries; each is likely to have a unique worldview.

Family Multicultural History

The members composing the family differ across ethnic groups. The intact nuclear family is associated with the Northern European culture. Italians extend the membership of the family to include three to four generations and may consider godparents and close friends as part of the family. The Chinese take this extended view one step further and include all living or deceased ancestors and descendants as members of the family. African-Americans also view the family from a multigenerational perspective. Some Native Americans consider the entire membership of their community as their family (Attneave, 1969).

Although these generalizations have been documented by sociologists, psychologists, and family researchers, we must remember that many families today are, in fact, a union of individuals from different cultures. Many marriages result from the attractive differences a person of another ethnic group offers (for example, Spanish expressiveness may combine with Norwegian stability). The role of the family counselor today is often to help the family explore the influence of ethnic heritage and belief systems, and to differentiate those thoughts and behaviors from personal attacks on the spouse (Falicov, 1983), as the following example illustrates.

Edward and Maria, an Italian/Greek couple, entered counseling because of the "constant conflict and tension" they were experiencing. In the first session, Edward provided a reserved critique of Maria's dramatic nature, labeling her as "hysterical and impulsive." Maria immediately countered with a louder complaint about Ed's "self-controlled, judgmental, and distant" way of talking with her. By the time treatment was initiated, both were convinced that their partners were being intentionally hurtful and wondered if they were still loved by the other. An essential component of treatment involved helping both Edward and Maria understand their behaviors within an ethnic context.

Although the list of examples of cultural differences could go on for chapters, it is important to note fundamental precepts that ground the work of a culturally sensitive therapist:

- Be aware of one's own ethnic heritage.
- Avoid stereotyping members of any ethnic background.
- Demonstrate empathy for members of other cultures.
- Realize that culture and ethnicity may be essential ingredients in a treatment plan.

The Family Genogram or Chart

The family genogram, or family chart, is one of the most useful diagnostic tools in the field. Once primarily the province of family therapists, individual counselors are increasingly using the genogram to help clients understand their past and present. Family genograms are useful in connection with the community genogram and provide the counselor and the client with additional vital data on the client's context. Often what was originally was thought of as an individual "problem" is reframed as a concern of the client in a family and community context.

The idea of a family genogram may be uncomfortable for some individuals. Those who come from adoptive families, gay or lesbian families, families considered dysfunctional, or other special situations (such as early parental death) may find the traditional term *family genogram* unsatisfactory. Thus, the term *family chart* can be used, with the understanding that what constitutes family will vary among individuals and cultural groups. The family chart or genogram can be a very personal and powerful exercise. Rather than follow the exact guidelines for genograms, you may find that charting clients in relation to others may be more appropriate. Flexibility and ability to work with varying client wishes are an essential part of the therapist's role.

The "cultural genogram" was developed by Hardy and Laszloffy (1995). Their approach to the family genogram reveals the importance of adding cultural issues. In addition, they provide a list of key questions to consider with individuals or families while developing a family chart. Among their list of twenty key questions are the following, which have been paraphrased and adapted for this book (Hardy & Laszloffy, 1995, p. 232):

1. How did your family enter the United States (Canada, Australia, New Zealand, etc.) and under what conditions?

2. What was your group's experience with oppression, and how did key family members respond to it? Was it identified in any way as oppression in the family?

3. How do issues of race and skin color, gender, and other multicultural issues, as listed in the multicultural cube, exist in your family of origin?

4. How does your group define family? Nuclear family? Extended family? Any special considerations?

The traditional genogram for Edward and Maria (the couple discussed in the preceding section) is presented in Figure 2.2. Several dimensions were at play, but the one that took the foreground early in the therapy was the conflict between the fraternal twins, who were constantly disrupting the family. The genogram revealed the extreme closeness of Maria to her father, which was also evident in an embedded relationship with one of the twins. As this situation was discussed, Maria was able to develop a more balanced relationship with the twins, although the conflict with Edward remained.

The counselor asked questions about the family of origin of each couple, and through this discussion, the different cultural patterns of Italian and Greek families

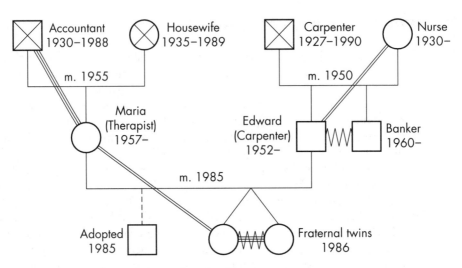

Figure 2.2 A Three-Generation Genogram

were clarified. Maria missed the closeness she had known with her father but at the same time admitted that she was drawn to Edward because he "allows me more space than my family did." The couple began to realize that their differences were not just individual but also the result of their unique family and cultural heritages.

There are other issues apparent in the genogram. Emphasis on academic achievement is common in Greek families, and Maria's father was an accountant. Edward is a carpenter. What implications might cultural views on education and achievement have for Edward and Maria's relationship? Might these influences relate to the conflict between Edward and his brother the banker? Maria and Edward had close, even enmeshed relationships with their opposite-sex parents. Would what they learned in their families be reflected in their own relationship? The family genogram opens up such questions as these.

Practice Exercise 2.4 asks you to develop a family chart with a volunteer client and write the chart on a large sheet of newsprint. Giving take-home assignments can help in elaborating and understanding family-of-origin issues and is a useful therapeutic technique. These exercises will help you understand clients more fully and help clients understand themselves more fully. The suggested symbols for a genogram should be adapted to meet the needs and wishes of each unique client, couple, or family. Posting family charts and community genograms on the wall throughout your sessions with a client will help both you and the client see the total context.

Children also respond well to a family genogram, which is usually presented in the form of a family tree. Working through family structure with a child can be very helpful in understanding the child's total context and can provide a way for a more complete understanding of any issues that may surface. For example, in developing a family chart, children may be encouraged to draw a tree. They then place themselves and family members in various places on the tree. Sometimes the closest per-

≡ Practice Exercise 2.4 ≡

Developing a Family Genogram or Chart

Complete the following yourself and with a volunteer "client."

Demographic Data

1. Write out the names of all family members for at least two or three generations.
2. Fill in the dates of birth, marriage, separation, divorce, death, and other significant life events.
3. Make notations regarding ethnicity, occupations, places of residence, and major life events.
4. The symbols used for a genogram should be negotiated with your client. Many clients object to the traditional "X" over those who have deceased, stating that the person "still lives in me." Other clients may prefer a road map, a network of rivers, or other symbolic framework to present their families and community heritage. The traditional model of genograms should not be imposed any more than we would impose a specific theory or counseling method on an unwilling client.

Basic Relationship Symbols

Close	═══
Enmeshed	≡≡≡
Estranged	—//—
Enmeshed and conflictual	∿∿∿

Distant	-----
Conflictual	MWW
Separated	—/—

Family Genogram Exercise

As a counselor, it is important to be aware of your own intergenerational issues, because these issues can affect your life and can be stimulated by your clients. To increase your conscious understanding of your family's legacy, take some time to complete a family genogram.

Begin by talking to your immediate and extended family. Go through family memorabilia. Then using the above symbols, begin mapping your family genogram. Be sure to include your own perceptions of the relationships with and between family members as well as those of other family members. It's always interesting to see how different family members view each other. Share the genogram with your family and look for patterns and themes. Then share it with a friend or someone who is not a member of your family.

Compare the insights gleaned from the family exploration and the nonfamily description. Which was easier? Which generated more emotions? What themes are important in your family? What personal and professional issues were raised by this exercise?

son to the child may be a grandparent, an aunt, or a godparent who is not biologically related to the child. The extended family may be more important than the nuclear family. A child's rendition of the family tree may give you a view of family structure that is very different than that of the traditional family genogram.

The authors' clinical experience is that some clients find traditional family genogram structures limiting. For this reason, we recommend flexibility when working with both adults and children in generating family charts. We suggest encouraging clients to use their own style of presenting their family. Nonetheless, traditional family genograms are often useful, as they provide additional information about family history and relationships.

Toward Multicultural Empathy and Competence

We are all individuals, and we also all have our origins in families. These factors impact our empathic understanding, as do the influence of our peer groups and friends, the neighborhood and community, and the overall culture. Throughout this book, issues relating to all of these areas are explored, although the primary focus is on *the individual developing in a family and multicultural context.*

The Professional Standards Committee of the Association for Multicultural Counseling and Development has generated a basic set of multicultural competencies and standards (Sue, Arredondo, & McDavis, 1992). Table 2.1 outlines some challenging goals that may be useful as you conceptualize your personal goals as a helper. Arredondo and others (1995) have operationalized these competencies in more detail. This elaboration may be found in brief form in Arredondo and D'Andrea (1995). These goals are briefly discussed as follows:

1. *Counselor awareness of own cultural values and beliefs.* If you are to be empathic with those of different backgrounds, it is essential that you become self-aware. The exercise in this chapter exploring your relation to your family of origin can be a step toward developing sensitivity about yourself as a cultural being. Other exercises in this book focus on helping you develop this type of self-awareness.

2. *Counselor awareness of client worldview.* Chapter 1 focused on this important concept, but it is important that you enhance this brief introduction by further reading and study. Being aware that worldviews and family experiences vary is a helpful beginning, but the next task is an in-depth study of the culture and worldviews of many other groups, including your own.

3. *Culturally appropriate intervention strategies.* This book is about the theory and practice of counseling and therapy. Thus, the authors have a special responsibility to present a variety of intervention possibilities and their appropriateness for various cultural groups. This book gives extensive attention to new work in multicultural counseling and therapy and feminist theory. We also attempt to provide a more culturally relevant portrayal of empathy, the microskills of listening and attending, and other dimensions.

Table 2.1   Multicultural Competencies and Standards

Goals	Attitudes and Beliefs	Knowledge	Intervention Strategies
Counselor awareness of own cultural values and beliefs	• Sensitive to one's own cultural heritage and how this influences thoughts, feelings, and behavior • Recognizes limits of abilities. • Comfortable with differences in race, ethnicity, culture, and beliefs.	• Aware of how background affects the definition of "normality" and the process of counseling • Understands concepts of racism, discrimination, and stereotyping. • Understands how one has benefited from above dimensions (for European-Americans). • Knows how one's own style may be inappropriate for culturally different clients.	• Seeks educational/ training experiences for continued learning, seeks consultation, and refers when necessary. • Seeks to understand oneself as racial/ cultural being and actively seeks a nonracist society.
Counselor awareness of client worldview	• Aware of negative emotional reactions and stereotypes relating to other groups; seeks to move to a nonjudgmental posture.	• Possesses specific knowledge of worldview, cultural style, and cultural identity levels of clients. • Understands how cultural issues relate to personal styles, help-seeking behaviors, and whether or not a particular helping intervention is suitable. • Familiar with what social and political influences such as poverty, racism, and powerlessness have on client development and how these influence the counseling process.	• Skilled in latest research and theoretical findings on groups culturally different from self. • Seeks appropriate educational experiences. • Actively involved with minority individuals in projects, friendships, social/ political functions, and celebrations so that perspective of minority experience is more than an academic or helping exercise.
Culturally appropriate intervention strategies	• Respects clients' religious/spiritual beliefs and values and understands how	• Understands how Eurocentric tradition in counseling and therapy may conflict	• Sends verbal and nonverbal messages accurately and appropriately.

Table 2.1   (continued)

Goals	Attitudes and Beliefs	Knowledge	Intervention Strategies
	these affect expressions of distress. • Respects indigenous helping practices and minority communities' natural help-giving networks. • Sees bilingualism as an asset rather than a liability.	with cultural values of other traditions. • Aware of institutional barriers and bias in assessment instruments and techniques. • Aware of the influence of varying family and community structures on the counseling process. • Understands issues of racism, oppression, and so on.	• Able to determine if clients' "problems" result from external factors, such as racism and bias in others. • Uses institutional interventions on behalf of clients. • Works with traditional healers and spiritual leaders as culturally appropriate. • Refers to good sources when own linguistic skills are insufficient. • Conducts training/educational interventions to combat oppression. • Educates clients to their personal and legal rights for effective multicultural intervention.

SOURCE: Adapted from ACA Professional Standards. Reprinted from *Journal of Counseling and Development,* 1992, *20,* 64–88. Reprinted by permission. No further reproduction authorized without written permission of the American Counseling Association.

Using Individual, Family, and Multicultural Empathy in the Interview

Your empathic response to one type of client may be inappropriate with another. How can you cope with the variety of clients and their many diverse cultures when no formula or theory provides an unfailingly reliable—that is, "correct"—response or action? The following three-step model of empathy provides you with a summary framework for balancing the uniqueness of the individual client with your own general knowledge and with counseling and therapy theory.

1. *Listen to and observe your clients' comments.* As you listen, recall that family and multicultural constructs may be an important part of their verbal or non-verbal behavior. As you listen, you can begin learning how your clients wish to be related to.

2. *Respond to clients' main words and constructs.* When in doubt, use attending and listening skills. When culturally and individually appropriate, add approaches based on your own experience, knowledge, and intuition. Also listen for and consider family and cultural issues.

3. *Check out your statements or interventions.* Ask "How does that sound?" "Is that close?" or some other statement that allows the client to respond to you. You may also indicate such a check of your perceptions by raising your voice at the end of your response in a questioning tone.

By checking out your approach with the client, you open the way for a more mutual, egalitarian dialogue. Although this is a good generic approach, some clients may prefer a more authoritative style, particularly those close to their traditional culture.

Use the perception check as a way to learn how to be with your client more empathically. Then return to the first step and change your style and comments as necessary until you and the client are both comfortable. Empathy is best cultivated as a process in which counselor and client together explore the nature of the client's worldview and beliefs about the problem. There is no final standard of "correct" empathy; rather, empathy requires that you constantly attune yourself to the wide variety of individual clients with whom you will work.

The importance of the perception check in building a solid, empathic counselor-client relationship cannot be stressed enough. By asking "Have I heard you correctly?" you show your empathy and respect for your client. Your client, in turn, will provide you with concrete data as to the effectiveness of your comment or intervention. If you respond accurately, your client will likely smile, say yes, and continue. If you are off target, your client will correct you, and you can use your new understanding to proceed with the session.

REFERENCES

AMERICAN COUNSELING ASSOCIATION. (1992). ACA professional standards. *Journal of Counseling and Development, 20,* 64–88.

AMERICAN COUNSELING ASSOCIATION. (1995). Summit results in formation of spiritual competencies. *Counseling Today,* p. 30.

ANTHONY, W., & CARKHUFF, R. (1977). The functional professional therapeutic agent. In A. Gurman & A. Razin (Eds.), *Effective psychotherapy* (pp. 103–19). Elmsford, NY: Pergamon Press.

ARREDONDO, P., & D'ANDREA, M. (1995, September). AMCD approved multicultural counseling competency standards. *Counseling Today,* pp. 28–32.

ARREDONDO, P., TOPEREK, R., BROWN, S., JONES, J., LOCKE, D., SANCHEZ, J., & STADLER, H. (1995, April). *Operationalization of multicultural counseling competencies*. Report submitted to the Association of Multicultural Counseling and Development, Washington, DC.

ATTNEAVE, C. (1969). Therapy in tribal settings and urban network interventions. *Family Process, 8,* 192–210.

AUERBACH, A., & JOHNSON, M. (1977). Research on the therapist's level of experience. In A. Gurman & A. Razin (Eds.), *Effective psychotherapy* (pp. 84–102). Elmsford, NY: Pergamon Press.

BAKER MILLER, J. (1991). The development of a woman's sense of self. In J. Jordan, A. Kaplan, J. B. Miller, I. Stiver, & J. Surrey (Eds.), *Women's growth in connection* (pp. 11–26). New York: Guilford.

BERGIN, A., & GARFIELD, S. (1986). *Handbook of psychotherapy and behavior change.* New York: Wiley.

BRASSARD, M., GERMAIN, R., & HART, S. (1987). *Psychological maltreatment of children and youth.* New York: Pergamon Press.

BUMPUS, G. (1991, October 25). Skin color doesn't determine culture. *Amherst Record*, p. 4.

CARKHUFF, R. (1969). *Helping and human relations* (Vols. 1 & 2). Troy, MO: Holt, Rinehart & Winston.

DINKMEYER, D., & DINKMEYER, D. (1995). *Client change through strength assessment.* Paper presented at the American Counseling Association Convention, Denver.

EGAN, G. (1994). The skilled helper (5th ed.). Pacific Grove, CA: Brooks/Cole.

FALICOV, C. (1983). *Cultural perspectives in family therapy.* Rockville, MD: Aspen Systems.

FIEDLER, F. (1950a). A comparison of therapeutic relationships in psychoanalytic, nondirective, and Adlerian therapy. *Journal of Consulting Psychology, 14,* 435–36.

FIEDLER, F. (1950b). The concept of an ideal therapeutic relationship. *Journal of Consulting Psychology, 14,* 239–45.

FIEDLER, F. (1951). Factor analysis of psychoanalytic, nondirective, and Adlerian therapeutic relationships. *Journal of Consulting Psychology, 15,* 32–38.

FLAHERTY, M. (1989). *Perceived differences in early family relationships and parent/child relations between adults diagnosed as borderline personality or bipolar disorder.* Unpublished doctoral dissertation, School of Education, University of Massachusetts, Amherst.

FUKUYAMA, M. (1990). Taking a universal approach to multicultural counseling. *Counselor Education and Supervision, 30,* 6–17.

GAVEY, N. (1991). Sexual victimization prevalence among New Zealand university students. *Journal of Consulting and Clinical Psychology, 59,* 464–66.

GENDLIN, E., & HENDRICKS, M. (1978). Changes. In E. Gendlin, *Focusing* (pp. 118–44). New York: Everest House.

GOLDFRIED, M., GREENBERG, L., & MARMAR, C. (1990). Individual psychotherapy: Process and outcome. In M. Rosenweig & L. Porter (Eds.), *Annual review of psychology* (pp. 659–88). Palo Alto, CA: Annual Reviews.

HARDY, K., & LASZLOFFY, T. (1995). The cultural genogram: Key to training culturally competent family therapists. *Journal of Marital and Family Therapy, 21,* 227–37.

IVEY, A. (1986). *Developmental therapy: Theory into practice.* San Francisco: Jossey-Bass.

IVEY, A. (1991). *Developmental strategies for helpers: Individual, family and network interventions.* North Amherst, MA: Microtraining.

IVEY, A. (1993). *Intentional interviewing and counseling: Facilitating development in a multicultural society.* Pacific Grove, CA: Brooks/Cole.

LAMBERT, M., & BERGIN, A. (1994). The effectiveness of psychotherapy. In A. Bergin & S. Garfield (Eds.), *Handbook of psychotherapy and behavior change* (4th ed.). New York: Wiley.

LAMBERT, M., DEJULIO, S., & STEIN, D. (1978). Therapist interpersonal skills. *Psychological Bulletin, 85,* 467–89.

LIEBERMAN, M., YALOM, I., & MILES, E. (1972). *Encounter groups: First facts.* New York: Basic Books.

LOCKE, D. (1990). A not so provincial view of multicultural counseling. *Counselor Education and Supervision, 30,* 18–25.

MARCOS, L. (1979). Effects of interpreters on the evaluation of psychopathology in non-English-speaking persons. *American Journal of Psychiatry, 136,* 171–74.

OGBONNAYA, O. (1994). Person as community: An African understanding of the person as an intrapsychic community. *Journal of Black Psychology, 20,* 75–87.

O'HANLON, W., & WEINER-DAVIS, M. (1989). *In search of solutions.* New York: Norton.

ORTIZ, V. (1978). *Let me speak! Testimony of Domitila, a woman of the Bolivian mines.* New York: Monthly Review Press.

OSHERTON, S. (1986). *Finding our fathers.* New York: Free Press.

RACHMAN, S., & WILSON, G. (1980). *The effects of psychological therapy.* New York: Wiley.

RIGAZIO-DIGILIO, S. (1989). *Developmental theory and therapy: A preliminary investigation of reliability and predictive validity using an inpatient depressive population sample.* Unpublished doctoral dissertation, University of Massachusetts, Amherst.

ROGERS, C. (1957). The necessary and sufficient conditions of therapeutic personality change. *Journal of Consulting Psychology, 21,* 95–103.

SLOANE, R., & STAPLES, F. (1984). Psychotherapy versus behavior therapy: Implications for future psychotherapy research. In J. Williams & R. Spitzer (Eds.), *Psychotherapy research: Where are we and where should we go?* (pp. 203–15). New York: Guilford.

SLOANE, R., STAPLES, F., CRISTOL, A., YORKSTON, N., & WHIPPLE, K. (1975). *Psychotherapy versus behavior therapy.* Cambridge, MA: Harvard University Press, 1975.

SUE, D., ARREDONDO, P., & MCDAVIS, R. (1992). Multicultural counseling competencies and standards: A call to the profession. *Journal of Multicultural Counseling and Development, 20,* 64–88.

TYLER, L. (1961). *The work of the counselor* (2nd ed.). East Norwalk, CT: Appleton & Lange.

CHAPTER

3

Conducting an Intentional Interview:
Theory, Skills, Decisions, and Solutions

CHAPTER GOALS

Clients' stories of their behavior, thoughts, and feelings are key to your understanding of their concerns. Intentional interviewing seeks to help clients tell their stories and, when necessary, facilitate their developing new understandings and actions.
This chapter seeks to help you:

1. Understand the basic theory of the microskills and decisional counseling approach and the microskills hierarchy, particularly as related to individual and multicultural differences.

2. Examine specific microskills and strategies of the microcounseling approach—attending, listening, and influencing, and, especially, focusing and confrontation.

3. Understand the five-stage structure of a well-formed interview and how this structure may be adapted in many theories of helping.

4. Use solution-oriented brief counseling and therapy to help clients find resolution to at least some of their issues within a relatively short time.

5. Through practice exercises, conduct or engage in
   • Drawing out the client's story or narrative using the basic listening sequence
   • Reframing a client's story through the use of the focusing skill
   • Basic decisional counseling using a five-stage interview structure
   • Brief solution-oriented counseling and therapy using a culturally aware five-stage interview structure

The Microskills and Decisional Counseling Worldview

Constructing an effective interview requires that you cultivate individual, family, and cultural empathy. At the same time, you must use effective, pragmatic skills to accomplish change. The microskills and decisional counseling framework is now considered to be a technology of constructivism, a systematic way to discover how clients make sense of the world and to act with clients to make a difference for the future. This approach poses the pragmatic question: How can we change our stories and act more effectively in the world?

Constructivism and Social Constructivism

George Kelly (1955) deserves credit for bringing constructivist thinking to counseling and therapy. Kelly argued that we are all are scientists in that we constantly test hypotheses about our world. For example, children or adults seeking to understand the world do not always immediately grasp what they see. Rather, they test their ideas (hypotheses) through actions (experiments) on the world, and the results (findings) lead to conceptualizations and ideas (theories) about the world.

Children constantly test their ideas—for example, by throwing balls into the air, building towers that do or do not fall over, and learning to ride tricycles and bicycles. According to Kelly, they develop an idea, try it out in the "real world," and, based on the results, change the way they think and act in the future. Adults trying to understand how to work effectively with children follow a similar pattern: start with an idea, test it out, see what the results are, and, based on the results, change behavior and thinking.

Kelly (1955) emphasized our "creative capacity . . . to represent the environment, not merely to respond to it. Because [people] can represent [their] environment, [they] can place alternative constructions upon it and, indeed, do something about it if it doesn't suit [them]" (p. 8). In effect, Kelly is suggesting that our clients are scientist-practitioners, much as we are ourselves as counselors and therapists. The storytelling process is our invention or hypothesis about ourselves.

People develop constructs about the world that organize and systematize events, people, and the environmental context. Constructs are hypotheses that are used to test some idea or behavior on the world and have been found in some way to be effective. Constructs are our ideas and representations of the world—in effect, our worldview. As counselors, we draw out and listen to clients' stories and hear their narratives or constructions of their experience.

Out of constructivist thought has come social constructivism, a frame of reference that encourages counselors and therapists to think about the social context in which clients' concerns developed. In short, what clients experience in their families of origin, their communities, and their cultures deeply affect the way they think about the world. External experience and reality is as important as internal thought.

The cultural and family genograms, for example, are two excellent tools for helping clients see how their constructions and meaning making relate to social and cultural history.

The Pragmatic Tradition— What Works

Social constructivist theory at first glance seems greatly removed from practice, but in truth it is closely allied to the American philosophical pragmatism of C. S. Pierce, William James, and John Dewey. Although the ideas of these philosophers are complex, pragmatism often amounts to "Let's find out what works and use it." Pragmatism has it roots in the utilitarian tradition that represents the basis of U.S. ideology. Pragmatism (as defined in the 1992 *American Heritage Dictionary*) is "distinguished by the doctrine that the meaning of an idea or a proposition lies in its observable practical consequences; and . . . a practical, matter-of-fact way of approaching or assessing situations or of solving problems."

Important to pragmatism is the idea that data obtained from experience must be used to revise meaning making. Constructivism and social constructivism are clearly allied with the practical tradition, but these newer traditions are much more complex and focus on thought processes. The microskills tradition described in this chapter originated in pragmatism and is based on "what works." Of course, "what works" must be modified by the complexity of the world, and it is here that ideas of social constructivism become central to microskills theory and practice.

This chapter introduces practical approaches and techniques in counseling and interviewing: microskills and decisional counseling and structuring an effective interview (Ivey, Normington, Miller, Morrill, and Haase, 1968; Ivey, 1971; Ivey, Gluckstern, and Ivey, 1992). As with pragmatism, the microskills approach developed out of practical observation in the real world and then was modified based on data from experience. The essence of the microskills and decisional tradition can be summarized in the following, which paraphrases Frank Parsons (1909/1967), a pioneer in vocational counseling:

> In counseling and therapy there are three main issues: (1) a clear understanding of how the thoughts, feelings, and actions with a client's story are constructed; (2) a clear understanding of how the client's story was constructed in a social context of family, community, and culture; and (3) an exploration of how the story might be changed and reconstrued by emotional and rational understanding and pragmatic action in the real world.

The term *microcounseling* encompasses the microskills approach. This counseling approach developed pragmatically by a focus on the observable actions of counselors and therapists in the interview that appeared to effect positive change in the session. This focus on "what works" led to the identification of the specific microskills described in this chapter and presented in the microskills hierarchy (see Figure 3.1). The decisional counseling frame was developed out of the five-stage interview presented later in this chapter. The microcounseling framework has recently moved toward a theory of helping through the specific connections to constructivist and social constructivist thought. Microcounseling thus represents both a technology for the interview and a social constructivist theory of what occurs between counselor and client.

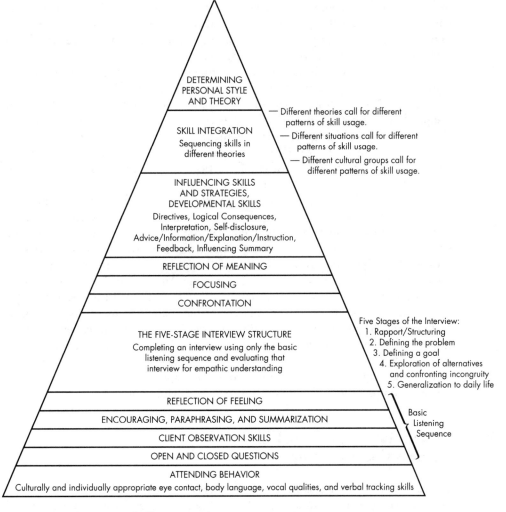

Figure 3.1 The Microskills Hierarchy

NOTE: The skill "reflection of meaning" is discussed in Chapter 12 in connection with the work of Viktor Frankl.

SOURCE: The Microskills Hierarchy is copyrighted by Allen E. Ivey, 1982, 1995, and is presented here by permission.

Pragmatism, Social Constructivism, and Practice

What is the connection between social constructivism and the pragmatic tradition? Both follow the scientific model—developing a hypothesis, testing it in the real world, and revising it based on available data. In other words, *if the counseling strategy or theory does not work, revise what you think you are doing and try again.* Social constructivism, however, provides an important modification missing in pragmatic, action-oriented approaches. Social constructivism reminds us that our theories and strategies are but narrative stories for describing our world. Our task as therapists is to help clients revise and act on new versions of their stories. The focus in social constructivism is on changing and revising theory to match new data, whereas the pragmatic approach can sometimes become encapsulated in old stories and fail to think in new ways about how to reach clients.

Social constructivism underlies the structure of this book and will be referred to from time to time. The authors believe that various theorists have written effective cognitive-behavioral, psychodynamic, humanistic, and multicultural stories about the psychotherapeutic and counseling process. All the stories have value for some clients. However, although a particular theory or strategy may work one time, it may not work the next time. If your first theory of choice does not work, consider trying another. No one theory or set of practice strategies provides all the answers.

Your task as a therapist/counselor is to construct your own organization of the complex world of professional helping. In effect, you are the author of your own story about counseling and therapy. The social constructivist view can offer an organizing frame for your story. Who are you going to select as the lead players in the story of psychotherapy (key theories)? What is the plot (which issues will you address—psychodynamic history, Rogerian relationship, specific observable behaviors)? Toward what ending is your story heading? And, in this framework, what is the context of your story (multicultural issues such as race, spirituality, gender)?

The microskills approach summarized in this chapter focuses on specific skills and strategies for identifying behaviors and actions useful in the interview, for drawing out and elaborating clients' stories, and for working with clients to change and reconstruct their stories and live more effectively and pragmatically. As you read the story of the microskills and decisional counseling approach, examine it for its relevance to your own narrative on the nature of the helping process.

Multicultural Issues, Microskills, and Decisional Counseling

The earliest work in microskills (Ivey, Normington, Morrill, Miller, and Haase, 1968) did not consider cultural issues, but this conceptual error was corrected in later work (Ivey and Gluckstern, 1974). This correction was a direct result of the constructivist/pragmatic tradition. It became clear very early that microskills had to be changed and shaped to meet the needs of culturally different individuals. However, many current standard texts in the field (or the popular press) still ignore the multicultural issues concerning interviewing skills. The microskills approach makes it clear that sometimes any intervention can be inappropriate for particular clients or groups.

Many in the helping profession still are using skills and theories that were found to be in need of change over twenty years ago. Again, *what works in one situation or with one client may not work with the next situation or client.* To be an effective counselor or therapist, you must observe what occurs in the interview and change your approach to meet the present situation. Environmental awareness is as important as individual perceptions. Social constructivist thought provides a clear basis for a theory that takes into account environmental and contextual factors. What we experience through being in the world informs our cognitions and emotions. We as unique beings make sense of the world in our own way, and the world provides basic data for our constructions and meaning making.

Cheatham (1990) focuses on the African-American experience, stating that "traditional concepts of psychological intervention ignore the cultural and contextual specificity of Black families and their members and thus are inadequate to serve these clients" (p. 388). Unless we as counselors consider social and environmental issues, we are very likely to fail with our clients. Davison (1991) addresses how societal descriptions of homosexuality as pathological become internalized in the worldview of the gay individual, thus begetting self-hate and internalized anxiety. If we are to work with gay or lesbian clients, it is vital that the social context and environment be considered an important component in therapy. Effective therapy with gays and lesbians requires that we examine society for its pathology and lack of understanding of the homosexual experience.

The decisional counseling and microskills approach, as with all other theories, also can fail to consider cultural and social contexts. However, microcounseling is recognized as the first skills-based system to take multicultural issues into account (see Ivey and Gluckstern, 1974). Chapter 5 introduces recent work by Nwachuku (1989, 1990) and Nwachuku and Ivey (1991) that further extends the microskills concept into the multicultural counseling and therapy approach. The ideas presented here are not final. We the authors invite you to join us as we move to change and adapt the current constructions and practices and obtain new data in the future.

The Microskills Approach: The Pragmatics of Constructivism

Microcounseling theory holds that all systems of counseling and therapy employ various patterns of skills. This is one of the dimensions that ties microskills to social constructivist thought. The process of identification and selection of specific skills of counseling is called the microskills approach. Using the microskills approach, we can break down the complex interaction of the counseling interview into manageable and learnable dimensions.

Underlying and shaping the interview are the nonverbal factors the helper brings to the interview. For instance, through body language and facial expression, the counselor expresses an attitude toward the client. Figure 3.2 shows a counselor listening to a client in two different ways.

Before reading further, take a moment to list on a separate sheet the specific nonverbal attitudes expressed in each photo. Be as precise as possible in identifying observable aspects of nonverbal behavior. Also note which counselor style would be more inviting to you if you were the client.

In the North American cultural context, the counselor's forward stance, direct eye contact, and relaxed body style in the first photo in the figure communicate interest and assurance. In the second photo, the counselor's poor eye contact, slouched body position, and closed arms and legs communicate a lack of interest.

Monitoring how you communicate nonverbally as you practice microskills is a complex challenge that can be further complicated by multicultural issues. For example, for clients of some cultures, the body language of the counselor in the first picture may be considered intrusive instead of inviting. A Navajo reported that the second photo was much more inviting and appropriate, although other Navajos might not agree. Each client will have different responses to nonverbal behavior. As you learn more about microskills and their application in multicultural settings, you will become more adept at choosing the appropriate nonverbal mode for the particular client. Research Exhibit 3.1 reviews findings on attending behavior and the microskills approach.

Attending Skills

When you interview or counsel another person, it seems obvious that you should look at them and maintain natural eye contact. Further, your body should communicate interest. It was once believed that counseling was solely a verbal occupation,

Figure 3.2 Counselor Listening Styles

Research Exhibit 3.1

Research on Attending Behavior and Interviewing Microskills

Prior to approaches such as microskills, counseling and therapy were considered almost mystical, and the idea of systematic definition of interview behavior did not exist. Where does a basic construct such as attending behavior come from? In their 1968 study, Ivey and colleagues Normington, Miller, Morrill, and Haase sought to identify foundational, specific skills of helping. After months of study and experimentation led only to failure, a simple experiment, described below, laid the foundation for the microskills approach discussed in this chapter. (The original work on microskills occurred in a European-American context. The findings would have been different had multicultural issues been considered.)

The basic breakthrough which resulted in the concepts of attending behavior and microcounseling occurred with one of our secretaries. The process consisted of five minutes of videotaping when she was interviewing a student volunteer. This was followed by a replay of the tape in which her behaviors, which reflected lapses of attending, were pointed out, and direction was given in how to increase identified attending behaviors. She returned to reinterview the student, and, after a moment of artificiality, began to respond in highly impactful ways. In fact, she performed like a highly skilled, highly experienced counselor. The change was not only dramatic, but, when we began to consider the twenty minutes of training, almost shocking! We have had less change of behavior in practicum students in an entire year.

When a hiatus was reached, the lack of training in counseling skills became apparent. The hiatus called for initiation of new areas, and the secretary did not follow one of our counseling traditions. If she had, she would have either waited for the client to respond (nondirective), initiated an expression of her own feeling state (recent client-centered), directed attention to early experience (analytic), presented a discriminative stimulus to elicit verbal responses which could be reinforced (learning theory), induced a trance state (hypnoanalysis), or brought out a Strong Vocational Interest Blank (vocational counseling).

The secretary actually began to talk about an interesting experience in her own immediate past (standard social behavior). However, since she still was attempting to engage in attending behaviors, this led rapidly to a new topic for the student, and she again resembled the highly skilled counselor.

As an indication of the relevance of attending and related constructs to behavior beyond the interview, our secretary entered the office on Monday and could not wait to tell us about attending to people over the weekend. She had developed an entirely new behavioral repertoire which was reinforced by a new kind of excitement and involvement with other people. The impact even on her husband was apparent. (Hackney, Ivey, & Oetting, 1970, p. 344)

This process of identification of researchable dimensions in counseling is cited in detail because it illustrates the sometimes whimsical nature of the research process in which discoveries are often made by chance rather than by choice. Since the original 1968 study on attending behavior, over 300 studies on the microskill of attending behavior have been completed (see Ivey, 1971; Ivey & Authier, 1978; Daniels, 1985; Daniels & Ivey, in press; Baker & Daniels, 1989; Baker, Daniels, & Greeley, 1990).

Following are some of the more important findings of microskills research:

1. Clients respond better and more positively, are more likely to verbalize at greater length, and indicate a greater willingness to return to attending counselors and therapists.

2. Experienced and sophisticated therapists and counselors seem to have good attending skills, whereas many beginning counselors score poorly on these dimensions.

3. Clients and therapists from varying cultures use microskills, but in a different fashion than presented in the original Eurocentric framework.

4. Different counseling theories use microskills, but focus on varying dimensions of client experience.

5. Training clients in microskills can be a useful part of a broader treatment program.

but with the advent of videotaping and the increased use of filming in interview training, it has become apparent that nonverbal communication is basic in any interviewing, counseling, or therapy session.

Eye contact and body language are the physical fundamentals of attending behavior. Another basic aspect of attending behavior is vocal tone. Does your voice communicate warmth and interest or boredom and lack of caring? Even though you may be physically attending, your voice often indicates the quality of your willingness and interest in listening.

Moreover, if you are to attend to someone, you must "listen" to them. Listening, however, is not an observable behavior. Intentional therapists not only maintain attentive body posture and facial expression, they also stay on the topic with the client and seldom interrupt or change topics abruptly. A major mistake of beginning counselors is to change the topic of discussion and ignore or fail to hear what the client has to say. For example:

Client: I've been downtown this afternoon, and I really got anxious. I even wanted to run when I saw a friend. I broke out in a sweat and felt I couldn't move. I've been in my room until just now.

Nonattending counselor: Let's see now, you're a sophomore this year?

Attending counselor: You say you wanted to run when you saw your friend. Could you describe the situation and what was happening in more detail?

It is seldom necessary or desirable to change the client's topic, particularly when a client such as the above is describing what most likely was a panic attack. Attend carefully, and the client will tell you all you need to know.

Attending and Cultural Differences

Attending behavior varies from culture to culture and from individual to individual (see Table 3.1). Data show clearly that individual differences among clients may be as important as cultural patterns. When reviewing such summaries of cultural pat-

Table 3.1   Nonverbal Attending Patterns in European–North American Culture Compared with Patterns of Other Cultures

Nonverbal Dimension	European–North American Pattern	Contrasting Example from Another Culture
Eye contact	When listening to a person, direct eye contact is appropriate. When talking, eye contact is often less frequent.	Some African-Americans may have patterns directly opposite and demonstrate more eye contact when talking and less when listening.
Body language	Slight forward trunk lean facing the person. Handshake a general sign of welcome.	Certain Eskimo and Inuit groups in the Arctic sit side by side when working on personal issues. A male giving a female a firm handshake may be seen as giving a sexual invitation.
Vocal tone and speech rate	A varied vocal tone is favored, with some emotionality shown. Speech rate is moderate.	Many Latina/o groups have a more extensive and expressive vocal tone and may consider European–North American styles unemotional and "flat."
Physical space	Conversation distance is ordinarily "arm's length" or more for comfort.	Common in Arab and Middle-Eastern cultures is a six- to twelve-inch conversational distance, a point at which the European-American becomes uncomfortable.
Time	Highly structured, linear view of time. Generally "on time" for appointment.	Several South American countries operate on a "being" view of time and do not plan that specified, previously agreed-upon times for meetings will necessarily hold.

NOTE: It is critical to remember that individuals within a single cultural group vary extensively.

terns, do not assume that one pattern of attending (or influencing) is appropriate for every individual of that cultural group you might interview.

Sue (1990) presents a framework for culture-specific strategies in counseling. He cites research showing that many minority clients terminate counseling early and suggests that more culturally sensitive approaches are needed. He summarizes literature demonstrating the vital importance of including spatial, nonverbal, and related dimensions in the helping process. Sue supports this by quoting a saying common among African-Americans: "If you really want to know what White folks are thinking or feeling, don't listen to what they say, but how they say it" (p. 427).

Mirroring Nonverbal Behavior

Examination of films and videotapes of interview sessions reveals fascinating patterns of nonverbal communication. In a successful, smoothly flowing interview, movement complementarity or movement symmetry often occurs between counselor and client. Movement complementarity is represented by a "passing" of movement back and forth between client and counselor. For example, the client pauses in the middle of a sentence, the counselor nods, and the client then finishes the sentence. Movements between counselor and client pass back and forth in a rhythm.

In movement symmetry, counselor and client unconsciously assume the same physical posture; their eye contact is usually direct; and their hands and feet may move in unison as if they were dancing or following a programmed script. Movement symmetry can be achieved in a rudimentary fashion by deliberately assuming the posture and "mirroring" the gestures of the client. This mirroring of nonverbal behavior often brings the therapist to a closer and more complete understanding of the client. The series of photographs in Figure 3.3 show a client and counselor discussing an issue of mutual interest. The time for the completion of this series of movements is about one second. Careful examination of helping interviews reveals many examples of movement symmetry as well as dissynchronous movement that often indicates failure to communicate effectively.

This lack of complementarity and symmetry is an important factor in counselor-client communication. For instance, the counselor may say something, and the client's head may jerk noticeably in the opposite direction. Dissynchronous body movements that occur between counselor and client can indicate that the interview is on the wrong track. A solid knowledge and awareness of body language is necessary to consistently observe dissynchronous behavior.

Once you become skilled in observing and practicing mirroring, it can be a valuable tool. If you note the general pattern of body language of your client and then deliberately assume the same posture, you will find yourself in better synchrony and harmony with the client. Through mirroring, new understandings and communication can develop. This tool should not be used manipulatively, but rather to develop increased awareness and new levels of insight.

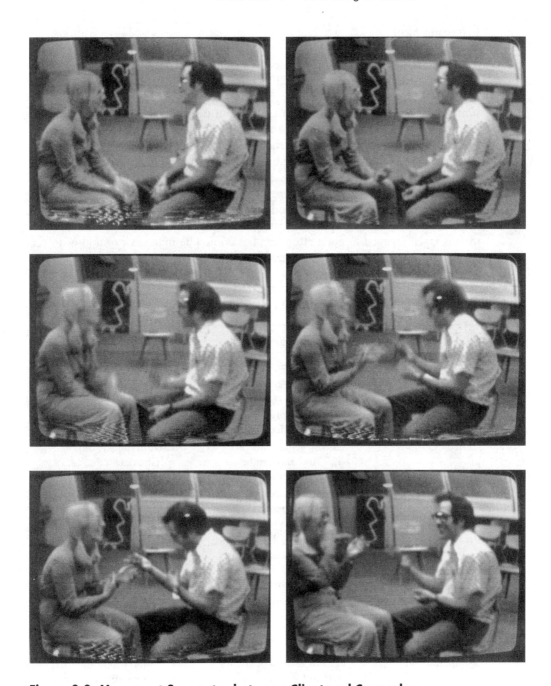

Figure 3.3 Movement Symmetry between Client and Counselor

SOURCE: Photos from *Microcounseling: Innovations in Interviewing, Counseling, Psychotherapy, and Psychoeducation* by A. Ivey and J. Authier, 1978, Springfield, IL: Thomas. Copyright 1978 by Thomas. Reprinted by permission.

Listening Skills

Attending skills can be organized into a coherent and systematic framework called the basic listening sequence. Table 3.2 identifies the specific microskills of listening: open and closed questions, encouraging, paraphrasing, reflection of feeling, and summarization. All these skills are intended to bring out clients' stories. The aim of listening skills is to discover how clients present their stories, with minimal intrusion on the part of the counselor or therapist.

The microskills of listening have been part of counseling and therapy for over thirty years but were not presented as an integrated sequence and theory until relatively recently (Ivey, 1988). The *basic listening sequence* (BLS) was first identified through direct observation by a skilled manager at Digital Computer Corporation. When an employee came up to the manager with a problem on the production line, the manager engaged in good attending behavior. The manager's responses to the employee included the following listening skills:

Table 3.2   The Basic Listening Sequence

Skill	*Description*	*Function in Interview*
Open questions	"What": facts "How": process or feelings "Why": reasons "Could": general picture	Used to bring out major data and facilitate conversation.
Closed questions	Usually begin with "do," "is," "are" and can be answered in a few words.	Used to quickly obtain specific data, close off lengthy answers.
Encouraging	Repeating back to client a few of the client's main words.	Encourages detailed elaboration of the specific words and their meanings.
Paraphrasing	Repeating back the essence of a client's words and thoughts using the client's own main words.	Acts as promoter for discussion; shows understanding; checks on clarity of counselor understanding.
Reflection of feeling	Selective attention to emotional content of interview.	Results in clarification of emotion underlying key facts; promotes discussion of feelings.
Summarization	Repeating back of client's facts and feelings (and reasons) to client in an organized form.	Useful in beginning interview; periodically used in session to clarify where the interview has come to date and to close the session.

Could you tell me about the problem on the production line? [*open question*]
The Zenos chip? [*encouraging*]
You say the supply department hasn't given you enough computer chips to keep your
    group moving smoothly? [*paraphrasing*]
Sounds like the situation really makes you angry. [*reflection of feeling*]

The manager then *summarized* the employee's view of the problem, and only then
did the interview start to move toward action.

Subsequent work has revealed the importance of the basic listening sequence in
a multitude of helping settings. Many counseling and therapy theories use the basic listening sequence to draw out information from the client. Although the skills
are not always sequenced as clearly as they are in the following example, most therapists and counselors use variations of this basic model as they get to know their
client and the client's life concerns.

Could you tell me about your family and how they react to your fear of going out in
    public? [*Open question—leads to drawing out how client organizes the problem*]
Protect you? [*Encourager—leads to exploring client's key words and underlying meanings*]
So, when you find yourself not wanting to go outside, the family goes out for you?
    [*Paraphrase—client knows she or he is heard*]
Is that right? [*Perception check—helps client know whether or not hearing has been ac-
    curate*]
And you seem to be feeling very sad/frightened/inadequate right now. [*Reflection of
    feeling—leads client to explore emotion*]
So this is what I'm hearing you say . . . [*Summarization—counselor emphasizes main
    points of the client's story to enhance understanding of the problem in a more organized
    fashion*]

The basic listening sequence has specific goals. It is vital that we bring out the
client's story by using these skills. In doing this we need to know the *main facts* as
described by the client, how the client *feels about those facts*, and how the client *or-
ganizes the story*.

In approaching these goals, it is good to take into account multicultural and gender issues. Men tend to ask more questions than women (and they also tend to interrupt more often). Women tend to use the techniques of paraphrase and
reflection of feeling more often than men. Then too, a European-American therapist working with a minority client may appear too intrusive if too many direct
questions are used. Although it is vital that you draw out the client's story and the
key facts, feelings, and organization of the story, the basic listening sequence must
be modified in the here and now of the interview.

Whether you are helping a client with a vocational decision, negotiating a divorce, or conducting a psychodynamic dream analysis, you will need to know the
facts and how the client feels about those facts and then organize them for further
analysis. The basic listening sequence and its accompanying microskills can be very
useful when you employ the different therapeutic approaches discussed later.
Whether you are a behavioral counselor, a reality therapist, or a family counselor,

the basic listening sequence is a critical therapeutic tool. Practice Exercise 3.1 discusses some techniques for listening to clients' stories.

Using Listening Skills with Children

The basic listening sequence and all the microskills are helpful in working with young children, with some modification. If you have a highly verbal child, perhaps even as young as five or six, listening skills work very effectively and you can follow the general rules presented here. But most children will need help in expressing information.

Many children will respond to an open question with confusion, looking puzzled and saying perhaps only a few words. Closed questions, phrased gently, often are useful in helping children express themselves. The danger, of course, is leading the child to a conclusion. The child may be anxious to please you as the counselor and follow your lead too easily. The danger closed questions pose for leading the child is especially critical when a child is being interviewed on issues of child abuse.

Paraphrasing can be especially useful in helping children talk. Effective classroom teachers constantly paraphrase comments of their students. Paraphrasing helps children keep on the topic, acts as a reinforcer, and indicates that you have heard them. Each child generates a unique construction, and if you use the key words of the child, you are more likely to learn how that child sees the situation.

MacFarlane and Feldmeth (1988, pp. 8–9) outline some key aspects of interviewing children. They point out that children's cognitive processes are different from adults' and that it is necessary to gear comments to the language and cognitive

---

=== **Practice Exercise 3.1** ===

 ## Using the Basic Listening Sequence to Draw Out Clients' Stories

Regardless of whatever theory you select, it is important that you draw out the client's story and the key facts, thoughts, and feelings within that story. With a real or role-played client, practice your listening skills and ability to draw out the client's story using the basic listening sequence. Audiotape this interview so you can examine and classify what listening skills you are using. Better yet, videotape the session so you can examine your own and the client's nonverbal behavior as well.

As a final check, give special attention to how you summarized the client's story at the end of the exercise. How accurately did you catch the story? Did you obtain the key facts as well as the client's thoughts and feelings?

level of the child. These researchers provide several useful guidelines for communicating with young children, which are summarized and paraphrased as follows:

1. Use short sentences and simple words.

2. Use concrete language and avoid abstractions. "Did he touch you?" is clearer than "Did he do something naughty?" The specifics of the touch may need to be clarified as well, perhaps through the use of anatomically correct dolls.

3. Avoid double negatives. Say "Did the teacher tell you not to do that?" rather than "Didn't the teacher tell you not to do that?"

4. Use names rather than pronouns. Children (and adults) under stress may confuse people and situations.

5. Be careful with closed questions that can be answered yes or no. This poses a challenge for many interviewers of children, as children's verbal skills may be quite limited. When you must ask such questions, follow up with paraphrasing and encouragers such as "Tell me more" to facilitate conversation. If you are called to court to testify in a case of child abuse, expect the attorney to quiz you thoroughly on whether or not you acted in a leading fashion in your interview procedure.

Beyond these guidelines, your personal ability to establish rapport and trust is essential. A pleasant office, small children's furniture, and suitable pictures and games can be helpful. Warmth and a cheerful smile are important to children. Most children talk more easily while playing games such as checkers or cards, molding clay with their hands, or drawing pictures. Children can readily do two things at once, so you can move easily between the game and your interview goals.

Influencing Skills and Strategies

Clients can profit and grow even if you use only attending behavior and listening skills. However, a strict listening approach fails to take advantage of the many possibilities for helping. Thus, the microskills system lists an array of skills and strategies that can be useful in guiding clients in changing their stories, thoughts, and feelings. Table 3.3 presents in summary form these key change strategies.

Interpretation and reframing are perhaps the central influencing skills, for in using these approaches the counselor or therapist most directly seeks to help clients find new meaning to old stories and behaviors. Although microcounseling theory argues for clients finding their own meanings via the basic listening sequence, many people will benefit from assistance and new ways of thinking. Those who have experienced harassment—women, gay individuals, or persons with AIDS, for example—need to tell their stories, but they may also benefit from the therapist's ideas and reframes. For example, many people who are harassed think of their issues as "their fault" and blame themselves. A basic reframe for helping clients see the social and contextual basis of their issues is to help them see how sexism, discrimination, and/or oppression are factors. Such observations are made from a multicultural counseling and therapy frame of reference.

Table 3.3   Influencing Skills

Skill	Description	Function in Interview
Interpretation/ reframing	Provides an alternative frame of reference from which the client may view a situation. May be drawn from a theory or from one's own personal observations. *Interpretation may be viewed as the core influencing skill.*	Attempts to provide the client with a new way to view the situation. The interpretation provides the client with a clear-cut alternative perception of "reality." This perception may enable a change of view that in turn may result in changes in thoughts, constructs, or behaviors.
Directive	Tells the client what action to take. May be a simple suggestion stated in command form or may be a sophisticated technique from a specific theory.	Clearly indicates to clients what action counselors or therapists wish them to take. The prediction with a directive is that the client will do what is suggested. Table 3.4 lists several specific directives drawn from different theories that will have differing anticipated results with clients.
Advice/information	Provides suggestions, instructional ideas, homework, advice on how to act, think, or behave.	Used sparingly, may provide client with new and useful information. Specific vocational information is an example of necessary use of this skill.
Self-disclosure	The interviewer shares personal experience from the past or may share present reactions to the client.	Emphasizes counselor "I" statements. This skill is closely allied to feedback and may build trust and openness, leading to a more mutual relationship with the client.
Feedback	Provides clients with specific data on how they are seen by the counselor or by others.	Provides concrete data that may help clients realize how others perceive behavior and thinking patterns, thus enabling an alternative self-perception.
Logical consequences	Interviewer explains to the client the logical outcome of thinking and behavior—if/then.	Provides an alternative frame of reference for the client. This skill helps clients anticipate the consequences or results of their actions.
Influencing summary	Often used at or near the end of a session to summarize counselor comments; most often used in combination with the attending summarization.	Clarifies what has happened in the interview and summarizes what the therapist has said. This skill is designed to help generalization from the interview to daily life.

Reframes from other theoretical approaches can also be helpful. Psychodynamic theory may be useful and can help clients see how their histories and past experiences relate to their present stories. Cognitive-behavioral reframes will often help clients think more effectively about their stories and provide action narratives for the future. The existential-humanistic reframe may help clients focus on their self-value. The point of reframing is to tell the story in a new way, one that is more functional and valuable to the client.

All influencing skills are oriented in different ways toward the same objective: finding new ways to think about, and then act on, old narratives and stories. Later, as you read through this book, you will find that Rogerian person-centered counseling employs very few of these influencing skills. Cognitive-behavioral theory, however, uses an extensive array of influencing change strategies. You as a professional counselor or therapist will want to find the balance and blend of listening and influencing that you believe to be most appropriate for your own practice.

Focus and Selective Attention

Beginning counselors and therapists often focus on problems instead of the people in front of them. It is generally (but not always) wiser to first focus on the client and later on the problem. The temptation is to focus on the problem and solve it, perhaps even disregarding the thoughts and feelings of the client in the process. This course should be avoided—for example:

Client: Yes, you've got it. I've got to cope with so many things, and it seems endless. I don't know where to turn. I've tried to get Chuck to Alcoholics Anonymous, but he only goes for a session or two and then quits. The school guidance counselor called me in because Joss got into trouble on the playground. They said he was bullying a smaller boy. How can I solve all these problems?

Counselor: I hear you as overwhelmed by it all. Let's start first with *you* and what's happening with *Suzanne.*

The counselor uses two personal pronouns and the client's name. Such naming of the client is an important personalizing technique seldom stressed sufficiently in the helping profession. By focusing on Suzanne, the counselor indicates an interest in the person and what that person feels and thinks. *Counseling is, after all, for the client.*

Although focus should usually be on the client, it can be invaluable to broaden the focus in a balanced fashion to include several additional dimensions. In working with a complex case such as Suzanne's, it should be clear that focusing just on Suzanne will not be sufficient in the long run. This client needs to work out her relationship with her husband, help her children, and resolve a wide variety of pragmatic problems. Thus, although counseling is indeed for the client, the ability to look beyond the client and focus the interview more broadly is also crucial.

Client-centered Rogerian theory and psychoanalytic theory treat the issue of focus differently. These systems of helping focus their interviewing leads almost totally on the client and give minimal attention to family issues or context. However, family, feminist, and multicultural theories hold that it is important to consider situational and contextual variables. It is also the case that some clients can best be reached by first focusing on the problem; only then will they be able to focus on themselves and their feelings.

Focus Analysis

It is apparent that focus can be approached in different ways. Thus, it is important that we consider all possible aspects of clients' problems. The seven dimensions of microskill focus analysis listed below are vital for understanding what is happening in any therapy session. Consider the following client statement:

> *Client:*   Yes, you've got it. I've got to cope with so many things, and it seems endless. I don't know where to turn. I've tried to get Chuck to Alcoholics Anonymous, but he only goes for a session or two and then quits. The school guidance counselor called me in because Joss got into trouble on the playground. They said he was bullying a smaller boy. How can I solve all these problems?

It is possible to respond to the client's statement in any of several ways:

1. *Client focus:* "Suzanne, you feel confused and lonely. You're unsure of what you want to do." This response contains four personal references to the client. Although counseling generally recommends a client focus, this may be culturally inappropriate in some situations. The client focus approach puts the problem squarely on Suzanne and tends to ignore family factors and gender issues.

2. *Other focus:* "Tell me more about your husband." In this case, the client likely will start telling about her husband and his drinking. The question "What's going on with Joss?" would result in a focus on the son. Both of these questions may lead to valuable information, but they do not tell us about the client and her reaction to the situation. For some clients, however, an other focus may be more appropriate than a client focus, as they may feel uncomfortable talking about themselves in the early stages of the helping process.

3. *Family focus:* Therapists are beginning to understand the importance of family history and family interaction and how these are played out in therapy with the individual client. A child who bullies on the playground may be acting out an abusive pattern at home. Responses that focus on the family include: "How would your son's bullying relate to what's going on in the family?" or "Family issues often reflect what happens in the individual. Tell me more about what's happening in your family" or (more historically oriented) "Let's go back to your own family of origin. Could you tell me what role alcohol played in your family while you were growing up?"

4. *Problem/main theme focus:* The presenting problem or main theme of the session could be said to be the general issue of how alcohol affects the client and her family. More specifically, this client seems to be nearing a crisis. Sample responses focusing on the problem and its solution would include: "What can I do to help you find housing so you could move out?" or "The situation sounds like an emergency. I'll call the women's shelter right now. You'll be safe there." or "Let's talk about how we could help your husband become more involved with AA." Clients often need concrete problems solved, particularly in times of crisis, and a focus on the individual client could be inappropriate at times.

5. *Interviewer focus:* "I grew up in an alcoholic family too. I can sense some of your issues." Focusing on your own experience may be useful as a self-disclosure or feedback technique, and it may help develop mutuality with the client. As rapport develops, such responses may be increasingly helpful. However, they must not be overdone. Counseling is for the client, not for the counselor.

6. *"We" focus:* "Right now we seem to be getting somewhere. The two of us ought to be able to generate some good ideas using what we know." This type of mutual sharing frequently appears in humanistically oriented interviews. It is also characteristic of feminist counseling and therapy in which the helper frequently joins the client as an advocate. This particular type of mutual focus leads toward a more egalitarian relationship between helper and helpee. (Note that "we" refers to the relationship between client and counselor or therapist.)

7. *Cultural/environmental/contextual focus:* "This is a concern facing many women. Society and its limited support systems do not always make things easy." Undergirding our client problems are long histories of interaction with sociopolitical systems. With some clients, this can become an important focus for discussion. Helpers with a multicultural or feminist orientation often effectively use this focus to produce change. Sample responses might include: "Many African-Americans feel a sense of rage because of discrimination. Racism is a fact of our society" or "You say that you can't speak assertively for yourself. This is a problem that many women have in our culture due to sexist conditioning." Most counseling theories, particularly the major ones, often overlook the cultural/environmental context and the historical background of the individual.

Focus analysis is concerned with the subject or main theme of the client-counselor interchange. Analyzing the grammatical subject of the client's sentences indicates the focus for the counseling intervention. Counseling is centrally concerned with getting clients to make "I" statements—statements in which they discuss themselves and their concerns. Counselors elicit "I" statements from their clients by using personal pronouns such as "you" and "your" and by using clients' names. It must again be emphasized that the other types of interview focus remain appropriate at times and, in fact, must be included if counseling is to be relevant to life experience. Practice Exercise 3.2 suggests steps for using the microskill of focusing with clients.

Practice Exercise 3.2

Focus Analysis: Reframing Clients' Stories

The microskill of focusing can be beneficial in helping clients gain multiple perspectives on their issues. The following steps are suggested for this exercise with a real or role-played client. Two discussion possibilities for this exercise are (1) an important story told in the family of origin that may have been repeated often, or (2) a story of a conflict in one's own present family or living situation. Specific steps for this exercise follow:

1. *Draw out the story using the basic listening sequence.* Be sure to summarize at the end of the story, paying particular attention to emotions.
2. *Tell the client that you are going to try to look in more detail at the story from several different perspectives.* Make this an egalitarian discussion involving the volunteer client. Clients often cooperate if they understand what and why you are using a particular strategy.
3. *Use focus analysis to help the client find multiple perspectives on the story.* Example questions or statements from each perspective follow. (If the client has already taken a particular focus, there is no need to repeat that one.)
   - *Client focus:* Please tell the story again, but this time let's focus on *you* and *your* feelings throughout.

I'd really like to know what the story means to *you.*
   - *Other focus:* How would your mother/father/sister/friend tell and think about this story or situation? How does the person you live with now think about and tell this story?
   - *Family focus:* How would your family think about this story?
   - *Problem/main theme:* This may seem a bit different, but this time I'd like you to tell the story using the problem named as the focus. If the problem were to tell the story, what would it say?
   - *Interviewer focus* (used in a brief, timely, and sensitive fashion): This is my view of this story.
   - *Relationship with interviewer* (*"we" focus*): How do you feel toward me or think about our relationship as you tell the story?
   - *Cultural/environmental/contextual focus:* How would this story be told from a man or woman's frame of reference? How would it be considered from the point of view of your spirituality or race/ethnicity?
4. Ask your client to summarize what he or she learns or observes from the multiple retelling of the story.

Confrontation

We often think of confrontation as a hostile and aggressive act. In counseling and therapy, confrontation is usually a far more gentle process in which we point out to the client discrepancies between or among attitudes, thoughts, or behaviors. In a confrontation, individuals are faced directly with the fact that they may be saying other than what they mean, or doing other than what they say.

Double messages, incongruities, and discrepancies appear constantly in counseling interviews. A client may present an open right hand and smile while the left hand is closed in a fist. The counselor may be sitting with an open posture while covering the genital area with both hands. The client may say, "I really like my parents" while sitting in closed posture with arms crossed over the chest.

One of the main tasks of counseling is to assist clients to work through, resolve, or learn to live with incongruities. Most counseling theories have as their main focus the resolution of incongruities. Freudians talk about resolving polarities and unconscious conflicts; Gestaltists, about integrating splits; client-centered therapists, about working through mixed feelings; rational-emotive therapists, about the need to attack incongruent irrational thinking; vocational counselors, about the distinction between unreal and real goals . . . the list could continue. The importance of identifying and resolving incongruities cannot be overemphasized.

Examples of ways to confront Suzanne, the client in the above examples, include:

Counselor: You're laughing, but I sense from the tone of your voice and the look on your face that underneath it isn't a laughing matter. [*Confrontation of discrepancy between verbal behavior and nonverbals*]

Counselor: On one hand, you say you want to get out of this relationship with Chuck, but on the other hand, you've been saying this for several months and you're still staying. How do you put that together? [*Confrontation of discrepancy between what is said and what is done*]

A useful model sentence for confrontation is: "On one hand, you think/feel/behave . . . but on the other hand, you think/feel/behave . . ." This model sentence provides the essence of the confrontation statement. It is nonjudgmental and helps clarify the confusing situation faced by the client. Using your hands in a gesture as if weighing the two alternatives can be very useful in emphasizing the contradiction.

An overly confronting, charismatic therapist can retard client growth, as can an overly cautious therapist. Intentional counseling requires a careful balance of confrontation with supporting qualities of warmth, positive regard, and respect. The empathic therapist is one who can maintain a balance, a "push-pull," of confrontation and support by utilizing a wide variety of counseling skills and theories.

Different Skill Patterns for Different Theories

Most systems of counseling and therapy give particular attention to the basic listening sequence. By mastering the foregoing specific skills, you can "mix and match" foundational patterns and apply alternative theories of therapy. Table 3.4 summarizes theoretical orientations in terms of their differential usage of microskills. In this table, it can be seen that client-centered theory primarily uses attending skills and very few questions. Psychodynamic theory makes extensive use of interpretation. Both tend to focus on individual issues. By way of contrast, multicultural therapy focuses on self-in-context and takes a more action-oriented approach.

Each therapeutic system has varying patterns that must be mastered if you are to work within that orientation. However, all systems use basic listening skills to some extent, and once you have mastered these skills, it is easier to move across theoretical orientations into new ways of functioning. When you learn new methods of therapy, you then can build on these skills and frame them into a wide variety of techniques and strategies appropriate to the system you are studying.

Using Microskills as a Treatment Supplement

The concepts of attending behavior (see Research Exhibit 3.1 on p. 57) can be brought into clinical use. Consider an early case example of counseling with a depressed college student who complained that he had no friends and was unable to talk to people. In the here and now of the interview, the counselor taught the student the four main dimensions of attending behavior and then role-played a conversation. The immediate change in the student was dramatic. He took these skills home and practiced them and returned the following week greatly improved. Like most depressed people, this client tended to talk too much about himself and his problems. This self-focus led to a continuous cycle of depression. Learning listening skills, particularly attending behavior and open questioning, helped him focus outwardly and gave him less time to focus narrowly on his own problems. Another benefit was that by listening to others, he was better able to build a solid base for friendships.

This first experience with microskills therapy was followed by several studies on teaching psychiatric patients listening skills (Donk, 1972; Ivey, 1973, 1991). The findings in each of these clinical evaluative studies were that patients could learn the skills that resulted in changes in behavior and were useful in learning job-related skills. This early work also included a major emphasis on family and multicultural issues (Ivey, 1973, p. 342):

> The more important issue in generalization of behavior, however, lies in transfer of the newly learned behavior to society at large. . . . Many families really don't want the

Table 3.4   Microskill Usage According to Theoretical Orientation

Microskill Category	Client-Centered Theory	Psychodynamic Theory	Multicultural Theory
Focus	*Primarily on individual client.* The problem will often be conceptualized as one of understanding one's own unique needs and wishes. A major goal is self-actualization.	*Primarily on individual client.* The problem is understanding how past experience affects what occurs in the present. A major goal is understanding unconscious mental functioning.	*Balance between the individual, family, and multicultural issues.* The problem is thought of as developed in a context. A major goal is helping the client understand self in relation to context and taking action for self and others.
Listening skills	*Central use of listening skills to facilitate client expression;* minimum use of questions. The therapist attempts to minimize influence on client constructions and meaning making. Major emphasis is on reflecting feelings.	*Basic listening sequence used to draw out data relating to psychodynamic theory.* Questions and encouragers are especially important to facilitate exploration of unconscious processes.	*Basic listening sequence used to facilitate client understanding of self-in-system.* The therapist will tend to listen for family and contextual issues that affect client expression of self.
Influencing skills	*Feedback and reflection of meaning most commonly used.* Interpretation and reframes are avoided. There is little or no attempt to lead the client to behavioral action.	*Interpretation is central skill.* In later stages of therapy, interpretations/reframes may be the only skill used. There is little or no attempt to lead the client to behavioral action.	*Varying use of the influencing skills depending on client's cultural context.* In general, there will be a greater emphasis on feedback and self-disclosure to build a more egalitarian relationship. Reframes will often focus on family and cultural issues. There may be an attempt to encourage the client to act on issues and to also consider action in the community and society as well.

behavior of psychiatric patients changed. Change simply disrupts the reinforcement balance within the home. Similarly, society does not necessarily want behavior change. One patient, for example, who had shown marked improvement from depression commented that he really couldn't see any meaning in his routine assembly job. . . . To meet this patient's needs, one can work on cognitive restructuring . . . or, better yet, work on changing the society that helped bring about the psychotic break.

Based on these and other findings, microskills and decisional counseling theory holds that individual change is insufficient. It is also necessary to do therapy, educate, and organize change in the family, the community, the workplace, and the broader cultural context. Training as a treatment modality in this broader change context can be an important part of counseling and therapy.

Decisional Counseling: Pragmatism in Action

As you work in the counseling and therapy field, you will encounter a multitude of theories and practices; some estimates are of over five hundred theories to date, and still increasing! One set of these theories focuses on decision making, although each theory uses similar but different language in its approaches.

The authors and others (e.g., Janis and Mann, 1977) argue that decisional counseling in its various guises dates back to Benjamin Franklin, who is credited for first outlining pragmatic decision making. Following are Franklin's approach to creative problem solving:

1. Define the issue or concern clearly.
2. Generate alternative possibilities for solution.
3. Weigh the positives and negatives of each alternative in a simple balance sheet.
4. Select one alternative for action and see how it works.

Franklin's system is perhaps the ultimate expression of the pragmatic worldview. His discovery of electricity by flying a kite is a particularly apt example of the testing of an idea to see if "it works."

Decisional counseling as presented in this chapter has two major criticisms of Franklin's problem-solving model. Social constructivist thought reminds us that the problem or concern can be defined in very different ways. If we defined a couple's difficulty as "his problem," then we would develop certain ways of approaching the "problem." But if we instead used multiple foci, we would consider the matter very differently. We might think of the issue as the partner's problem, or as a family concern, or as related to the cultural or environmental context (for example, unemployment). If we take a psychodynamic approach, we might view the problem as an issue of development in the family of origin; cognitive-behavioral theory might connect the issue to a lack of skills or some irrational thought pattern. As you work with the pragmatic decisional counseling model, remember that how you define the problem, issue, or concern may be as important as the issue itself.

The decisional model presented here is one of many models found in the field. For example, Egan (1994) has built a theory of helping in the interview based on a three-stage model: reviewing the problem, developing the preferred scenario, and determining how to get there. Each of the three stages are in turn divided into substages, including storytelling, setting up goals, and brainstorming possible resolutions. D'Zurilla (1986) has developed a theory of helping entitled *Problem-Solving Therapy.* Carkhuff (1987) has long been known for his problem-oriented model, and Brammer (1990) has been particularly influential in orienting beginning professionals to creative problem solving. Hansen (1991) draws from the Minnesota trait-and-factor model to derive a gender- and culture-sensitive model of decisional counseling she calls "integrated life planning." The following five-stage microskills model was influenced by the work of Leon Mann (Mann, Beswick, Allouache, & Ivey, 1982) and by the structure for the five-stage interview developed by Ivey and Matthews (1984). Nonetheless, Franklin must be credited as the originator of all these ideas.

The Five-Stage Interview Model: Pragmatic Decisional Counseling

The central theoretical and pragmatic point of the five-stage decisional interview is that *counseling and therapy are not only about decisions, but the interview itself also may be structured using a decision-making framework.* Drawing from social constructivist theory, the five-stage interview is also a way to consider how interviews are conducted through many forms of therapy. This later point will be elaborated as alternative theories are discussed throughout this book.

Table 3.5 presents the five-stage interview model in brief form, identifying key counselor leads for each stage. Vocational counseling, employment counseling, family problem solving, issues of conflict between disputing parties, life planning, retirement counseling, financial advisement, management discussions, nutritional counseling, compliance with medical advice, and even legal counsel can be carried out effectively using this model. In fact, the microskills approach and the five-stage interview model have been used for all of the above purposes and more. Moreover, psychodynamic, cognitive-behavioral, and existential-humanistic theory can be understood in terms of practice if you have mastered this basic model. Later chapters show how to use the five-stage model with other theoretical orientations.

The model as presented is linear, is oriented toward specific problem solving, and moves step by step. The model has been translated into at least fourteen languages and has been proven useful in settings as diverse as alcohol counseling in the central Arctic, manager relations at Mercedes-Benz in Germany, and peer counseling in Hong Kong. In each setting, adaptations must be made for the particular cultural framework. When working with the five-stage decisional counseling model, the following stages and guidelines for individual and multicultural adaptation are important:

Stage 1: Rapport and structuring. The microskills particularly important at this stage are culturally and individually appropriate attending behavior and the ability to observe client reactions, particularly the ability to change the structure and pace

Table 3.5   The Five-Stage Structure of the Interview

Definition of Stage	Function and Purpose of Stage	Cultural and Individual Issues
1. Establishing rapport and structure "Hello. This is what we'll be doing today."	To build a working alliance with the client and to enable the client to feel comfortable with the interviewer. Structuring may be needed to explain the purpose of the interview. Structuring functions to help keep the session on task and to inform the client what the counselor can and cannot do.	With some clients and some cultural groups, rapport development may take a long time so that trust can grow. Methods of rapport development and decision making will vary with individuals and cultures.
2. Gathering data and identifying assets "Tell me your story." "What's your concern?" "What are your strengths?"	To find out why the client has come to the interview and how he or she views the concern. Skillful problem definition will help avoid aimless topic jumping and give the interview purpose and direction. Also to identify clearly positive strengths of the client.	Not all clients appreciate the careful delineation of issues typical of middle-class helping. Solution-oriented approaches minimize this stage.
3. Determining outcomes/ goal setting "What do you want to have happen?"	To find out the ideal world of the client. How would the client like to be? How would things be if the "problem" were solved? This stage is important in that it enables the interviewer to know what the client wants. The desired direction of the client and counselor should be reasonably harmonious. With some clients, skip stage 2 and define goals first.	If work is clear and concrete here, specific resolutions may be immediately apparent. Many cultural groups and individuals prefer to start here. If we know goals, the concern may be clear and we can move to stage 4. This is also characteristic of solution-oriented therapy.
4. Generating alternative solutions "What are we going to do to generate new ideas?" "How could we look at the story differently?"	To work toward resolution of the client's issue. This may involve the creative problem-solving model of generating alternatives (to remove stuckness) and deciding among those alternatives. It also may involve lengthy exploration of personal dynamics. This phase	It is critical that individual and cultural differences in decisional style be acknowledged. What is the "correct" decision from your point of view may be highly inappropriate to another. With some groups, a highly directive style on the counselor's part may be appropriate. In general, listen

Table 3.5   The Five-Stage Structure of the Interview

Definition of Stage	Function and Purpose of Stage	Cultural and Individual Issues
	of the interview may be the longest.	and let the client decide.
5. Generalizing and transferring learning "Will you do it?"	To enable changes in thoughts, feelings, and behaviors in the client's daily life. Can the new story be generalized to the real world?	The degree of generalization will also relate highly to how effectively you took cultural and individual differences into account in the early stages of the session(s).

of the interview to meet individual and cultural needs. Your ability to establish rapport both early in the session and later will be important in establishing an empathic bond between you and the client.

When working with delinquent acting-out youngsters, this stage may take weeks before trust is developed. In Aboriginal Australia, social workers often spend more than half of the interview focusing on family and social interconnections before even asking about the issue to be discussed. With many middle-class people in North America, this stage almost can be omitted, as clients often start talking about their problems quickly. Nonetheless, continual development of rapport and trust throughout the session is vital.

Stage 2: Gathering data and identifying assets. The microskills most associated with this phase of the interview are those of the basic listening sequence. Use the BLS to draw out clients' narratives or stories and also to draw out clients' strengths. Focus analysis can be helpful in enabling clients to see their concerns from varying perspectives. Your ability to summarize clients' stories or issues in their own words is an important part of empathic understanding.

Social constructivism and focus analysis remind us that defining the problem is not as easy as it seems. The pragmatic model of Franklin gives insufficient attention to the fact that the way we define and tell stories of an issue often decide how the issue will be resolved. Is the problem "in the client" and thus an issue of internal locus of control, or is it "in the environment" and thus concerned with contextual issues? Feminist theory, for example, points out that environmental contingencies of sexism are vital issues in any work with women. Some rational-emotive theorists, on the other hand, make the point that "it is not things, but how we think about things." Different approaches to problem definition obviously result in very different ways of constructing the meaning of a "problem."

Some point out that the very use of the word *problem* starts decisional counseling off on the wrong foot. Decisional counseling argues strongly that counseling and therapy are too much about "problems" and suggests that counselors and therapists use the words *issues* or *concerns*. Lanier (1991) notes that many African-Americans object to the concept of "problem" and respond more readily to the use of words such as *issues* or *concerns*. Experience with other racial and ethnic groups reveals that many clients prefer the more open and positive language suggested by Lanier.

Decisional counseling argues for the need to identify positive client strengths in each session. These strengths may include such things as positive childhood experiences, accomplishments in sports or the arts, something the individual is proud of doing, images of supportive relatives, times things were "going right" in the person's life, or the ability to survive a trauma. Positive stories and images help center clients and give them strength to delve more deeply into the difficult areas of their lives.

Stage 3: Determining outcomes. The basic listening sequence and focus analysis are also central tools at this stage. However, at this point the listening sequence focuses on helping the client find positive, clear, and reachable goals. Concreteness, as described in Chapter 2, is essential. Too often counselors fail in this area, as clients are often willing to talk endlessly about their issues but reluctant to talk about what they want to have happen.

Many clients can benefit from an immediate focus on goals. Solution-oriented therapy (O'Hanlon and Weiner-Davis, 1989) gives minimal attention to stages 1 and 2, choosing instead to find out what the client wants to have happen. This approach makes the excellent point that if clients can achieve what they want, there is no need to bother with long stores and definitions of problems and concerns. Solution-oriented therapy, like decisional counseling, focuses on client strengths—what they are already "doing right"—and identifies specific wishes of the client.

Moving directly to goal setting and establishing a story of mutual goals for the interview may help you work more effectively with clients who are culturally different than you. Clients often find it difficult to tell a counselor their stories of life issues and problems if there is a lack of trust due to a history of racism or spiritual oppression.

Finally, the goals of counseling are sometimes established by theorists before the client walks in the door. There are some practitioners who believe that every client needs to understand the unconscious, become self-actualized, or "really look at themselves" in a gender-fair society. Although all of these goals may be laudable, the field increasingly is moving away from this "top-down" approach and is involving clients in establishing their own goals.

Stage 4: Generating alternative solutions. Influencing skills and focus analysis become more important at this stage. Any of a variety of skills or theoretical alternatives may be employed to help clients create new ways of thinking about their stories. Clear discussion of clients' stories and strengths, followed by precise goal setting, is often enough to help clients brainstorm their own solutions. Implied in this is the basic confrontational statement "On the one hand, your issue/problem/concern is . . . and on the other hand, your goal is . . ." Images and stories of strengths may be brought in to help clients act on their issues.

Leon Mann and his colleagues (Mann, Beswick, Allouache, and Ivey, 1982, 1989) used a more sophisticated version of Franklin's model in their balance grid sheet (see Figure 3.4). When clients have important decisions to make, working carefully through each alternative with the balance sheet can clarify actions. The balance sheet considers the effects of decisions on others, not just on the individual. Due to its inclusion of relational issues, the balance sheet has some multicultural and gender validity. The challenge of the balance grid sheet is getting both counselors and clients to "stand still" and actually do it, even though it is demonstrably effective. Thus, talking about alternatives and consequences in a less structured way may be necessary at times. A good question to keep in mind is, Who is resisting the structure—you or the client?

Stage 5. Generalization and transfer of learning. Influencing skills are particularly important at this stage, as you want to ensure that the client actually does something as a result of the session. Special attention to *relapse prevention* (Marlatt &

ALTERNATIVE # _____

GAINS	LOSSES
Material gains for me	Material losses for me
Material gains for others	Material losses for others
Gains in self-approval	Losses in self-approval
Approval by others	Disapproval by others

Figure 3.4 Balance Sheet Grid

SOURCE: From *Decision Workshops for the Improvement of Decision Making Skills* by L. Mann and others, 1982, Adelaide, Australia: Flinders University. Copyright 1982. Used by permission.

Gordon, 1985) is given in Chapters 9 and 10 on cognitive-behavioral methods. Unless you plan for the transfer of decisions and actions in the session, much of your work will be for naught.

One useful strategy at the end of the session is to ask the client the questions: What stands out for you today from our session? or What one thing might you remember from today? These open-ended questions often have surprising results. What we thought was our brilliant intervention may not have even been noticed by the client. Data obtained from these questions often tell us what to do next to ensure that the client returns and/or takes action on the decisions reached.

Mann and colleagues (1982) have used the *future diary* as a technique to facilitate generalization and transfer of learning. Decisions are not just rational but are also deeply linked to emotions. Keeping a future diary helps clients think through the emotional aspects of decision making. In the diary, clients describe a typical day one year in the future, based on the circumstances that might evolve from a particular decision. Future diaries often bring out feeling issues that were not brought out by the more cognitive decisional balance sheet.

These emotional issues can be more easily identified by helping clients generate visual, auditory, or kinesthetic images of their futures. Guided imagery works well as a supplement to decisional counseling, particularly in aiding clients to think ahead to the future.

Decisions do not occur in a vacuum in the counseling office. You and your relationship with the client will impact the client's life. The five-stage model presented here—when coupled with specific decisional research and other models of systematic decision making—can make an important difference in clients' lives. Clients can become vigilant decision makers as a result of your own vigilance and intentionality in the helping process. Practice Exercise 3.3 presents steps in decisional counseling.

Practice Exercise 3.3

 An Exercise in Decisional Counseling

Find a friend or family member who has a decision to make. Ask your "client" if you may take him or her through a systematic decisional program. Good topics for your first attempt include a major purchase, a forthcoming job search, or how to resolve a current problem with a friend or colleague. The following exercise includes the five-stage structure of the interview.

1. *Rapport/structuring.* Spend some time developing rapport and telling your client about the structure of the session that will follow.

2. *Data gathering.* Define the problem clearly and include a positive asset search. You will want to ask about the client's past history with this problem and how he or she has gone about making decisions. Consider

other problem descriptions using focus analysis.

3. *Determine outcomes.* Ask the client what an ideal and specific solution to this problem might be.

4. *Generate alternative solutions.* Use creative decisional models presented in this chapter. Given the clear definition of the problem and the ideal outcome, what alternatives can you and the client generate? Brainstorm as many ideas as possible.

Then, systematically list the alternatives generated and fill in balance sheets as presented in Figure 3.4. Follow this by prioritizing the goals and selecting one alternative for action.

Ask your client to think ahead a year from now and to creatively anticipate how life would be, given the implementation of the favored alternatives. This future diary may be written if you wish. Talk with the client about the future diary and give special attention to the emotions the client has toward this alternative.

Will the client be satisfied and comfortable? You may find that serious examination of the future may bring up new issues and new concerns. For the purpose of this exercise, stay with the original problem as defined and note other problems for a possible follow-up chat.

If the alternative selected does not *feel right* emotionally, consider other alternatives in the client list of priorities.

Finally, ask the client to select one possibility for implementation.

5. *Generalization.* Make a contract with your client to implement the decision or a part of the decision. This may itself take some creativity. Follow up with your client in the next few days to see how the decision is going and, if necessary, encourage the client to "fine-tune" the decision so that minor problems and setbacks do not undermine the total effort. Depending on the issue, develop a systematic long-term plan for generalization.

Microskills and Brief Solution-Oriented Counseling and Therapy

We live in an age that emphasizes accountability and results. Many professionals working in mental health agencies, private practice, and schools are increasingly asked to shorten their time with clients and provide clear evidence of counseling effectiveness. Clients can get lost in this "rush to results," and solution-oriented approaches can sometimes be inadequate substitutes for more intensive therapy and counseling.

Despite these criticisms, brief solution-oriented counseling and therapy (SOCT) is considered an important strategy for counseling and therapy professionals. Authors writing on this strategy all focus on positive strategies and emphasize client respect (de Shazer, 1985; O'Hanlon & Davis, 1989; Talmon, 1990; Berg, 1994; White & Epston, 1992). Brief (one- to ten-session) therapy is not a cure-all but rather a concrete way of providing clients with useful approaches to specific issues and problems that clients can then use in resolving other issues.

SOCT is less useful with clients who have issues concerning the meaning of life or who want to examine their life histories. Clients with these goals may be better served by existential-humanistic or psychodynamic therapy. Clients suffering from severe depression may benefit from some of the short-term solutions offered by SOCT, but cognitive-behavioral or developmental counseling and therapy methods may be of more benefit for these clients. Each of these models can be enhanced by the brief therapy approach to help clients realize specific goals in longer-term therapy.

The purpose of this section is to show how the microskills approach and the five-stage interview structure can enhance SOCT. In addition, by using community and family genograms (see Chapters 1 and 2), SOCT can be made more culturally relevant and sensitive (Kuehl, 1995). However, the efficiency of SOCT may be inappropriate with some cultural groups whose view of time is different than that of European-American culture. In this regard, LaFromboise (1996, p. 5) comments on Native American culture:

> The idea of time is quite different—elongated and more subtle. It's important that you be there when you are needed rather than relying on artificial boundaries. The time for termination needs to be extended. In a sense, your being as a person will be tested more completely than it was in any counseling degree program. There is a tendency to prefer open directive approaches to helping. The reflective, client-centered approach is often viewed with suspicion.
>
> Working with Native American Indians is a wonderful opportunity for counselors and therapists to learn what community means and what it means by waiting for the right time and working with the client's frame. This is a real test of discipline—a chance to be a true friend when you are really needed. You'll also learn humility.

Social constructivists might point out that the meaning of time, of a "problem-oriented" focus, and even of what a "solution" is will be heavily dependent on multicultural issues.

Practice Exercise 3.4 presents the specifics of SOCT from the perspective of microskills and the five-stage interview process, This exercise provides you the opportunity to integrate and practice the ideas presented in the first three chapters. Solution-oriented theorists constantly emphasize the importance of strengths; thus, this practice exercise starts with positive images and stories from the family and community genograms. Microskills theory holds that we can find our greatest strengths as selves-in-relation and that we can draw on our networks of family and community in our search for solutions.

Rapport and structuring are often accorded less time in SOCT. However, relationship is vital, for without a caring, empathic relationship, the chances of finding solutions are reduced. Talmon (1990) stresses that we must structure the interview very early in our search for solutions and suggests that a positive attitude on the part of the counselor is essential in communicating that something

=== **Practice Exercise 3.4** ===

 # Solution-Oriented Counseling and Therapy

The following structured exercise may be used with a volunteer or real client. You should photocopy the following and share it with your client before so that he or she knows very specifically what is going to happen and why. This sharing of interview plans moves you toward coconstruction in the interview (see Chapter 4) and often provides the client with a feeling of safety.

This exercise seeks to integrate the first three chapters of this book. As such, this exercise represents a written outline of all of the practice exercises. It may take you more than an hour to complete, or you may wish to have a second session with your client. Recall that brief therapy is considered anything less than ten sessions.

Stage 1. Rapport and Structuring

Spend some time making the client comfortable in your own way. Share the interview plan in writing and talk about what is to happen.

"What would you like to have happen today?" is a suggested opening question. This opening implies that something is indeed going to happen. Usually the client will express a concern or issue. Use the basic listening sequence to hear the client's story briefly.

Stage 2. Gathering Data and Identifying Assets

Community and Family Genograms
Tell the client that before you go further, you'd like to learn more about his or her family and community situation. Develop on-the-spot brief family and community genograms. This can be done in fifteen minutes as a beginning step. Make it clear that you want to avoid negative stories at this time and that you will focus only on strengths. Later in this session or following sessions, you can focus on other issues that may arise.

It is particularly important to generate two to three positive family and community images and to locate the feelings associated with these images in the body. These are resources and strengths that can be developed later.

Listening to the Client's Concern
Briefly return to the original concern and use the basic listening sequence to draw out the issue in more detail. Even at this early stage, ask questions that focus on positives and may serve as resources. For example: Are things any better now? What's keeping it from getting worse? Are there any good things you observe in the situation?

An essential part of this process is clarifying the narrative. Part of this process is making sure that the concern is presented in a specific, concrete fashion and that clearly observable behaviors are identified. If thoughts or emotions are the issue, being clear and specific is equally important. (Skills in applied behavioral analysis can be particularly useful; see Chapter 9.)

Positive Asset Search

Any of the techniques of the positive asset search (see Chapter 2) may be used here. "What are you already doing right?" is a particularly helpful question. Many clients have strengths that can be drawn on to help them find solutions. You may need to help them define these strengths by giving feedback based on your observations. The community and family strengths should again be noted. If you cannot find something positive in the client—refer!

Stage 3. Determining Outcomes

"What do you want to happen?" is the basic question of the third stage of the five-stage structure and is even more important in SOCT. Be aware of your client. You may want to introduce this central question even in the first phases of rapport and structuring. Your task as counselor or therapist is to clarify, specify, and concretize goals. Without clear-cut directions and goals, SOCT will not succeed. It may be helpful to write down with your client the specific *achievable* goal(s) you have defined. The goal should be simple. If the problem or issue is large, work only on a part rather than the whole.

After goal setting, the major focus of your session will be on how to achieve those goals. Use the client's own main words and language for the goals. If the client's first language is other than English, write the goals in the client's language as well.

Stages 4 and 5. Generating Alternative Solutions

In SOCT, the stages of generating alternative solutions and generalizing and

transferring learning are combined. This combination stage focuses on brainstorming possibilities that meet client goals and requires a good deal of creativity from you and your client. Essentially, your joint task is to create new solutions to old issues and to act on these solutions—ideally in the near term.

Throughout the following steps, draw on strengths and positive assets noted earlier in the session. Both you and your client should feel free to refer to this list, especially during your first attempts at SOCT.

Brainstorming Suggestions

Some examples of questions that may be useful include:

- Tell me about times when the problem is absent or less strong. What is happening?
- What are exceptions to the problem? When does the problem not happen?
  What is different about those times?
  How do you get to that more positive result?
  What did you do (they do) to get a more satisfactory ending?

From a different vantage point, the following questions are sometimes helpful:

- What do you do for fun? (This breaks the mind-set and may provide surprising answers.)
- What could be funny about the issue? (Using humor and surprise in a culturally sensitive fashion may be exceptionally helpful.)
- How does your family and culture relate to these issues?
- What supports or answers do they provide?

Family and Multicultural Issues
The family and community genograms often provide new ideas, positive assets, and support at this stage. The following questions can be based on these charts:

- Drawing on your image of the elder in your family, how would he or she look at this issue?
- Imagine the elder is standing at your shoulder. What would he or she say to you right now?
- Your community (or group) has many strengths. Where would you go for support with some of these issues?

Taking It Home
Aim constantly for generalization of new ideas about and resolutions to issues in daily life. The more specific the joint solution, the more possibility there will be of something actually happening as a result of this session. You may even want to write a contract for action in both English and your client's own language (if it is different).

As part of the brainstorming and transfer-of-learning process, the following questions may be helpful:

- How will your life be different?
- Who will be the first to notice change?
  What will he or she do or say?
  How will you respond?
- What would you like to happen?
- How can we make that happen?

Rehearsal and role-playing, using the concepts of assertiveness training (see Chapter 9) are useful here. The specificity and immediacy of these techniques are helpful because assertiveness training in itself is a brief therapy. Do not hesitate to add other theories and strategies according to the needs of your client. Relapse prevention, another cognitive-behavioral strategy, may be very useful at this point to ensure generalization and transfer of learning.

Follow-up
Use the telephone or e-mail to follow up and provide support. Encourage the client to call in and tell you how things are going. Remind the client that he or she can contact you later for another session to work on another part of the issue.

can be done to help. Thus, in Stage 1, during the first few minutes of the session, the counselor should emphasize that something can be done, both in the short and longer term, to make a positive difference in the client's life. Although the basic listening sequence remains important, SOCT holds that most counselors and therapists spend too much time listening to problems and issues. Therefore, the second stage—gathering data and identifying assets—should be brief and to the point. Although feelings are noted and reacted to sensitively, solution-oriented counselors are more focused on concrete and specific action. As part of this action approach, the positive asset search and emphasis on client strengths are emphasized constantly in the session.

"What do you want to have happen?" is the essence of the third stage of the five-stage interview structure. In SOCT, goal setting is the centerpiece of effective intervention. Practice Exercise 3.4 provides several specifics for setting goals and determining outcomes with clients. Stages 4 and 5 of the five-stage structure are often combined into one stage in SOCT. As each solution is brainstormed, the therapist immediately focuses on how the client could take the problem resolution into the real world of daily life. Transfer of training is particularly important in solution-focused counseling.

Solution-oriented counseling and therapy is keenly aware that resolving issues in a limited number of sessions does not remake the client. Therapy does not seek "cures." Rather, SOCT often asks clients to think about counseling and therapy sessions as similar to stopping for gas at a service station. This attitude might be expressed as follows: "All of us problems and concerns from time to time. We've worked on this issue over three sessions, and you've achieved some real progress. But new issues will present themselves again in the future. Think of me and our center as a place to come back to when new concerns arise. It may be six weeks or six months or six years, but I look forward to seeing you again when you'd like to explore what is happening in your life."

The idea that "there is no life-long cure" seems a useful one. All of us face issues constantly, and long-term therapy may help us find meaning or understand our developmental history. But, even with the best long-term therapy, specific issues (divorce, death, living with a serious illness) may lead a client back to therapy again and again. SOCT offers a useful model to be used in conjunction with traditional methods. At times we need to examine life in depth, but often many clients will do well with short-term specific efforts to resolve their concerns.

Limitations and Practical Implications of the Decisional and Microskills Approach

The decisional and microskills approach is noted for its precision and clear description of behavior. Although early presentations of the model did not take cultural issues into account, the precision of the approach led to its current, hopefully more culturally sensitive, presentation. It is now an axiom of the microskills approach that all interviews must take into account both individual and multicultural differences.

The microskills of attending and listening "work" and are clear and teachable. They should, however, be used in a culturally and individually appropriate fashion. There is a danger in teaching culturally inappropriate skills to trainees, particularly those skills that are effective and precise in description.

The first author of this book worked with Matthew Rigney, a highly skilled Aboriginal social worker in Australia, in jointly examining the multicultural implications of attending. Matthew was videotaped interviewing a client in the "Aboriginal way," which involved limited eye contact and a more self-disclosing and participative style of interviewing. On reviewing the tape, Matthew commented, "You mean it's OK to do counseling in our people's way?" Despite his obvious skill, Matthew had come to believe that only the European-Australian style of listening was appropriate. Needless to say, he was encouraged to maintain and sharpen his traditional ways of listening. Matthew Rigney is very much alive in the ideas presented in this chapter and in this book.

And at the present time, many people in Australia, Canada, and the United States continue to teach and use microskills and decisional counseling in a culturally insensitive manner. Some books still discuss attending without attention to cultural differences. Needless to say, this gap between theory and practice is not solely associated with the microskills approach. Individualistic psychodynamic and client-centered theories are also transported to relational cultures and presented as "the way to conduct interviewing and therapy." Powerful and intrusive Gestalt techniques may be highly effective in North America, but they can be highly inappropriate in other settings. Cognitive-behavioral techniques, like microskills, are often useful in other cultural settings, but require serious cultural modification to ensure that they are appropriate.

REFERENCES

BAKER, S., & DANIELS, T. (1989). Integrating research on the microcounseling program: A meta-analysis. *Journal of Counseling Psychology, 35*, 213–22.

BAKER, S., DANIELS, T., & GREELEY, A. (1990). Systematic training of graduate-level counselors: Narrative and meta-analytic reviews of three major programs. *Counseling Psychologist, 18*, 355–421.

BERG, I. (1994). *Family-based services: A solution-based approach.* New York: Norton.

BERMAN, J. (1979). Counseling skills used by Black and White and male and female counselors. *Journal of Counseling Psychology, 26*, 81–84.

BRAMMER, L. (1990). *The helping relationship.* Englewood Cliffs, NJ: Prentice-Hall.

CARKHUFF, R. (1987). *The art of helping VI.* Amherst, MA: Human Resource Development Press.

CHEATHAM, H. (1990). Empowering Black families. In H. Cheatham & J. Stewart (Eds.), *Black families* (pp. 373–93). New Brunswick, NJ: Transaction Press.

DANIELS, T. (1985). *Microcounseling: Training in skills of therapeutic communication with RN department program nursing students.* Unpublished doctoral dissertation, Dalhousie University, Halifax, Nova Scotia.

DANIELS, T., AND IVEY, A. (in press). *Microcounseling* (3rd ed.). Springfield, IL: Thomas.

DAVISON, G. (1991). Constructionism and morality in therapy for homosexuality. In J. Gonsiorek & J. Weinrach (Eds.), *Homosexuality: Research implications for public policy.* Newbury Park, CA: Sage.

DE SHAZER, S. (1985). *Keys to solution in brief therapy.* New York: Norton.

DONK, L. (1972). *Attending behavior in mental patients: Dissertation Abstracts International, 33* (Ord. No. 72-22, 569).

D'ZURILLA, T. (1996). *Problem-solving therapy.* New York: Springer.

EGAN, G. (1994). *The skilled helper.* Pacific Grove, CA: Brooks/Cole

HACKNEY, R., IVEY, A., & OETTING, E. (1970). Attending, island, and hiatus behavior: A process conception of counselor and client interaction. *Journal of Counseling Psychology, 17*, 342–46.

HANSEN, S. (1991). Integrative life planning: Work, family, community. *Futurics, 15*, 80–86.

IVEY, A. (1971). *Microcounseling: Innovations in interviewing training.* Springfield, IL: Thomas.

IVEY, A. (1973). Media therapy: Educational change planning for psychiatric patients. *Journal of Counseling Psychology, 20,* 338–43.

IVEY, A. (1988). *Managing face-to-face communication.* Lund, Sweden: Studentlitteratur, Chartwell Bratt.

IVEY, A. (1991, October). *Media therapy reconsidered.* Paper presented at Veterans Administration Conference, Orlando, FL.

IVEY, A. (1994). *Intentional interviewing and counseling* (3rd ed.). Pacific Grove, CA: Brooks/Cole.

IVEY, A., & AUTHIER, J. (1978). *Microcounseling: Innovations in interviewing, counseling, psychotherapy, and psychoeducation* (2nd ed.). Springfield, IL: Thomas.

IVEY, A., & GLUCKSTERN, N. (1974). *Basic attending skills.* North Amherst, MA: Microtraining.

IVEY, A., GLUCKSTERN, N., & IVEY, M. (1992). *Basic attending skills* (3rd ed.). North Amherst, MA: Microtraining.

IVEY, A., & MATTHEWS, W. (1984). A meta-model for structuring the clinical interview. *Journal of Counseling and Development, 63,* 237–43.

IVEY, A., NORMINGTON, C., MILLER, C., MORRILL, W., & HAASE, R. (1968). Microcounseling and attending behavior: An approach to pre-practicum counselor training. *Journal of Counseling Psychology, 15,* 1–12.

JANIS, I., & MANN, L. (1977). *Decision making: A psychological analysis of conflict, choice, and commitment.* New York: Free Press.

KELLY, G. (1955). *The psychology of personal constructs* (Vols. 1 and 2). New York: Norton.

KUEHL, B. (1995). The solution-oriented genogram: A collaborative approach. *Journal of Marital and Family Therapy, 21,* 239–50.

LAFROMBOISE, T. (1996). On multicultural issues. *Microtraining Newsletter,* p. 5.

LANIER, J. (1991). Personal communication, Sangamon State University, Springfield, IL.

MACFARLANE, K., & FELDMETH, J. (1988). *Child sexual abuse: The clinical interview.* New York: Guilford.

MANN, L., BESWICK, G., ALLOUACHE, P., & IVEY, M. (1982). *Decision workshops for the improvement of decision making skills.* Adelaide, Australia: Flinders University.

MANN, L., BESWICK, G., ALLOUACHE, P., & IVEY, M. (1989). Decision workshops for the improvement of decision making: Skills and confidence. *Journal of Counseling and Development, 67,* 478–81.

MARLATT, G., & GORDON, J. (1985). *Relapse prevention: Maintenance strategies in the treatment of addictive behaviors.* New York: Guilford.

NWACHUKU, U. (1989). *Culture-specific counseling: The Igbo case.* Unpublished doctoral dissertation, University of Massachusetts, Amherst.

NWACHUKU, U. (1990, July). *Translating multicultural theory into direct action: Culture-specific counseling.* Paper presented at the International Roundtable for the Advancement of Counseling, Helsinki, Finland.

NWACHUKU, U., & IVEY, A. (1991). Culture specific counseling: An alternative approach. *Journal of Counseling and Development, 70,* 106–11.

O'HANLON, W., & WEINER-DAVIS, M. (1989). *In search of solutions.* New York: Norton.

PARSONS, F. (1967). *Choosing a vocation.* New York: Agathon. (Original work published 1909)

SUE, D. (1990). Culture-specific strategies in counseling: A conceptual framework. *Professional Psychology, 21,* 424–33.

TALMON, M. (1990). *Single session therapy.* San Francisco: Jossey-Bass.

WHITE, M., & EPSTON, D. (1992). *Narrative means to therapeutic ends.* New York: Norton.

Developmental Counseling and Therapy: Individual and Family Therapy

Sandra A. Rigazio-DiGilio, Allen E. Ivey,
Mary Bradford Ivey, Lynn Simek-Morgan

CHAPTER GOALS

This chapter seeks to help you:

1. Identify the postmodern holistic worldview underlying DCT.
2. Use DCT assessment and treatment strategies, which can be used to classify emotions, cognitions, and behaviors in the immediacy of the interview, and help clients[1] understand and work with their issues from multiple perspectives.
3. Understand systemic cognitive-developmental therapy (SCDT), which provides assessment and treatment strategies that can be used to work with couples and families.
4. Examine DCT and SCDT metatheory, which can be used to design comprehensive, developmentally oriented, culturally sensitive treatment plans by organizing strategies—within and across various psychotherapy models—in a coconstructive, developmental, and integrative metaframework.
5. Through practice exercises, to
   - Assess client meaning making within four cognitive-developmental orientations
   - Utilize specific questions to facilitate client conversation and narratives within the four cognitive-developmental orientations
   - Examine your own family of origin and how family members and you have coconstructed meaning, thoughts, behaviors, and relationships

- Utilize specific questions to facilitate family conversation and narratives within the four cognitive-developmental orientations
- Identify your own personal style, present competencies, and counseling and therapeutic goals

The five practice exercises in this chapter (plus those of the preceding three chapters) will enable you to approach the four major counseling and psychotherapy forces—psychodynamic, cognitive-behavioral, existential-humanistic, and multicultural counseling and therapy—with rigor and understanding. Moreover, you will be able to engage in the strategies these theories offer with more expertise, confidence, and skill.

A Figure to Figure: What Is Your Perspective?

What occurs for you when you focus on the Gestalt image in Figure 4.1? Take a moment to record your perspective.

This figure is usually described as reflecting an "old woman" and a "young woman." At first glance, some see the older woman, whereas others see the younger. Take some time until you can see both. Some individuals find it difficult to see the second woman, which can indicate a form of "stuckness" that reflects a lack of intentionality or an inability to take an alternative perspective.

As you focus on the figure more intensely, you will find that the images alternate, and you can see both figures move from one to another as if in a motion picture. With further concentration, you can obtain a "still photo" and see both women at once.

There are also multicultural implications in the figure. Why, for example, is the woman with the larger nose often considered "ugly," whereas the woman with the smaller nose is often considered "beautiful"? There are no "real" reasons that one woman is more beautiful than the other. In fact, in ancient Greece, a large nose was deemed a sign of beauty, and in Italy, a sign of strength. Our perceptions and interpretations often come from our cultural perspectives and learnings. We may think we "see what is real," yet we may fail to realize that our environment affects the way information enters our minds. *At times our existing culturally based assumptions and learnings direct our sense impressions and the meaning we make of these impressions.*

This chapter is about *multiple seeing*, or the ability to take several perspectives on the psychotherapy process. Whether you work from a single theory, adopt an eclectic approach, or develop your own integrative framework, the ability to apply theories and see clients from multiple perspectives is invaluable.

The DCT Postmodern Worldview

Developmental counseling and therapy (DCT) (Ivey, 1986, 1991) is an integrated theory of assessment and treatment that is representative of postmodern thought. Typically, Western and European psychotherapy theories seek to discover the

Figure 4.1 A Figure to Figure: What Is Your Perspective?

SOURCE: From original drawing by W. E. Hill, published in *Puck*, November 6, 1905. First used for psychological purposes by E. G. Boring, "A New Ambiguous Figure," *American Journal of Psychology*, 1930.

unique, "true" nature of the self. Postmodern theory instead argues that the self constantly changes in interaction with different contexts over time. DCT provides tools and strategies that can assist clinicians to identify the unique ways individuals think, feel, and act while in interaction with their environment and while dealing with particular life tasks. By understanding how people construct meaning, practitioners can design treatment plans that are in concert with each individual's personal way of understanding and operating in the world.

Philosophical Base

Conceptually, the support for viewing issues from multiple perspectives is grounded in postmodern theory. Rather than advocating for a single best theory or approach, the postmodern paradigm rests on the *narrative of possibility* (e.g., Gergen, 1994; Polkinghorne, 1992). Traditional psychological theory draws from Descartes in that it searches for a single narrative and the ultimate truth. Alternatively, postmodern theory draws from Kant in its focus on the many selves that interact and shift in relation to differing contexts. Miller (1991) uses the term *self-in-relation* to address the issue of multiple selves in multiple relations. Postmodern theory reminds us that these selves change continuously in different contexts over time.

How does the postmodern view relate to psychotherapy? DCT theorists suggest that all assessment and intervention strategies represent one part of a larger network of possibilities that changes throughout the therapeutic process. The client, the psychotherapist, and the therapeutic relationship also change over time and in response to different circumstances (Ivey, 1986, 1991). Individuals, families, groups, communities, and cultures are simultaneously seen as entities, and as part of a broader interdependent whole. DCT provides a coherent framework from which to view these multiple aspects of psychotherapy within a unified, developmental, and co-constructive perspective.

Theoretical Base

The pragmatics of DCT rest on an adaptation and reinterpretation of Piagetian theory (Piaget, 1926/1963, 1965). Piaget found that children construct knowledge within four levels of thought. Historically, Piaget's observations have had only limited use in adolescent and adult psychotherapy. More recently, however, there has been a gradual burgeoning of conceptual work with adults using Piagetian constructs (see Basseches, 1984; Kegan, 1982, 1994; Loevinger, 1976; Rosen, 1985). The language of these theorists may differ, but all ultimately adapt and extend Piaget's work.

DCT's central assumption is that children, adolescents, and adults *metaphorically* repeat Piagetian stages of development (i.e., sensorimotor, concrete, formal, post-formal) as they encounter different contexts and life tasks over time. However, although Piaget stressed the importance of moving to higher, more complex forms of thinking, DCT values each style of cognition, emotion, and behavior. There is as much value in experiencing the world directly at the sensorimotor level as there is at complex, abstract levels. According to DCT, *a higher developmental level is not better; each perspective is different and clarifies the whole, and, in turn, the whole is changed by each new perspective.*

DCT translates Piaget's stages to represent four "orientations" that need to be considered and worked through during the psychotherapy process: sensorimotor/elemental, concrete/situational, formal/reflective, and dialectic/systemic. Each orientation taps different frames of reference within the whole, and together all four orientations provide an organizing framework for the psychotherapy field.

Practical Base

DCT is a holistic framework that depends on multiple perspectives. For example, DCT, as a model of treatment, suggests that effective practice is based on a synthesis of the following psychotherapy dimensions: (1) an empathic relationship with a skilled clinician, (2) the inclusion of decisional counseling issues, and (3) theoretical and multicultural variables that modify these two dimensions and offer alternative perspectives. Additionally, as an integrative metaframework, DCT offers a paradigmatic bridge that connects supposedly antagonistic worldviews. In this regard, DCT finds value in individualistic psychodynamic and cognitive-behavioral approaches as well as in interdependent feminist, systemic, and multicultural approaches. Multiple seeing demands multiple realities in order to maintain a holistic view.

DCT and Multicultural Counseling and Therapy

Basic to DCT is that multicultural issues deeply influence the way we think about and coconstruct our reality. Psychotherapy is usually thought of as a two-person relationship—specifically, a relationship between a clinician and a client. More recently, we have come to see that the therapeutic relationship is broader. For example, some suggest that the interview is not just a relationship between individuals physically present in the session (see Clement, 1983; Lacan, 1966/1977). When you think you are reacting to the client or the client is reacting to you, each person may actually be acting from their own encapsulated historical and cultural background (see Figure 4.2).

Most traditional psychotherapy frameworks focus solely on the client-practitioner relationship. DCT and multicultural theory also stress that understanding the wider context (e.g., family, groups, community, culture) is essential if clinicians are to work effectively and holistically. The DCT community genogram (see Chapter 1) is designed to bring these tacit influences to the surface.

DCT was influenced by many of the ideas of multicultural counseling and therapy (Chapters 5 and 6). For example, Cross (1995) suggests that along with personal

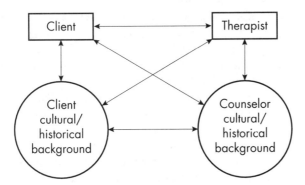

Figure 4.2 The Influence of Cultural/Historical Background on the Interview

SOURCE: From *Developmental Therapy: Theory into Practice* (p. 321) by A. E. Ivey, 1986, San Francisco: Jossey Bass. Copyright 1986 by Jossey-Bass, Inc. Used by permission.

identities, individuals also possess multiple identities of self (e.g., a racial/ethnic self, a gender-related self, a spiritual self). As people, we are complex, and DCT assists clinicians to explore the multiplicity of selves present in the psychotherapy relationship within a culturally sensitive frame, as contrasted with traditional models of psychotherapy, which seek to find the "real" self within a culturally neutral frame.

Central DCT Constructs of Integrating Skills and Theory

Drawing from a holistic worldview that is developmental and focuses on self-in-relation, DCT is based on three central constructs: (1) the coconstructive nature of relationships and knowledge, (2) a reformulation of Piagetian cognitive stages for use in the immediacy of psychotherapy sessions, and (3) a spherical metaframework that integrates the multiple voices of psychotherapy.

Coconstructing Our World through Assimilation and Accommodation

Our minds, through interaction with our environments, build structures or theories about our world. Piaget (1985) used the concept of schema[2] theory to describe the development and modification of these mental structures. Each client has developed schema about the world that they coconstructed in relation to others (e.g., family, culture) over time. DCT posits that the clinician's task is to understand clients' current schema and to appreciate the family and cultural influences evident in such conceptions of the world. At times, it is also the clinician's task to help clients generate enhanced or transformed schema, thus providing for a wider range of cognitive, affectual, and behavioral options.

Piaget used the processes of assimilation and accommodation to explain how schema are created and modified. Assimilation and accommodation represent two sides of the same process. Through accommodation, we receive (and possibly transform) stimuli from the environment, whereas through assimilation, we act on and impose our perspectives on the environment. Like yin and yang, both are inseparable, even though one may be primarily operative at a certain time. Piaget hypothesized that balancing these two aspects of operating within the world constitutes the adaptive process of development.

Through assimilation and accommodation the individual seeks to balance intrapersonal, interpersonal, and environmental pressures. Sociocultural factors may force an imbalance, which results in an increase of pain and suffering. DCT provides a wide framework in which to consider these factors as well as other situations directly affecting our clients. For instance, sociocultural, political, and environmental tragedies often result in an increase in people seeking psychotherapy. By way of illustration, mental health referrals increased after the assassination of Israeli prime minister Yitzhak Rabin, and the environmental disruption caused by the flooding of the Mississippi River resulted in an increase in suicide and abuse referrals. A clinician must be aware that issues affecting the client, the client's social network, and the client's wider community may cause an imbalance between assimilation and accommodation.

In assimilation we use our constructions of knowledge—our schema—to understand and act on our world. For example, Freud and Skinner used tightly organized schema to explain human behavior. An abused child may use a rigidly assimilated schema about the world in relationships with others. Assimilated knowledge represents what we have internalized over time as a result of our interactions with our environments.

One task of psychotherapy is to help clients who are overly reliant on assimilation to identify more adaptive schema by accommodating alternative views of the world. When clients who overassimilate encounter new events or stimuli, they first try to fit these into their existing schema. Sometimes the data do not fit, and clients cannot or will not integrate the new information. This represents rigid assimilated schema. Accommodation occurs when clients can use alternative data to modify old schema or build entirely new schema. A danger here, of course, is that we might inadvertently help clients accommodate or adapt to oppressive systems or situations. This is a danger we as therapists should be aware of and try to avoid. Interculturally focused supervision and collaboration are recommended for all counselors until their ability to view treatment planning from a multicultural frame of reference becomes commonplace.

The empathic attitude defined in Chapter 2 and the microskills framework outlined in Chapter 3 are oriented toward helping clinicians enter the client's coconstructed worldview. Simply listening to and hearing how clients experience, interpret, and act on the world may be sufficient for change. This point is made clearly by Rogers (see Chapter 11). In such cases, clinicians focus on accommodating to and learning from their clients. Moreover, when practitioners repeat back (i.e., encourage, paraphrase, reflect feelings, and summarize) what clients say, they will be able to accommodate the new ideas and modify or transform their schema. Rogerian client-centered therapy, for example, may be described as a primarily accommodative theory, as the focus is on clients' constructions of the world.

Some theories and clinicians, however, use a primarily assimilative mode. In these instances, the therapeutic task is to encourage clients to enter the worldview of the clinician. For example, you will find that many clients in behavioral therapy tend to talk about their lives using the language of behaviorism. DCT argues for a balance between accommodative and assimilative approaches to human change.

Coconstructing Relationships and Knowledge

DCT posits that clients and clinicians learn together. The word *coconstruction* is similar to the "self-in-relation" concept of feminist and systemic psychotherapies and of holistic Afrocentric theory in that coconstruction emphasizes the importance of interdependence between therapist and client. Thinking of relationships and knowledge as coconstructed represents a move toward less hierarchical, more egalitarian clinician-client relationships. This type of relationship is difficult to achieve and maintain and requires counselors to consciously monitor the interactive process of the psychotherapeutic alliance and to guard against superimposing their own perceptions, or the perceptions of the dominant society, onto their clients.

Psychotherapy theory traditionally starts with the worldview of the theorist. Therapists later apply the theory, and its associated set of techniques, to clients. For example, when clients go through psychoanalysis, a Freudian worldview likely will influence the process and outcomes. Through free association, dream analysis, and related techniques, clients gradually learn to talk about their problems in Freud's language and eventually may come to accept the Freudian worldview as truth. In essence, Freud's voice becomes the client's voice.

In a landmark film, a client named Gloria is interviewed by Carl Rogers, Fritz Perls, and Albert Ellis (Shostrum, 1966). Through a detailed linguistic analysis, researchers found that Gloria assumed the language pattern of each clinician (Meara, Shannon, & Pepinsky, 1979; Meara, Pepinsky, Shannon, & Murray, 1981). She used client-centered language with Rogers, Gestalt language with Perls, and rational-emotive language with Ellis.

In a variation on this theme, Chasin, Grunebaum, and Herzig (1990) show how family clinicians influence client conceptualizations, experiences, and actions. A couple, Larry and Jennifer, met with four clinicians (James Framo, Peggy Papp, Norman Paul, Carlos Sluzski), each of whom represented different vantage points in systemic therapy. The authors show how each interview "led" to a different "reality" about the couple. As the work was not intended to demonstrate the superiority of any one approach, a context was set for the couple, with each clinician, to coconstruct multiple perspectives on the issues. The couple recognized that each interview offered only a partial approximation of reality and noticed the expanded range of options created by the combination of all four sessions. This research demonstrates the conceptual possibilities and practical limitations inherent in any one perspective and emphasizes the need to guard against imposing one's personal reality as the truth. DCT and the family oriented SCDT model provide conceptual tools to develop multiple perspectives about clients' issues and to examine the interchange between clinician and client. In this way, the application of DCT and SCDT works toward a more egalitarian integration of client and clinician perspectives.

Translating Piagetian Cognitive Stages to Adolescent and Adult Development

Learning how to recognize client cognitive-developmental orientations in the here and now of the interview can facilitate a clinician's assessment and treatment planning abilities. This skill also can help clinicians to guard against the unintentional imposition of their constructs on the clients they serve. In DCT, cognitive-developmental orientations are defined as the different types of cognitive, emotional, and behavioral reference points that individuals rely on to experience, understand, and operate in their worlds.

The DCT counseling process consists of (1) identifying the primary and secondary cognitive-developmental orientations used by clients to describe their treatment issues and (2) constructing developmentally appropriate, culturally sensitive treatment plans tailored to the unique needs of each client.

Identifying Client Cognitive-Developmental Orientations

Piaget talks of four major stages of cognitive development. DCT uses Piagetian thinking as a metaphor and speaks of four cognitive-developmental orientations that appear and reappear within individuals as they understand and operate in their worlds. Clients function within sensorimotor/elemental, concrete/situational, formal/reflective, and/or dialectic/systemic orientations. Although clients may have access to cognitive, emotional, and behavioral resources inherent in several orientations, most tend to rely on a primary orientation to understand and react to their specific issues.

An important task for DCT practitioners is to enter the world of the client—to understand and appreciate how the client makes sense of and operates in that world. Clients make meaning within four cognitive-developmental orientations (see Table 4.1).[3] Each orientation involves a different complexity of language that represents the client's meaning-making process. Clients talk about their experiences within these different orientations. Some clients will operate within only one orientation (*rigid access*). Others will randomly or haphazardly present several orientations (*diffuse access*). Still others will move, in an organized way, from orientation to orientation throughout an interview or treatment series (*flexible access*).

For example, consider counseling work with Michael, a client going through a divorce. During the treatment process, he talks about the divorce from several orientations. As you read the following, keep in mind that it is likely that clients who use several orientations will need you to provide therapeutic environments that offer varying types of psychotherapy strategies corresponding to each orientation being accessed.

- *Sensorimotor/Elemental*—Tears are present. Michael talks in a random, confused fashion and simultaneously denies feelings of hurt and anger. However, there are times when Michael is able to directly experience his hurt and confusion.

- *Concrete/Situational*—Michael gives many details and tells many stories related to the divorce. He names feelings around situations, but there is an absence of self-reflection as well as considerable blaming and anger toward his spouse.

- *Formal/Reflective*—Michael talks more abstractly. He seldom discusses the specifics of what happened between him and his wife. Rather, he defines repeating patterns and is able to reflect on himself and his feelings.

- *Dialectic/Systemic*—Michael sees multiple perspectives regarding his pending divorce and can see his wife's frame of reference. He realizes how he learned

Table 4.1   Cognitive-Developmental Orientations and Associated Psychotherapy Issues

Cognitive-Developmental Orientations	Emotional Expressions	Psychotherapy Issues	Associated Interventions and Goals
Sensorimotor/Elemental			
(What are the *elements of experience?*) Clients are able to experience life directly in the immediate here and now. They can become enmeshed in sensory experience and in what they directly see, hear, and feel. They may show randomness in their conversation and behavior. They may lack conscious awareness of environmental issues.	Two types of emotion represent the sensori-motor orientation: (1) emotion is integrated with cognition—"I am my emotions"—with direct access to affective experience; and (2) emotions are split off and unrecognized, as can happen with an adult survivor of child abuse or of an alcoholic family, or a person who is unaware of or denies family/cultural issues.	Counselors and therapists, who are often primarily formal operational, may be weak in skills within this level. They may prefer to talk *about* feelings rather than experience them *directly.* A trainee once said, "I used to think I was good with feelings. Now I know I use formal operational thought and reflect on my feelings rather than experiencing them."	*Interventions:* Focus on the here and now and bring the client to awareness—Gestalt exercises, body work, Freire's (1972) use of images to expand consciousness of cultural issues are all helpful. *Goal:* To help client experience the world directly; remove denial and splitting; accept randomness.
Concrete/Situational			
(What are the *situational descriptions?*) Clients may describe their life events in great detail—"This happened . . . , then this . . . and so on." They are concerned with action in the world and with objective, observable events. Some clients will be able to establish cause and effect—if/then—thinking.	Clients can name emotions but are unable to reflect on them. In the early phases, naming of emotions will be all that can be done. Later, clients will begin to realize that emotions are related to events in a "causal" fashion. The classic counseling response "You feel . . . because . . ." is a particularly clear example of concrete emotions.	Many formal operational counselors often become bored and frustrated with concrete stories and details. However, Piagetian scholars estimate that from 25 to 40 percent of North American adults do not primarily access full formal operations (G. Forman, personal communication, 1985).	*Interventions:* Focus on action—assertiveness training, decision making on a specific issue, reality therapy, and many behavioral techniques can be useful. *Goal:* To draw out the specifics of a situation and later cultivate if/then thinking and predictable actions.
Formal/Reflective			
(What is the nature of *self* and repeating *patterns of self, thought, and*	Clients working within this orientation can reflect on their feelings	Much counseling and therapy theory exists primarily within the	*Interventions:* Focus on analysis—Rogerian, psychodynamic,

Table 4.1   (continued)

Cognitive-Developmental Orientations	Emotional Expressions	Psychotherapy Issues	Associated Interventions and Goals
action?) Clients are able to move out of the concrete world and deal with abstractions. They like to think about themselves and their personal patterns of feeling and thinking. They can reflect on their feelings (but may not be able to experience them in the here and now of sensorimotor experience). They are able to analyze and look at their problems with more distance.	and examine patterns of feelings. They may even be able to examine patterns of patterns. But this ability to reflect on self and feelings may make it difficult to experience emotion in the sensorimotor here and now. Also, despite their ability to analyze feelings, the formal client may be unable to act on them.	formal orientation. For example, Rogerian client-centered theory requires one to be able to reflect on feelings, although the microskill of reflection of feelings can be useful within all cognitive orientations. Many therapists and counselors like to work with formal operational clients, as they tend to be verbal and see patterns. The danger is in a client-therapist relationship that is all talk and no action.	and much of cognitive theory are useful. *Goal:* To help clients look at themselves and their life patterns.
Dialectic/Systemic			
(How did all this develop in a *system* or how is it *integrated?*) Clients are able to reflect on reflections and can work with comfort on systems of operations. They are capable of multiple perspectives and are able to identify how family and cultural pressures affect them and their thinking processes. They may become enmeshed in abstract cognitive processes, with emotion markedly split off from experience.	Clients will see emotions changing with situational context (for example, sadness about death when faced with the immediacy of a loss, but also happiness that a terminally ill parent no longer has to suffer). Emotions are multidimensional and complex. At the same time, this awareness may interfere with an ability to experience feelings directly or to act on these.	More and more counselors and therapists are moving beyond formal thinking to this broader, more contextual and multiculturally aware frame of reference. The dialectic/systemic frame of reference allows one to take a more metatheoretical, integrative approach to the field. When you generate your own theory or metatheory of helping, you are engaged in dialectic/systemic thought.	*Interventions:* Focus on construction. Consciousness-raising theories—multicultural counseling and therapy, feminist therapy, and much of family therapy is useful here. *Goal:* To facilitate integrative and multiperspectival thought and awareness of self-in-relation to others and the system.

patterns in his family of origin that are repeated in his relationships. Multicultural issues of gender, ethnicity, and religion become part of his awareness.

It is important that clinicians match their language and treatment techniques with the orientation primarily influencing a client's feeling, thinking, acting, and response to certain issues. For example, it would not be effective to try to have a male client working within a sensorimotor framework to formally analyze how he contributed to a pending divorce. DCT suggests the need to first join clients where they are in their own emotional, cognitive, and behavioral development. The term *predominant cognitive-developmental orientation* is used to signify the orientation a person is primarily using to make sense of a particular situation or issue.

Table 4.1 illustrates the strengths and weaknesses of each orientation. Full development of human potential occurs by expanding client awareness and potential within each orientation. Individuals who work within several orientations have access to the strengths inherent in each orientation. Those who rely on one orientation can be limited by the weaknesses of that orientation.

Clients usually present their issues within several orientations but tend to rely on a predominant orientation to frame their understanding of their experiences. For example, Susan, a teenager with bulimia, is enmeshed in the sensory world of food and bodily sensations. She also is a gymnast and is able to compete successfully in the world of athletics. She is skilled in formal thinking and is an excellent student, yet she also has low self-esteem. Her family blames her for her negative thoughts and eating patterns while denying that the family and athletic cultures also influence her thoughts, feelings, and behavior. Susan primarily discusses her issues from a sensorimotor/elemental orientation, usually emphasizing her frustrations and disappointments. The DCT model contains a systematic classification system to help therapists assess the predominant and secondary cognitive, emotional, and behavioral orientations a client uses throughout the course of treatment. Research Exhibit 4.1 summarizes research on the DCT model and the importance of multiplicity for mental health. Practice Exercise 4.1 provides you with an opportunity to practice assessing cognitive, emotional, and behavioral orientations.

DCT Orientations and Cultural Identity Development Theory

The four cognitive, emotional, and behavioral orientations can be related to cultural identity development theory (see the discussion in Chapter 5). Cultural identity theory can be thought of as a model of the evolution of consciousness. The embedded consciousness of stage 1—naiveté, or passive acceptance of the status quo—is parallel to many of the cognitions and emotions that occur within the sensorimotor/elemental orientation. Stages 2 and 3—encountering and naming action—have parallels with concrete/situational thought, emotion, and action. Stage 4—focusing on reflection—has much in common with formal/reflective thought patterns. Finally, the multiple perspective of stage 5—internalization—is integrative and simultaneously demands multiperspective thought; it is thus similar to the dialectic/systemic frame of reference.

=== **Research Exhibit 4.1** ===

Defining Cognitive-Developmental Orientations

Do the constructs of DCT really exist? Can they be identified and measured reliably? Does the claim that clients have the ability to take multiple perspectives hold? Is there a relationship between the ability to hold multiple perspectives and health? All of these questions were answered in the affirmative in work with inpatient depressed clients (Rigazio-DiGilio & Ivey, 1990). Independent raters were able to classify patient cognitive-developmental orientations with high reliability (0.98 kappa = 0.87). When answering standard questions from the DCT model, both short- and long-term depressed clients responded consistently with the theory (99 percent). Informal clinical data revealed cognitive and behavioral changes in family therapy sessions after the brief treatment.

Mailler (1991) found that instruction in the DCT model was useful with students preparing for the workplace. He applied the DCT questioning model to conceptualize a program for burnout prevention, personal growth, and organizational change.

Heesacker, Pritchard, Rigazio-DiGilio, and Ivey (1995) conducted a factor analytic study of DCT constructs with 1,700 subjects. The factor structure for the four orientations was again validated. An even more important part of the study found that people who were able to function within multiple orientations had fewer psychological and physical problems than those working within single orientations. In effect, an individual capable of functioning with sensorimotor, concrete, and formal styles showed more positive indications of mental and physical health than a person who functioned solely or primarily with a single style

---

Beyond the parallel structure of DCT and MCT, another bridge between the two is offered by Brooks (1990). Brooks notes that both models suggest that emotions are manifest in each orientation or stage, albeit from different vantage points or frames of reference. Both models emphasize that a major goal of treatment is to help clients liberate, or enhance and expand, their emotions and consciousness and then to act on this alternative awareness.

The DCT Sphere: A Metatheoretical Integration of Psychotherapy

Along with being a theory in its own right, DCT is metatheoretical in that it provides an integrative framework for combining different psychotherapy perspectives and approaches throughout the treatment process. DCT requires clinicians to master not

Practice Exercise 4.1

Assessing Predominant Cognitive-Developmental Orientations

This practice exercise provides a sample of how raters were trained in the DCT classification system. It provides you with an opportunity to test your own ability to rate client statements.

Task

Define the *predominant* cognitive-developmental orientation of Ricardo in each of the following four statements. Expect to find dimensions of other levels, but determine if Ricardo talks in a *primarily* sensorimotor, concrete, formal, or dialectic/systemic fashion. Ricardo is a depressed inpatient who is talking about the death of his sister and his current marital problems. The information is randomized from varying parts of the interview.

1. I'm reacting this time very similarly as I did to my sister's death. I guess everyone saw her as ill but me. I didn't see anything wrong. And when she died I was completely shocked. I fell apart just like I'm falling apart now. Everyone else had to take care of things.

2. I feel paralyzed . . . petrified. I feel like my legs are stiff and still . . . great weights keeping me stuck . . . I feel empty . . . dead inside.

3. What I learned when I was growing up has not prepared me for dealing with loss. My parents did everything to protect me and my sister. . . . We were never taught to look for problems and try to fix them, or that nat-

ural things would occur and we would have to adjust. This talk is making it clear that I don't know what to do, so I completely pull into myself and become paralyzed.

4. She came home from work and rather than having dinner on the table, she was sitting at the table looking distraught . . . upset. She said, "We have to talk," and I thought maybe someone died. Then she told me she wanted to leave . . . she was unhappy for five years. I collapsed. I didn't see it coming. I didn't know what to do. That's why I'm here . . . she brought me to the hospital 'cause I didn't know what to do.

Analysis

Statement 1—formal/reflective
Ricardo is reflecting on himself and is contrasting his reactions with others. A concrete/situational client would have difficulty with this cognitive task.

Statement 2—predominantly sensorimotor/elemental with some concrete/situational elements
Ricardo usually feels emotions directly ("great weights keeping me stuck," "dead inside") and sometimes names or describes emotions ("I feel paralyzed") instead of experiencing them at a fuller sensorimotor level.

Statement 3—dialectic/systemic
Statement 4—concrete/situational

SOURCE: From "Developmental Therapy and Depressive Disorders: Measuring Cognitive Levels through Patient Natural Language" by S. A. Rigazio-DiGilio and A. E. Ivey, 1990 (p. 474), *Professional Psychology: Research & Practice, 21.* Copyright 1990 by American Psychological Association. Reprinted by permission.

only DCT, but also as many alternative helping styles as possible. Anderson (1983) describes "style-shift counseling," emphasizing counselors' need to accommodate to clients' assimilated schema, to choose an approach that matches clients' primary orientations, to evaluate the effectiveness of the approach, and to "shift style" to other approaches when clients have grown or if the chosen intervention is ineffective.

Given that clients will work within several orientations during the course of treatment, DCT clinicians need to employ multiple theories and skills. For example, a single client might need sensorimotor relaxation training to combat tension, concrete assertiveness training to prepare for a job interview, formal client-centered work to facilitate increased self-esteem, and dialectic systems reframes to understand the family and cultural issues underlying all of the above issues. Multiple treatment for a single client, even using seemingly antagonistic theories and methods, is basic to the practice of the integrative DCT model.

DCT theorists identify four types of psychotherapy styles and therapeutic environments that are associated with each of the four cognitive-developmental orientations: environmental structuring, coaching, consulting, and collaborating. These are summarized in Figure 4.3, which illustrates the integrated, spherical model of development and adaptation represented by DCT. Client orientations are represented by the spiral, and corresponding psychotherapy styles and therapeutic environments are represented by the four planes. Examples of interventions for the four therapeutic environments are presented in this figure and in the fourth column of Table 4.1.

The *structuring environment* (S1) provides firm and gentle parameters that permit therapists and clients to explore the sensory-based experience generated during the therapeutic encounter. A *coaching environment* (S2) helps therapists and clients clearly delineate thoughts, feelings, and behaviors from a linear, interactive frame in order to act more predictably within and outside of the therapeutic encounter. A *consultative environment* (S3) stresses the facilitation of reflective and integrative skills and is used to assist therapists and clients to identify patterns of behaviors, thoughts, and feelings across individuals, systems, and situations. Finally, a *collaborative environment* (S4) focuses on the cognitive and metacognitive processes supporting therapists' and clients' belief systems.

The sphere is placed at an angle to emphasize that DCT is a nonhierarchal model and that learning and development are balanced within all four orientations. The list of therapeutic environments is only partial, as there are many routes toward development. In addition, many techniques and theories are indeed multioriented, and the clinician's intention for each intervention will determine which orientation is being accessed.

Movement through the Sphere

Following style-shift theory, the first task for the clinician is to assess the client's primary cognitive-developmental orientation and to match interventions to this orientation. Horizontal development helps clients expand their exploration of issues within their predominant orientations. This assists clients to expand and master the

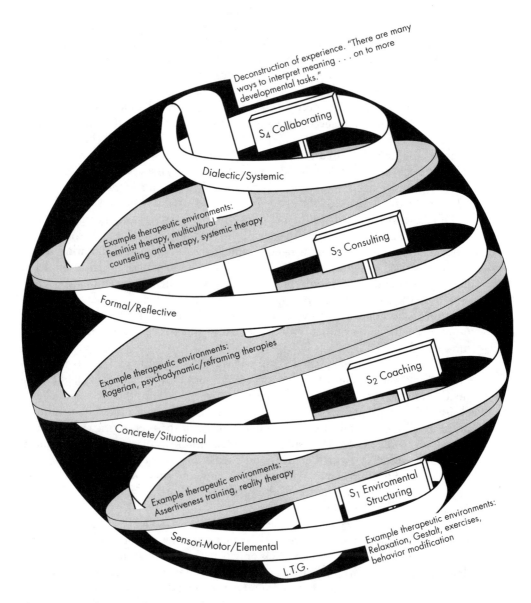

Figure 4.3 The Developmental Sphere: The Four Psychotherapy Styles and Therapeutic Environments

NOTE: The four cognitive-developmental orientations can be further divided into eight orientations (see Ivey, 1991).

SOURCE: The developmental sphere was first drawn by Lois T. Grady and is used here with her permission.

use of resources within the primary orientation, providing a firm foundation that can then be used as a stepping-stone to access other orientations.

For example, Chadra, an Iranian-American female, describes an incident in which her Arabic background was insulted. She enters psychotherapy at a stage 2 level of consciousness—resistance and anger—which corresponds to the concrete/situational DCT orientation. The first task is to help Chadra expand awareness and competence within the concrete/situational orientation. In this case, Cheek's (1976) culturally aware cognitive-behavioral approach (see Chapter 9) may be appropriate. As another example, Patrick, a formal/reflective European-American male, enters psychotherapy with self-doubts and might profit from horizontal development within a client-centered or psychodynamic frame of reference.

Vertical development, in the DCT spherical framework, can be either up or down. As all dimensions of consciousness are considered important for holistic development, higher is not better; rather, inclusive is better.

Both Chadra and Patrick might benefit from imaging, relaxation training, and other sensory-based techniques that correspond with the sensorimotor/elemental orientation. These techniques might help Chadra get in closer touch with her feelings about oppression and racism. Patrick might use imaging to better understand the roots of his self-doubt. Once vertical development is activated, the new orientation will provide the focus for new horizontal growth. Both Chadra and Patrick might benefit from horizontal development within the sensorimotor/elemental orientation to directly experience emotions related to personal and cultural issues.

In short, DCT recommends both horizontal and vertical development within as many orientations as feasible for each client. Helping clients experience, discuss, and work on their issues from multiple perspectives can assist them in developing a range of options and resources to draw on along their developmental journeys. In fact, Heesacker, Prichard, Rigazio-DiGilio, and Ivey (1995) found that individuals able to access multiple orientations report fewer physical and emotional symptoms than individuals who rely on one orientation to understand and operate in their world.

DCT in Applied Practice

As a metatheoretical approach, DCT draws from all the theories and strategies presented in this book. DCT reflects an integrated practice wherein expanding consciousness and action based on these expansions is a major treatment goal. DCT also has generated constructions and techniques of its own, which can be a useful part of the therapeutic process. Two dimensions of DCT are explored here: developmental questioning strategies and DCT treatment planning.

DCT Questioning Strategies

We all like to be heard. When you accommodate to clients by listening, not only are you able to understand their perspectives, but you also have given them a rare gift.

Through the simple act of listening, clients see and understand themselves clearly and holistically. Listening well at times can be enough in itself to promote change.

At the same time, as a clinician, you have immense influence, so much so that clients will take on your language and perspectives. Further, because we cannot integrate everything, we selectively attend to what our clients say. We may focus only on negative issues or only on positive ones. A Rogerian psychotherapist may focus on individual issues, a family clinician on family concerns, and a feminist practitioner on gender socialization. All clinicians, with the best of intentions, inevitably lead clients to emphasize certain issues. *Not only do clients talk about what you show interest in, they also tend to talk and act using the orientation from which you frame your questions and conduct your interventions.*

It is not enough to discover that your client is using a concrete frame of reference. Once this is known, you need to encourage horizontal movement by asking concrete questions and conducting concrete interventions (concrete decision making or assertiveness training). Over the course of treatment, you may encourage vertical movement within sensorimotor (imaging, body work), formal (self-examination of repeating patterns), and dialectic (how issues are influenced by multicultural, family, or systemic variables) orientations.

Using DCT Questions to Explore Issues within Several Orientations

Your style of selective listening and focusing, along with the questions you ask, affects how clients present their issues. If a woman talks about job-related difficulties and you ask her concrete questions, she will give you specific details. If you focus on formal thoughts, she may examine patterns in her thoughts, feelings, and behavior. If you focus on issues of job discrimination, she may operate within the dialectic/systemic orientation.

DCT uses specific questioning strategies to help clients explore their issues within each orientation. Practice Exercise 4.2 contains an abbreviated version of DCT questions related to each orientation. These questions may already be familiar to you, as such questions are commonly used to structure interviews. Such questions can facilitate understanding of naturally occurring events in the session and provide an organized way to integrate different voices during the therapeutic process.

A Caution about the Sensorimotor/Elemental Orientation

On sensitive topics, clients may become tearful when responding to simple, direct, here-and-now, sensorimotor questions. You and your clients may be surprised at the strength of these deeper emotions. Your own comfort level will be an important determinant as to how well your clients cope with emotions in sessions. If either of you has difficulty being with the immediacy of emotions, you may want to use the struc-

Practice Exercise 4.2

 ## The DCT Questioning Sequence (abbreviated)

A useful practice exercise is to take a volunteer "client" through the four cognitive-developmental orientations. Begin your exercise by informing your client what you are planning to do and share the following list of questions with your client. Once you or your client has selected a topic for discussion, ask the first question. Try to assess the client's primary and secondary orientation, as these can be identified in the language used to discuss the selected topic.

Once you have done this, work through each phase of the DCT questioning sequence slowly, giving your client time to experience each orientation fully. Use particular care within the sensorimotor/elemental orientation to respect your client's privacy.

Open-Ended Questions for Preliminary Assessment
(assessing the primary cognitive-developmental orientation)

1. Can you tell me what occurs for you when you focus on (the selected topic)? (A useful topic is "your family of origin.")

   Goal: To obtain a short story of about 100 to 200 words.

   Skills: To encourage, paraphrase, and summarize to bring out the story; try to limit your impact on the story.

   Sum: Summarize the client's example, story, or issues. Pay special attention to developmental orientation(s) presented in client's story.

Cognitive-Developmental Questioning Sequence
(assessing the client's ability to access each orientation)

Sensorimotor/Elemental Explorations
(key words: see, hear, feel)
1. What is an image that you come up with when you focus on (the selected topic)?
   a. Describe this image for me.
      (1) What are you seeing?
      (2) What are you hearing?
      (3) How are you feeling right now?

   Goal: To elicit one image and ask what is seen, heard, and felt. The aim is for here-and-now experiencing; accept randomness.

   Skills: Only ask questions that maintain a focus in this orientation. Do not ask for facts, descriptions, or interpretations; use encouraging, paraphrasing, and summarizing approach.

Sum: Summarize key elements of the experience. Be sensitive to client's emotional world.

Concrete/Situational Explorations
(key words: do, if/then)
1. Choose an example that highlights (the selected topic). Give me an illustration of what occurs in relation to (the selected topic), focusing on what I would see if I were there with you.
    a. Ask various behavioral tracking questions, such as
        (1) Who was involved?
        (2) What happened first? Next?
        (3) What did he/she do then?
        (4) What did you do? How did you feel?

Goal: To obtain a linear description of the chosen example or story.
Skills: Only ask questions that maintain a focus in this orientation. Do not ask for feelings, here-and-now experiencing, or interpretations; use encouraging, paraphrasing, and summarizing approach.
Sum: Summarize key descriptors of the example.

Formal/Reflective Explorations
(key words: reflect, patterns, self, relationship)
1. Can you describe other situations in which you take on roles or positions similar to the ones you just described?
2. Can you describe other situations that seem to generate the same set of behaviors, even when you wish it would happen differently?
3. Is this a pattern for you?
4. Has anything like this ever happened before? Does it happen a lot?

Goal: To talk about and reflect on repeating patterns of thoughts, feelings, and behaviors as these occur within the self or within different contexts.
Skills: Only ask questions that maintain a focus in this orientation. Do not ask for feelings, here-and-now experiencing, or descriptive events; use encouraging, paraphrasing, and summarizing approach.
Sum: Summarize key reflections.

Dialectic/Systemic Explorations
(key words: integrate, challenge, change-in-context)

Integration
1. Looking back on what we've talked about today, what stands out for you? What central themes do you notice?

Coconstruction
1. How would you define the rules or assumptions that influence how you think, feel, and act in relation to this story or these issues?

2. Where did these rules come from? Where did you learn these rules? Who taught you these rules? For example, did these rules come from your family of origin?
3. What role did/does your wider context (e.g., gender-role socialization, culture, community, religion) play in the development and maintenance of these rules?

Multiple perspectives
1. Are there other ways to look at these rules that you live by?
2. How might someone else see things differently? A friend? Your family?

Deconstruction
1. Can you identify ways that these rules may not be working effectively for you right now?
2. Do you notice any flaws or constraints in these rules—ways that these rules do not get you what you need?
3. How do these rules help or hinder your current way of understanding and acting?

Reconstruction and action
1. If you could add to or change these rules, how would you do it?
2. Based on these possibilities of change, is there anything you could do differently right now to see the issues that brought you here from a different perspective?
3. Based on these possibilities of change, is there anything you could do differently right now to work on the issues that brought you to treatment?

> *Goal:* To obtain an integrated summary of the conversation; facilitate an understanding of coconstruction; obtain different perspectives; note parameters in how one understands, experiences, and operates; and review alternatives for thinking, feeling, and acting.
>
> *Skills:* Only ask questions that maintain a focus in this orientation. Use encouraging, paraphrasing, and summarizing approach.
>
> *Sum:* Summarize key elements of the experience.

ture of concrete and formal questioning procedures. For example, you could say empathically, "Tell me what happened when you were feeling that" (concrete/situational) or "Is that way of feeling a pattern for you?" (formal/reflective). These questions move the client gradually away from direct sensorimotor experiencing. Ethics, professional standards, and careful supervision are especially important when working within the sensorimotor/elemental orientation. DCT recommends that you share the purpose of your questions with your clients and let them know ahead of time what may happen. If you have shared what will happen with your client in a coconstructive fashion, you can make a joint decision as to how to proceed.

If you take a client through the standard questions in Practice Exercise 4.2, you and the client will gain new perspectives on the issues that promoted treatment.

Things seem very different when viewed from sensorimotor/elemental, concrete/situational, formal/reflective, or dialectic/systemic perspectives. Integrating questions about the family of origin into the standard series of questions is particularly valuable. For example, you could begin Practice Exercise 4.2 by asking, Could you tell me what happens for you when you focus on your family of origin? Additionally, you could begin the coconstruction segment of the dialectic/systemic orientation by asking, How is it that your family of origin may have taught you these rules or assumptions?

You also can deviate from the sequence of the DCT standard questions. Building on the work of Cheek (1976), it may be useful with African-American clients, for example, to focus first on dialectic questions and to follow up later with more individually oriented questions. MCT (see Chapters 5 and 6) might go so far as to turn the DCT questioning sequences "upside down," placing the emphasis on cultural and systemic issues (e.g., "How might your gender/ethnicity/sexual orientation relate to these issues?"). Starting an interview by exploring how individuals are affected by the systems and relationships in their lives is very different from client-centered, cognitive-behavioral, or psychodynamic orientations.

Finally, knowledge of DCT assessment and questioning strategies will likely be helpful as you work with other theoretical approaches. Clinicians who use many approaches and modalities often follow the DCT sequences. For example, the cognitive-behaviorist Beck (1967) (see Chapter 8) often asks clients to picture early life images (sensorimotor/elemental). Clients are then encouraged to describe happenings from that time (concrete/situational) and to observe patterns in later life that are derived from these images (formal/reflective). Finally, Beck asks clients to reflect on systems of operations (dialectic/systemic). Through this process, clients obtain an alternative integration that can lead to new thoughts, feelings, and behaviors. Beck, however, tends not to discuss multicultural issues as an inherent part of his systematic procedures. Rogers and Perls have followed similar questioning sequences in their work, but again with the emphasis on an individual focus (Ivey, 1986, pp. 112–16). Shapiro's (1994) promising new strategy for working with individuals dealing with trauma—eye movement desensitization and reprocessing—also integrates images, thoughts, and physical sensations in a manner consistent with the DCT questioning sequence (see Chapter 9).

Developing an Integrated Assessment and Treatment Plan

This section focuses on the DCT treatment planning process. The issue of depression will be used for illustrative purposes. DCT suggests that there are multiple narratives or stories in depression. The task of psychotherapy is to discover, sort out, and work with the multiple voices underlying the depression. DCT shows how a variety of strategies discussed in this book can be arranged to construct developmentally oriented treatment plans for working with depression. Clients who are severely depressed may require inpatient treatment and medication. Milder forms of depression will be evident in many clients with whom you work. Although those with serious depression usually require more extensive treatment planning, the inclusive framework of DCT can provide a useful way to think about all forms.

DCT Treatment Planning: Integrating Alternative Theories and Strategies

Our first task is to join the language system used by clients to understand their distress. Individual, family, and cultural empathy, along with effective listening skills, are needed to learn clients' ways of voicing their stories. The first task is to assess clients' predominant orientation and to then match your language and early interventions to their ways of being.

As clients' stories unfold, DCT questioning strategies are used to mismatch their predominant orientation and facilitate an exploration of the same story from different orientations or vantage points. For example, a man may be depressed and sad over the loss of his friend. The first task would be to join him within the sensorimotor/elemental orientation and allow him to work through his emotion by adapting many of the strategies identified in Table 4.2 that are associated with the sensorimotor/elemental perspective, such as imagery and body work. Once a firm foundation of understanding has been established at the sensorimotor/elemental orientation, the clinician could use other DCT questioning strategies or interventions associated with predominantly concrete/situational strategies, as noted in Table 4.2, to assist the client to move on to detailed examples and linear stories. Strategies, such as automatic thoughts charting or decisional counseling, might be utilized to elicit concrete/situational perspectives.

After a deep understanding of the client's issues has been developed at the concrete/situational orientation, vertical movement to the formal/reflective level can be effected by posing questions aimed at that orientation or employing strategies from the formal/reflective category (see Table 4.2). Dream analysis and pattern analysis of depressive behavior, cognitions, and affect would be typical of interventions within the formal/reflective orientation. Once sufficient abstract reflection on the stories has been achieved, a broader analysis at the dialectic/systemic orientation can be initiated by using techniques listed in Table 4.2, such as explorations of family and community genograms. Note that the same story can be told by using emotion, by using concrete stories and examples, and by using reflections on patterns and meanings of loss.

Movement through the various orientations is not as easy as it sounds. Individuals working within the concrete/situational orientation may have difficulty with formal reflection, thereby requiring you to adapt your questions and interventions carefully and to build on concrete skills. Similarly, those with predominantly abstract resources may have difficulty providing concrete examples or may be unable to access the catharsis and direct experiencing associated with the sensorimotor/elemental orientation. Interestingly, many psychotherapy theories

Table 4.2   Illustrative Strategies Corresponding to Each DCT Orientation

Predominantly Sensorimotor/Elemental Strategies

Body work—acupuncture, acupressure, massage, yoga
Emotional catharsis
Gestalt "hot seat"
Imagery
Medication
Meditation
Relaxation training

Predominantly Concrete/Situational Strategies

Automatic thoughts chart
Assertiveness training
Concrete telling of stories and narratives
Crisis intervention
Decisional counseling
Desensitization therapy
Rational-emotive analysis of a single event
Solution-oriented therapy
Thought stopping

Predominantly Formal/Reflective Strategies

Client-centered therapy
Cognitive therapy
Dream analysis
Logotherapy treatment of hyperreflection
Pattern analysis of stories or narratives, or other concrete strategy
Psychodynamic therapies
Malaysian dream analysis
Rational-emotive therapy

Predominantly Dialectic/Systemic Strategies

Analysis of projective identification
Analysis of transference
Community genogram
Family genogram or chart
Family dream analysis
Introspective developmental counseling
Trauma treatment

Theories and Strategies Applied across Orientations

Cognitive-behavioral therapy
DCT and SCDT
Systemic therapies
Feminist therapy
Multicultural counseling and therapy
Self-help groups (e.g., AA, ACOA, Eating Disorders)

are predominantly formal and abstract; relatively limited attention is given to exploring concrete specifics, and even less attention is given to sensorimotor issues. In this regard, we as counselors must develop a repertoire of concrete and sensorimotor skills that we can use to assist clients in accessing skills in these orientations.

A single intervention may encompass numerous orientations. For example, dream analysis is a predominantly formal intervention that requires clients to tell their dreams in considerable detail (concrete/situational). In the process of their dream narratives, clients may be moved to tears as they express themselves within the sensorimotor/elemental orientation. Additionally, they may consider family, gender, and ethnic/racial issues and images as these are related to their dreams (dialectic/systemic). Thus, analyzing dreams can include an infinite array of meanings and voices. The last category in Table 4.2 lists some strategies that lend themselves to work across all orientations and help foster numerous narratives about the issues surrounding clients' depression.

Often, depressed patients internalize anger and loss and blame themselves for their situations. A goal of DCT is to include social history, family, community, and multicultural issues (dialectic/systemic) in working with these clients. Additionally, it may be necessary to block or modify severe depressive symptoms with medication (sensorimotor/elemental). Concrete psychotherapies may include cognitive-behavioral thought stopping or assertiveness training. Formal action can include analysis of cognitive patterns or client-centered work on self-esteem. DCT sees all of these strategies as potentially beneficial and holds that effective resolution of clients' issues occurs by working within each orientation. No form of cognitive, emotional, or behavioral expression is considered "best," and the perspective provided by working through issues within multiple orientations is recommended.

DCT clinicians hold that a change in any part of the whole usually results in change throughout. Thus, a mildly depressed client who constantly repeats negative self-statements might profit from the cognitive-behavioral strategy of thought stopping (Chapter 10) and require no other treatment. Another client might obtain sufficient support from participating in a psychoeducational group on stress management. The full utilization of treatment strategies within all developmental orientations may not be necessary.

In summary, DCT treatment plans help clients talk about and work on their issues within multiple orientations. It is helpful to examine clients' stories from more than one perspective, as this usually highlights expanded options for understanding and change. The field of psychotherapy is moving away from the idea of a "single best" theory or practice and moving toward a postmodern integrative view of psychology and therapy. The integrative metatheoretical framework of DCT affords the clinician a wide repertoire of strategies and interventions to help clients explore the multiple facets of depression or of any issue.

The focus thus far has been on conceptualizing the use of DCT in the assessment and treatment of individuals experiencing distress. However, DCT constructs have also been effectively extended to work with couples and families, and this extension is called systemic cognitive-developmental therapy (SCDT) (see Rigazio-DiGilio, 1994a; Rigazio-DiGilio & Ivey, 1991, 1993).

Systemic Cognitive-Developmental Therapy and Family Systems

Systemic cognitive-developmental therapy (SCDT) considers family development as a holistic process. Like DCT, this family oriented model offers guidelines and strategies for assessing and treating families within a coconstructive, developmental, and integrative framework. SCDT also provides a metaframework that can be used to organize family systems interventions into developmentally appropriate and culturally sensitive treatment plans.[4]

Using SCDT to Understand Family Meaning Making

Individuals do not develop in a vacuum, disconnected from others and their culture. We all participate in and are influenced by a meaning-making process that evolves within our family as we learn to understand and relate to others. SCDT uses the term *collective cognitive-developmental orientations* to identify this aspect of family influence. The family's collective orientation affects how individuals make sense of themselves, others, relationships, families, communities, the world, and developmental tasks. In this way, the family's collective orientation, which reflects how the family assimilates and/or accommodates to wider cultural values and mores over time, becomes a significant filter that individual members and the family as a whole use to understand and operate within the world.

A family's way of coconstructing meaning can be demonstrated by analyzing how family members relate to one another. Practice Exercise 4.3 can be used to decipher how your family's way of coconstructing meaning affects your experiences, thoughts, behaviors, and relationships. As you complete this practice exercise, you may notice that your views of yourself and your world reflect collective meanings established across family generations and wider environments. You may notice influences related to (1) culture (e.g., assumptions regarding "belongingness" inherent in Italian-American cultures or "self-responsibility" inherent in midwestern cultures), (2) community (e.g., assumptions regarding small town living versus inner city living), (3) socioeconomic status (e.g., assumptions related to issues of survival versus issues of privilege), (4) gender socialization (e.g., assumptions regarding traditional versus nontraditional roles), or (5) family interaction (e.g., assumptions regarding the utility or futility of arguing). Even individuals who no longer live "at home" operate in ways that reflect basic premises coconstructed in their families of origin. For this reason, clinicians must be conscious of the cultural and family influences affecting their clients' behaviors, thoughts, and feelings. Convening sessions that include members of the family of origin (the families individuals were raised in) or the fam-

Practice Exercise 4.3

The Family of Origin and Coconstruction of Meaning, Thoughts, Behaviors, and Relationships

Draw a large floor plan of the home you lived in that was most significant to you and your family while you were growing up. Place the home in the context of your immediate neighborhood. Once you have drawn this floor plan, complete the following:

1. Put a 1 in rooms you were allowed in and a 2 in rooms you were not allowed in for any significant length of time without another family member present.
2. Put a 3 in rooms that family company was allowed in and a 4 in rooms that this company could not enter for any significant period of time without another family member.
3. Put a 5 in rooms your friends could enter and a 6 in rooms they were not allowed to enter for any significant period of time without another family member besides yourself.
4. Put a 7 next to the entrances family could use and an 8 where family could be in relation to the exterior of the home. Place a 9 next to the entrances company could use and a 10 where they could be in relation to the exterior of the home.
5. Now respond to the following questions:
   Did you have a space that was your own? If so, how did this space become yours?
   How much time did you spend in this space? Who could enter this

space without permission? Who needed permission? If you did not have a space, how could you be alone, and how was this need responded to?

Was there a space where the family spent significant amounts of time together? If so, how did this space become identified as the family's and what activities took place in that space? If not, how did collective family activities occur?

Was there a place in your home where loud arguments occurred? If so, who had permission to be there during arguments, and who was usually absent?

Was someone in charge of maintaining the interior and exterior of the home? If so, did this person(s) take care of this alone or delegate responsibility, and was the process used successful? If not, how did the family maintain the home?

This abbreviated memory search illustrates one way to remember significant relational patterns that were a part of your growing up. Once you finish the exercise, review the process. Then ask yourself the following questions to get to the collective meanings that evolved in your family:

1. Looking at all of this, what "rules," or ways of doing things, do you think were established in your family?

What were the rules about privacy and togetherness?

What were the rules about company and friends?

What were the rules about conflict and conflict resolution?

What were the rules about decision making and responsibility?

2. What variables (intergenerational, cultural, community) influenced the establishment of these rules?

3. How does or did your family react when attempts were made to change these rules?

4. How do these rules currently influence

Your view of yourself, and how you present yourself

Your view of and interaction with family members

Your view of and interaction with others outside your family

Your view of and interaction with the wider environment in which you live

5. If you could add to or change these rules, what modifications would you make at this time in your life? Why?

ily of procreation (the families that individuals construct) is one way to assess the collective meaning-making processes affecting individuals, relationships within families, and families as a whole. By observing the interactive dialogue among family members, the collective orientations that are influencing and influenced by clients' presenting issues can be ascertained.

In the case of depression, family sessions can provide information about who else shares the depression, what individuals and relationships influence the depression, where the depression is directed, and what rules are used to govern the expression and acceptance of depressive feelings, thoughts, and behaviors. Sometimes the whole family will share the depression toward society as a whole. Other times, one individual may be the standard bearer of the depression for the family. Only by observing a family's collective meaning-making processes can a therapist determine how the family, its relational systems, and its members understand and operate in the world. Clinicians should have a basic understanding of the observation and conceptual tools associated with marriage and family psychotherapy in order to fully interpret family processes related to collective meaning making and collective orientations.

Understanding Collective Cognitive-Developmental Orientations and Adaptation

A family's collective meaning-making process can be classified in terms of four cognitive-developmental orientations. Just as with individuals, the collective meaning of families changes over time, in different contexts, and in response to different life tasks. Also, as with individuals, families tend to rely on a predominant cognitive-developmental orientation when dealing with specific issues. This predominant orientation may shift according to the situation. For example, a family may use concrete skills to plan a cross-country journey and then use formal reasoning strategies to persuade their youngest member not to engage in aggressive acts with others. Adaptive families tend to be able to use several orientations and therefore to call on a wide variety of resources to respond to developmental and situational tasks. Nonadaptive families, however, are less able to effectively access several orientations and therefore have fewer resources on which to draw.

Because families are composed of individuals with unique ways of experiencing the world, it is difficult to imagine that a family can actually coconstruct primary and secondary collective orientations. Nonetheless, families do use primary collective views as filters to respond to life's demands. It is not required that individual family members show loyalty to the family's collective orientation. Sometimes a family's collective meaning is a blending of each member's cognitive-developmental orientation or a combination of the orientations of subgroups of family members. Also, the orientation of a particularly dominant family member may shape the family's way of looking at issues. Only by directly interviewing and observing the family can the coconstructive process, as well as the predominant family orientation, be assessed. Table 4.3 provides a brief description of the four collective cognitive-developmental orientations, including both the strengths and weaknesses inherent in each orientation. Appropriate psychotherapeutic interventions are included for each orientation.

Families experiencing distress may present in the treatment session in various ways. Two of the most common ways are (1) families who rigidly attempt to hold to a single perspective and (2) families whose collective orientation is so scattered across the four orientations that it is too diffuse to identify. Rigid family orientations sacrifice all others' ways of perceiving the world to one view, which often leaves the family with a narrow range of thoughts, emotions, and behaviors not in sync with the current circumstance. Diffuse family orientations often reflect a family that has entered treatment because of an inability to efficiently master resources in any of the orientations. These families tend to haphazardly and ineffectively react to demands for change.

To provide an illustration, families seeking assistance with depression that have become immobilized in one orientation will share a narrow range of thoughts, emotions, and actions. A family operating within the sensorimotor/elemental orientation will share feelings of sadness and detachment. Families primarily functioning within a concrete/situational perspective will share stories about the helplessness and hopelessness of their situations. Formal/reflective families will present the recurring patterns of loss they attribute to their depressive state. Dialectic/systemic families will discount their own ability to alter larger societal and cultural conditions and envelop their depression in cynicism and powerlessness.

Using SCDT in Applied Practice

SCDT, like DCT, offers a developmentally and culturally sensitive approach to treatment and a metatheory that can be used to integrate intervention strategies and techniques from various schools of family psychotherapy. The therapeutic goals of

Table 4.3   The Four Collective Cognitive-Developmental Orientations

Sensorimotor/Elemental Orientation

These families are prone to chaotic functioning that is guided by affect over reasoning. Strengths include an ability to directly experience emotions. Families who overly rely on this orientation are overwhelmed by slight variations and have difficulty sustaining a coherent sense of identity and organizing their lives. Interventions are initially geared to helping families structure their environment, establish a sense of identity, and gain control over their emotional lives.

Concrete/Situational Orientation

These families tend to depend on a predictable set of beliefs and behaviors to understand and operate in their world and to maintain a sense of identity. Strengths include developed problem-solving skills and strong recall for details. Families rigidly stuck in this orientation may overly rely on well-known solutions to maintain continuity. They are less likely to see salient themes or to revise their thinking and behavior. They use outdated beliefs and behaviors that are not effective. Interventions are initially geared to set and carry out revised goals and to transfer this learning to new situations.

Formal/Reflective Orientation

These families tend to analyze the relational patterns and events in their lives and find it easy to generate alternative solutions within their current way of filtering data. However, it is difficult for them to challenge their basic assumptions. They can intellectualize, yet find it difficult to translate thoughts into action or to directly experience emotion. Interventions initially access the family's analytic skills with the goal of generating effective action plans.

Dialectic/Systemic Orientation

These families recognize intergenerational and contextual issues and how these issues influence their lives. They can challenge and revise their assumptions in response to changing circumstances. Under stress, they find it hard to put their thoughts into action and can become overwhelmed by the influences affecting their lives. Initial interventions are aimed at assisting these families to examine these influences in a more organized fashion.

SCDT are to assist families to function effectively within and among the different collective orientations, to empower them to view their issues from multiple perspectives, and to generate solutions that are appropriate to their developmental and situational needs.

SCDT emphasizes the importance of coconstructing suitable therapeutic environments for facilitating family growth and adaptation. As such, SCDT provides (1) an assessment phase for identifying collective orientations, (2) a set of questioning strategies to be used during treatment, and (3) an organizing metaframework that can be used to integrate other models of family work into coherent treatment plans.

The SCDT Assessment Phase and SCDT Questioning Strategies

During the SCDT assessment phase, a family is asked to discuss the issues that prompted treatment or is invited to talk about how members would like to change. To identify the predominant collective orientation being accessed, different types of open-ended questioning strategies are used while the clinician assumes a participant-observer role, trying to only minimally influence the flow of communication. The practitioner observes the family's interaction and notes within what orientation the family comes to agreement. Additionally, watching who participates and how this happens provides the therapist with some initial hypotheses regarding the degree of investment each member has in the problem, in change, and in the family's collective meaning-making process.

Practice Exercise 4.4 provides the questions you can use to assess orientation. Ask two of your family members to go through the SCDT questioning strategy outlined in this exercise. A good beginning question would be "Could the two of you talk together and reach some consensus about a significant issue in your lives as members of this family?" Ask two members of your own family to work with you, and assist them to step through the SCDT questioning sequence. This should take approximately one hour. Then ask them what they learned from the experience.

To take an example, the counselor or therapist might note that the parents of a client named Jeff form the dominant relational system that enforces the family's collective understanding of and response to his depression and suicidal thoughts. Jeff's parents formally reflect on their son's behavior across situations, noting that in most situations he tends to lose confidence and withdraw rather than trying to master the tasks he encounters. Some of Jeff's brothers and sisters also talk with their parents within the formal/reflective orientation, sharing reflective insight into Jeff's presenting problem. However, it is also the case that the family members who participate in this formal/reflective dialogue, although able to understand and reflect on the patterns Jeff is exhibiting, have no idea what part they may be playing in what is occurring or how to effectively take action to assist Jeff. An older sibling who is less invested in the family's view may attempt to share some concrete suggestions (e.g., "Jeff is using a lot of drugs and alcohol, and we should help him to stop. This might be the cause of his depression."). Another sibling may suggest that self-confidence is not the issue at all but rather that the parents did not help Jeff to grow up by allowing Jeff to be irresponsible because of his history of chronic illness (leukemia) and frailty (a dialectic/systemic perspective of the presenting problem). However, because the dominant members rigidly adhere to formal/reflective dialogue, these precursors to concrete or dialectic dialogue would not be collectively explored. Jeff's sensorimotor symptoms of distress also would not prompt movement outside the predominant formal/reflective dialogue. A clinician observing this

Practice Exercise 4.4

 The SCDT Questioning Sequence (abbreviated)

The following exercise will take you approximately an hour. However, it can be of major benefit to you in increasing your understanding of how different interviewing styles lead to different types of client conversations. Not only will you gain an understanding of DCT, you also will develop skills in other orientations to helping. You may learn from this exercise that you need to be able to talk with clients at multiple levels of meaning.

As you work through the steps, share the list of questions with your client. Work together and coconstruct alternative ways of looking at your client's life. We recommend that you focus on the question "What occurs for you when you focus on your family?" as it helps the client see issues of self-in-relation. If the focus is solely on the individual, we tend to miss contextual and relational issues. However, any topic is suitable for this interaction.

Do not rush through this exercise. Allow your client time to tell stories and experience each orientation fully. Use particular care within the sensorimotor level so that client privacy is respected.

Open-Ended Questions for Preliminary Assessment (assessing the primary cognitive-developmental orientation level)

Select the topic to be discussed in the session. For the first phase of the interview, follow the wording carefully. The first question is the one we recommend.

1. Could you tell me what occurs for you when you focus on your family? (or Could you tell me what occurs for you when you focus on [the selected topic]?)
2. Can you talk together and come to some consensus regarding the issues that have brought your family to treatment?
3. Can you talk together and come to some consensus regarding what occurs for the family when you focus on these issues?
4. Can you talk together and reach some consensus about what your family envisions will come out of the therapy process?

Cognitive-Developmental Questioning Sequence (assessing the family's ability to access each orientation)

Sensorimotor/Elemental Explorations
1. Choose an image that the family can generate when members focus on the issues that promoted treatment.
   a. Describe the image that you are generating. How does it look? What are the sounds? How do you feel as you generate this image?

2. *Summation question:* What does this image and the feelings it generates say about your family?

Concrete/Situational Explorations
1. Choose an example that highlights what occurs in the family in relation to the issues that brought you here.
   a. Once an example is chosen, ask a variety of behavioral tracking questions such as: Who is involved? What happened next? What did he or she do then? How did your parents react? Who steps in at that point? What happens afterward?
2. *Summation question:* Given the way these facts emerged, what are you learning about how you influence one another?

Formal/Reflective Explorations
1. Can you describe other situations that require family members to take on roles or positions similar to the ones you just described?
2. Can you describe other situations that seem to generate the same set of behaviors even when you wish it would happen differently?
3. *Summation question:* What are you learning about the similar ways you all act in seemingly different situations?

Dialectic/Systemic Explorations
1. Based on what we have been discussing, can you define some of the rules that seem to operate in your family—that influence how each of you thinks, feels, and acts?
2. Where do you think these rules came from?
3. Are there other ways to look at these rules that have come to influence your family so much? How might another family see the same thing?
4. Can you identify ways that these rules may not be working so effectively for you now? If you could change the rules, how might you do this?
5. *Summation question:* Based on all this, is there anything your family might try a little differently to work on the issues that have brought you here?

SOURCE: From "Systemic Cognitive-Developmental Therapy: Training Practitioners to Access and Assess Cognitive-Developmental Orientations" by S. A. Rigazio-DiGilio, 1994b, *Simulation and Gaming: An International Journal of Theory, Design, and Research,* 25. Copyright 1994. Reprinted by permission.

---

family's communication and interaction would note the predominant formal/reflective orientation and would further note that the family could not collectively address and accommodate alternative views held by other family members.

To continue the assessment process, the counselor or therapist would then use the SCDT questioning sequence (see Practice Exercise 4.4) to determine the degree to which family members can collectively discuss their issues using the four orientations and the degree to which the family system will allow members to share alternative perspectives. Although these questions are used to determine the range of access a family has to each orientation, the questions can also be used to facilitate family dialogue in each orientation during the treatment phase of psychotherapy. Most families, for example, have the ability to sustain dialogue in each orientation when their conversation is guided by the counselor. By assisting families to explore issues from within each orientation, clinicians can help family members gain multiple perspectives and access more avenues for change.

In Jeff's family, the counselor's use of the SCDT questioning sequence might encourage those members with alternative perspectives to voice these more fully. Such sharing would be a clue that, given a therapeutic environment that allows for exploration within alternative orientations, the family may be able to embrace different ideas held silently by other members.

The SCDT Metaframework

As with DCT, SCDT suggests that throughout the course of treatment the clinician should coconstruct therapeutic environments that match and shift in response to the changing developmental needs of the family. Also, as with DCT, an SCDT metaframework has been developed that can be used to organize strategies from various schools of psychotherapy into developmental treatment plans. This metaframework provides a way for clinicians to access an organized set of interventions and strategies that can be used to assist families to explore and act on their issues within a variety of orientations. These strategies can be used during the actual session or assigned to families to work on between sessions. As it is not the intent of this chapter, or this book, to provide an overview of systemic psychotherapy strategies, a brief listing of some of the more well-known family treatment activities and exercises is offered in Table 4.4 to illustrate the concept of the SCDT metaframework. The intention of each activity is provided to assist you in understanding its objective.

SCDT Treatment Planning

As with DCT, SCDT treatment is initiated within the family's predominant collective orientation. The clinician matches the therapeutic environment to fit with the family's primary perspective. Using interventions from across the field of family psychotherapy, activities and tasks are coconstructed to assist the family to fully develop and extend their behavioral, cognitive, and affective repertoires within their primary orientation.

For an example, the Arial family came to treatment because of a suicide attempt by their fourteen-year-old son. On initial assessment, the family's predominant collective orientation was classified as concrete, with secondary formal/reflective and sensorimotor/elemental perspectives. The initial phase of treatment, emphasizing horizontal development, assisted the family to develop and secure an effective method for identifying and reducing the stress level within the family, to create time

Table 4.4   Illustrative Strategies Corresponding to Each SCDT Orientation

Cognitive-Developmental Orientation	Therapeutic Environment	Structured Activity/ Exercise	Intention
Sensorimotor/Elemental Interactions are often influenced by affect over logic or reasoning.	*Structuring* Provide a context that directs the client to immediate sensory data.	Ritual Drama Genogram Sculpting Interactional letter writing Modeling fantasy alternatives	To intensify and enhance immediate emotional experience To reduce and inhibit chaotic emotional experience
Concrete/Situational Linear reasoning is used to explain discrepancies and there is reliance on well-known solutions to maintain continuity.	*Coaching* Provide assistance to examine thoughts, feelings, and behaviors from a linear perspective.	Ritual Communication skills training Conflict skills training Genogram Sculpting	To describe and/or enact family rituals To learn and practice skills To describe family relations To organize and demonstrate family relationships
Formal/Reflective Reflective thinking is used to examine interactional patterns, interpret events, and generate solutions.	*Consulting* Encourage reflection and recognition of patterns.	Ritual Family mapping Programmed writing Genogram Video playback	To facilitate analysis of and reflection on interactional patterns To encourage examination of intergenerational patterns To facilitate examination of patterns of communication
Dialectic/Systemic Clients have the ability to be aware of and to realize the influence that various contexts have on the	*Collaborating* Promote examination of reality constructions and the coconstruction of new meanings and actions.	Ritual Genogram	To examine the influence of culture and intergenerational domains on family meanings To examine the influence of intergenerational domains on the construction of family meanings

Table 4.4   (continued)

Cognitive-Developmental Orientation	Therapeutic Environment	Structured Activity/ Exercise	Intention
construction of meanings and actions.		Extended family reunion	
		Family reconstruction	
		Interactional letter writing	To examine personal assumptions and their influence on patterns of interaction

SOURCE: From "Systemic Cognitive-Developmental Therapy: Organizing Structured Activities to Facilitate Family Development" by K. P. Kunkler and S. A. Rigazio-DiGilio, *Simulation and Gaming: An International Journal of Theory, Design, and Research*, 25, 75–87. Copyright 1994. Reprinted by permission.

management plans to increase the amount of family time per month, and to assist the son to develop new and more supportive friendships.

As families develop a more expanded repertoire of skills within their predominant orientation, a shift in environment is effected to stimulate vertical development. The plan for the Arial family was first to look for patterns of depressive behaviors within the family unit and across multiple generations of the family. The results of their family genogram analysis (a formal/reflective activity) suggested that depressive symptoms were a common coping mechanism for family members who found it difficult to handle more complex tasks along their developmental journey. Remaining within a formal/reflective environment, family members engaged in pattern analysis and reframing activities to enhance the family's ability to understand and communicate more abstract ideas about the role of depression in their family's history.

The formal/reflective exploration and subsequent understanding of the historical and intergenerational nature of depression paved the way for a shift to the sensorimotor/elemental orientation to more directly examine the feelings associated with these patterns. Interventions included some individual work for each family member and some Gestalt family psychotherapy strategies, which emphasized sculpting and direct confrontation of feelings.

Treatment was mutually terminated after work within the dialectic/systemic orientation was completed. The shift to this orientation was initiated by questions that examined more effective ways to learn and master developmental tasks. Horizontal development helped the family to restructure their communication style and to have greater tolerance for a wide variety of personal interpretations by each family member. By being able to employ numerous interventions across treatment approaches within a developmental treatment plan, the therapist was able to tap a wide array of resources to help the Arial family work through developmental blocks and thereby enrich the lives of all of its members.

Developing a Generalized Plan for Treatment

DCT and SCDT suggest that assessing client cognitive-developmental orientations and matching environments to client needs and style are basic to all treatment planning. For example, if you are doing vocational counseling and focusing on a concrete plan for action, clients may also benefit from reflective analysis of their behavior via formal reflection of patterns in past work experience. The vocational client also needs to look at self-in-system and the nature of the broad job market.

Alternatively, you may be working with a couple distressed over the possibility of divorce. They may present within the formal/reflective orientation, communicating with each other in an analytic fashion. The practitioner should initially join them within this orientation, using DCT and SCDT questioning strategies and corresponding techniques. The couple may, however, be avoiding the emotional component. In such cases, drawing out concrete examples of each partner's narrative can be helpful as can asking them to generate consensual images of difficult or traumatic situations. In this way, you may help the couple experience emotion that had heretofore been denied. Referral to a support group of partners dealing with stress also may be useful, as will a combination of individual and couple psychotherapy. Multicultural issues of gender, spirituality, and socioeconomic status may need to be considered within the dialectic/systemic orientation. Practice Exercise 4.5 asks you to generate a list of your own present competencies within each of the cognitive-developmental orientations. What theories, strategies, and skills do you presently have for work within each orientation? Consider these as you develop your own list of competencies for working with clients.

Limitations and Practical Implications of an Integrative Approach to Psychotherapy

The DCT and SCDT frameworks present a special challenge to the practitioner, as both demand expertise in multiple theories and interventions. Very few of us are equally expert in all modes of helping. One way to meet this challenge is to work in multidisciplinary teams. DCT and SCDT also stress including community support groups, such as Alcoholics Anonymous, cancer support groups, and Parents With-

Practice Exercise 4.5

 ## Identifying Your Own Personal Style, Present Competencies, and Goals

None of us can be fully versed in all helping techniques and theories. This exercise asks you to examine yourself—your personal style and your present competencies—within the DCT and SCDT orientations, as well as your goals for developing additional skills.

What is (are) your preferred cognitive-developmental orientation(s)?
You have been introduced to the importance of direct sensory experience, the usefulness of storytelling, the value of a reflective consciousness, and the significance of balancing all these orientations with self-in-relation and self-in-system.

Reflect back on your life experience and identify meaningful events or situations that relate to each of the cognitive-developmental orientations. Can you identify a general preferred style? How able are you to operate within each orientation? Are there some orientations that are less comfortable for you?

What is your present knowledge base and skill level in the strategies, techniques, and theories presented in Table 4.1 and Table 4.4?
These two tables cover many skills and strategies of individual and family counseling and psychotherapy. Examine them

both and consider your present level of skills and knowledge. Return to this exercise when you have completed this text.

In addition, be sure to register other areas of personal expertise not represented in this list, such as techniques in marriage and family therapy and group counseling. List areas in which you have some competence, and classify these in relation to your level of expertise. Rank yourself on a five-point scale (1 as high, 5 as low).

Do your areas of expertise match your own preferred cognitive-developmental style? Most counseling and therapy students appear to be most comfortable within the formal/reflective orientation and often find themselves impatient with the repetition of examples and stories by clients working within a predominantly concrete/situational orientation. How effective will you be with clients who are different than you?

What are your goals for the future in terms of developing further expertise?
Again, review the listings in Tables 4.1 and 4.4 and consider methods associated with other treatment modalities. What areas do you see as needing further development as you work through this text and plan your professional career?

NOTE: Self-assessment instruments are available for this exercise (Ivey, 1991) and are included in the *Instructor's Resource Manual*.

out Partners, in the treatment approach. Only the rare clinician can be an equally effective individual, family, and community intervention specialist.

Although early clinical and research findings are promising, much study and experience will be needed to more fully verify the DCT and SCDT frameworks. Fortunately, both DCT and SCDT were designed as open systems and as such are constantly subject to change and modification. Furthermore, DCT and SCDT represent only two integrated approaches to psychotherapy. Multimodal therapy (Lazarus, 1981), psychosynthesis (Assagioli, 1976), and the metaframeworks process of family therapy (Breunlin, Schwartz, & MacKune-Karrer, 1992) are just some of the metatheoretical models currently being advanced.

DCT and SCDT do not reject any form of psychotherapy. Rather, both seek to find competencies in each therapeutic orientation and to determine how each model can be tailored to the needs of diverse clients living within a wide contextual milieu.

DCT and SCDT also offer a theoretical framework for integrating diverse helping approaches. Their roots in Piagetian thinking lead to a focus on client cognition, emotion, and behavior and an attempt to move away from imposing the clinician's frame of reference on clients toward more egalitarian, coconstructive relationships. The overriding objective of both DCT and SCDT is to work "with the client" rather than "on the client."

NOTES

1. Clients include individuals, partners, families, and wider systems seeking the services of a clinician.
2. Varying grammatical forms of *schema* and *schemata* (the plural of *schema*) are used by different authors, including *scheme*, *schemes*, and *schemas*. Here the word *schema* will be used as both singular and plural.
3. The four cognitive developmental orientations are further divided into eight orientations. The standard cognitive-developmental interview and the standard cognitive-developmental classification system may be viewed in Ivey, 1991. The eight orientations have many parallels to Cross's (1995) and Freire's (1972) integration (see Chapter 5).
4. The term *family system* refers to the various forms committed relationships can take, including, but not limited to, partnerships, intact families, blended families, single-parent families, intercultural families, adoptive families, and community families.

REFERENCES

ANDERSON, T. (1983). *Style-shift counseling* [Internal government publication]. Ottawa: Correctional Service of Canada, Staff Training and Development Branch.

ASSAGIOLI, R. (1976). *Psychosynthesis.* New York: Penguin.

BASSECHES, M. (1984). *Dialectical thinking and adult development.* Norwood, NJ: Ablex.

BECK, A. (1967). *Depression: Clinical, experimental and theoretical aspects.* New York: Harper & Row.

BORING, E. G. (1930). A new ambiguous figure. *American Journal of Psychology.*

BREUNLIN, D., SCHWARTZ, R., & MACKUNE-KARRER, B. (1992). *Metaframeworks.* San Francisco: Jossey-Bass.

BROOKS, E. (1990). *Emotions and identity.* Unpublished paper, University of Massachusetts, Amherst.

CHASIN, R., GRUNEBAUM, H., & HERZIG, M. (Eds.). (1990). *One couple, four realities: Multiple perspectives on couples therapy.* New York: Guilford.

CHEEK, D. (1976). *Assertive Black . . . puzzled White.* San Luis Obispo, CA: Impact.

CLEMENT, C. (1983). *The lives and legends of Jacques Lacan.* New York: Columbia.

CROSS, W. (1995). The psychology of Nigrescence: Revising the Cross model. In J. Ponterotto, M. Casas, L. Suzuki, & C. Alexander (Eds.), *Handbook of multicultural counseling* (pp. 93–122). Newbury Park, CA: Sage.

FREIRE, P. (1972). *Pedagogy of the oppressed.* New York: Herder & Herder.

GERGEN, K. J. (1994). *Toward the transformation of social knowledge* (2nd ed.). London: Sage.

HEESACKER, M., PRICHARD, S., RIGAZIO-DIGILIO, S., & IVEY, A. (1995). *Development of a paper and pencil measure on cognitive-developmental orientations.* Unpublished paper, Department of Psychology, University of Florida, Gainesville.

IVEY, A. (1986). *Developmental therapy: Theory into practice.* San Francisco: Jossey-Bass.

IVEY, A. (1991). *Developmental strategies for helpers: Individual, family and network interventions.* Pacific Grove, CA: Brooks/Cole.

IVEY, A. E., & RIGAZIO-DIGILIO, S. A. (1991). The standard cognitive-developmental classification system. In A. E. Ivey, *Developmental strategies for helpers: Individual, family and network interventions* (pp. 301–6). Pacific Grove, CA: Brooks/Cole.

IVEY, A. E., RIGAZIO-DIGILIO, S, A., & IVEY, M. B. (1991). The standard cognitive-developmental interview. In A. E. Ivey, *Developmental strategies for helpers: Individual, family and network interventions* (pp. 289–99). Pacific Grove, CA: Brooks/Cole.

JACKSON, B. (1975). Black identity development. *Journal of Educational Diversity and Innovation, 2,* 19–25.

KEGAN, R. (1982). *The evolving self: Problem and process in human development.* Cambridge, MA: Harvard University Press.

KEGAN, R. (1994). *In over our heads.* Cambridge, MA: Harvard University Press.

KUNKLER, K. P., & RIGAZIO-DIGILIO, S. A. (1994). Systemic cognitive-developmental therapy: Organizing structured activities to facilitate family development. *Simulation and Gaming: An International Journal of Theory, Design, and Research, 25,* 75–87.

LACAN, J. (1966/1977). *Écrits: A selection.* New York: Norton.

LAZARUS, A. (1981). *The practice of multimodal therapy.* New York: McGraw-Hill.

LOEVINGER, J. (1976). *Ego development.* San Francisco: Jossey-Bass.

MAILLER, W. (1991, October). *Preparing students for the workplace: Personal growth and organizational change.* Paper presented at the North Atlantic Regional Association for Counselor Education and Supervision, Albany, NY.

MEARA, N., PEPINSKY, H., SHANNON, J., & MURRAY, W. (1981). Semantic communication and expectation for counseling across three theoretical orientations. *Journal of Counseling Psychology, 28,* 110–18.

MEARA, N., SHANNON, J., & PEPINSKY, H. (1979). Comparisons of stylistic complexity of the language of counselor and client across three theoretical orientations. *Journal of Counseling Psychology, 26,* 181–89.

MILLER, J. (1991). The development of women's sense of self. In J. Jordan, A. Kaplan, J. B. Miller, I. Stiver, & J. Surrey (Eds.), *Women's growth in connection* (pp. 11–26). New York: Guilford.

PIAGET, J. (1963). *The origins of intelligence in children.* New York: Norton. (Original work published 1926)

PIAGET, J. (1965). *The moral judgment of the child.* New York: Free Press.

PIAGET, J. (1985). *The equilibration of cognitive structures.* Chicago: University of Chicago Press.

POLKINGHORNE, D. E. (1992). Postmodern epistemology of practice. In S. Kvalve (Ed.), *Psychology and postmodernism* (pp. 146–55). London: Sage.

RIGAZIO-DIGILIO, S. A. (1994a). A co-constructive-developmental approach to ecosystemic treatment. *Journal of Mental Health Counseling, 16,* 43–74.

RIGAZIO-DIGILIO, S. A. (1994b). Systemic cognitive-developmental therapy: Training practitioners to access and assess cognitive-developmental orientations. *Simulation and Gaming: An International Journal of Theory, Design, and Research, 25,* 61–74.

RIGAZIO-DIGILIO, S. A., & IVEY, A. E. (1990). Developmental therapy and depressive disorders: Measuring cognitive levels through patient natural language. *Professional Psychology: Research & Practice, 21,* 470–75.

RIGAZIO-DIGILIO, S. A., & IVEY, A. E. (1991). Developmental counseling and therapy: A framework for individual and family treatment. *Counseling and Human Development, 24,* 1–20.

RIGAZIO-DIGILIO, S. A., & IVEY, A. E. (1993). Systemic cognitive-developmental therapy: An integrative framework. *The Family Journal: Counseling and Therapy for Couples and Families, 1,* 208–19.

ROSEN, H. (1985). *Piagetian dimensions of clinical relevance.* New York: Columbia University Press.

SHAPIRO, F. (1994). EMDR. *Behavior Therapist, 17,* 153–56.

SHOSTRUM, E. (1966). *Three approaches to psychotherapy* [Film]. Santa Ana, CA: Psychological Films.

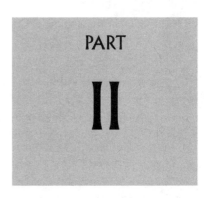
MULTICULTURAL COUNSELING AND THERAPY
The Fourth Force

Historically, we talk of first-force psychodynamic, second-force cognitive-behavioral, and third-force existential-humanistic psychology. Counseling and psychotherapy really began with Freud and psychoanalysis. James Watson and later B. F. Skinner challenged Freud's emphasis on the unconscious and focused on observable behavior. Carl Rogers, with his person-centered counseling, revolutionized the field of helping by focusing on caring and the relationship. All three approaches are still alive and well and are discussed in detail in Chapters 7 through 12. Multicultural counseling and therapy (MCT) has been described as the fourth force. There is really no one person or group representing this approach to helping. MCT is the shared product of many men and women from widely varying cultural backgrounds. MCT is not in opposition to the historical forces of coun-

seling and psychotherapy. Rather, MCT seeks to enrich and broaden psychodynamic, cognitive-behavioral, and existential-humanistic thought by focusing on issues of culture, ethnicity/race, gender, and other factors. At the same time, MCT benefits from the rich history of the field.

Six major theoretical propositions underlie multicultural counseling and psychotherapy. Chapter 5 outlines the first three: (1) MCT as an integrative metatheory of psychotherapy and counseling in general; (2) the multiple levels of experience we all encounter; and (3) cultural identity development theory. Chapter 6 then addresses the other three propositions: (4) developing theories and strategies that match the individual and cultural background of the client; (5) expanding counseling and therapy to include the multiple helping roles of family, community, and cultural groups; and (6) utilizing specific interviewing skills to liberate client consciousness of self-in-relation or self-in-context. The focus in both chapters is on applying MCT theory in practice, and with this goal each chapter includes a number of practical exercises.

Multicultural Counseling and Therapy I: Metatheory—Taking Theory into Practice

Harold Cheatham, Allen E. Ivey, Mary Bradford Ivey, Paul Pedersen, Sandra Rigazio-DiGilio, Lynn Simek-Morgan, Derald Wing Sue

CHAPTER GOALS

This chapter seeks to help you:

1. Understand the multicultural worldview from a universal and culture-specific perspective.

2. Identify and understand three central theoretical propositions of multicultural counseling and therapy.

   I. MCT is an integrative metatheory of counseling and therapy.

   II. Counselor and client identities are formed within multiple levels of experience (individual, group, and universal) and contexts (individual, family, and cultural). The totality of experiences and contexts is a central focus of treatment.

   III. Cultural identity development is a major determinant of both counselor and client attitudes toward the self, others of the same group, others of a different group, and the dominant group.

The authors of Chapters 5 and 6 are presented alphabetically. Multicultural counseling and therapy is not associated with any one key figure, as Freud is with psychodynamic therapy or Rogers is with person-centered therapy. Rather, MCT was developed in many settings by men and women of widely varying cultural background. Accordingly, these chapters have multiple authors. The six propositions of MCT were developed by Derald Wing Sue (1995). If citations of the six propositions are made, please reference his work. Key explanatory paragraphs are taken from D. W. Sue, A. Ivey, and P. Pedersen (1996) *A Theory of Multicultural Counseling and Therapy* (Pacific Grove, CA: Brooks/Cole) by permission of the authors and the publisher. H. Cheatham, M. Ivey, L. Simek-Morgan, and S. Rigazio-DiGilio have contributed to these two chapters through writing and editing portions of the chapters.

3. Examine your own level of cultural identity development and awareness of cultural issues in the helping process.

4. Learn some key MCT techniques and strategies that can be integrated into daily clinical practice.

5. Through practice exercises, conduct or engage in
   - Generating your own counseling and therapy theory for a multicultural group
   - A beginning exercise in Japanese Naikan therapy
   - Life-span review through developmental mapping and storytelling
   - Basic consciousness raising
   - Using the circle of life for decision making
   - Learning your personal place in cultural identity theory

Approaches to Multicultural Counseling and Therapy

Multicultural counseling and therapy (MCT) may best be described as a metatheoretical approach that recognizes that all helping methods ultimately exist within a cultural context. MCT stands as a theory in its own right, with a large array of therapeutic strategies. It also serves as an integrative framework for counseling and therapy in general.

MCT starts with awareness of differences among and within clients and is thus person centered. However, MCT also stresses the importance of family and cultural factors affecting the way clients view the world and is thus also culture centered (Pedersen & Ivey, 1993). MCT challenges practitioners, theoreticians, and researchers to rethink the meaning of counseling and psychotherapy and to give attention to unique individuals and their family and cultural contexts.

In 1976 Cheek commented on the counseling and psychotherapy field: "I am advocating treating one segment of our population quite differently from another. This is implicit in my statement that Blacks do not benefit from many therapeutic approaches to which Whites respond. And I have referred to some of these approaches of counselors and therapists as 'White techniques' " (p. 23).

In the years following, increasing attention was gradually paid to generating culturally appropriate theory. Cheatham (1990, pp. 380–81) comments first on the danger of therapy that is culturally insensitive and then suggests fundamental changes needed for truly multicultural counseling and therapy:

> The helping professional doubtless will violate the Black client's sense of integrity or "world view." . . . Blacks are products of their distinct sociocultural and sociohistorical experience. Counseling and therapy are specific, contractual events and thus may proceed more effectively on the basis of understanding of the client's cultural context.

Cheatham argues that the role of the therapist is not just to work with an individual, but also to work with the family and with extended networks that may be important to the client. An African-American client who suffers from depression should be treated both as an individual and as an individual within a cultural context. The existence of racism in the culture often can contribute to depression. According to Cheatham (1990), Cheek (1976), and White and Parham (1990), multicultural counseling and therapy will not be effective until the counselor focuses on and intervenes in issues of racism, sexism, and oppressive societal elements.

Sue (1992) states that "counseling has been used as an instrument of oppression, as it has been designed to transmit a certain set of individualistic cultural values. Traditional counseling has *harmed* minorities and women. Counseling and therapy have been the handmaiden of the status quo and, as such, represent a political statement" (p. 6). Sue (1995) has gone on to generate the basics of MCT theory. These ideas, in turn, have been expanded into a detailed metatheory by Sue, Ivey, and Pederson (1996), which forms the basis of the organization of these two chapters.

Freire (1972) uses the term *conscientizacào* as a general goal of education and, by extension, of counseling and therapy as well. *Conscientizacào* is focused on the liberation of the individual from personal, social, and economic oppression. Many clients come to therapy blaming themselves for their conditions. Your task is to liberate these clients from self-blame, encourage them to see their issues in a social context, and facilitate personal action to better their situations.

The multicultural counseling and therapy framework is concerned with counseling and psychotherapy as liberation—the viewing of the self in relation to others and to social and cultural contexts. Interdependence is basic to philosophy and action in MCT. MCT seeks to work with the individual and family in an egalitarian fashion. Furthermore, MCT hopes to see clients and therapists cooperatively working together in the community and society to alleviate and prevent future concerns and problems.

The Universal Approach to Multicultural Counseling

Fukuyama (1990) argues for a transcultural, universal approach to multicultural counseling and therapy, meaning that certain factors are important regardless of culture. Foremost is the fact that historically, traditional counseling theory has been unaware of culture. Fukuyama might point out that the theories presented in this book focus on values of individualism, rationalism, and self-determination. In research on counseling and therapy, the typical client is European-American, educated, middle class, and female (even though these theories were predominantly generated by European-American males).[1]

The universal approach recommended by Fukuyama challenges the field to become aware of multicultural issues and to recall that all counseling and therapy is culturally based. Fukuyama (1990, p. 9) argues for a counseling curriculum that:

- Defines culture broadly (including gender, affectional orientation, age, etc., as well as ethnic/racial issues)
- Teaches the danger of stereotyping
- Emphasizes the importance of language as the vehicle of counseling and therapy
- Encourages loyalty and pride in one's own culture and family ties
- Provides information on the processes of acculturation and oppression
- Discusses the importance of gender roles
- Facilitates each individual's identity development as a member of a culture
- Builds self-esteem and awareness
- Facilitates the understanding of one's own worldview and how it relates to family and cultural history

Client-centered Rogerian theory, psychodynamic theory, and cognitive-behavioral theory have all tended to focus on the individual, with minimal attention to contextual issues. Decisional counseling directs attention toward environmental action but also focuses primarily on individual issues.

The MCT universal approach focuses on cultural issues in each counseling contact. Rather than solely emphasizing individual issues, counselors should explore the multicultural context and environment of each client. MCT treatment often goes beyond individual therapy and may involve a network of interventions and even community action. For example, in counseling a Puerto Rican male who had just lost his job, a common approach would be to assess and address individual concerns and plan for a new work setting. An MCT therapist would do the same but would also encourage awareness of the person-in-context by such questions as: What are the implications of job loss as they relate to cultural issues such as *machismo* and *respecto?* Are issues of real or perceived discrimination present? What is the family context of the individual? What was the context of the work setting? Were cultural differences or lack of understanding part of the dismissal?

Fukuyama believes that the universal approach can change the field by challenging the foundations of traditional counseling and therapy. In this approach, one starts with awareness of culture and then later seeks to understand how individual or family issues grow out of and relate to cultural background.

The Focused Culture-Specific Approach

Locke (1990) challenges the universal approach, pointing out that the multicultural approach can become too overarching.

> I went to the class and made a formal presentation about culturally different students, focusing primarily on African-Americans. Finally, I asked the students about what they had read. To my chagrin I discovered that not one student in the class had selected an article about African-American students or any other group likely to be in their special education classes.

Locke states that it is incumbent on the counselor or therapist to gain cultural expertise in specific groups likely to be encountered. If the multicultural approach becomes too general, specific cultural groups will suffer from inefficient and oppressive methods of counseling and therapy. Taking the universal approach can weaken and dilute efforts for change. Given the history of racism in North America, Locke argues that multicultural counseling should focus primarily on African-American, Asian-American, Latina/o, and Native American cultures.

Locke (1990) argues for what he calls a "focused approach" in which it is important "to see people *both* as individuals and members of a culturally different group" (p. 23). This approach requires us to

- Examine our own racial beliefs and attitudes as they relate to culturally different individuals and groups
- Discuss racially relevant topics at an institutional level and be willing to work on issues of oppression beyond the individual and family session
- View our clients both as individuals and members of groups

The universal versus focused debate is a very real one. Some authorities feel that concerns of women, gays and lesbians, and other special populations are used to dilute what they consider the central issue in society—racism. However, those with feminist, gay/lesbian, or religious orientations have been known to criticize books on multiculturalism that focus primarily on racial/ethnic differences and give less attention to these particular issues. This debate can and has become heated.

One way to resolve this debate in practice is to focus on the issue that is most salient and important to your client. For example, if a person with a developmental disability is concerned over issues of discrimation or lack of access, focus on this issue. At a later time, racial/ethnic and other issues can be considered. Even this resolution, however, fails to consider the matters of community action and societal education.

MCT as Metatheory

MCT can be discussed in many ways. The propositions presented in Chapters 5 and 6 describe one way to approach this complex field. These ideas are drawn from the work of Sue (1995) and will need to be refined as MCT continues to grow and develop. (See Sue, Ivey, & Pederson [1996] for a detailed elaboration of these ideas.) As much as possible, these propositions and corollaries are based in available research and theory of multiculturalism.

Proposition I. MCT is a metatheory of counseling and psychotherapy. It is a theory about theories and offers an organizational framework for understanding the numerous helping approaches humankind has developed. It recognizes that theories of counseling and psychotherapy developed in the Western world, and those indigenous helping models intrinsic to other non-Western cultures, are neither inherently "right" or "wrong" or "good" or "bad." Rather, MCT holds that each theory represents a different worldview.

MCT has evolved from a method of helping members of one cultural group relate to members of different cultural groups into a metatheoretical perspective that recognizes the centrality and primary importance of culture as an internalized, subjective perspective constructed in response to contact with persons of contrasting cultural backgrounds. MCT rests on the assumption that all theories of counseling are culture specific and that values, assumptions, and philosophical bases need to be made clear and explicit.

Each theory of counseling and psychotherapy was developed in a particular cultural context. To the extent that each theory is appropriate to a particular cultural context, it will likely be biased toward contrasting cultural contexts. Different worldviews lead to different constructions of client concerns. For example, in traditional Western psychotherapy, psychodynamic approaches may view client issues as originating in unconscious developmental history, whereas cognitive-behavioral approaches may see the same issues as a result of social learning. These differing worldviews (or stories) result in different modes of conceptualizing and treating clients.

MCT recognizes the utility of Eurocentric theory and practice and recommends using all traditional and innovative theories drawn from this frame. In addition, MCT points out the importance of seeing the individual-in-context—considering the cultural background of the client and finding culturally appropriate solutions. This approach may involve changes in the way therapy is conducted. Specifically, MCT therapists help individuals see their problems in context, draw group or family members into the treatment, and use non-Western therapeutic approaches as appropriate to the client. Historically, traditional Western diagnosis and therapy (such as that in DSM-IV) see the "problem" in the client and fail to consider contextual issues.

MCT theory is ultimately concerned with cultural intentionality. The goal of MCT is to free individuals, families, groups, and organizations so that they can generate new ways of thinking, feeling, and acting and thereby live intentionally. This needs to happen within the clients' cultural frameworks and with understanding and respect for other worldviews. In this sense, MCT is not in opposition to cognitive-behavioral, psychodynamic, or existential-humanistic approaches but rather seeks to add culture as a center while respecting older traditions.

Theories of human behavior are defined by their ability to predict future behavior and explain past behavior. By these parameters, MCT qualifies as a theory in that it predicts failure as resulting from either the overemphasis of cultural differences or of culture similarities and predicts success as resulting from a simultaneously combined perspective. When cultural differences are overemphasized, the result is a stereotyped, exclusionary, politicized, and antagonistic perspective. When cultural similarities are overemphasized, the result can be the exploitation of less powerful by more powerful groups and a pretense of a melting pot environment that disregards essential features of cultural identity.

Generating New Theory from an MCT Perspective

Although the structure presented here for generating more culturally relevant theory and practice has been derived from Afrocentric theory, this structure can be adapted to other cultural frameworks. A practice exercise on generating culturally relevant theories of helping is included after Afrocentric theory is discussed (see Practice Exercise 5.1).

The Afrocentric Worldview

The Afrocentric worldview proposes that the African-American experience in the United States continues African history and culture. Years of slavery and racism have not dimmed the African intergenerational legacy of family relationship and group solidarity. Molefi Kete Asante's (1987) controversial and influential book *The Afrocentric Idea* has brought this concept to national prominence. However, many other authors have also emphasized these ideas (for example, Blassingame, 1972; Gutman, 1976; and Myers, 1988).

Cheatham (1990, p. 375) elaborates on the Afrocentric idea:

> Unlike the Western philosophic system, the African tradition has no heavy emphasis on the individual; the individual's being is authenticated only in terms of others. Nobles writes that there is a sense of corporate responsibility and collective destiny as epitomized in the traditional African self-concept: "I am because we are; and because we are, therefore I am" (1972).

Further, Cheatham, synthesizing available sources, argues that the philosophic linkages with Africa were retained even with transplantation to the United States, that this country's particular physical features facilitated retention of African ethos, and that rigidly enforced isolation of Blacks allowed (perhaps even required) retention of their orientation toward self-in-connection.

The Afrocentric or African worldview is holistic, emotionally vital, interdependent, and oriented toward collective survival. Additionally, the Afrocentric view emphasizes an oral tradition, uses a "being" time orientation, focuses on harmonious blending and cooperation, and is highly respectful of the role of the elderly (White & Parham, 1991, p. 15). In doing therapy with African-American or African clients or those of African descent from the Carribean, the therapist or counselor should consider this worldview and be aware that each individual client will be affected by this worldview differently.

In contrast, the North American Eurocentric worldview tends to divide the world into discrete, "knowable" parts; handles emotion somewhat carefully, even to the point of emotional repression; focuses on self-actualization and independence as a goal of life; emphasizes the clarity and precision of the written word; is oriented toward a linear "doing" view of time; stresses individuation and difference rather than collaboration; and is more oriented toward youth than toward the elderly. Traditional counseling theories tend to support this orientation.

Neither frame of reference or worldview is "right" or "wrong." Rather, each represents a way of constructing the world and making meaning. What can be harmful is to impose an Afrocentric frame on a Franco-American client or to impose a Eurocentric framework on an African-American client. However, clients will at times benefit from exposure to a culturally different frame of reference. Thus, sharing new perspectives and narratives from other cultures at times may be beneficial to clients, but imposing a worldview is to be avoided.

Moreover, each individual you work with is likely to have some mixture of cultural frames of reference. An African-American or Japanese-American client, for example, is likely to have been influenced by North American culture and may have incorporated many values of the Eurocentric frame. Many women who take a feminist orientation have consciously or unconsciously joined the Afrocentric worldview.

The Afrocentric Worldview Related to Other Cultures

Many of the sons and daughters of families of southern Italian, Chinese or Japanese, and Puerto Rican and Mexican origin have a life orientation closer to the Afrocentric worldview than to the European–North American worldview. Sue and Sue (1990) provide an important summary of key issues in multicultural counseling and development. They point out that constructions of the world are very different among Asian, African-American, European-American, and Native American populations, but that issues of relationship are often more important in non-Eurocentric cultures.

Also, we should recall that each individual is unique and special. There are some African-American clients whose worldview is more similar to midwestern culture than to that of their ethnically related brothers and sisters. Similarly, there are some religious cultures that adopt a more relational and family-centered orientation than do some African-Americans. *As always, never stereotype your client.* If you do not begin your interview by learning from the client, your "culturally aware" helping may be more oppressive than if you knew nothing about cultural differences at all.

Nwachuku's Theory: Developing New Theoretical Approaches from an MCT Perspective

Again, recall the importance of biculturality and multiculturality. Many of your clients will identify with more than one cultural or ethnic tradition. As stated in Chapter 2, multiple cultural identities can be a major strength. Due to conflicting cultural expectations, racism, and/or social status differences, at times bicultural or multicultural experience becomes a counseling issue in itself that you will need to help the client sort out.

Can the microskills approach (see Chapter 3) offer some direction in generating more culturally relevant theory and practice? One route toward this objective is to examine a specific African culture and then see how the findings may relate to African-Americans, European-Americans, and other groups.

Uchenna Nwachuku, a Nigerian Igbo, has explored the above question in some detail and has generated the important concrete beginnings of a specifically Afro-centric theory and method of helping (Nwachuku, 1989; Nwachuku, 1990; Nwachuku and Ivey, 1991). Nwachuku's methods are highly instructive for those who seek to make broad concepts of multicultural helping workable for the practicing counselor or therapist.

Drawing on his personal experience and knowledge of Western helping methods, Nwachuku evolved the following specific steps in generating an Afrocentric theory oriented toward the Igbo. Nwachuku's specific steps follow and provide ideas for generating theory and practice in cultures other than the Nigerian Igbo. For example, many dimensions of feminist theory can be explained by Nwachuku's method.

1. *Examine the culture itself. What are important personal and interpersonal characteristics in this culture?*

This goal entails field research, interviews with those in the cultural group, and reading from an anthropological frame of reference. From such work, Nwachuku noted five key characteristics of the Igbo: individual versus group orientation, decisional style, developmental progressions, attitude toward change, and language. These key characteristics formed the foundation of his Afrocentric theory, and will be of greater or lesser importance in varying cultures. As you work with different groups, you may want to add additional dimensions related to a particular group's special interests. For example, in developing a theory for gays, the process of "coming out" as gay may be one dimension. For the deaf, developing a positive awareness of deafness as a culture can be an issue.

For example, Nwachuku, reflecting on his own developmental history, talks about going for walks with his mother. Rather than running ahead or holding his mother's hand as a Western child might, Nwachuku recalls walking with his hand held close under his mother's armpit and feeling the beat of her heart. He comments that that beat is still with him. This particular vignette provides an interesting example of how a relational culture, such as that of the African Igbo, uses the developmental process to foster cultural goals. In this case, the focus is on the child in relation to the community and the mother. The Western child may have been oriented to individualism by moving ahead separately. In one society, children are kept closer to the mother; in another, children are encouraged to go out on their own.

The Igbo have much in common with other African cultures, but there is much that is distinctive about their own group as well. Thus, generalizations drawn from the Igbo cannot be applied to the Nigerian Yoruba, for instance. African cultures differ, just as do French and German or Haitian and Cuban cultures.

An important contribution of MCT to counseling and therapy theory is the awareness that all not client issues are internal. The rational emotive behavior therapy and the cognitive-behavioral Stoic traditions (i.e., It is not things but what I think of things that is most important) face a major challenge here. Those who adopt an MCT perspective recognize that external reality at times may be far more important than internal cognitive structures, unconscious processes, or even empathic conditions. For example, racism, sexism, and discrimination are external conditions that cannot be dealt with solely by internal cognitive change.

To date, issues of dominance and power have been insufficiently considered in helping theory. The very terms *counselor* and *client* or *therapist* and *patient* imply an important hierarchy of power. Historically, much of traditional Western therapy has served as the handmaiden of a racist, sexist, homophobic, and classist culture. MCT therapists recognize the problems inherent in power imbalance. Much of feminist therapy and culturally sensitive therapy focuses on client and counselor coconstruction of issues and a basic egalitarian approach to the therapy and counseling process and treatment planning.

2. *Identify concrete skills and strategies that can be used in helping relationships.*

Drawing out the client's story using empathic listening skills is a central part of an Igbo theory of helping. However, traditional Igbo culture often worked to solve personal problems by telling another story or through metaphor. The task of the Igbo helper was to "help," which traditionally meant taking a more authoritarian and directive approach to helping once the client's issues were understood.

The microskill of focus is particularly important in Nwachuku's theory and practice. Whereas most counseling theory focuses on the individual client, Nwachuku's Afrocentric theory recommends a focus on the extended family and the community, with a secondary focus on the individual and the nuclear family. For instance, in the Igbo culture, the paternal uncle is a particularly important figure whose opinion needs to be considered.

Applications of the Igbo model to African-Americans and other nonmajority populations should be considered. Berman (1979) found that a "we" focus was used in counseling sessions with Blacks considerably more often than with Whites, suggesting more mutuality between client and therapist than is usually recommended by traditional counseling theory. Roberts (1982) replicated these findings among African-American managers. Working with culturally distinct Arabian groups in Lebanon, Kikoski (1980) also found a more mutual focus and an orientation toward a more directive approach to helping.

Practice Exercise 5.1 outlines other issues for you to consider. The example here works on the individual level. The community and family genograms remind us constantly of the context in which we work. If we are dealing with issues of oppression, it is important to listen and hear the client's story, but our theory of action may have to move far beyond traditional individual counseling and therapy.

≡ Practice Exercise 5.1 ≡

 ### Generating Culturally Relevant Theories of Helping

Select a specific group of interest to you and practice building culturally relevant theory. You are not expected to generate a fully developed theory. Rather, this exercise is designed as a beginning set of steps to help you think about the possibility and need for generating new theory to meet the special needs of any group with which you may work. A possible topic for the theory includes any group defined by language, gender, ethnicity/race, affectional orientation, age, physical challenge, socioeconomic status, or trauma. In addition, you may wish to consider geographical locations and how regional differences might affect the counseling process.

Step 1. Examine the group culture. What are the important personal and interpersonal characteristics?

a. *What is the cultural attitude toward individual and relational issues?* Traditional European theories tend to focus on the individual. The African Igbo is both individualistic and oriented to the group, and thus both individual and relational issues need to be considered. Similar issues come to the fore with African-Americans, Asian-Americans, Latinas/os, and Native Americans, although each group has its unique patterns.

b. *How are decisions made, and who are the natural helpers?* The attitudes and wishes of extended family and the entire community are central to individual decision making in African Igbo culture. This suggests that decisions need to focus not only on the client, but also on these other influences as well. This is in direct contrast to the locus of individualistic decision making stressed in European-American theories. Native American culture, in particular, may be described as more similar to the Igbo style than it is to Eurocentric helping. The extended family and elders are seen as "natural helpers" in one group, whereas "professionals" may be the natural helpers in another.

c. *What are the developmental progressions?* You may wish to review Tamase's life-span theories as a new way to consider developmental issues. Childrearing is balanced between the nuclear family, the extended family, and the community in African Igbo culture, as contrasted with the nuclear family of traditional European-American culture. Developmental theory and the concept of healthy adjustment in one culture cannot be generalized immediately to another.

d. *What is the attitude toward change, both from within and from without?* The Igbo are receptive to change, but they also value age and respect elders. For counseling purposes, this suggests that some Western techniques and ideas may indeed be appropriate but also that the age of the counselor may be important. The attitude toward change varies among groups. South Pacific Islanders and many Native American Nations value harmony with the environment and do not uphold the values of change, which may have been imposed on them by colonizing peoples.

e. *How is language used?* Figures of speech, complex communication, proverbs, and quotations are used frequently in Nigerian Igbo communication. These complex language patterns suggest that Igbo clients should respond well to metaphorical orientations and that the straightforward style of European-American counseling approaches may be resisted. It therefore may be better to tell clients a story or have them join you in storytelling. Cheek (1976) and White and Parham (1991) stress the importance of bidialectic communication with African-Americans. Important stories may need to be told first in the primary language of clients, and then they can translate the story for you.

f. *What are some key issues that people deal with in the cultural group, especially in relation to power?* If you are working with a client who is a minority in a majority culture, how might issues of social oppression be manifested? How does the group deal with racism, sexism, homophobia, or classism? In working with Vietnam veterans, cancer survivors, or a homeless population, what are the key issues? It is important to note that the concerns presented are related to external pressures and power. An important addition of MCT to counseling and therapy theory is the awareness that all not client issues are internal.

Step 2. Identify concrete skills and strategies that can be used in helping relationships.

This will be a cumulative process, and you will want to review ideas in Chapters 5 and 6 on MCT before developing a preliminary answer. The first place to look, however, is in the natural helping style of the group. Search out the informal networks of helpers. Who goes to whom for assistance and under what conditions? The community genogram and family genogram can be useful tools in understanding broader helping frameworks beyond individual counseling. How are nonverbal and verbal attending behaviors and listening and influencing skills played out in this group?

You may wish to draw on adaptations of microskills, specific techniques, and strategies presented in Chapters 5 and 6 and adapt ideas from psychodynamic (Chapters 7 and 8), cognitive-behavioral (Chapters 9 and 10), and existential-humanistic (Chapters 11 and 12) approaches. You may also want to include family and community action as part of your set of skill strategies.

Step 3. Test your new helping theory and skills in a coconstructive process with your client or clients.

Coconstruction and mutuality are vital. Too often there exists a "top-down" approach in which the theorist or clinician takes seemingly excellent ideas to clients and then is surprised when the theories do not work. When you approach culturally appropriate counseling and therapy in a coconstructed manner with your clients, you will likely find that there is more in client wisdom than we usually acknowledge.

3. *Test the new helping theory and its skills in action.*

Nwachuku used the microtraining format to generate traditional Western and Afrocentric videotaped examples of culturally appropriate helping. Both videotapes focused on the same question: Should an African student return home from graduate school in the United States and meet family responsibilities? In the traditional model, the helper focused immediately on the problem, used an "I" focus, and encouraged the client to make an independent autonomous decision. As excellent listening skills were demonstrated, most counseling experts would consider the model a fine example of how counseling should be approached. The client was supported in finding his own independent decision.

The Afrocentric Igbo videotaped model of helping was quite different. More time was spent at the beginning of the session as the counselor helped the client feel comfortable. Although a "we" focus was used, it was also clear that the Igbo helper was establishing himself as an authority who expected to take charge of the session. The client's story was drawn out by the Igbo helper through questioning. After briefly probing the client's thoughts about the issue, the interviewer then focused on the extended family and asked questions about the client's uncle. It soon was apparent that a broader network of decision makers was involved. The African Igbo client had obviously been influenced by North American individualism and needed some help from the counselor—specifically, a reminder that more people than just the client were involved in his important life decision.

The counselor then told the client a traditional Igbo story about family values and looked at the client. The client understood the meaning of the story and acknowledged that he had lost some of his traditional values in the more individualistic United States. Discussion followed on how to balance the strengths of an individualistic culture with the different strengths of a relational culture. Being able to see both perspectives helped clarify decision making.

Implications of Nwachuku's Model

Beginning or experienced professionals in counseling and therapy may not be comfortable with Nwachuku's model. The idea that the family and the counselor lead the client in making decisions may seem directly antagonistic to the traditional goals of counseling and therapy. Moreover, clients may not agree with all the values of their cultures. Many clients from other cultures may find strengths in European–North American culture that they will want to adapt to their own lives. Similarly, as European-Americans learn about other cultural traditions, they may want to adapt Afrocentric or other frames to their own lives. Helping clients sort out these issues will be an important part of therapy.

Counseling theory is in a time of change and revision. Nwachuku's framework can be applied to a variety of cultural contexts, and this application may prompt a new view of European-American theory and practice. Understanding multiple worldviews from Afrocentric, European-American, Native American, Asian-American, and other perspectives will lead to new levels of understanding that can change your practice.

Research Exhibit 5.1 discusses the development of psychotherapy for ethnic minorities.

Research Exhibit 5.1

Psychotherapeutic Services for Ethnic Minorities: Twenty-Five Years of Research Findings

Sue (1988) reviewed the literature on helping services for ethnic minorities, stating that services for minorities are frequently considered ineffective. Leong, Wagner, and Piroshaw Tata (1995) updated this literature with similar observations. Their findings follow:

1. *There are important differences in conceptualization of psychological issues.* Many minority groups conceptualize psychological difficulties as more organic in nature and believe that "mental health is enhanced by will power and the avoidance of morbid thinking" (Sue, 1988, p. 302). Thus, understanding cultural differences is an important feature in counseling and therapy. For example, what is a concern for a European-American client may not be an issue for an Asian-American.

2. *Majority counselors often hold negative stereotypes toward the ethnically different.* "These stereotypes tend to reflect the nature of race or ethnic relations in our society" (Sue, 1988, p. 302). Leong and others (1995) also found that the Afrocentric versus Eurocentric discussion illustrates how differently the world is viewed by these two groups. If we consider these differences as constructions rather than as "reality," we may make an important advance toward multicultural understanding.

3. *Despite these issues, there is some research evidence that minority clients do benefit from therapy, even with European-American helpers.* Sue cites the work of Jones (1978, 1985), among others, showing this encouraging finding. African-American clients were more often likely to discuss issues about race during the therapy process. Leong and others (1995) note similar findings and discuss the importance of the African-American church.

Griffith and Jones (1978) state: "Unquestionably, race makes a difference in psychotherapy. Still, this is not to say that the skillful and experienced White therapist cannot effectively treat the Black client. Rather the critical requisite is that the White therapist is sensitive to the unique ways in which . . . race affects the course of treatment" (p. 230). These comments are upheld by Leong and others (1995).

4. *The degree of acculturation is important in client-therapist matching.* Sue (1988) presents extensive research that reveals that many minority group members prefer a counselor of their racial/ethnic background. However, data also exist that a highly acculturated minority counselor may be ineffective with a less acculturated client of the same race or ethnic group. Also, some minorities will not be willing to consult with majority counselors.

It seems likely that cultural identity theory may explain these sometimes contradictory results. If clients are matched with therapists who have similar cultural awareness (and the therapists are competent), a good result may be expected. A sensitive, European-American therapist may be equally effective if the client is at a level of cultural identity development that makes seeing a White counselor a viable alternative. "Ethnicity is important, but what is more important is its meaning" (Sue, 1988, p. 307). Leong and others (1995) stress the need for "culturally responsive" counseling and therapy, the need for more prevention work on the part of professionals, and the need for more effective health policies, thus making helping available to those who presently do not have the choice of seeking psychological or counseling assistance.

The Multiple Contexts and Experiences of MCT

Proposition II. Counselor and client identities are formed and embedded in multiple levels of experiences (individual, group, and universal) and contexts (individual, family, and cultural). The totality and interrelationship of experiences and contexts need to be considered in any treatment.

MCT therapists acknowledge that all individuals possess an individual, group, and universal level of identity. Even though we are unique individuals, we share commonalties with our multicultural reference groups (cultural, racial/ethnic, gender, religion, sexual orientation, etc.) as well as the universal identity that we are all human beings. These levels of identity are fluid and ever changing so that the salience of one over the other is also changing. An individual client may at one moment focus on individual needs, at another moment on a issue related to multicultural reference group identity, and at still another time on universal human experience. The effective helping professional validates all levels and strives to relate to that which is most salient and important to the person at the time of contact. Unfortunately, traditional counseling and psychotherapy have tended to relate at primarily the individual or universal levels, thereby negating multicultural reference group identities.

In contrast, MCT theory stresses the importance of the person-environment interaction. Working effectively with clients requires an understanding of how the individual is embedded in the family, which in turn requires an understanding of how the family is affected by a culturally diverse society. The family-culture interface is often best approached through emphasis on community by using such approaches as the community genogram (Chapter 1).

MCT therapists presume that the salient cultural feature (individual, multicultural group identification, or universal) will change in a psychodynamic fashion for the client during the interview and that a skilled counselor will be able to accurately track the change from one cultural referent to another. Counselors should remember that not all of clients' cultural affiliations will be equally important all of the time. Also, as noted before, counselors should be aware that they bring their own families, communities, and cultural backgrounds to sessions and that their worldviews affect the way they conduct therapy.

The Microskill of Focusing and MCT

In traditional counseling, counselors are accustomed to making "I" statements and focusing on what individual clients can do to help themselves. It is important to realize that this attitude may clash with the worldviews of many minority people, whose traditions focus on the family. It may be difficult for these individuals to separate themselves from their families and just think of themselves. Their sense of self is often collective in nature, and their being may be authenticated mainly in terms of others. In counseling clients from various cultures, an individually balanced focus among individual, family, and cultural expectations is needed. The emphasis on each aspect will naturally vary with the particular client.

Thus, a portion of any counseling session should address the influence of significant others and of cultural, environmental, and contextual issues. Counseling and therapy have been in the past focused on the individual. Asking questions about, paraphrasing, and interpreting individual's worldviews as they relate to family and cultural issues will make a significant difference in the way helpers and clients conceptualize and consider concerns. For example, traditional psychology and psychiatry once considered Vietnam veterans with psychiatric distress to be malingerers seeking benefits from the government. This condition is now recognized as posttraumatic stress disorder (PTSD), a natural result of extreme battle stress. PTSD was once considered an individual problem, and it took considerable effort on the part of Vietnam veterans to demonstrate that PTSD is, for many, a consequence of being exposed to an incredibly stressful environment. Many now would consider it inappropriate to consider Vietnam veterans with PTSD as suffering primarily from individual and internal conflicts.

Another way to approach counseling the individual in context is to adapt existing counseling theories to include a multicultural focus. In addition to the concepts of self-actualization, autonomy, and independence of traditional therapy, MCT would also add the concepts of self-in-relation, connectedness and relationship, and interdependence. For example, with humanistic theory the microskill of focus would be employed. Most of the traditional Rogerian skills and values can be enhanced if the words "You feel . . ." are changed to "You feel this in relationship to . . . (family and/or cultural background)." The precise phrasing may vary, but the usefulness of reflective listening skills and the goals of traditional Rogerian theory can be enhanced by adding a focus on relational and cultural issues. Often clients mention family and cultural issues; we can ignore these issues if we constantly focus on the individual. Placing the individual in context can be an important way of honoring and enhancing individuality.

Cognitive-behavioral theory is an effective treatment modality with many clients but can be only partially effective if insufficient attention is paid to environmental determinants. For example, counselors often attack the "irrational" ideas of clients without first looking for possible rational elements, as can be discovered when client statements are considered from a cultural perspective. Similarly, therapy from rational-emotive or cognitive stances often neglects how family and cultural issues affect clients' being in the world. Focusing specifically on the individual in an irrational context may be a way to reframe cognitive theory and practice. Behavioral programs, such as stress management techniques that focus on meditation, relaxation, and cognitive issues, may overlook the fact that the client is reacting normally to environmental stressors.

Life-Span Review: Introspective Developmental Counseling

Introspective developmental counseling (IDC) seeks to learn how clients' life histories affect their present experiences. This theory was generated from a multicultural framework in Japan by Tamase (1991). IDC draws on past and present strengths in working on and resolving problematic life issues. IDC is Tamase's integration of Japanese Naikan therapy (Reynolds, 1990), Erikson's life-span theory (1950/1963), and developmental counseling and therapy theory. Tamase's theory will be presented in more detail after first examining some concepts of Japanese Naikan therapy.

Naikan Therapy

Naikan therapy is aimed at assisting clients to discover meaning in their lives and repair damaged relationships with others (Murase & Reynolds, 1972; Reynolds, 1990). This system seeks to help clients move from narrow self-centeredness to awareness of how the individual was and is formed by important relationships. Naikan therapy points out that a narrow focus on the self leads to neurotic and painful outcomes.

For example, most depressed clients in North American culture focus very much on themselves and can benefit from focusing outward and seeing themselves in a relational context. Rigazio-DiGilio and Ivey (1990) found that DCT questions helped inpatient depressed clients see themselves more in context. This focus on the self-in-relation proved to be therapeutic and resulted in better feelings toward self and others.

An example adapted from Naikan therapy is presented in Practice Exercise 5.2 and reveals a very different view of therapy than usually experienced in the Western world. Much of this therapy involves silent meditation on how the individual depends on others throughout the life span and thus is focused on relationship to others. This practice exercise can seem strange to individualistically oriented Western-trained counselors. Likewise, Eurocentric ideas may seem odd to some Japanese clients and counselors.

Naikan therapy usually is conducted in residential week-long sessions in which clients review their experiences throughout the life span. The therapy consists of alternating meditative sessions and debriefing discussions with the therapist. One of the major goals of Naikan therapy is to help clients realize the importance of other

Practice Exercise 5.2

 # Naikan Therapy and Self-in-Relation

Either by yourself or with a volunteer client, you may experience the powerfulness of Naikan therapy through this introductory exercise. You can expect a very different emphasis with European-American methods.

1. *Establish a meditative state.* Sit in a comfortable chair or cushion; relax and focus on your breathing. Allow a minimum of five minutes for this preliminary process to ensure solid focusing on the issue at hand.

2. *Think about yourself in relation to your most significant caregiver who nurtured you as a child.* Meditate on the following three dimensions of the relationship: (a) how the caregiver has given to you and cared for you, (b) what you have given in return, (c) the trouble you have caused the caregiver. Find concrete examples for each dimension, and, if you wish, accompany each example with a sensorimotor image. Develop the image specifically in your mind. What are you seeing, hearing, feeling? Locate the feelings associated with the image in your body.

3. *Debrief the meditative exercise by asking the following questions:*

   a. What do you notice about this experience? How are we formed in relationship?

   b. How has your development been influenced in a positive way by your relationship with your caregiver?

   c. What is your responsibility to your caregiver? Your responsibility to others?

people throughout the life span and to accommodate to cooperative existence. Naikan therapy is particularly interesting in that it offers a complete contrast to the theories presented in this book. For instance, assertiveness training is virtually antithetical to Naikan, and humanistic and psychodynamic self-examination would be considered selfish from the Naikan perspective.

Introspective Developmental Counseling and Life Review

Tamase's work is unique in that it combines Eastern and Western frameworks. Erikson's life-span theory (summarized in Table 5.1) has been severely criticized on the grounds that it is based on a Northern European/U.S. White male model (Gilligan, 1982). Nonetheless it remains a useful framework when modified by IDC and MCT theory.

Erikson defines the developmental task of early childhood (ages 2 through 4) as developing a sense of autonomy. However, elsewhere, such as in Africa, Japan, or South America, the goal of this period is not autonomy but rather a sense of connectedness to the caregiver. In fact, overemphasis on autonomy and separation is considered pathological in many cultures.

Tamase avoids labeling any developmental period as being focused on a particular task, maintaining instead that different cultures will focus on different issues at different stages than those proposed by Erikson. Tamase points out that individuals find their own unique life paths but always within a network of relationships. Furthermore, as life experience expands and contracts through the processes of accommodation and assimilation, different individuals make different meanings.

Tamase's Basic Life Stages.   Tamase identifies four age-related developmental phases in IDC: (1) birth through preschool, (2) elementary school, (3) adolescence, and (4) present-day life. Tamase has thus far focused primarily on the early life stages. As this model expands, additional questions will be raised about later life stages. Early research and clinical practice, however, reveal that the first four phases produce a substantial base of information and insight (Tamase and Kato, 1990; Tamase, 1991). Tamase has developed specific questions for each life period, which may be found in more detail in Ivey (1991).

In response to developmental questions for the birth-to-preschool period, Tamase has found that clients tend to discuss random, disconnected images and fragments of events. At the elementary school stage, concrete stories are related, whereas adolescent-stage questions elicit self-examination and the beginning of pattern identification. In the present-day life stage, clients become aware that their present modes of functioning are deeply related to their past developmental histories.

Tamase's framework offers some advantages over Eriksonian life stages in that Tamase does not impose a set of culturally bound expectations such as "autonomy

Table 5.1   Erikson's Developmental Stages throughout the Life Span as Modified by Multicultural Counseling and Therapy

Life Stage (approximate age and major developmental crises derived from Eurocentric norms)	Key Environmental Systems (will vary with the cultural experience of the individual)	Developmental Tasks (will vary with family, community, and culture)	Example of How Life Stages Differ among Multicultural Groups
Infancy (birth–2) Balancing trust in others vs. mistrust	Caregiver and family. Families may be traditional, single-parent, blended, grandparent, adoptive, gay or lesbian, rich or poor. Seek out the nature of the early attachment experiences and how they may be unique to the person, family, and culture.	Attachment to caregiver, individual, or network. Sensorimotor intelligence. Basic motor coordination.	Caregiver and nuclear family are the focus in European-American situations, but extended family may be central in many groups. The "holding environment" of Japan may produce closer attachments than in Eurocentric cultures.
Early childhood (2–4) Autonomy vs. shame and doubt (learning one's responsibility to others)	Family, extended family, preschool play group.	Need to determine how much emphasis is to be placed on individual needs vs. the group. Self-control. Language learning. Attachment to family is basis for developing a beginning sense of self and others. Walking and play activities are central.	Autonomy is a Eurocentric construct. In Japan, for example, the child is often encouraged to develop a sense of closeness and dependence on others. Too much autonomy is viewed as selfishness in some cultures.
Middle childhood (5–7) Initiative vs. guilt (responsibly representing one's family and culture—initiative exists within a context)	Family, neighborhood, school.	Gender identity. First stages of moral development. Concrete mental operations.	Boys and girls have been taught since infancy to behave differently and dress differently and are rewarded for different types of behaviors in virtually all cultures. Initiative may be defined as aggressiveness in some groups.

Table 5.1   (continued)

Life Stage (approximate age and major developmental crises derived from Eurocentric norms)	Key Environmental Systems (will vary with the cultural experience of the individual)	Developmental Tasks (will vary with family, community, and culture)	Example of How Life Stages Differ among Multicultural Groups
Late childhood (8–12) Industry vs. inferiority. Most cultures expect some form of productivity from the child at this stage, yet the focus is on doing. Some cultures would emphasize the importance of "being vs. doing."	Family, neighborhood, school, and peer group.	Basic time of learning social relationships through work and play. Team membership may be as important as building self-esteem and feelings of competence. Egocentric learning. Learning of many basic life skills in the culture.\n\nLate concrete mental operations. "If . . . then" reasoning. Moral development in terms of right vs. wrong.	Children of poverty may not be surrounded by a stimulating material environment and may have less chance to learn self-esteem and basic skills, which are considered natural to children of a more economically advantaged background. The word *industry* is related to a "doing orientation" of Eurocentric culture, as contrasted with Afrocentric and Arabic ideas of "being."
Puberty and adolescence (12–18) Identity vs. role confusion. Role confusion might be translated by feminist theory as a time of developing multiple roles and recognizing that identity can be only defined in relationship to others.	Peer group, school, family, neighborhood, work setting.	Sexual maturation. Formal operational thought. Generation of self-concept and awareness of personal identity in Eurocentric culture as a move toward independent living. In traditional Latina/o experience, the movement may be toward taking one's place in organized society and recognizing relational responsibilities.	Piagetian theorists estimate that between 25 and 40 percent of the population never reaches full formal operations. Gay or lesbian adolescents may have a particularly difficult time at this stage due to cultural expectations.

(continued)

Table 5.1   (continued)

Life Stage (approximate age and major developmental crises derived from Eurocentric norms)	Key Environmental Systems (will vary with the cultural experience of the individual)	Developmental Tasks (will vary with family, community, and culture)	Example of How Life Stages Differ among Multicultural Groups
Young adulthood (20–30) Intimacy vs. isolation. Intimacy may be defined in Chinese culture as being part of a larger extended family. Most cultures focus on issues of connection, but in varying ways.	In Eurocentric culture, new family and living mate(s) may become central. Friendship network, may move away from family of origin. Work setting becomes more important.	Finding one's own sense of self in a family relationship of love and commitment. Initial parenting. A new relationship with parents and extended family. Major career decisions and financial decisions.	Adolescent women in U.S. culture work on issues of intimacy during adolescence, perhaps even more so than identity. In some African and Italian cultures, the extended family remains especially important in living and decision-making arrangements.
Adulthood (30–65) Generativity vs. stagnation. The definition of generativity in one culture may focus on work, whereas in another it may be on family. Stagnation may be interpreted by some as a contemplative state of being.	Family and children, friendship network, work setting, community.	Reworking of all the issues above from a new perspective of maturity. Special emphasis on career and family changes. Particularly important are the physical, cognitive, and emotional changes that come with each new decade.	Women's career and life patterns do not easily fit into Erikson's framework. Rather than move systematically through the stages one by one, as suggested by Erikson, some women work on many at once. Maturity may be flexibility in the use of all stages. Each culture will define maturity differently. The thirty years of adulthood are more complex than allowed for in the Erikson time frame.
Old age (65–death) Ego integrity vs. despair. The concept	Family, friendship network, community, caring and health	Reworking all previous developmental crises	Experts now concede that many are still in middle age at 70. A

Table 5.1   (continued)

Life Stage (approximate age and major developmental crises derived from Eurocentric norms)	Key Environmental Systems (will vary with the cultural experience of the individual)	Developmental Tasks (will vary with family, community, and culture)	Example of How Life Stages Differ among Multicultural Groups
of ego again focuses on the individualistic aspects of Erikson's framework. Is integrity to be defined by an individual or a self-in-relation?	agencies (as one faces illness and nears death).	once again. Life review and finding meaning in what one has done. Coping with physical changes and illness. Dealing with the death of family and friends. Financial/living concerns and decisions.	new and rapidly increasing category is the "old old" who are 85 and over, many of whom still have good health and enjoy full lives, contrary to cultural stereotypes. Age is valued far more in Native American Indian culture.

versus shame and doubt" or "identity versus role confusion." By emphasizing age periods without prior constructions of meaning, Tamase offers a more multiculturally viable life-span review process. Whereas traditional life review focuses on the individual, IDC demands a focus on self-in-relation and a more complex view of identity development than that proposed by Erikson.

Making Meaning from the Past.   Drawing from Naikan therapy, the goals of IDC are in some ways similar to psychodynamic formulations in that the past is believed to affect the present. However, Tamase avoids giving theoretical interpretations for the client. Rather, the IDC interviewer simply listens and helps the client review the past. Often, if the counselor listens to past events carefully, clients begin to discover repeating patterns and make their own interpretations. When the interviewer adds the sensorimotor, concrete, formal, and dialectic/systemic DCT questions (see Chapter 4), IDC can be a powerful therapeutic tool. Also, whereas Erikson's work is solely descriptive, Tamase provides room for specific action and treatment. Practice Exercise 5.3 presents a shortened version of IDC. This exercise can be helpful in thinking about your clients from a more developmental and multicultural perspective.

Tamase's adaptation of life-span theory will become most meaningful if you devote some care and time to this practice exercise. DCT theory and method (Chapter 4) can help explain some of your discoveries. Most adults recall the early

≡ Practice Exercise 5.3 ≡

An Exercise in Developmental Mapping and Storytelling

This exercise will help you understand how you or your client has generated key construct systems and beliefs about the world. The exercise can be quite lengthy, and a review of each life stage can take an hour or more. Alternatively, you can relate a brief story from each stage to help you understand how some life patterns have developed.

Review one life stage or more by asking yourself or your client the following questions:

1. *Key environmental systems.* The focus here is on the individual and key environmental support systems.

   a. What was the family situation during this life stage?
   b. What important life events or stressors affected your family or caregivers during this period?
   c. What is the nature of family or extended family in your personal history?
   d. Where did you obtain your support during this life stage?

2. *Life stage developmental story.* The focus here is on the individual recollections, although the recollections are usually in a context.

   a. Tell me a story and/or significant event that stands out for you from this life stage. (Examples might be a birth story, a fragment of a childhood memory, a repeatedly told family story.)
   b. What are additional stories from this life stage?

3. *Multicultural issues.* The focus here is on the individual and how he or she relates to the community and the multicultural environment.

   a. How did gender, religion, ethnic/racial status, or other multicultural issue affect your development during this period?
   b. Tell me a story you recall about the role of men or women, a religious figure, or ethnic/racial figure from that time period.
   c. Who were your heroes?
   d. Whom did you look up to and respect?

4. *How does the past relate to the present?* The focus here is on balancing the individual with family and multicultural issues.

   a. Given the data you've discussed during this time period, how does this relate to your present life experience?
   b. Do you see any patterns that relate to how you are now and/or how you relate to others?
   c. What do you see as the influence of family and culture on where you are now?

If you wish to work through the framework at a deeper level, add the four-level questioning framework of DCT to your interview. For example, in discussing the family situation in the first question, ask for an image and what is seen, heard, and felt; then ask for a concrete situation; then ask for what patterns there are. End with a systematic multicultural examination of the family system.

years of their lives in random sensorimotor feelings, images, and short descriptions. Clients may even return experientially to early happenings. When you review with clients their early school-age experiences, they usually provide concrete descriptors of specific situations and events. When you turn to the adolescent period, clients tend to talk about their experiences and become more reflective and formal operational. Using DCT questions, you can bring out sensorimotor, concrete, formal/reflective, and dialectic/systemic thought to enrich the review of each life stage.

The dialectic/systemic perspective applied to life-span theory asks you and the client to reflect on life and its multiple systems. Rather than define each stage within a specific theoretical framework, Tamase encourages clients and counselors to coconstruct new, culturally specific and culturally appropriate stages of life development.

Focus and Consciousness-Raising Groups

The essence of consciousness-raising is group discussion of stories, which can help individuals plan action for the future. An example can be found in the project initiated by the Aboriginal Educational Foundation to help native people discuss their issues, strengths, and desires for the future, with the goal of empowering families and groups. The Aboriginal project brought families and groups together to tell their stories in an intensive two-hour session. The objectives were to draw out their daily life struggles as they related to schooling or study and employment. The task of the leaders was simply to listen and learn. There was an emphasis on group sharing of experiences in a safe atmosphere. As the group members discussed their concrete issues, they soon discovered many commonalities and patterns, as described in the report of the Aboriginal Educational Foundation (1992, p. 1):

> Most have strong criticisms of their schooling.
> All are very critical of the employment choices open to them.
> Few reported satisfaction with their current employment and training situation.
> Many hoped that their children and grandchildren could be spared similar experiences.

These comments might be similar to those of many nonmajority people throughout the world. Irish migrant workers in Britain, Ukrainian farmers in Canada, and African-Americans in the United States might have similar concerns.

Group consciousness-raising can also be the foundation for theory development. For example, feminist theory and practice evolved out of women's consciousness-raising groups and their concrete naming of common experiences. Consciousness-raising can be conducted in groups and can also be an addition to individual counseling and therapy. Practice Exercise 5.4 provides a specific set of strategies that can be employed with either individuals or groups.

Practice Exercise 5.4

 Basic Consciousness-Raising

1. *Establish a group of at least three participants.* The topic for your session can be as broad as what it means to be male or female; gay, lesbian, bisexual, or heterosexual; or some other racial/ethnic or multicultural group. Being a White Canadian or White U.S. citizen also represents a multicultural group. You might have groups share an experience they have had with oppression.
2. *Discuss the general issue.* Begin by asking members of the group to tell a story that represents what group membership means to them. Allow time for sharing after each story. The group likely may find common patterns in their experiences.
3. *Divide the time by focusing on three dimensions.* In a consciousness-raising session, one-third of the time may be profitably spent on focusing on personal stories and narratives of oppression or group identity, one-third on group process and reactions of members to one anothers' stories, and one-third on the cultural/environmental contexts surrounding the issues. The microskill of focus is particularly helpful for the group leader. Time may be structured formally along these three dimensions, or you may wish to simply balance discussion along the three dimensions from time to time.
4. *Establish an action commitment.* Ask your participants for one thing they might do differently as a result of this interaction. Examples could be a new behavior or a new way of thinking about things.

The Integrative Life Patterns Model

Hansen's (1990, 1991) integrated life patterns (ILP) model is a decisional counseling model that raises consciousness of multicultural issues. Hansen's framework is more relational and comprehensive than most decisional theory and provides a useful framework for considering the importance and place of the decisional process in professional counseling and therapy.

Integrative life patterning has been defined as the "lifelong process of identifying our primary needs, roles, and goals and the consequent integration of these within ourselves, our work, and our family" (Hansen, 1990, p. 10). ILP is a comprehensive model of decisional counseling in which individuals make decisions about their total development—physical, intellectual, social/emotional, vocational/career, sexual, and spiritual.

The concept of life patterns, or patterning, within ILP is particularly important. Formerly, ILP was called "integrative life planning" and was focused more on decision making. The concept of patterning puts emphasis on relationships and life-span issues. A decisional focus tends to emphasize outcomes, whereas patterning stresses that decisions are a process and are made contextually in relation to others—the community and society at large.

Four Major Life Patterns

ILP focuses on four major life roles—loving, learning, labor, and leisure—as the expression of life patterns. In each of these life areas, individuals make decisions. For example, a decision for labor or work affects present and future decisions in other areas in that it can result in less time for relationships, learning, and leisure. ILP expands decisional theory by pointing out the systemic impact of any decision.

A problem with decisional theories is their emphasis on the linear decisional process. Hansen, although working within the decisional tradition, maintains that a more comprehensive developmental view is needed. Although individual decisions are clearly important, Hansen points out that counselors and therapists need to help their clients consider the impact of their decisions on important relationships. Hansen's model expands the trait-and-factor tradition. Being more relational in nature, it tends to be accepted more readily by, for example, women, Latinas/os, and Asian-Americans.

Decisions in Relationship

ILP suggests the need for planning and making decisions about life roles and the need to focus not only on achievement and success, but also on achievement in relationship to others. The life patterns of both women and men, individually and in relationship, are examined in ILP, and the importance of self-sufficiency and connectedness for both is affirmed. The ILP model encourages decision making that moves from dominant-subordinate relationships to equal partners, and ILP encourages intuitive decision making as well as rational thought. ILP emphasizes the importance of understanding the changing life contexts in work, family, education, and the larger society.

Hansen suggests a variety of individual and group or workshop strategies appropriate for implementing the ILP model. These include various forms of lifelines in which one examines one's personal history, present and future risk-taking exercises, visualization and imagery, life role identification, and journal writing.

The Circle of Life

In Hansen's circle of life (see Figure 5.1 and Practice Exercise 5.5), note that the lifetime of decision making is presented as a circle. Varying decision styles that may be useful over the life span are respected, and integrated life planning is done in relationship to others and as an exercise in self-awareness. The circle of life concept pro-

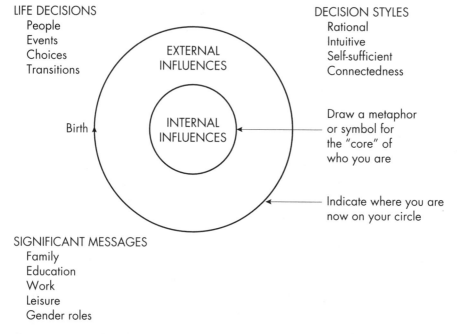

LIFE DECISIONS
  People
  Events
  Choices
  Transitions

DECISION STYLES
  Rational
  Intuitive
  Self-sufficient
  Connectedness

EXTERNAL INFLUENCES

INTERNAL INFLUENCES

Birth

Draw a metaphor or symbol for the "core" of who you are

Indicate where you are now on your circle

SIGNIFICANT MESSAGES
  Family
  Education
  Work
  Leisure
  Gender roles

Figure 5.1 Circle of Life: An Integrated Life Patterns Example
SOURCE: Adapted from S. Hansen's Integrative Life Planning Exercise, 1991. Used by permission.

≡ Practice Exercise 5.5 ≡

Using the Circle of Life for Decision Making

Identify a decision you or a client wishes to make. Does your decision concern loving, learning, labor, or leisure? Is it one relating to people, events, choices, or transitions? Then examine the multiple issues that might be affected by this decision, as follows:

1. What is your decisional style? What are its strengths and weaknesses? Can you allow yourself to use multiple decisional styles?

2. How does your decision relate to people, events, choices, or transitions?

3. What are the significant messages you have received related to this decision from your life context—from family; school or work environment; or leisure, gender, or multicultural groups?

4. A decision involves your own internal influences and wishes as well as external messages and demands. What is your core self, and how does it relate to external factors?

5. Can you make a decision that successfully involves you and the broader context of key relationships?

vides a more holistic framework for considering person-environment counseling and action. Hansen (1990) draws from trait-and-factor history, adds her own model of decision making, and demonstrates that decisions are an integral part of an individual's life and being—"the deep integration, wholeness, a source of the interrelatedness of all life."

Cultural Identity Development Theory

Cultural identity self-development represents a cognitive, emotional, and behavioral progression and expansion through identifiable and measurable levels or stages of consciousness. Although theorists vary in the specific characteristics, these stages appear to follow a sequence of (1) naiveté and embedded awareness of self as a cultural being, (2) an encounter with the reality of cultural issues, (3) the naming of these cultural issues, (4) reflection on the meaning of self as a cultural being, and (5) some form of internalization and multiperspective thought about self-in-system. Each stage of development involves different attitudes toward oneself (self-identity) and others (group identity and/or differences). This leads us to the third proposition underlying MCT:

> *Proposition III.* Cultural identity development is a major determinant of both counselor and client attitudes toward the self, others of the same group, others of a different group, and the dominant group. These attitudes, which may be manifested in affective and behavioral dimensions, are strongly influenced not only by cultural variables, but by the dynamics of a dominant-subordinate relationship among culturally different groups. The level or stage of racial/cultural identity influences how clients and counselors define the problem and dictates what they believe to be appropriate counseling and therapy goals and processes.

Each client (individual, family, group, organization) has multiple cultural identities that likely will not progress or expand at the same rate. Different clients have different salient issues. For example, an individual's identity as a Navajo may be quite high, whereas awareness of self as a heterosexual or Vietnam veteran may be less developed. Or, in another example, African-American college students may be expected to focus on issues of racial identity, whereas other issues may be less central.

MCT counselors and therapists constantly seek to expand awareness of cultural identity issues, both for themselves and for their clients. There is no end to cultural identity development; MCT affirms the difference between individual differences and cultural differences. Skin color at birth is a clear, unambiguous example of an individual difference, whereas the meaning of that skin color to self and others as it has evolved over time is a clear, unambiguous example of a cultural difference. MCT affirms that cultural identities are complex and that culturally learned patterns relate to issues of multiple identities. However, the client takes the lead as to which issue of identity is foremost.

The Specifics of Cultural Identity Development Theory

The essential idea of cultural identity theory is that individuals have varying levels of consciousness about their ethnic/racial backgrounds. As counselors and therapists we must be able to recognize cultural identity level or awareness. Then it is helpful to be able to match our interviewing style to the level of client awareness. The most highly developed models of cultural identity have been generated by African-Americans (Cross, 1971, 1991, 1995; Helms, 1990, 1995; Jackson, 1975, 1990) and Asian-Americans (Sue & Sue, 1990). Cultural identity theory has come to be used for many other multicultural groups, including Latinas/os (Casas & Pytluk, 1995), biracial groups (Kerwin & Ponterotto, 1995), and Whites (Helms, 1995). Myers and others (1991) present a comprehensive universalist approach to these issues. Thomas (1971) and Cross (1971, 1995) are generally regarded as the originators of the model, although the foundational ideas were generated independently in many settings.

A summary of the five-stage model of cultural identity development is presented in Table 5.2. In this model, the movement of consciousness is from naive lack of awareness to action and awareness of self in relation to society. Jackson and Hardiman's (1983) Black identity development theory emphasizes evolution of consciousness—the growing awareness of oneself in relationship to others and society. Cross (1995) points out that each developmental stage has a special value. Jackson (1975) would argue that all but the first and second stages are of particular value for African-Americans. However, for individuals subject to constant oppression, denial of the naiveté stage may be necessary for survival and sanity.

The counterpoint to the advantages in the fifth level of consciousness is that it involves a multiperspectival division of consciousness that sometimes makes action in a racist society difficult. Furthermore, this level of critical consciousness can be emotionally and cognitively exhausting. Parham (1989) points out that each of us will constantly cycle through the five levels again and again as new issues are discovered. Again, there is no end to development of consciousness as a cultural being.

Table 5.3 presents the cultural identity model and three of its related frameworks. The first, women's identity theory, illustrates how both European-American and minority women develop consciousness. The second speaks to how these constructs can be related to Vietnam veterans who may be suffering from trauma. It should be pointed out that survivors of trauma experiences are themselves a special culture and need highly sensitive treatment designed for their levels of awareness.

Any individual may have more than one set of multicultural issues. For example, if you are working with an African-American or Chinese-American nurse who suffered posttraumatic stress disorder from working in Vietnam, this woman will not only have issues around posttraumatic stress disorder, but also will have been treated differently by the bureaucracy, colleagues, and others because she is a woman and a minority person. Her level of consciousness may be high in terms of her African-American or Asian-American identity, but she may be at different levels on awareness of women's issues and the meaning of the Vietnam War.

Table 5.2   Cultural Identity Development Theory

Stage 1. Naiveté. The individual has little focused awareness of self as a cultural being. This is most clearly represented by children who do not distinguish skin color as an important feature. Helms (1995) points out that many White individuals lack awareness of the meaning that "Whiteness" has in our society. Naive understanding can also be manifested by successful and educated professionals who fully or partially deny that they have been oppressed and discriminated against.

Stage 2. Encounter. Despite lack of contact or efforts to shield oneself from racism, sexism, or other discrimination, the individual encounters experiences in the environment that clearly demonstrate that the earlier naive view was inadequate. For example, the African-American goes through a critical transformation and recognizes that discrimination is real and that being African-American is different than being White or Asian.

Stage 3. Naming. The act of naming is transformative. When Betty Freidan (1963) named the "problem that has no name" as sexism, she forever changed the way women viewed themselves and their issues. The gay liberation movement named itself gay, and thus took on what was previously a negative slur as its own positive identity. At this stage, the individual may feel much anger and may actively or passively refuse to work with those considered oppressors—most often European White males. For White and majority people seeking to support liberation of consciousness, the naming phase represents a real challenge, as it often leaves the White person without any sense of a positive identity.

Stage 4. Reflection on self as a cultural being. The development of a keener awareness of being Asian-American, bisexual, or culturally deaf continues. However, at stage 3, the Black individual may turn away from White culture and become totally immersed in reflecting on African-American history and the Black community. The lesbian may move away from confronting men and focus within her own community. At this point, the majority society is less relevant. The developmental task is the establishment of a definite cultural consciousness.

Stage 5. Multiperspective internalization. The individual develops pride in self and awareness of others. This individual makes use of the important dimensions of all stages of development and thus recognizes and accepts the worthwhile dimensions of predominant culture; fights those aspects that represent racism, sexism, homophobia, and oppression; and integrates all the stages in a transcendent consciousness. The individual is able to view the world through multiple frames of reference.

Identity Development Theory for European–North American Counselors and Therapists

Ponterotto (1988) has developed a theory of identity development for White counselor trainees. His four-stage model is similar to those described above, particularly that of Jackson. The European–North American counselor trainee often works through the following stages when confronted with multicultural concerns:

Table 5.3   Cultural Identity Developmental Theory as Related to Women and Vietnam Veterans

Cultural Identity Development Theory	Women's Developmental Identity Theory	Vietnam Veterans' Developmental Identity Theory
Naiveté	Lacks awareness of system; "buys into the status quo."	Feels guilty and at fault for participation in war; frequent physical/emotional concerns.
Encounter	Becomes aware of women's oppression through contact with multiple issues that illustrate the failure of naiveté.	Becomes aware that he or she is not "at fault." Begins to see a new and broader picture of the war.
Naming	Identifies issue as sexism; angry with men and takes action to produce change.	May become angry at being a tool for the system. Becomes angry with governmental lack of support and sensitivity.
Reflection on self as cultural being	Pride in being a woman. Often separates from men to find self and self in relation to other women.	Generates increased pride for role in defending country. Often with the help of other veterans, develops an understanding of self in relation to others and the war.
Multiperspective internalization	Views male-female relationships in cultural/historical perspective. Values aspects of maleness, sees men selectively, is able to take parts of women's identity theory interchangeably and accept, act, and reflect, as the situation warrants.	Multiperspective—sees war and participation in war as both an individual and social phenomena. Able to accept the status quo at times, able to become angry and use action when appropriate, and can reflect on both self and situation from multiple perspectives.

Stage 1. Preexposure. The White counselor trainee has not thought about counseling and therapy as a multicultural phenomena. The trainee may say that "people are just people" and in counseling practice may engage in unconscious racism and sexism or, more positively, try to treat all clients the same.

Stage 2. Exposure. When multicultural issues are introduced, the White therapist trainee (or experienced professional) learns about cultural differences and matters of discrimination and oppression and realizes that previous educational experiences have been incomplete. The trainee at this stage may become perturbed and confused by the many incongruities that exist.

Stage 3. Zealotry or defensiveness. Faced with the challenge of multicultural issues, students and professionals may respond in different ways. Some become angry and active proponents of multiculturalism, even to the point of offending their colleagues. Another common response to the incongruities experienced in stage 2 is to retreat into quiet defensiveness. Criticisms of European-American culture, "the system," and therapeutic theory are taken personally. These students become passive recipients of information and "retreat back into the predictability of the White culture" (Helms, 1985, p. 156).

Stage 4. Integration. The counselor acquires a respect for and awareness of cultural differences and becomes aware of personal family and cultural history and how this might affect the interview and treatment plan. There is an acceptance that one cannot know all dimensions of multicultural counseling and therapy at once, and plans are made for a lifetime of learning.

Although the above model was generated for White European Americans, it can also have implications for counselor and therapy trainees of other cultural backgrounds. For example, a Lakota Sioux counselor may be aware of issues for the Sioux and midwestern European-American cultures but may have had limited contact with Mexican-American and African-American cultures. Practice Exercise 5.6 outlines an way to facilitate your personal awareness of multicultural issues as a counselor and therapist.

Advantages and Limitations of MCT

The most important implication of MCT is that it is a distinct and growing theoretical orientation in itself and has as much as or more potential than traditional therapies. As it is a developing orientation, MCT will continue to be defined by further theory, research, and practice. Because MCT is a highly diverse approach to the field, no clear direction can be defined at this time. Whereas it once seemed that MCT was in opposition to traditional theory, it now seems that bridges between traditional therapy and MCT are being explored. Most likely, multicultural issues will change traditional theory and practice, and MCT will continue to draw many ideas from existing theory.

Perhaps the major limitation of this newest approach to therapy is that it challenges so many traditional approaches to helping. Thus, MCT concepts are particularly difficult to accommodate for established professionals, who already have "concepts and methods that work." MCT suggests that "what works" actually may

=== **Practice Exercise 5.6** ===

Your Personal Journey as a Therapist or Counselor in Terms of Cultural Identity Theory

Following are some questions to consider as you think about the role of multicultural counseling and therapy in your own practice:

1. *Ethnic/racial identity*

    a. Given the five stages (or the four of Ponterotto), at what stage are you in your own personal journey as an African-American, Japanese-American, Cuban-American, German-Canadian, Mexican-American, Alberta-Ukranian-Canadian, French-Canadian, or other ethnic/racial identity?

    b. Think back on yourself at earlier stages of life during which your identity as a ethnic/racial human being might have been different than what it is now. How did you think and feel then? What led you to change?

    It may be useful to review your community and family genograms. The other practice exercises in this chapter may also be useful, particularly Practice Exercise 5.4.

2. *Counselor or therapist identity and multiculturalism*

    a. Trace your personal path in your counseling and therapy training program.

    b. Can you identify dimensions of preexposure, exposure, zealotry/defensiveness, and integration in your way of being and thinking?

be harmful with some clients and that relying on one approach is never appropriate for a well-intentioned professional helper.

The concepts of cultural identity theory suggest that many of our present systems of therapy are incomplete and perhaps more limited than we would like to admit. These new theories are, of course, subject to limitations and dangers in the hands of overly zealous and charismatic practitioners who may force their ideas on clients. Yet, the very nature of these theories suggests that coercion is contrary to the goals and values of MCT. It is anticipated that as our world becomes more global and multicultural, the contributions of MCT will become increasingly important.

NOTE

1. Grosskurth (1991) states that many ideas generated by women have been incorporated by men before they were accepted. In the psychoanalytic field, for example, the ideas of

Melanie Klein, Helene Deutsch, Anna Freud, and Karen Horney preceded the constructs of D. W. Winnicott, Otto Kernberg, and Heinz Kohut. In the same vein, Parham (1990) points out that African-American scholars generated many concepts of multicultural counseling that were ignored until White males started presenting similar ideas, often without recognizing African-American contributions.

REFERENCES

ABORIGINAL EDUCATIONAL FOUNDATION. (1992). *Aboriginals respond to the Royal Commission into Aboriginal deaths in custody.* Bedford Park: Flinders Press.

ASANTE, M. (1987). *The Afrocentric idea.* Philadelphia: Temple University Press.

BERMAN, J. (1979). Counseling skills used by Black and White male and female counselors. *Journal of Counseling Psychology, 26,* 81–84.

BLASSINGAME, J. (1972). *The slave community.* New York: Oxford University Press.

CASAS, M., & PYTLUK, S. (1995). Hispanic identity development: Implications for research and practice. In J. Ponterotto, M. Casas, L. Suzuki, & C. Alexander (Eds.), *Handbook of multicultural counseling.* Thousand Oaks, CA: Sage.

CHEATHAM, H. (1990). Empowering Black families. In H. Cheatham & J. Stewart (Eds.), *Black families* (pp. 373–93). New Brunswick, NJ: Transaction Press.

CHEATHAM, H., & STEWART, J. (Eds.). (1990). *Black families.* New Brunswick, NJ: Transaction Press.

CHEEK, D. (1976). *Assertive Black . . . puzzled White.* San Luis Obispo, CA: Impact.

CROSS, W. (1971). The Negro to Black conversion experience. *Black World, 20,* 13–25.

CROSS, W. (1991). *Shades of Black.* Philadelphia: Temple University Press.

CROSS, W. (1995). The psychology of Nigrescence: Revising the Cross model. In J. Ponterotto, M. Casas, L. Suzuki, & C. Alexander (Eds.), *Handbook of multicultural counseling.* Thousand Oaks, CA: Sage.

ERIKSON, E. (1950/1963). *Childhood and Society* (2nd ed.). New York: Norton.

FREIDAN, B. (1963). *The feminine mystique.* New York: Dell.

FREIRE, P. (1972). *Pedagogy of the oppressed.* New York: Herder & Herder.

FUKUYAMA, M. (1990). Taking a universal approach to multicultural counseling. *Counselor Education and Supervision, 30,* 6–17.

GILLIGAN, C. (1982). *In a different voice.* Cambridge, MA: Harvard University Press.

GRIFFITH, M., & JONES, E. (1978). Race and psychotherapy: Changing perspectives. In J. Masserman (Ed.), *Current psychiatric therapies* (Vol. 18) (pp. 225–35). Orlando, FL: Grune & Stratton.

GROSSKURTH, P. (1991, September 29). Mothers of psychoanalysis. *New York Times Book Review,* p. 12.

GUTMAN, H. (1976). *The Black family in slavery and freedom: 1750–1925.* New York: Harper-Collins.

HANSEN, S. (1990, July). *Work and family roles: An integrated context for career planning.* Paper presented at the International Round Table for the Advancement of Counseling, Helsinki, Finland.

HANSEN, S. (1991). Integrative life planning: Work, family, community. *Futurics, 15,* 80–86.

HARDIMAN, R. (1982). *White identity development: A process oriented model for describing the racial consciousness of White Americans.* Unpublished doctoral dissertation, University of Massachusetts, Amherst.

HELMS, J. (1985). Toward a theoretical explanation of the effects of race on counseling: A Black and White model. *Counseling Psychologist, 12,* 153–65.

HELMS, J. (1990). *Black and White racial identity.* Westport, CT: Greenwood.

HELMS, J. (1995). An update of Helm's White and People of Color identity models. In J. Ponterotto, M. Casas, L. Suzuki, & C. Alexander (Eds.), *Handbook of multicultual counseling.* Thousand Oaks, CA: Sage.

IVEY, A. (1991). *Developmental strategies for helpers: Individual, family and network interventions.* Pacific Grove, CA: Brooks/Cole.

JACKSON, B. (1975). Black identity development. *Journal of Educational Diversity and Innovation, 2,* 19–25.

JACKSON, B. (1990, September). *Building a multicultural school.* Paper presented to the Amherst Regional School System, Amherst, MA.

JACKSON, B., & HARDIMAN R. (1983). Racial identity development: Implications for managing the multiracial work force. In R. Vitvo & A. Sargent (Eds.), *The NTL managers' handbook* (pp. 107–19). Arlington, VA: NTL Institute.

JONES, E. (1978). Effects of race on psychotherapy process and outcome. *Psychotherapy Theory, Research, and Practice, 15,* 226–36.

JONES, E. (1985). Psychotherapy and counseling with Black clients. In P. Pedersen (Ed.), *Handbook of cross-cultural counseling and therapy* (pp. 173–79). Westport, CT: Greenwood.

KERWIN, C., & PONTEROTTO, J. (1995). Biracial identity development. In J. Ponterotto, M. Casas, L. Suzuki, & C. Alexander (Eds.), *Handbook of multicultural counseling.* Thousand Oaks, CA: Sage.

KIKOSKI, K. (1980). *A study of cross-cultural communication, Arabs and Americans: Paradigms and skills.* Unpublished doctoral dissertation, University of Massachusetts, Amherst.

LEONG, F., WAGNER, N., & PIROSHAW TATA. (1995). Racial and ethnic variations in help-seeking attitudes. In J. Ponterotto, M. Casas, L. Suzuki, & C. Alexander (Eds.), *Handbook of multicultural counseling.* Thousand Oaks, CA: Sage.

LOCKE, D. (1990). A not so provincial view of multicultural counseling. *Counselor Education and Supervision, 30,* 18–25.

MURASE, T., & REYNOLDS, D. (1972). *Naikan therapy.* Psychological Research Division monograph. Ichikawa City, Japan.

MYERS, L. (1988). *Understanding an Afrocentric world view: Introduction to an optimal psychology.* Dubuque, IA: Kendall/Hunt.

MYERS, L., SPEIGHT, S., HIGHLEN, P., COX, C., REYNOLDS, A., ADAMS, E., & HANLEY, P. (1991). Identity development and worldview: Toward an optimal conceptualization. *Journal of Counseling and Development, 54,* 54–55.

NOBLES, W. (1972). African philosophy: Foundation for Black psychology. In R. Jones (Ed.), *Black psychology* (pp. 19–22). New York: Harper & Row.

NWACHUKU, U. (1989). *Culture-specific counseling: The Igbo case.* Unpublished doctoral dissertation, University of Massachusetts, Amherst.

NWACHUKU, U. (1990, July). *Translating multicultural theory into direct action: Culture-specific counseling.* Paper presented at the International Round Table of Counseling, Helsinki, Finland.

NWACHUKU, U., & IVEY, A. (1991). Culture specific counseling: An alternative approach. *Journal of Counseling and Development, 70,* 106–51.

PARHAM, T. (1989). Cycles of psychological Nigresence. *Counseling Psychologist, 17,* 187–226.

PARHAM, T. (1990). *Do the right thing: Racial discussion in counseling psychology.* Paper presented at the American Psychological Association Convention, Boston.

PEDERSEN, P., & IVEY, A. (1993). *Culture-centered counseling.* New York: Greenwood.

PONTEROTTO, J. (1988). Racial consciousness development among White counselor trainees. *Journal of Multicultural Counseling and Development, 16,* 146–56.

REYNOLDS, D. (1990). Morita and Naikan therapies—Similarities. *Journal of Morita Therapy, 1,* 159–63.

RIGAZIO-DIGILIO, S. A., & IVEY, A. E. (1990). Developmental therapy and depressive disorders: Measuring cognitive levels through patient natural language. *Professional Psychology: Research & Practice, 21,* 470–75.

ROBERTS, W. (1982). *Black and White managers in helping: Interaction effects of managers in responding to culturally varied subordinate vignettes.* Unpublished doctoral dissertation, University of Massachusetts, Amherst.

SUE, D. (1990). Culture-specific strategies in counseling: A conceptual framework. *Professional Psychology, 21,* 424–33.

SUE, D. (1992). Derald Wing Sue on multicultural issues: An interview. *Microtraining Newsletter* (North Amherst, MA), p. 6.

SUE, D. W. (1995). Toward a theory of multicultural counseling and therapy. In J. Banks & C. Banks (Eds.), *Handbook of research on multicultural education.* New York: Macmillan.

SUE, D. W., IVEY, A., & PEDERSON, P. (1996). *A theory of multicultural counseling and therapy.* Pacific Grove, CA: Brooks/Cole.

SUE, D., & SUE, D. (1990). *Counseling the culturally different* (2nd ed.). New York: Wiley.

SUE, S. (1988). Psychotherapeutic services for ethnic minorities: Two decades of research findings. *American Psychologist, 43,* 301–8.

TAMASE, K. (1988). *Introspective-developmental counseling.* Unpublished manuscript, Nara University of Education and the University of Massachusetts, Amherst.

TAMASE, K. (1991, April). *The effects of introspective-developmental counseling.* Paper presented at the American Association of Counseling and Development. Reno, Nevada.

TAMASE, K., & KATO, M. (1990). Effect of questions about factual and affective aspects of life events in an introspective interview. *Bulletin of Nara University of Education,* pp. 153–63.

THOMAS, C. (1971). *Boys no more.* Beverly Hills, CA: Glencoe.

WHITE, J., & PARHAM, T. (1991). *The psychology of Blacks: An African-American perspective* (2nd ed.). Englewood Cliffs, NJ: Prentice-Hall.

Multicultural Counseling and Therapy II: Integrative Practice

Harold Cheatham, Allen E. Ivey, Mary Bradford Ivey, Paul Pedersen, Sandra Rigazio-DiGilio, Lynn Simek-Morgan, and Derald Wing Sue

CHAPTER GOALS

This chapter seeks to help you:

1. Identify and understand three further propositions of the MCT integrative metatheory:

    IV. The effectiveness of counseling and therapy is enhanced when the counselor uses techniques, strategies, and goals consistent with the life experiences and cultural values of the client. No single helping approach or intervention strategy is equally effective across all populations and life situations.

    V. The traditional approach to counseling and psychotherapy is only one of many theoretical techniques and strategies available to the helping professional. These strategies go beyond one-on-one therapy to involve larger social units, systems intervention, and prevention.

    VI. The liberation of consciousness is a basic goal of MCT. Whereas self-actualization, discovery of how the past affects the present, or behav-

The authors of Chapters 5 and 6 are presented alphabetically. Multicultural counseling and therapy (MCT) is not associated with any one key figure, such as Freud is with psychodynamic therapy or Rogers is with person-centered therapy. Rather, MCT was developed in many settings by men and women of widely varying cultural backgrounds. Accordingly, these chapters have multiple authors. The six propositions of MCT were developed by Sue (1995). If citations of the six propositions are made, please reference his work. Key explanatory paragraphs are taken from Sue, Ivey, and Pedersen's (1996) *A Theory of Multicultural Counseling and Therapy* (Pacific Grove, CA: Brooks/Cole) by permission of the authors and the publisher. H. Cheatham, M. Ivey, L. Simek-Morgan, and S. Rigazio-DiGilio have contributed to these two chapters through writing and editing portions of the chapters.

ioral change have been traditional goals of Western psychotherapy and counseling, MCT emphasizes the importance of expanding personal, family, group, and organizational consciousness of self-in-relation, family-in-relation, and organization-in-relation. Thus, MCT is ultimately contextual in orientation and also draws on traditional methods of healing from many cultures.

2. Learn key MCT techniques and strategies that can be integrated into daily counseling and therapy practice.

3. Consider how techniques and strategies of other theories described in this book may be adapted to multicultural counseling and therapy practice.

4. Through practice exercises, conduct or engage in

- An introductory exercise in feminist therapy and analysis of client stories and narratives from a multicultural perspective
- Analysis of yourself as a multicultural being and your potential ability to work with individuals culturally different than you
- Basic meditation for your personal benefit and/or as a client treatment strategy
- The examination of family rules and roles and how they may play out in the client's life today
- Psychotherapy as liberation through a structured approach to help clients cope with oppression, see their issues in a social context, and act on them

Coconstructing Culturally Appropriate Techniques and Strategies

The fourth proposition of MCT considers the development of theories and strategies that match the culture of the client:

Proposition IV. Counseling and therapy's effectiveness is enhanced when the counselor uses techniques, strategies, and goals consistent with the life experiences and cultural values of the client. No single helping approach or intervention strategy is equally effective across all populations and life situations. The ultimate goal of multicultural counselor and therapist training is to expand the repertoire of helping responses available to the professional, regardless of theoretical orientation.

Coconstruction of the goals and strategies of therapy implies a nonhierarchical relationship with the client. The search for an egalitarian client-counselor relationship, of course, must be modified when working with individuals from traditional cultures in which the counselor is expected to take the expert or leader role. This issue will be explored later in this section.

Interventions that may be appropriate for one client in one cultural context may be inappropriate for another client in another cultural context. It is important to increase your repertoire of various counseling skills and then match the right skill in the right way with the right client at the right time. Feminist therapy offers perhaps the most complete framework for considering how to mutually coconstruct a working alliance with the client.

Feminist Therapy

Feminist therapy theory focuses on mutual education and psychoeducation. Both the client and the counselor, in an egalitarian relationship, need to analyze their worlds and educate each other about them. Teaching clients multiple ways to view the world is an important part of feminist therapy. In this sense, feminist theory promotes a mutual dialogue (as does Paulo Freire, who is discussed later in this chapter). Through posing questions and sharing information, client and therapist can grow together.

Social context and oppression are particularly key issues in feminist therapy. It is not enough that counselors help clients feel better about themselves; helpers also must become aware of themselves in a social context. The focus in traditional therapy is typically on the individual rather than the person-in-relation. Ignoring context is considered by feminist therapists to be a failure of traditional therapy. As intentional therapists, we must include the concepts of oppression, system, family, and context in our approaches. Cognitive-behavioral, humanistic, and psychodynamic therapy can be enriched by adding contextual concepts to theory and practice.

Gender issues and sexism are, of course, central to feminist therapy, as noted by Ballou and Gabalac (1984):

> Feminist therapy holds that traditional systems of psychotherapy are in serious error which stems from traditional sexist assumptions about women. Therefore, research paradigms, personality theory, clinical practices . . . are all suspect. . . . The feminist orientation to therapy is eclectic, endorsing theoretical positions which postulate external factors as causative in the client's problems. . . . The client's strengths rather than her weaknesses are emphasized. . . . An egalitarian relationship between therapist and client is demanded by feminist therapy. (p. 31)

It is also important to take into account the interface between gender and other forms of diversity. Islamic women will have different issues than those of Jewish or Christian women; African-American men will have differing ideas on the pace of therapy than will Native American Indian or Irish-American men. Those with physical issues, gay or lesbian identity issues, spiritual issues, or other issues also have unique perspectives. We must not assume a common context for all client concerns and issues.

Many of the constructs and theories discussed in this book are open to feminist critique. Also, the structural parallels between feminist therapy and the Black or

Asian identity development movements are apparent. However, the movement toward women's rights is distinct from movements toward more extensive rights and equal treatment for culturally different groups. Each group has its own struggle and unique set of cultural/historical factors.

Ballou (1996b) and Ballou and Gabalac (1984) have summarized the major areas of feminist therapy, which are paraphrased as follows:

1. *Egalitarian relationship.* The feminist therapist considers herself as a partner with the client and values women and their need for mutual support and exploration. Self-disclosure of one's own personal experiences as a woman is a particularly important part of the therapeutic process. Important here is the concept of power. Feminist therapy emphasizes sharing power and working against domination by any group.

2. *Pluralism.* Feminist theory values difference. Although focused on women, the feminist approach also recognizes the many dimensions of MCT. Again, the issue of power is critical. One cannot be free if others are restricted. A basic tenet of feminist therapy and of MCT is the awareness of the need to respect others.

3. *External emphasis.* Whereas much of cognitive-behavioral theory focuses on internal thoughts, feminist therapy and MCT stress that oppressive aspects of reality (such as sexism and homophobia) may need to be addressed directly—"It is not what we think of things, but rather what *is* which must be addressed" (M. Ivey, 1994).

4. *Use of community resources.* Therapy does not end with the completion of an interview. Many clients are referred to women's support groups, community action work, legal aid, and other relevant community services.

5. *Active, participatory counseling style.* Feelings are considered important, but confrontation of discrepancies in the client and between the client and society are important. For example, the therapist might work with a client who is full of conflict to understand emotions but also confront the client with the need for growth and resolution. Although the therapist may be warm and supportive, a gradual move toward independent thought is emphasized. The therapist is likely to use most of the techniques discussed in this book (such as assertiveness training, Frankl's dereflection, dream analysis, and so forth) but will do so with an awareness of the feminist context of the helping process.

6. *Information giving.* A strong educational component exists in feminist counseling. The client may be instructed in social/historical facts concerning sexism and the impact of cultural conditioning. Sex-role analysis (Carter & Rawlins, 1977) may be used so that women can understand how they have become culturally conditioned to respond in certain ways.

7. *Personal validation.* Many women come from oppressed situations in which they have little or no awareness of their own inherent personal worth.

Feminist therapy seeks to validate the individual and her cultural heritage as unique and valuable.

A particular value conflict within feminist theory focuses on the issue of when and how women should be confronted with issues of sexism. Clearly, a fragile individual could be overwhelmed and disturbed if suddenly confronted with the social facts of her life. Marriages can be broken by the anger that often comes as a client moves from lower to higher levels of feminist consciousness. One group believes that traditional therapy is more appropriate for the "traditional woman" and that feminist therapy can be used later, when the individual has achieved some social insight. Alternatively, some see difficulty and personal pain as a necessary part of the route toward a larger, evolving feminist consciousness and would seek to bring all women to a feminist awareness.

This brief summary of feminist therapy illustrates that it is a clearly articulated alternative approach to counseling and therapy. The following typescript from an interview conducted by Mary Ballou (1996a) illustrates some of the issues and the therapeutic approach of this orientation. The method here is different than other theories of helping, particularly in the mutual exploration of both therapist and client and the manner in which cultural factors undergirding the interview are included.

Client: Yes it is, but what should I do?

Counselor: Let's see if we can explore this a bit more. For example imagine what would happen if Joe was an apartment-mate not a boyfriend/partner?

Client: His demands for so much attention and sex would go away, and the help with the money and kid would still be there. My family and church would approve. But I would be lonely, and you are supposed to love and give sex to your boyfriend.

Counselor: Let's look at your hidden views under your ideas. One is your family and the church can and should define your choices. Another is that male-female relationships are a bargain—money and childcare for attention and sex—made OK if you love him. A third is that you cannot make new choices about how to meet your own needs. The final one is that there are realities outside of our control, for example, money needed for food, rent, medical care. These factors affect us deeply but are outside of our control. Do I understand correctly?

Client: I think so but I never thought of it that way.

Counselor: In fact many social and economic arrangements often benefit one party over the other. Many people just follow the rules, assuming it's the way it is. Often the reasons behind the rules and just who benefits are not very clear. Options are not talked about. I think the key is to see all the reality and make our own choices. How does this strike you?

Client: It means I have to think about everything and then decide. That's scary and hard.

Counselor: Making decisions about what to value and how to live instead of following preset answers and patterns is difficult, and yet it can be exciting.

There are conditions that are given, like responsible childcare and needing money, about which there is little real choice. But there are also some options to sort through and choices to be made. The decisions are yours to make, and although it is hard, whatever you decide is not cast in stone. Decisions can be looked at and remade. I think the keys are to claim the power to make decisions and to make them carefully and with complicated pieces in mind. Now, these are my ideas and I have been talking a lot. I want to listen to your ideas.

Client: I'd like to talk about deciding about Joe, especially the apartment-mate idea and relationships being mutual rather than bargains. Both are very different from the way I've thought about things.

Counselor: Maria, last week we talked about your relationship with Joe, the baby's father. You said he is living with you and the baby again. We identified the positives as meeting your family's wishes, more money to pay the bills, help with childcare and transportation, and your sense of rightness as defined by the church rules and your community's standards. We also identified the negatives as more yelling at home, which is disliked by you and upsetting for your daughter; more physical and emotional caretaking responsibilities for you; conflict about sexual demands and other relationships; a recent episode of his hitting you; and your sense of Joe's immaturity and dependence rather than experiencing him as a partner. Is this how you remember our session, and is there more to add from your thinking this week?

Client: That covers last week pretty well. This week I've been thinking that I do not love him but I need him and think he should be here. I just don't know what to do.

Counselor: What is the need to do something?

Client: I must love him and make him be a partner or have him leave and raise my kid alone.

Counselor: Are those the only options?

Client: What do you mean? I don't love him so he should go, but we need him to make it as far as money, babysitting, and transportation.

Counselor: What I mean is, you are thinking of the situation as either/or. Maybe there are some other ways to think about it. It seems instead of mutuality your relationship is a bargain, with lots of tension and conflict.

Feminist Therapy and MCT

The above discussion can be applied to much of MCT practice. For example, the emphasis on external reality and its impact on the individual is central to the theory of MCT. *Power* is a word most often missing in psychodynamic, cognitive-behavioral, and other psychotherapeutic vocabularies. The idea that working in a community context can be more important than one-on-one counseling is challenging to the psychotherapy and counseling establishment. Kirby and McKenna (1989) provide an important model for thinking in new ways about using research and practice to promote social change. Practice Exercise 6.1 is useful for adapting the ideas of feminist and MCT theory in the interview setting.

Applying MCT with Culturally Different Clients

To the extent that the client is culturally different than the counselor in ethnographic, demographic, status, or affiliation variables, the counseling process will likely encounter some difficulties. To the extent that the counselor and client are similar, the counseling process will likely be facilitated. Sometimes too much similarity can produce blind spots. At issue is finding the appropriate blend of similarity and difference. In matching and blending client and counselor styles, considerations of cultural similarity must be secondary to client preferences. For example, clients may prefer a counselor who is culturally different. Automatically assuming that clients will prefer culturally similar counselors is itself an example of stereotyping and should be avoided.

Counselors who are culturally different than their clients can learn multicultural skills and become effective with these clients despite the cultural differences. Under some conditions, cultural differences may actually enhance the counseling relationship, providing that the counselor has developed multicultural counseling skills. It is a fact, however, that many clients who are culturally different than the counselor may not return for a second interview (Sue & Sue, 1990). Reasons for this vary with the cultural group, but often the issue relates to the formality of counseling, counselor-client hierarchy, and, particularly, the lack of sensitivity to varying cultural norms on the part of the helper.

Paniagua (1994) provides some general guidelines for preventing attrition and establishing appropriate relationships with African-American, Hispanic, Asian-American, and Native American Indian clients. Although these guidelines are not all inclusive, they clearly point to the need to modify the helping approach to address multicultural dimensions and to not stereotype clients.

In working with African-American clients, Paniagua recommends that counselors discuss racial differences early in the session. It is important to focus on environment and context, as many issues will be considered to be externally related. It may be useful to involve the church as part of the counseling process. Paniagua states that medication is considered impersonal and may be seen as a way for the therapist to avoid the client. Following the principles of coconstruction, any referral should be in full consultation with the client.

Hispanic clients often feel more comfortable with a formal approach *(formalismo)* at the beginning, followed by a gradual introduction of a more personal style *(personalismo)*. Again, the church may be important in assessment and treatment, and spiritual issues may need to be addressed. The father will often need special regard, owing to issues of respect *(respecto)* and manhood *(machismo)*. Paniagua suggests that specific recommendations be made for action on the problem even in the

Practice Exercise 6.1

 Applying Feminist Theory in Practice

The following exercise can be useful in beginning to adapt the ideas of feminist theory and MCT in the interview when focusing on issues of reality and possible oppression. You can go through the following exercise on your own or with a volunteer client.

1. *Storytelling.* Recall an incident in which you (or the client) feel vaguely uncomfortable. For example, you may think of an incident in which you felt embarrassed about your appearance, awkward in your behavior, or perhaps a time you felt somewhat inferior to others. One specific example might be a situation in which you encountered people of a different social class or cultural background than yourself.

2. *Identifying themes.* Draw out the story of the embarrassing incident from the client using the basic listening sequence. Be sure to summarize key facts, feelings, and thoughts.

3. *Gender analysis.* First, conduct a feminist or gender analysis of the story by asking "How does being a man or a woman affect this narrative?" Often people tend to first look internally and "blame" themselves for what happened. The general purpose of reviewing the story from a gender perspective is to consider how these issues might change the way we look at reality.

4. *Oppression/harassment analysis.* It is particularly important to look for real issues of oppression or harassment that may occur in the story. Oppression may come from others to the client or can originate unconsciously as self-oppression. It also can be helpful to review the same story from an ethnic/racial perspective. Religious or spiritual dimensions may provide still other views of the same story.

5. *Informing the other about oppression or other contextual issues.* One of the major tenets of feminist and MCT theory is that it is at times appropriate to tell our clients how their behavior may be influenced by external factors. Many times clients will continue to blame themselves when it is obvious that responsibility for the events lies outside the person. The counselor can carefully assist the client to construct alternative views about contextual reality. In this process, you as the helper have an important opportunity to coconstruct a new cognitive view of reality with your client.

first session. Medication may be expected, and the counselor should be prepared to discuss this matter early in treatment. Time is not viewed as specifically as it is in North American culture, and so the counselor should not make an issue of a client's being late for a session.

Paniagua suggests a more formal approach with Asian-American clients throughout the interview series. It may be useful to discuss your educational background and certification. He particularly stresses the importance of waiting for the client to share problems, as shame often accompanies having problems and the need to see a professional. Asian-American clients often have positive dependent relationships with their parents, and these relationships should be supported rather than be seen as pathological. It may be important to refer Southeast Asian clients to social service agencies for housing or school-related issues. Also, clients from Cambodia, Laos, or Vietnam may have a history of trauma, and these issues must be addressed carefully.

Native American Indian clients, according to Paniagua, tend to prefer a listening rather than talkative counselor. Time is viewed very differently than it is in a Eurocentric context, with the focus on being-in-time rather than on a linear "on time" frame. Coconstruction of plans and actions is often important, and your participation in the community is as important as your behavior in the interview. Medication may be viewed with suspicion. Particularly, you should avoid overuse of authority. It is important to be respectful and not overly personal.

These suggestions above include four broad cultural groupings and do not allow for individual, gender, or regional factors or length of time spent in contact with North American culture. There is an emphasis on respect for humankind and a clear indication that standard Eurocentric norms of behavior and action must constantly be modified as counselors work with those who are culturally different.

Dealing with Personal Ethnocentrism

MCT recognizes that sympathy, which is focused on how the counselor would feel in the client's situation, is less appropriate than empathy, which is focused on the client's feelings in the particular situation. In MCT therapy, the Golden Rule might be revised to read: Do not do unto others as you would have them do unto you because they might want something different.

Understanding and acknowledging your own personal biases and possibly ethnocentric attitudes is an important part of MCT. The first step toward becoming culturally empathic is to be aware of yourself as a multicultural being. The community and cultural genograms are tools for gaining this awareness, as is the multicultural cube (see Chapters 1 and 2). Also, Practice Exercise 6.2 provides some beginning steps for examining your understanding of yourself as a multicultural being. If you are to be empathic rather than sympathetic with clients, you must first examine your own life. If you have a solid beginning of multicultural understanding, then you will be better prepared for the lifetime effort of developing increased multicultural competence.

Becoming versed in the tenets and techniques of MCT can help in developing an empathic understanding of others. The MCT approach prompts a rethinking of traditional modes of helping. The European-American approach is highly internally

Practice Exercise 6.2

 ### The Counselor or Therapist as a Multicultural Being

Counseling historically has focused on learning about clients and theories that may help clients. Issues concerning the professional helper have always been a concern and have focused on helpers' mental health, quality of training, and support services. Counseling and therapy have developed in a White European–North American context, and relatively little attention has been paid to cultural assumptions on which theory and practice are based.

The following exercise asks you to identify yourself as a multicultural being and then to consider how your own background gives you natural expertise as well as limitations. What is appropriate in your cultural background may be totally inappropriate in another. How knowledgeable and effective are you in cultures different than your own?

1. The nine dimensions of the multicultural cube (see Chapter 2) are listed below. The key ideas of cultural identity development presented in Chapter 5 will become more powerful and meaningful to you if you identify your level of cultural identity development on each dimension.

    a. Identify, and provide examples of, your cultural identity development at each developmental stage—naiveté, encounter, naming, reflection on self as a cultural being, multiperspective internalization—on the multicultural cube

dimensions of language, gender, ethnicity/race, religion/spirituality, affectional orientation, age, physical ability, socioeconomic status, experience with trauma.

    b. Review your family of origin. How would you classify your family as a whole on their awareness of these cultural identity issues? What are the personal implications for your own life. (This exercise can be useful with clients in therapy and counseling as they seek to understand family conflict.)

2. Generally speaking, counseling and therapy theories have been generated by heterosexual, middle-class, middle-aged White males of Christian and Jewish background who speak European languages and devote little or no attention to physical issues or their personal experiences with trauma.

    a. How universal do you believe these theories are?

    b. How well can you work with people whose life experience is different than your own? (For example, if you speak English, how effective are you going to be with those whose primary language is Spanish? Or if you are a woman, how effective are you counseling men?)

3. Review the section on applying MCT with culturally different clients

in this chapter, specifically Paniagua's suggestions for counseling
with African-Americans, Asian-
Americans, Latinas/os, and Native
Americans.

a. Using these same dimensions,
   what would help you personally
   benefit from counseling?
b. Notice where you are similar and
   where you are different from the

listings, whether you are from one
of these four groups or not.
c. If you are from one of the four
   groups listed, which suggestions
   do you agree with and which do
   not apply to you personally?
d. Given your own preferences and
   beliefs, how able are you to move
   beyond them to work with others
   different than you?

oriented, with an emphasis on how one thinks about the world rather than what is
in the world.

This approach is effective with both those who have a predominant North
American–European background and those who do not, since the latter still often
are affected by Eurocentric ways of being. Nonetheless, the internal approach can
be enhanced by an increased awareness of multicultural realities and strategies. As
society becomes more multicultural, European-Americans likely will respond positively to a variety of multicultural approaches, such as the cognitive-behavioral
strategy of meditation, which is an Asian tradition.

Meditation

Meditation, derived from Asian methods and psychology (Kabat-Zinn, 1990;
Ram Dass, 1971; Suzuki, 1970), has moved to center stage in North American
psychology. For example, stress management programs and cognitive-behavioral
psychology have adopted meditation as an important tool (Davis, Robbins, &
McKay, 1995; Meichenbaum, 1993, 1994). Also, meditation is an increasingly
respected option in the management of anxiety and pain and for coping with various kinds of stress.

Research indicates that meditation and yoga affect physical as well as mental
health. Ornish (1990) has demonstrated that these techniques (combined with diet
and exercise) actually reverse atherosclerosis and heart disease. There is also evidence
that immune system function may be improved by meditation (Kabat-Zinn,
1990).

Practice Exercise 6.3 was developed by Lynn Simek-Morgan (Ivey & Simek-
Downing, 1980) and can be used with clients or for yourself as an introduction to
meditative procedures. Works by Ornish (1990), Kabat-Zinn, (1990), and Smith
and Wilks (1988) are only several of a multitude of presentations on approaches to
meditation.

Practice Exercise 6.3

 ## Basic Meditation

This is a useful exercise for any student of counseling and therapy. Counseling and therapy can at times be very stressful, and learning to cope with this stress in difficult times is an important skill. Meditation can be most helpful when made a part of your daily routine.

Basic Meditation

1. Sit or lie.
2. Close eyes or fix eyes on one point.
3. Relax all muscles.
4. Concentrate on breathing in and out.
5. Breathe with diaphragm—concentrate on breathing.
6. Let thoughts slip in and out of your mind.
7. Always return your concentration to your breathing.

Process

1. You may sit with your legs crossed on the floor, lie or sit on floor or a bed, or sit in a lotus position. The important thing is that you are in a position where you are comfortable and able to relax your muscles.

2. You may close your eyes to eliminate visual distractions, or you may leave your eyes open and fix them on one point on the wall or anywhere in front of you. You may want to focus on a flower if you are outdoors or on a meaningful object. You should choose a vision that will not be distracting.

3. You may use a systematized relaxation system, as described in Chapter 10 on behavioral counseling, for relaxing all of your muscles, or you may choose to devise your own. You may use yoga, karate, a period of quiet reading, or a variety of other alternatives to relax prior to meditation.

4. Concentrating on your breathing requires finding your "breathing center." Get into the rhythm of your breath and feel the oxygen going in and out of your body. You may even wish to repeat the words "in" and "out" to yourself as a chant.

5. Deep breathing with the diaphragm is important because it expends the least amount of energy and you obtain the most value from the exercise. You can tell if you are breathing with your diaphragm if your stomach moves in and out. Breathing with the lungs is an up-and-down motion, but breathing with the diaphragm is an in-and-out motion.

6. Meditation affords us the luxury of taking a break from thinking. As thoughts appear in your mind, reflect on them for a few seconds and then let them drift from your mind. The object here is to not become attached to any one thought, because doing so will remove your concentration from your breathing. When you let go of a thought, bring your concentration back to the motion of your breathing. As you learn how to return your attention to your breathing, you will find that the spaces of time between thoughts shorten and your ability to become engaged in meditation increases.

Meditation is perhaps best described as an intensified relaxation technique coupled with an effort to center or cleanse the mind. Meditation can develop a sense of well-being, a creative reflectiveness on the meaning of life, and a sense of physical harmony. The instructions for meditation are simple and can serve as a useful adjunct to virtually any therapeutic or counseling effort, regardless of theoretical orientation. You may use the instructions above for elementary meditation or for clients who may be in need of centering or slowing down their pace.

MCT Practice and Multiple Helping Roles

Community resources can enrich therapy. A network of treatment alternatives that can support individual or family therapy may include the extended family, people in the neighborhood, spiritual advisors, government officials, and many others. This is the basis of the fifth proposition of MCT:

> *Proposition V.* MCT stresses the importance of multiple helping roles developed by many culturally different groups and societies. Conventional counseling and psychotherapy are only one approach of many theoretical techniques and strategies available to the helping professional. These approaches extend beyond one-on-one therapy and involve helping strategies, systems intervention, and prevention approaches developed by the family, community, and larger social units.

The traditional one-directional description of counseling emphasizes the outcome measures of pleasure, happiness, or good feeling. A multidirectional MCT description of counseling might emphasize the importance of meaning that incorporates both pain and pleasure, happiness and sadness, good and bad. In addition, successful outcomes consider the individual-in-context. Counseling includes the whole system of individuals, families, groups, and communities. If we see ourselves as people-in-community, then new types of meanings and outcomes emerge. The concept of mental health might even be expanded to include satisfaction within one's community.

Network Therapy

From a multicultural therapeutic orientation, there is something paradoxical about working with the individual alone when that person comes from a relational culture. Carolyn Attneave originated network therapy as a way to integrate Native

American concepts of relationship and community with family therapy (Attneave, 1969, 1982; Speck & Attneave, 1973).

Attneave was not satisfied to limit her interventions to the individual. For example, if the presenting problem was alcoholism, Attneave brought the individual together with the family and community network, which included the nuclear family, the extended family, important neighbors, and key figures from the community such as the priest, the teacher, the police, and perhaps even the local bartender. These group meetings generated a network of helpers who were aware of the individual alcoholic's problem. Alcoholism is often a hidden behavior, and family and community members often remain silent, even if they suspect the problem. Attneave's network approach brings group awareness and help for the individual's issues.

Attneave's community interventions inevitably changed the way those in the community thought about themselves and their relationships. For example, the bar owner could not sell drinks to the alcoholic without being aware that the priest or a neighbor might observe this and inquire. The teacher, now aware of the family difficulty, could not simply dismiss the acting-out child. The police would be more aware of their responsibility as community support agents and might be motivated to work more closely with the community.

Network therapy addresses the individual and the family, but it also relates the community and the environment. Underlying the network approach are Native American conceptions of interdependence as the basis of therapy, as contrasted with the independent orientation. La Fromboise and Low (1989) explain the Native American traditions underlying network therapy:

> Traditionally, Indian people live in relational networks that serve to support and nurture strong bonds of mutual assistance and affection. Many tribes still engage in a traditional system of collective interdependence, with family members responsible not only to one another but also to the clan and tribe to which they belong. The Lakota Sioux use the term *tiospaye* to describe a traditional, community way of life in which an individual's well-being remains the responsibility of the extended family. . . . When problems arise among Indian youth, they become problems of the community as well. The family, kin, and friends join together to observe the youth's behavior, draw the youth out of isolation, and integrate that person back into the activities of the group. (p. 121)

As with Afrocentric and feminist orientations, the network approach stresses the importance of interdependence and self-in-relation (Cheatham & Stewart, 1990). This multilevel intervention approach to change has been applied to the treatment of child abuse by Ivey and Ivey (1990). Individually focused counseling and therapy interventions tend to be ineffective, especially when working with children, and a network approach can make a difference. Although it is not always possible to bring together a full network, several types of intervention with children can be used to produce change, as explored in Research Exhibit 6.1.

For those oriented toward individual intervention, Attneave's network therapy approach seems almost overwhelming. However, with children and many adult clients, taking the time to establish multiple levels of intervention early will be more

Research Exhibit 6.1

Adaptations of Network Intervention Treatment with Children

Multilevel network interventions may make a difference in the life of a child, adolescent, or adult. The following specific interventions have been combined in an overall treatment plan.

1. *Individual therapy.* Individual sessions allow children to tell and/or enact their stories. Interviews are conducted with an awareness of self-in-relation to others, family, and culture.

2. *Small group work.* Friendship, social skills, and sharing groups can be useful for children, such as groups of children who all experience alcoholism in the home or self-esteem groups focused on the values of varying cultural groups.

3. *Classroom observation and teacher consultation.* Children spend much of their day in the classroom. Unless behavioral programs and teacher support are provided, the results of small group work and individual therapy will be lost. Classroom instruction is often European-American in orientation. A vital helping intervention may be to change the curriculum to a more balanced, culturally sensitive approach.

4. *Educational support team.* Children in counseling often also have academic difficulties. Many schools now have special education and treatment teams available to support the overall treatment plan for the child. Special education efforts, of course,

need to be undertaken in concert with family and cultural expectations.

5. *Family therapy and counseling.* If a child has difficulties, the family often has multigenerational difficulties as well. For example, in a case of child abuse, members of the abusing family may themselves have been abused in their own family of origin.

6. *State and government intervention.* It is legally mandated that state agencies must be involved with abused children and their families. At times, economic support may be required, as financial issues often bring about abuse in the family.

7. *Community/multicultural intervention.* Some children need mentors or older friends from the community to give them attention that has been unavailable at home. In addition, the family may be refugees, and children may have suffered multiple traumas before entering the school situation. In addition, they may face discrimination and prejudice in the community. In such cases, action to institute better housing options and to change community attitudes may be necessary.

8. *Large group/network meetings.* In some cases, it is possible to assemble network meetings of many individuals in the community. In these sessions, the approach is very similar to that endorsed by Attneave (1974) in that a general "community plan" is

agreed to by participants. When it is not feasible for the full network to meet, bringing together the extended family, the employer, a religious figure, and perhaps some key friends and neighbors can be a powerful supplement to individual and group work.

---

efficient than long-term one-on-one or family work. It is crucial that the key interventions discussed in Research Exhibit 6.1 be in place and coordinated; otherwise change will occur more slowly.

Where to Start with Network Therapy

When you work with a European-American child, it is likely that you can start network therapy with the individual and the family, later expanding to larger networks. However, if you are working with a Laotian or Cambodian child, for example, you may want to start by going into the community and learning about the customs of the group. You may find that developing an understanding relationship with a Buddhist monk is more important in helping you understand how to help the child solve problems than doing play therapy.

Similarly, with African-American clients, there will likely be some measure of distrust if you are of a different cultural group (Solomon, 1990; White & Parham, 1990). Working in the community to combat racism may be a step you can take that will aid you in developing a meaningful counseling relationship with a child or adolescent. Cooperation is often best developed by framing your intervention in terms of an egalitarian relationship with the African-American client or family.

The following guidelines can be helpful when using the network approach:

1. *Don't expect to do it all by yourself.* As a counselor or therapist, you cannot personally be expected to do all that is involved in the network approach on your own. Network therapy relies on a treatment team working together. Case management skills and the ability to work with organizations can be as important as your individual helping skills.

2. *Use multiple theoretical approaches.* Also implied in the network approach is that different theories may be useful at different times with different clients. At one time a child may need art therapy to work out certain issues, play therapy at another, and traditional talk therapy at still another. Surprisingly, most adult therapy techniques work well with children if you use appropriate language.

3. *Consider the value of network treatment for all clients.* If you work with a traumatized individual, you can expect that the family is also traumatized in some way. In addition, anticipate that the extended family as well as the neighborhood and community are influenced as well by your client. Network therapy

has value for adult European-American clients just as it does for Native American and other groups.

Family Therapy and Multicultural Issues

Many clients may prefer to work with their families on issues of concern. It is not within the scope of this book to provide an in-depth introduction to family therapy, but the MCT frame requires that special attention be paid to this important part of treatment. The multicultural treatment of choice is often family therapy. Practice Exercise 6.4 provides a list of questions that you can use to identify family rules in counseling with clients and their families.

As discussed in Chapter 2, the definition of family varies across cultures. The family as a system with specified relationships, roles, and rules applies to a wide variety of family types (gay and lesbian, single-parent, blended, and nuclear). Furthermore,

---

Practice Exercise 6.4

 Examining Family Rules in Individual Counseling

Many techniques and strategies of family therapy are also effective in one-on-one counseling and therapy. The following exercise, taken from structural theory, can be helpful with clients of varying cultures and backgrounds.

1. Ask your volunteer client to tell you a family story that concretely represents the family style. Use the basic listening sequence to draw out the story, and be sure to summarize what you have heard to the client's satisfaction.

2. Ask your client to reflect on this story and to search for a family rule that the story might exemplify. For example, do certain family members have typical standardized roles? Who is expected to take on key duties?

3. What specific behaviors, thoughts, and feelings did this client have in this story? Are the behaviors, thoughts, and feelings the client has similar to what the original experiences were? Most important, does the client repeat the family rule or role with other people in daily life?

Family theory reminds us that we learn much of our behavioral and emotional styles in our families of origin. This exercise can be helpful in enabling clients to see how their present behavior relates to experiences in the family and can help them realize that the way they treat or react to other people relates to their learned family rules and roles.

in African-American, Latina/o, and Native American cultures, the extended family and even the broader network of relationships may represent the family. Family dynamics also exist in such living arrangements as college dormitories and group homes. A promising new area of consultation and treatment is in the business community, where many work groups operate much like dysfunctional families.

Cultural expectations infuse every family and group experience. Children in Western society are encouraged to excel on an individual basis, be it in sports, school, charm, or physical looks. Children in China are encouraged to excel in cooperative activities that benefit first the community, then the family, and then the self. Culture, because it is manifest in all that we are exposed to, becomes a significant ingredient in our construction process.

As also emphasized in Chapter 2, a significant component of our self-concept is derived from our ethnic heritage. Often, when asked to describe ourselves, we use our family's nationality as a primary descriptor: "I am Irish, Jewish, Puerto Rican, Japanese, African-American." Research indicates that ethnicity is a filter through which families and individuals understand and interpret their symptoms, their beliefs about the cause of their illness, their attitudes toward helpers, and their preferred treatment methods (Giordano & Giordano, 1977; Tseng & McDermott, 1981). For example, Italian and Jewish family members may use their tendency toward emotional expressiveness in sharing suffering, whereas those from Irish and British backgrounds may tend to pull into themselves and not discuss their feelings with others.

Attitudes toward mental health professionals also vary. Italians, in general, rely primarily on the family and seek professional assistance only as a last resort. The church is the only extrafamilial institution that many African-Americans trust and feel safe with when they are in need of help (Cheatham, 1990; Hines & Boyd-Franklin, 1982). Research Exhibit 6.2 explores family therapy in the African-American context. Many Puerto Ricans, Chinese, Norwegians, and Iranians experiencing psychological stress often report physical symptoms and seek medical rather than mental health services. Research indicates that Irish, African-Americans, and Norwegians tend to place blame for their issues on themselves, whereas Greeks, Iranians, and Puerto Ricans tend to blame others for their issues (McGoldrick, Pearce, & Giordano, 1982).

Traditional Healing

Although what has been called counseling developed in a European-American academic setting in the twentieth century, the function of counseling has occurred historically whenever individuals have found it necessary to help other individuals with their emotional and personal problems. Formal methods in formal settings or informal methods in informal settings have been applied depending on the cultural setting. Traditional healing is a form of informal counseling. It is important that the multicultural therapist develop an understanding and awareness of indigenous helping and traditional healing approaches

=== **Research Exhibit 6.2** ===

Family Therapy with African-American Families

Cheatham (1990) suggests that therapies best tailored to African-American families are those that do not rely on theoretical notions of how therapy should be conducted. The most beneficial therapies provide counselors and therapists with access to active, intervention-oriented treatment plans and strategies that give prominence to social functioning over internal thoughts and emotions. In addition to drawing from these tailored forms of treatment, the effective counselor or therapist also must attend to the historical and cultural experiences of African-Americans and gain specific knowledge about the history and presence of racism in North America.

Additionally, therapists working with African-American families need to understand the prominent values that are reflected in the family's organization and functioning. For example, the counselor should understand the importance of the extended family, the community, and the church. These intrafamilial and extrafamilial variables can be causes of stress or support and, as such, need to be given central attention in the problem-definition and solution-determination processes inherent in the therapeutic relationship.

Cheatham (1990) offers five central elements in his family therapy model that address the type of framework best tailored to the needs of African-American families seeking therapeutic services.

1. *Discussion of counselor and client roles and expectancies.* It is essential that the therapist draw from each member of the family the expectations regarding the therapeutic encounter. This should be done in a way that allows family members to clearly spell out what they expect to happen during sessions and as a result of the therapeutic encounter. Issues of power and influence also must be recognized, discussed, negotiated, and revised if necessary. Cheatham (1990) suggests that in working with African-American families therapists refrain from familiarity with the family until or unless the family offers permission for informal contact. For example, formal salutations and given names should be used; nicknames should be avoided. He also suggests that therapists or counselors be flexible in terms of times and locations for therapy, thus providing evidence of their willingness to revise the power differential inherent in many traditional therapeutic venues. Finally, cultural differences, and how these can both enhance and restrict the therapeutic process, must be discussed.

2. *Identification and interpretation of the situation promoting therapy.* Cheatham (1990) suggests that counselors and therapists keep central the importance of the family's cultural norms and values and also remain mindful that undergirding these norms and values is a strong sense of pride and respect. The culturally sensitive therapist or counselor should draw out the family's story in a manner that does not violate the family's sense of cultural propriety. As such, any construction of the issues that promoted treatment should include an understanding of how family members evaluate the presenting issues within their wider cultural context.

3. *Coconstructing a resource inventory.* Cheatham (1990) describes how to assist families to coconstruct a resource inventory that includes those persons, institutions, family members, and other networks that may be able to assist in problem resolution. The list can be considered similar to microskill's positive asset search.

4. *Practicing for legibility.* As therapy continues, the practitioner should provide a facilitative environment that assists family members to practice and own their plan of action. In systemic therapies, this is generally labeled "enactment." The basic question to be addressed is whether or not the family is able to state, understand, and implement the plan. The process that must occur is for the family to practice the plan, receive corrective feedback, repractice

the plan, and then be able to transfer any newly obtained or modified skills outside of the therapeutic context. The therapist or counselor can facilitate this generalization of skills by ensuring that culturally relevant and culturally specific reinforcers and suggestions are coconstructed during the therapy sessions.

5. *Evaluating the legitimacy of the plan and the result.* Once a family has practiced and generalized new or modified knowledge and skills, the therapist and the family need to evaluate the adequacy of the solutions they coconstructed. The key question to address is whether or not the new or modified thoughts and behaviors effectively diminish the reasons for seeking treatment. It is also important, at this stage, to determine if the family wishes to address any additional issues before terminating treatment. If so, the phases of the therapeutic process may be repeated. Finally, the family should be assisted to consider how relapses will be handled and when or if the family should engage again the services of the therapist.

Achebe's Structural Model of Traditional Healing

Achebe (1986) provides an unusually clear example of how traditional healing is structured by diviners in African Igbo culture. Her model helps explain the almost universal acceptance of traditional healers by native peoples. Furthermore, her summary reveals parallels between traditional and modern approaches. Achebe's model presents traditional methods in a clear and comprehensive fashion, bridging the gap between older systems and our newer "more scientific" modes of therapy.

First, Achebe notes that it is important for professionals to understand the worldview of the client. In African cultures, the extended family is central, and humans and nature compose one interrelated system. Part of this system is the world of the spirits. Traditional healing seeks to reestablish harmony in the whole system.

The combining of individual, family system, culture, and spirituality of traditional healing can be foundational for multicultural counseling and therapy with European-American clients as well as with those of other cultures.

According to Achebe, the elements of traditional healing are as follows:

1. The healer invokes the spirit of the gods through traditional practices, which can range from dancing to candle lighting to whatever is appropriate in the culture.

2. The process of helping is clearly structured. Often, the healer explains his or her credentials and develops rapport with the client. This process is particularly important in that it provides the healer with authority. Dancing, drumming, incense, fires, or specific shamanic ceremonies may be part of this process.

3. The client is asked to share the problem or concern.

4. The healer diagnoses the problem through divination. Divination activities vary with the cultural setting and help establish the credibility of the healer.

5. Interventions suggested by the healer tend to be time limited and to involve the client and often the client's family. These interventions, being culturally based, make sense within the worldview of the client.

The parallels between the traditional healing process and Western psychotherapeutic practice should be apparent. Traditional healers work within the worldview and beliefs of the client. Similarly, cognitive-behavioral and other techniques represent a menu of prescriptions for healing and therapy within the North American worldview. As an example of structural similarity, the following discussion of rational-emotive behavioral therapy suggests how Western-oriented theories of helping (for example, psychodynamic, existential-humanistic, cognitive-behavioral, and the microskills five stages) may not be too different from traditional healing. The five steps outlined by Achebe can be used to structure a rational-emotive behavior therapy (REBT) session that considers cultural and community issues, as follows:

1. The REBT healer invokes the spirit of rationality in accordance with Western culture. An attractive office, with appropriate credentials on the wall, establishes credibility. (The traditional healer gains the same status and power through dancing and invoking the power of the gods.)

2. The REBT healer structures the session clearly and thus gains authority.

3. The client is asked to share the problem or concern.

4. The REBT healer diagnoses the problem through Western linear logic and searches for irrational ideas.

5. REBT interventions tend to be time limited and focused. In a broader community orientation, homework would include the family and key social networks.

Important in traditional healing and REBT is the psychological relationship between therapist and client. Given enough belief in therapist power, many cognitive and behavioral changes can occur in either system.

Traditional Healing and the Psychotherapeutic Process

In their classic study, Strong and Schmidt (1970) showed that perceived counselor expertness, attractiveness, and trustworthiness have much to do with client change in counseling and therapy. Rational-emotive behavior therapy (REBT), for example, is seen as expert and trustworthy. REBT depends very much on client belief systems and focuses on the linear rationality of these systems. Many traditional cultures might consider this reliance on rationality to be irrational because it overlooks spiritual dimensions. Again, the influence of culture on client belief systems must be taken into account in therapeutic practice.

Traditional healing paradigms as well as those of European–North American culture have similar structures and are both based on the epistemology and belief systems of the culture. Achebe's description of traditional healing in other cultures describes divination processes focusing on spiritual-human connections in the world. The European–North American traditions of cognitive-behavioral, existential-humanistic, and psychodynamic helping similarly have developed divination processes based on the individual self—the object of value in this culture. Both paradigms have value, and both are deserving of respect.

Recognizing parallels between Western and traditional healing opens the way for cooperation between the two areas of helping. Modern psychotherapy generally would uphold the emphasis on community and family inherent in the traditional approach described by Achebe. Increasingly, it is accepted that effective therapy sometimes requires that the therapist work in concert with a traditional healer. However, many professionals may object to doing so. For example, Attneave (1974, p. 53) quotes a psychiatrist on working with Native American Indian medicine men:

> I'm a careful, hard-working, scientific physician. I don't prescribe medications I don't know about or use therapies that haven't got substantial evidence that they do some good. . . . These medicine men aren't about to tell me what they do or how they did it. No! I can't refer my patients to them. That would be unethical.

Attneave goes on to point out that the clients of this psychiatrist seldom returned for additional sessions. She strongly recommends that professionals learn to work within the community and states that it is especially important to develop a respectful relationship with traditional healers such as medicine men.

In his study of traditional healers, Lee (1996) recommends that therapists be aware of the work of herbalists, fetish men or women, mediums, and mystics. For instance, in Mexico, the *curandera/o* specialize in herbalism and massage as part of their practice. In many Islamic countries, healers recite verses from the Koran as part of the healing ritual. Consideration of religious and spiritual systems is important in MCT, and spiritual and cultural images can be integrated naturally into the interview as positive resources for personal development.

Traditional healers are not as removed from scientific methods as most Western professionals might think. Both traditional and modern approaches are heavily based on belief systems. As modern approaches have become more inclusive of family, community, and culture, the larger social system has entered the healing process. Achebe notes that traditional healers have always included the family and the larger community in developing effective treatment plans.

Although MCT encourages awareness and inclusion of traditional healers, it is important to define boundaries. For example, the Native American Indian sweat lodge has become popular in the treatment of posttraumatic stress disorder. This may be an effective addition to treatment if a Native American Indian healer is consulted about the sweat lodge procedure. The sweat lodge also has played a part in men's movement gatherings. For many Native Americans, such usage of one of their spiritual traditions is considered insulting. Many people have adopted traditional practices without first consulting with the host culture. If you plan to use nontraditional approaches in your work, it is important to collaborate with traditional healers and show respect for their traditions.

The Liberation of Consciousness: Self-in-Relation

The sixth MCT proposition concerns the awareness of self-in-relation:

> *Proposition VI.* The liberation of consciousness is a basic goal of MCT. Whereas self-actualization, discovery of how the past affects the present, or behavioral change have been traditional goals of Western psychotherapy and counseling, MCT emphasizes the importance of expanding personal, family, group, and organizational consciousness of self-in-relation, family-in-relation, and organization-in-relation. Thus, MCT is ultimately contextual in orientation and also draws on traditional methods of healing from many cultures.

Paulo Freire, a leading Brazilian educational and political theorist, has had a great impact on helping people develop an understanding of themselves in a social context. Whereas Brazilian peasants had been used to blaming themselves and "fate" (*fatalismo*) for their situation, Freire pointed out that their position was "the direct product of a whole situation of economic, social, and political domination—and of the paternalism—of which they were victims" (Shaull, 1970, pp. 10–11). Freire (1972) developed a specific method to help these people name their situation as resulting from oppression and eventually to act against their oppressors. He was exiled from Brazil for his work, but his writings had an immense influence throughout Central and South America and are considered integral in the democratic movement there.

Freire's theoretical educational processes closely correspond to those of cultural identity theory as presented in Proposition III (see Chapter 5). The cultural identity model concerns consciousness-raising—helping individuals become more aware of themselves in social systems—and movement away from an embedded self to an awareness of self-in-relation or self-in-system.

Freire's Five Levels of Consciousness

Freire notes a "culture of silence" among the dispossessed. For counseling purposes, the dispossessed can include any group—women, religious groups, ethnic/racial groups, survivors of trauma—that considers itself oppressed by others. In his work to help Brazilian peasants become conscious of their dispossession and to act positively for their own futures, Freire's first task was to address what he called "naive consciousness," which is similar to the first level of embedded consciousness in cultural identity theory. The dispossessed at this level of consciousness tend to blame themselves for their condition and do not see themselves in social context.

At a second level, Freire notes that the people often seek to identify with the oppressor. "During the initial stage of their struggle, the oppressed find in their oppressor their model of *personhood*" (Freire, 1970, p. 30). This identification with the oppressor is similar to some of the later aspects of naiveté and early dimensions of naming. As the peasants discovered and named their condition, anger was often the result. Women or African-Americans struggling for personal and group identity also may operate at this level. At issue is how anger can be directed in a positive direction. Anger at the discovery of how one has been dispossessed by racism, sexism, or economic oppression is a common result of consciousness-raising.

The fourth level occurs when the individual begins to reflect on the self as a cultural being. "The insistence that the oppressed engage in reflection on their concrete situation is not a call to armchair revolution. On the contrary, reflection—true reflection—leads to action" (Freire, 1970, p. 52). Personal identity is made by the self in relation to, rather than the self in opposition to, the oppressor. In the final level, noted by Freire, the person becomes project: "There would be no human action if [humankind] were not a 'project,' if he [or she] were not able to transcend him (or her) self" (p. 38). At this fifth level, the person sees self-in-system and is ready to move to action. Theory has become practice.

Freire's Psychoeducational Method

There is often a strong psychoeducational component to MCT. The role of the counselor or therapist often involves teaching the client about the underlying cultural dimensions of present concerns. Feminist theory argues that counselors and therapists must help women see their issues as not just located in the individual but also as related to external conditions—the self-in-context. Cultural identity theorists have the same objective: to teach clients that what they see as their concerns are not just personal issues but also the result of what occurs in the social context. Because the counselor or therapist adopts a leader role, it is particularly important that ideas of coconstruction and equality be addressed regularly throughout the therapeutic process.

When Freire worked with peasants who could not read, he developed "culture circles" in which peasants sat together in a relationship of equality between instructor and student. (This approach mirrors the egalitarian structure of feminist therapy and MCT as well as consciousness-raising principles.) Freire wanted his students to develop reading skills in relation to their natural environment. Thus, he used the images (visual, pictorial, graphic, tactile, auditory, and compound) to elucidate their experience. He elicited direct sensory experience first, before inviting stories.

As the peasants shared their images and experiences, Freire helped them name their experiences and then write the words in Portuguese. This process resulted in more concrete storytelling so that eventually the peasants could reflect together on what their lives meant. If the peasants developed, for example, images of the good life of the plantation owner, they would name these images. In turn, these affluent images could be contrasted with their own lives of poverty. This concrete naming could lead to anger as the peasants developed an identity in opposition to the plantation owner. Reflective consciousness then developed as the peasants began to see similarities in their stories and plan for action. Thus, although the peasants began instruction with an embedded naive consciousness, Freire's method led them to increased awareness of alternative perspectives on their situation and eventually to action.

Relating Educational Method to Counseling and Therapy Practice

Despite being exiled, Freire returned to Brazil and has become an international figure who is influential in many fields. What does he offer for the practice of counseling and therapy? Ivey (1994, 1995) suggests that there are several practical specifics Freire offers for therapeutic practice. Theoretically, there are significant parallels among DCT, cultural identity theory, and Freire's approach. For example, the techniques and strategies of developmental counseling and therapy closely parallel Freire's teaching methodology. Freire used sensorimotor images to bring out holistic summaries of the peasants' condition. This was followed by concrete naming and storytelling. Freire's reflective consciousness level corresponds to the formal operational aspects of DCT, and his contextual fifth level closely corresponds to DCT's dialectic/systemic theory and methods. DCT provides a link to traditional psychological theory and practice, and Freire provides an overarching frame for further integration. Cultural identity theory focuses on the cognitive/emotional development of people-in-context, which is the basis of Freire's approach. The following subsections offer examples of how the examination of cultural identity can be used in the interview to facilitate awareness of self-in-relation.

Inviting a Narrative

In this example, a client, traumatized over an incident involving racial or sexual harassment, has come for counseling. The following presents two possible client responses:

Therapist: Could you tell me what occurred for you? (*Drawing out the client's story is facilitated by using the basic listening sequence in Chapter 3. What are the main facts, feelings, and thoughts of the client?*)

Client 1: I don't know, perhaps it was my fault. Maybe I shouldn't have dressed as I did.

Client 2: They called me a _____. I hate that name. I would have liked to kill them.

Here the therapist has asked for the narrative or story of the event. The discussion can go on at some length as the client explores issues in depth, as therapist and client feel appropriate. The second client seems ready for action (albeit inappropriate), whereas the first takes on a great deal of unnecessary personal responsibility.

Often, counseling and therapy take an issue orientation to clients' narratives and may seek to resolve the problem. The psychotherapy-as-liberation perspective maintains an interest in the problem but also seeks to help individuals see their issues as systemic. This approach closely approximates that of Freire, DCT, and cultural identity theory. In addition, Freire provides a framework for examining cultural identity.

If we apply cultural identity concepts to this exchange, we see a level 1 or level 2 naive acceptance in client 1 and a level 3 resistance or angry consciousness in client 2. Consider next that the narrative has been developed sufficiently for each client, and each agrees to explore the issues in more depth. The questioning styles in the following subsection are *not* appropriate for all cultural groups but are provided to indicate one way to facilitate new ways of making meaning of experience.

Reexperiencing the Sensory Dimensions of Cultural Identity Issues

Recall that Freire began discussion in his cultural circles with auditory, visual, olfactory, kinesthetic, and even gustatory images. A narrative of a story, valuable and central as it is, nonetheless separates the client from the direct experience of the event, which originally was experienced in a sensory fashion. An important part of Freire's naming process was enabling clients to know and learn the sensory elements in their experiences. Similarly, if we are to help clients experience their stories—and eventually the cultural implications of these stories—we need to help them get in touch with the original sensory experiences. Such emotional learning here can help clients move from the naive level to other levels of consciousness.

The following approach can help clients explore the sensory dimensions of their narratives:

Take one dimension of the story that struck you as especially important.

Focus on that dimension and allow yourself to reexperience the event.

Make an effort to develop an image of the event.

As you focus on the event, what are you seeing, hearing, feeling?

This emphasis on sensory aspects is also characteristic of DCT and Freire's work. This approach involves the complex techniques of regression, in which clients go back to old events and reexperience them with sensory awareness in the present moment with a supportive helper. These techniques can be powerful and should be used carefully so that the past negative experience is not repeated with the counselor or therapist. Practice Exercises 2.1 and 2.2 in Chapter 2 provide specific guidelines for using sensory-oriented questions in a way that is ethical and protects the client.

The value of moving the narrative to a sensory orientation is that the event is holistically and directly reexperienced in the body rather than as an intellectual construct. This technique corresponds to Freire's codification and use of images in teaching reading to Brazilian peasants and is an important part of the psychotherapy of liberation.

Making the Narrative Concrete and Specific

After sensory experiencing, Freire would then have his groups tell concrete stories about how their lives had been affected by the events. These concrete narratives provided a structure and a way to share meaning. As people hear stories from others, they begin to realize that their images, experiences, and stories are at least partially shared with others.

Working with a single client, it may be useful to encourage storytelling around the theme of the primary event. When clients tell several concrete and situational stories, they are better prepared for formal operational reflective consciousness. The telling of stories is similar to the naming stage of cultural identity theory. A client who tells an angry story is most likely working with issues at the resistance stage. A client who tells a story of accommodation to a racist or sexist situation may be at the passive acceptance stage.

The therapist can help clients express their narratives and then provide gentle confrontations to help them examine inconsistencies in their story lines, as follows:

Tell me a story of what happened.

What happened first, next, and how did it end?

Tell your story in as much detail as possible.

Tell me another story that occurs to you and give me as many details as possible.

Applied behavioral analysis (see Chapter 9) is important here.

Another approach is to have the client describe how another person would tell the story. The process of naming can be approached by asking the client to provide a title for the story. Suggestions may be provided by the therapist. Through questions that focus on the client's story, the counselor can obtain more details. Often the client's story is enriched by the sensory imaging experience. Furthermore, emotion seems to be more connected to the story as it is repeated.

The cognitive-behavioral methods of Ellis, Beck, and Glasser (see Chapter 10) may be useful, as there may be irrational or illogical aspects to the story. The emphasis, however, is on helping clients see their stories in social context. Traditional cognitive-behavioral work focuses on irrationality in the individual, whereas the MCT frame focuses on irrationality in the context.

Moving to a Reflective Consciousness

In group work, the sharing of stories almost automatically leads to a reflective consciousness. As people share their stories, they note similarities and differences. The story begins to be put into cultural and social context, moving from "my story" to "our story." In cultural identity terms, this process deals with issues around introspection. Helms (1990, 1992) mentions disintegration and reintegration. Through the reflective process, old ideas are taken apart and examined and new meanings are developed. The individual or the group looks at stories, patterns of stories, and perhaps even writes a metastory in a reflective mode.

In individual counseling and therapy, a variety of cognitive and reflective techniques are used to help clients reflect on the meaning and patterning of their stories. For example:

Is that a pattern?
Does that happen a lot?
As you reflect on it now, what sense do you make of it?
How are you feeling and thinking right now?

What is common to these stories?
As you look at the story now, old meanings seem to be breaking down.
How is this process of disintegration for you?
How could a new integration be generated?

What common themes do you see in these stories?
How do these themes relate to gender, racial, or cultural issues?

A number of these techniques are from DCT. Also, the techniques of cognitive-behavioral examination of cognitive and emotional style can be beneficial.

Through such formal operational questions and strategies, clients learn to think about their situations and issues more broadly. They see patterns where before only separate, unconnected situations existed. They start seeing their own behavior in relation to the system. In short, they are beginning to see themselves in context.

Seeing Self-in-Relation or Self-in-System

Freire was especially concerned that clients see themselves in a social context. The sharing and identifying of patterns and themes described above still tend to focus on individual or group perceptions. Freire (1970) was interested in fostering debate around the concept of culture: "As they discuss the world of culture, they express their level of awareness of reality, in which various themes are implicit. Their discussion touches upon other aspects of reality, which comes to be perceived in an increasingly critical manner" (p. 117).

Ivey (1995) has generated a set of questions that can be used to facilitate client consciousness. The purpose of these types of questions is to encourage the client to examine self-in-relation to system.

> As we look back on all we've talked about and/or done, what stands out for you? How? Why?
>
> How do you/we put together all we've talked about?

These questions help individuals or groups look back and reflect on their cognitive and emotional operations. The questions may loosen old thought patterns and constructs and lead to a new integration or belief system.

> How might cultural, gender, or racial issues relate to this issue?
>
> Under what rule(s) were you (or the other person or group) operating?
>
> Where did that rule come from?
>
> How might someone else (another family member, a member of the opposition, someone from a different cultural background) describe this situation?
>
> How do these rules relate now?

> How might we describe this from the point of view of some other person, theoretical framework, or language system?
>
> How might we put it together using another framework?

> How is your experience part of a cultural theme? A family theme?
>
> What do experiences in your family of origin have to say to this?

> What shall we do? How shall we do it together?
>
> What is *our* objective and how can we work together effectively?

In working through these questions, techniques such as the microskill of focusing and the family and community genograms can be helpful. Also, behavioral techniques (see Chapter 10) may be employed to help the client plan specific actions for the future.

Freire, of course, was centrally concerned with generalization, with having the peasants take learnings from the cultural groups back to life within the community. Words and thoughts need to be enacted in concrete practice. In counseling terms, the issue is finding techniques to encourage "homework" and doing something with the changed narrative. Freire's concept of human projects—helping clients project their new selves in a concrete fashion through action—is important here.

Parham (1989) talks about the idea of recycling in cultural identity theory. An individual may be able to view self-in-system—to achieve the "highest" level of cultural identity—but then a new challenge or event may result in the individual's recycling through the entire process. In this recycling, many new learnings in more depth are likely to occur. Again, there is no end to cultural identity development.

Practice Exercise 6.5 provides a summary of the psychotherapy-as-liberation process. This exercise is particularly important as an integrative framework for

===== **Practice Exercise 6.5** =====

 Psychotherapy as Liberation

The following exercise is an abbreviated version of the detailed questioning strategies presented in the section on relating educational method to counseling. You may wish to refer to this section so you can supplement this exercise with the more detailed questions. Allow at least an hour for this process and ensure that you are available to your client/consultant for follow-up support.

Seek a volunteer client who has experienced some form of oppression, discrimination, or harassment. The client should be an equal coparticipant in the process and will be referred to as the "client/consultant" in order to emphasize the mutuality of the process. Share the general structure of the interview plan and the theoretical rationale for psychotherapy as liberation with your client/consultant. The general purpose of the session is to see a past experience with oppression from several perspectives and perhaps to act in a new way on the issue.

Together generate a topic that is important to both you and the client/consultant. For example, many women have suffered sexual harassment. This type of oppressive experience is often helpful to review from a psychotherapy-as-liberation perspective. You and the client/consultant should be aware that retelling the old story may reawaken troubling memories. Other topics might include experiences with racism, homophobia, insensitivy to disability, or other types of discrimination. Together, choose a topic

that you both feel equipped to handle. Feel free to stop at any time during the session to discuss the process with your client/consultant. The specific steps of this process follow:

1. *Preliminary steps.* Use the community genogram and/or family chart/genogram to draw out strengths and support systems in the client/consultant's background. Use imaging to make specific support systems and strengths from the cultural background concrete and available as positive resources. Do not begin exploration until a solid base of positive strength and mutual respect is developed.

2. *Opening.* Begin by asking the client/consultant to tell you a narrative of the story: "Could you tell me what occurred for you?" Draw out the story by using the basic listening sequence (Chapter 3). What are the main facts, feelings, and thoughts of the client/consultant?

3. *Sensorimotor exploration.* Take one dimension of the story that impresses you and the client as especially important. Focus on that dimension and ask the client/consultant to reexperience the event. Have the client/consultant make an effort to develop an image of that event and ask: "As you focus on the event, what are you seeing, hearing, feeling?" This can be a powerful experience and can often bring tears; inform your client/con-

sultant of this potential. Draw on positive resources and images as necessary to remind the client/consultant of strengths.

4. *Making the narrative more concrete and specific.* It is often helpful to retell the story a second time by asking: "Tell me a story of what happened. What happened first, next, and how did it end?" If the incident has been repeated several times, draw out more related stories in concrete detail by asking: "Tell me another story that occurs to you and give me as many details as possible." Another approach is to ask the client/consultant to describe how another person would tell the story.

The Freirian process of naming might be approached by asking the client/consultant to provide a title for the story. Certain titles may be suggested by the therapist.

5. *Moving to a reflective consciousness.* The discussion with the client/consultant now focuses on looking back, reflecting on, and thinking about the story. The following questions can guide this process:

   a. As you reflect on it now, what sense do you make of it? How are you feeling and thinking right now?

   b. What common themes do you see in story 1 and story 2? Between your stories and those of other women (gays, people of your race, etc.)? How do these themes relate to gender, racial, and cultural issues?

   c. What is common to these stories? As you look at the story now, old

meanings seem to be breaking down. How is that process of disintegration or decentering for you? How could a new integration or center be generated?

6. *Seeing self-in-relation or self-in-system.* The final step for your client/consultant and you is to think about the entire interview, how it relates specifically to multicultural issues, and the actions that might be taken to address the oppressive incident by using the following questions as a guide:

   a. As we look back on all we've talked about and/or done, what stands out for you? How? Why? How do you/we put together all we've talked about?

   b. How might cultural, gender, or racial issues relate to this issue? What rule(s) were you (or the other person or group) operating under? Where did that rule come from? How might someone else (another family member, a member of the opposition, someone from a different cultural background) describe that situation? How do these rules relate to us now?

   c. How is your experience part of a cultural theme? A family theme? What do experiences in your family of origin have to say to this? (The family and community genograms may be useful here.)

   d. What shall we do? How shall we do it together? What is *our* objective and how can we work together effectively? (The behavioral techniques in Chapter 10 may be employed to help the client/consultant plan specific actions for the future.)

7. *Following up with your client/consultant and seeking supervision.* Some client/consultants will need additional emotional support, whereas others may appreciate assistance in

following up their discussions with plans for behavioral action. MCT suggests that at times you may have to leave the office setting and take action in the community itself. It is also important to have suitable supervision through this process.

---

many of the ideas presented in this book. This exercise points up the idea of psychotherapy as liberation—helping clients see their issues in a social context. This contextual emphasis sets multicultural counseling and therapy apart from most counseling and therapy theory, although there are ways that the idea of context can be included in traditional psychotherapeutic theory.

Adapting Existing Theories, Skills, and Strategies to the MCT Counseling Session

Traditional first-, second-, and third-force counseling and therapy theory has a place in MCT. It must be acknowledged that many useful theories, skills, and strategies exist within traditional and popular theoretical frameworks. Paniagua (1994) reviews existing theory and makes specific recommendations for using these theories in practice with non-European clients. His general conclusion is that these theories are helpful but require careful monitoring and consideration regarding the experience and needs of each client. Paniagua stresses the importance of concrete, cognitive-behavioral techniques and strategies as contrasted with the humanistic or the psychoanalytic approaches.

Cheek (1976), a pioneer in assertiveness training, clearly demonstrates the validity of traditional behavioral concepts with African-American clients. He is also an early proponent of cognitive methods being used concurrently with assertiveness training, calling this "didactic assertiveness training." The didactic process is similar to the dialectic dialogue approach of Freire. For example, the following interview focuses on the complex issue of male-female African-American relations.

Therapist: I understand you have trouble rapping with sisters [Black women].

Patient (African-American male):   Yeah, that's right. I can seem to talk with White women, but I can't seem to get across to sisters. Like at the last social we had—there was this fine number I wanted to rap with—you know—just get to know her—but I didn't know how to go about it.

Therapist: What if the woman was White?

Patient: Well, I would put on my gentleman act and break it on down.

Therapist: And with a sister?

Patient: Well, I'd either just go along with the program or cuss her . . . out.

Therapist: OK, then maybe you're satisfied with that approach.

Patient: No—that's not the way it should be. I've got feelings and ideas that I really would like to get across—but I don't want her laughing at me or thinking I'm . . . square—you dig?

Cheek interprets this behavior as representative of underlying anxiety and the need for assertiveness. Cheek (1976) starts the session at the point where the client is most uncomfortable in order to get therapy moving, as "Blacks have little time (or money) to fool around" (p. 67). In this example, some standard techniques of cognitive-behavioral approaches are used, but gender and cultural issues are attacked directly and economically. The cognitive work in this dialogue provides a base for the assertiveness training to follow.

Although there is insufficient space in this book for presenting the specifics for adapting existing methods to culturally diverse clients, Cheek (1976) and Paniagua (1994) address this topic. However, there is a need for more theory and methods on adapting Eurocentric psychotherapy to other cultural groups. Throughout this book, the authors seek to provide specific ideas on how to do this. Following are some general principles that can help guide the adaptation of psychotherapeutic theories and practices to issues of diversity:

1. The general principles of Rogerian respect and empathy for the client seem to hold broadly across cultural groups, whereas the reflective listening style is not always appropriate. A more active counseling style than one usually associates with Rogerian theory seems to be called for with some cultures. At the same time, being willing to be silent at times with some Native American Indian clients may be particularly important, for respect may be communicated best at times through saying nothing.

2. It is important to be willing to move out of the office and work in the community. The counselor or therapist should be seen at key community gatherings, festivals, and celebrations. As counselors gradually develop trust through being in the community, clients may be willing to try some traditional strategies, especially if they are explained clearly and approached cooperatively.

3. Concrete approaches with an action orientation often seem to be accepted better than abstract talk. Thus, the cognitive-behavioral tradition seems to offer many useful methods for MCT, as long as they are adapted in a culturally sensitive fashion. Solution-oriented therapy, with its specific focus, can be useful if adapted for varying orientations to time and cultural style.

4. Family approaches are often suitable. Given this, more emphasis on family issues in counselor training curricula is necessary. The importance of integrating family issues into individual interviews is emphasized in this book.

5. Counselors must continually educate themselves on new thinking about traditional practice as well as about multicultural counseling and therapy.

Advocates of MCT have commented that many of the principles and methods of feminist therapy also apply to counseling for diversity. Particularly important is the concept of egalitarian relationships—the equal distribution of power. All too often traditional theory and therapy accord power to the helper. The egalitarian principle can be used to advantage as traditional therapy techniques are adapted to diverse clientele. MCT specifically endorses this point in its theory, assumptions, and corollaries. The issue of power must be more centrally addressed, not only by MCT, but also by all theories and practice of counseling and therapy.

Feminist theory also focuses on mutual education and psychoeducation. Both the client and the counselor, in an egalitarian relationship, need to analyze their worlds and educate each other about them. Teaching clients ways to view the world is an important part of feminist therapy. In this sense, feminist theory depends on developing a dialogue similar to that used by Freire. Through posing questions and sharing information, clients and therapists can grow together.

Social context and oppression are special issues in feminist therapy. MCT believes that it is not enough to help clients feel better about themselves; they also need to become aware of themselves in social context. The failure to consider context is one example of the limitations of traditional therapy. Liberation requires massive, yet simple and concrete, change. Cognitive-behavioral, humanistic, and psychodynamic theories can all be enriched by adding contextual considerations to practice and theory, always keeping in mind the diversity of contexts. The therapist or counselor should not assume that there is only one context common to all clients.

Limitations and Practical Implications of MCT

There are many challenges in using the MCT approach, and these challenges represent limitations of the theory. MCT asks the helping practitioner to (1) be highly competent in traditional theory, (2) have developed an understanding of MCT metatheory, and (3) to over time develop an understanding of the specific needs, wishes, and developmental histories of many highly diverse multicultural groups. Added to these demands is the limitation of a relatively small research base on which to establish the claims of MCT. The research base is constantly expanding, and evidence shows that adding multicultural issues to practice improves effectiveness.

We live in a world of cultural differences. MCT thus is extremely practical, as it forces us to deal with the realities of difference. The very complexity and high demands of MCT are simultaneously its strength and weakness. Chapters 5 and 6 have provided a number of practical experiential exercises to illustrate that there are a substantial number of interventions that can be applied in multicultural counseling and therapy. There are also a large number of specific helping interventions used by various cultural groups. Unfortunately, space limits the consideration of the contributions of specific groups in more detail. However, the examples discussed, such as Freire's work with Brazilian peasants and Achebe's work with traditional healers, point to the significant contributions such culturally specific interventions can make to therapy and counseling. MCT provides us with challenge and opportunity. Clearly, one cannot master its many concepts without extensive time and study. However, MCT likely will have an increasing influence on psychotherapeutic thinking and practice over time.

REFERENCES

ACHEBE, C. (1986). *The world of the Ogbanje*. Enugu, Nigeria: Fourth Dimension.

ATTNEAVE, C. (1969). Therapy in tribal settings and urban network interventions. *Family Process, 8*, 192–210.

ATTNEAVE, C. (1974). Medicine men and psychiatrists in the Indian health service. *Psychiatric Annals, 4*(9), 49–55.

ATTNEAVE, C. (1982). American Indian and Alaskan native families: Emigrants in their own homeland. In M. McGoldrick, J. Pearce, & J. Giordano (Eds.), *Ethnicity and family therapy* (pp. 55–83). New York: Guilford.

BALLOU, M. (1996a). Interview transcript (Manuscript). Boston: Northeastern University.

BALLOU, M. (1996b). Multicultural counseling and women. In D. Sue, A. Ivey, & P. Pedersen (Eds.), *A theory of multicultural counseling and therapy*. Pacific Grove, CA: Brooks/Cole.

BALLOU, M., & GABALAC, N. (1984). *A feminist position on mental health*. Springfield, IL: Thomas.

CARTER, D., & RAWLINS, E. (Eds.). (1977). *Psychotherapy for women*. Springfield, IL: Thomas.

CHEATHAM, H. (1990). Empowering Black families. In H. Cheatham & J. Stewart (Eds.), *Black families: Interdisciplinary perspectives*. New Brunswick, NJ: Transaction.

CHEATHAM, H., & STEWART, J. (Eds.). (1990). *Black families: Interdisciplinary perspectives*. New Brunswick, NJ: Transaction.

CHEEK, D. (1976). *Assertive Black . . . puzzled White*. San Luis Obispo, CA: Impact.

DAVIS, M., ROBBINS, E., & McKAY, M. (1995). *The relaxation and stress management workbook* (4th ed.). Oakland, CA: New Harbinger.

FREIRE, P. (1970). *Pedagogy of the oppressed*. New York: Continuum.

FREIRE, P. (1994). *Education for critical consciousness*. New York: Continuum.

GIORDANO, J., & GIORDANO, G. (1977). *The ethno-cultural factor in mental health: A literary review and bibliography*. New York: Committee on Pluralism and Group Identity, American Jewish Committee.

HELMS, J. (1990). *Black and White racial identity: Theory, research, and practice*. Westport, CT: Greenwood.

HELMS, J. (1992). *A race is a nice thing to have*. Topeka: Content Communications.

HINES, P., & BOYD-FRANKLIN, N. (1982). Black families. In M. McGoldrick, J. Pearce, & J. Giordano (Eds.), *Ethnicity and family therapy*. New York: Guilford.

IVEY, A. (1994, Fall). *Multicultural counseling and therapy: A contextual approach*. Paper presented at Wing Memorial Hospital, Palmer, MA.

IVEY, A. (1995). Psychotherapy as liberation. In J. Ponterotto, M. Casas, L. Suzuki, & C. Alexander (Eds.), *Handbook of multicultural counseling and therapy*. Thousand Oaks, CA: Sage.

IVEY, A., & IVEY, M. (1990). Assessing and facilitating children's cognitive development: Developmental counseling and therapy in a case of child abuse. *Journal of Counseling and Development, 68*, 299–306.

IVEY, A., & SIMEK-DOWNING, L. (1980). *Counseling and psychotherapy: Skills, theories, and practice.* Englewood Cliffs, NJ: Prentice-Hall.

IVEY, M. (1994, April). *Developmental counseling and therapy: Feminist issues.* Paper presented at Hong Kong Polytechnic University.

KABAT-ZINN, J. (1990). *Full catastrophe living.* New York: Delta.

KIRBY, S., & MCKENNA, K. (1989). *Experience, research, social change: Methods from the margins.* Toronto: Garawood.

LAFROMBOISE, T., & LOW, K. (1989). American Indian adolescents. In J. Gibbs & L. Hwang (Eds.), *Children of color* (pp. 114–47). San Francisco: Jossey-Bass.

LEE, C. (1996). Implications for indigenous healing systems. In D. Sue, A. Ivey, & P. Pederson (Eds.), *Toward a theory of multicultural counseling and therapy.* Pacific Grove, CA: Brooks/Cole.

MCGOLDRICK, M., PEARCE, J., & GIORDANO, J. (Eds.). (1982). *Ethnicity and family therapy.* New York: Guilford.

MEICHENBAUM, D. (1993). Stress inoculation training: A twenty-year update. In R. Wolfolk & P. Lehrer (Eds.), *Principles and practices of stress management.* New York: Guilford.

MEICHENBAUM, D. (1994). *A clinical handbook/practical therapy manual for assessing and treating adults with post-traumatic stress disorder (PTSD).* Waterloo, Ontario: Institute Press.

ORNISH, D. (1990). *Dr. Dean Ornish's program for reversing heart disease.* New York: Ballantine.

PANIAGUA, F. (1994). *Assessing and treating culturally diverse clients.* Thousand Oaks, CA: Sage.

PARHAM, T. (1989). Cycles of psychological Nigrescence. *Counseling Psychologist, 17*(2), 187–226.

RAM DASS, BABA. (1971). *Be here now.* New York: Crown.

SHAULL, R. (1970). Foreword. In P. Freire, *Pedagogy of the oppressed.* New York: Continuum.

SMITH, E., & WILKS, N. (1988). *Alternative health meditation.* London: Macdonald.

SOLOMAN, B. (1990). Counseling Black families at inner-city church sites. In H. Cheatham & J. Stewart (Eds.), *Black families* (pp. 353–73). New Brunswick, NJ: Transaction Press.

SPECK, R., & ATTNEAVE, C. (1973). *Family process.* New York: Pantheon.

STRONG, S., & SCHMIDT, L. (1970). Expertness and influence in counseling. *Journal of Counseling Psychology, 17,* 81–87.

SUE, D. W., IVEY, A., & PEDERSEN, P. (Eds.). (1996). *A theory of multicultural counseling and therapy.* Pacific Grove, CA: Brooks/Cole.

SUE, D. W., & SUE, D. (1990). *Counseling the culturally different.* New York: Wiley.

SUZUKI, S. (1970). *Zen mind, beginner's mind.* New York: Weatherhill.

TSENG, W., & MCDERMOTT, J. (1981). *Culture, mind, and therapy: An introduction to cultural psychiatry.* New York: Brunner/Mazel.

WHITE, J., & PARHAM, T. (1991). *The psychology of Blacks: An African-American perspective* (2nd ed.). Englewood Cliffs, NJ: Prentice-Hall.

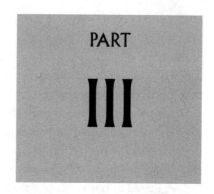

HISTORICAL THEORIES OF COUNSELING AND PSYCHOTHERAPY
The First, Second, and Third Forces

Although more than 250 theories of change exist, psychodynamic, cognitive-behavioral, and existential-humanistic theories remain the most influential. This part considers these theories and how you may take them into concrete practice in real situations. Two chapters are devoted to each of the major historical forces.

First-force (psychodynamic) theory is primarily associated with its founder Sigmund Freud. Although Freud remains influential, it is clear that the many derivatives of his theory have the most immediate impact on practice today. At this time, the work of John Bowlby, as supported by the researcher Mary Ainsworth, is especially important. There is much that is practically useful in their work on attachment theory. Understanding the basic concepts of attachment theory presented here will give you a solid foundation on which

to study object relations theory, ego psychology, and the many permutations of psychoanalytic thought. Drawing from an African and a multicultural orientation, Bruce Taub-Bynum gives special attention to integrating family and ethnic/cultural issues into practice.

Second-force (cognitive-behavioral) theory has long been associated with B. F. Skinner, but, once again, his concepts have been extended and modified. Skinner preferred to identify himself as a behaviorist rather than a cognitive-behaviorist, believing the mind and cognition to be relatively unimportant constructs. Researchers such as Donald Meichenbaum, Albert Ellis, Aaron Beck, and William Glasser have extended Skinner's foundational work in important ways and have shown the importance of mind as well as behavior. The cognitive-behavioral tradition is currently the most frequently practiced of all orientations. Donald Cheek is noted as one of the earliest practitioners of cognitive-behavioral therapy, and his applications of this theory to multicultural populations is important in broadening an understanding of the second force.

Third-force (*existential-humanistic*) *theory* originated in European philosophy but achieved its maximum influence in counseling and therapy through the basic work of Carl Rogers. The work of Viktor Frankl and Frederick "Fritz" Perls is presented in detail, as they represent two important extensions of this third-force orientation. The third force has deeply influenced the way all other theories are currently practiced. Clemmont Vontress speaks to the existential-humanistic perspective from an African and African-American framework and shows how spiritual issues can be considered in more detail in the counseling and therapy process.

Fourth-force (*multicultural counseling and therapy*) *theory* relates to these historical theories. MCT recognizes that traditional theories of helping developed in a predominantly Northern European and North American context. As such, these traditional theories are relevant for working with clients from these cultures but have limitations with other clients of other cultures. For example, most of the historical theories have been generated by European-American White males and as such

tend to have gender and cultural limitations. Moreover, there is relatively little consideration of family issues in the first-, second-, and third-force orientations.

The multicultural counseling and therapy approach may be described as unifying in that it seeks to respect multiple perspectives and use different approaches in individually and culturally appropriate treatment. MCT draws heavily on first-, second-, and third-force theory in its actual practice but constantly adapts these constructs to meet the diverse needs of clients. The United States and Canada, as culturally diverse nations, increasingly are finding it necessary to explore new ways to think about delivery of counseling and therapy services. In this process, MCT recognizes the value of traditional approaches.

The following six chapters focus on describing psychodynamic, cognitive-behavioral, and existential-humanistic thinking and include a large array of useful practical exercises that you likely will be drawing on throughout the rest of your student and professional life. Although these techniques have been found to be effective over time, many will require adaptation as you work with culturally diverse peoples. It is your opportunity and challenge to help the field grow as the world becomes increasingly multicultural and global.

Psychodynamic Counseling and Therapy I: Conception and Theory

CHAPTER GOALS

This chapter seeks to:

1. Summarize the worldview of psychodynamic theory and illustrate that it is far from a single orthodox framework.

2. Give special attention to multicultural issues and the psychodynamic frame of reference.

3. Present some central theoretical constructs, giving special attention to the object relations developmental framework and focusing on the work of Bowlby and Ainsworth.

4. Extend this framework through consideration of Taub-Bynum's view of the family unconscious, a theory and practice that help relate psychodynamic theory to current multicultural trends.

5. Enable you, through a practice exercise, to generate a positive developmentally oriented treatment plan that takes past individual, family, and cultural history into account.

The Psychodynamic Frame of Reference

Freud brought order out of chaos. Until his brilliant and insightful work was publicized, mental operations and behavior seemed unknowable and almost mystical. His place in history ranks with the major influences of Darwin, Einstein, and Marx. Although discussions of his legacy sometimes bring more heat than light, there can be no disputing his importance in the development of Western psychological thought.

What does Freud offer us today? First, his extensive writings organize human functioning and conceptualize the emotional and irrational feelings underlying behavior. Second, his many disciples provide a constant impetus for change in psychotherapy through addition to and modification of his concepts. Those who started from a Freudian orientation include close followers such as Ernest Jones and revisionists and neo-Freudians such as Alfred Adler, Eric Erikson, Karen Horney, Melanie Klein, and Harry Stack Sullivan. When names such as Fritz Perls (Gestalt therapy), Alexander Lowen (bioenergetics), and Eric Berne (transactional analysis) are added, it is easy to see how profound Freud's influence remains.

The psychodynamic frame of reference presented in this chapter starts with Freud but then moves to the more multiculturally relevant attachment theory of John Bowlby, which is supported by the research of Mary Ainsworth. The innovative work of Bruce Taub-Bynum is then presented, as it shows how family and multicultural influences can be made more explicit in the psychodynamic model. Just as the entire field of counseling and therapy is changing, so can we anticipate major new constructions of psychodynamic theory in the future.

The Psychodynamic Worldview

"If Freud's discovery had to be summed up in a single word, that word would without a doubt have to be 'unconscious,'" wrote Laplanche and Pontalis (1973, p. 474). The word *unconscious* means lack of awareness of one's own mental functioning. More broadly, it also means all things of which we are not aware at a given moment—both biological and psychological. Individuals are unaware (unconscious) of what is impelling and motivating them toward action.

Psychodynamic theory needs to be contrasted with *psychoanalytic theory*. As used here, the term *psychoanalytic* refers specifically to Freud's theory and orientation. Psychodynamic theory is a broader set of constructs that includes psychoanalytic theory as an important foundation. Some key aspects of the definition of psychodynamic theory used in this chapter follow:

1. *Client developmental history is important and needs to be considered for full client understanding.* Freud is often considered the first developmental psychologist. Basic to his orientation and the psychodynamic frame of reference is the importance of childhood experience in determining how we act and behave in the present.

2. *Important in our developmental history are the key people we have related with over time—our object relations.* In psychodynamic language, *object relations* is the term given to relationships with people and important objects in our life. We develop in relationship to people—our family, friends, and peers.

3. *We are unaware (unconscious) of the impact of biological needs, of past developmental object relations, and of cultural determinants on our present behavior.* The unconscious is the reservoir of our memories and biological drives, most of which we are unaware of.

4. *We constantly act out in our daily lives our developmental history and our unconscious biological drives.* From the psychodynamic frame of reference, we are heavily ruled, sometimes even completely determined, by forces outside our awareness. However, some psychodynamic theories claim biology is central in unconscious development, whereas others focus more on life-span developmental issues. Increasingly, the influence of multicultural factors in unconscious development is being recognized.

5. *The task of counseling and therapy is to help the client discover how the past influences the present.* Although this is a common issue, the designation of which part of the past we need to pay attention to varies. Orthodox psychoanalysis gives special attention to sexual development, particularly during the Oedipal period (ages 5 through 7), whereas attachment theory and object relations theory focus on infancy and early childhood. Feminist theory concentrates on how cultural gender roles influence our present, whereas Jungians search for cultural archetypes in history that determine how we live our lives today. Those oriented toward family therapy are interested in how intergenerational family issues affect the way we are today, as are many of those in recovery movements such as Adult Children of Alcoholics.

Psychodynamic methods have been called an "uncovering therapy," because the focus is often on discovering how the past affects present behavior. However, rational-emotive theory holds that it is an "irrational idea that *the past has a lot to do with determining the present*" (Davis, Eshelman, & McKay, 1995, p. 143). Thus, it seems clear that what is an accepted truth in one theoretical orientation is not considered so in another.

Each of the above points would be modified greatly if one were to assume an ego psychology position (Freud, 1982; Erikson, 1950/1963; Hartmann, 1958), a more classic object relations orientation (Guntrip, 1968; Klein, 1975; Winnicott, 1988), a linguistic interpretation (Lacan, 1966/1977), a feminist orientation (Chodorow, 1978; Baker Miller, 1976; Okun, 1992), or a family/multicultural orientation (Taub-Bynum, 1980, 1992). Within each of the groups, there are sharp differences, and the authorities just listed are but a small part of a vast array of scholars and clinicians whose opinions vary widely.

Clearly, there exist differences of opinion within the psychodynamic establishment, but all in the field agree on the central importance of the unconscious. The position emphasized in this chapter is basically that of Bowlby's (1969, 1973, 1988) attachment theory, a variation of the object relations orientation. Attachment theory takes an ecological person-environment approach to psychodynamic thought and is currently rapidly increasing in influence. Ainsworth has conducted the basic research supporting the theory, and she and Bowlby (1991) won the American Psychological Association Award for Distinguished Scientific Contributions.

The chapter will close with consideration of Taub-Bynum's psychodynamically oriented work (1984, 1992), which builds on Jungian theory and shows how family and multicultural forces are in action at the conscious and unconscious levels.

Multicultural Issues and the Psychodynamic Tradition

Psychodynamic theory has received a great deal of criticism,[1] much of it from women and minority groups. Psychoanalytic theory tends to be seen as male and elitist in origin. Many still think of psychoanalytic theory as a monolith, with orthodox interpretations based on libido theory and unconscious sexuality. Given its sexist concepts such as penis envy, a highly verbal intellectualized orientation, and a reputation for long periods of treatment, psychodynamic theory has been viewed by many as therapy only for the wealthy.

Patriarchy and domination are often associated with the psychoanalytic framework. Sayers (1995) argues that these oppressive concepts are also buried in the unconscious as a part of developmental history. Multicultural and feminist theorists hold that a critical issue in modern psychodynamic therapy is helping women and other groups learn how their present concerns are related to past histories of oppression and domination. From this frame of reference, insight becomes a valuable tool leading to new actions and behaviors in the future. Instead of blaming the family, the client learns to see self in social context.

Integrating Multicultural and Feminist Issues with a Psychodynamic Approach

Comas-Diaz and Minrath (1985) urge that issues of ethnicity and race become part of the psychodynamic treatment process. Rather than separate multicultural issues from therapy, the modern psychodynamic approach encourages you as a counselor to use these issues as part of therapy. If there is some form of prejudice in your background, it will show in countertransferential form in the interview. If you have done work on multicultural issues, you may be able to use multicultural factors as part of the free association and insight processes, which is effective psychodynamic therapy.

Taub-Bynum (1984, 1992) makes the above general points more explicit. He points out that we learn about ourselves and our culture in the family and proposes, in his complex extension of the psychodynamic model, that we need to focus on the *family unconscious*. From the family unconscious perspective, each individual is a specific focus of experience in the family and culture, but much of that experience is also shared with others. Family experience is implicated in the inner landscape of *each person who shares the same family*, both unconsciously and consciously.

Jean Baker Miller's *Toward a New Psychology of Women* (1976) has been particularly influential as what could be considered psychodynamic criticism from a women's frame of reference (also see Baker Miller, 1991). Women's sense of self has been generated in a family and cultural context, and Baker Miller argues that many women "do good" while "feeling bad." Society has placed conscious and unconscious roles on women that restrict their ability to cope with conflict. In terms of therapeutic work with women, Baker Miller would point out that the psychodynamic techniques are dangerous unless issues of gender are considered.

Psychodynamic Theory and Insight

Psychodynamic approaches are oriented to understanding and insight. Sue and Sue (1990) comment:

> We need to realize that insight is not highly valued by many culturally different clients. There are also major class differences as well. People from lower socioeconomic classes frequently do not perceive insight as appropriate to their life situations and circumstances. . . . Insight assumes that one has time to sit back, to reflect and contemplate about motivation and behavior. . . .
>
> Likewise, many cultural groups do not value insight. In traditional Chinese society, psychology is not well understood. . . . Many Asian elders believe that thinking too much about something can cause problems. . . . "Think about the family and not about yourself" is advice given to many Asians as a way of dealing with negative affective elements. *This is totally contradictory to Western notions of mental health—that it is best to get things out in the open in order to deal with them.* (pp. 38–39) (Emphasis added)

Psychodynamic approaches are indeed focused on insight. The required self-disclosure and interpersonal openness are sometimes seen as immaturity by Asian cultures. Many African-Americans, Native Americans, and other minority members would strongly endorse variations of these statements. Sue and Sue's comments should give us all reason to pause as we review some central constructs of psychodynamic theory.

Central Constructs of Psychodynamic Theory

As mentioned earlier, psychodynamic methods have been described as an "uncovering therapy," in that the goals of therapy are focused on discovering the unconscious processes governing behavior. Once these unconscious processes are discovered in their full complexity, the individual is believed able to reconstruct the personality.

Id, Ego, and Superego

Id.   Imperative for uncovering unconscious functioning is an understanding of id, ego, and superego functioning. As Laplanche and Pontalis (1973) observe: "The id constitutes the instinctual pole of the personality; its contents, as an expression of the instincts, are unconscious, a portion of them being hereditary and innate, a portion repressed and acquired" (p. 197). It may be noted that the id is almost totally unconscious and may be either playful and creative or destructive. Biological drive theory is important for those who focus on the id.

Superego.   By way of contrast, the superego is totally learned as the child matures in the family and society. Conscience, ideals, and values are within the realm of the superego. Whereas the id is uncontrolled, the superego may seek to control.

In the superego may be found internalized rules of the family and cultural history. It is in superego functioning that issues of gender roles, attitudes toward one's affectional orientation, and other multicultural issues are most relevantly explored. For example, the homeless, the Vietnam veteran suffering from posttraumatic stress disorder, or the gay male afraid to "come out of the closet" may have incorporated society's discriminatory attitudes at an unconscious level and blame themselves for their problems.

Ego.   The ego serves as a mediator between the superego (conscious rules from family and society) and the id (unconscious rebellion or playful storehouse). In traditional Freudian theory, the ego is sometimes seen as being at the mercy of these two competing forces. Modern ego psychology theorists, such as Erikson, talk about increasing ego functioning and giving the person more power to control her or his own life.

Ego strength may be increased through assisting the client to understand the interplay of ego with id and superego. The ego operates at conscious, preconscious, and unconscious levels of experience, although it is primarily manifested in counseling at the conscious level.

Balancing Id, Ego, and Superego: The Role of Anxiety

Anxiety and tension may result from the conflicts between the id, ego, and superego; from fear caused by conscious or unconscious memories of past experiences from childhood development; from dangerous impulses of the id, such as sexual desires that may be taboo; from superego-derived guilt; or from the inadequacies of the ego to resolve conflict.

Anxiety may be attached to a specific object or cause so that the reason for anxiety may be clear, or anxiety may be "free floating," in that the reason for anxiety is lost in the unconscious. A sense of free-floating anxiety without rational explanation is particularly threatening and may be repressed into the ego defense mechanisms described in the following subsection. The complex task of the therapist or counselor is to uncover the structure of anxiety so that personal reconstruction can begin.

If you work psychodynamically, you will have to take a position on the respective roles and importance of id, ego, and superego dimensions. If you place the id as central in importance, you will find orthodox, traditional analytic theory most helpful to you in uncovering the roots of anxiety. If you take an id, or drive-oriented, position, you may be more interested in and supportive of medication. If you place the ego as central to your theory, you will find ego theorists such as Erikson (1963) or Hartmann (1958) most helpful.

The position stressed in this chapter is that of Bowlby and Taub-Bynum, who recognize the importance of id and ego functioning but are more oriented to the superego and environmental/contextual issues. This balance of person and environment is likely to be more in accord with evolving fourth-force multicultural counseling and therapy.

Ego Defense Mechanisms

What is the ego defending itself from? Generally speaking, the answer is anxiety. But where does the anxiety come from? It tends to come from conflicts between internal biological drives and wishes (id) and demands of the environment (superego). Thus, ego defense mechanisms are oriented to protecting and strengthening the ego, which somehow has to balance these competing demands.

How Defense Mechanisms Arise

The specific role of defense mechanisms is well illustrated through Bowlby's (1940, 1951, 1988) observations of British children separated from their parents during World War II. The children were taken from their homes in London to protect them from the intense German bombing and placed in homes in the countryside. Needless to say, this was a highly anxiety-provoking time for the children.

Bowlby observed that the young children who were separated from their parents became depressed and morose but gradually learned to cope and to behave more "normally." When their parents visited them, most children did not greet them enthusiastically; rather, they edged toward their parents carefully. Some might display anger and even seek to hurt their parents.

Bowlby points out that the anxiety associated with the loss of the caregiver was so intense that the children defended themselves against another loss. *Avoidant behavior* and *acting-out* behavior are two types of defense mechanisms that protect not only children but also adults from deeper internal conflicts and the experience of anxiety. Bowlby notes that it was functional for the children to defend themselves against further anxiety—specifically a reexperience of loss when the parents returned to London. The defense mechanisms worked effectively to protect against emotional pain.

Bowlby may be considered a *developmental ecologist* in that he recognizes that each unique individual develops in relationship to the environment. Bowlby takes biology as a given but provides clear evidence that environmental factors shape the nature of individual uniqueness.

A family and multicultural view would extend the concepts of defense mechanisms, maintaining that varying family backgrounds and varying cultural issues will have relevance to the type of defense mechanism selected (Taub-Bynum, 1992). For example, an older child taken from London might use the more positive defense mechanism of sublimation (discussed in Research Exhibit 7.1) and survive the emotional trauma by taking care of and supporting other younger children. This child may have learned such behavior and thinking patterns in the family of origin. Family-of-origin patterns, then, are transferred as survival defense mechanisms in later life.

Imagine you are a therapist working with one of these children years later. As an adult, the individual may be suffering from deep anxiety that may play itself out in many ways (defense mechanisms and an array of pathologies such as depression, phobias, and so on). The client may talk to you about "not caring about the loss of parental support and nurturing" years ago. One of your therapeutic tasks, according to psychodynamic theory, is to uncover the historic roots of present anxiety, depression, or other ineffective current behavior.

The Antisocial Personality as a Defensive Structure

Nowhere is the importance of underlying mechanisms of defense more key than in your understanding of the antisocial personality. This diagnostic classification is often considered the most difficult to treat. Following from Bowlby, it is important to think of such behavior as a set of defense mechanisms used to protect the individual from harm.

Underlying the antisocial client's bravado and manipulation is a person whose dependency needs were never met. Although there is evidence that some antisocial behavior has a genetic foundation, family environments of antisocial individuals frequently are full of neglect and abuse (Brassard, Germain, & Hart, 1987). When you do establish a relationship with an antisocial client, he or she unconsciously fears the loss of this relationship and thus strives to avoid or to destroy it.

The child diagnosed with conduct disorder often reappears in later life as the antisocial personality. You can safely assume that many children who are difficult to manage experience abusive and assaultive home lives. The conduct disorder and/or antisocial client has learned that the "best defense is a good offense." Thus, when you work with difficult clients, recall that you are working with defensive structures (their offensive behavior) that cover up underlying issues.

*The Existence of Multiple
Defense Mechanisms*

The antisocial's attempts to leave a healthy therapist relationship can be considered a defense mechanism, which might be termed a reaction formation (doing the opposite of the desired) to the client's own underlying dependency needs. When you confront such clients, they will often use denial as a major way to protect themselves. Their repressed behavior is a continuation of past issues.

Your difficult task as a psychodynamic therapist is to break through the defensive structure and work for understanding of how the present situation was influenced by past history. *More than one defense mechanism may be represented by a single episode of behavior, feeling, or thought.* Research Exhibit 7.1 lists examples of defense mechanisms.

Research Exhibit 7.1

 Examples of Defense Mechanisms

Following are examples of defense mechanisms, how these might be employed by varying types of clients, and possible positive benefits of each defensive structure. These interpretations are derived from Laplanche and Pontalis (1973).

1. *Repression and continuation.* An underemphasized generic concept of the defense mechanism is that our behavior, thoughts, and actions are repressed developmental continuations from the past. Winnicott (1988) maintains that all defense mechanisms are methods the child (and adult) uses to repress pain. These mechanisms stem either from denial of internal drives (id wishes) or hurts from external reality (superego pressures).

Therefore, in a broad sense defense mechanisms are all repressed continuations of past biological and environmental issues and stressors. Many, perhaps even most, of your clients will be continu-

ing old behavior, thoughts, and emotions in some form from their developmental past.

The remainder of the defense mechanisms are elaborations of this basic point. Your task as a therapist, as both Winnicott and Bowlby imply, is to find the underlying structure of the anxiety and the purpose of particular defense mechanisms used by the client.

2. *Denial.* This is the most difficult and troublesome defense mechanism. Many of your clients will refuse to recognize their traumatic and troublesome past. Vietnam War veterans often psychologically split off and deny the origins of their distress in combat; antisocial clients will deny needs for dependency and attachment; and survivors of abuse or rape may unconsciously forget (deny) that they were abused.

Denial, at the same time, can be healthy. If we allow ourselves to be in touch with our past and present pain all the time, we can only become depressed. From this frame of reference, then, depression is at least a partial failure of the positive aspects of the defense mechanism of denial.

3. *Projection.* When clients refuse to recognize behavior or thoughts in the self and see, or project, this behavior onto someone else, the defense mechanism of projection is likely to be in operation. We are most often troubled by behavior in others that is similar to our own behavior.

At an extreme level, you will find projection in the paranoid client. Individuals with a paranoid style often have a history of real persecution in the family of origin or developmental past. They have learned to project onto others anticipated persecution. As it happens, anticipating persecution often results in a self-fulfilling prophecy. However, there can be positives to paranoia. For example, when buying a used car, it might help to be a bit paranoid.

Similarly, one of the most important helping skills may be related to projection. In empathy, we try to see the world as others see it and project ourselves into the client's worldview. Some of us become so empathic and entwined with others that we literally project ourselves into the client and fail to see the client. This relates closely to the Kleinian concept of projective identification, which is discussed in detail in Chapter 8.

4. *Displacement.* This defense mechanism is a variety of transference in that the client's feelings or thoughts are transferred or directed toward a person other than the originating source. The worker who has a bad day on the job and then treats her or his spouse badly is a common example of displacement. If antisocial clients act out against you for no apparent reason, they are likely to be displacing anger and aggression around past maltreatment onto you.

You may notice that each of the defense mechanisms relates to others. In a sense, displacement is behavior *repressed and continued* from the past. Displacement *denies* what is really happening and often *projects* onto others the events of the day or the past. The displacement may enact itself in an opposite form of the conscious intent—that is, *reaction-formation.* These defense mechanisms are not clearly distinct entities. Rather, defense mechanisms are simply alternative constructions of the same continued event from the past. You will find that one defense mechanism construction is more useful at times, and that another, at first seemingly totally different, mechanism is useful at others.

5. *Sublimation.* A more positive defense mechanism, sublimation takes repressed instinctual energy and unconscious continuations from the past and channels them to constructive work such as artistic, physical, or intellectual endeavor. A person who is frustrated sexually or a survivor of abuse may turn to movie making, athletics, or creative writing and be rewarded well by society for these efforts.

Sublimation, however, may fail in the long term as repressed anger and hurt well up in surprising places. Many survivors of child abuse sublimate past hurt and become counselors and therapists (see Miller, 1981). The danger here is that wounded helpers who have denied or sublimated their own history of abuse may unconsciously prevent clients who have been abused from looking at their own past history.

6. *Other mechanisms.* The five mechanisms here represent only a beginning. Other mechanisms include: *fixation* (being immobilized at an earlier level of development), *rationalization* (the making up of rational reasons for irrational or inconsistent behavior), *regression* (returning to early childhood behavior when faced with a life event somehow resembling an old traumatic injury), *conversion* (translating unconscious mental functioning into physical symptoms such as headaches), *identification* (acting and behaving like someone else), *reaction-formation* (doing the opposite of unconscious wishes), and *provocative behavior* (acting in a way such that others are provoked to do to one what one is unable to do to oneself, such as showing anger or love), among other mechanisms.

Counselors and therapists tend to think about defense mechanisms as abstract ideas. In truth, clients indicate again and again in very concrete ways their defensive style. Bowlby's attachment theory provides some very concrete ways in which you can use defense mechanisms to assist in understanding clients and in helping them break out of inefficient patterns of thinking, feeling, and behaving. These defense mechanisms are learned through our developmental history in the culture.

Developmental Roots of Behavior, Emotion, and Thought

Freud has been termed the first developmental psychologist because he made sense out of childhood by pointing out that distinct patterns and problems can be associated with each developmental stage. One of Freud's tenets is that each stage of development requires us to face key developmental tasks, as illustrated in the following subsections. Drawing from Taub-Bynum, Bowlby, and feminist theory, some additional perspectives on development in a multicultural society are also included.

The Issue of Trust

The child in the oral period (roughly 0 through 2 years) must learn how to be dependent, trust, and relate with the primary caregiver, usually the mother. If the child does not accomplish age-related developmental tasks adequately, interpersonal relationships will likely be disturbed and appear as adult problems.

From an id-oriented biological dynamic frame, children are dominated by internal dynamics. Taub-Bynum (1984), speaking more from a superego perspective, would emphasize what happens in the family of origin. The multicultural and feminist frames would also be superego focused, pointing out that what occurs in the societal context heavily influences individual and family behavior. The task of the ego is to balance internal (id) and external (superego) forces.

The Issue of Control

The developmental task of the anal period (2 through 4 years) is that of control. The child must move away from the primary caregiver, take control over his or her own life, and become a separate, eventually individuated person. The "terrible two's," with characteristic strife and temper tantrums, are illustrative of the child's struggle to become her or his "own person." Freud (1925/1964) points out that the individual is often constituted in negativity or opposition. A child may have developed the capacity for relationships in the oral period, but unless separation occurs at this age, the individual may remain overly fused or overly distant from others as an adult.

It is a vast oversimplification to talk about the control of feces as the major issue of this period. This type of conceptualization is naive and makes it easy for many to reject the Freudian framework. The task of this period focuses on control and becoming a separate human being. This separateness is built on the earlier attachments of the oral stage.

Sex Role Development

The Oedipal period (4 through 7 years) is the time when children learn to understand the sex roles they are to undertake. As can be seen in the oral and anal periods, the child has already received considerable training in sex roles through the holding environment and the manner in which the control issues of the anal period have been handled by the culture. What is distinctive about the Oedipal period is that the child develops awareness of the meaning and importance of sex roles themselves and brings together all previous learnings in a total gestalt.

The interpretation of the Oedipal period has given rise to controversy. Chodorow (1978) has been particularly critical of the overly male interpretation of this period. Bragg and colleagues (1987) criticize traditional Oedipal theory from a lesbian frame of reference. Erikson's (1950/1963) formulations (see Chapter 5) have been an important influence on the way development has been viewed, but his framework, like Freud's, has been generated from a predominantly Eurocentric, White male frame of reference (see, for example, Neugarten, 1979).

Limitations of the Freudian View

Freud first pointed out the importance of early life stages and human development. His framework, however, is basically biological, and he gives relatively little attention to issues of caregiving, mothering, and the family. If something goes wrong with the child in the developmental process, the fault is seen in the child rather than in the system of interpersonal relationships.

One example of the limitation of the Freudian view is found in the Oedipal drama. Freud talks about Oedipal issues as if the five-year-old is the most pivotal and influential family member. The role of possibly oppressive and immature parents tends to be minimized in classical Freudian drive theory. Traditional id-oriented drive theory has historically tended to minimize child abuse and child assault.

The developmental stages above and the key tasks associated with each need to be adjusted to address variations in gender and culture and developmental tasks. What is needed is a culturally relevant developmental framework similar to that proposed by Tamase (1991), described in Chapter 5, that allows for the fact that different cultures have differing needs at differing times in the developmental process.

Object Relations Theory

Object relations theory, an offshoot of psychoanalytic theory, leads to a new precision invaluable to all counselors and therapists in understanding the key word *relationship*.[2] Object relations (OR) could be translated as "people relations." OR theory is concerned with examining the relations between and among people and how the history of interpersonal relationships is transferred from the past to present behavior. The major object or person in a client's history is the caregiver, most often the mother.

However, depending on social, economic, and cultural considerations, the caregiver may be the father, a couple, or a grandmother. In traditional rural Puerto Rican culture, the caregiver is really the entire extended family. In Africa and Aboriginal Australia, the primary caregiver may be anyone in the extended family or the whole community. Issues of single parenthood, adoption (especially when the birth mother remains involved with the adoptive parents), and same-sex parents further change the concept of caregiver. Some would even argue that day-care workers need to be considered part of the caregiver complex. Regardless of terminology, all are important objects in the development of the child.

OR theory shows us how to study the relationship we have with our clients. With that developmental knowledge and the multiple frameworks of the family/cultural perspective, it is often possible to assess client developmental history. With this knowledge, you can predict with more accuracy how your interventions will be received by your clients.

John Bowlby and Developmental Ecology

John Bowlby (1969, 1973, 1988) presents one of the clearest expositions of object relations theory, although he does not follow the traditional individualistic points of view. Bowlby (personal communication, January 1987) describes his ideas as having developed in opposition to Melanie Klein, the first major OR theorist. Bowlby is also interested in information-processing theory, social ecology, and psychological science. He may be construed as a developmental ecologist, as he stresses the importance of the child developing in relation to context and environment.

Attachment

Bowlby's concepts are often described as *attachment theory*. The primary task in the mother-child relationship[3] is for the child to learn how to become securely attached. If the child can become attached, it has a secure base for exploring. Using an attachment framework clarifies the developmental tasks specified in Freud's oral stage.

As a developmental ecologist, Bowlby emphasizes the joint construction of the mother-child relationship: the child is not only affected by the environment, but the child also impacts that same environmental context. For example, some children seem to be neurologically equipped for closer relationships than others. Moreover, Bowlby points out that the child's natural biological endowment develops in relationship with the mother. Child and caregiver grow (or deteriorate) in an ecological process of mutual social influence.

Bowlby points out that three major patterns of attachment exist: securely attached, anxious resistant (generated by an ambivalent and alternating accepting-and-rejecting mother-child relationship), and anxious avoidant (generated by a rejecting and impoverished relationship). Research by Ainsworth and others (Ainsworth, 1985; Ainsworth & Bowlby, 1991) has verified these attachment patterns.

Most important in supporting Bowlby's theories, however, is longitudinal research that shows that children's pattern of attachment assessed in the early months is highly predictive of later adjustment. Some specific examples follow:

1. The pattern of attachment identified at twelve months is still present at six years (Main & Solomon, 1986).

2. Children identified as securely attached are found to be described in nursery school three and a half years later as cheerful, cooperative, and popular, whereas anxious avoidant and anxious resistant patterns of attachment are described as emotionally insulated, hostile, and antisocial (Bowlby, 1988).

3. Children who are securely attached in early life are later found to respond to failure with increased effort, whereas the less securely attached do the opposite (Lütkenhaus, Grossman, & Grossman, 1985).

These are but a few examples, and a strong base of research literature supporting Bowlby's theories is developing (see Research Exhibit 7.2).

Separation

There is also a second task related to attachment, that of separation. A securely attached child is able to separate and individuate. The task of separation may be con-

Research Exhibit 7.2

The Ainsworth-Bowlby Connection: How Research Validates a Theory

John Bowlby's theory has had immense influence. However, it is Mary Ainsworth who has verified Bowlby's work in a variety of cultural situations, including Africa (1967) and Europe (1977). Currently, Bowlby's attachment theory has more direct empirical validation than any other psychodynamic theory.

Essentially, what Ainsworth (1979) has verified is that children need secure attachments with the caregiver if they are to develop and eventually become separate human beings in accord with cultural expectations.

The Ainsworth Strange Situation Procedure (Ainsworth, Blehar, Waters, & Wall, 1978) provides a laboratory situation for testing the nature of a child's attachment. The child is videotaped with toys in situations in which the mother is first present and then absent. The focus is on how the child responds when the mother returns.

Securely attached children tend to smile and hug the returning parent. *Anxious resistant* children tend to show angry resistance on the mother's return. *Anxious/avoidant attached* children ignore or even back away from the mother and may show as much interest in a stranger as they do their own mothers. (These patterns of child interaction are similar to those observed by Bowlby in his work with children during World War II and discussed earlier in this chapter.)

Using the Strange Situation as a baseline, researchers have found that securely attached infants are (1) more cooperative, enthusiastic, and compliant at two years (Main, 1973; Matas, Arend, & Sroufe, 1978); (2) more competent with peers at age 3 (Waters, Wippman, & Sroufe, 1979); and (3) in better self-control in preschool (Egelund, 1983).

Bowlby (1988) cites research in Germany replicating these findings (Wärtner, 1986) and indicating that patterns of attachment tend to remain stable over time. A wide variety of studies exist that lend increasing support for Bowlby's descriptions. Needless to say, the data are not yet complete that will prove that the tenets drawn from Bowlby's early work will hold true through adulthood.

Ainsworth and Bowlby (1991) update these findings and provide an overview of the development of their theory and research.

sidered roughly analogous to the sense of autonomy and personal control associated with Freud's anal period. Other object relations theorists, particularly Margaret Mahler (1975), give detailed attention to this aspect of development. It is particularly important to note that Freud, Erikson, Mahler, and Klein tend to focus on individuation and separation. Bowlby recognizes the importance of these concepts but stresses attachment and a stable base in the family as critical for human development.

In summary, Bowlby's ecological/ethological position contrasts rather markedly with that of Freud but does not deny the validity of much of Freud's biological determinism. It can be argued that Freud did not give adequate attention to the fact that the child develops in a person-environment social context and that Freud and many of his followers have failed to consider the very real and demonstrated impact of the mother, the father, and other significant caregivers, such as the extended family, nursery school, child care providers, and so on. All these caregivers can and do affect children's growth and development.

Practical Implications

Bowlby's work has practical implications for counselors and therapists in the following ways:

1. Building an awareness of the importance of early child relationships for later development
2. Suggesting that psychoeducational interventions in terms of family education are critically important
3. Indicating the importance of infant child care (including extended family, babysitters, and infant school) as important areas of counseling intervention
4. Enabling us as counselors and therapists to identify likely early childhood experiences of our clients, thus underlining the importance of varying our style of therapeutic interaction and relationship according to the developmental history of our client. (For example, an adult who was insufficiently attached as a child may need support and empathy from us, whereas an adult who was overly attached may need encouragement to individuate and separate.)

This introduction to the complex, and sometimes esoteric, world of object relations is but a beginning. Although focused on self-in-relation to other contexts and of demonstrated cultural relevance, Bowlby's framework may still give insufficient attention to multicultural issues. The following discussion adds a family and multicultural focus to understanding and treatment from a psychodynamic perspective.

The Family Unconscious and Multicultural Psychodynamic Theory

Taub-Bynum (1984) identifies three interrelated levels of unconscious functioning—the individual, the family, and the collective or multicultural unconscious. The individual unconscious is similar to that described in earlier portions of this chapter and is characteristic of most individualistic, Eurocentric approaches to psychodynamic thought.

The Family and
the Multicultural Unconscious

According to Taub-Bynum (1984), "The Family Unconscious is composed of extremely powerful affective (emotional) energies from the earliest life of the individual" (p. 11). This statement is in accord with object relations theory but reframes and extends these concepts. Essentially, our life experience in our family of origin enters our being in both positive and negative ways. Experience in the family (as contrasted with experience solely with a single caregiver) is transmitted to the child and becomes very much a part of the child's being (and later, of course, the adolescent and adult being).

Thus, the construction, development, and recognition of the family of origin become of key importance in understanding the individual's development. There is a marked relationship between these formulations and those of Tamase (1991; Tamase & Kato, 1990), as presented in Chapter 5. Both are telling the field that many of the social and environmental constructions of reality the individual absorbs come from the family, which itself is located in a cultural context.

Taub-Bynum draws from Jungian psychology for his concept of the multicultural or collective unconscious (see Jung, 1935). Jung describes the collective unconscious as drawing on all the thought and behavior patterns over time. Jung's constructs have been clarified by Fordham (1957), who points out that much of the collective unconscious is the repository of client experience in the family. As indicated in Chapter 2, when you work with an individual, the family and the culture are also present. From this frame of reference, this construct of the collective unconscious becomes closely allied with issues of multicultural empathy and understanding.

Family and Culture

The family is where we first experience and learn the culture. The family unit is the culture bearer, and the nature of the family and its functions varies widely among cultures. Taub-Bynum (1984) speaks of the "powerful affective . . . energies" we experience in the family. The interplay between individual and family affective experience is the formative dialectic of culture. It is not really possible to separate individuals, families, and culture, for their interplay is so powerful and persistent.

The interaction of family and culture is also reflected in the composition and psychodynamic life of the individual. Furthermore, when that individual is considered within the expanded context of the family unconscious, we readily see how each person's psychodynamic functioning is implicated in the functioning of significant others who share the same field of consciousness, energy, and experience. This interrelationship can be seen in the choice of symptoms and behavior, both somatic and psychological.

A hologram provides a useful analogy. In a hologram, each image and area in the overall field reflects and dynamically enfolds each other area but from a slightly different angle. That different angle significantly can be seen as the perception and experience of "individuality" in the interdependent family system. Each family member contains the experience of the family and the culture, but each member has varying perceptions and experiences.

Unconscious mental functioning and constructs are heavily influenced by culture. For example, at birth the Japanese child is immediately placed on the mother's body, and the two mold—or bond—together as one. In European cultures, the newborn traditionally has been taken from the mother and held separately. Emotional body attachments and relational thinking are thereby reinforced in Japanese childrearing practices, whereas the focus in European societies is on separation and autonomy. This small example illustrates that individual constructions of self (or self-in-relation) depend very much on family and cultural conditions.

Taub-Bynum's family and multicultural constructions are in some ways similar to those of the French psychoanalyst Jacques Lacan (1966/1977). Lacan disagrees with ego psychologists, whom he considers naive in their interpretations of Freud. Lacan argues for interdependence as the goal of psychotherapy rather than the traditional autonomy so often associated with ego psychology.

A classic statement of Lacan is that we do not even own our personal unconscious. Rather, we are the "discourse of the Other." The Lacanian view of development and ego psychology stresses that influences of the family and the culture are so profound that the ego itself is "very feeble." A major goal of Lacanian-style psychoanalysis is to help the client discover how much of the so-called self is indeed the result of a lifetime of interactions in the family and the culture.

Therapeutic Implications of the Family and Multicultural Unconscious

You as counselor or therapist can assume that the client is in some way acting out the family and multicultural unconscious. In some cases, the client will present a unique personal construction of the problem, but in others, family or cultural influences are more powerful and important than are individual forces.

The microskill of focus is a simple introduction to a very complex issue. If a client presents an issue and you focus on the issue by emphasizing personal pronouns ("*You* seem to feel . . .") and "I" statements, the client will talk about the problem on an individual basis. If you focus on the family in connection with the individual, the process of therapy changes ("How did *you* learn that in your *family?*" "How does that experience relate to *your family of origin?*"), and the client will talk about issues from a family orientation.

At the multicultural level, the focus changes to the impact of the context and culture on the client's development and present worldview ("How does the *Irish* experience of Yankee oppression in Boston relate to how *your* family generated its ideas in the world and how does that play itself out in *you?*" "What does being *African-American* [or other minority group] have to do with your *family* experience and *your* own view of *yourself?*"). (These example questions are designed to be illustrative of the interrelationship of the individual, the family, and the cultural context; specific questions and clarifications should be appropriate to the context of the interview.)

Cheatham (1990), however, would challenge the above constructions, suggesting that we not only need to understand what is happening in the client's family and multicultural context, but we also need to take action. We as therapists need to work to help the family deal with the culture, and even more important, we as therapists need to work to change a culture that often is more responsible for problems and pathology than are individuals or families.[4]

At a more complex level, Taub-Bynum talks about the intergenerational transmission of symptoms in a family. If you construct a family history/genogram of an alcoholic client, you often find several alcoholics in the family over the generations. Family theory (see Chapters 4 and 6) gives central attention to this dynamic.

The story of Kunta Kinta in Alex Haley's popular book *Roots* (1977) illustrates the above point. Kunta Kinta, taken into slavery from Africa, provided his family with an image that played itself out over generations, right to the time when Haley wrote his book. Family members acted out this story over the generations in differing ways, but much of their thinking and behavior could be traced to this ancestor. For example, an upstanding member of the family might be acting out the positive intergenerational family script, whereas another family member might be in trouble with the law and acting out the negative family script. Each of these family members could be said to be engaging in a set of defense mechanisms that could be explained by tracing individual, family, and cultural history.

The Family Dream

Dreamwork is an important part of psychodynamic practice (see Chapter 8), and Taub-Bynum's (1980) conception of the family dream adds an important and interesting dimension. Traditionally, dream interpretation focuses on the meaning of the dream in the individual life context, with minimal attention given to family and cultural issues.

In family dreamwork, the focus is on how the dream represents not just individual life experience, but also family intergenerational themes. For example, a client may have an anxious dream about the loss of some object—perhaps in the dream the client searches for the holy grail. A common interpretation that focuses on the individual would be that the client fears loss of important attachments, perhaps through the parents' old age and impending death. This interpretation might be useful, but it would also be important to explore the meaning of loss in the client's family over the years.

To continue the example, loss to a Jewish-American client might be much more than an individual issue, perhaps representing broader intergenerational issues around the holocaust. It is clear that those who survived the holocaust experienced considerable trauma that shows up in unconscious grief reactions. These experiences do not end with the immediate survivor, but are transmitted to the children and grandchildren (for example, see Rosenthal & Rosenthal, 1980).

Family dreamwork with German holocaust survivors would include individual interpretations but would also focus on complex intergenerational family issues. Furthermore, the cultural symbol of Jewish loss and persecution over time might be stressed as well. Therapy includes individual, family, and cultural grieving and appreciation work. Appreciations might include the strengths of the Jewish family over the generations, pride in religious heritage and symbolism, and values of cultural cooperation as represented by the kibbutz.

Multicultural and Gender-Related Implications of Family Unconscious Theory

A system as complex as that of Taub-Bynum's is difficult to summarize in a few words. What he is saying is that the basic ideas of Freud (and Bowlby and others) have immense relevance in a multicultural practice of counseling and therapy. The limitation of traditional psychodynamic practice is that it has not gone far enough nor has it focused on positive cultural dimensions and issues that can help clients face their lives more courageously and with a greater sense of pride.

An African-American, Puerto Rican, or Chinese-American client who seeks therapy needs help in handling day-to-day issues. Taub-Bynum would endorse humanistic and concrete cognitive-behavioral approaches as most immediately practical to the client. However, if clients are dealing with more complex and long-term issues, psychodynamic techniques can be highly beneficial as part of a general treatment plan. It is important to help clients look at themselves from the perspectives of their developmental history and the influence of family and culture on present-day life. Developing this perspective will help many clients move to the fourth level of multiperspective awareness suggested by cultural identity developmental theory.

Okun's (1992) review of object relations theory and psychodynamic practice raises many similar issues from a feminist frame of reference. She particularly stresses the need to look at issues of development and object relations from a perspective of gender roles and women's development in an often sexist society. She points out that "object relations and self-psychology are too dependent on inference and confuse data with interpretation" (p. 37) and that insufficient attention is given to the father's role. The latter point is one that Taub-Bynum's family-oriented approach speaks to directly. Rather than place responsibility for the child's psyche on one person (the mother), this approach shows us how the individual and a variety of family possibilities are generated in a multicultural context.

Using Psychodynamic Theory for Case Conceptualization

When asked how he worked with clients in therapy, Bowlby (personal communication, January 1987) replied clearly and directly: "Clients treat us as they were treated—this is our guide for treatment." What Bowlby is saying is that you can expect clients to repeat their developmental history with you. Their developmental history in their family of origin is particularly important, and you can anticipate that many client behaviors with you in the here and now of the interview may be traced back to past experience.

For example, if the client is narcissistic and attention seeking, you can anticipate that somehow this behavior relates to what happened in the family. Most likely, as children narcissistic clients were rewarded by parents for certain types of behavior. In therapy, this client will likely seek the same type of admiration from you, even though you and many others in the client's life find such behavior undesirable. Moreover, narcissistic clients often have developmental histories in which they were only rewarded by parents and others for certain types of achievement; the child's very real need for admiration and support for just being a child was not met.

Miller (1981) addresses the importance of meeting the healthy narcissistic needs of the child. If these needs are met, the child will have a secure, attached base as described by Bowlby and Ainsworth. However, many children become instruments of their parents' desire. Narcissistic, obsessive-compulsive, and many other types of clients are often in varying ways trying to meet unmet needs from the past, as can be seen in the following discussion of the dependent client. For example, overidentification and projection defense mechanisms are at play for some parents in their demands for achievement by their children in athletics, academics, or the arts. Crespi (personal communication, New Hartford, Conn., 1995) calls these children "tool children," as they are "acting out the conscious and unconscious needs and dynamics of their parents."

The Dependent Client: A Case Conceptualization

In the interview, you can expect the client with problems of dependency to treat you in a dependent fashion. Expect dependent clients to ask your opinion and advice, attempt to please you, be very demanding of your time, and when especially needy, appear on your doorstep asking for special help. Think about your own experience of dependent and needy people. What are your own thoughts and feelings toward this type of individual? Take a moment and write down some of these thoughts and feelings.

Dependent clients treat you as they were treated in their family of origin. Psychodynamic theory suggests that clients repeat their developmental history again and again. When clients respond in a dependent, needy way in the interview, you can anticipate that somehow this behavior can be traced back to the past and their family of origin. How do you imagine dependent clients might have been treated in their families? Allow yourself a moment to think about the possible developmental antecedents in the family of origin for the dependent client.

Dependent clients can come from a variety of family backgrounds, but certain typical patterns may be anticipated. Many have had parents who modeled dependency. If the client is female, the client had a mother and a father who, owing to cultural conditioning and stereotypes, modeled dependency and dominance, respectively. The dependent client was often not allowed to make decisions but rather learned it is safer to do what one is told. Such people have never had real personal needs met, and in working with you, they will often seek to have old unmet dependency needs filled.

Dependency as a Multicultural Issue

In North American culture, dependency tends to be seen inherently as a "problem." Given a cultural setting that focuses on autonomy, excessive dependency and neediness certainly can result in difficulties. However, it is important to recall that in Japan and much of Asia, dependence on others is taken for granted and one can even express love (in Japanese, *amae*) as integral to interdependent relationships. What results in difficulty in one society can be an asset in another.[5]

Dependency is reinterpreted as a positive experience of caring and relational behavior by Stiver (1991), who defines it as "a process of counting on other people to provide help in coping physically and emotionally with the experiences and tasks encountered in the world when one has not sufficient skill, confidence, energy and/or time" (p. 160).

The basic need for self-in-relation is foundational to our being. An individual needs others to depend on from birth. The failure to meet these needs can result in severe emotional difficulties. Developmental counseling and therapy suggests that dependency issues are important in all the personality styles/disorders of DSM-IV (Ivey, 1991).

Dependency and its variations are the focus for this interpretation of Bowlby's treatment philosophy. For the purposes of this discussion, it is assumed that the client has dependency issues that result in problematic functioning in both family and society.

Anticipating Developmental History

In the here and now of the therapeutic relationship, you as a therapist learn about the past relationships of the client. Needless to say, your dependent client will not always follow the stereotyped pattern described above, but if you use good listening and observation skills and ask questions about the family of origin, you can discover the unique historical developmental path of the client.

Similarly, antisocial clients will likely treat you as they were treated. When they manipulate and abuse you, you can postulate their likely family history. Most antisocial adults or conduct disorder children have histories of severe abuse. In therapy, they challenge you to treat them again and again as they were treated. Their dependency needs clearly were not met, and they react to this lack by attacking or manipulating you and others in the same way they experienced life as a child and adolescent.

Most of your clients will have histories of relationship problems. The confusing pattern of seduction followed by sudden vicious rejection that you will experience with borderline clients represents their likely past history of sexual abuse. Such a developmental past is common with borderlines, as demonstrated by Flaherty (1989), who found that nineteen of twenty borderline clients had clear indications of sexual abuse. Clients who respond to you with depressed affect and show signs of clinical depression will tell you that they have something to be depressed about from the past. Rigazio-DiGilio and Ivey (1990), for example, found that seventeen of twenty inpatient depressed clients had severe histories of varying types of trauma in their developmental history.

Anticipating Current Problems

You can also anticipate what some of the dependent client's present difficulties are likely to be. For example, in their current relationships, dependent clients can be expected to play out their dependency in self-destructive ways. Whether male or female, dependent clients tend to attach to people who are stronger than they are and who will make their decisions for them. The stronger person initially enjoys the feelings of adulation and power the dependent person gives them but later finds the neediness too much and starts rejecting the dependent individual.

When dependent individuals feel rejected in a relationship, they tend to try harder, complain, or otherwise exaggerate their dependent style. Women who have relationships with males who have the need to dominate (for example, antisocial or narcissistic personality styles) are in danger of abuse. In many dependent cases, you can expect a history of family abuse that will tend to be repeated in the current relationship—that is, female dependent clients are especially subject to abuse. The antisocial client, by way of contrast, often acts out past history of abuse by abusing others. Clearly, difficulties will likely occur when the antisocial male establishes a relationship with a dependent female.

The personality style will also be repeated on the job. The dependent person may constantly ask the boss for directions; the narcissist will want attention for achievements; the antisocial type may use manipulative techniques developed over a lifetime and leave the job abruptly. Clearly, vocational counseling could profit by more attention to personality style/disorder.

Personality Disorder/Style: A Developmental View of Complex Defense Mechanisms

Developmental counseling and therapy summarizes the preceding interpretation of attachment theory in Table 7.1. DCT emphasizes the importance of the *Diagnostic and Statistical Manual* Axis II personality disorders, but reinterprets the word *disorder* as learned "developmental personality style mechanisms." In effect, personality disor-

Table 7.1   Developmental Personality Styles

Style and Positive Aspect	Behavior/Thoughts in Session	Possible Family History	Predicted Current Relationships	Possible Treatment Approach
Paranoid				
It is important to watch out for injustice.	Suspicious, takes remarks out of context and interprets them to support own frame of reference	Probable history of persecution, active family rejection	Controlling behavior; anticipates exploitation, may mistrust friends and family; quick to anger	Always be honest, never defensive; structure ahead of time; don't argue, you'll only lose
Schizoid				
It is useful to be a loner or independent of others at times.	Relationship with therapist fragile; constricted body stance; little emotion shown; problems accepting support	Cold family; received little affection; rewarded for being alone and on own; may be identified patient in otherwise normal family	Loner; few friends; superficial relationships	Be consistent, warm, supportive—no pressure; social skills training may be helpful
Antisocial				
It is sometimes necessary to be impulsive and take care of our own needs.	Acts out; cannot sustain task; involved in crime, drugs, truancy, physical fights; cruel, maltreats family; tries to "con" therapist	Probable abuse as child; avoidant family forced child to take matters into own hands; little affection in home	Abusive, exploitive relationships; fear of abandonment	Be open, honest, and set clear limits; avoid entanglement; expect client to leave treatment if you get close
Borderline				
Intensity in relationship is desirable at times.	Pushes therapist's "buttons" skillfully; impulsive; intense anger or caring; suicidal gestures	Enmeshed family during early childhood; lack of support for individuation; probable sexual abuse	Serial, intense relationships; may have close friends; relationships may move rapidly between extreme closeness and distance	Confront engulfment and support individuation—that is, do opposite of family; group/systems approaches are useful

Histrionic				
All could benefit at times with open access to emotions.	Seeks reassurance; seductive, concerned with appearance, too much affect; self-centered, vague conversation	Enmeshed, engulfing family, with little support for indivduation; possible sexual abuse/seduction; little family expectation for accomplishment; aware of others, not of self	Similar to the borderline without the externalized anger; actions directed inward rather than outward	Encourage individuation; use assertiveness, skills training, consciousness raising; examine history of problem; use cognitive-behavioral and systems interventions
Narcissistic				
A strong belief in ourselves is necessary for good mental health.	Grandiose, self-important, sees self as unique; sense of entitlement; lacks empathy; oriented toward success and perfection	Received perfect mirroring for accomplishments rather than for self; engulfing family; child enacts family's wishes; anxious/ambivalent caregiver	Focuses on selfish needs, tends to engulf others with needs; is charming to get wishes met, Don Juan type; may pair with borderline	Interpret behavior; look to past; employ cognitive-behavioral, systems, sensitivity training in a group
Avoidant				
It is useful to deny or avoid some things.	Avoids people, shy, unwilling to become involved, distant; exaggerates risk	Either engulfing family or avoidant family; enacting what the family modeled	Not many friends; easily becomes dependent on them or therapist	Use many behavioral and cognitive techniques; assertiveness training and relaxation training useful
Dependent				
We all need to depend on others.	Dependency on therapist even outside of session; indecision; little sense of self	Engulfing, controlling family; not allowed to make decisions; rewarded for inaction; told what to do	Dependent on friends; drives people away with demands	Reward action; support efforts for self; use paradox, assertiveness techniques

(*continued*)

Table 7.1 (continued)

Style and Positive Aspect	Behavior/Thoughts in Session	Possible Family History	Predicted Current Relationships	Possible Treatment Approach
Obsessive-compulsive				
Maintaining order and a system is necessary for job success.	Perfectionistic and inflexible; focuses on details, making lists; devoted to work; limited affect; money oriented; indecisive	Overattached family that wanted achievement; oriented to perfection, like narcissist, but keenly aware of others, with a limited sense of self	Controlling; limited affect; demands perfection from others; hard worker; cries at sad movies	Reflect and provoke feeling; orient to client's personal needs; support development of self-concept; orient to body awareness
Passive-aggressive				
All of us are entitled to procrastinate at times.	Procrastinates; seems to agree with therapist, then undercuts; seems to accept therapist, then challenges authority	Perhaps obsessive family; individual instead moves away from perfectionism and fights back; a more healthy defense needs to be developed	"Couch potato"; skilled at getting back at and at criticizing others; defends by doing nothing; resents suggestions; not pleasant on the job	Let client learn the consequences of behavior; do not do things for client, but confront and interpret and pay special attention to client reactions

SOURCE: From *Developmental Strategies for Helpers* (pp. 164–65) by A. Ivey, 1991, North Amherst, MA: Microtraining. Copyright 1991 by Microtraining. Used by permission.

der/styles are considered systems of defense used by the client to cope with environmental stressors. In turn, Axis I disorders are seen as a reaction to immediate trauma or, more commonly, failure of the defensive structure around the personality style.

Table 7.1 summarizes the DCT approach to personality disorder/style. DCT suggests that it is important to note behavior, thoughts, and feelings in the session. These elements are indicative not only of diagnosis, but also possibly of family history and current life relationships, including interaction style on the job. With this knowledge, you will soon learn that client behavior in the interview is not necessarily directed at you personally but rather is a continuation of past life events.

Using DCT questions (Chapter 4) and the psychodynamic constructs presented in this chapter, you will likely be able to uncover and understand client dynamics. Perhaps most important, however, is that this information can lead you to an informed choice of treatment options. These treatment possibilities can, and likely should, include multicultural and cognitive-behavioral as well as psychodynamic, developmental, and other interventions.

Using Psychodynamic Theory for Treatment of Personality Style/Disorder

When conceptualizing a case, it is important to first note how the client is treating you in the here and now of the interview. The ways clients treat you provide clues to (1) developmental history in their family of origin, (2) the nature of their current interpersonal relationships, and (3) likely functioning in their work environment. This information gives you some indication of the future life of the client as concerns specific problems that may be anticipated in relationships, work, and child-rearing. *Keep in mind, however, that most clients are mixtures of varying personality styles/disorders.* In a single interview, various pieces of developmental history will be manifested in the ways the client treats you.

Behavior in the session represents a continuation of past defense mechanisms, and you will need to sort through with clients the more precise nature and underlying meaning of their surface defensive behavior. In this section, we consider some specifics of interviewing and treatment planning based on the psychodynamic frame of reference (Ivey, 1991).

A basic rule of thumb in psychodynamic therapy is to *treat clients differently than they were treated in the past.* The most obvious and elementary point is that if clients are treating us as they were treated in the past, our task is to treat them differently in the interview, even though they may try our patience and understanding and perhaps even threaten us personally. For example, a conduct disorder child or an antisocial adolescent or adult is particularly problematic for many in the helping field. Professional helpers are usually "nice" people and find it difficult to work with those who are not nice. (Miller [1981] suggests one of the reasons for this is that counselors' own survival in their families of origin often required them to be nice.)

As noted earlier, conduct disorder children and antisocial personality clients tend to have serious histories of abuse, and therefore these clients will often treat you in some sort of an abusive fashion. *If you react to these clients as others in their history have, you can expect them to continue their behavior.* If you react differently—specifically, if you treat them differently than they were treated in the past—there is some possibility that they will develop a useful relationship with you, which can make a difference in their lives.

In short, to help clients you must react to client maltreatment of you with patience, firmness, a clear sense of boundaries, and evidence of caring. This approach describes the Rogerian relationship, but with these differences. It is your task to think quickly on your feet and not allow yourself to be taken in by the client's presentation. Simply seeing antisocial clients' worlds as they present them to you is likely to fail, since they can use your empathy and understanding to manipulate you.

Another important rule to remember is to *treat the dependent client differently.* With dependent clients you must offer a solid relationship. Do not run from dependent clients' demands, but remember to maintain your boundaries. In the beginning stages, allow some dependent behavior and then gradually lead clients toward more independence or interdependence. Encourage clients to share their feelings and thoughts toward you. Providing these clients with accurate nonjudgmental feedback on the nature of the relationship can be helpful. Practice Exercise 7.1 provides steps for generating a treatment plan for dependent as well as other client personality styles.

These therapeutic efforts are designed to move dependent clients away from a hierarchical relationship. The dependent client has been at the low end of a relationship hierarchy for long time, and moving them toward an egalitarian orientation in which plans for change are coconstructed can be extremely beneficial. Multicultural therapy, feminist therapy, and developmental counseling and therapy all place special emphasis on the egalitarian relationship as basic to change processes. Practice Exercise 7.1 provides ideas to help you generate a psychodynamic developmentally oriented treatment plan.

From a psychodynamic frame of reference, the relationship you establish with the client is of key—perhaps of crucial—importance. Your understanding of your own developmental history plays a vital role. If you do not understand and accept your own relationship history, you are more likely to find yourself "triggered" by difficult clients and reacting to them ineffectively.

Limitations and Practical Implications of Psychodynamic Approaches

Psychodynamic approaches require and demand extensive study, reading, and supervised practice by carefully trained individuals who have completed years of study. Full-blown psychodynamic practice is not for the beginner in that psycho-

Practice Exercise 7.1

Generating a Psychodynamic Developmentally Oriented Treatment Plan

In reading through this chapter, you have hopefully already generated ideas for a treatment plan for a dependent personality style. It is also useful to develop a treatment plan for another personality style. You can do this exercise individually or in a small group. Members of your group probably will have slightly different treatment plans, depending on their own life histories and their counseling and therapy knowledge and competencies. Summarize your treatment plan and compare it with those of others. The steps in generating a treatment plan follow:

1. Decide on a specific developmental personality style.
2. Using your intuition, work through the following six steps to define that style and then consult DSM-IV and other sources to add to or modify your original impression.

    a. What are the positives and survival skills in the personality style of the client? These skills should be identified clearly, respected, and supported. The goal of therapy is to balance, not eliminate, these key personality qualities.
    b. What is the anticipated family history? How was client treated at home?
    c. What is the expected nature of current personal relationships?
    d. How are the ways the client relates to others likely to manifest in interviews with you?

    e. How is the client likely to react in the vocational world?
    f. What possible Axis I problems may be anticipated if the client's defensive structure fails?

3. Generate a treatment plan for the developmental personality style.

    a. How will you develop a positive base for treatment in current interviews and over the long term?
    b. What are the key relationship issues for you for this style? What is your personal history and attitude surrounding this issue? How might this style "push your buttons"? How will you change the relationship as the client develops? What balance of attachment and separation behaviors does this client need?
    c. How will you generate an integrated treatment plan at the sensorimotor, concrete, formal, and dialectic/systemic levels? How would you use the specific questioning and intervention strategies of DCT with this type of client? (How might the cultural genogram and family genogram be used to further client understanding of how the issues developed in a social context?)

4. What are the key multicultural and contextual issues that must frame the analysis and treatment plan?

dynamic training requires the most rigorous intellectual discipline of all methods. The ideas presented in this chapter represent the most complex organization of human experience of any set of theories.

Nonetheless, this approach can be helpful to counselors and therapists in that it can create an awareness that what a client presents as a surface problem, concern, or behavior may not be the issue. Underlying the description of a problem may be a vast array of unconscious or unknown forces, ideas, and thoughts. As Bowlby, Ainsworth, Miller, and Lacan remind us, the force of unconscious experience is extremely powerful and should not be overlooked.

Psychodynamic approaches have been criticized as antithetical to and irrelevant for any other than highly verbal middle-class clients. Furthermore, there are many practicing psychodynamic therapists who have yet to come to terms with the family and multicultural challenge. Focusing solely on the individual, they may miss issues critical for client change and growth. Miller (1981) has pointed out the pitfall of failing to be aware of the therapist's own issues, and Taub-Bynum reminds us that cultural and family roots must be part of an overall treatment conceptualization.

NOTES

1. Psychodynamic theory has long been criticized as self-referential and tautological—a needless repetition of the same thoughts in different words. However, it is a holistic framework, and each alternative language frame gives a new perspective on the client and the client's developmental framework. Examination of the important book *The Language of Psychoanalysis* (Laplanche & Pontalis, 1973) helps explain this basic, but often misunderstood, point. Begin with any basic psychoanalytic construct (repression, Oedipal complex, transference, projective identification) and read the definition carefully. Starting with transference, for example, you will be referred to countertransference and projective identification for further information. Moving there, you will be referred back to transference, but also to new concepts that will ultimately enlarge your understanding of the place you started. Psychodynamic theory is like a dictionary: every word defines other words. In the process of studying the psychoanalytic "dictionary," you begin to understand the complex whole of psychodynamic thinking.

One is reminded of the story of the blind men and the elephant. How one defines the elephant depends on which piece of the elephant you touch. The world is a totality, but we can only grasp a piece of its complexity. The more ways we look at the elephant, the better we can understand the whole, which, in truth, is beyond language.

2. The presentation here is based on A. Ivey (1989). A general model of object relations is proposed. The focus is on the work of John Bowlby and Alice Miller in the belief that these two theorists provide the clearest, most multiculturally relevant, and most available introduction to what is a very complex set of theories (such as Klein, 1975; Guntrip, 1968; Kernberg, 1980; Mahler, 1968; Masterson, 1981).

3. Bowlby and his colleague Ainsworth have both been criticized severely by some in the women's movement as focusing almost solely on the mother as caregiver. This criticism has some merit. For example, Bowlby's 1958 article was entitled "The Nature of the Child's Tie to His Mother." More recently, however, Bowlby seems to have come to terms with a broader definition of caregiver. For example, in 1988 he said, "Looking after babies and

young children is no job for a single person. If the job is to be well done, the caregiver herself (or himself) needs a great deal of assistance. From whom that comes will vary: very often it is the other parent; in many societies, including more often than is realized, it comes from a grandmother" (p. 2). Bowlby goes on to point out that the concept of caregiver varies from culture to culture.

4. Cheatham's comment is challenging to the field. The first author of this book has worked with a number of minority students who have had difficulty in practicum or internship settings. The cause of the difficulty was that these students often spend time outside the clinical or counseling settings helping troubled individuals or families find shelter, work through financial difficulties, and so on. Many practicum and internship settings consider the act of "doing something" to be an inappropriate professional role. They have criticized minority clinicians severely for "countertransference."

This, of course, is a reasonable construction if one takes the traditional psychodynamic ego psychology model. If one assumes the broader frames of Miller, Taub-Bynum, and Cheatham, then community action is relevant, and it is the ego psychologists and practica/internship supervisors who suffer the pains of "countertransference" owing to their blindness to obvious family and cultural contextual issues. It may be anticipated that such issues will be debated more openly in the next decade.

5. Excessive dependency, of course, can be an issue in any culture. In Japan, which values dependency and interdependence, difficulty still can occur when a child who has an especially close relationship with the mother has to leave for school.

REFERENCES

AINSWORTH, M. (1967). *Infancy in Uganda: Infant care and the growth of love.* Baltimore: Johns Hopkins University Press.

AINSWORTH, M. (1977). Social development in the first year of life. In J. Tanner (Ed.), *Developments in psychiatric research.* London: Hodder & Stoughton.

AINSWORTH, M. (1979). Attachment theory and its utility in cross-cultural research. In P. Leiderman, S. Tulkin, & A. Rosenfeld (Eds.), *Culture and infancy: Variations in the human experience* (pp. 47–67). San Diego: Academic Press.

AINSWORTH, M. (1985). I. Patterns of infant-mother attachment; II. Attachments across the life-span. *Bulletin of the New York Academy of Medicine, 61,* 771–812.

AINSWORTH, M., BLEHAR, M., WATERS, E., & WALL, S. (1978). *Patterns of attachment.* Hillsdale, NJ: Erlbaum.

AINSWORTH, M., & BOWLBY, J. (1991). An ethological approach to personality development. *American Psychologist, 46,* 333–41.

BAKER MILLER, J. (1976). *Toward a new psychology of women.* Boston: Beacon.

BAKER MILLER, J. (1991). The development of women's sense of self. In J. Jordan, A. Kaplan, J. Baker Miller, I. Stiver, & J. Surry (Eds.), *Women's growth in connection* (pp. 11–26). New York: Guilford.

BOWLBY, J. (1940). The influence of early environment in the development of neurosis and neurotic character. *International Journal of Psycho-Analysis, 21,* 154–78.

BOWLBY, J. (1951). *Maternal care and mental health.* Geneva: World Health Organization.

BOWLBY, J. (1958). The nature of a child's tie to his mother. *International Journal of Psycho-Analysis, 39,* 350–73.

BOWLBY, J. (1969). *Attachment.* New York: Basic Books.

BOWLBY, J. (1973). *Separation.* New York: Basic Books.

BOWLBY, J. (1988). *A secure base.* New York: Basic Books.

BRAGG, M., DALTON, R., DUNKER, B., FISHER, P., GARCIA, N., OBLER, L., ORWOLL, L., PAISER, P., & PEARLMAN, S. (1987). *Lesbian psychologies.* Urbana: University of Illinois Press.

BRASSARD, M., GERMAIN, R., & HART, S. (1987). *Psychological maltreatment of children and youth.* New York: Pergamon Press.

CHEATHAM, H. (1990). Empowering Black families. In H. Cheatham and J. Stewart (Eds.), *Black families* (pp. 373–93). New Brunswick, NJ: Transaction Press.

CHODOROW, N. (1978). *The reproduction of mothering: Psychoanalysis and the sociology of gender.* Berkeley: University of California Press.

COMAS-DIAZ, L., & MINRATH, M. (1985). Psychotherapy with ethnic minority borderline clients. *Psychotherapy, 22,* 418–26.

DAVIS, M., ESHELMAN, E., & McKAY, M. (1995). *The relaxation and stress reduction workbook* (4th ed.). Oakland, CA: New Harbinger.

EGELUND, B. (1983). Comments on Kopp, Krakow, and Vaughn's chapter. In M. Perlmatter (Ed.), *The Minnesota symposia on child psychology* (Vol. 16, pp. 129–85). Hillsdale, NJ: Erlbaum.

ERIKSON, E. (1963). *Childhood and society* (2nd ed.). New York: Norton. (Original work published 1950)

FLAHERTY, M. (1989). *Perceived differences in early family relationship and parent/child relations between adults diagnosed as borderline personality or bipolar disorder.* Unpublished doctoral dissertation, School of Education, University of Massachusetts, Amherst.

FORDHAM, M. (1957). *New developments in analytical psychology.* London: Routledge.

FREUD, A. (1982). *Psychoanalytic psychology of normal development: 1970–80.* London: Hogarth.

FREUD, S. (1964). Negation. In S. Freud, *On metapsychology* (pp. 435–42). London: Penguin. (Original work published 1925)

GUNTRIP, H. (1968). *Schizoid phenomena, object relations, and the self.* New York: International Universities Press.

HALEY, A. (1977). *Roots: Saga of an American family.* New York: Doubleday.

HARTMANN, H. (1958). *Ego psychology and the problem of adaptation.* New York: International Universities Press.

IVEY, A. (1989). *Object relations: An introduction.* Unpublished manuscript, University of Massachusetts, Amherst.

IVEY, A. (1991). *Developmental strategies for helpers: Individual, family and network interventions.* Pacific Grove, CA: Brooks/Cole.

JUNG, C. (1935). The personal and collective unconscious. In C. Jung, *Collected works* (Vol. 7, pp. 87–110). New York: Pantheon.

KERNBERG, O. (1980). Developmental theory, structural organization and psychoanalytic technique. In *Rapprochement.* New York: Aronson.

KLEIN, M. (1975). *Envy and gratitude and other works, 1946/1963.* London: Hogarth.

LACAN, J. (1977). *Ecrits: A selection.* New York: Norton. (Original work published 1966)

LAPLANCHE, J., & PONTALIS, J. (1973). *The language of psychoanalysis.* New York: Norton.

LÜTKENHAUS, P., GROSSMAN, K. E., & GROSSMAN, K. (1985). Infant-mother attachment at twelve months and style of interaction with a stranger at the age of three years. *Child Development, 56,* 1538–42.

MAHLER, M. (1975). *The psychological birth of the human infant.* New York: Basic Books.

MAIN, M. (1973). *Play, exploration and competence as related to child-adult attachment.* Unpublished doctoral dissertation, Johns Hopkins University, Baltimore.

MAIN, M., & SOLOMON, J. (1986). Procedure for identifying infants as disorganized/disoriented during the Ainsworth Strange Situation. In M. Greenberg, D. Cicchetti, & M. Cummings (Eds.), *Attachment in the preschool years.* Chicago: University of Chicago Press.

MASTERSON, J. (1981). *The narcissistic and borderline disorders.* New York: Brunner/Mazel.

MATAS, L., AREND, R., & SROUFE, L. (1978). Continuity of adaptation in the second year: The relationship between quality of attachment and later competence. *Child Development, 49,* 547–56.

MILLER, A. (1981). *The drama of the gifted child.* New York: Basic Books.

NEUGARTEN, B. (1979). Time, age, and the life cycle. *American Journal of Psychiatry, 136,* 887–94.

OKUN, B. (1992). Object relations and self-psychology: Overview and feminist perspective. In L. Brown & M. Ballou (Eds.), *Theories of personality and psychopathology: Feminist reappraisals* (pp. 20–45). New York: Guilford.

RIGAZIO-DIGILIO, S., & IVEY, A. (1990). Developmental therapy and depressive disorders: Measuring cognitive levels through patient natural language. *Professional Psychology: Research and Practice, 21,* 470–75.

ROSENTHAL, P., & ROSENTHAL, S. (1980)). Holocaust effect in the third generation. *American Journal of Psychotherapy, 34,* 572–79.

SAYERS, J. (1995). Consuming male fantasy: Feminist psychoanalysis retold. In A. Elliott & S. Frosh (Eds.), *Psychoanalysis in contexts.* New York: Routledge & Kegan Paul.

STIVER, I. (1991). The meanings of "dependency" in female-male relationships. In J. Jordan, A. Kaplan, J. Baker Miller, I. Stiver, & J. Surry (Eds.), *Women's growth in connection* (pp. 143–61). New York: Guilford.

SUE, D., & SUE, D. (1990). *Counseling the culturally different* (2nd ed.). New York: Wiley.

TAMASE, K. (1991, April). *The effects of introspective-developmental counseling.* Paper presented at the American Association of Counseling and Development, Reno, NV.

TAMASE, K., & KATO M. (1990). Effect of questions about factual and affective aspects of life events in an introspective interview. *Bulletin of Nara University of Education, 24,* 153–63.

TAUB-BYNUM, E. B. (1980). The use of dreams in family therapy. *Psychotherapy: Theory, Research, and Practice, 17,* 227–31.

TAUB-BYNUM, E. B. (1984). *The family unconscious.* Wheaton, IL: Quest.

TAUB-BYNUM, E. B. (1992). *Family dreams: The intricate web.* Ithaca, NY: Haworth Press.

WÄRTNER, U. (1986). *Attachment in infancy and at age six, and children's self-concept.* Unpublished doctoral dissertation, University of Virginia.

WATERS, E., WIPPMAN, J., & SROUFE, L. (1979). Attachment, positive affect, and competence in the peer group. *Child Development, 50,* 821–29.

WINNICOTT, D. (1988). *Human nature.* New York: Schocken.

Psychodynamic Counseling and Therapy II: Applications for Practice

CHAPTER GOALS

This chapter seeks to:

1. Discuss the central psychodynamic technique of free association and how it serves as the foundation for all other dynamic practice.

2. Provide some guidelines and suggestions for a more multiculturally oriented psychodynamic practice.

3. Enable you, through practice exercises, to conduct or engage in
   - Focused free association as a basic psychodynamic technique and strategy
   - An array of free association exercises and techniques—tapping unconscious experience via everyday symbols and the "Freudian slip," dream analysis, analysis of resistance, and analysis of transference—that provide an experiential basis to the theory presented in these two chapters
   - Guided imagery with gender, spiritual, and cultural symbols
   - A complete psychodynamic interview using the five-stage model in Chapter 3

The complexities of the psychodynamic frame of reference are virtually infinite, and thus the discussion in Chapter 3 is only a beginning. Some of the exercises in this chapter can be quite powerful, particularly when combined with the imagery and sensorimotor techniques of developmental counseling and therapy (see Chapter 4), and therefore should be used with a sense of ethics and under appropriate supervision.

Free Association:
The Central Strategy

Free association, the basic technique of the psychodynamic approach, is the "method according to which voice must be given to all thoughts without exception which enter the mind, whether such thoughts are based on a specific element (word, number, dream-image, or any kind of idea at all) or produced spontaneously" (Laplanche & Pontalis, 1973, p. 169). Just as the word *unconscious* represents Freud's contribution, so does the technique of free association stand as a symbol of dynamic methodology. Basically, free association encourages the client and the counselor to say anything that comes to mind.

Freud developed free association in his early work on hysteria as a way to encourage patients to search for underlying unconscious factors, and he refined this technique in his own self-analysis, particularly of his dreams. Through using dream analysis, Freud discovered the "royal road to the unconscious." He found that allowing oneself to say anything that came to mind (no matter how seemingly irrelevant) would often reveal a pattern that helped explain the meaning of a behavior, dream, or seemingly random thought.

Practice Exercise 8.1 introduces you to the technique of focused free association. This simple, but often very powerful, exercise encapsulates both the theory and practice of the psychodynamic approach to counseling and therapy, being based in the idea that whatever comes to mind from the past is important and somehow connected to current life issues. Free association can be made more powerful and understandable if sensorimotor elements involving images and bodily sensations are added, as is done in this practice exercise. The exercise asks you to concretely describe your present issues and relate these to past events—that is, to make connections or patterns. Making connections is a formal operational process that is basic to the psychodynamic approach. Such formal operational thought requires verbal ability and depends on a relationship of trust between therapist and client.

Therapists and counselors often ask questions in their interviews that relate to the concept of free association. For example, when you ask a client such questions as: What comes to your mind? What do you think of next? or even What is the *last* thing that comes to mind? you are inviting the client to freely associate to an idea. Free association is an invaluable technique, regardless of the theoretical orientation, because it focuses on clients' constructions of issues and provides you the therapist with access to clients' inner dialogues, thoughts, and feelings that you might miss when using other techniques. Free association gives you and your clients access to often surprising and valuable information, such as indicators of otherwise unsuspected abusive history. Practice Exercise 8.2 acquaints you with an array of free association exercises and techniques as a way of illustrating the practical aspects of psychodynamic counseling and therapy.

Practice Exercise 8.1

Focused Free Association

Engaging in the following exercise will help make the material and concepts of this chapter more useful and understandable. Furthermore, this exercise can be used with your clients, not only in psychodynamic practice, but also in conjunction with other theories of helping. Think about the points in each of the following steps before moving on:

1. Focus *now* on a current concern or issue. Take time and consider it fully. It sometimes helps to visualize an image of the problem—What are you seeing, hearing, and, *especially*, feeling as you think about the issue? Make this exercise as " here and now" as you can.

2. What emotions do you have around this issue? Focus now on your feelings. Locate this feeling physically in your body and really focus on it.

3. Allow your mind to drift to an earlier time in your life—the earlier the better—associated with this feeling. What comes to your mind? You may experience visual images or fragments of feelings or remember a specific situation. Allow yourself to experience these old thoughts and feelings once again. When using this technique in therapy with a client, be careful not to suggest specific possibilities. These should be the client's associations, not yours.

4. How do you *connect* your present concern with the past? How are the past and present similar? Does the *association* between past and present give you some new thoughts about the meaning of the present concern?

5. Think about your gender, family of origin, and your cultural/ethnic identification. How do these factors relate to your experience? (Free association too often focuses just on the individual. If you ask your client to free associate to gender, family, or cultural issues, you have moved a long way to adapting psychodynamic theory to multicultural issues.)

Practice Exercise 8.2

Free Association Exercises and Techniques

The purpose of the following exercises is to illustrate some basic and practical aspects of psychodynamic functioning. The person who moves through each exercise carefully will have a more complete sense of the importance of free association and its potential implementations in the counseling interview. These exercises are only an introduction to an incredibly complex theory.

1. *The symbols of everyday life.* Much of Freudian and psychodynamic thought is based on sexuality and sexual symbolism. A good way to understand symbols and their meanings is to go through a few basic free association/creativity exercises. Take a separate sheet of paper and brainstorm as many words as you can think of when you hear the word *penis.* Make this list as long as you can. Now take the word *vagina* and make as extensive a list as you can.

Now having made the two lists, expand them further. What objects in everyday life remind you of the penis and the vagina? What about types of people, the universe, things in your own living room? Make this list as long and extensive as you can. It can be suggested that brainstorming and creativity are closely allied to the processes of free association. Having completed your list, you may find it helpful to turn to the tenth lecture in Freud's *A General Introduction to Psychoanalysis* (1920/1966). Many of the words and symbols you generated will likely be listed in this chapter. It was in a similar, but less structured, fashion that Freud slowly constructed his entire theory of personality.

As time and interest permit, consider the words *intercourse, death, love, hate, breast, masturbation, birth, body,* and other specific words of interest to you. In each case, brainstorming a list of words will reveal a general pattern of the symbols that represent that idea or concept in everyday life.

2. *The "Freudian slip."* Slips of the tongue are often small windows on the unconscious. A student once walked into our office and asked if we gave "objectionable" tests. It takes but a very quick free association to understand this student's unconscious feelings. Not all such slips are as easily understood. But if one allows oneself to free associate, it is often possible to find the meaning of the error in speech. Think back on your own speech errors or those of your friends, then free associate to their meanings.

The process of examining the psychology of errors may be studied in more detail in Freud's second, third, and fourth lectures (1920/1966). Errors also show in our forgetting appointments, dropping things at crucial times, behavior that seems to repeat itself unnecessarily, and in many other ways. Again, free association is a route toward understanding the meaning of these errors.

3. *Dream analysis.* Recall and write down a dream you have had. Then sit back, relax, and focus on one aspect of that dream. Letting your free associations lead you, open your mind to whatever comes. Then see if any patterns or new ideas emerge that help you understand the dream.

As an alternative, keep the whole dream in mind and relax. This time, free associate back to an early childhood experience. Then follow that experience and go back to an even earlier childhood experience. In some cases, a third experience association may be helpful. Return to your dream and determine if the dream related to your associations.

The preceding processes are similar to those employed in analysis of dreams. An examination of Freud's lectures five through fifteen will reveal that you have anticipated some of his constructs and ideas. It is possible, using free association techniques, to realize intuitively many of Freud's concepts before you read them. This direct experiencing of free association should help you to understand the intellectual aspects of his theory more fully.

4. *Analysis of resistance.* Resistance is the name given to "everything in the words and actions of the . . . [client] that obstructs his gaining access to his unconscious" (Laplanche & Pontalis, 1973). Most likely, in one of the preceding exercises you "blocked" at some point and couldn't think of a word. Your free associations stopped for a moment. These blockages are miniexamples of resistance and illustrate the operation of the general defense mechanism of repression. To recover the lost association that was blocked, it is important that you first focus on the block itself. The following example may prove helpful. Let us assume you want to understand your feelings toward your parents or some other important person in your life in more depth. One route to this is free associating a list of words that come to your mind in relation to this individual. For example, suppose that one free associates to one's lover the following: "warmth, love, that hike to Lake Supreme, bed, touching, sexuality, (block), tenderness, an argument over my looking at another person, anger, frustration, (block)." First, one can get a general picture of feelings and important thoughts via this free association exercise. It is next appropriate to turn to the block and to use one of the following techniques to understand the block (or resistance): (1) free associate, using the block as a starting point (a clue may come via this route); (2) sing a song, let it come to your mind as you relax, then free associate from that song; (3) draw a picture, and once again free associate; (4) go to the bookshelf and select a book, or go to a dictionary and select a word, and free associate from what you select (sometimes the answer will be there immediately).

This small set of exercises does not explain resistance in its full complexity. If you have entered into it fully and flexibly, you may have broken through one of your own blocks or resistances and developed a slightly better understanding of yourself. An examination of Freud's nineteenth lecture will amplify these concepts and perhaps suggest additional exercises for you.

5. *Analysis of transference.* We sometimes find people we immediately dislike. Psychodynamic theory suggests that we have transferred feelings related to someone from our past onto this new individual. Select someone you have problems with and try some of the free association exercises already suggested. Later, examine Freud's twenty-seventh lecture and compare what you anticipated with what he said.

Free Association and Multicultural Images

Psychodynamic thought has been criticized as overlooking issues of social justice and as "alien" to those of other cultures who may not wish to disclose personal feelings and issues (Ponterotto & Casas, 1991). However, it is quite possible to blend multicultural issues with psychodynamic techniques. Practice Exercise 8.3 presents

Practice Exercise 8.3

Focused Free Association and Guided Imagery with Gender, Spiritual, and Cultural Symbols

The following exercise is designed to help clients recognize and use strengths from their gender, religion, and/or cultural backgrounds.

1. *Inform your client about your process and intent.* Rather than surprise the client, tell the client what is about to happen and why it is potentially helpful. For instance, you can say that we can carry images around with us that can be personally helpful and supportive when we recall them in stressful situations.

2. *Generate an image.* Ask your client to relax and then to generate a positive image that can be used as a resource. Suggest that the image be related to gender, religion, or cultural background. It is possible that a single image may encompass all three dimensions. A Franco-American woman, for example, might focus on Joan of Arc. Alternatively, a Jewish-Canadian might focus on the Star of David; a Navajo, on a mountain or religious symbol; a Mexican-American, on the Christian cross or the pyramids near Mexico City.

3. *Focus on the image.* Using developmental counseling and therapy techniques, ask your client to see the image in the mind's eye. What is seen, heard, felt? Locate the positive feelings in the body. Identify the image and body feeling as a positive resource always available to the client. (Body anchoring of resources will make them more readily available when needed in counseling and therapy.)

4. *Take the image to the problem.* Using relaxation and free association techniques, guide the client to the previously discussed issue or to any issue of choice. Suggest that the client use the positive resource image to help work with the issue. It is important to stress to the client that the image can be a resource, although it may or may not resolve the concern. If the issue seems too large, the image can be used in working on a smaller part of the problem rather than in finding a complete solution.

an exercise in free association and imagery that uses gender-related, spiritual, or cultural symbols. This exercise, if presented well and timed carefully, can be helpful in bringing to the fore important images from the past that can help clients think about issues from new perspectives. The fourth item in the exercise is not associated with dynamic theory, as it leads clients to talk about the systems in which they develop their ideas. However, at this systems level the combination of psychodynamic thought and the multicultural approach has real value.

The Importance of Free Association

In the following sections on the basic techniques of psychodynamic counseling, one central fact should stand out: *free association is the basis for all the techniques discussed*. Free association is the most direct route to reach unconscious experience. The techniques discussed (interpretation, dream analysis, regression, analysis of resistance, analysis of transference and countertransference, and projective identification) all rely on free association in some way.

Interpretation

Psychodynamic counseling approaches are interpretive. Interpretation is a sophisticated and complex skill in which intellectual knowledge of psychodynamic theory is integrated with clinical data about the client. In Chapter 3, the microskill of interpretation was defined as the renaming of client experience from an alternative frame of reference or worldview. Applied specifically to dynamic approaches, the skill of interpretation comes from the worldview of psychoanalysis and seeks to identify and give meaning to wishes, needs, and patterns from the unconscious world of the client.

There are some specific guidelines the therapist may follow in interpretation. First, the counselor must use attending skills carefully so that the data point clearly to the interpretation. Next, the interpretation should be stated and the client given time to react. The helper may "check out" the client by asking such questions as: How do you react to that? or Does that ring a bell? or Does that make sense? Such questions encourage the client to think through and assimilate or reject the interpretation.

One of the goals of intentional psychodynamic therapy is to encourage clients to make their own interpretations. When clients interpret their own stories, they often gain insight, or the ability to look at old information from new perspectives. Insight is directly related to intentionality and creative responding. The person who is able to interpret life experience in new ways through insight is able to generate new ways of describing the world.

These new descriptions are almost invariably verbal. A verbal insight or new description is most useful if the client is able to take the new information out of the session and use it in daily life. A criticism of some psychodynamic approaches is the emphasis on insight, which produces clients who search diligently in the past while continuing to have difficulty coping with present-day living.

Interpretation in the psychodynamic model has traditionally been made from an individualistic, ego psychology frame of reference that locates the problem and decision making in the individual. There is an increased awareness of how the psychodynamic model can be extended by including interpretations made from a family or multicultural frame of reference. The following example illustrates multicultural interpretation with a client suffering from depression, a common symptom for the dependent personality style:

Client: I'm really depressed. It's taken a long time for me to understand myself. I can only be happy if I do something for others, but they always seem to want more. I feel I'm never liked for myself.

Counselor (individualistic interpretation):   Your pattern seems to be to try to do things for others with little attention to yourself. That would seem to go back to the way you solved problems as a child. You didn't feel adequate, so you tried to please others. Here again we see you continuing the behavior now.

Counselor (family interpretation):   Your role in your family was the placater. Everyone else was arguing, and you took it on yourself to take this role. Then they kept you in it and still do even today. You're very good at keeping your new family flowing smoothly.

Counselor (gender-oriented multicultural interpretation):   Women in North American culture are expected to take the caring role. We've learned to define ourselves through relationships with others. It's natural, but the question is what do you want?

Counselor (ethnic/racially oriented multicultural interpretation):   Puerto Rican women are expected to put the family interests ahead of their own—it's in our tradition of *Marianismo.* How can we respect that tradition and find a place in U.S. society?

Each of these interpretations of the client's issue might be helpful and might even be useful with the same client at various points in the interview or treatment series. The danger of taking a strictly individualistic psychodynamic approach and ignoring family, gender, and multicultural issues is that it places the primary burden on the individual and ignores self-in-relation.

The assumptions on which psychodynamic interpretations are based are often Eurocentric in origin. This limitation can result in harm for minority clients (see Sue & Sue, 1990), and possibly for North Americans of European origin as well. It seems time to expand our conception of the psychodynamic approach to therapy.

Dream Analysis

Dream analysis is another important technique of the psychodynamic approach. Dream analysis can be conducted at a surface level, which means that the manifest, or observed, content of the dream is examined. Underlying the conscious parts of the dream is the latent content, which relates to deeper structures of meaning. Free association can be used by psychodynamic counselors in the analysis of dreams at either level.

In conducting a dream analysis for the first time, the five-stage structure of the interview is useful. Practice Exercise 8.4 presents an example of psychodynamic interviewing that focuses on a dream. The same structure provided in this example can be useful for working with a variety of other issues as well.

=== **Practice Exercise 8.4** ===

 # An Exercise in Psychodynamic Interviewing

The purpose of this exercise is to illustrate how the skills and concepts explored in this text may be used to conduct a basic interview from a psychodynamic perspective. Analysis of a dream or a client's reaction to an authority figure works well in the following framework. Alternatively, you may have identified a repeating life pattern in which the client tends to have a certain style of response, thought, feeling, or behavior in several situations.

If you wish, you can go through the stages by yourself, thinking to yourself about one of your own dreams, your reactions to authority, or your own repeating patterns.

The framework presented here provides an introduction to how psychodynamically oriented counseling and therapy may be conducted.

Stage 1. Rapport and Structuring

Develop rapport with the client in your own natural way. Inform the client that you will work through some basic psychodynamic understandings about a dream, a relationship with authority, or a life pattern. Decide the issue to be worked on mutually.

Stage 2. Data Gathering

Use the basic listening sequence (BLS) of questioning, encouraging, paraphrasing, and reflection of feeling to bring out the issue in detail. If you are working with a dream, be sure that you bring out the facts, feelings, and the client's organiza-

tion of the dream. If you are working with an authority issue, draw out a concrete situation and obtain the facts, feelings, and organization of the issue. In the case of repeating patterns, draw out several concrete examples of the pattern. Once you have heard the issue presented thoroughly, summarize it using the client's main words and check it out to ensure that you have understood the client correctly.

At this point, it is often wise to stop for a moment and use the positive asset search. Specifically, use the BLS to draw out the facts, feelings, and organization of something positive in the client's life. This may or may not be related to the dream or authority figure. Clients tend to move and talk more freely from a base of security.

Stage 3. Determining Outcomes

Setting up a specific goal of understanding may be useful. A general goal may be to find earlier life experiences that relate to the dream, authority issue, or repeating life pattern. Use the BLS to specify what the client would like to gain from this interview.

Stage 4. Generating Alternative Solutions

Depending on your purpose and your relationship with this client, there are three major alternatives for analyzing the problem that may be useful.

Alternative 1: Summarize the dream, authority issue, or pattern, and then summarize the desired outcome of the session. Ask your client "What comes to mind as a possible explanation?" If you have communicated the fact that you have been listening, you will often find that clients generate new ideas and interpretations on their own. The structure provided by the interview decisional model and by listening is often sufficient to help clients analyze and understand their own problems.

Alternative 2: Summarize the issue and then reflect the central emotion you may have noted in the conflict or ask the client what one single emotion stands out from the first part of the interview. Ask the client to focus on that emotion and stay with that feeling. Through the use of the focused free association exercise, direct the client to concentrate on that emotion and then to free associate back to an earlier life experience—the earlier the better. (Free associations are more valuable if made from an emotional state rather than from a state of clear cognitive awareness.) Most clients' first association is with some experience in their teenage years, whereas others associate to a recent event. In either case, draw out the association using the basic listening sequence.

You now should have the facts, feelings, and organization of the dream, reaction to authority, or pattern and the facts, feelings, and organization of the first association. Based on a clear summary of these two, you and the client should be able to find some consistent pattern of meaning. The discovery and notation of these patterns are an example of a basic psychodynamic interpretation.

Key words will often be repeated in both the association and the original dream or problem. Deeper understandings may come from continuing the exercise as below.

Alternative 3: Continue as in alternative 2, but ask your client to free associate to an even earlier life experience. Again, use the focused free association technique. Draw out these earlier free associations with the BLS. You may assemble over time a group of recollections, and you will find several patterns in the associations that repeat themselves in daily life.

At this point, the client may make interpretations of meaning or you may add your own interpretations. Generally speaking, interpretations generated by the client are longer lasting.

Stage 5.   Generalization

Psychodynamic therapy is not typically oriented to transfer of learnings from the interview to daily life. However, it may be helpful to ask the client to summarize the interview. What did the client summarize as the main facts, feelings, and organization of the interview? As appropriate, you may want to add to the client's perspective and work toward some action.

Comment

The five-stage structure of the interview plus the microskills discussed earlier are basic to a successful psychodynamically oriented interview. However, cultural and individual empathy, client observation skills (both of verbal and nonverbal behavior, incongruities, pacing, and leading), and the positive asset search are all critical dimensions in a successful session. What psychodynamic theory adds to the process is a content, a specific direction and purpose for which to use the skills—the uncovering of life patterns and relating them back to earlier life experiences with specific theoretical interpretations.

Dream Analysis and Current Real Issues

Although dream analysis can be a good place to start practicing psychodynamic interviewing, a more effective approach is to use the five-stage interview structure and emphasize focused free association on any important client topic. Although dreams may be "the royal road to the unconscious," free association is too useful a technique to be reserved only for dreams.

For example, you may have an adult child of an alcoholic (ACOA) as a client. Many ACOAs have "split off" and forgotten their painful childhood experiences. Once you have developed a trusting relationship with your ACOA client, focused free association techniques can be very useful in helping the client recover lost childhood experiences, as the following example shows. The client is going through his second divorce; both of his marriages were to alcoholics, although the client himself does not drink. The repetition by the counselor of key words, as in Gestalt therapy, intensifies the experience for the client.

Client: Yes, I tried so hard to please Joanie, but she continued to drink no matter what I did. Everyone at the office says I'm good at getting along with people, but I simply could never please her.

Counselor (using nonverbal observation):   I notice that when you said, "I could never please her" you seemed to almost cringe at that moment. Could you go back and visualize an image of Joanie and say, "I could never please her"?

Client: I can see her. "I could never please her."

Counselor: Again.

Client (more weakly):   "I could never please her."

Counselor: Again.

Client (almost inaudible and near tears):   "I could never please her."

Counselor: What are you feeling in your body right now?

Client: My head aches. It hurts.

Counselor: Could you get in touch with that feeling in your head? (pause) What comes to your mind as you think about your childhood in an alcoholic family? Can you get an image of yourself in your family?

Client: (pause) I see myself cringing in my bedroom. Mom is standing over me. She's drunk and she's going to hit me. I never could please her either.

A common pattern among children of alcoholics is to repeat the family structure they grew up with. In the example above, the client has played the peacemaking or placating role in the family of origin and repeats this pattern in present-day relationships. After the session, the counselor in the above case noted that the client was trying to please the counselor in the interview. Much like the example of the depressed dependent-style client discussed above, ACOA clients will repeat with you in the interview how they themselves were treated in the past. The free association technique can lead to an understanding of the parallels between the client's past and the present.

The Family Dream

Taub-Bynum (1980, 1992) maintains that dreams should also be related to the family structure, not just to individual experience. He cites the following examples of dreams in a family context:

> In one family, the following dream recurred often to a fifteen-year-old female. She dreamed that she "escaped" from her parents' house and jumped into their car. As she drove away, the father would run toward her but would never manage quite to catch her. The closer he got, the faster the car went. Finally, the fifteen-year-old female fully escaped only to run headlong into a telephone pole.
>
> In this family's therapy session, the themes of autonomy and separation, accompanied by a great deal of anxiety, occurred repeatedly. This fifteen-year-old fought continuously with her parents over her own intense involvement with a young man of whom the family did not approve. The girl felt dominated by and rebellious toward her parents, in particular her father. However, when she stayed away from home too long, she began to experience somatic problems and wanted to "lose" herself in other males.
>
> The younger sibling dreamed that a large "awful" man ran around screaming at her mother, her oldest sister, and herself. Finally, the man stepped on all three but did not kill them. The dream recurred several times.
>
> The family that provided this dream series was composed of a father who had a manic/depressive illness, an extremely religious compulsive mother, and two adolescent siblings. All three females in the family had psychosomatic problems, i.e. stomach cramps, persistent gas pains, migraine, and frequent depressive episodes. (p. 228)

Taub-Bynum suggests that dreams are not just individual events but are also related to issues in the family. In the family presented above, it is apparent that the two daughters have shared images of the family gestalt and that the dysfunctional family interaction has resulted in somatic symptoms.

Treatment for such a complex of issues could follow a variety of paths. The therapist could take either of the daughters through the individualistic dream analysis of Practice Exercise 8.4. Alternatively, the therapist might work through the dreams using similar procedures with the two young women or the family itself. The procedures and techniques of dream analysis remain essentially the same, but the focus of interpretations and body sensation (particularly somatic symptoms) is interpreted in the context of the family unconscious as a whole.

Multicultural Issues in Dreaming

Dreams have different values in different cultures. For instance, Australian Aboriginals consider "dreamtime" more real than daily "reality." Dreams are an important and useful avenue to spiritual issues. Too often psychodynamic work is drawn from traditional Freudian terminology, which often focuses on psychopathology rather than health. Many dream and life experiences can be interpreted from a spiritual or cultural perspective. Roman Catholic, Baptist, Mormon, Moslem, or Buddhist clients will tend to have dreams that relate to their particular spiritual tradition. We do not just incorporate individual interpretations of the world; we also make family, spiritual, and cultural experience part of our being.

Imagine that your Jewish client is facing a major difficulty in the family and dreams of Massada, a mountain in Israel where the Jews established a heroic defense. A typical individualistic interpretation might be that the dream represents some sort of defense mechanism and the individual is defending himself from some underlying issue, possibly sexual in nature. A multicultural interpretation might make the connection that the client is drawing on the natural bravery and selflessness of his culture. Further exploration may reveal that both the individual and the cultural interpretation provide deeper understanding of the dream and/or issue. If so, the cultural metaphor may provide a way of working with the underlying concern.

The Senoi of Central Malaysia believe that dreams provide the dreamer with positive ideas for more effective living (Stewart, 1951). The Senoi believe that dreams are real and are most helpful when viewed as providing clues that dreamers can use to help themselves or others. For example, a frightening dream of falling may be viewed by the Senoi as "flying," and the dreamer may be told, "Next time you dream, imagine you are flying. Note the joyous feeling and see where you go." The dreamer often incorporates this positive suggestion and develops a way to be in control while dreaming. Senoi dreamwork provides an important contrast to traditional psychotherapy. Instead of concerns being "problems," they are reinterpreted by the Senoi as part of the "solution." This idea is related to the point made earlier in this chapter that all behavior, thoughts, and feelings have a purpose and tell clients something about themselves.

Using Regression Techniques to Reexperience Past Trauma

Regression occurs when you help clients return to old negative experiences, particularly to images of trauma, and encourage them to "relive" the event by describing to you what they saw, heard, and felt at that time. Regression theory holds that talking about an old difficulty that may have been long repressed in unconscious memory in the safety of the therapeutic setting can help clients "work through" their traumas.

Survivors of trauma—be they children of alcoholic or abusive families, rape survivors, or Vietnam veterans—have all benefited from going back to old traumas and talking about these issues with an understanding and supportive counselor. In regression, clients can examine issues at varying cognitive-developmental levels. The most powerful reexperiencing of trauma is at the sensorimotor level, particularly when the therapist asks the client to envision images connected with the event. Concrete description of specific events also can be powerful, but often is less so. Formal operational and dialectic/systemic reflection on the experience helps put the situation in perspective.

Needless to say, regression work, particularly the intense reexperiencing at the sensorimotor level, should be done with care. It would obviously be unwise to encourage a rape survivor to go back and relive the experience if she was not ready to do so. A basic rule of psychodynamic therapy is *to not push clients further or faster than they want to go.* Regression techniques should only be used when the client is ready; otherwise there is the danger of pushing the client more deeply into depression or even triggering a psychotic break.

In the ACOA example discussed above, the free association techniques uncover the forgotten physical trauma. Through the use of imagery and the here-and-now emphasis—What are you seeing? Feeling? Hearing?—the ACOA client brings the repressed memories and feelings to awareness at the sensorimotor level. Through discussing thoughts and feelings, the trauma can gradually be brought into focus and made part of conscious experience. However, before you engage in regression and reliving, it is important to have a solid relationship and to understand the issues the client faces.

Concrete Storytelling and Therapist Listening Skills

People who have gone to the hospital for a major operation or who have been in a car accident are often eager to tell their stories in considerable concrete detail, outline how they felt, and relate the meaning of the experience for them. They also want to tell their stories several times. People who have gone through traumas need to tell the concretes and specifics of their stories. If they are not allowed to tell their stories soon after the events have occurred, the memories can become repressed and "pop up" in later life through flashbacks, nightmares, or, more likely, behavior and thoughts in their relationships with significant others. For example, the ACOA client discussed earlier repeated the past relationship with his mother with his wife. Psychodynamic theory holds that these *repetition compulsions* will repeat again and again until they are brought to consciousness and worked through.

With many clients who have experienced trauma, concrete discussion and formal reflection on the experience will be safer and wiser than direct and powerful age regression techniques. As understanding and trust are developed, the client may later decide to explore the more powerful aspects of regression and reexperiencing with you. Empathy and the basic listening sequence are particularly important in working with survivors of trauma. You need to listen to the client's story carefully—perhaps several times over several interviews—before you encourage regression and reliving of the old experience. Regression is different than storytelling in that the story is not talked about but rather lived. This reliving occurs in a new and safe context with the therapist.

Putting the Trauma in Perspective

Another alternative for working through past trauma is group therapy. In the supportive and understanding environment of people who have suffered similar traumas, the client can hear from and talk with others. Out of such experiences, clients often discover systemic issues underlying their feelings around the trauma. Adult children of alcoholics and incest survivors may discover how their family system related to and now relates to their current issues. Rape survivors may find themselves working to change a culture that in many ways promotes rape. War veterans may work to help others suffering from similar issues. These adjuncts to traditional one-on-one therapy can be as important and even more important than regression techniques in individual therapy.

Through one-on-one therapy and group work, the trauma survivor's reaction and behavior in the situation can be *normalized.* Many clients are troubled by their behavior in the traumatic situation. Incest survivors, for example, may feel that they somehow "caused" the sexual abuse. A common reaction during rape is for women to depersonalize the situation by "floating out of their bodies." Vietnam veterans may feel that they "chickened out" during a time of particularly fierce combat. Trauma survivors tend to feel that they are alone in their reactions. In group therapy, they can find personal validation and support for what they have done.

The word *survivor,* rather than *victim,* is used when discussing varying types of trauma. This usage frames individuals not as passive objects but rather as having the personal strength to take action on their own behalf. A general rule of trauma work, which also applies to regression techniques, is that *whatever the client did or experienced was what the individual needed to do to survive.* This positive reframe, or interpretation, normalizes what clients often think was abnormal behavior.

Freud's Damaging Error

Freud's early writings give considerable attention to the early abusive experiences of his clients; he discovered that many of his clients had been sexually, emotionally, or physically abused as children. His writings even include the following statement: "Unfortunately, my own father was one of these perverts and is responsible for the hysteria of my brother" (Masson, 1985, pp. 230–31).

Shortly after the death of of his father, Freud moved away from acknowledging the fact of child abuse and instituted his "fantasy theory" in its place. In the fantasy theory, which has been so highly influential in this century, the child is believed to have imagined the abuse. This idea that child abuse is the child's fantasy remains predominant in much of today's psychoanalytic practice. Society somehow feels more comfortable blaming the child rather than acknowledging the reality of child abuse and child assault.

It could be argued that Freud almost single-handedly set back the cause of child rights at least a century when he abandoned his early stance on the reality and dangers of child abuse. McGrath (1986) provides the specifics of this important piece of psychodynamic history. Other important sources are Freud's letters to Fliess on this topic (Masson, 1985) and Malcolm's (1985) fascinating account *In the Freud Archives.*

Alice Miller (1981, 1984) also attacks basic psychoanalytic theory, but from another perspective. She presents evidence that many of Freud's interpretations were designed to avoid the truth rather than to face up to realities that might negate his basic theoretical points. For example, she points out that the famous case of the Wolf Man is discussed with no real attention to the sexual abuse the Wolf Man experienced as a child. Obholzer (1982) interviewed the Wolf Man, and from her account it is apparent that Freud distorted the truth and that treatment was a failure. Fortunately, Miller, Bowlby, Taub-Bynum, and others have worked toward redressing this particular error of Freud's. Nonetheless, there are still many practicing therapists who remain unaware of weaknesses in Freud's conceptions and prefer to work within the fantasy theory.

Analysis of Resistance

Another important theoretical and methodological issue in psychodynamic approaches is analysis of resistance. Resistance includes everything in the words and behaviors of the client that prevents access to unconscious material. The temptation in many approaches to helping is to avoid areas of resistance and find other routes toward client verbalization. The effective psychodynamic counselor or therapist, by contrast, often pays prime attention to areas of resistance. In the process of counseling clients often fail to hear important statements from the counselor. The client may say "What?" and look puzzled. Alternatively, the client may hear the therapist but forget what was said within a minute or two or between interviews. Such behavior can indicate an area of resistance. Other indicators of resistance can be when the client blocks while trying to say something, leaves out a key part of a dream, comes late to an interview, or refuses to free associate. Resistance shows up in many ways as the client unconsciously tries to sabotage the treatment process.

The "Freudian slip," in which the client substitutes one word for another or mixes two words together, often provides a clue as to underlying issues and resistance. For example, a client reported that he had recently visited his mother-in-law, with the goal of tape recording her comments on family history, and had told her "I want to record you for mortality." The implications of such slips go beyond being amusing and can offer useful access to unconscious functioning.

The German word Freud used for resistance is better translated as a rheostat that controls the amount of electricity available. Thus, Freud was telling us that resistance is the amount of unconscious psychic energy the client can allow out at a particular time. Unfortunately, the common English definition of resistance is most often thought of as "working against" something, in this case the therapist. This is a serious misconception, as the client is making an effort to communicate with, not to work against, the counselor. It is helpful to view resistance as an opportunity for a deeper understanding. The task of the psychodynamic counselor is to decide whether or not to confront resistance immediately or at a later point. The resistance often represents a major incongruency or discrepancy in the client or in the relationship between the counselor and client. One approach to analyzing resistance is to label or interpret the resistance and then encourage the client to free associate to the facts and feelings associated with the resistance. The exercises in Practice Exercise 8.2 provide some specifics for working with client resistance positively.

Analysis of Transference and Countertransference

Transference refers to feelings and thoughts clients have toward the counselor. Clients do not have a clear picture of the nature of the helper due, in large part, to the neutrality and objectivity of the counselor. Clients will thus likely project an imagined image on the therapist, literally transferring feelings and thoughts they have toward other people onto the therapist. These data provide the therapist with here-and-now information on the life experience of clients. For example, a client may relate to the therapist as a parental figure, revealing that the client is struggling with family-of-origin issues.

The techniques for coping with a transference situation are similar to those for dealing with resistance. The transference is identified and labeled, and free association techniques are used to clarify meaning. Premature and too direct an examination of transference feelings can confuse and trouble the client, so analysis of transference is usually done in the middle or later stages of therapy. Virtually all counselors and therapists, regardless of their theoretical orientation, observe transference in their clients' comments. However, differing theories vary widely in their use of analysis of transference, and some ignore this area completely.

A nontraditional but perhaps more multiculturally relevant approach is to consider transference through family-of-origin work. Many of the examples in this chapter focus on how clients transfer learnings from their families to their daily lives through personality style and/or defense mechanisms. Clients often feel more comfortable talking about how they experienced life and learned modes of behavior in their families. Thus, analysis of transference often works more smoothly if discussed from a family frame of reference (e.g., Taub-Bynum, 1984).

Countertransference, defined broadly, consists of feelings and thoughts the therapist has toward the client. Countertransference often results in counselor "blind spots" and can be destructive and disruptive to the interview process. Feelings the counselor has toward the client must be isolated, identified, and worked through. A major portion of training in psychoanalytic work is devoted to a form of counselor therapy in which the counselor shares feelings, attitudes, and fantasies held toward the client with a psychodynamically trained supervisor. The supervisor also analyzes countertransference feelings through use of free association and the various concepts and methods of psychodynamic counseling.

Supervision for the psychodynamic therapist is very much like that of the counselor-client interview. Strong countertransference feelings and feelings of resistance toward the client may preclude counselors working with some clients until personal counseling or therapy is undertaken. Awareness of feelings toward the client and ability to cope with these feelings are essential to any therapist. Supervision when dealing with complex issues of tranference and countertransference is particularly important for any professional, beginning or advanced.

Projective Identification

One of the most important and difficult psychodynamic concepts is that of projective identification (Klein, 1975; Segal, 1986). Projective identification carries the concepts of transference and countertransference to a new level of complexity and conceptual power. The formal definition of projective identification provided by Laplanche and Pontalis (1973, p. 356) follows:

> [A] term introduced by Melanie Klein: a mechanism revealed in phantasies in which the subject inserts [the] self—in whole or in part—into the object in order to harm, possess or control it. . . .
>   Projective identification may thus be considered as a mode of *projection* . . . the ejection into the outside world of something subject refuses in [her- or] himself—the projection of what is bad.

In counseling and therapy, it is important to remember that all of us project our unconscious wishes onto others. We see in others parts of ourselves we want to deny or of which we are unaware. We attribute qualities of ourselves to others, and we identify in them parts of ourselves. This projective identification, whether it is on our part or the client's part, can interfere with and derail the therapeutic process.

The Family and Projective Identification

It is crucial for you as a therapist to watch for projective identification not only in your clients but in yourself. The patterns learned in the family of origin lead to projective identification; therefore, examining the psychodynamics of this family is important. For example, you may be the child of an alcoholic or abusive parent. In your family of origin, you learned at an unconscious level that the way for you to survive was to watch out for danger, keep quiet, and, above all, be a peacemaker in the family. Other children of alcoholics may take different roles. For example, some act out and later become alcoholics themselves; others become passive, quiet, and withdrawn; others become psychically numbed and depressed. Varying patterns exist in alcoholic families. In your case, however, given that your experience of abuse led you to become a peacemaker, you will be likely to enact this style in a variety of situations in later life.

But underlying the peacemaker role is unconscious rage, hurt, and frustration over never having been allowed to be one's real self as a child. The peacemaker role may be termed a false self. The angry, frustrated parts of the child are denied in the unconscious and are split off from awareness. Inside many "good children" are considerable feelings of hurt and rage.

Projective Identification in the Therapeutic Session

Projective identification occurs in your relationships when you produce in others your own unacknowledged feelings. With the best of intentions and behavior, you may project your unconscious hurt or anger onto your spouse, lover, or child, who will enact your feelings for you. These others actually embody what is occurring inside you. It is well known in family systems theory that certain family members enact certain behaviors and feelings for the entire family. The concept of projective identification is closely related to this systemic view.

Continuing the above example, the peacemaker role "works" and helps you make it through high school and college. In your relationships, you tend to continue the peacemaking function you learned in your early family situation, but the underlying rage and hurt are still there in your unconscious.

Like many who learn the peacemaker role, you are drawn to the helping professions and become a therapist. Despite your desire to make peace and help clients live and work in harmony, you find yourself working with very angry, hostile, difficult clients. But, having learned how to deal with such difficult people in your family of origin, you are very skilled in calming and managing these clients. Owing to your success with these clients, you receive rewards from your profession and are acknowledged as a skilled therapist. You enjoy this adulation but at times worry that some of your clients may be acting out your own unconscious rage by abusing their spouses. You have had three completed suicides among your clients over the past ten years, and this concerns you and ultimately leads you to question your "success" as a therapist.

This scenario reminds us that our unconscious desires can become the very life of our clients. We as therapists can remain "good" while our clients are "bad." Clients enact those split-off parts of ourselves of which we are unaware.

Of course, projective identification can also work from the client to the therapist. The borderline client is particularly masterful at the art of projective identification—placing their feelings of love and/or rage in counselors and therapeutic staff. These clients are sometimes so effective that they can split psychiatric staffs into warring groups of "good" and "bad" team members. When the developmental history of the borderline client is examined, it becomes clear that their skills of projective identification were learned as survival techniques in their families of origin.

Melanie Klein and Projective Identification

Klein's concept of projective identification is not always popular or accepted in the field. Esman (1985, pp. 303–4) presents a representative critique of Klein's thinking:

> Her theories of development and psychopathology are characterized by incredible complexity [and] idiosyncratic language. . . . Further, her work rests on certain basic assumptions, that to say the very least, are not fully shared by those who work outside

her theoretical framework—which means virtually all other psychoanalytic and non-analytic students of child development.

When one encounters a critique of such vehemence, one senses that perhaps Klein has been able to project some of her own unconscious rage into the strong reactions of others—and this, without their awareness.

You and Projective Identification

Assuming that the concept of projective identification has meaning to you, what can you do about it and its obvious dangers? First, you need to cultivate an awareness of the concept and the potential for your desires and wishes for the client becoming the client's wishes and behavior. Most of us do not consciously want clients to act out our own life scripts. Second, therapy for you as the therapist or counselor may help you understand how your own life history relates to your work with clients. Third, supervision and consultation with colleagues can help you understand your motivation and what is going on in the helping process, but you must be open to some surprise discoveries about yourself.

Finally—and this is not as difficult and mystical as it sounds—notice your body. When borderline or other problematic clients seem difficult or you find yourself particularly entranced or attracted by a client, focus on your felt body sense. Where do you have a feeling? What are you feeling? Then free associate back to your own current and past situations. Very likely there is something occurring in the interview that relates to something in you and your developmental past. Such self-awareness can free you for more intentional responding.

Treating the Family/Multicultural Unconscious

All of the above constructs can be adapted and applied to Bruce Taub-Bynum's ideas of the family unconscious. For example, instead of making interpretations from an individual basis, the therapist can interpret the client's behavior from a gender, family, or multicultural frame. The following are examples of each frame for a dependent client:

Gender interpretation (to European-American female client): Your dependency on others seems to make a lot of sense. Perhaps we can start by valuing a woman's ability to care and be in relationship, and you have this ability. Now, what would seem an appropriate balance of your ability to care and of being dependent in the relationship you're in now?

Family interpretation (male or female from most cultural backgrounds): Dependent behavior is learned in the family of origin. Dependency there worked well for you to survive, but now it isn't working in your new relationships.

Multicultural interpretation (to Japanese student in North America from abroad): As I listen to you, you say you find it lonely in the individualistic culture of Canada. It must be painful for you. Many Japanese find our society troublesome. It is indeed difficult for a person from a more interdependent culture to be comfortable here. There are some ways I can help you cope with this different type of culture.

Needless to say, each interpretation must be sensitively used and timed to the needs, interests, and backgrounds of different clients. The microskill of focus is again important in this type of interaction. Rather than focusing on the individual person, the attempt in gender, family, and multiculturally oriented responding is to help clients see themselves in context. Similarly, dream analysis, transferential, and projective identification issues can be made more relevant to gender, family, and multicultural practice by adding a different focus.

Limitations and Practical Implications of Psychodynamic Methods

One of the major problems of the psychodynamic approach to counseling has been that amateurs who know a little about the concepts apply them freely to friends and clients with no real understanding of the meaning and force of these techniques.

Interpretation and Wild Analysis

Laplanche and Pontalis (1973), who have made a careful study of the derivation and meaning of key psychoanalytic concepts, discuss this idea of "wild" analysis:

> Broadly understood, this expression refers to the procedure of amateur or inexperienced "analysts" who attempt to interpret symptoms, dreams, utterances, actions, etc. on the basis of psychoanalytic notions which they have as often as not misunderstood. In a more technical sense, an interpretation is deemed "wild" if a specific analytic situation is misapprehended in its current dynamics and its particularity, and especially if the repressed content is simply imparted to the client with no heed paid to the resistances and to the transference.

All of gender, family, and multicultural interpretations of the preceding section could be helpful, or they could be wild analysis. As you move your psychodynamic practice past traditional individualistic approaches, there is a danger that you may miss the unique individual before you. The reverse is also true: failing to consider possible multicultural interpretations when they are appropriate also may make you guilty of wild analysis. Considering Freud's mishandling of the critical issue of child abuse and child assault, perhaps it is the traditional Freudian interpretations still prominent in much of today's therapeutic practice that truly represent wild analysis.

The Importance of Transferential Issues

The concept of transference in the therapeutic relationship represents one of the central contributions of psychodynamic theory to the field of professional helping. It is highly likely your clients will transfer their past history of interpersonal relationships into the interview. You may or may not choose to work on these issues, but awareness of transferential patterns is essential regardless of your theoretical orientation.

The repetition of your own life patterns and feelings in relationship to the client—or countertransference—is equally possible. The complex issues of transference and countertransference can be dealt with best through supervision and consultation with colleagues and superiors and by cultivating an awareness of clients' transference and your own countertransference.

Uses and Limits

The psychodynamic approach can be very useful for understanding clients and *why* they behave as they do. At the same time, psychodynamic therapists may spend so much time on endless analysis of behavior that they never move toward change. Thus, it is sometimes recommended that psychodynamic theory be considered primarily as a useful frame of reference for conceptualizing clients and for helping clients think about themselves in new and more positive ways. However, this approach can be even more effective if coordinated with other theories, particularly cognitive-behavioral interventions, so that behavioral as well as intellectual change is facilitated.

The therapist is often established in the psychodynamic system as the center of power. Modern psychodynamic and feminist psychodynamic frames of reference are increasingly seeking ways to share information and data on a more egalitarian basis. The positive use of family, gender, spiritual, and cultural symbols can be helpful in achieving this goal.

Going beyond all theories, however, is what you as a person bring to the therapeutic relationship. Research Exhibit 8.1 presents provocative information suggesting that the characteristics the counselor or therapist brings to therapy are more important than the therapeutic approach.

Research Exhibit 8.1

The Vanderbilt Psychotherapy Studies: How Personal Characteristics Affect the Therapy Process

Hans Strupp (1993), working primarily from a psychodynamic frame, examined behaviors and thoughts of therapists of varying persuasions for forty years. As he examined therapist responses to various patients, he first noted in the late 1950s that "therapists who expressed a positive attitude toward the patient tended to give the patient a more favorable prognosis, assigned a more benign diagnostic label, and the tone of their communication was more empathic" (p. 431). In short, who you are and how you act as a person may be more important than your theory of choice. This initial finding has been elaborated in the years since, with the following additional findings:

1. Untrained college professors noted for their warmth were as effective as highly trained professionals (Strupp & Hadley, 1979). Strupp (1993) points out that this study did not have sufficient time for the effect of training to be evident, but the results suggest that the "working alliance" between client and therapist is a most essential dimension in the helping relationship.

2. Professional and lay therapists did poorly with clients who entered therapy with negative attitudes. Moreover, therapists unconsciously seemed to blame such clients in subtle ways. However, experienced therapists were demonstrated to develop significant gains with patients who were motivated for change. Again, the importance of a positive working alliance is apparent.

3. The above findings led Strupp and Binder (1984) to focus on the thera-

peutic relationship in its own right. They found that the nature of the working alliance and dealing deftly with resistance and other complicated dynamic issues are important. The Vanderbilt Psychotherapy Study II examined "manualized" treatment for time-limited psychodynamic therapy in which specific suggestions for the therapeutic process and how to work through difficult issues were defined precisely.

4. In an evaluation of the Vanderbilt study, Henry and others (1993) found that therapists adhered to the specifics of the manual and that deterioration in interpersonal relationships occurred. In effect, being very specific as to treatment procedures seemed to get in the way of the most effective therapeutic alliance.

From these data it seems clear that relationship remains central, whether one works psychodynamically, cognitive-behaviorally, humanistically, or from a multicultural frame of reference. Moreover, the characteristics that the therapist and client bring to the session are extremely important. Although specific exercises and techniques for conducting interviews presented in this or any other text can be very useful, it seems essential that you consider your own attitude and motivation for being a professional helper.

REFERENCES

ESMAN, A. (1985). Kleinian theory revisited. *Contemporary Psychology, 30,* 303–4.

FREUD, S. (1966). *A general introduction to psychoanalysis.* New York: Norton. (Original work published 1920)

HENRY, W., STRUPP, H. H., BUTLER, S., SCHACHT, T., & BINDER, J. (1993). Effects of training in time-limited dynamic therapy: Changes in therapist behavior. *Journal of Consulting and Clinical Psychology, 63,* 434–40.

KLEIN, M. (1975). *Envy and gratitude and other works, 1946/1963.* London: Hogarth.

LAPLANCHE, J., & PONTALIS, J. (1973). *The language of psychoanalysis.* New York: Norton.

MCGRATH, W. (1986). *Freud's discovery of psychoanalysis: The politics of hysteria.* Ithaca, NY: Cornell University Press.

MALCOLM, J. (1985). *In the Freud archives.* New York: Vintage.

MASSON, J. (ED.). (1985). *The complete letters of Sigmund Freud to Wilhelm Fliess: 1887–1904.* Cambridge, MA: Harvard University Press.

MILLER, A. (1981). *The drama of the gifted child.* New York: Basic Books.

MILLER, A. (1984). *Thou shalt not be aware.* New York: Signet.

OBHOLZER, K. (1982). *The wolf-man: Sixty years later: Conversations with Freud's controversial patient.* New York: Continuum.

PONTEROTTO, J., & CASAS, M. (1991). *Handbook of racial/ethnic minority counseling research.* Springfield, IL: Thomas.

SEGAL, H. (1986). *The work of Hanna Segal: A Kleinian approach to clinical practice.* London: Free Association Books.

STEWART, K. (1951). Dream theory in Malaya, *Complex, 6,* 21–34.

STRUPP, H. H. (1993). The Vanderbilt psychotherapy studies: Synopsis. *Journal of Consulting and Clinical Psychology, 61,* 431–33.

STRUPP, H. H., & BINDER, J. L. (1984). *Psychotherapy in a new key.* New York: Basic Books.

STRUPP, H. H., & HADLEY, S. W. (1979). Specific versus nonspecific factors in psychotherapy: A controlled study of outcome. *Archives of General Psychiatry, 36,* 1125–36.

SUE, D., AND SUE, D. (1990). *Counseling the culturally different* (2nd ed.). New York: Wiley.

TAUB-BYNUM, E. B. (1980). The use of dreams in family therapy. *Psychotherapy: Theory, Research, and Practice. 17,* 227–31.

TAUB-BYNUM, E. B. (1984). *The family unconscious.* Wheaton, IL: Quest.

TAUB-BYNUM, E. B. (1992). *Family dreams: The intricate web.* Ithaca, NY: Haworth Press.

Cognitive-Behavioral Therapy and Counseling I: Behavioral Foundations

CHAPTER GOALS

This chapter seeks to:

1. Describe the evolving worldview of CBT, which has moved from an emphasis on observable behavior and action to include the inner world of cognitions.

2. Point out some multicultural implications of CBT and its practice.

3. Present central constructs of CBT, such as applied behavioral analysis, that are basic to both behavioral and cognitive interventions.

4. Present key behavioral techniques, including relaxation training, systematic desensitization, social skills training, assertiveness training, and relapse prevention.

5. Enable you, through practice exercises, to conduct or engage in
   - Applied behavioral analysis, a foundational skill for behavioral counseling and therapy
   - Relaxation training
   - Systematic densensitization and the construction of an anxiety hierarchy
   - Elementary social skills training
   - Assertiveness training
   - Relapse prevention
   - Your own stress management program

The Cognitive-Behavioral Frame of Reference

Cognitive-behavioral therapy and counseling (CBT) is currently the "treatment of choice" for a wide array of client problems and concerns and is especially important in today's managed care. Regardless of your theory of choice, the well-researched and effective skills and strategies of CBT will be a required part of your practice at some point in your career. CBT is centrally concerned with concrete change and empowerment of clients—giving clients control over their own actions and destiny.

Traditionally, counseling and therapy texts have separated behavioral and cognitive theory and methods. During the past two decades, however, those interested in behavioral change have developed a more cognitive orientation. Simultaneously, the more cognitive theorists have integrated behavioral techniques as part of a broader treatment series. The conceptions of the integrative cognitive-behavioral theorist Donald Meichenbaum will be discussed in this chapter; the more cognitively oriented theorists Albert Ellis, Aaron Beck, William Glasser, and Arnold Lazarus will be featured in the following chapter. All five use many of the techniques and ideas discussed in both chapters. Finally, the multicultural critiques and analyses of Cheek (1976) and Kantrowitz and Ballou (1992) provide CBT with some important additional challenges.

The Power of Reinforcement: A Case Example

Historically, behavioral therapy is rooted in the work of the behaviorists John Watson, Ivan Pavlov, and B. F. Skinner. In Skinner's view, our behavior is determined by what happens to us as a result of our behavior. If we are reinforced for what we do, then likely we will continue to engage in that behavior. If we are ignored or punished, the behavior is likely to cease. In its purest form, behavioral therapy seeks to help control the consequences of our behavior, thus leading us to change our actions.

Consider the following true scenario, as outlined in Ivey and Hinkle (1968), and its implications:

The cast: (a) A professor noted for the quality of his knowledge of subject matter. He understands that he will make a presentation and be video-recorded, but is unaware of the purpose of the session. (b) Six students trained in "attending behavior" and who know "how to pay attention" to the professor.

Outline of plot: The students are told to engage in "typical" classroom behavior for the first portion of the lecture. Then at a signal, they are to "attend" to the professor physically through eye contact and manifestations of physical interest. At another signal, they are to return to typical student nonattending behavior.

The question: What happens to the professor? And the students?

The play in synopsis form: The professor enters the room carrying his notes. He looks up at the T.V. camera peering into the room, then at his notes. He does not look at the assembled students. There is a 30-second pause and he begins. The lecture is heavily laden with references to "exciting" research and clearly shows extensive preparation. Occasionally, the professor looks up from his notes and observes the students engaging in typical classroom behavior of notetaking. He then returns to his paper and continues on. For ten minutes his hands remain motionless and do not rise above the seminar table.

The signal comes and the students are alerted. They are now focusing all attention on the professor. He, however, is deeply in his notes and does not look up for 30 seconds. When he does, it is only briefly, but he apparently notes a student attending and gazing at him. Shortly he looks up again briefly at the same student and is again reinforced. Again, he looks up for a longer time and sees the student following him closely. He next raises his head and looks around to the rest of the class. They too are attending to him. Immediately, he becomes animated, he gestures for the first time. His verbal rate increases, his physical involvement through gestures and other characteristics is obvious. The students raise a few questions and the professor continues his discussion without notes. The quality of his knowledge of the material is still apparent as the flow of content is constant, but with less reference to specific research. However, a new classroom scene emerges. He is involved and the students are involved.

At another signal, the students stop attending and return to their notepads. The professor continues his talk uninterrupted. He does not stop; but he noticeably slows down. He looks to the students for further support and reinforcement which is not forthcoming. His verbalization slows down further. Resignedly, he returns to his notes and continues through the rest of his lecture once again resting his presentation on others' knowledge instead of his own.

The students comment later that it was difficult to stop attending and return to typical student behavior as they had found the material most stimulating. The students state they had enjoyed his presentation while they had attended and felt they had deserted the professor who needed them as they needed and wanted him.

This is nothing but a simple exercise in what psychologists call the "Greenspoon Effect," after Dr. Joel Greenspoon of Temple Buell College. Psychology classes have for years reinforced their professors by alternately smiling and ignoring the professor. Typically, the students have used this as a game to get a professor to stand in a certain place in the classroom or perhaps get [her or] him walking back and forth in front of the class much like one of B. F. Skinner's pigeons. Students have not typically reinforced or rewarded a professor by attending to the presentation. (p. 4)

The power of such shaping techniques and positive reinforcement can never be forgotten. If you work *with* your clients, these concepts can be invaluable. Innumerable concepts and programs for modifying the behavior of children, prisoners, couples, athletes, overeaters, smokers, alcoholics, drug addicts, and many others have been based on the elementary ideas of positive reinforcement and reward.

The above description is *not* representative of cognitive-behavioral psychology today. After considerable theorizing, political struggle and infighting, research, and careful evaluation of clinical results, behavioral counseling and therapy now focus on personal choice and the value of collaboration. Furthermore, with the evolution of what is now termed *cognitive-behavioral therapy and counseling* (CBT), the role of cognition and thought (internal speech) has become important in the practice of most behavioral clinicians. Emotion has gained a new center stage, and CBT has become a major force in counseling and psychotherapy.

The Evolving Cognitive-Behavioral Worldview

Behavioral psychology is related to the concept of modernity, which is a philosophic approach that emphasizes the impact of science. Modernity and behavioral psychology are rooted in the ideal of progress—the faith that science can solve human problems—and in a devaluation of the past (Woolfolk & Richardson, 1984). The worldview of behaviorism may be described as antithetical to the psychodynamic approaches, which emphasize the idea that history drives and directs the present.

Behavioral psychology developed primarily in the United States and is very typically North American in that it is scientific, forward-moving, optimistic, and concerned with "what works." The worldview presented by B. F. Skinner suggests that we humans can have the closest approximation to "freedom" through recognizing that we can control and shape behavior in our culture and our families if we choose. We can choose what behavior to reinforce. The question, of course, is, Who decides?

Albert Bandura, one of the most prominent behavioral psychologists, helped move the field to an evolving "behavioral humanism" and emphasizes that the client should be deeply involved in the choice and direction of treatment. Behavioral psychology now emphasizes individual rights and collaboration in the treatment process. Bandura's work on self-efficacy (1982, 1989), a concept very similar to intentionality, stresses that individuals grow best when they feel they are in control of their own destiny.

In the classical Skinnerian view, internal mental processes and cognitions are given little attention; the focus has been instead on direct, observable behavior. Bandura's work was key in the shift to a more cognitive orientation. Cheek (1976) presents an important early statement of the cognitive-behavioral framework, and Meichenbaum (1991) is perhaps most prominent in solidifying what has become a major change in behavioral psychology.

Meichenbaum (1991) emphasizes person-environment interaction. He believes behavior to be reciprocally influenced by thoughts, feelings, physiological processes, and the consequences of behavior. This approach may be contrasted with the behavioral tradition, which placed the locus of control in the external environment. Clients assume a much more important role in this newer tradition.

> *CBT does not hold that there is "one reality,"* nor that the task for the therapist is to educate or correct clients' misperceptions (errors in thinking, irrational thoughts). Rather in the tradition of the Kurosawa movie, *Rashomon, CBT holds that there are "multiple realities."* The collaborative task for clients and CB therapists is to help clients appreciate how they create such realities. (p. 4)

The idea of multiple realities, of course, brings us back to the Escher print of Chapter 1. Changing the way we view that print brings a new meaning. Meichenbaum reminds us clearly that one of the important tasks of psychotherapy and counseling is helping clients find new perspectives on their situations. The idea of helping clients see their worlds from new frames of reference is becoming an increasingly central idea to all theoretical approaches to the field.

The Multicultural Approach and Cognitive-Behavioral Issues

Kantrowitz and Ballou (1992) applaud the shift of behavioral theory from a strict individual orientation to awareness of how the social context affects development. For example, if a woman has a behavioral difficulty, no longer can we find "fault" with the person. Therapists can more accurately see how environmental interactions affect behavior and internal thought.

However, Kantrowitz and Ballou point out that "individuals are expected to improve their adaptive capacities to meet the environmental conditions, which serve to reinforce the dominant (male) social standards" (p. 79). Assertiveness training is insufficient help for a woman suffering harassment in the workplace. Kantrowitz and Ballou state that action in the community and challenging standard social norms must be considered part of the therapeutic process.

CBT uses the word *cognitive* and as such gives primacy to thinking over feeling. How a person develops in the culture, particularly around issues of gender, is given relatively little attention in CBT theory. In short, despite its many positive qualities, Kantrowitz and Ballou maintain that CBT needs to be used with caution and sensitivity. Cheek's (1976) early work, discussed below, and Meichenbaum's newer construction of CBT are important in addressing these issues.

The origins of behavioral psychology obviously lie in concrete behavior, with minimal attention given to philosophic constructs. Thus, behavioral counseling and therapy has presented somewhat of a puzzle to those committed to a multicultural approach. Behavioral techniques tend to be successful in producing change and, owing to their clarity of direction and purpose, are often understandable and acceptable to minority populations.

At the same time, the behavioral approach can run into problems in multicultural situations over the issue of *control*. Early ventures in behavioral psychology often gave the therapist, counselor, or teacher almost complete power, and decisions sometimes focused on controlling clients rather than helping them control themselves. Behavioral psychology has been forced to overcome some of these early problems and the resultant fears among minority clients and their advocates.

Making CBT Culturally Relevant

Probably no one person has done more to make behavioral counseling and therapy multiculturally relevant than Donald Cheek, whose pioneering book *Assertive Black . . . Puzzled White* (1976) shows how to use assertiveness training in a culturally relevant way with African-American clients. In an imaginary introductory dialogue, Cheek speaks directly to some of the problems and issues underlying assertive behavior (comments from the authors in italics):

Me [*Cheek*]:   . . . A Black person has got to know when to be assertive and when to kiss ass.

[*Knowing is a cognitive act. Cheek focused not just on assertive* behavior, *but also on the* thinking, cognition, and emotion *that guide that behavior. Cheek's 1976 book can now be read as one of the clearest early presentations of cognitive-behavioral counseling.*]

You: But so does everybody.

Me: I mean it in terms of survival baby—survival—I mean whether or not the man even lets you live. Ain't that many Whites who got to worry about being killed because they want to be assertive enough to vote. . . . You see the authors on assertiveness have not sufficiently considered the social conditions in which Blacks live—and have lived. That blind spot in many ways alters or changes the manner that assertiveness is applied. . . . Current assertive authors have a great approach—it's an approach which can really aid Black folks, in fact they need it—but at the time these authors are unable to translate assertiveness training into the examples, language and caution that fit the realities of a Black lifestyle. (pp. 10–11).

Cheek calls his approach to assertiveness and behavioral methods *didactic assertiveness training.* He points out that assertive behavior varies between African-American and White cultures and that both groups need to understand the frame of reference of the other. He also points out that the passive nonviolent stance of the Black freedom movement represented a particularly powerful type of Black assertiveness. Assertiveness is not aggression; rather, it is culturally relevant behavior and thinking in which people or groups stand up for their rights.

Meichenbaum (1985) also speaks to multicultural issues:

Given the marked variability of reactions to stressful events, stress training programs should take into consideration cultural differences in determining adaptive coping mechanisms. Attempting to train clients to cope in ways that may violate cultural norms could actually aggravate stress-related problems. In some cultures, people tend to cope with stressors passively, by trying to endure them rather than viewing them as challenges and problems to be solved. Stress management training must reflect these cultural preferences. (p. 17)

As early as 1976 Cheek said much the same thing. A culturally relevant cognitive-behavioral practice requires that you be able to work with the way your clients think as well as the way they behave. Both Cheek and Meichenbaum stress the importance of full collaboration with the client in the conduct of the interview and treatment series.

Meichenbaum's Construction of Cognitive-Behavioral Therapy

Donald Meichenbaum (1985, 1991, 1994) has been one of the primary forces in moving behavioral therapy to its present cognitive-behavioral orientation. In Meichenbaum's view, CBT is concerned with helping the client define problems cognitively as well as behaviorally and with promoting cognitive, emotional, and behavioral change and preventing relapse.

Meichenbaum's conception of CBT summarizes many of the ideas of this book: Our task as therapists is to define the problem (and goals) with our clients; we then apply a wide variety of techniques to produce cognitive, emotional, and/or behavioral change. Finally, we must act if we are to ensure that behavioral change is to be maintained in the environment of the real world. Whether we commit ourselves to psychodynamic, behavioral, existential/humanistic, or some other orientation, meeting the criteria of this brief outline should be useful.

Meichenbaum's Central Constructs

Meichenbaum (1990, 1991) outlined ten central tenets of CBT. As you read the following, note how his modern view, based on traditions of behaviorism, expands our conception of the helping process. The following ten points are abstracted and paraphrased from Meichenbaum's presentation to the Evolution of Psychotherapy Conference in 1990 (published in 1991).

1. *Behavior is reciprocally determined by the "client's thoughts, feelings, physiological processes, and resultant consequences"* (p. 5). No one of these elements is necessarily most important. Thus, the therapist can intervene in the interacting system by focusing on thoughts or feelings, using medication, or changing consequences. Meichenbaum points out that with clients suffering from depression, the amount of criticism coming from the spouse (resultant consequences in the environment) is the most important predictor of relapse.

2. *Cognitions do not cause emotional difficulties; rather, they are part of a complex interactive process.* A particularly important part of the cognitive process is "metacognitions" in which clients learn to comment internally on their own thinking patterns and thereby act as their own mentor or therapist. "Moreover, CB therapists insure that clients take credit [for] behavioral changes they implement" (p. 6).

The cognitive structures we use to organize experience are our *personal schemas.* We learned these constructions from past experience, and changing ineffective schemas is an important part of therapy. For example, clients who are diagnosed with anxiety disorders have particular concerns about issues of loss of personal control and physical well-being. Depressed individuals are prone to be concerned about issues of loss, rejection, and abandonment. Individuals who are particularly concerned about the issues of equity, fairness, and justice are prone to have problems with anger.

Meichenbaum and Gilmore (1984) describe the case of a lawyer who was the only son of an immigrant father. The lawyer, who evidenced problems with controlling his anger and experienced accompanying hypertension, marital discord, and depression, reported that he would "never allow anyone to take advantage of

[me] like people who took advantage of [my] father. Got that!" The lawyer carried with him a personal schema concerning the issues of fairness and equity that colored the way he appraised events. This personal schema not only contributed to his short fuse and anger problem, but it also played a role in his altruistic behavior as reflected in his being active in such movements as Amnesty International, a world agency for protecting human rights.

The cognitive-behavioral therapist helped this lawyer appreciate how he viewed the world and the impact of his personal schema (issues about fairness) on how he appraised events. Over the course of therapy, the client came to see the price he paid, the toll taken, both interpersonally and intrapersonally, for his particular way of viewing the world and himself. Collaboratively with the therapist, the lawyer came to better understand and alter his way of thinking and to cope with personal concerns.

3. *"A central task for the CB therapist is to help clients come to understand how they* construct and construe reality" (p. 7). In this statement Kelly's (1955) personal construct theory has been joined with the behavioral tradition. Meichenbaum stresses that clients and counselors can work collaboratively to explore cognitions and desired changes.

4. *"CBT takes issue with those psychotherapeutic approaches that adopt a rationalist or objectivist position"* (p. 8). This is an important and radical position that challenges the concepts of Ellis (Chapter 10). Meichenbaum's approach is more existential-humanistic in nature and is directed toward how clients subjectively experience the world. He stresses the importance of reflecting key words and phrases of clients and of mirroring their feelings back to them "in an inquiring tone" (the microskills of encouraging and reflection of feeling). By mirroring, Meichenbaum seeks to help clients understand how they have constructed reality.

5. *"A critical feature of CBT is the emphasis on* collaboration *and on the* discovery *processes"* (p. 8). Meichenbaum talks about the importance of having clients make their own discoveries. He recommends using a variety of behavioral techniques, such as those presented in this chapter, to facilitate the discovery process.

6. *Relapse prevention is a central dimension of CBT.* Marlatt and Gordon's (1985) model has become central to the thinking of many different approaches to counseling and therapy. Unless we specifically help clients generalize, the effects of counseling will wear away.

7. *"CBT holds that the* relationship *that develops between the client and the therapist is critical to the change process"* (p. 10). Empathy and listening skills (Chapters 2 and 3) are critical as well as the important relationship dimensions stressed by Rogers (Chapter 11).

8. *"Emotions play a critical role in CBT "* (p. 11). Much like psychodynamic theory, Meichenbaum's view of CBT suggests that clients bring into the therapy session the emotional experiences they have had with others. Past life experiences

are seen as affecting how clients react with you in the session, and emotions are the route toward understanding the nature of the relationship.

9. *"CBT therapists are now recognizing the benefits of conducting CBT with couples and families"* (p. 12). In this sense, CBT is moving toward the network treatment constructions of Attneave (see Chapter 6).

10. *CBT can be extended beyond the clinic setting for both prevention and treatment.* Meichenbaum points out that CBT techniques have been used in probation offices, schools, hospitals, the military, and infant home visitations. It is becoming clearer that psychoeducational work is an important part of preventing drug and alcohol abuse and that it can be a useful part of any treatment program.

In summary, it can be seen that cognitive-behavioral therapy and counseling build on a behavioral foundation and provide an integrating framework for many differing and seemingly oppositional forms of therapy and counseling. Research Exhibit 9.1 presents an example of the application of cognitive-behavioral techniques in the treatment of agoraphobia.

Research Exhibit 9.1

Cognitive-Behavioral Assessment and Treatment of Agoraphobia

Behavioral and cognitive-behavioral techniques are by far the most extensively and carefully researched in the field of counseling and therapy. This exhibit focuses on one area of research—agoraphobia. Agoraphobia is described in DSM-IV (American Psychiatric Association, 1994) as follows:

> A marked fear of being alone, or being in public places from which escape might be difficult or help not available in case of sudden incapacitation. Normal activities are increasingly constricted as the fears or avoidance behavior dominate the individual's life. The most common situations avoided involve being in crowds, such as on a busy street or in crowded stores, or being in tunnels, on bridges, on elevators, or on public transportation. Often these in-

dividuals insist that a family member or friend accompany them whenever they leave home. (p. 227)

The following comments illustrate how the cognitive-behavioral tradition has integrated epidemiological research, research on assessment, and research on treatment effectiveness. This comprehensive approach is common to research reviews on cognitive-behavioral methods and is probably one of the main reasons for its gradual gain in popularity in the field.

Incidence and Related Problems

Agoraphobia is an anxiety disorder and may occur with or without panic disorder.

Females predominate over males by a ratio of four to one (Michelson, 1987; Dionne, 1990). It is important to look for related depression and panic attacks when agoraphobia appears, particularly so as up to 20 percent of those with panic attacks may have attempted suicide at some point in their lives (Dionne, 1990). Generally, the onset of the disorder is seen in the mid-twenties, but child school phobics are now being recognized as an early form of agoraphobia. In addition, there is some evidence of family transmission of the set of disorders, but not agreement on genetic versus environmental causation (Dionne, 1990).

Cognitive-Behavioral Assessment

Beyond DSM-IV criteria, there are a number of standardized assessment instruments. One good example is the Standardized Behavioral Avoidance Course (S-BAC), which has the client walk through a standard course alone, beginning at the front door of the hospital and ending at a crowded shopping mall (Agras, Leitenberg, & Barlow, 1968). The actual measures on the S-BAC are distance traveled, psychophysiological monitoring (heart rate, breathing), and *in vivo* discussion of client cognitions and thoughts as they go through the process. (This example shows how applied behavioral analysis can be very systematically used.)

At a more general level, the A-B-C techniques of applied behavioral analysis presented later in this chapter can be used to determine more precisely what occurs before, during, and after an attack of agoraphobia (see Michelson, 1987, for a review of alternative clinical

and research methods). In addition, CBT stresses the importance of assessing emotion and cognition.

Treatment

Graduated exposure has been found to be a highly useful strategy for the treatment of agoraphobia. Graduated exposure is similar to systematic desensitization described in this chapter except that clients are actually taken out into the field for graduated practice exercises. (For comprehensive treatment reviews, see Emmelkamp & Mersh, 1982; Michelson, 1987; Dionne, 1990). Another form of treatment is to have a family member or partner help the client work through graduated exposure. Deep muscle relaxation (as described later in this chapter) is helpful as part of a treatment program. Although controversial, the general feeling in the psychological field is that medication is not necessary for treatment.

The pinpointing of specific behaviors, positive reinforcement, and the concepts of charting are important skills for establishing a comprehensive treatment plan for agoraphobics. Social skills training and stress inoculation are obvious treatment adjuncts.

Cognitive techniques are described in more detail in Chapter 10, but Michelson (1987) reviews cognitive studies in detail, and this type of work appears to be effective with agoraphobics. For example, Emmelkamp et al. (1986) compared *in vivo* graduated exposure with two types of cognitive therapy and found all three groups improved, with the greatest improvement in the graduated exposure groups. This study was further validated in a major study by the National Institute of Mental Health, which compared a cognitive intervention with psychophysiological and behavioral interventions. Clients in all approaches showed significant improvement (Michelson et al., 1985).

There is also some evidence that family treatment (Chapter 4), problem-solving training (Chapter 3), and other forms of helping can be useful. Logic suggests that a multidimensional treatment plan in-corporating several of the methods discussed above may be useful. It is not which treatment is best, but which set of treatments is best. This latter interpretation allows us to think of comprehensive treatment plans in the hope that cognitive, behavioral, family systems, and other methods can be integrated more broadly than our "single-shot" interventions of the past. Family treatment may be a direction of the future owing to increasing evidence of intergenerational family issues (Dionne, 1990).

Applied Behavioral Analysis: Foundation of Cognitive-Behavioral Therapy

Behavioral counseling rests on applied behavioral analysis, a systematic method of collaboratively examining the client and the client's environment and jointly developing specific interventions to alter the client's life conditions. Successful applied behavioral analysis rests on four foundations: (1) the relationship between the counselor and the client, (2) the definition of the problem through operationalization of behavior, (3) the understanding of the full context of the problem through functional analysis, and (4) the establishment of socially important goals for the client.

Central Constructs of Applied Behavioral Analysis

Client-Counselor Relationship

It was once thought that those who engaged in behavioral approaches were cold, distant, and mechanical. A classic research study in 1975 by Sloane and others forever changed this view. This research examined expert therapists from a variety of theoretical orientations and found that behavioral therapists exhibited higher levels of empathy, self-congruence, and interpersonal contact than other therapists and that levels of warmth and regard were approximately the same. Behavioral therapists may be expected to be as interested in rapport and human growth as those working from any other orientation.

Behavioral therapists have very specific methodologies and goals. In addition to working toward rapport, behavioral therapists engage in careful structuring of the interview. They are willing and eager to share their plans collaboratively with the client in the expectation that the client will share with them in the therapy process.

Relationship variables have differing meanings, according to individual and cultural background. It is important that eye contact, body language, vocal tone, and verbal following be culturally appropriate. Too many reflective listening skills can result in mistrust unless culturally appropriate sharing is included. A relationship can develop slowly or quickly.

For instance, working with urban Aboriginals in Australia or with the Inuit or Dene in the Arctic, the professional helper may take half an interview or more simply to become acquainted, learn the family system, share personal anecdotes, and so on before trying to find out what the client wants to talk about. At the other extreme, a relationship can develop quickly with many urban White professionals who can be fully intimate and open with a therapist immediately on entering the room.

If you have some skill in observation and listening, some beginning knowledge of multicultural differences in style, and a willingness to share at least part of yourself, you have the basics to establish yourself as a helper in multicultural settings.

Operationalization of Behavior

Clients often bring to the therapist clouded, confused, and abstract descriptions of their issues. You can help clients become much clearer if you focus on concreteness and specifics of behavior. The temptation for many formal operational counselors is to think and talk abstractly. Operationalization of behavior will help you and the client "get down to cases" and discover what is really happening.

An Example. Let us assume that you have a client who is depressed and talks about feeling sad. In psychodynamic therapy, you might seek to discover the roots of the sadness, whereas in cognitive or humanistic therapies, you might want to help the client alter the way he or she thinks about the world. However, in behavioral therapy, particularly with applied behavioral analysis, the task is to determine what the patient does specifically and concretely when he or she feels depressed, as the following dialogue illustrates:

Counselor: You say you feel depressed. Could you tell me some of the specific things you do when you are depressed?

Client: Well, I cry a lot. Some days I can't get out of bed. I feel sad most of the time.

Counselor: How does your body feel?

[*Contrary to some stereotypes, behaviorally oriented therapists are very attuned to emotions and stress the importance of emotional issues. Many therapists would settle for "sad," but here special effort is taken to make the emotion more based in actual sensorimotor experience.*]

Client: It feels tense and drawn all over, almost like little hammers are beating me from inside. It gets so bad sometimes that I can't sleep.

The counselor's two questions have made the behaviors related to the general construct of depression far more obvious. Crying, failure to get out of bed, feelings of bodily tension, and inability to go to sleep are operational behaviors that can be seen, measured, and even counted. The feelings of sadness, however, are still somewhat vague, and further operationalization of the sentence "I feel sad most of the time" might result in the following, more specific, description of behaviors:

> *Counselor:*   A short time ago you said you feel sad much of the time. Could you elaborate a little more on that?
>
> *Client:*   Well, I cry a lot and I can hardly get moving. My wife says all I do is whine and complain.
>
> *Counselor:*   So sadness means crying and difficulty in getting moving . . . and you complain a lot. You also said you felt tense and drawn inside . . . hammers, I think you said.

Here the counselor ties in the vague feelings of sadness with the more concrete operational behaviors mentioned by the client and locates them more specifically in sensorimotor space.

Making the Behavior Concrete and Observable.   The objective of operationalization of behavior, then, is the concretizing of vague words into objective, observable actions. Virtually all behavioral counselors will seek this specificity at some point in the interview, believing it is more possible to work with objective behavior than with vague nonspecific concepts such as depression and sadness.

A simple but basic clue when engaging in operationalization of behavior is to ask "Can I see, feel, hear, or touch the words the client is using?" The client may speak of a desire for a "better relationship" with a partner. Since the behavioral therapist cannot see, feel, hear, or touch "better relationship," the therapist would seek to have this concept operationalized in terms of touching, vocal tone, or certain verbal statements (e.g., "I wish my partner would touch me more and say more good things about me").

Again, it is important to note that making vague terms as specific as possible can be useful in other theoretical orientations. The clarity that comes with a careful behavioral analysis often provides a basic understanding for truly appreciating the client's worldview and environmental situation.

Functional Analysis

The A-B-Cs of Behavior.   An individual's behavior is directly related to events and stimuli in the environment. Another task of the behavioral therapist is to discover how client behaviors occur in the "natural environment." Behavioral counselors and behavioral therapists talk about the "A-B-Cs" of functional analysis—that is, the study of antecedent events, the resultant behavior, and the consequence(s) of that behavior. The behavioral counselor is interested in knowing what happened just prior to a specific behavior, what the specific behavior or event was, and what the result or consequence of that behavior was on the client and the environment. Chapter 10, which will focus primarily on cognition, explores parallel "A-B-Cs" for inner thoughts and feelings.

In the following examination of functional cause-and-effect relationship, the counselor comes to understand the sequence of events underlying the overt behavior of a client. Out of such functional patterns, it is possible to design behavioral programs to change the pattern of events.

Counselor: So far, I've heard that you are generally depressed, that you get these feelings of tiredness and tension. Now could you give me a specific example of a situation when you felt this way? I want to know what happened just before the depression came upon you, what happened as you got those feelings and thoughts, and what resulted after. First, tell me about the last time you had these feelings.

Client: Well, it happened yesterday . . . (sigh) I came home from work and was feeling pretty good. But when I came in the house, Bonnie wasn't there, so I sat down and started to read . . .

Counselor: (interrupting) What was your reaction when your wife wasn't home?

Client: I was a little disappointed, but not much, I just sat down.

Counselor: Go ahead . . .

Client: After about half an hour, she came in and just walked by me. . . . I said hello, but she was angry at me still from last night when we had that argument. Funny, I always feel relieved and free after we have an argument . . . almost like I get it out of my system.

Counselor: Then what happened?

Client: Well . . . I tried to get her to talk, but she ignored me. After about ten minutes, I got really sad and depressed. I went to my room and lay down until supper. But just before supper, she came in and said she was sorry, but I just felt more depressed.

Counselor: Let's see if I can put that sequence of events together. You were feeling pretty good, but your wife wasn't home and then didn't respond to you because she was angry. You tried to get her to respond and she wouldn't [*antecedents*]. Then you got depressed and felt bad and went to your room and lay down [*resultant behavior*]. She ignored you for a while, but finally came to you and you ignored her [*consequences*]. The pattern seems to be similar to what you've told me about before: (1) you try something; (2) she doesn't respond; (3) you get discouraged, depressed feelings and tensions—sometimes even crying; and (4) she comes back to you and apologizes, but you reject her.

From a cognitive-developmental frame, the counselor summarized concrete cause-and-effect sequence through the A-B-C analysis. This awareness of sequence is characteristic of late concrete operations. Then, the counselor used the word *pattern*, thereby helping the client see that this one concrete example is representative of repeating behavior. If the client is not cognitively able to think in patterns (formal operations), it is preferable to stay with a single example and work on that specific situation.

Reinforcers and Reinforcement Patterns.   Important in performing functional analysis is being aware of how behavior develops and maintains itself through a system of rewards or reinforcers and punishments. At the simplest level, whatever follows a particular piece of behavior will influence the probability of that behavior happening again. In the above case, the husband gained no attention from his wife until he became depressed. At this point, and at this point only, she came to him. Therefore, the wife's behavior heavily influences the probability of his becoming depressed. On this subject, Skinner (1953) notes:

> Several important generalized reinforcers arise when behavior is reinforced by other people. A simple case is attention. The child who misbehaves "just to get attention" is familiar. The attention of people is reinforcing because it is a necessary condition for other reinforcements from them. In general, only people who are attending to us reinforce our behavior. . . . Attention is often not enough. Another person is likely to reinforce only that part of one's behavior of which he approves, and any sign of his approval becomes reinforcing in its own right. (p. 78)

Patterns of attention are particularly important in understanding human relationships. In the above case, the husband gets attention only when he becomes depressed, and his wife's attention at that time only reinforces further feelings of depression and hopelessness. If she were to attend to him when he initiated behavior, it is possible—even likely—that certain portions of his pattern of depression would be alleviated. However, neither does the husband attend to (reinforce) his wife's coming to him in the bedroom. He ignores her and thereby continues the pattern of mutual lack of reinforcement. Either individual could break the self-defeating pattern of antecedents, behavior, and consequences.

Any meaningful functional analysis must examine the reinforcement patterns maintaining the system of an individual or couple. The word *pattern* is formal, and with many clients, it will be necessary to work only with one single situation and examine in detail the concrete A-B-C sequence. Once several single situations have been mastered by the client, it may then be possible to examine formal patterns of behavior.

The social reinforcers of attention and approval are particularly potent and vital in human relationships. However, other reinforcers (money, grades, or other tangibles, as well as social rewards such as smiles, affection, and recognition) must be considered in any functional analysis. In many cases, negative attention (punishment) is often preferred to being ignored. Ignoring a human being can be a very painful punishment.

Establishing Behavior Change Goals

If a counselor is to help a client, the intended behavior change must be relevant to the client, as Sulzer-Azaroff and Mayer (1977) point out:

> Applied behavior analysis programs assist clients to improve behaviors that will promote their own personal and social development. Consequently, prior to its implementation, a program must clearly communicate and justify how it will assist the client to function more effectively in society, both in the near and distant future. It also must show how any changes that accompany the behavior change of focus will not interfere with the client's or the community's short- and long-range goals. . . . It does not deal with bar pressing. . . . Nor should it serve individuals or agencies whose goals are to the detriment of either clients or their immediate and broader societies. (p. 7)

Making the Goals Concrete.   During the goal-setting phase of the interview, the counselor works with the client to find highly specific and relevant goals (Sulzer-Azaroff, 1985). Rather than setting a generalized goal such as "My goal is not to be depressed anymore," the behavioral counselor will work toward detailed specific plans. One early goal might be as basic as going to a movie or learning to dance. Later goals might be to join a community club, start jogging, and find a job. Applied behavioral analysis breaks the abstract idea of depression down into manageable behavioral units and teaches clients how to live their lives more happily and effectively. One can do something about specifics; as concrete goals are achieved, the depression lifts.

Throughout applied behavioral analysis, there is an emphasis on concrete doing and action. The individual must do something that can be seen, heard, and felt. Thoughts are less important, but these become central in behavioral psychology's offshoot, cognitive psychology (discussed in Chapter 10). Interestingly, behavioral psychotherapy often tends to be especially effective with depressed clients, as its emphasis on doing and acting rather than on self-reflection gets the client moving. The emphasis on movement, action, and doing, again, tends to be typically North American and pragmatic in orientation.

Behavioral psychology is concerned with *doing*. Functional analysis will have a more lasting meaning for you if you actually practice it. Practice Exercise 9.1 provides you an opportunity to do so.

Cognitive-Behavioral Treatment Techniques

Intentional CBT often starts with careful applied behavioral analysis. The central constructs and exercises presented earlier are essential assessment prerequisites for the following treatment techniques. A critical task of the behavioral counselor is to select from among the many possibilities now existing the most appropriate behavioral change procedure for the individual client. Some key behavioral change procedures follow.

Practice Exercise 9.1

 Applied Behavioral Analysis

The following exercises have been chosen as basic to successful behavioral and cognitive-behavioral practice.

Operationalization of Behavior

The following are vague statements a client might present in the interview:

> "I'm depressed."
> "I'm no good as a parent."
> "He argues all the time."
> "I'm unhappy."
> "She doesn't love me anymore."
> "The boss doesn't like me."
> "The boss harassed me."

When clients give you vague statements such as the above, your task is to help them become more concrete and specific. For example, if the client said, "The boss harassed me," your task would be to obtain the concrete specifics of "harassment." You can obtain these concrete specifics by asking:

> "Could you give me a specific example of what the boss did?"
> "What do you mean, all the time?"
> "What happened specifically?"
> "What words does he use?"
> "How loudly does he talk?"
> "Where did he touch you?"
> "Who holds the power?"
> "What's the boss's behavior toward other men/women/minorities?"

Interview a friend or colleague. When you hear a vague statement such as those described above, ask open questions, using the above guidelines, until you get the concrete specifics of the behavior.

At times, you will want to concretize a sequence. In the example below, the focus is on making an argument specific. You can do this simply by asking:

> "What happened in the argument?"
> "What did she or he say?"
> "What did you say?"
> "What happened before?" (*to obtain antecedents*)
> "What happened afterward?" (*to obtain consequences*)

To ensure that you have heard the client correctly, use the microskill of summarization to lay out the sequence of events. Also be aware of the social context of your analysis. Your efforts will often be most effective if conducted with contextual awareness and action.

Again with your friend or colleague, using these ideas, draw out the sequence of events.

Functional Analysis

A functional analysis is a systematic and sequential operationalization of behavior. The questioning techniques above are basic to a functional analysis. In conducting a functional analysis, think about the A-B-Cs of behavior. In the following examples, note the importance of the word *do*, which focuses on action, so characteristic of behavioral counseling and therapy.

A—Antecedent events
Examine preceding behavioral facts as well as feelings and emotions.

"What happened just before the argument?"

"What were you doing?"

"What were they doing?"

"Could you just step back and describe the event step by step—give me lots of details?"

"What did you feel beforehand?"

"How did the other person seem to feel?"

It may also be useful to explore the environment.

"Where did this occur?"

"What else was going on?"

"Who else was there?"

You may think of the newspaper sequence of "who, what, when, where, why, and how" questions to enrich the background.

A critical question that should be asked at each segment of any careful functional analysis is "*Have we missed anything important?*" Summarize the antecedents to ensure that you have heard them correctly.

B—Behavior that occurred (resultant behavior)

Here you focus on the immediate argument and important sequence of events or interaction during the critical period. Use variations of the same questions suggested above and pay special attention to feelings and emotions that accompanied the behavior.

Again summarize the behavior and check to see if you missed something important.

C—Consequences

Most essential here is what specifically happened as a result of A and B. Some possible helpful questions include:

"What was the end result of the whole event?"

"Could you explore what happened for you as a result and what happened for the other person?"

"How did you feel when it was over?"

"Are there situational, environmental checks on you or others that may have power and influence over the total situation?"

Again, summarize the behavior and check to see if you missed something important.

This completes the A-B-C analysis of behavior, which will give you a good conception of what occurred for the client or clients in many varying types of problem situations.

Establishing Behavior Change Goals

Once having completed an A-B-C functional analysis, the task is to establish, with the client's participation, specific goals for behavioral change.

Many clients can participate very effectively in analyzing behavioral sequences, but when you ask them "What is your goal for change?" they often will return to vague, nonspecific concepts. Clients who have just been depressed, suffered sexual harassment, or experienced an argument may say "I want things to be better," which is too abstract for any real action. Your task as a therapist is once again to help them become more specific about their goals for change. Some helpful types of questions follow. This information provides you with data revealing that change can be sought in the areas of antecedents, the behavior itself, the consequences, or some combination of these three.

"Given that we have discussed your parental argument (your depression, the issue of harassment) and conflict in detail, what specifically would you like to change?"

"We could work on how you behave before the argument occurs, how you talk and behave when one does occur, or what you do after an inevitable argument happens."

This example is likely to be too complex for most clients, and thus the following types of questions may be more useful.

"Ideally, what one single thing would you most like to change?"

"Let's explore that in more detail. What would you have to do differently?"

It is helpful to use a fantasy directive such as "Fantasize an ideal solution if everything were exactly like you'd wish it to be."

A situational question such as "What can we do to help change the system in which this happened?" will help add a multicultural focus.

Again, take a friend or colleague through the specifics of operationalizing behavior, defining the A-B-C sequence, and establish clear, measurable goals for behavioral change.

Regardless of whatever behavioral technique or strategy you chose to use from the several included in this chapter, your interventions will be most effective if they include a carefully constructed functional analysis and operationalization of behavior. Including situational/environmental issues in your functional analysis will help keep you aware of possible multicultural issues

Pinpointing Behavior, Positive Reinforcement, and Charting

Pinpointing Behavior

Assume, for example, that you are working with a hyperactive child. A teacher or parent may complain about the child's overactivity and tell you that the child is "difficult to control." These are not directly observable behaviors. Your task is to pinpoint very precise behaviors, such as the number of times the child interrupts a classmate or teacher, the number of times the child leaves his or her seat during a specified time period, or the child's "time on task" (percentage of time the child is actually working on schoolwork).

Your skill in applied behavioral analysis is basic to pinpointing specific behavioral targets for change or reinforcement. You can use operationalization of behavior concepts to pinpoint very specific behaviors associated with depression, arguments, or sexual harassment (Practice Exercise 9.1).

Positive and Intermittent Reinforcement

Perhaps the most direct behavioral technique is the provision of rewards for desired behavior. The systematic application of positive reinforcement to human beings began with an important experiment by Greenspoon (1955), who demonstrated that it was possible to condition people to "emit" more plural nouns whenever the "counselor" smiled or nodded his head. In the context of what appeared to be a normal interview, Greenspoon conducted a typical interview with the exception that whenever the client uttered a plural noun, the interviewer smiled and nodded. Very soon the client was providing him with many plural nouns.

Smiles, nods, and the attention of others are particularly reinforcing events. We all seek reinforcement and reward. Those who provide us with these rewards tend to be our friends; those who do not we tend to ignore or avoid. Money is another powerful positive reinforcer. It may be said that we work because we are rewarded or reinforced with money. In any applied behavioral analysis that is fully effective, the counselor will be able to note the positive reinforcers and rewards that maintain the behavior. The search for the A-B-Cs of behavioral sequences will often unravel seemingly complex and mystical behavior.

When learning theory concepts, such as extinction, shaping, and intermittent reinforcement, are joined together, extremely powerful and effective programs of human change can be developed. At the most sophisticated level, elaborate economies have been developed in prisons, psychiatric hospitals, schools, and other settings in which tangible reinforcers in the form of tokens are given for desired acts immediately after they have been performed. At a later point the tokens may be exchanged for candy, cigarettes, or privileges. Important to the success of positive reinforcement and token economies is the clear identification, by the client, of the desired behavior with the reward. Too long a delay in reinforcement dulls its effectiveness in changing behavior.

Intermittent reinforcement is another behavioral concept that is helpful in understanding client behavior. For example, a woman may suffer from spousal abuse but refuse to leave the home, even if in danger of her life. From a behavioral frame of reference, this behavior could be explained as follows: (1) the woman has a strong history of positive reinforcement from the male in some form; (2) many abusive men apologize and provide immediate promise of positive reinforcement, even after dangerous physical incidents; (3) the woman has no place else to go for positive reinforcement if she leaves the male; and (4) behavior research indicates that a random mixture of negative and positive events at times can be even more powerful in maintaining behavior than unmixed positive reinforcement. Thus, the intermittent reinforcement pattern in abusive relationships is one of the hardest to break whether one works from a behavioral, humanistic, feminist, or other frame of reference.

Charting

One route toward identifying whether or not progress is being made with a behavioral change program is charting the changes made by a client. Charting is the specific recording of the number of occurrences of important behaviors before, during, and after treatment. For example, a teacher may be concerned with "out-of-seat behavior" of a hyperactive child. The goal of the behavioral program is to reduce this behavior using a modified token economy in which the child is rewarded for staying at the desk.

The chart in Figure 9.1 illustrates the daily frequencies for out-of-seat behavior before the intervention was instituted, during the treatment, and after treatment was terminated. It is important to record behavior before the program is instituted so that the effectiveness of the behavioral program can be examined. Charting after program completion is important because when the intervention is removed, the behavior sometimes returns to the previous level, indicating that the behavioral program was unsuccessful in maintaining desired outcomes. When charts indicate failure, another type of behavioral program (or even another type of counseling intervention, such as psychodynamic or humanistic) needs to be instituted. In such cases relapse prevention programs can be particularly useful.

Charting is often used in weight control programs, family communication skill training, aiding a child in keeping a room clean, stop-smoking programs, and in a wide variety of interpersonal or classroom situations. The very act of self-recording (charting) sometimes helps an individual modify her or his behavior without further instruction or counseling.

Many therapists, particularly those who work with children and adolescents, find that pinpointing behavior and conducting a thorough A-B-C analysis, as in Figure 9.1, are vital if change is to occur. Once a change plan has been collaboratively agreed to with the client (and parents, if you are working with a child), charting is

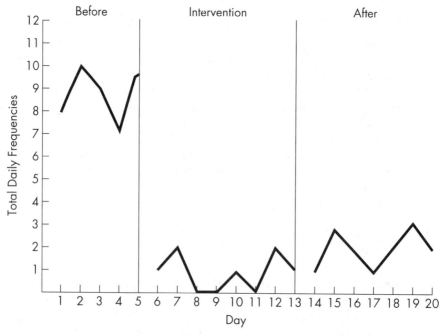

Figure 9.1 Charting Out-of-Seat Behavior

helpful for studying whether or not your intervention is effective and whether or not change is maintained after the intervention ceases.

Relaxation Training

Physical body tension is characteristic of many clients who enter counseling or therapy. This tension may show itself in a variety of ways, including statements of fear or tension in social situations; direct complaints of sore, constantly tense muscles; impotence and frigidity; difficulties with sleep; and high blood pressure. There is clinical evidence that borderline clients will reduce the number of suicidal gestures and "cutting" if they are supported with a relaxation training program. Most seriously depressed clients can benefit from relaxation training as part of their treatment regimen.

Surprisingly, simply teaching people the mechanics of systematic relaxation techniques has been sufficient to alleviate many seemingly complex problems. Rather than search for the reasons that a client is unable to sleep, for example, behavioral counselors have found it more effective in many cases to teach the client relaxation techniques. The simple procedure of training clients in relaxation can be an important way to bring totally new views of the world to them. Through finding that they can control their bodies, clients can move on to solve many complex personal difficulties.

For this reason, virtually all counselors and therapists today are becoming skilled at training clients in relaxation techniques similar to the exercises presented in Practice Exercise 9.2. A client may learn the rudiments of relaxation training in a fifteen-minute session, but careful planning and training are needed if relaxation techniques are to become part of a client's life.

A variety of systematic relaxation tapes is now available commercially, making it possible for the busy behavioral counselor to delegate this training to the machine and to spend more time training the client how to use relaxation in specific situations. Relaxation may, for example, be an important part of assertiveness training. If a client describes physical tension in the stomach when talking with members of the family or the boss, it is possible to teach the client to deliberately relax the stomach muscles and remain calm as part of a larger program of assertiveness training.

Biofeedback and Self-Regulation

It is now possible to use instrumentation to monitor tension in muscles, heartbeat, and blood flow as part of a treatment plan to help clients alleviate tension. Biofeedback combines many of the relaxation procedures of behavioral psychology for analysis and treatment of a variety of client tension patterns.

Biofeedback has become an increasingly popular treatment technique for tension headaches (Grazzi et al., 1990) and general stress reactions. It has been used to sup-

===== **Practice Exercise 9.2** =====

 # Two Relaxation Exercises

Most programs of relaxation are based on a tension-relaxation or direct relaxation procedure. The two systems discussed here usually will be found in some form among the many relaxation exercises, training programs, and audiotapes available in the counseling field. To use the following exercises most effectively, have a friend or family member read them to you slowly while you go through the procedures yourself. Then change roles and help the other person enter the same relaxed state you have just enjoyed. As a final step, adapt the material below into your own relaxation program and place it on audiotape for your own and others' use.

Tension-Relaxation Contrast

Many people exist at such a high level of tension that they find it difficult to start relaxing. Tension-relaxation contrast shows the beginner in relaxation what tension is and how it may be controlled systematically. As a first step, the person who is to go through relaxation training should be seated comfortably in a chair or be lying on the floor. An easy, casual manner and good rapport are essential for the counselor.

1. Start the procedure by suggesting that the client close her or his eyes and take a few deep breaths, exhaling slowly each time.

2. Tell the client, "We are going to engage in a systematic relaxation program. You'll find it's something you'll enjoy, but we must go at your pace. If you find I'm

moving too fast or too slowly, let me know. In general, I'll know how you are doing as I can watch your response and will time what I'm doing to where you are. First, I'd like you to tighten your right hand—that's right—hold it tight for about five seconds—one, two, three, four, five. Now let it go, and notice the difference between relaxation and tension. Notice the feeling of ease as you let your hand go. What we'll do is go through your body in much the same fashion, alternatively tightening and letting go of each muscle group. Let's begin . . ."

3. Continue by having the client tighten and loosen the right hand once again. Remember to have the client notice the difference between relaxed and tense body states. Awareness of muscle tension is one key goal of relaxation training. After you have done the right hand for a second time, continue through the rest of the body in the order suggested in number 4, below. Each time, have the client (1) tighten the muscle group, (2) hold the tension approximately five seconds, (3) let the tension go, and (4) notice the difference between tension and relaxation. As the training progresses, it is not necessary to comment on awareness at each muscle group, but mention awareness of the contrasting feelings from time to time. Occasionally, it is helpful to suggest taking a deep breath, holding it, and then exhaling while noting the contrast between tension and relaxation.

4. A suggested order for muscle groups follows:

right hand
right arm
left hand
left arm
neck and shoulders together
neck alone
face and scalp
neck and shoulders again
chest, lungs, back
abdomen-stomach
entire upper body—chest, back, lungs, abdomen, face, neck, both arms, followed by a deep breath held and then exhaled slowly and gently
abdomen-stomach again
buttocks
thighs
feet
entire body

5. Complete the exercise by suggesting that the client continue to sit or lie still, enjoying the feelings of relaxation and ease. When he or she wishes, suggest opening the eyes and returning to the world.

Direct Relaxation

Many people prefer this form of relaxation if they find the alternative tensing and loosening tiring and/or uninteresting. However, it has been found that the tension-relaxation procedure is often a good place to start with the beginner in relaxation. Eventually, many people will want to shift to some form of direct relaxation.

One form of direct relaxation is to use the above order of muscle groups and go through them one at a time. However, no tension is used, and the client simply lets each muscle group go, one at a time. With practice and experience, the relaxation can be as complete without the practiced tension.

A second form of direct relaxation involves visualization and imagery. Following is one brief example of this approach to relaxation. As in tension-relaxation contrast, the client may sit or lie down. In this form of relaxation, the relationship between the counselor and client is even more important.

1. Start the procedure by suggesting that the client close her or his eyes and notice the feelings inside the body. Take some time and suggest that the client notice the breath going in and out, the feeling of the chair or floor on the buttocks and back, the feeling of the temperature in the room. All this should be done slowly, easily, and comfortably. The effort focuses on bringing the client to a here-and-now awareness of body experience.

2. Then suggest that the client freely think about a scene in the past where he or she felt at ease and comfortable and happy. Suggest that the client go to the scene and enjoy the feelings and thoughts that go with that happy time, noticing as many details and facts as possible. The client may wish to notice the feelings in the body at that time, such as movement of the air, temperature, and body movements. Let the client continue with the visualization as long as desired and then become silent, letting him or her determine when to come back.

3. Alternatively, let the client know that he or she will have some time to enjoy the scene and experience, but that you'll come back in a while. After about ten minutes, gently say that it is time to return to this room. Suggest that the eyes remain closed and that he or she note once again the feelings in the body connected with this room, as in the first part of the exercise. Suggest that the eyes may open when the client wishes.

port behavioral treatment of patients on insulin (Bailey, Good, & McGrady, 1990) and in many cases of pain control (Hatch & Saito, 1990). Biofeedback may have an important future in medicine and stress control. When faced with stress, blood vessels constrict. Relaxation training, biofeedback, and stress management all can help people relax and ease blood flow.

There are some important multicultural issues around stress control. African-Americans, for example, suffer from hypertension, with all the resulting complications. Leary (1991) reports that the blood vessels of African-Americans who went through a stress test took ten times longer to return to normal levels than did those of Whites. An ongoing stressor for African-Americans (and, most likely, other minorities as well) is a general environment that is nonsupportive to their cultural differences.

If the data and several studies reported by Leary hold true, it then follows that biofeedback, relaxation, and stress management may be important programs to facilitate not only mental health, but also physical health for minorities. Cheek (1976) might add that cognitive consciousness raising about issues of powerlessness and how to work effectively to promote change could be useful parts of such health-oriented programs. Cheatham (1990) and Parham (1990) would state that direct action by the therapist or counselor in the community that produced the stress is what is needed.

Eye Movement Desensitization and Reprocessing

Eye movement desensitization and reprocessing (EMD/R) is a set of strategies developed by Shapiro (1991, 1994) for work with those with experiences of trauma. Research results are promising for EMD/R, although the strategy remains controversial. This complex method has eight phases that integrate many cognitive-behavioral techniques. These eight phases include client history taking and involving the client in planning treatment. The first and second phases involve empowering clients and making them aware of how "dysfunctional material from the past is arising internally" (Shapiro, personal communication, December 1995). During these first two phases, the traumatic memory is identified.

The third phase asks clients to develop an image of their traumatic experience and then make a statement summarizing their thoughts and feelings about the trauma (e.g., "I should have done X" or "It was my fault" or "I'm helpless"). A positive self-statement is generated to replace the negative cognitions, and a scale (similar to the anxiety scale of systematic desensitization) is developed for levels of discomfort. This scale serves as a means to measure the immediate progress of clients and, later, clients' generalization to the real world.

In the fourth phase, desensitization, the client does three things simultaneously (e.g., generates an image, identifies thoughts, and notes physical body sensations) while the therapist moves the index finger in front of the eyes. Then, the client empties the image from the mind and focuses on physical sensations and a positive self-statement ("I did the best I could" or "It was not preventable" or "I'm capable"). The reprocessing continues through variations on the above.

The fifth phase focuses on "installation" during which the new positive cognitions are given more force. The sixth phase is a body scan in which the client holds the negative event in mind and searches for remaining bodily tension. These body feelings are also examined carefully. The seventh and eighth phases work on issues of closure and reevaluation of treatment progress.

There is definite clinical evidence that EMD/R is effective with some clients. However, some theorists, such as Meichenbaum (1994), conclude that the method is not yet proven. EMD/R seems to work best with those who have had a single trauma (accident, burglary, flood). Nonetheless, some who experienced severe trauma and suffer from post-traumatic stress disorder (PTSD) claim benefits from this approach. Shapiro (personal communication, December 1995) responds with citations of a number of papers and presentations attesting to the EMD/R's effectiveness. Wilson, Becker, and Tinker (1995) have conducted a fifteen-month study that provides useful evidence supporting Shapiro's claims. Work by Carlson and others (1995) and by Rothbaum (1995) also seems to support the effectiveness of this new procedure.

In EMD/R, images and body sensations are focused on, as are cognitive-emotional self-statements. There is also a focus on positive experiences. These principles and structure are similar to the positive asset search of the empathic and microskills approaches. The positive use of images is similar to developmental counseling and therapy (DCT) as well as many techniques of cognitive-behavioral therapy. Although more research is needed, it is possible that the overlaying of positive images and experiences on negative ones, particularly with an emphasis on body sensations, will be an increasingly important technique.

Systematic Desensitization

Systematic desensitization is a useful technique to solve more complex personal issues surrounding anxiety and tension. Many people feel anxious in specific situations or in relation to certain objects, animals, or people—that is, they have phobic difficulties that cause extreme anxiety.

The assessment portion of systematic desensitization is useful in helping you understand the specific nature of a wide variety of client difficulties. The collaborative generation of an anxiety hierarchy will help you identify the client's issues in a very concrete way. This information can be combined with typical behavioral change methods or with psychodynamic, decisional, and other treatment alternatives.

Systematic desensitization consists of three primary steps: (1) training in systematic deep muscle relaxation, (2) construction of anxiety hierarchies, and (3) matching specific objects of anxiety from the hierarchies with relaxation training. It is impossible to be simultaneously relaxed and anxious; thus, the purpose of systematic desensitization is to train an automatic relaxation response in conjunction with a previously feared object. Systematic desensitization has proven effective with anxieties or phobias such as those about snakes, heights, death, sexual difficulties, and examinations.

Examination anxiety is particularly appropriate for desensitization, as the procedure has proven useful with innumerable students in many academic institutions. The first steps in systematic desensitization involve training in relaxation and applied behavioral analysis of the antecedents, resultant behavior, and consequences relating to the student's examination problems. A typical problem is the student who, on thinking of a forthcoming examination, experiences mild anxiety, with gradually increasing anxiety and tension until the examination itself occurs; at this point the student might block facts important in the examination, feel physically ill, or even leave the examination room.

Constructing an Anxiety Hierarchy

In the construction of an anxiety hierarchy, it is helpful to develop an anxiety scale. Wolpe and Lazarus (1966) suggest: "Think of the worst anxiety you have ever experienced or can imagine experiencing, and assign to this the number 100. Now think of the state of being absolutely calm, and call this 0. Now you have a scale. On this scale how do you rate yourself at this moment?" (p. 73).

Two things can be accomplished with this type of scale: (1) the counselor and the client develop a common understanding of how anxious the client was or is at any time in the past or present, and (2) the beginning and end points of an anxiety hierarchy have been established. Then, through questioning and further applied behavioral analysis, it is possible to fill in and rate stress-producing experiences. An example anxiety hierarchy for a student suffering from examination anxiety is presented below:

____ 0 School is over and I have no more exams for another year.

____ 10 On the first day of class, the professor tells us the course plan and mentions examination plans.

____ 30 About a week before the examination, I realize it is coming.

____ 50 Two days before the examination, I get particularly nervous and begin to find it hard to concentrate.

____ 70 The day before the examination, I get sweaty palms and feel I am forgetting things important to me.

____ 85 The night before the exam, I find I can't sleep and wake up in the middle of the night.

____ 90 As I walk to the exam, I find myself shaking and feeling almost ill.

____ 95 As I enter the room, my hands sweat; I fear I am forgetting everything; I want to leave.

____ 99 When the tests are passed out, I feel totally tense, almost unable to move.

____100 As I look at the examination I see a question or two that I really don't know and I absolutely panic. I leave the room.

The importance and value of this type of individualized, collaborative assessment cannot be overstressed. It is important that you personally take time to practice the construction of anxiety hierarchies, and Practice Exercise 9.3 can help you become familiar with this tool as well as with desensitization techniques.

Practice Exercise 9.3

Constructing an Anxiety Hierarchy and Systematic Desensitization

One of the most valuable tools a counselor or therapist can have is the anxiety hierarchy. Making a hierarchy provides awareness of how anxiety plays itself out in the interview and in the daily life of the client. Brief, solution-oriented therapy also uses an anxiety hierarchy, although it is called the process of "scaling." You can practice constructing an anxiety hierarchy or scale using the following approach.

1. Develop rapport with a volunteer or real client. Again, work mutually and tell the client what to expect. Ask the client to tell you about something that is anxiety producing. Good topics include examinations, specific fears (heights, animals, public speaking), and even the degree of physical tension and anxiety felt in the "here and now" of the therapeutic interview.

2. Coconstruct with the client an anxiety scale numbered from one to ten. The lowest point should represent a feeling of calmness; the highest, a feeling of maximum anxiety or tension. Define specific situations and behaviors for points one and ten. You may find applied behavioral analysis helpful in this process. Then, identify specific behaviors, situations, and feelings for the remainder of the scale.

3. A second anxiety scale is often helpful. You and your client may also want to modify the above scale so you are able to communicate about the level of tension in your interview. For example, it is often helpful to ask clients how physically tense and anxious they are as you move from topic to topic. An occasional question about where the tension is located in the body will help you understand the client's emotional state more clearly.

Desensitization can be done most effectively by either teaching brief relaxation methods or by asking the client to develop a positive image along with focusing on positive body sensations, as follows:

1. Ask the client to relax and/or visualize the positive image while simultaneously viewing the absence of the problem at zero on the anxiety scale. Check to make sure that the client feels calm before moving on.

2. Work through the anxiety hierarchy in a similar fashion, making sure that the positive visualization and body sensation are paired with the negative. Gradually, the client often will be able to monitor and control anxiety levels throughout the hierarchy. Some peo-

ple can construct and work through a full anxiety hierarchy and desensitization in one session. More likely, several sessions may be needed.

3. In actual therapy, you may want to add live experience in the environment to the use of imagery and relaxation. For example, if the client is fearful of crowds, you may jointly plan homework exercises in which the client gradually moves into larger groups of people. In some cases, you may want to go with the client to the place in which anxiety is greatest and practice the new behavior in the "real world."

Using the Hierarchy for Treatment

Following completion of the anxiety hierarchy, the client is asked to sit with eyes closed and visualize a variety of scenes close to the 0 point of anxiety. These scenes may be of school being over or of an enjoyable activity, such as a picnic or walking in the woods. The therapist asks the student to note the easy feelings of relaxation and then moves gradually up the hierarchy, having the client visualize each scene in the hierarchy. If tension is felt, the client may indicate this by a raised finger. For example, if tension was experienced as the student visualized the situation two days before the examination, the therapist and student would work to note the tense muscles and relax them while still thinking of the usually tension-producing scene.

Gradually, the client learns to visualize all the scenes in the anxiety hierarchy while relaxed. This type of training may take several interviews, but it has been demonstrated to be effective. When students find themselves in similar tension-producing situations, they are able to generate relaxation behaviors to counteract the feelings of tension.

Similar work with anxiety hierarchies has proven equally effective in many anxiety and phobic situations. Some of the most dramatic demonstrations of desensitization procedures have been with snake phobics who, as a final test, allowed a snake to crawl over them (Bandura, Blanchard, & Ritter, 1969).

Frigidity and impotency also have been successfully treated with this method. In these cases, couples construct anxiety hierarchies related to sexual experimentation and the sex act. Generally, it is found that the sex act is the most tension-producing experience of all. Assuming there is no biological component, couples are instructed in systematic relaxation and go through the anxiety hierarchy visualization, much as did the student with examination anxiety. When transferring the newly learned behavior to the bedroom, the couple is often instructed to stop further sexual experimentation until full relaxation is regained.

Modeling and Social Skills Training

Seeing is believing, it is said, and behavioral psychologists have found that watching films or videotapes of people engaging in successful behavior is sufficient for clients to learn new ways of coping with difficulties. For example, Bandura (1976) found that live modeling of snake handling was even more effective than systematic desensitization in teaching snake phobics to cope with their anxieties.

> After observing the therapist interacting closely with the snake, clients were aided through other induction procedures to perform progressively more frightening responses themselves. At each step the therapist . . . performed the activities fearlessly and gradually led the clients to touch, stroke, and hold the midsection of the snake's body with gloved and then bare hands for increasing periods. . . . As clients became more courageous, the therapist gradually reduced [the] level of participation and control over the snake until eventually clients were able to tolerate the squirming snake in their laps without assistance, to let the snake loose in the room and retrieve it, and to let it crawl freely over their bodies. (p. 256)

In a sense, modeling is one of the most simple and obvious ways to teach clients new behaviors. Seeing and hearing directly, either live or via film or tape, brings home a message much more clearly and directly than direct advice and description. Modeling can be combined with relaxation, assertiveness training, and other behavioral techniques in developing uniquely individualized programs for clients. Modeling is a key ingredient in social skills training.

Social Skills Training

An increasingly important part of cognitive-behavioral methods is that of skills training—teaching clients and others specific modes of responding. Skills training is the subject of three important books (Hargie, Saunders, & Dickson, 1987; Larson, 1984; Marshall, Kurtz, & Associates, 1982), which present a wide variety of systematic formulations for teaching communication skills, life skills for difficult/delinquent adolescents, marital skills, skills for psychiatric patients, among others. Skills training, in fact, is beginning to present itself as a theory of psychotherapy and change in its own right.

Most often, skills training involves the following cognitive-behavioral components:

1. *Rapport/structuring.* Clients/trainees are prepared cognitively and emotionally for the instruction.

2. *Cognitive presentation and cueing.* Usually, some form of explanation and rationale for the skill is presented. In stress inoculation, Meichenbaum (1985), using Socratic-type questions, helps clients in a collaborative fashion better understand the nature of stress and why it is important to learn stress management.

3. *Modeling.* Role-plays, videotapes, audiotapes, and demonstrations are commonly used so that trainees can see and hear the behaviors of the skill in action. Cognitions from earlier stages are paired with specific observable behaviors.

4. *Practice.* One does not always learn a skill by cognitive understanding and watching. Most skills trainers require their clients/trainees to engage in the skill

through role-played practice possibly supplemented by videotape and audiotape feedback. It is important that the skill be mastered to a high level or it is likely to be lost over time.

5. *Generalization.* All skills training emphasizes the decision to take the learning outside and beyond the immediate situation of the training session. In some cases, a full relapse prevention worksheet will be employed. The cognitive-behavioral therapist works with the client (or clients if the treatment is conducted on a group basis) to anticipate possible barriers or obstacles that might interfere with their employing coping skills. In this way, clients become their own therapists.

One cognitive-behavioral skills training program is that of the microskills framework of Chapter 3 in which counseling and communication skills are taught. It has been found that teaching these skills is not only useful for training in counseling and therapy, but also for a wide variety of patient and client groups.

More specifically, Ivey (1971, 1991) videotaped depressed psychiatric patients talking about their issues with a therapist. The patients then viewed the videotape and observed and counted behaviors they themselves selected (for example, poor eye contact, slumped body posture). The patients practiced the skills in role-plays with the therapist and counted and charted changes in pinpointed behaviors. This "media therapy" project proved effective in helping patients who had been in the hospital for up to four years move out of the hospital within from one to two months.

In addition to psychiatric patients, others have benefited from this form of training, including management interns, medical personnel, and hospice workers. Skills training itself is a major theoretical and practical form of treatment and is closely related to assertiveness training. Practice Exercise 9.4 presents the structure for teaching social skills to clients.

Assertiveness Training

Some individuals passively accept whatever fate hands them. You may know someone who acts as a "doormat" and allows friends and family to dominate. This person may allow others to make decisions, let strangers cut in front while standing in line, or accept being ignored by a waiter for an hour. Individuals who may be overly passive in their behavior can benefit from assertiveness training and learn to stand up for their rights.

You may also know someone who is overly aggressive and dominating, who tells others what to do and what to think. This person may interrupt conversations rudely, cut in front of others in line, and yell at waiters. This aggressive individual can also benefit from assertiveness training.

Assertiveness training involves learning to stand up for your rights—but simultaneously to consider the thoughts and feelings of others. While emphasizing overt behavior, assertiveness training also focuses on client cognitions.

Practice Exercise 9.4

 An Exercise in Social Skills Training

An effective behavioral technique is direct instruction of how to behave in a variety of social situations. One of the most common, yet important, social skills is the microskill of attending behavior. Culturally appropriate eye contact, body language, vocal tone, and verbal following behavior are often missing in depressed, shy/avoidant, angry/resistant, and many other clients. Teaching these clients the basics of attending, as follows, often can make a significant difference:

1. Establish rapport and tell your client what to expect. Although you are planning to teach a skill, take a mutual coconstructive approach, ensuring that what you are about to share has some positive meaning for your client.
2. Tell your client about the primary dimensions of attending behavior. Discuss their value, and be sure that you maintain awareness of and respect for cultural differences.
3. Conduct a role-play in which the client talks to you using poor attending skills. Or you may want to role-

play the negative behavior yourself so that the client can get an image of what failure to attend looks like. Discuss this negative model.
4. Have the client engage in a positive role-play. If the client has difficulty, focus on a single dimension of attending—for example, eye contact. Continue practicing until the client masters the skill.
5. Plan for generalization to real-life situations and follow up to see if the skill has been mastered.

This same structure can be used to teach a wide variety of social skills. In drug education, refusal skills are very important. The specific social skill in this case is the ability to say no. Another example is working with teens on dating skills. Social skills training is also important with perpetrators of violence. These individuals often lack attending and listening skills, may not be able to recognize when another person says no, and may lack many other basic skills of living. This approach also is effective with large or small groups in workshop settings.

Alberti and Emmons (1970/1990) are recognized as the pioneers of assertiveness training. Bower (1990) and Bower and Bower (1985) have written highly useful statements on the framework. Bower (1976) and Phelps (1987) specifically apply the model to women. Cheek (1976) first discussed the multicultural implications of the framework and provided important linkage for more cognitively oriented assertiveness training.

The specifics of assertiveness training are outlined in Practice Exercise 9.5. If you can conduct a basic applied behavioral analysis and can pinpoint behavior with some precision, you should be able to conduct assertiveness training with some understanding and skill. This practice exercise is oriented toward behavioral assertiveness training, with minimal attention to internal cognitive states. If your depressed, agoraphobic, or normal clients do not have some attention paid to their internal states of thinking and feeling, change is much less likely to occur and be maintained. The cognitive dimensions of CBT stressed in Chapter 10 are critical for producing enduring change.

Practice Exercise 9.5

 An Exercise in Applied Behavioral Analysis and Assertiveness Training

The purpose of this exercise is to integrate the concepts of this chapter in a practical format that you can use to implement assertiveness training in your own counseling practice. With a role-played client who is willing to discuss a specific situation in which he or she may have been too passive or too aggressive, work carefully through the following interview:

1. *Rapport/structuring.* Remember that data indicate that behaviorally oriented counselors and therapists offer as much or more warmth than other orientations to helping. Establish rapport with your client in your own unique way and use attending behavior to "tune in" to the client and client observation skills to note when you have established rapport.

Give special attention to structuring the interview and telling your client ahead of time what to expect. Behavioral counseling operates on mutuality between counselor and client.

2. *Data gathering.* Your goal is to get a clear, behavioral definition of the problem. The basic learning sequence (BLS) will help you draw out the specific

behavior. Identify a clear, specific instance in which the individual was not sufficiently assertive. Asking for concrete examples will facilitate operationalizing the present overly passive or overly aggressive behavior.

Use applied behavioral analysis to find out the antecedents of the behavior. What was the context, and what happened before the behavior occurred? Define the problem behavior even more precisely. Finally, what were the consequences after the behavior? In each case, use questioning skills to help the client describe the behavior.

A role-play is a particularly useful way to obtain further behavioral specifics. Once you have a clear picture of antecedent-behavior-consequence, have your client role-play the situation with you acting as the other person(s). Make the role-play as real and accurate as you can.

Finally, draw out positive assets of the client and the situation. What strengths does the client have that will be useful in later problem solution? You may find it necessary to provide your client with positive feedback, as nonassertive clients often have trouble identifying any positives in themselves or the situation.

3. *Determining outcomes.* Develop clear, specific behavioral goals with your client. You will want to use listening skills and operationalization of behavior methods. Is the goal established by your client clear, specific, and attainable? Will it lead to change?

4. *Generating alternative solutions.* At this point you have the goals of the client that can be contrasted with the problem as defined. In addition, you have some positive assets and strengths of the client.

With your client, review the goals and then practice in a role-play the new behaviors represented by those goals. Continue practicing with your client until the client demonstrates the ability to engage in the behavior.

You may find that relaxation training, charting, modeling, cognitive-behavioral therapy, and other behavioral techniques may be useful to supplement and enrich your behavioral program.

5. *Generalization.* It is easy for the successful therapist to stop at the fourth stage. Here it is critical that specific behavioral plans be made with your client for generalization of the behavior beyond the session. Use the relapse prevention form (presented later in this chapter) with your client. Be clear and specific with your behavioral goals and anticipate the likely relapse potential. Behavior that is not reinforced immediately after training is likely to be lost two weeks later.

6. *Follow-up.* One week after the interview, follow up with your client and determine if behavior actually did change. Later follow-ups can be useful to both you and the client. As necessary, use the relapse form to analyze any difficulty with behavioral generalization.

Multicultural Dimensions

Imagine you are working with a woman or minority who is dealing with discrimination and the associated stress. One important dimension of being able to engage in assertiveness training is feeling good about oneself. Sometimes people who experience discrimination believe that the problems they suffer are "their fault" and that "if only" they behaved more effectively, their problems would resolve.

In addressing these attitudes, cognitive instruction, as discussed in Chapter 10, can be a vital part of assertiveness training. Furthermore, the ideas of multicultural counseling and therapy (Chapters 5 and 6) clearly show that the focus of your intervention must often be on changing the environment, not just the individual. In assertiveness training language, there is a need to help individuals change cognitions about themselves and their environments so that they can be more effective and assertive.

Cheek (1976), for example, talks of the importance of "a foundation for the Black perspective." Assertiveness training does not seek to have African-Americans behave or think like European-Americans or to have women think like men. Assertiveness training seeks to recognize the perspective and worldview of different multicultural and gender groups. Cheek (1976) notes that the African-American cognitive perspective includes

- Familiarity and experience in both the African-American and European-American perspectives
- A frequent distrust of European-Americans, with accompanying emotions such as anger and rage
- An emphasis on race and its importance
- Internal conflict as to whether to talk in "White" or "Black"; African-Americans are often bidialectical
- An ability to "fake it" with European-Americans

Fifteen years later, Cheatham (1990), Parham (1990), and White and Parham (1990) addressed many of the same issues, leading to the conclusions that behavioral change is insufficient and that cognitive work on societal issues must be part of any treatment program with minorities. Focusing on the individual solely will often be seen as "blaming the victim." Cheatham argues that techniques such as assertiveness training, although useful, beg the question of causation: Did the problem originate in the client or society? If the latter is the issue, Cheatham advocates action by the counselor in the community or society as the best route toward individual change. Given this, the non-African-American therapist or counselor must put behavioral treatment in context. Clearly, the techniques and ideas of this chapter have multicultural relevance, but they can only be accepted as part of the solution.

Similar issues of the meaning of assertiveness training with various groups can be raised. For example, assertiveness training for Latinas needs to be conducted with cultural sensitivity, for women from a Spanish-speaking tradition face different problems when they act assertively than do most European-American women. What is assertive for European-American cultures may be considered intrusive and aggressive by those from other cultural groups. This latter point it especially true for those who may come from more sensitive cultures.

European-American women usually find assertiveness training helpful, but it is most helpful if combined with issues around being a woman in a sexist society. Kantrowitz and Ballou (1992) give special attention to assertiveness training, stating that in a practical setting, assertiveness training should not be used to teach women a man's style of being. Cheek (1976) supports this point, noting that assertiveness training should be oriented to the African-American culture and not "make Blacks White." Individual and societal issues have clearly become part of the assertiveness training movement. Assertiveness will appear in different forms in, for example, New York City and Charleston, S.C.

Relapse Prevention

Relapse prevention (RP) is a set of cognitive-behavioral techniques and strategies developed by Marlatt and Gordon (1985) that have become foundational to counseling and therapy. It is an axiom of therapy that clients often will lose insights, behaviors, and new skills gained from therapy if the counselor does not take specific action to help clients maintain these gains.

In your client sessions, you may see some changes taking place. Then the client returns to the home environment and faces the same problems that led to therapy. For example, an alcohol abuser or a teenager suffering from bulimia must live with the same family and/or job circumstances that likely played an important part in generating the original difficulties. Your task in relapse prevention is to work with clients to help them find workable strategies for the future.

Research on Relapse Prevention

General findings on relapse prevention show that single efforts at maintaining client behavior change are weaker than more broad-based comprehensive programs. The RP model is a comprehensive program based on Marlatt's work with alcohol addiction (Daley, 1989; Marlatt & Gordon, 1985) that was later extended to weight control (Rosenthal & Marx, 1979) and to the maintenance of skills training (Marx, 1982, 1984).

Research on relapse has shown that the initial lapse in treatment is particularly important in the likelihood of future and continued lapses. For example, in weight control therapy, the way the overeater handles the first failure to stay on the diet is highly predictive of what will happen in the future. Because skills developed in therapy have not yet been tested in real-life situations, we can expect relapse in nearly 100 percent of our clients in some form. Our task as therapists is to help our clients construct relapse prevention programs (generalization programs in the fifth stage of the interview) to ensure that newly learned behavior and insights are not lost shortly after the interview. Research in RP clearly indicates that a systematic program can help clients learn more from their therapy and training programs and maintain their behavioral change for a longer time.

Helping the Client Cope with the Environment

Environmental realities (family, job, the availability of cigarettes, drugs, and so on) often conspire to make long-term behavioral maintenance almost impossible. To combat the difficulties of the environment, Marx developed a four-point program to help clients become more prepared to manage the postcounseling environment.

1. *Anticipate difficult situations.* Clients can often predict the circumstances likely to be threatening to their resolve to maintain their behavioral change program. Clients, with the counselor's assistance, can identify high-risk situations that might sabotage new learning and serve as an early warning system so that they will be on guard against relapse.

2. *Regulate thoughts and feelings.* Emotions can sometimes get out of control and make us feel incompetent, upset, or temporarily irrational. Relapses are less likely to occur if clients expect these temporary responses and then return to a rational approach and learn from their mistakes.

3. *Diagnose necessary support skills.* Although we may help clients change behavior, their old patterns may reemerge when they are in a hurry or when faced with other stressors. Techniques such as assertiveness training, time management, or key cognitive skills may be useful in helping clients avoid eventual relapse.

4. *Regulate consequences.* A key behavioral concern is to provide appropriate consequences for behavior. When a client maintains a new behavior, there will be no thunderous applause. That support must come from the client, who must learn how to create meaningful rewards for good actions and behavioral maintenance.

Making RP Work for You

Practice Exercise 9.6 summarizes the RP program so you can use it with a real or role-played client. Note that RP is skill specific. For example, a client may want to stop overeating. The task of the therapist is to help the client understand the several strategies that are available for controlling overeating. Once clients have learned the behavioral techniques to slow down the rate of eating (that is, eat only in specified places and times, monitor calories, understand how emotions affect eating, and eliminate discretionary eating), they are ready to begin preparing for the hurdles in the environment once counseling is over and they must manage on their own.

Stress Management

Stress management training programs involve three distinct phases: (1) helping clients develop a cognitive understanding of the role stress plays in their lives, (2) teaching specific coping skills so they can deal with stress effectively, and (3) working with thoughts and feelings about the stressful situation so they will be motivated to do something about stress. Meichenbaum (1985, 1993) makes the important point that cognitive awareness of stress is not enough to produce change, nor are learning skills. One must actually decide to do something. Ultimately, a change in behavior as well as in thoughts and feelings must occur.

An Example

A professional couple may be faced with difficulties in their lives and may very frequently argue with each other. Their problem could be defined as a "marital difficulty," or it could be defined as a problem in coping with stress. The couple both may work and have two children and be active in the community. There simply is

▰▰▰ Practice Exercise 9.6 ▰▰▰

 ## Relapse Prevention Worksheet

Self-Management Strategies for Skill Retention

by Robert Marx

(Go through this worksheet by yourself, perhaps using a behavior you have difficulty in maintaining. Alternatively, use the form to go through the danger of relapse with a real or role-played client.)

I. Choosing an Appropriate Behavior to Retain

Describe in detail the behavior you intend to retain:

_____

_____

How often will you use it? _____

How will you know when a slip occurs?

_____

II. Relapse Prevention Strategies

A. Strategies to help you anticipate and monitor potential difficulties—regulating stimuli

1. Do you understand the relapse process? What is it?
2. What are the differences between learning the behavioral skill or thought and using it in a difficult situation?
3. Support network? Who can help you maintain the skill?
4. High-risk situations? What kind of people, places, or things will make retention especially difficult?

B. Strategies to increase rational thinking—regulating thoughts and feelings

5. What might be an unreasonable emotional response to a temporary slip or relapse?
6. What can you do to think more effectively in tempting situations or after a relapse?

C. Strategies to diagnose and practice related support skills—regulating behaviors

7. What additional support skills do you need to retain the skill? Assertiveness? Relaxation? Microskills?

D. Strategies to provide appropriate outcomes for behavior—regulating consequences

8. Can you identify some likely outcomes of your succeeding with your new behavior.
9. How can you reward yourself for a job well done? Generate specific rewards and satisfactions.

Predicting the Circumstance of the First Lapse

Describe the details of how the first lapse might occur, including people, places, times, emotional states.

SOURCE: Adapted from R. Marx, University of Massachusetts. Used by permission.

not time to "do it all" effectively, and this becomes a major stressor in itself. The first task in stress management is to help the couple define the problem as one of stress. This itself can be useful, as they no longer have to "blame" each other for their difficulties and now can see the impact of their environment on the marriage.

Second, this couple needs to learn stress reduction procedures (such as relaxation training) and decision making and social skills (often via a form of assertiveness training) so that they might learn alternatives to constant work. These behavioral skills can lead to important changes and will likely involve techniques of modeling, role-play, and direct instruction.

Finally, knowing one has a problem with stress and having some skills are not enough. Will the couple decide for action? At the point of generalization, their emotional and cognitive world may again become stress engendering, and maladaptive thinking (and the accompanying dysfunctional emotions) will prevent them from a decision to act. Relapse prevention may be employed to ensure action. The therapist may follow up with this couple to ensure that they actually do implement the systematic plan of behavioral change that has been pinpointed.

Racism and Stress

Racism can produce damaging stress. For example, McNeilly (1996) found that racist comments from Whites "triggered significant rises in blood pressure and heart rate in 30 Black women. . . . Racism can act as a potent stressor that may contribute to hypertension and heart disease" (p. A7). Similarly, a woman who encounters sexual harassment, a gay or lesbian who is attacked for sexual preference, and other groups that experience either short-term or systematic discrimination also suffer physically from stress. Stress management can be an important component in multiculturally respectful counseling and therapy.

Stress Management Training

Most therapists and counselors today find themselves required to do some sort of stress inoculation or stress management training as part of individual therapy. Moreover, as a therapist you might well be called on to conduct a group training program in stress management. Stress management programs combine many of the behavioral techniques described in this chapter plus important cognitive techniques of the next chapter. Assertiveness training is often an important part of stress management, as are the microskills of listening (Chapter 3). Practice Exercise 9.7 asks you to generate your own stress management program for use with clients and in training small groups.

Stress Management Training and Trauma.   The concepts of stress management and stress inoculation have been expanded to include specific suggestions on how to work with survivors of trauma (rape, abuse, terrorist attacks). Stress management is increasingly vital as a treatment framework in its own right. Meichenbaum (1993) elaborates his innovative ideas and includes suggested clinical interventions for work-

Practice Exercise 9.7

Developing Your Own Stress Management Program

You may use any of a large number of strategies in individual counseling and therapy for helping clients deal with stress. For example, you might teach a lonely or shy person the microskills of listening and then use assertiveness training to help this individual become more socially effective. You can teach relaxation training or desensitization to phobic clients to help reduce their stress level. Most cognitive-behavioral techniques can be used for individual or group stress management programs.

To experience the powerfulness of stress management, get together a small group of three or more individuals with similar issues and spend at least two hours teaching them some of the basic principles of stress management. A model group stress management program includes, but need not be restricted to, the following:

1. *Establish rapport and relate program goals to your group's special needs.* Usually, there is a special topic or need the group shares. For example, your group might be teenagers, adult children of alcoholics, women dealing with job stress, or an inpatient group diagnosed as borderline. Spend time with your group so that they feel part of the process.

    Your task at this stage is to share your program goals and to learn the individual needs of your members. Modify your program to meet their wishes and needs.

2. *Provide cognitive instruction as to the origins of stress and what it does to people.* Following the collaborative model, draw out from your group the nature of stress in their lives. Story-

telling and personal sharing will draw your group together and help define a common purpose.

You can share a brief lecture on the nature of stress and what it does to the body and to our minds. An analysis of the antecedents, behaviors, and consequences of stress can be especially helpful. In addition, you may want to brainstorm the many stressful events we all face in our daily lives. This list may include various stressors, such as commuting, conflict with supervisors, family arguments, loss of a job, medical issues, or the neighbor's dog barking.

3. *Stress management training.* Select your own favorite stress management techniques for this first session. Review your own special skills and experience, and make your first try at stress management from what you know best. Usually, stress programs include some form of relaxation training, meditation, or yoga, personal sharing of coping mechanisms, listening skills training, and assertiveness training. Do not overplan, and be sure your program itself is not rushed and stressful. You will also want to tailor your stress management program to the special needs of your group.

4. *Homework.* Relapse prevention techniques are an important part of a stress management program. Unless your trainees are encouraged to "take home" what they have learned, the experience with you is likely to be forgotten. Follow up with your workshop participants a week later to see how effective your program was.

ing with posttraumatic stress clients. Stress management will not "cure" extremely severe stress issues, but it can be an important part of the therapeutic approach.

For example, a nine-session stress inoculation was used with rape survivors by Foa and others (1991) and was found to be more effective than traditional counseling in that long-term follow-up revealed significant improvement in posttraumatic stress disorder. The overall content of the sessions was similar to the general concepts presented in this chapter, although considerable emphasis was also given to cognitive variables as well, such as those described in Chapter 10.

More recently, Foa, Hearst-Ikeda, and Perry (1995) examined the effectiveness of brief cognitive-behavioral therapy with recent assault survivors and found that a combination of education about common reactions to assault plus CBT resulted in significantly fewer symptoms of posttraumatic stress disorder five and a half months after the assault.

Working with clients who have experienced trauma requires special training beyond the scope of this book. Further direction for work with these clients can be found in Donald Meichenbaum's *A Clinical Handbook/Practical Therapist Manual for Assessing and Treating Adults with Post-Traumatic Stress Disorder (PTSD)* (Meichenbaum, 1994).

Limitations and Practical Implications of Practicing Cognitive-Behavioral Therapy

Ineffective and careless counseling can endanger clients. No matter how good the theory or the potential power of a counseling or treatment intervention is, the counselor has the professional and ethical responsibility to be aware of manifestations of false practice. The term *manipulative behavioral counseling* can be used to describe the misuse of these techniques.

Manipulative behavioral counseling occurs when the counselor makes a decision for the client without client awareness or when the counselor has so much power in the client's life that the client has no choice but to go along with the behavioral program whether or not he or she agrees. For example, a focus of behavioral counselors has been to increase "time on task" (amount of time spent working at one's desk) in elementary classrooms. This can be a desirable educational goal, but sometimes these behavioral interventions have been implemented without child or parent awareness that anything was being changed.

Cognitive-behavioral techniques are often readily accepted by minority clients due to their clarity and effectiveness. At the same time, effectiveness does not equate with cultural appropriateness. As Cheek reminds us, cognitive-behavioral techniques need to be applied with the gender and culture of the client in mind.

The several practice exercises in this chapter provide a solid beginning in cognitive-behavioral counseling and therapy. Relapse prevention is an especially useful set of techniques to add to the final stages of the interview, regardless of what therapeutic technique or theory you are using. The fifth stage of the interview (generalization), follow-up with clients after the interview, and relapse prevention are critical elements for therapy.

Behavioral techniques "work," and clients often benefit from and enjoy the specificity of these techniques. At the same time, some clients will change their behavior but still feel that "something is missing." These clients may benefit from the addition of more cognitive methods (Chapter 10) to your treatment plan, or some may want to examine the reasons their behavior developed as it did. In short, you may find that behavioral counseling benefits from association with other helping theories.

REFERENCES

AGRAS, S., LEITENBERG, H., & BARLOW, D. (1968). Social reinforcement in the modification of agoraphobia. *Archives of General Philosophy, 19,* 423–27.

ALBERTI, R., & EMMONS, M. (1990). *Your perfect right* (6th ed.). San Luis Obispo, CA: Impact. (Original work published 1970)

AMERICAN PSYCHIATRIC ASSOCIATION. (1994). *DSM-IV.* Washington, DC: Author.

BAILEY, B., GOOD, M., & McGRADY, A. (1990). Clinical observations on behavioral treatment of a patient with insulin-dependent diabetes mellitus. *Biofeedback and Self Regulation, 15,* 7–13.

BANDURA, A. (1976). Effecting change through participant modeling. In J. Krumboltz & C. Thoresen (Eds.), *Counseling methods* (pp. 248–64). Troy, MO: Holt, Rinehart & Winston.

BANDURA, A. (1982). Self-efficacy: Mechanism in human agency. *American Psychologist, 37,* 122–47.

BANDURA, A. (1989). Human agency in social cognitive theory. *American Psychologist, 44,* 1175–85.

BANDURA, A., BLANCHARD, E., & RITTER, B. (1969). The relative efficacy of desensitization and modeling approaches. *Journal of Personality and Social Psychology, 13,* 173–99.

BOWER, S. (1976). Assertiveness training for women. In J. Krumboltz & C. Thoresen (Eds.), *Counseling methods* (pp. 467–74). Troy, MO: Holt, Rinehart & Winston.

BOWER, S. (1990). *Painless public speaking.* Northhamptonshire, U.K.: Thorsons.

BOWER, S., & BOWER, G. (1985). *Asserting yourself.* Reading, MA: Addison-Wesley.

CARLSON, J. G., CHEMTOB, C. M., RUSNAK, K., & HEDLUND, N. L. (1995, June). *A controlled study of EMDR and biofeedback assisted relaxation for the treatment of PTSD.* Paper presented at the fourth European Conference on Traumatic Stress, Paris, France.

CHEATHAM, H. (1990). Empowering Black families. In H. Cheatham & J. Stewart (Eds.), *Black families* (pp. 373–93). New Brunswick, NJ: Transaction.

CHEEK, D. (1976). *Assertive Black . . . puzzled White.* San Luis Obispo, CA: Impact.

DALEY, D. (Ed.). (1989). *Relapse: Conceptual, research, and clinical perspectives.* New York: Haworth.

DIONNE, H. (1990, October). *Parents with panic disorder: The impact on their children.* Unpublished comprehensive paper, University of Massachusetts, Amherst.

EMMELKAMP, P., BRILMAN, E., KUIPER, H., & MERSH, P. (1986). The treatment of agoraphobia. *Behavior Modification, 10,* 37–53.

EMMELKAMP, P., & MERSH, P. (1982). Cognition and exposure *in vivo* in the treatment of agoraphobia. *Cognitive Research and Therapy, 6,* 72–90.

FOA, E., HEARST-IKEDA, D., & PERRY, K. (1995). Evaluation of a brief cognitive-behavioral program for prevention of chronic PTSD and recent assault victims. *Journal of Consulting and Clinical Psychology, 63,* 948–55.

FOA, E., ROTHBAUM, B., RIGGS, D., & MURDOCK, T. (1991). Treatment of post-traumatic stress disorder in rape victims: A comparison between cognitive-behavior procedures and counseling. *Journal of Clinical and Consulting Psychology, 99*, 715–23.

GRAZZI, L., LEONE, M., FREDIANI, F., & BUSSONE, G. (1990). A therapeutic alternative for tension headache in children: Treatment and one-year follow-up results. *Biofeedback and Self Regulation, 15*, 1–6.

GREENSPOON, J. (1955). The reinforcing effect of two spoken sounds on the frequency of two responses. *American Journal of Psychology, 68*, 409–16.

HARGIE, O., SAUNDERS, C., & DICKSON, D. (1987). *Social skills in interpersonal communication.* Cambridge, MA: Brookline.

HATCH, J., & SAITO, I. (1990). Growth and development of biofeedback: A bibliographic update. *Biofeedback and Self Regulation, 15*, 37–46.

HOOLEY, J., ORLEY, J., & TEASDALE, J. (1987). Levels of expressed emotion and relapse in depressed patients. *British Journal of Psychiatry, 7*, 643–47.

IVEY, A. (1971). Media therapy: Educational change planning for psychiatric patients. *Journal of Counseling Psychology, 20*, 338–43.

IVEY, A. (1991, September). *Developmental therapy and media therapy: An update.* Presentation to Veterans Administration Conference, Orlando, FL.

IVEY, A., & HINKLE, J. (1968). Students, the major untapped resource in higher education. *Reach* (a publication of the Colorado State University *Collegian*), *6*, 1, 4.

KANTROWITZ, R., & BALLOU, M. (1992). A feminist critique of cognitive-behavioral therapy. In L. Brown & M. Ballou (Eds.), *Theories of personality and psychopathology: Feminist reappraisals* (pp. 70–87). New York: Guilford.

KELLY, G. (1955). *The psychology of personal constructs.* New York: W.W. Norton.

LARSON, D. (Ed.). (1984). *Teaching psychological skills.* Belmont, CA: Wadsworth.

LEARY, W. (1991, October 22). Black hypertension may reflect other ills. *New York Times*, p. C3.

MARLATT, G., & GORDON, J. (1985). Relapse prevention: Maintenance strategies in the treatment of addictive behaviors. New York: Guilford.

MARSHALL, E., KURTZ, P., & ASSOCIATES. (1982). *Interpersonal helping skills.* San Francisco: Jossey-Bass.

MARX, R. (1982). Relapse prevention for managerial training: A model for maintenance of behavior change. *Academy of Management Review, 7*, 433–41.

MARX, R. (1984, August). *Self-control strategies in management training: Skill maintenance despite organizational realities.* Symposium chaired at the annual meeting of the American Psychological Association, Toronto, Canada.

MCNEILLY, M. (1996, March 18). Stress of racism may kill, study finds. *Honolulu Advertiser*, p. A7.

MEICHENBAUM, D. (1985). *Stress inoculation training.* New York: Pergamon Press.

MEICHENBAUM, D. (1990, December). *Evolution of cognitive behavior therapy: Origins, tenets and clinical examples.* Paper presented at the second conference on the Evolution of Psychotherapy, Anaheim, CA.

MEICHENBAUM, D. (1991). Evolution of cognitive behavior therapy. In J. Zeig (Ed.), *The evolution of psychology, II.* New York: Brunner/Mazel.

MEICHENBAUM, D. (1993). Stress inoculation training: A twenty-year update. In R. Wolfolk & P. Lehrer (Eds.), *Principles and practices of stress management.* New York: Guilford.

MEICHENBAUM, D. (1994). *A clinical handbook/practical therapy manual for assessing and treating adults with post-traumatic stress disorder (PTSD).* Waterloo, Ontario: Institute Press.

MEICHENBAUM, D. & GILMORE, J. (1984). The unconscious reconsidered: A cognitive behavioral perspective. In K. Bowers & D. Meichenbaum (Eds.), *The unconscious reconsidered.* New York: Wiley.

MICHELSON, L. (1987). Cognitive-behavioral assessment and treatment of agoraphobia. In L. Michelson & L. Ascher (Eds.), *Anxiety and stress disorders* (pp. 213–70). New York: Guilford.

MICHELSON, L., MAVISSAKALIAN, M., & MARCHIONE, K. (1985). Cognitive-behavioral treatment of agoraphobia. *Journal of Consulting and Clinical Psychology, 53*, 913–25.

PARHAM, T. (1990). *Do the right thing: Racial discussion in counseling psychology.* Paper presented at the American Psychological Association Convention, Boston.

PHELPS, S. (1987). *The assertive woman.* San Luis Obispo, CA: Impact.

ROSENTHAL, B., & MARX, R. (1979, December). *A comparison of standard behavior and relapse prevention weight reduction programs.* Paper presented at the meeting of the Association for the Advancement of Behavior Therapy, San Francisco.

ROTHBAUM, B. O. (1995, November). *A controlled study of EMDR for PTSD.* Paper presented at the twenty-ninth annual convention of the Association for the Advancement of Behavior Therapy, Washington, DC.

SHAPIRO, F. (1991). Eye movement desensitization: A new treatment for post-traumatic stress disorder. *Journal of Behavior Therapy and Experimental Psychiatry, 20*, 211–17.

SHAPIRO, F. (1994). EMD/R. *Behavior Therapist, 17*, 153–56.

SKINNER, B. F. (1953). *Science and human behavior.* New York: Free Press.

SLOANE, R., STAPLES, F., CRISTOL, A., YORKSTON, N., & WHIPPLE, K. (1975). *Psychotherapy vs. behavior therapy.* Cambridge, MA: Harvard University Press.

SULZER-AZAROFF, B. (1985). Achieving educational success. Troy, MO: Holt, Rinehart & Winston.

SULZER-AZAROFF, B., & MAYER, G. (1977). Applying behavior-analysis procedures with children and youth. Troy, MO: Holt, Rinehart & Winston.

WHITE, J., & PARHAM, T. (1990). *The psychology of Blacks.* Englewood Cliffs, NJ: Prentice-Hall.

WILSON, S. A., BECKER, L. A., & TINKER, R. H. (1995, May). *EMDR: Fifteen-month follow-up of a controlled study.* Paper presented at the annual conference of the American Psychiatric Association, Miami, FL.

WOLPE, J., & LAZARUS, A. (1966). *Behavior therapy techniques.* Elmsford, NY: Pergamon Press.

WOOLFOLK, R., & RICHARDSON, F. (1984). Behavior therapy and the ideology of modernity. *American Psychologist, 39*, 777–86.

Cognitive-Behavioral Therapy and Counseling II: Cognitive and Integrative Approaches

CHAPTER GOALS

This chapter seeks to:

1. Present the worldview provided by the more cognitive portion of the cognitive-behavioral tradition.

2. Relate the cognitive orientation to multicultural counseling and therapy.

3. Describe the key ideas of three important cognitive-behavioral theorists—Ellis, Beck, and Glasser—and illustrate some of their work with case examples.

4. Provide an integrative view of CBT through the lens of Arnold Lazarus's multimodal therapy.

5. Enable you, through practice exercises, to conduct or engage in

   - Ellis's rational-emotive behavioral analysis of cognitions
   - Beck's analysis of automatic thoughts
   - Glasser's reality therapy, adapted to include contextual and multicultural cognitive issues
   - Lazarus's BASIC ID assessment and treatment planning

The Cognitive Worldview and Its Relation to Cognitive-Behavioral Tradition

Integration of thought, feeling, and action is the task of cognitive-behavioral therapy and counseling (CBT). In this chapter, the focus is on the work of therapists whose writing primarily emphasizes cognition. Yet, it is critical to recall that thought without accompanying action (cognition without accompanying behavior) is considered empty by CBT and integrative theorists.

Chapter 9 has shown the evolution of behavioral psychology to a more cognitive orientation. In different ways, three figures—Albert Ellis, Aaron Beck, and William Glasser—have been leaders in this direction. All three stress the importance of two goals in counseling and therapy: (1) to examine how clients think about themselves and their world and, if necessary, to help them change these cognitions; and (2) to ensure that clients act on those cognitions through behavior in their daily life—thus the term *cognitive-behavioral*.

Most reviewers of the cognitive frame of reference trace the history of the movement to the stoic philosopher Epictetus, who noted that people "are disturbed not by events, but by the views they take of them." Changing how one thinks about the world, then, becomes a major goal of the cognitive-behavioral point of view.

A worldview in which thinking and ideas about the world are central can be traced beyond stoicism to Plato and also to the philosophies of idealism. The philosophies of idealism emphasize that the idea one has about the world is more important than what is "real." In fact, the concept of "reality" may be dismissed by the idealists as a mere "idea about things." More recent adaptations of the idealistic philosophic tradition are manifested in the work of Kant and Hegel. The work of Freud may be described as being in this tradition. Freud in some ways was a stoic, as he felt that little could be done about the human condition except to know it and understand it. Behavioral change may be helpful in this frame of reference but is still viewed as relatively limited in scope.

But what about "reality"? The British and American logical positivists and pragmatists (Bentham, Mill, James, Russell) have questioned that cognition and good thinking are meaningful or sufficient for living in the real world. Out of their philosophic work has arisen the optimistic scientific tradition of hypothesis testing and direct action on the world. Behavioral psychology, as represented by Skinner and the cognitive-behavioral work of Meichenbaum, is an obvious extension of this scientific, realistic orientation.

Existentialist philosophers such as Kierkegaard, Tillich, and Sartre question both idealistic and realistic philosophers and emphasize the act of individual choice and the process of intentionally choosing and deciding. Rogers and Perls clearly represent this orientation to helping.

The cognitive-behavioral worldview may be described as a beginning attempt to integrate the three major philosophic traditions of idealism, realism, and existentialism. Ellis, considered a pioneer of cognitive-behavioral theory, first maintained a psychodynamic practice. He then started work on his theory of rational-emotive therapy and was classified in the existential-humanistic tradition for many years. However, he continued to emphasize the importance of action in his practice. Many of his ideas were adopted by behavioral psychology, and Ellis considers himself a cognitive behaviorist.

The worldview of cognitive-behavioral therapy, then, may be described as an evolving synthesis of the three major philosophic and psychological traditions of the Western world. The cognitive-behavioral theorist will ultimately be interested in knowing how the individual developed ideas or cognitions about reality, chooses and decides from the many possibilities, and acts and behaves in relationship to reality.

Multicultural Issues in Cognitive Therapy

Kantrowitz and Ballou (1992) critique and challenge the cognitive-behavioral worldview:

> Challenging beliefs and thoughts may not fit well with many cultural and gender socialization patterns. Asians, for example, have been taught to create emotional harmony and avoid conflict in accord with their cultural norms. . . . Women's perceptions have been minimized and misunderstood. (p. 81)
>
> There is nothing in the theory which enhances sensitivity to gender, race, and class issues. . . . The lack of careful consideration of gender, class, race, and ethnic factors as well as contextual information, specific antecedents, and consequences of specific beliefs and behaviors is a problem in cognitive-behavioral conceptualizations of pathology. Also problematic is their attribution of responsibility, implied by their goal of changing the individual client. (pp. 82–83)

The last point is of particular importance. Multicultural counseling and therapy focuses on the importance of working with the client on issues of oppression and of seeking to change environmental context. One of the great cognitive shifts of this century has been the self-awareness movement of African-Americans, women, gay men and lesbians, the deaf, those who face physical issues, the aged, and others. It can be argued that the changes in consciousness brought about the Black identity movement have done more for African-American mental health than all counseling theories combined.

Although the consciousness-raising movement has resulted in the development of multicultural theories of helping, their relationship to cognitive theories discussed here and in the preceding chapter should be mentioned. Cheek (1976), in his pioneering work on assertiveness training (see Chapter 5), gave equal attention to the way African-American clients viewed themselves and their condition as he did to assertiveness training techniques themselves. Indeed, it could be argued that Cheek was the first cognitive-behavioral theorist. Moreover, he is very likely the first person in the CBT movement who included multicultural cognitive issues as an explicit part of the treatment process.

Consciousness-raising techniques, feminist therapy, and psychotherapy as liberation all use various forms of cognitive techniques and strategies. As such, they have much in common with the ideas presented in this chapter. MCT strategies focus on helping individuals see themselves in social context (self-in-relation), whereas the cognitive techniques of this chapter focus more on the individual self. MCT benefits from the well-researched strategies of this chapter but puts such concepts as irrational ideas, automatic thoughts, and the nature of reality in a contextual framework. Sometimes it is the environment that is irrational, not the individual. This is the point that Cheek made in 1976 in his pioneering book *Assertive Black . . . Puzzled White.*

All four theorists discussed in this chapter—Albert Ellis, Aaron Beck, William Glasser, and Arnold Lazarus—have used their techniques successfully with culturally different clients. Part of what is involved in surmounting discrimination, prejudice, and unfairness is generating a new cognitive view of self and the ability to change situations. In the first case example in this chapter, Albert Ellis helps a young gay male come to terms with his affectional orientation.

Albert Ellis and Rational-Emotive Behavior Therapy

Albert Ellis's rational-emotive behavior therapy (REBT) originated in the mid-1950s as he became increasingly aware of the ineffectiveness of psychoanalysis to produce change in his patients. He had an extremely successful private psychoanalytic practice, yet he was dissatisfied with the results he was obtaining. Gradually, he found himself taking a more active role in therapy, attacking clients' logic, and even prescribing behavioral activities for patients to follow after they left therapy (Ellis, 1983). Ellis must be credited as the pioneer who provided us with a method of cognitive therapy that connected to classic behavioral theory and method.

In 1994 in a new edition of his classic *Reason and Emotion in Psychotherapy,* Ellis changed the name of his forty-year-old therapeutic method from rational-emotive therapy (RET) to rational-emotive behavior therapy (REBT). He provides a detailed explanation for this name change, including the following illustrative summary (Ellis, 1995):

> RET is . . . a misleading name because it omits the highly behavioral aspect that rational-emotive therapy has favored right from the start. . . . RET has always been one of the most behaviorally oriented of the cognitive-behavior therapies. In addition to employing systematic desensitization and showing clients how to use imaginal methods of exposing themselves to phobias and anxiety-provoking situations (Wolpe, 1982), it favors in vivo desensitization or exposure. . . . [It is] more behavioral than the procedures of other leading cognitive-behavioral therapies. RET has really always been rational-emotive behavior therapy (REBT). (pp. 86–89)

It should be noted that there is no "battle" between or among theories. Rather, the issue is how to integrate the many techniques of behavioral and cognitive therapy. Donald Meichenbaum may be identified primarily with the behavioral side of the cognitive-behavioral continuum, but he has a cognitive orientation in many ways as strong as that of Albert Ellis. Aaron Beck is identified most clearly with cognitive methods, but he too uses most of the behavioral techniques. At issue for you is how you decide to integrate this powerful methodology in your own thinking and practice. Ellis's approach to therapy in action is best illustrated in the following case example. Then the constructs and systems underlying his interviewing style are outlined.

Case Presentation: Am I Gay?

Ellis's early work in sexuality and sexual counseling is particularly noteworthy (Ellis, 1958). He was one of the first to recognize that being a gay male or a lesbian may be an alternative life-style rather than a "clinical problem." Ellis may or may not spend time developing rapport. He has a unique personal style and is known for starting the interview with a direct, rather confrontative challenge. Ellis is nonjudgmental about life-style issues. But he would urge that the individual make a decision based on personal preference rather than absolute musts and learn to live with that decision comfortably.

The following transcript[1] illustrates how Ellis (1971) rapidly moves into direct action with the client, with the goal of eventually helping the client decide how he wants to live with the idea of being gay. Ellis's work on this case is typical of much of his thinking. If the same client were treated today using REBT, we might anticipate that some attention would also be paid to the issue of discrimination against gay men and lesbians.

1. *Therapist:*   What's the main thing that's bothering you? [*Open question*]
2. *Client:*   I have a fear of that I'm gay—a *real* fear of it!
3. *Therapist:*   A fear of *becoming* a gay? [*Encourager*]
4. *Client:*   Yeah.
5. *Therapist:*   Because "*if* I were gay—," what? [*Open question, oriented to helping the client think in terms of logical consequences, a skill basic to RET work. Note that Ellis here focuses on thoughts or cognitions about being gay rather than on behavior. "It is not things, but how we view things" that is most important.*]
6. *Client:*   I don't know. It really gets me down. It gets me to a point where I'm doubting every day. I do doubt everything, anyway.
7. *Therapist:*   Yes. But let's get back to—answer the question: "If I were gay, what would that make me?" [*Directive, open question*]
8. *Client:*   (pause) I don't know.
9. *Therapist:*   Yes, you do! Now, I can give *you* the answer to the question. But let's see if you can get it. [*Opinion, directive*]
10. *Client:*   (pause) Less than a person?
11. *Therapist:*   Yes. Quite obviously, you're saying: "I'm *bad* enough. But if I were gay, that would make me a *total* shit!" [*Interpretation, logical consequences. Ellis*

often uses language to shock, and in this process, the client realizes that even if the "worst" is said, the client still survives and is respected by Ellis. Underneath the "tough" demanding exterior, Ellis demonstrates immense positive regard for the strengths within each individual.

This particular interpretation also focused on the logical consequences of the client's thinking. Note that A = the possible facts, B = the beliefs about the facts at A, and C = the emotional consequence. Ellis is particularly skilled at drawing out the cognitive thought patterns or sequences in client thinking and emotion.]

12. *Client:*   That's right.

13. *Therapist:*   Now, why did you just say you don't know? [*Open question*]

14. *Client:*   Just taking a guess at it, that's all. It's—it's just that the fear really gets me down! I don't know why.

15. *Therapist:*   (laughing) Well, you just gave the reason why! Suppose you were saying the same thing about—we'll just say—stealing. You hadn't stolen anything, but you thought of stealing something. And you said, "If I stole, I would be a thorough shit!" Just suppose that. Then, how much would you then start thinking about stealing? [*Expression of content—sharing information/instruction, closed question*]

16. *Client:*   (silence)

17. *Therapist:*   If you believed that: "If I stole it, I would be a thorough shit!"— would you think of it often? occasionally? [*Closed question*]

18. *Client:*   I'd think of it often.

19. *Therapist:*   That's right! As soon as you say, "If so-and-so happens, I would be a thorough shit!" you'll get obsessed with so-and-so. And the reason you're getting obsessed with being gay is this nutty belief, "If I were gay, I would be a total shit!" Now, look at that belief for a moment. And let's admit that if you were a gay, it would have real disadvantages. Let's assume that. But why would you be a thorough shit if you were gay? Let's suppose you gave up girls completely, and you just screwed guys. Now, why would you be a thorough shit? [*Encourager, interpretation, directive, open question. Here we see the more inclusive microskill of logical consequences, as discussed in Chapter 3, used in its fullest sense.*]

20. *Client:*   (mumbles incoherently; is obviously having trouble finding an answer)

21. *Therapist:*   Think about it for a moment. [*Directive*] (pp. 102–3)

In later stages of the interview, Ellis seeks to have the client decide what he wants to do for logical reasons that are satisfactory emotionally—thus the terms *rational* and *emotive*. The individual must think and feel a decision is correct. This interviewing style may be most appropriate for Ellis, as it is congruent with his personality, which is often associated with the culture of New York City. It is not wise that you be as forceful and direct if this style is not personally authentic for you. Some confuse Ellis's personal style with his theory. It is possible to use the theory of rational-emotive therapy in a fashion that is authentic to you.

Integrating Theory and Action

The goal of the client and therapist in this session was to change cognitions about the idea of being gay (cognitive), to make decisions about how one wants to live (cognitive-existential), and to then act/behave according to those decisions (behavioral). This preceding sentence reflects the integration of the three basic philosophic traditions of idealism, existentialism, and realism.

When encouraging the client to act on his cognitions, Ellis is likely to use role-plays similar to those of social learning theory (modeling) or Kelly's (1955) fixed-role therapy. He almost certainly would recommend "homework" in the final stages of the interview to ensure that the client does something different as a result of the session. In the follow-up interview, Ellis would likely check carefully on whether or not the client had done anything differently in the time between sessions.

Current therapeutic work with clients debating sexual orientation would possibly include homework assignments to help build awareness of the gay pride movement and examine the role of media in stereotyping and bibliotherapy. Ellis has a long history of tolerance for difference. He would support a gay male or lesbian client in activities oriented toward helping the community become more aware of the group's special needs. While working with a client, Ellis would continue to challenge the basic assumptions and logical structure of the client's thinking. He would never hesitate to challenge any client whose thought and emotional patterns were self- or socially defeating.

REBT and MCT

Chen (1995) provides an important counterpoint and supplement to Ellis's system. Chen states that Chinese philosophy values rationality and stresses the importance of perception over real events, as does Ellis. Given this, REBT may have value for traditional Chinese clients. However, Chen notes that the confrontational style of some REBT practitioners may be personally and culturally offensive to Chinese clients. Chen suggests an emphasis on relationship and a soft, yet strong, approach to challenging a client's rationality. Trust is foundational in this approach.

By way of contrast, Scorzelli and Reineke-Scorzelli (1994) studied cognitive therapy in India and found that the cognitive approach conflicted with clients' spiritual beliefs and their connections with family and culture. In fact, religious beliefs were a particularly important factor in those cases in which REBT was found to be less effective.

The comments of these researchers suggest that REBT does have multicultural relevance but that major changes in how the interview is conducted may be required. Moreover, clients' strong cultural or spiritual orientations may necessitate changes in the way REBT is conducted. Later in this chapter, Glasser's reality therapy is explored as a way to work through some of these issues from a cognitive perspective.

Central Theoretical Constructs and Techniques of REBT

Ellis and the REBT approach focus more on dysfunctional thoughts than do other therapies, although the importance of emotional foundations is also stressed. The REBT view is that people often make themselves emotional victims by their own distorted, unrealistic, and irrational thinking patterns. Ellis takes an essentially optimistic view of people, but criticizes some humanistic approaches as being too soft at times and failing to address the fact that people can virtually "self-destruct" through irrational and muddled thinking. The task of the REBT therapist is to correct clients' thought patterns and minimize irrational ideas, while simultaneously helping them change their dysfunctional feelings and behaviors.

Emotion and REBT

Emotion is central in REBT theory. Unless the "E" in REBT is present, change is unlikely to occur. Ellis, himself, is often seen personally as a highly rational and logical person. Yet, awareness of others' emotions and constructions of reality is central to his approach. For example, Weinrach (1990) provides a personal anecdote in which he describes his observations of Ellis in action as he supervises a beginning helper:

> One of the students played a tape which reflected virtually no mastery of the RET concepts or techniques which had been exhaustively taught and demonstrated over the previous three days. . . . As the tape played, other group members and I expected Al to show some understandable frustration or exasperation. To the contrary, Al proved to be the ever-patient, tender, and gentle master teacher. He started at the very beginning and taught this student the basics of RET, step-by-step. That experience forced me to reconcile the discrepancy between Al's public and private personae. (p. 108)

Ellis unconditionally accepts all manner of clients, just as does Rogers. And, like Perls, Ellis is searching for authenticity. Ellis encourages clients to think rationally and be in touch with their emotions. He may use bibliotherapy and ask clients to write journals to increase their understanding. He may use humor or sarcasm, as appropriate, with the client. He constantly stresses "homework" as important to the change process, seeking to have clients generalize ideas from the interview to their daily lives.

Examining Philosophy and Belief Systems

Ellis distinguishes REBT from other cognitive-behavioral theories, putting an emphasis on philosophy (Ellis, 1994):

> CBT of course emphasizes cognitive processes, but it does not have a specific philosophic emphasis, as REBT does. Donald Meichenbaum, a leading proponent of CBT, covers many techniques, but often significantly omits any stress on a distinctly philosophic outlook. REBT, on the other hand, emphasizes that humans are born (as well as reared) as philosophers and that they are natural scientists, creators of meaning, and users of rational means to predict the future. One of its main goals, therefore, is to help clients make a *profound philosophic change* that will affect their future as well as their present emotions and behaviors. (pp. 241–47)

Important in understanding REBT is the idea of belief systems. Belief systems are organized ways of thinking about reality and one's personal experience. Belief systems are the concrete operations of abstract formal philosophy. The gay male in the case example unfortunately had adopted oppressive ideas from society. This belief system, in turn, resulted in a negative self-view. It is important in a cognitive approach to this negative belief system to examine the system and seek to find positive ways of thinking about self. Moreover, as one goes further and in more depth, it becomes possible to examine overarching belief systems and personal philosophy of life.

The language clients use constantly tells us about their personal philosophy and belief systems. Ellis (1994) believes in free will, pointing out that clients "*create* their own emotional disturbances by strongly believing in absolutistic, irrational Beliefs"(p. 248). Clients can actively choose their belief systems and philosophies, but all too often, they choose a language and philosophy that are irrational and cause them cognitive and behavioral difficulties. REBT is an attempt to bring these irrational views to consciousness and effect change.

If clients are to change, Ellis suggests that it is important to examine their systems of thinking, or cognitions, and to place these on a more rational basis. As the counselor or therapist works with irrational thoughts, it becomes possible to organize these ideas into larger philosophic patterns. Effective REBT can help clients solve specific, concrete problems and later to examine their overall philosophies of life. For the gay client in the above case, we might expect that attacking single specific irrational ideas would eventually lead to a new philosophy of being gay in a homophobic society. The first step in developing skills in REBT is to learn how to identify irrationality in the actual language of the client.

Identifying Irrational Statements

In the interview, clients will frequently use such irrational statements as "If I don't pass this course, it is the end of the world," "Because my parents have been cruel to me as a child, there is nothing I can do now to help myself," "As the economy is lacking jobs, there is no meaning to my life," "If I can't get that scholarship, all is ended," and "The reason I have nothing is that the rich have taken it all." All of these statements at one level are true, but all of them represent "helpless" thinking, a common end result of irrational thought.

For example, the gay client presented in the foregoing transcript began with an irrational statement that Ellis helped extend and clarify. For example, "Therapist: Yes. Quite obviously you're saying: 'I'm *bad* enough. But if I were gay, that would make me a *total* shit.'" Here Ellis identifies a key irrational statement that will be the focus of the ensuing interview and treatment series. This challenging of the irrational statement is key to changing an entire philosophy of self later in the session.

There are many irrational or disfunctional ideas. Following are five particularly common ones identified by Ellis (1967). In these statements there is also an underlying demand for perfection accompanied by a denial of the impossibility of that perfectionist demand. Read these examples carefully and think about those that might apply to you.

1. It is a *necessity* to be loved and approved of by *all* important people around us. "If he (or she) doesn't love me, it is awful."
2. It is *required* that one be *thoroughly* competent, adequate, and achieving if one is to be worthwhile. "If I don't make the goal, it's all my fault."

3. Some people are bad and *should* be punished for it. "He (or she) did that to me and I'm going to get even."
4. It is better to *avoid* difficulties and responsibilities. "It won't make any difference if I don't do that. People won't care."
5. It is *awful* or *catastrophic* if things are not the way they are supposed to be. "Isn't it terrible that the house isn't picked up?" (p. 84)

This list can be amplified, but more at issue is your ability to recognize irrational thinking in whatever form it takes. Listen carefully to those around you, and you'll discover that the world is full of irrational ideas and thoughts. Particularly, search the above statements for "all-or-none" thinking—irrational thinking that helps the client avoid the complexity of life. The words *should, ought, never,* and *must* are useful indicators of irrational thinking.

The basic therapeutic maneuver is always to be on the alert for irrational thinking and when it is observed, to confront it directly, concretely, and immediately. REBT counselors vary in their use of microskills, but Ellis uses a large number of open and closed questions, directives, interpretation, and advice and opinion. The listening skills of paraphrasing and reflection of feeling play a less prominent role in his therapy. Confrontation of cognitive discrepancies is central.

An abbreviated REBT self-help form is presented in Practice Exercise 10.1. This form may be useful in aiding you to identify your own and your clients' faulty thought patterns. In addition, this exhibit summarizes the A-B-C/D-E-F patterns discussed in the following subsection.

The A-B-Cs of Cognition

Perhaps Ellis's most important concrete methodological contribution is his A-B-C theory of personality,[2] which can be summarized as follows:

A—the "objective" facts, events, behaviors that an individual encounters

B—the person's beliefs about A

C—the emotional consequences, or how a person feels and acts about A

People tend to consider that A causes C, or that facts cause consequences. Ellis challenges this equation as naive, pointing out that it is what people think about an event that determines how they feel. Applying the A-B-C framework to the preceding interview with the gay client, we see that:

A—The "objective fact" is the possibility of being gay.

B—The client believes being gay is bad and self-denigrating.

C—Therefore, as an emotional consequence, the client experiences guilt, fear, and negative self-thoughts.

In this case the client has short-circuited B, concluding that "if I am a gay, I am bad. Thus . . ." Ellis's goal is to attack this belief system. What the client thinks about being gay causes his anxiety and difficulties, not the objective facts of the situation. There are obviously numerous gay, lesbian, and heterosexual people who be-

=== **Practice Exercise 10.1** ===

 Rational-Emotive Behavior Therapy Self-Help Form

This form can be used for examining yourself. It also can be used with equal effectiveness in the interview with your clients and/or as a homework assignment for them.

A. *Objective fact, event, or behavior.* List and describe the activating events, thoughts, or feelings that happened just before you felt emotionally disturbed or acted in some self-defeating way.

B. *Identify the irrational beliefs.* Look at your description of events, thoughts, or feelings and examine them for irrational thinking. Circle all those that apply or add irrational beliefs. Examples:

1. I MUST do well or very well.
2. I am a BAD or WORTHLESS PERSON when I act weakly or stupidly.
3. I MUST be approved or accepted by people whom I find important.
4. I NEED IMMEDIATE GRATIFICATION for my needs.
5. Other people MUST live up to my expectations or it is TERRIBLE.
6. It's AWFUL or HORRIBLE when major things don't go my way.
7. I CAN'T STAND IT when life is really unfair.
8. Additional irrational beliefs.

C. *Emotional consequences.* How did you feel after the fact, event, or behavior? What did you do to produce it? How would you like to change?

D. *Disputes.* Look at the irrational belief and then challenge it. Examples: "Why MUST I do so very well?" "Where is it written that I am a BAD PERSON?" "Where is the evidence that I MUST be approved or accepted?"

E. *Effective rational beliefs.* These can replace irrational beliefs. Examples: "I would prefer to do well, but I don't HAVE TO BE that perfect." "I am a person who acted badly, but not a BAD PERSON." "There is no evidence that I HAVE TO BE approved, although I would like to be."

F. *More positive and rational feelings and behaviors.* Finally, place here the feelings, behaviors, and thoughts you are experiencing after challenging and working on your irrational beliefs.

Can you make the following commitment? "I will work hard to repeat my effective rational beliefs forcefully to myself on many occasions so that I can make myself less disturbed now and act less self-defeatingly in the future."

SOURCE: This form is summarized from a longer form authored by Joyce Sichel and Albert Ellis (1984) copyrighted by and available from the Institute for Rational-Emotive Therapy, 45 East 65th Street, New York, N.Y. 10021. It is used here by their permission.

lieve that alternative life-styles are valid and who do not come to the same conclusion at C that this client does.

Ellis's approach in this case, then, was to challenge the client's logic: "If I were gay, I would be a total shit." He points out the A-causes-C conclusion and challenges the irrationality of this "logic." Again, it can be seen that it is not the specific beliefs that are challenged, but rather the unfoundedness of those beliefs, which leads to illogical conclusions.

Ellis does not challenge the client's goals and values (that he doesn't *want* to be gay) but instead attacks his *absolute demands* about achieving these values (that under *no* conditions *must* he be gay; that he would be a worthless "shit" if he were gay). The emphasis of the therapy is on changing the way the client thinks about the behavior, rather than on changing the behavior itself. Recall Epictetus—it is not events but our view of events that is critical.

The A-B-C framework is really the nugget of Ellis's theory. It is not the event that really troubles us, but instead the way we think about the event. Ellis's theory is closely akin to humanistic therapies that focus on meaning and the importance of how a person interprets the world. Frankl (Chapter 12), for example, survived the horrors of a Nazi concentration camp. He comments on how his survival depended on his ability to believe certain things about the events around him and to find something positive on which to depend. Beliefs were more important to survival than objective facts.

The D-E-Fs of Promoting and Maintaining Change

"D" stands for disputing irrational beliefs and thinking. It is at this point that Ellis's work first became controversial. When the logic of the client's A-B-C thought patterns is ineffective, Ellis becomes directly challenging and confrontative: "But why would you be a thorough shit if you were a gay? Let's suppose you gave up girls completely, and you just screwed guys. Now, why would you be a thorough shit?" This language and style offended many people in the 1950s and 1960s, a time when Rogerian listening and respect were at their greatest influence. Furthermore, Ellis's tolerance and openness to cultural difference were ahead of his time.

It is now widely recognized that disputing and challenging clients' logical systems is an effective mode of intervention and that rational disputation is an important therapeutic strategy. In the later sections of this chapter, you will see that Beck and Glasser both use disputation, but in a more gentle manner than that associated with Ellis.

"E" is the effect that disputation (or other interventions) has on the client. At this point, the client generates a more effective belief system or philosophy about the situation. In the above example, the fact of being gay has not been changed, but the client generates a new way of thinking about himself: "It's OK to come out of the closet and be a gay man—if I wish to take that direction."

"F" stands for new feelings and behaviors. The client has new emotions associated with the situation. "I'm gay and I'm proud and I feel good about myself." REBT emphasizes emotional change as foundational. Although much of REBT work focuses on logical thinking, unless logic is ultimately integrated with emotion, change will be unlikely to last. Emotional change is basic if we are to prevent relapse into old ways of thinking and feeling. Behavior change follows from new feelings about the self.

Summary

The following summarizes the basic tenets of REBT:

1. Expect your clients (and yourself, your family, and your friends) frequently to make impossible, perfectionistic statements about themselves and others.

2. The basic treatment rule is to dispute the rationality of the perfectionistic cognition and to teach clients how to do their own realistic, open-minded disputation.

3. In therapy, it may be useful to work through several irrational statements in a step-by-step A-B-C process and search for repeating patterns of thought and emotion.

4. Agreed-upon homework can help your clients take their new knowledge into the real world.

5. Do not hesitate to add Gestalt, behavioral, or other techniques to the REBT structure if you feel it helps you and your client reach your joint goals.

Rational Recovery: REBT's Approach to Alcoholism

Theories of psychotherapy have given insufficient attention to treatment issues around alcoholism. It is important to remember that at least half of the clients that come to counseling and therapy are affected in some significant way by alcohol or drugs. Clients may be addicted themselves, be in a relationship with a substance abuser, or be the child or grandchild of an alcoholic. Alcohol can be described as an unseen dimension in much of psychotherapy and counseling.

There are now over three hundred groups using REBT as a system of treating alcoholism, and Rational Recovery (RR) is becoming an alternative to Alcoholics Anonymous. Founded in 1986 by a licensed social worker, Jack Trimpey, Rational Recovery recognizes that substance abuse may have many biological foundations (Trimpey, 1989). Nonetheless, treatment can be facilitated by an REBT approach. Ellis (1992) comments:

> Many (not all) problem drinkers first tend to bring out dysfunctional Consequences (C's), such as anxiety and depression, when unfortunate Activating Events or Adversities (A's) occur in their lives; mainly by constructing irrational or self-defeating Beliefs (B's). Second, they then tend to construct more irrational beliefs (B's) about their feelings of depression and anxiety—especially, "I must not be anxious! I can't stand this anxiety!"—and consequently (C) take to drinking in order to allay their pain. Third, problem drinkers often take their secondary Consequence, "alcoholism," and

create more irrational Beliefs about that—such as, "I must not be an alcoholic. What a worm I am for drinking too much." This creates a tertiary Consequence (C), self-damnation, that frequently drives them to drink even more. (p. 5)

Treatment involves analysis and disputation, usually done in groups with the support of professionals. RR diverges from AA in its attempt to bring professionals more directly into the treatment process, although RR members pay no fees. Although both AA and RR emphasize an educational approach, RR differs from AA in that spiritual concepts such as a "Higher Power" are not emphasized. Ellis (1992) comments that many clients are nonreligious and thus seek help in groups such as RR, Secular Organizations for Sobriety (SOS), and Men and Women for Sobriety (MFS and WFS).

As a counselor and therapist, it is vital that you bring an understanding of the many effects of alcohol and substance abuse into the therapeutic hour. If you have an understanding and appreciation of the value of the Alcoholics Anonymous twelve-step program, Rational Recovery, and other treatment programs, you can conduct counseling and therapy as part of an overall treatment program that includes and does not deny the issues of substance abuse in this society.

Aaron Beck and Cognitive Therapy

Aaron Beck, a major cognitive-behavioral therapist, first became known for his success in treating depression. The personal strength and warmth of Beck are perhaps best illustrated by a case from his well-known book *Cognitive Therapy and the Emotional Disorders* (1976). He describes a depressed patient who had failed to leave his bedside for a considerable period of time. Beck asked him if he could walk to the door of his room. The man said he would collapse. Beck said, "I'll catch you." Through successive steps and longer walks, the man was shortly able to walk all over the hospital and in one month was discharged.

Relationship as Central to Change

How are such "miracles" accomplished? First, Beck is a powerful and caring individual who himself believes that change is possible. He is willing to provide himself as a support agent for the client and has specific goals and behaviors in mind for the client. In this case, he sought to change the way the depressed person thought about himself. Through slow, successive approximations, from shorter to longer walks with Beck's help, the client was able to change his behavior.

This case illustrates the importance of relationship and behavior as well as cognitive change. It also points out that you may at times need to move out of the office and work in the community. In Beck's framework, this basic cognitive change would be a move from "I can't" to "I can." Basic to much of behavioral work is to take small steps toward success. Somewhere along the continuum of change, clients will likely realize that they *can* do something to help themselves. It is this attitude of "I can" that is basic to generalizing learned behavior and ways of thinking from the therapy hour to real life.

Clearly, someone who facilitates this type of change for clients has something special, a charisma as full of impact in its way as that of Ellis. Beck's approach is compared, using meta-analysis, with Ellis's in Research Exhibit 10.1.

Beck has outlined important principles for working with many types of patients. Since his early work with depression, he has demonstrated that his concepts are equally effective with anxiety disorders (Freeman & Simon, 1989), personality disorders (Beck, Freeman, & Associates, 1990), and many other issues. The following transcript reveals some of the characteristics of Beck's interviewing style.

Research Exhibit 10.1

Meta-Analyses of Ellis's RET and Beck's Cognitive Therapy

Two major reviews of research studies on these two important techniques have recently been completed. The findings on both rational-emotive therapy (RET), now called rational-emotive behavioral therapy (REBT), and cognitive therapy are encouraging. There are fewer studies on Beck's more recent cognitive therapy.

Rational-Emotive Therapy

Lyons and Woods (1992) have reviewed seventy outcome studies involving RET and conducted a meta-analysis. General results indicate that clients who receive RET benefit from the process. Of special interest is the fact that experienced therapists were more impactful than beginners. Those clients who experienced short-term treatment of one or two interviews did not change as much as clients who experienced RET for a longer time period.

Of special interest in the above study is that cognitive-behavioral and behav-

ioral therapy methods were equally effective in RET. The authors of the study comment, "RET was shown to be an effective form of therapy. Perhaps it is time to stop the needless and inefficient discussion of the efficacy of this therapy. Rather a better focus of investigations and reviews would be to determine which factors, or combinations thereof, contribute most to the effectiveness of RET" (pp. 20–21). In effect, perhaps the answer is not which therapeutic method is best or most effective but which combination of therapies will be most helpful to our clients.

Cognitive Therapy

Twenty-eight studies of Beck's cognitive therapy for depression were examined through meta-analysis (Dobson, 1989). There were clear indications that cognitive therapy was more effective than a waiting list or no-treatment control groups, pharmacotherapy, behavioral therapy, or other psychotherapies. Of particular importance, Dobson found eight studies comparing cognitive therapy with medication. "Cognitive therapy clients, on average, did better than 70 percent of drug therapy patients" (p. 415).

Beck's cognitive therapy was built on clinical work and theorizing around depression. The research evidence is that the therapy works. Beck (1991) himself provides a thirty-year perspective on theory and research in cognitive therapy. Five studies indicate that cognitive therapy prevents relapse better than do antidepressant drugs (Hollan & Najavits, 1988).

Similarly, the important National Institute of Mental Health study of depression found cognitive therapy superior to antidepressant drugs and interpersonal therapy in terms of recurrence of depression during follow-up (Shea et al., 1990).

Beck summarizes additional studies showing that cognitive therapy is particularly effective with clients suffering panic attacks and generalized anxiety disorder. There is promising evidence that the system is effective with clients experiencing eating disorders, heroin addiction, couple's problems, and schizophrenia. The data seem clear that cognitive therapy and cognitive-behavior modification have both immediate and lasting value for clients.

Case Presentation: Depression

In the following session, Beck uses a relatively direct interviewing style. When the client says "Now I'm all alone!" Beck probes this statement for underlying meaning and logic. In this search for meaning, there are clear parallels to the approach of Frankl. By implicitly questioning the logic underlying the client's overgeneralization or automatic thought, Beck attempts to produce change in cognitive processes similar to Ellis's attack of irrational thought patterns.

In theory and practice, Beck focuses on identifying automatic thoughts, internal self-statements that help clients organize their thinking patterns. This is a critical difference from the approach of Ellis. Beck does not focus on unconscious motivation; nonetheless, his psychodynamic roots still influence his work to some extent. For example, he considers automatic thoughts to be rooted in early parent-child interactions and to repeat in adulthood.

In the following vignette (Diffily, 1984), Beck uses many questions to encourage clients to explore themselves and their situations.

Strain grips the face of the young woman on the television monitor. Hers would be a pretty face were it not for the puffy, reddened eyes, and the glistening tear-tracks splotched on her cheeks.

"My husband wants to leave me," Linda is saying to someone out of camera range. "He wants to go for an unspecified length of time. Then maybe he'll come back. He says it's non-negotiable; he wants no more commitment." She has difficulty controlling her voice; breathy sobs punctuate her recitation.

"I've gotten more and more depressed," Linda continues. "It felt like I had a guillotine over me, or like I had cancer. I told him maybe he'd better leave. And now—" (she begins sobbing in earnest) "—now I'm all alone!"

The camera draws back, bringing into view a man seated at the table with Linda. His most striking feature is a thatch of thick white hair smoothed back from his face. Behind his glasses the psychiatrist's eyes are at once gentle and probing. He regards Linda calmly.

"What do you mean, all alone?" asks Beck.

[*This is the first step toward searching for automatic thoughts. By asking "What do you mean, all alone?" Beck is moving beneath the surface structure sentence to find the underlying thinking patterns.*]

"I don't have Richard!" she gasps, mopping at her eyes with a tissue from the box on the table. "Life wouldn't mean anything without him. I love him so much."

[*Here we see A—the objective facts, "I don't have Richard"—and C—the emotional consequence, a classic Ellis irrational thought pattern. Beck, however, is searching for the automatic thought patterns underlying the depression.*]

"What do you love about him?" Beck asks.

"I don't know," Linda says, shaking her head, confused. "I guess I live for him. He's so rotten. But I remember the good stuff."

[*In this exchange, the client begins to examine her own faulty automatic thoughts.*]

CLICK. In the darkened viewing room, Beck pushes a switch and freezes the images of Linda and himself on the monitor. He turns to a visitor and explains his strategy for this emergency therapy session. "First, you always summarize the patient's thoughts to her. This gives clarity and reassures her that you understand. Second, you have to figure out where you're going to move in. It's very difficult in a crisis situation. You have to think on your feet." Beck explains that according to his theory of depression, the patient will underestimate herself and exaggerate her degree of loss and a negative view of the future. "You have to explore these channels and work it through."

CLICK. The video images move and talk. On the screen, Beck summarizes for Linda his first therapy session with her six weeks earlier, reminding her that Richard had made certain promises and commitments regarding their marriage. "What happened between then and now?"

[*Highly characteristic of the cognitive-behavioral approach is the search for sequence. Much like the antecedents, behaviors, and consequences of functional analysis explored in Chapter 9, CBT is concerned with ordering of events but gives much more stress to internalized thoughts and feelings than do behavioral methods.*]

"I don't know. I really think he lied to me." She begins to sob again. "This is like a bad dream."

"Richard deceived you?"

"He did. I feel like a fool," Linda cries, "for believing him."

CLICK. To his visitor, Beck says, "This is aggravating the problem; she is feeling deceived, feeling foolish. Which angle am I going to explore—her actual loss, or the hurt to her pride? You have to make a split-second decision."

CLICK. On the screen, Beck is talking quietly to Linda. "What have you lost?" He is going for the loss angle first.

"I lost my best friend, someone to talk to." She pauses and adds ruefully, "Even though he didn't want to listen to me." What else? "I've lost the father of my children. Financial support, security."

[*Note the "all-or-none" thinking on the part of the client. The CBT therapist will recognize the very real hurt, but will not accept that all is lost. Common to irrational ideas and automatic thoughts is overgeneralization of negatives and deletion of possible positives.*]

"What hurts you most?" Beck wonders. "The money?"

"No—losing him. I've lost all my hopes." What hopes? "That things would work out for us." "Aren't there other hopes?" Beck asks. Linda looks doubtful. "I guess I'm not letting them come in. But who would want me? He rejected me. I'm not lovable."

[*The above is a good example of rational disputation in which the client's faulty thinking patterns are challenged by the therapist. Note below how humor can be used to challenge patterns of thinking.*]

"Do you really believe that? Is Richard the supreme arbiter of that?" Beck says. "Should we trust his judgment?" Laughter. Linda, incredibly, is laughing. "Don't make me laugh when I'm crying!" she is saying through a mixture of giggles and sobs.

A brief smile plays across Beck's face; he continues pressing his point. "Richard broke promises to you on and off for months. And you feel terrible that a guy like that doesn't love you? Why should his problem be reflected in your self-image?"

Beck asks Linda to list her husband's good and bad qualities. He records them on a long sheet of lined paper divided into two columns. When Linda finishes her list, the "bad" column is twice as long as the "good" column.

[*This may be recognized as a variation of the decisional balance sheet of Chapter 3. Problem-solving techniques are often used in CBT.*]

"Is this the kind of man you'd want for a mate?" the psychiatrist asks.

"It really sounds dumb when you write it out," she admits.

Eventually Beck elicits another admission from Linda: Even though she is suffering from dire emotional stress and pain, she can endure it and even adopt a more positive view of her future. "I guess I've been standing it so far," Linda says, "so I can stand it now."

[*The faulty automatic thoughts about her husband have been adequately challenged, and Linda can now revise her personal constructions of herself, her ex-mate, and her situation.*]

CLICK. Beck's visitor, moved by the emotions and the glimpse of hope she has viewed on videotape, has a question for him.

"Didn't you want to hug Linda, to comfort her, instead of just asking questions?"

"Empathy and understanding," the psychiatrist answers, "are not enough in therapy. As in any branch of medicine, you tend to empathize with the patient. But most reassuring to the patient is your understanding of her problem and your ability to give her a mastery of the situation." In no way, Beck emphasizes, was Linda's depression "cured" by this one session; she had to come back for therapy on a regular basis for a while. But using his therapeutic approach—one that has inspired considerable interest and excitement among mental health professionals worldwide—a therapist can "snap people out of a severe depression very quickly" and help them start coping with their problems in a constructive, rewarding way. (pp. 39–46)

Beck's Central Theoretical Constructs and Techniques

Beck gives central attention to the cognitive process. He points out that there is a constant stream of thoughts going through our minds, not all of which we listen to. These thoughts move so rapidly that Beck calls them "automatic thoughts" and points out that it is difficult to stop them. In the case of the woman described in the transcript, she automatically thought her life would be "over" and she would be "alone" without her husband. Beck is concerned with stopping such harmful automatic thoughts and having the person examine his or her mode of thinking and eventually develop new forms of cognition.

Changing Faulty Thought Patterns

In Beck's model, the therapist seeks to change the clients' thinking patterns and way of constructing their worldviews. This requires the following steps, all of which may be identified in the case example above:

1. *Recognize maladaptive thinking and ideation.* The woman in the case example above felt that "all was lost" because of her husband leaving.

2. *Note repeating patterns of ideation that tend to be ineffective.* Beck terms such repeating patterns *automatic thoughts.* You may, for example, have been frightened by a dog and now all dogs are scary for you. You "automatically" think all dogs are dangerous. The therapeutic task is to break down the illogical thinking patterns to help you realize the distinctions between safe and unsafe dogs. With the depressed woman, the task becomes to help her recognize that her present difficulties do not mean that she needs to be totally depressed.

3. *Distance and decenter to help clients remove themselves from the immediate fear, thought, or problem so they can think about it from a distance.* This results in obsessive thinking becoming less of a "center" in the person's life. When Beck asked, "Do you really believe that? Is Richard the supreme arbiter of that?" and the client laughed, she was clearly decentering her thoughts about the issue.

4. *Change the rules.* This is important in working with faulty thinking and automatic thoughts. The therapist talks with the client about the logic of the situation. For example, you may rethink your dog phobia through realizing that the chances of being bitten by a dog are at best one in a thousand. When Beck had his client fill out an elementary problem-solving balance sheet of the pros and cons of her husband, he helped her change the rules of her thinking.

Beck's system has proven particularly effective with depressed clients whose worldview is full of pessimistic automatic thoughts that forcefully affect their behavior. Beck (1972) has a list of "faulty reasonings" that in many ways is similar to Ellis's conceptualizations of irrational ideas. Beck's list includes such concepts as dichotomous reasoning (assuming things are either all good or all bad—"I'm either perfect or I'm no good"), overgeneralization ("If my husband leaves me, I'm totally alone"), magnification (Ellis terms this *catastrophizing*), and flaws in inference or logic.

Clients will manifest a multitude of variations on perfectionism. Automatic thoughts and irrational ideas tend to be obsessive in nature, as they are repeated over and over again. An underlying structure of obsessive behavior and thought is often perfectionism. However, what makes ideas irrational are their unattainability, overgeneralization (one *must* reach 100 percent of everything), or significant distortion of occurrences.

Beck's cognitive therapy assumes that clients can examine themselves. Many patients, particularly the depressed, are embedded in their own construction of the world. Beck recognizes that their particularly self-centered worldview may indeed be accurate, but if one thinks about alternatives, these alternatives may be even more useful and certainly more growth producing. In this area, important parallels to Kelly's (1955) personal construct theory should be noted. The depressed individual has a set of ineffective personal constructs, which are hypotheses this person uses to frame the world. The task of the therapist is to change the client's constructs in the expectation that if the way one views the world is changed, the way one acts in the world will also change.

The Daily Record of Automatic Thoughts

As indicated in the case example above, negative automatic thoughts often take time to alleviate and change. One technique Beck recommends is the use of the daily record of automatic thoughts. Table 10.1 depicts a portion of the record of the automatic thoughts of a male who was diagnosed as having an obsessive-compulsive personality disorder. Using the daily record method can help the client learn how to identify thinking patterns using one or more of the four steps indicated above.

Table 10.1   An Obsessive-Compulsive Personality's Daily Record of Automatic Thoughts

Date	Situation (describe briefly)	Emotions	Automatic Thoughts	Rational Response	Outcome
5/12	Office	Anxiety, fear	If I don't do the report perfectly, I'll get fired.	Do the best you can. Nobody's perfect.	Felt better. Boss liked report.
	Dinner	Anger	Why doesn't my wife have things ready on time?	I'm lucky she cooks at all. I need to help her more.	I helped with meal.
	Movie	Tears, sadness	Why am I doing this? It always happens in sad places.	Just enjoy the movie. It's OK to cry.	More tears? Why?

Experience has shown that automatic thoughts often reappear unless closely monitored for a period of time outside of the interview. The client is instructed to mark on the daily record each time an automatic thought intrudes and the client feels uncomfortable. Just the act of recording in itself reinforces and promotes change.

It is crucial that the therapist monitor this form and encourage clients to continue using the form for a sufficient time period to ensure that automatic thoughts do not relapse. If the daily record is discontinued too soon, the client will likely relapse into old patterns of automatic thoughts. Table 10.1 reveals that the obsessive-compulsive client was able to monitor emotions and thoughts in two situations and change the outcome to a more positive one. For example, his record notes he was in tears at the movie. Many obsessive-compulsive types, contrary to popular stereotype, cry easily yet feel uncomfortable about it. The data gained from the daily record provide the counselor with new information for further cognitive-behavioral treatment. At this point, the cognitive therapist can focus on a variety of techniques to understand the meaning of the tears, such as the use of images at the sensorimotor level.

The daily record can also provide the counselor or therapist specifics of client behavior and thinking for further diagnosis and assessment. This is an important technique and one highly useful in counseling and therapy from many theoretical orientations. It is recommended that you use this format in several practice exercises so that you can master this important part of cognitive theory.

Adding Family/Multicultural Dimensions.   The chart of automatic thoughts tends to put the responsibility for most change within the client. As such, multicultural theory would point out that this method fails to consider contextual issues. Gender and multicultural dimensions can be added to the automatic thoughts chart by adding a column focusing on context. In the above example, the obsessive-compulsive male could review the entire record as an example of sex-role stereotyping learned in the family of origin. In this case, cognitive consciousness raising about the oppressiveness of male roles may be beneficial.

For many individuals, reviewing automatic thought patterns from a gender, family, or multicultural perspective can be very helpful. Women and minorities, for example, may sometimes blame themselves for lack of job advancement. If the record of automatic thoughts is reviewed for examples of sexism or racism, this may change the meaning and the cognitions of the client. At the same time, it is important to balance internal and external responsibility for change. Information gained from such analysis may require you as counselor or therapist to take action in the environment. We must never forget that many, perhaps most, of our clients are in some way harmed by context. To place internal responsibility for change on one person is sometimes highly naive. Practice Exercise 10.2 provides an opportunity to explore automatic thoughts in a multicultural context.

Practice Exercise 10.2

 Automatic Thoughts within Gender and Multicultural Contexts

With yourself or a real or role-played client, work through an automatic thoughts record around an issue of concern. To make the task clear at the beginning, use only one specific situation. Later, identify more situations so that you can search for patterns. Note that the search for one situation is an example of concrete thought processes. When we combine several situations, we develop formal operational thought patterns.

For this practice exercise, ask yourself or the client to develop a sensorimotor image of the situation. Imaging will help concretize the situation and make emotion more accessible. The addition of gender and multicultural contexts enables a dialectic/systemic view of the cognitive process.

1. *Situation.* Ask the client to tell you a brief story or narrative of the situation. Ask the client to identify the emotions associated with the narrative.

2. *Emotions.* If appropriate, seek an image of the situation by asking the client to select one key scene and keep it in mind. Through the use of images the past situation can be brought into the here and now. Again, ask the client to identify the emotions associated with the image. Usually, this will be a more powerful experience than that in item 1; as such, special care should be taken. Do not lead the client, but simply ask for whatever image comes to mind.

3. *Automatic thoughts.* Ask the client, "What occurs in your mind during the situation?" or "What thoughts go through your head when you experience that image?" Discovering automatic thoughts requires questioning skills. Clients who have been used to external control will require considerable help in looking inside themselves. Automatic thoughts analysis forces overexternalized clients to look inward.

4. *Rational response.* Think of a logical response as you or the client reflect on the situation, the resulting emotions, and the automatic thoughts. This process will involve some coconstruction with the client. Whereas REBT tends to dispute client cognitions, cognitive therapy is more likely to work with the client in generating a rational approach to reality. This rational response provides the foundation for a new stylistic approach to life.

   When working with a daily record of automatic thoughts, you have the opportunity to generate patterns of thought and action and to then examine broader life-style issues and move to more comprehensive change.

5. *Gender and multicultural issues.* There is a pronounced tendency in cognitive-behavioral psychology to ignore gender and multicultural matters. However, multicultural theorists

often stress that external reality must be dealt with if clients are to achieve mature cognitions and emotions.

Ask yourself or your client, "Reflect back on your system of emotions and automatic thoughts. How do your gender and cultural, religious, and other frameworks speak to these issues?" Through adaptations of this core question, your clients will be able to see their situations in a broader context. In this way, external reality can be brought into the cognitive paradigm. Is the client or the external situation irrational?

6. *Outcome.* Ask clients what occurs for them if they change their rational responses to the situation. Also, you may wish to encourage them to think about whether or not gender and multicultural issues are related to the entire process. At issue in this approach to automatic thoughts is balancing internal and external reality.

The Use of Images

Our clients have basic images of themselves and situations and are often unaware of these images. These images are usually the basis for automatic thoughts. The importance of visual images in developmental counseling and therapy and in psychodynamic therapy was stressed in Chapters 4 and 8. Beck often searches for client images as he seeks to understand automatic thoughts and behavioral patterns. Many of your clients' automatic thoughts are images that can be accessed for better understanding, as with the following client with an avoidant history discussed by Beck, Freeman, and Associates (1990):

> During the first few sessions with the therapist, she received the standard cognitive therapy for personality problems. In one visit, after she had been given a homework assignment that she failed to follow through with, she told her therapist that she was feeling particularly upset over not having done the homework. The therapist asked her where the feeling was localized. The patient responded that she felt it somewhere in her "stomach." The therapist then asked her whether she had an image in reference to what was upsetting her. She then said the following, "I see myself coming into the session. You are larger than life; you are critical and demeaning; you are like a big authority."
>
> The therapist then asked when this had occurred previously. The patient responded that she had experienced this many times during childhood when she had unpleasant encounters with her mother. Her mother drank a good deal and was frequently irritable toward the child when she had been drinking. One day the child came home from school early, and the mother "blasted her" for waking her up. (pp. 92–93)

This example reveals psychodynamic thought in Beck's system, although Beck tends not to use psychodynamic labels or explanations. In her past, the client learned to avoid authority figures because they were painful. This past experience was the origin of automatic thoughts such as "I am a bad person" and "I am wrong because I upset my mother." This learned pattern of automatic thoughts was transferred to the interview with the therapist. Clients' automatic thoughts will appear with you as well as with others. Again, this can be thought of not so much as transference but as learned cognitions and behaviors.

Reliving Childhood or Other Traumatic Experiences

In what is termed *regression* in psychodynamic therapy, the client returns to painful, often traumatic scenes via images and "relives" them again in the safety of the therapeutic hour. The avoidant client above was encouraged by the therapist to relive the past situation with her possibly alcoholic mother. Through the use of images, role-plays, and even the Gestalt empty chair technique ("talk to your mother as if she were sitting there"), clients are able to reexperience old, often forgotten and repressed events.

Reliving old situations can be highly dramatic and emotionally draining. In a situation of trust and safety, the client can release emotional energy and "work through" the trauma more completely. Psychodynamic theory talks of removing the repressed event, whereas cognitive theory focuses on completing the learning involved in the event. For example, the automatic thoughts of a child of an alcoholic parent often involve varying forms of unrealistic perfectionism. Through the use of images and by working through old events, the client is often able to develop more rational and effective ways of behaving, and automatic thought patterns can be changed.

Beck points out that depressed clients first need to have their depression removed before they can encounter the challenge of reworking issues through extensive use of images. He recommends using images and reliving old events particularly for clients with personality disorders. The techniques discussed in these sections are powerful and should be used only by those with considerable experience or those who are under clinical supervision.

Many of your depressed clients will likely have serious histories of abuse, neglect, and trauma. For example, Rigazio-DiGilio (1989) found that seventeen of twenty inpatient depressives had serious instances of family trauma. Given Miller's (1981) observations on the incidence of child abuse and Brassard, Germain, and Hart's (1987) convincing summary of child and adolescent maltreatment literature, it is likely that use of images and reliving of old traumatic events will play an increasingly important part in your practice.

Past traumatic issues that clients bring to therapy are complicated by the fact that 50 percent of psychiatrically diagnosed clients have some serious alcohol or drug problems—that is, they have a dual diagnosis (Evans & Sullivan, 1990). It is critical that you have some form of substance abuse treatment options available as well as the more traditional counseling theories. Integrating cognitive-behavioral, developmental, and family systems concepts (Chapter 13) is useful in generating treatment programs for dual diagnosis clients and those who have drug and alcohol problems, including a family history of substance abuse.

Potential Issues with Images and Regression

Anytime we ask clients to use images to help them think back to situations from the past to understand automatic thoughts or other issues, we employ the technique of regression—making the past powerfully present in the here and now of the clinical session. Currently in the field, there is conflict around these matters, particularly as concerns the "false-memory syndrome." If imaging and regression techniques are used in an overly directive or insensitive manner, it is possible to implant your ideas and theories in clients, thus giving them a false memory of their past.

How can you avoid unconsciously putting your ideas into clients? It is most important to be client-centered and to put clients in control, work with, and not on, them. Asking leading questions or suggesting types of images clients should develop should be avoided, as should a continual focus on the negative. The issue in counseling and therapy is moving forward, not in retrieving multiple examples of negative experiences and trauma.

Positive images from the culture, community, and family are suggested as a way to balance and counteract negative images. Ellis and Beck both stress the need for a forward-moving therapy that emphasizes action as well as cognition. Those who mistakenly use these powerful techniques to focus primarily on past issues do their clients damage.

Summary

The following lists some basic tenets of Beck's system:

1. Everyone forms patterns of automatic thinking that can be irrational.
2. These automatic thoughts can be observed and identified in the therapeutic interview. Clients can be taught skills for identifying misleading thought patterns—for example, making a daily record of automatic thoughts.
3. Beck believes that automatic thoughts are continuations of old issues from the past that are transferred to the present. This stance places him closer to the psychodynamic orientation. His focus, however, is on direct behavior and thoughts rather than on abstract theorizing.
4. Images may be useful in concretizing situations and obtaining a better understanding of emotional experience.
5. Beck's ideas about depression and its treatment have been particularly influential. His balance of cognitive and behavioral approaches is a model for many professionals.
6. As in REBT, Beck's cognitive system often includes relaxation training, systematic desensitization, and all the techniques and strategies of cognitive-behavioral modification.

William Glasser and Reality Therapy

If Albert Ellis's rational-emotive behavior therapy could be summarized as "Be rational and think about things logically," William Glasser's reality therapy could be summarized by saying, "Take responsibility and control of your own life and face the consequences of your actions." Glasser's reality therapy can be considered a cognitive-behavioral therapy, but one that focuses very much on realism and how to treat difficult clients. Although research on reality therapy is limited, it is a frequent treatment of choice in working with difficult clients, particularly acting-out or delinquent youth or adults. In reality therapy, there is more focus on external reality than in the approaches of Beck and Ellis.

Especially in the early stages of therapy, some younger clients, particularly those who are acting out or delinquent, will not "stand still" for the approaches of Ellis and Beck. However, after you establish a working alliance with such clients, perhaps through reality therapy, you can return successfully to cognitive-behavioral techniques. A case study of reality therapy with an acting-out younger client is presented, followed by a discussion of theoretical constructs.

Case Presentation: Probation Client

Counseling sessions within reality therapy can range from a regularly scheduled fifty-minute hour to brief personal encounters in the dining room, classroom, or other setting. Many clients do not want to come to the office for the highly verbal and sophisticated treatments that we as therapists might prefer to offer. Reality therapy offers a viable alternative that you can use as a basis for working with difficult clients; later, other forms of helping can be incorporated.

The following interview shows the second phase of reality therapy. The client is an eighteen-year-old young man on probation for repeated offenses of a minor nature, including selling alcohol to minors, assault, and petty theft. The counselor in this case is a county probation officer, and the meeting occurs in the community half-way house. They are just finishing a game of Ping-Pong.

1. *Counselor:*   Got ya! 21 to 18. Took me three games, but I finally got one.
2. *Client:*   Yeah, you pulled it off finally. Man, I'm pooped. (They sit down and have a cup of coffee.)
3. *Counselor:*   So, how have things been going? [*Open question*]
4. *Client:*   Well, I looked for jobs hard last week. But nothing looked any good. The bastards seem to know I'm coming and pull the help wanted sign down just as I come walking in.
5. *Counselor:*   So, you've been looking hard. How many places did you visit? [*Paraphrase, closed question; note search for concrete behavior*]
6. *Client:*   Oh lots. Nobody will give me a chance.

7. *Counselor:* Maybe I can help. Tell me some of the places you've been. [*Directive, with continued emphasis on concreteness. Where Beck and Ellis often move clients to formal operational thought, the Glasser approach focuses on specifics—one of its values for the many concrete operational clients you will encounter.*]

8. *Client:* I tried the gas station down the street. They gave me a bad time. Nobody wants me. It's really tough.

9. *Counselor:* Where else did you go? [*Closed question*]

10. *Client:* I tried a couple other stations too. Nobody wants to look at me. They don't pay too good anyway. Nuts to them!

11. *Counselor:* So you haven't really done too much looking. Sounds like you want it served on a silver plate, Joe. Do you think looking at a couple of gas stations is really going to get you a job? [*Paraphrase, interpretation, logical consequences. Here we see a lead, particularly typical of reality therapy, that places considerable emphasis on the consequences of actions. The point is similar to applied behavioral analysis, but the way of reaching consequences is quite different.*]

12. *Client:* I suppose not. Nobody wants to hire me anyway.

13. *Counselor:* Let's take another look at that. The economy is pretty rocky right now. Everyone is having trouble getting work. You seem to think "they" are after you. Yet, I've got a friend about your age who had to go to thirty-five places before he got a job. How does that square with you looking at three places and then giving up? Who's responsible—you, the service station owners, or the economy? [*Directive, information giving, open question; note confrontation and emphasis on the word* responsible. *Responsible action is the formal operational concept toward which most of reality therapy aspires.*]

14. *Client:* Yeah, but, there's not much I can do about it. I tried . . .

15. *Counselor:* Yeah, at three places. Who's responsible for you not getting a job when you only go to three places? At a time like this you've really got to scramble. Come on, Joe! [*Interpretation plus logical consequences*]

The interview continues to explore Joe's lack of action, with an emphasis on responsibility. At points where a Rogerian counselor might have paraphrased or reflected feelings and attitudes (such as at Client 4, 8, and 10), the reality therapist opted for more behavioral specifics through questions and interpretation. The process of examining Joe's behavior is closely akin to that of the behavioral counselor using applied behavioral analysis. However, the use of the behavioral data is quite different in reality therapy. Instead of seeking to change behavior, the reality therapist works on changing awareness of responsibility. Once the focus of responsibility has been acknowledged and owned by the client, it is possible to start planning a more effective job search. Later in the interview, the process of planning evolves.

51. *Counselor:* So, Joe, sounds like you feel you made a decision this past week not to really look for a job . . . almost as if you took responsibility for

not getting work. [*Reflection of meaning, interpretation. Note that placing the locus of decision in the client can be a helpful strategy in any approach to helping. It is here that reality therapy truly becomes cognitive-behavioral. At the same time, this is a clear example of moving away from a societal, contextual focus.*]

52. *Client:*   Yeah, I don't like to look at it that way, but I guess I did decide not to do too much.

53. *Counselor:*   And what about next week?

54. *Client:*   I suppose I ought to look again, but I really don't like it.

The reality therapist at this point moved to a realistic analysis of what the client might expect during the coming week on the job market, constantly emphasizing the importance of the client, Joe, taking action and responsibility for his life. A practice role-played job interview was held, and several alternatives for generating a more effective job search were considered. Joe tried to escape responsibility at several points ("I couldn't do that"), but the counselor confronted him and allowed no excuses or ambivalence.

A reality therapist will use skills and ideas of other theoretical orientations when they serve the purpose of assisting the client to confront reality more effectively. More likely, the reality therapist will be her or his natural self and use humor, sarcasm, and confrontation in very personal ways to assist the client in understanding behavioral patterns and developing new action approaches. Role-playing, systematic planning, and instruction in intentional living are important tools in reality therapy.

Although many who practice reality therapy approaches may be in power situations (guards, principals, rehabilitation counselors), they still tend to be themselves and to use reality therapy as an extension of themselves; this adds a tone of genuineness and authenticity to the process at a more significant level than would be possible with other approaches. For example, a prison guard trained in reality therapy can simply state his position realistically as one of power and control. Then, with the role relationships clearly established, the process of involvement, teaching of responsibility, and relearning can occur.

Reality Therapy and MCT

Reality therapy has much to offer multicultural counseling and therapy, for the emphasis on responsibility to others and society is in accord with Native American Indian and Asian and Asian-American value systems. Reality therapy's focus on the relationship between external and internal cognitions provides an important balance to the internality of the approaches of Ellis and Beck. Practice Exercise 10.3 illustrates how reality therapy can be tied to multicultural counseling and therapy.

=== **Practice Exercise 10.3** ===

 Facing Reality: Adding Context to Cognitive Therapies

Most work in cognitive therapies and constructivist theory focuses on the internal thoughts and feelings of the client. Reality therapy adds an important dimension in that it balances person-environment interaction. Not only is the client looking at self, but also the client is challenged to see self-in-context. In this sense, reality therapy offers some useful ideas for a multiculturally sensitive approach. The following exercise illustrates this point.

1. *Find a volunteer client.* Ask a friend or classmate to volunteer as a client. Show your volunteer this exercise so that you are working mutually in a coconstructive relationship. A suggested topic for this exercise is examining an interpersonal conflict.

2. *Use the basic listening sequence to draw out the client's story.* Be sure to obtain the central facts and emotions and clearly summarize what you have heard. You may also wish to use the concepts of applied behavioral analysis so that the story is really clear.

3. *Review the story from three perspectives—client, other person, and context.* First, point out that the client has told the story from a personal perspective. Ask the client to describe how the other person would tell the same story. Give special attention to what the client and other person need to have happen. Finally, consider with the client how multicultural or other contextual is-

sues, such as gender, socioeconomic status, sexual preference, religion, race/ethnicity, workplace, and physical space might affect the conflict. Specifically, if a person from one or more of these backgrounds described the story, which elements might be the same and which might change?

4. *Introduce the issues of responsibility and what is realistic in this situation.* Reality therapy stresses that we must look beyond clients' internal needs and also examine the facts of external reality. Traditional cognitive therapy does not deal with external facts as directly. In this practice exercise, explore with your client issues of personal responsibility and how best to face the realities of this context. Encourage the client to seek fulfillment for self, others, and the broader context.

5. *Review possible consequences of cognitive and behavioral change.* You may wish to brainstorm the future results of varying actions on the part of the responsible client. Encourage your client to take specific behavioral action on the conflict. Or you may even encourage your client to take action on the context affecting the problem. Here you may wish to utilize some of the behavioral techniques of Chapter 9 or the community action programs of multicultural counseling and therapy (Chapter 6).

Central Theoretical Constructs of Reality Therapy

In describing the basic tenets of reality therapy, Glasser (1965) states that all clients have been unsuccessful in meeting their needs and that in attempts to meet their needs, they often tend to select ineffective behaviors that virtually assure their failure. Further,

> All patients have a common characteristic: they all deny the reality of the world around them. Some break the law, denying the rules of society; some claim their neighbors are plotting against them, denying the improbability of such behavior. Some are afraid of crowded places, close quarters, airplanes, or elevators, yet they freely admit the irrationality of their fears. Millions drink to blot out the inadequacy they feel but that need not exist if they could learn to be different; and far too many people choose suicide rather than face the reality that they could solve their problems by more responsible behavior. Whether it is a partial denial or the total blotting out of all reality of the chronic backward patient in the state hospital, the denial of some or all of reality is common to all patients. Therapy will be successful when they are able to give up denying the world and recognize that reality not only exists but that they must fulfill their needs within its framework.
>
> A therapy that leads all patients toward reality, toward grappling successfully with the tangible and intangible aspects of the real world, might accurately be called a therapy toward reality, or simply Reality Therapy. (p. 6)

Reality therapy can best be described as a commonsense approach to counseling. What Glasser advocates is finding out what people want and need, examining their failures and their present assets, and considering factors in the environment that must be met if the needs are to be satisfied. One cannot meet needs except in a real world; people must face a world that is imperfect and not built to their specifications and must act positively in this world. The worldview of reality therapy is that people can do something about their fate if they will consider themselves and their environment realistically. In this sense, reality therapy has much in common with decisional counseling. (Variations of decisional counseling are often used in work in correctional facilities.)

The Importance of Responsibility

As might be anticipated, reality therapy focuses on conscious, planned behavior and gives relatively little attention to underlying dimensions of transference, unconscious thought process, and the like. The goal is to consider the past as being past and done with; the present and the future are what are important. Yet reality therapy does not emphasize applied behavioral analysis or the detailed plans of assertiveness training or systematic desensitization. Rather, almost like rational-emotive therapy, reality therapy focuses on responsibility and choice. What is central is that clients examine their lives to see how specific behavior is destructive. The more important step, however, is to take responsibility, which Glasser (1965) defines as "the ability to fulfill one's needs and to do so in a way that does not deprive others of the ability to fulfill their needs" (p. 13). Learning responsibility is a lifelong process.

Given the population that reality therapy often serves (clients of street clinics, prison inmates, school children, and others in institutional settings), it is clear that relationship and trust are particularly important. The institutions with which children and prisoners cope do not engender the trust that often is a given in a traditional client-therapist setting. The *personhood* of the reality therapist becomes especially important. The qualities of warmth, respect and caring for others, positive regard, and interpersonal openness are crucial.

Reality therapy is much more likely to be practiced in settings other than the counseling office, although this method is also used in the standard clinical setting. The individual practicing reality therapy likely may be out on the playground or in a delinquent detention center or may be a classroom teacher or perhaps a prison guard. The possible multiplicity of relationships requires a special type of person to maintain consistency. This challenge provides an opportunity for the reality therapist to serve as a continuing model of personal responsibility to the client outside the counseling environment.

Cognitive Trends in Reality Therapy

A critical part of reality therapy is client awareness of consequences of actions: "If you do X, then what is the consequence?" Reality therapy, in a highly nonjudgmental fashion, attempts to help individuals learn what they can expect when they act in certain ways. In this sense, you may again note a similarity and a difference from rational-emotive behavior therapy. In REBT, the consequences are those inside the person (feeling depressed, and so forth), whereas in reality therapy, the consequences may indeed be inside, but the emphasis is on what happens in the outside world when the client fails to face reality and be responsible.

Glasser has continually expanded his thinking but has remained true to the basic constructs of the method and theory described above. In his 1981 book, *Stations of the Mind*, he builds a comprehensive picture of the workings of the "internal world" of the mind. Glasser notes that the "internal reality" of the mind (cognitions) must be able to understand how the individual relates to external reality.

Control is an increasingly important aspect of Glasser's thinking. "We Always Have Control Over What We Do" is a chapter heading in Glasser's book for the popular market, *Take Effective Control of Your Life* (1984). At issue is how the individual exercises that control. One can choose misery as a way of life because it is an excuse from trying harder and may win help or pity from others, and so on. Psychosomatic illness is considered a specific type of internal control to help individuals avoid reality. "Headaching" individuals may benefit because having a headache gives them a reason to lie down and rest. Drugs and alcohol are still other ways people exert control to avoid facing reality.

Careful analysis of Glasser's recent work suggests that he is moving closer to the position of Ellis and the cognitive-behavioralists in that he gives increased attention to the way people think about things. However, he still uses the basic structure of reality therapy to produce change. His theory of control provides an important additional tool for therapists working with individual clients. The therapist insists that the client "own" thoughts, behavior, and feelings and be responsible for them. The logic is that if one can exert control toward seemingly unsatisfactory ends such as drugs, headaches, stealing, and interpersonal conflict, then one can reframe control more positively.

Glasser talks about "positive addictions," which range from spending time with friends to jogging to movies to meditation—anything through which an individual can obtain a "high" in a more satisfactory and healthy way. The world offers us the opportunity for negative addiction or for positive addiction. We choose our addictions and our fate. We can choose headaches or we can choose joy. The choice is ours. We are in control.

Glasser's new emphasis on control indicates that he is moving toward a more immediate, confrontational, and cognitive point of view. With certain clients, we may expect direct and forceful confrontations of thought patterns, active teaching of alternative perceptions of reality, and an emphasis that focuses more on internal states and thoughts. Needless to say, the client must be ready for this new challenge. The "how" of control theory has not really been addressed, except by implication. At the moment, traditional reality therapy and the new dimensions of control theory seem somewhat at odds. We may anticipate for the future, however, a more complete integration of Glasser's thinking with illustrations of how a new theory of reality therapy may be used in more practical ways. In the past, Glasser seemed to stress the importance of the client adapting to the world as it is. He now appears to be adding the dimension of internal cognitive states to his basic view.

Summary

The following summary reviews some key aspects of reality therapy:

1. We need to consider the behavior and cognitions of other people than just the client. We need also to assess the facts of cognitive and behavioral consequences in person-environment interactions. This dimension moves reality therapy close to multicultural counseling and therapy.

2. The typical office setting of most counseling and therapy may not reflect the reality of life. If counselors and therapists move out into the real world, they will quickly find that even the best theory must change in practice.

3. Responsibility for our actions is central. Adding dimensions of personal ethics and analysis of consequences for our behavior is a particular strength of reality therapy.

Arnold Lazarus and the Multimodal Approach

How can the ideas of the cognitive-behavioral approach be integrated in a meaningful assessment and treatment plan? Arnold Lazarus (1992) has addressed this question in what he calls multimodal therapy. This framework allows for the integration of multiple techniques and strategies to meet unique client needs. The multimodal approach holds that there are ten issues to consider if any treatment is to be fully comprehensive (Lazarus & Fay, 1993):

1. Biological factors
2. Conflicting or ambivalent feelings or reactions
3. Misinformation, especially to irrational beliefs
4. Missing information or lack of skills
5. Maladaptive habits, behavioral or cognitive
6. Negative social or traumatic past experience
7. Present social support network
8. External stressors
9. Self-concept and self-esteem issues
10. Existential and meaning concerns (pp. 37–38)

Although this listing focuses on problems, it is also important to stress positive aspects of the client. Multicultural counseling and therapy (MCT) suggests a focus on the positive aspects of the client's cultural background. Although Lazarus has not yet given extensive attention to gender and multicultural issues, there are some ways in which these matters may be approached within his framework. There is a tendency in the cognitive-behavioral tradition to focus on individual deficits and to ignore the role of the family in the present and also in the past. Nonetheless, the above factors are valuable and important if you can remember to also bring a positive dimension to your assessment. Assessment of strengths can be as important as diagnosis of problems. Clients will often find solutions to issues in positive behaviors, cognitions, and family and cultural support systems.

If you work within the Lazarus framework, you might begin your series of sessions with the Comprehensive Multimodal Life History Questionnaire. This twelve-page inventory is completed with the client and elaborates the ten points above. Again, family and multicultural issues could enrich this inventory. In addition, the BASIC-ID would be added as an individual style assessment mechanism.

The BASIC-ID

The BASIC-ID was designed to help assess clients' ways of being-in-the-world. It is a comprehensive framework that can be invaluable in making sure that you have considered all important issues. As above, the BASIC-ID does not consider environmental, multicultural, and contextual issues fully. Lazarus (1995) presents the BASIC-ID system as follows:

B   Behavior—as in applied behavioral analysis

A   Affect—feeling and emotions

S   Sensation—senses of sight, sound, smell, touch, and taste plus sensuality and sexuality

I   Imagery—ability to form mental pictures of events, plus amount of daydreaming and fantasy engaged in

C   Cognitions—self-talk and thoughts about self, ideas, and philosophy

I   Interpersonal relationships—general style plus how much of a "people" person the individual is

D   Drugs and biological/health factors

If you work through the BASIC-ID carefully, you will have a good sense of your client, and this understanding can help you plan your treatment series. Lazarus (1986) considers treatment planning as developing a "modality firing order." He suggests that treatment usually begins with awareness of client style and personal needs. For example, a client who seems to have issues around being able to experience affect and sensation might benefit from instruction in learning to name and recognize emotions plus work with body awareness. A client with primarily behavioral concerns might be given any of a number of strategies from the previous chapter. If a client has a drug or health concern, this is the obvious place to start. After you have resolved the initial key issue, you can turn to other aspects of the BASIC-ID.

Sometimes the initial firing order doesn't work. Then Lazarus suggests using another related approach. For example, if the client's issue is lack of being in touch with affect and sensation and your early therapeutic efforts have not been successful, then work with imaging techniques or cognitive methods may be employed. In short, you may be able to improve client functioning in one modality by using a secondary method.

Coconstruction and mutuality are important parts of Lazarus's technical eclecticism. The careful and somewhat lengthy evaluation process of the BASIC-ID involves clients in their own treatment. Lazarus takes a particularly broad and open approach to treatment. Due to this openness, the multimodal approach may be especially helpful when other methods have failed. Practice Exercise 10.4 may be useful in generating a deeper understanding of the potential of Lazarus's framework.

Summary

Following are some of the most important aspects of Lazarus's framework:

1. The multimodal approach provides a comprehensive view of the client and the client's style.

2. A particularly important aspect of this broad-based system is that it encourages therapist and client mutual assessment and construction of a treatment plan.

=== **Practice Exercise 10.4** ===

 Exploring the BASIC-ID

With a volunteer or a real client, test some of the ideas of a BASIC-ID assessment. Begin by telling your client about the BASIC-ID and why you are engaging in this exercise so that the client can be a full mutual participant with you. Stress that you are exploring the general style of the client.

Jointly decide on a specific issue your client finds of interest. Ask the client to tell you a brief story or narrative about the issue. Use the basic listening sequence to make sure you have summarized the major facts and feelings.

1. *Behavior.* Focus on the story from a behavioral perspective. Using applied behavioral analysis, obtain the A-B-Cs of the story. What behaviors in this situation would the client like to increase or decrease? Is this a typical behavior for the client?

2. *Affect.* Identify the client feelings clearly. Is this client able to identify emotions and experience them fully? Would the client like to increase or decrease emotional experience around this issue? In general, how emotionally expressive is the client?

3. *Sensation.* Talk with the client about the modalities—visual, auditory, olfactory, kinesthetic, or taste—experienced in this story. Also, ask the client about bodily sensations during the telling of the story. In general, how in touch is the client with what is going on in the body?

4. *Imagery.* Ask the client to generate an image of the story. This will provide a second opportunity to examine sensation. Ask your client where the images are experienced in the body. From this account you can obtain a deeper felt sense of affect and, later, of cognitions, as images tend to be holistic. Also, this experience can be an opportunity to learn how the client uses imagination and fantasy.

5. *Cognition.* What was going on in terms of thoughts and ideas in the client's head throughout the story? Here you have the opportunity to learn about the client's self-talk while the action was happening. If appropriate, conduct an REBT or automatic thoughts analysis. Finally, is this client primarily a "thinker" or a "doer"?

6. *Interpersonal relationships.* Discuss the nature of personal relationships exemplified in this story. What generally is the interpersonal style and competence of this client? How might this client like to change?

7. *Drugs and biological/health factors.* Review this area with your client. Are drugs, alcohol, or medication an issue in this client's life? Is the person active or passive physically? What are important current and past health issues? Would any of these affect what happened in the story?

When you have completed the BA-SIC-ID analysis, take some time to consider with the client gender, family, and other multicultural issues that might affect the story. Then review together the total assessment and talk about various cognitive and behavioral strategies that might be employed if a comprehensive treatment plan were developed for change in any one of the seven areas.

3. Lazarus speaks especially effectively to often-overlooked biological and health factors.

4. The firing order concept reminds us that matching treatment with client needs is vital. If our original match for treatment is ineffective, we can draw on other parts of the BASIC-ID framework.

5. Multimodal assessment and treatment may profit from consideration of gender and multicultural factors. Moreover, the BASIC-ID may give insufficient attention to positive assets of the client.

Limitations and Practical Implications of Cognitive-Behavioral Counseling and Therapy

In general, the same limitations of the cognitive-behavioral tradition cited in Chapter 9 and discussed in other chapters hold true here. Specifically, a charismatic "high-powered" therapist may dazzle and harm an unsuspecting client. Similarly, a warm and gentle therapist also can emotionally "seduce" clients and manipulate them, either consciously or unconsciously. Some would like to think that therapists do no harm. However, advertent or inadvertent harm occurs again and again in all forms of therapy.

Ellis's personal style is considered by some to be abrasive, and thus some people have discounted his important and seminal work. However, it would be a mistake to confuse personal style with theoretical merit. As with any therapy, it is important that you find your own way of integrating Ellis's work into your array of skills and theories.

The constructs of REBT have been vastly influential. Ellis's three major tenets are critical additions to the skills and understandings of any professional helper, regardless of theoretical orientation: (1) REBT points out to us that it is possible to change the ways we think about things and that cognitive change is often sufficient for significant improvement; (2) the A-B-C and D-E-F frameworks for analyzing client irrational cognitions have become a standard in the field; and (3) Ellis has provided significant leadership in generating a more culturally equitable approach to helping.

Beck developed his cognitive framework independently from Ellis, and Beck's work currently appears to be increasingly influential and to be gradually developing a significant research base. Beck's concept of automatic thoughts is a significant extension of Ellis's framework. Whereas Ellis appears to deny the importance of developmental history and psychodynamic formulations, Beck seems able to integrate these ideas comfortably. Beck points out to us clearly that early client history can often influence cognitive patterns, and his use of imagery in accessing both thoughts and past experiences is important. However, Beck, Ellis, Meichenbaum, and Glasser would all agree that it is not always essential to delve into past history.

For some, including Glasser's reality therapy as a cognitive-behavioral technique may seem unusual, as Glasser tends to work outside the therapeutic mainstream. Glasser tends to discount early childhood experience and focus practically on what needs to be done now. With its clear emphasis on logical consequences of personal actions and the importance of personal control, Glasser's reality therapy will remain appropriate in work with difficult clients or in institutional settings in which regular interviews and time-intensive treatment plans are not always feasible.

All four of the cognitive-behavioral approaches discussed in this chapter tend to put the problem "in the client." This, of course, is true for most individualistically oriented helping theories. Reality therapy, for example, stresses the need for the client to adapt to necessary environmental contingencies. Sometimes clients come from oppressive family, neighborhood, and cultural histories. Although it is important that the client adapt to reality, such adaptation can result in clients returning to oppressive systems with the idea that the "fault" is in them rather than in the environment. REBT and Beck's cognitive approach also can fall prey to what some call "blaming the victim" and to a focus on curing the "ills" of the client, when family and society are also responsible.

The discussion of the work of Lazarus provides a useful conclusion to these two chapters on cognitive-behavioral theory and strategies. His multimodal approach has helped organize the complexity of counseling and therapy issues, and his BASIC-ID has become virtually a standard assessment tool in the field. Lazarus, however, like many theorists described in this book, focuses primarily on problems, with relatively little attention given to client strengths or multicultural issues.

Cognitive-behavioral methods and strategies often make quick and decisive change possible and are especially emphasized in this era of managed care and emphasis on results. Thus, responsible professionals should be conversant with and competent in this framework.

NOTES

1. This transcript was edited for clarity. The italics are Ellis's.
2. An earlier chapter discussed the A-B-Cs of behavior—the antecedents, behaviors, and consequences. It is helpful to be skilled in both types of A-B-C analysis. At times, the more behaviorally focused analysis can be used to clarify the cognitive thought processes. Similarly, if you can understand the client's cognitive patterns, you will have some ability to predict what actually happens behaviorally.

REFERENCES

BECK, A. (1972). *Depression: Causes and treatment.* Philadelphia: University of Pennsylvania Press.

BECK, A. (1976). *Cognitive therapy and the emotional disorders.* New York: International Universities Press.

BECK, A. (1991). Cognitive therapy: A 30-year retrospective. *American Psychologist, 46,* 368–75.

BECK, A., FREEMAN, A., & ASSOCIATES. (1990). *Cognitive therapy of personality disorders.* New York: Guilford.

BRASSARD, M., GERMAIN, R., & HART, S. (1987). *Psychological maltreatment of children and youth.* New York: Pergamon Press.

CHEEK, D. (1976). *Assertive Black . . . puzzled White.* San Luis Obispo, CA: Impact.

CHEN, C. (1995). Counseling applications of RET in a Chinese cultural context. *Journal of Rational-Emotive and Cognitive-Behavior Therapy, 13,* 117–29.

DIFFILY, A. (1984). Aaron Beck: A profile. *Brown Alumni Monthly.* Providence, RI, pp. 39–46.

DOBSON, K. (1989). A meta-analysis of the efficacy of cognitive therapy for depression. *Journal of Consulting and Clinical Psychology, 57,* 414–19.

ELLIS, A. (1958). *Sex without guilt.* Secaucus, NJ: Lyle Stuart.

ELLIS, A. (1967). Rational-emotive psychotherapy. In D. Arbuckle (Ed.), *Counseling and Psychotherapy.* New York: McGraw-Hill.

ELLIS, A. (1971). *Growth through reason.* Palo Alto, CA: Science and Behavior Books.

ELLIS, A. (1983). The origins of rational-emotive therapy (RET). *Voices, 18,* 29–33.

ELLIS, A. (1992). *Rational recovery systems: An alternative to Alcoholics Anonymous.* Unpublished manuscript, Institute of Rational-Emotive Therapy, New York.

ELLIS, A. (1994). *Reason and emotion in psychotherapy.* New York: Birch Lane.

ELLIS, A. (1995). Changing rational-emotive therapy to rational-emotive behavior therapy. *Journal of Rational-Emotive and Cognitive-Behavior Therapy, 13,* 85–90.

EVANS, K., & SULLIVAN, M. (1990). *Dual diagnosis: Counseling the mentally ill substance abuser.* New York: Guilford.

FAY, A., & LAZARUS, A. (1993). On necessity and sufficiency in psychotherapy. *Psychotherapy in Private Practice, 12,* 33–39.

FREEMAN, A., & SIMON, K. (1989). Cognitive therapy of anxiety. In A. Freeman, K. Simon, L. Beutler, & H. Arkowitz (Eds.), *Comprehensive handbook of cognitive therapy* (pp. 346–66). New York: Plenum.

GLASSER, W. (1965). *Reality therapy.* New York: HarperCollins.

GLASSER, W. (1981). *Stations of the mind.* New York: HarperCollins.

GLASSER, W. (1984). *Take effective control of your life.* New York: HarperCollins.

HOLLAN, S., & NAJAVITS, L. (1988). Review of empirical studies of cognitive therapy. In A. Frances & R. Hales (Eds.), *American Psychiatric Press Review of Psychiatry* (Vol. 7, pp. 643–66). Washington, DC: American Psychiatric Press.

KANTROWITZ, R., & BALLOU, M. (1992). A feminist critique of cognitive-behavioral theory. In L. Brown & M. Ballou (Eds.), *Personality and psychopathology: Feminist reappraisals.* New York: Guilford.

KELLY, G. (1955). *The psychology of personal constructs* (Vols. 1 and 2). New York: W.W. Norton.

LAZARUS, A. (1986). Multimodal psychotherapy. *International Journal of Eclectic Psychotherapy, 5,* 95–103.

LAZARUS, A. (1992). *I can if I want to.* New York: Morrow.

LAZARUS, A. (1995). Adjusting the carburetor: Pivotal interventions in marital and sex therapy. In R. Rosen & S. Leiblum (Eds.), *Case studies in sex therapy* (pp. 81–95). New York: Guilford.

LYONS, L., & WOODS, P. (1992). The efficacy of rational-emotive therapy: A quantitative review of the outcome literature. *Clinical Psychology Review.*

MILLER, A. (1981). *The drama of the gifted child.* New York: Basic Books.

RIGAZIO-DIGILIO, S. (1989). *Developmental theory and therapy: A preliminary investigation of reliability and predictive validity using an inpatient depressive population sample.* Unpublished doctoral dissertation, University of Massachusetts, Amherst.

SCORZELLI, J., & REINEKE-SCORZELLI, M. (1994). Cultural sensitivity and cognitive therapy in India. *Counseling Psychologist, 22,* 603–10.

SHEA, M., ELKIN, I., IMBER, S., STOSKY, S., WATKINS, J., COLLINS, J., PILKONIS, P., LEBER, W., KRUPNICK, J., DONAN, R., & PARLOFF, M. (1990). *Course of depressive symptoms over follow-up: Findings from the National Institute of Mental Health Treatment of Depression Collaborative Research Program.* Manuscript submitted for publication cited in A. Beck, Cognitive therapy: A 30-year retrospective. *American Psychologist,* 1991, *46,* 368–75.

TRIMPEY, J. (1989). *Rational recovery from addiction: The small book.* Lotus, CA: Author.

WEINRACH, S. (1990). Anecdotes. In D. DiMattia & L. Lega (Eds.), *Will the real Albert Ellis please stand up?* (pp. 42–43, 108–9, 124–25). New York: Institute for Rational Emotive Therapy.

WOLPE, J. (1982). *The practice of behavior therapy* (3rd ed.). New York: Pergamon.

The Existential-Humanistic Tradition I:
Existential-Humanistic Theory and
Person-Centered Theory and Practice

CHAPTER GOALS

This chapter seeks to:

1. Describe the general worldview of existential-humanistic theory. This orientation greatly influences the practice of most counseling and therapy, even though the practitioner may follow another theoretical direction.

2. Examine person-centered theory and its possible relevance for work with multicultural populations.

3. Present central theoretical and practical constructs from the work of Rogers.

4. Present the work of the multicultural humanist Clemmont Vontress, which integrates existential, Rogerian, and multicultural thought.

5. Enable you, through practice exercises, to conduct or engage in
   - A complete interview using a "nondirective" approach
   - A complete interview integrating existential-humanistic and multicultural issues

The Existential-Humanistic
Frame of Reference

The existential-humanistic tradition has two aspects in counseling and psychotherapy. First, it is a group of major theories—existential, person-centered, logotherapy, Gestalt, and other related systems. Second, it is an attitude toward the human condition and the interview that now permeates virtually all practice, regardless of theoretical persuasion. The foundational concepts of empathy (Chapter 2) are derived from Carl Rogers's person-centered theories, and the listening microskills (Chapter 3) are closely allied with his early work in nondirective counseling. Cognitive-behavioral, psychodynamic, and multicultural approaches often draw from existential-humanistic theory and practice when they address the importance of relationship. More than any other group of theories, the existential-humanistic tradition focuses on the nature and meaning of the client and counselor relationship.

Although the roots of the existential-humanistic tradition lie in philosophy, Rogers and his person-centered counseling have been most influential in popularizing the existential-humanistic point of view and making it accessible and relevant to clinical and counseling practice. Rogers's techniques are designed to help you enter the worldviews of your clients and then to facilitate clients finding their own new directions and frames of thinking.

The ideas of Clemmont Vontress are also discussed in this chapter. His ideas of relationship differ somewhat from those of Rogers and add a new dimension to the constructs of existential-humanism. Vontress (1995b) speaks of the relationship as central in existential-humanistic counseling and therapy:

> The existential counseling relationship is an interaction in which two co-equal humans benefit from the encounter. The focus is on one of the interactants only because that one declares him- or herself to be in need of help from the other. Undergirding the relationship are existential ideas such as death, sympathy, psychotherapeutic eros, and an I-Thou personal relationship. (p. 1)

The Rogerian and the existential-humanistic perspective delves into the rich, complex, and, at times, disturbing elements of human experience. The existential-humanistic tradition does not have all the answers for helping victims and survivors, but its deep tradition of caring and of individual free choice is an important part of any treatment you may engage in. The philosophic aspects of this theoretical approach are well received in virtually all cultures, and its major theorists have had wide impact and acceptance throughout the world.

The Existential-Humanistic Worldview

The existential-humanistic view focuses on men and women as people who are empowered to act on the world and determine their own destiny. The locus of control and decision lies within the individual, rather than in past history or in environmental determinants. At the same time, the humanistic aspect of this tradition focuses on *people-in-relationship* one to another. It is this combination of individual respect and the importance of relationship that gives this framework its long-lasting strength.

Existentialism's roots may be traced to the Danish philosopher Kierkegaard, but the movement came into full bloom following World War II with the writings of Sartre (1946, 1956) and Camus (1942, 1958). Heidegger (1962), Laing (1967), Husserl (1931), and Tillich (1961) loom large among the many existential philosophers, psychologists, and theologians that influenced this approach. May (1969, 1958, 1961) has played a key role in bringing existential thought to the awareness of counselors and psychologists in the United States.

However, Binswanger (1958, 1963) and Boss (1958, 1963) have been particularly instrumental in pulling together the many threads of existentialism into the practice of counseling and therapy. *Being-in-the-world* is regarded as the most fundamental concept of existentialism. We are in the world and acting on that world while it simultaneously acts on us. Any attempt to separate ourselves from the world alienates us and establishes a false and arbitrary distinction. Alienation results either from separateness from others and the world or from our inability to choose and act in relationship. The central task of therapy and counseling, then, is to enable alienated clients to see themselves in relationship to the world and to choose and act in accordance with what they see. Racism, sexism, homophobia, and the failure to understand difference lead to alienation by producing separation from others, a main cause of existential anxiety and aloneness.

Being-in-the-World

To facilitate analysis, existentialists often think of the individual in terms of the *eigenwelt* (the person and the body), the *mitwelt* (other people in the world), and the *umwelt* (the biological and physical world). The *überwelt* (spiritual dimension) is added to this framework by Vontress (1995b), who states that assessing the client's relationship to larger issues is a vital part of counseling and therapy. Spirituality and religion connect the individual to the past and to spiritual images and traditions and provide a way to address some of the largest issues clients face.

Alienation can be experienced in one or more areas: the person may be alienated from self and body, from others, or from the world. A general process of existential analysis is to enable individuals to study what the world (both *mitwelt* and *umwelt*) and their relationship to that world are like. Then, having examined the world, individuals are assumed free to act, rather than only to be acted upon.

The issue of action, however, brings with it the possibility of existential anxiety. Although existential anxiety may result from alienation, it may also result from failure to make decisions and to act in the world. Choices and decisions are often difficult; any time we choose, we must accept the fact that by choosing we deny other alternatives and possibilities. Although choice may be painful, it is likely to be less so than the anxiety created by not choosing.

Existential Commitment, Intentionality, and the I-Thou Relationship

Existential commitment is the decision to choose and to act; such action can be expected to alleviate anxiety. Yet because of our being-in-the-world we must constantly make choices, which reactivates anxiety. This circle of choice and anxiety causes some existentialists (such as Sartre and Kierkegaard) to become pessimistic and dubious. Others (such as Buber and Tillich) regard the issue of choice as opportunity rather than as problematic.

As used throughout this book, intentionality is a key existential construct that holds that people can be forward moving and act on their world, yet must remain keenly aware that the world acts on them as well. Intentionality provides a bridge to humanism, a worldview that finds its full bloom in Carl Rogers and Martin Buber. As Abbagnano (1967) puts it: "Humanism is . . . any philosophy which recognizes the value and dignity of [the person] and makes [her or] him the measure of all things" (p. 69). The existential-humanistic tradition recognizes the infinite variety of life experience and being-in-the-world as an opportunity rather than as a problem. Basic to this philosophy is assuming responsibility for choice and acting intentionally in the world.

The person who adopts the existential-humanistic position has made an intentional commitment toward what is positive and possible in human relations. Buber (1970) talks of the importance of "I-Thou" relations between people—that is, a relationship in which others are seen as people rather than as objects:

> Whoever says [Thou] does not have something for his [or her] object. For wherever there is something, there is also another something; every It borders on other Its; It is only by virtue of bordering on others. But where [Thou] is said, there is no something. [Thou] has no borders. (p. 55)

The intentional individual seeks I-Thou relationships as opposed to it-it relationships, in which people are seen as things. Buber's concept of I-Thou relationships speaks directly to multicultural concerns: How can we learn to stand in relationship to those different from ourselves?

Summary

The existential-humanistic point of view is an attitude toward the counseling interview and the meaning of life. The main point of this mode of counseling can be summarized as follows:

1. We are in the world; our task is to understand what this means. It is clear that the meanings we generate vary from culture to culture.

2. We know ourselves through our relationships with the world, and in particular through our relationships with other people.

3. Anxiety can result from lack of relationship (with ourselves, with others, or with the world at large) or from a failure to act and choose.

4. We are responsible for our own construction of the world. Even though we know the world only as it interacts on us, it is we who decide what the world means and who must provide organization for that world.

5. The task of the existential-humanistic therapist or counselor is to understand clients' worlds as fully as possible and ultimately to encourage them to be responsible for making decisions. However, existential counselors will also share themselves and their worldviews with clients as is appropriate.

6. A special problem is that the world is not necessarily meaningful. Existentialists such as Sartre and Kierkegaard often develop a negative and hopeless view of what they observe to be the absurdity and cruelty of life. However, humanistic existentialists such as Buber and May suggest that the very confusion and disorder in the world are an opportunity for growth and beauty.

7. The spiritual dimension (*überwelt*) is given credence by the work of Clemmont Vontress, who suggests that a truly holistic experience must include something beyond the individual (*eigenwelt*), the relationship (*mitwelt*), and the cultural/environmental context *(umwelt).*

8. The distinction between existential and existential-humanistic positions can be defined as one of philosophy or faith. If individuals see the many possibilities in the world as a problem, they have a problem. If individuals see the array of possibilities as infinite opportunity, they will choose to act.

The Rogerian Revolution

The word *self-actualization* is now a basic part of North American culture and can be traced to Rogers's influence, as can be seen in the following comments of Rogers and Wallen (1946):

> Counseling . . . [is] a way of helping the individual help [the] self. The function of the counselor is to make it possible for the client to gain emotional release in relation to . . . problems and, as a consequence, to think more clearly and more deeply about . . . self and . . . situation. It is the counselor's function to provide an atmosphere in which the client, through . . . exploration of the situation, comes to see . . . self and . . . reactions more clearly and to accept (personal) attitudes more fully. On the basis of this insight [the client] is able to meet . . . life problems more adequately, more independently, more responsibly than before. (pp. 5–6)

This worldview, now commonplace in counseling and therapy and in Western society as a whole, represented a radical departure from the psychodynamic tradition following World War II. Whereas psychodynamic and behavioral counseling and therapy viewed humankind as the often unknowing pawn of unconscious forces and environmental contingencies, existential-humanistic psychology, particularly as interpreted by Rogers, stressed that the individual could "take charge" of life, make decisions, and act on the world.

Undergirding this worldview is a faith that people are positive, forward moving, basically good, and ultimately self-actualizing. Self-actualization, or mental and emotional health, may ultimately be defined as experiencing one's fullest humanity. Self-actualizing people enjoy life thoroughly in all its aspects, not only in occasional moments of triumph. The task of the counselor is to assist clients in attaining the intentionality and the health that are natural to each individual. When a person becomes truly in touch with the inner self, that individual will move to positive action and fulfillment.

Adding Multicultural Dimensions to Self-Actualization Theory

Lerner (1992) notes that the positive view of human nature and the desire for an egalitarian approach make much of existential-humanistic theory and practice appealing to women and other multicultural groups. However, she criticizes the view of Rogers as particularly limited in terms of placing responsibility for development, growth, and change almost totally within the individual. Rogers "pays almost no attention to the so-called 'real world' or 'reality' " (p. 11). For women and other groups, Lerner maintains that Rogers's and other humanistic practice is potentially harmful: "No person constructs their own reality without external influences. The theories did not take in account exactly how influential external forces really are" (p. 13).

Some might propose that Rogers would agree with Jean Baker Miller's (1991) concepts of self-in-relation. Rogers, after all, was a relationship therapist. At the same time, the very term *self-actualization* could be read as self-centered and self-focused, even though this was not Rogers's meaning or desire. Thus, Rogers's work has meaning as well as limitations when applied to multicultural counseling and therapy.

Different cultures and social classes place different emphasis on *eigenwelt* (the person and the body), *mitwelt* (other people in the world), and *umwelt* (the biological and physical world). Some upper- and middle-class clients have learned to believe that the *eigenwelt* is perhaps the only desirable mode of being. This focus has led to some alienation of women and others from self-actualization counseling and therapy.

The microskill of focus can be a simple, but effective, way to balance *eigenwelt*, *mitwelt*, and *umwelt*. Assume the following lesbian client is oriented to relationship as well as self-actualization. Note the variation in responses as the therapist focuses on different dimensions.

> *Client:* The professor just doesn't understand. He keeps talking about self-actualization and finding one's own way. I can't find my own way. My lover, Jenny, and I are very close. I don't want to be separate from her—we are as one. Right now she's sick and how can I find my own way if she's not OK? I don't even feel able to go out and work right now.

Therapist: (focusing on *eigenwelt*) *You're* feeling overwhelmed, and *you* don't quite know what to do. What can *you* do to work through *your* present difficulties?

[*The italics highlight* you *as representative of a possible* eigenwelt *response that may lead the client to self-actualization.*]

Therapist: (focusing on *eigenwelt* and *umwelt*) Jenny's terribly important to *you*. The *relationship* sounds like the most important thing in *your* life right now. The question is how the *two of you* can survive this difficult time. *You're both* worried and upset and feel lost.

Therapist: (focusing on *umwelt*) The possibility of losing your *job* sounds very worrisome. You are wondering if issues of discrimination aren't part of the picture as well. Tell me some more about what's going on *at work*.

Therapist: (focusing on *überwelt*) I've heard your pain and sense your confusion. Tell me about your spiritual history. Where do you find strength and power outside and beyond yourself? What values or concepts are most meaningful to you?

The first three therapist responses can be useful in a Rogerian existential approach. Rogers constantly sought to help people work together. In some ways, the very terms *person-centered* and *client-centered*, attractive though they may be, can obscure the theoretical and practical value of Rogerian theory for non-middle-class and non-European–North American clients.

The fourth therapist response addresses the *überwelt* of Vontress as a way of enriching and expanding the therapy and counseling process. Vontress suggests that truly multicultural counseling and therapy must consider *überwelt* issues.

Fusion and Boundaries in Relationships

The foregoing example focused on an issue in relationship—namely, fusion—that has controversial interpretations in the field. Fusion is an important concept in counseling and therapy with lesbian clients (Mencher, 1990) as well as heterosexual couples. Fusion represents deep closeness between individuals so that at times the two individuals feel as one. This is seen by Mencher as a strength of lesbian relationships. This closeness is very reassuring, giving each individual a sense of being-in-relationship. However, much of traditional theory holds that fusion is pathological and something to be avoided and that what is important is maintaining firm interpersonal boundaries.

Fusion operates in many, perhaps most, heterosexual relationships as well. The best human relationships include some dimension of fusion. However, just as with all dimensions of human experience, one can experience "overfusion" and lose a sense of self. What is desirable is a balance. Moreover, what in some cultures is considered fusion may be normal closeness of relationship in another. For instance, the well-defined boundaries of a New England Yankee or a German-American may be seen as "overly distanced" from another cultural standpoint.

If, as a therapist, you focus totally on the primarily North American male values of individuation, self-actualization, and autonomy, you will view things in terms of boundary and distancing issues and may miss important relational issues of interpersonal closeness. Because he was always open to expanding his approach, Rogers would likely now argue that a balance of self-actualization (*eigenwelt*) and relationship (*mitwelt*) is required.

Rogerian therapy is a highly verbal approach and may require complex cognitive skills on the part of the client. As such, the theory tends to be less effective in actual practice with children, adolescents, and less verbal clients. The economically disadvantaged often find most immediate benefit from a direct action approach rather than a self-reflective one. Behavioral, family systems, consciousness-raising, community organization, and developmental methods and techniques therefore are often the treatment of choice for these groups.

The Influence of Rogers

Despite the above-mentioned difficulties, the humanistic philosophy remains important in all counseling and therapy and has been supported by research over the years (see Research Exhibit 11.1). Most practitioners who have adopted other theories or taken an eclectic or metatheoretical approach still employ Rogers's interviewing skills and humanistic attitudes.

Rogers was never content with the status quo. He constantly changed, shaped, and adapted his ideas over the years, increasingly emphasizing in his later years the importance of awareness and action on issues. The following case example presents three views of Rogers: nondirective, client-centered, and person-centered. Although his methods changed at each stage of his development, his underlying faith in humanity and the individual-in-relationship remained constant.

Case Examples from Three Periods of Rogers's Work

Rogers believed in and acted on his theories. His life was a personal demonstration of intentionality and self-actualization, as he constantly changed and grew. Three main stages[1] of his process have been identified, as follows:

1. *Stage 1: Nondirective (1940 to 1950).* This stage emphasizes the acceptance of the client, the establishment of a positive nonjudgmental climate, trust in the client's wisdom, and permissiveness. It uses clarification of the client's world as the main technique. Rogers's writings give a central emphasis to skills in the counseling process.

2. *Stage 2: Client-centered (1950 to 1961).* This stage centers on reflecting the feelings of the client, incorporates resolving incongruities between the ideal self and real self, avoids personally threatening situations for the client, and uses reflection as the main technique. Skills are not emphasized; rather, a major emphasis on the counselor as a person is evolving.

Research Exhibit 11.1

 ## Research on Person-Centered Theory

Because Rogers's methods have deeply influenced other approaches to helping, detailed attention will be given to research on his framework.

Landmark Research

A landmark series of studies by Fiedler (1950a, 1950b, 1951) sought to define the ideal therapeutic relationship and studied therapists of psychoanalytic, Rogerian, and Adlerian persuasion. Fiedler found that expert therapists of these various persuasions appeared more similar to each other than they did to inexperienced therapists within the same theoretical orientation. An equally important study was conducted by Barrett-Lennard (1962), who found higher levels of facilitative conditions among experienced therapists.

Relationship as Central in Many Theories

The above-mentioned studies prompted an avalanche of studies of the Rogerian qualitative dimensions during the ensuing years. Useful reviews of this research may be found in Anthony and Carkhuff (1977), Auerbach and Johnson (1977), and Garfield and Bergin (1986).

The influential study by Sloane et al. (1975) found that behavioral therapists exhibited higher levels of empathy, self-congruence, and interpersonal contact than did psychotherapists, whereas levels of warmth and regard were approxi-

mately the same. There was no relationship, however, between these measures and eventual effectiveness of the therapy.

Therapist Warmth

It is interesting to note that behavioral therapists, often thought of as cold and distant, proved warmer than did psychotherapists. Sloane and Staples reviewed this landmark study in 1984 and made this critical summarization: "Successful patients in both therapies rated their personal interaction with the therapist as the single most important part of treatment" (p. 225). It is difficult to deny or disregard such a powerful statement by clients.

Research Findings

In a comprehensive review of psychotherapy research, Strupp (1989) comments: "The first and foremost task for the therapist is to create an accepting and empathic context" (p. 718). The Psychotherapy Research Project of the Menninger Foundation, which compared different types of therapy, finds that "supportive mechanisms infiltrated all therapies, psychoanalysis included, and accounted for more of the achieved outcomes (including structural changes) than anticipated" (Wallerstein, 1989, p. 195). Coming nearly forty years after the Fiedler studies, the consistency of research on the Rogerian model is notable.

A Different View

However, Mitchell, Bozarth, and Krauft (1977) read the literature on Rogerian theory quite differently, concluding: "The recent evidence, although equivocal, does seem to suggest that empathy, warmth, and genuineness are related in some way to client change, but that their potency and generalizability are not as great as was once thought" (p. 483). Work by Lambert, DeJulio, and Stein (1978) severely criticizes empathy research, suggesting that methods have not always been adequate. A major study using person-centered methods with schizophrenics (Rogers et al., 1967) was not truly successful.

Matching Therapeutic Style to Client Needs

Rogers pointed out that many therapists fall short of offering empathic conditions and that therapy and counseling can be for better or worse. Strupp and Hadley (1976) and Strupp (1989) have illus-trated this point. They reviewed a large number of studies indicating possible deterioration as an effect of the psychotherapeutic process and point out the importance of a solid relationship appropriate to the need level of the client. Strupp (1977) catches the essence of his argument, saying that "the art of psychotherapy may largely consist of judicious and sensitive applications of a given technique, delicate decisions of when to press a point or when to be patient, when to be warm and understanding, and when to be remote" (p. 11). Strupp suggests that simple application of a few empathic qualities is not enough. These qualities also must be in synchrony with the client, at the moment, in the interviewing process (see especially Strupp, 1989).

Lambert and Bergin (1994) conducted a careful review of process and outcome variables in counseling and therapy and found, once again, that the Rogerian conditions of relationship are vital to the interview.

3. *Stage 3: Person-centered (1961 to 1987).* This stage is characterized by increased personal involvement, with more stress on relational issues. While maintaining consistency with all past work, Rogers moved increasingly to emphasizing present-tense experience, a more active and self-disclosing role for the counselor, group as well as individual counseling, and consideration of broader issues in society, such as cultural differences and the use of power. The focus on skills has remained minimal, and there is instead a stress on counselor attitudes. Coupled with this is an emphasis on experiencing oneself as a person-in-relation to others. A review of Rogers's transcripts reveals an interpretative helping style.

In the following subsections, examples of each of the three major phases of Rogers's growth and development will be explored through the presentation and analysis of brief excerpts from interview sessions typical of each period.

The Nondirective Period
(1940 to 1950)

Rogers brought a new openness to the interview process. Through detailed notes and discussion and the then-new medium of audiorecording, Rogers shared in great detail what he did in the counseling interview. Up to that time, the training of counselors and therapists had taken place in formal classrooms and through lectures and discussion of what a therapist remembered from an interview.

A classic research study by Blocksma and Porter (1947) revealed that what therapists say they do in an interview and what they actually do are two different things. Rogers's ability to share what he was doing, coupled with the work of Blocksma and Porter, has forever changed the nature of counseling and therapy training. There remains, however, strong resistance to this openness, particularly among some psychoanalytic therapists, who often prefer more abstract discussions of underlying unconscious conflicts to what actually happens in the session.

Gendlin (1970) summarizes in a few brief words the change process of person-centered therapy throughout its periods and changing styles:

> By saying what the client said, something new will occur, the client will soon say something new, and then we can respond to that. By featuring responsivity at every small, specific momentary step, . . . the therapist carries forward not only what the client verbally stated, but also the client's experiential process. . . . This responsivity to specific felt meaning at each step engenders, carries forward, and changes the individual's ongoing experiential process. This is the underlying principle that is implicit in client-centered therapy and its early quaint rules for therapist responding. (pp. 32–33)

In effect, Gendlin suggests that when clients share their experiences with the counselor and the counselor responds with accurate listening, clients are moved forward by the interaction. Even if the counselor just directly repeats what clients say, clients' worlds will have been changed by the very act of being heard. Being heard by another person can thus be considered an action on the world.

Many, perhaps most, clients do not feel they have power and influence on others or their surroundings. By the giving of themselves to their clients through empathic attending skills, counselors empower their clients. Clients speak; therapists listen carefully and attempt to understand clients' perceptions of the world. Having been heard and understood, clients can move forward.

Interview Example

In the following typescript, taken from Rogers's nondirective phase, he is explicitly trying to draw out the client and impose as little of his orientation as possible (Rogers & Wallen, 1946). His belief was that interference from the counselor would only slow natural client growth. The microskills used in this interview are all attending skills. As a useful practice exercise, fill in the blank space to the left of the counselor response with both the focus and the microskill(s) being used. (A listing of the microskills used can be found at the end of the chapter.)

Focus	Microskill	
		1. *Client:* I wish I knew how to pray.
___	___	2. *Counselor:* Do you want to tell me some more about that?
___	___	3. *Client:* I'm all in a mess. I can't sleep. Last night I walked the streets most of the night in a pouring rain. I haven't been able to sleep all the time I've been on leave. I was home for awhile, and I couldn't even talk to my folks there. You see, my buddy was killed, and I just can't get over it.
___	___	4. *Counselor:* That's been a pretty upsetting blow to you.
		5. *Client:* Well it has. You see, my buddy was my only real friend—I don't make friends easily, never have had very many—and he and I always stuck together. [Tells how they met and some of the things they had been through.] We worked on the same gun crew, and we knew each other so well we never had to tell each other what to do. We could just signal by the way we looked. In this particular scrap the enemy planes were coming over plenty. It was pretty hot. The ammunition box was getting empty, and I just glanced at my buddy. He knew what I meant, and he went to get another box. While he was doing that a shell exploded right near him and killed him. (pause) I just can't get over it. I feel—I feel as though I caused his death.
___	___	6. *Counselor:* You feel that somehow you are to blame for the fact that he was killed.
		7. *Client:* Yes I do. I don't see why. Well, there's one thing I haven't mentioned. Maybe that has something to do with it. My buddy and I, we got along swell. We hardly ever quarreled, but just the day before this all happened we had quite an argument. [He relates the details of the argument.] We really got sore at each other. I wouldn't even speak to him for several hours afterward. You know, I think that does have something to do with it. I guess that quarrel makes me feel that I am to blame for what happened.
___	___	8. *Counselor:* You feel that your being angry at him in some way was responsible for killing him.
		9. *Client:* You know, I think that's it. I haven't thought that through before. Maybe I was scared to think it through. Somehow it helps to talk about things like this. You see, I didn't usually quarrel with my buddy, and I guess it hit me hard to think that we had an argument just the day before he was killed. It doesn't seem so bad when you tell about it. He was really a great guy. [He goes on to tell at some length about his buddy and his buddy's accomplishments and the good relationship they had together. The conversation then turns into other channels, and he talks about his own family and again mentions the fact that he had been very upset while home on leave.] I don't know what you've done sir, but this has sure helped me a lot. I don't see why I felt so much to blame as I did.
___	___	10. *Counselor:* It seems to have helped to get it off your chest. Is that it?
		11. *Client:* It sure has. I wonder, sir, if it would be too much if I could write to you if I ever feel this way again. I'm probably shipping out pretty quick so I don't think I'll have a chance to see you again, but maybe I could write you a letter.

12. *Counselor:*   I'd be delighted to get a letter from you even if you're not feeling upset. I hope you will write to me.
13. *Client:*   Well, thanks a lot for talking with me. I've got to go now but you may be hearing from me. (pp. 120–21)

Commentary on the Nondirective Period

It seems most likely that the foregoing exchange was really the summary of a longer session. Note that every one of Rogers's leads was a listening skill much like the basic listening sequence (Chapter 3). The above example also illustrates issues of focusing on the *eigenwelt* and *umwelt*. Rogers's leads at numbers 2, 4, and 10 focus solely on the client (*eigenwelt*). Critical leads at numbers 6 and 8 focus on the client-in-relation to his buddy. Rogers's last statement (number 12) brings the counselor directly into the relationship.

Rogers provides an interesting personal analysis of this interview and points out that the counselor does not direct the depth of the interview but rather attempts to establish conditions so that the client can determine how far or deep to go. Whereas many counselors might have wanted more concreteness and specifics about the situation, the counselor in this case accepts the sailor's definition of what has happened.

Another view of this same interview is that Rogers is more directive than he thinks. By focusing on the individual and selecting certain key words (e.g., *blame* and *anger*), Rogers actually does shape the interview. If the interviewer had been an antiwar activist and had focused on the *umwelt* and the horrors of war, the interview likely would have been very different. Reinforcement theorists suggest that even in the nondirective and listening approaches, we unconsciously encourage clients to talk about their issues in certain ways. Practice Exercise 11.1 can help you become aware of your listening style and how it might shape the interview.

Rogers tended to reply in a particularly disarming fashion to those who criticized his work. He suggested that therapists must find their own ways of being authentic with another person and that those whose views differed from his would select counseling theories that worked best for them. Thus, Rogers exhibited unusual congruence within himself. Not only did he emphasize and respect clients' rights to determine what was appropriate for themselves, but he also respected his critics' ability to determine what was right for themselves.

The importance of listening is illustrated dramatically in studies by Inbar et al. (1989) of soldiers who experience combat stress. These researchers found that combat-stressed soldiers benefited from talking about their difficulties with supportive staff personnel. Because combat stress was treated as a normal response to an abnormal situation, these soldiers were able to return to their posts with minimum long-term effects. If combat difficulties are ignored, as they were in the Vietnam war, there is evidence that stresses will reappear later as posttraumatic stress disorder.

Rogers's nondirective style has continuing relevance. When clients are involved in their own experiences, it is important to focus totally on them. Clients need to be

Practice Exercise 11.1

An Exercise in Nondirective Counseling

The basic listening sequence (Chapter 3) focuses on drawing out client stories with minimal influence on the part of the helper. Yet, most researchers now recognize how very much we influence client stories just by the way we listen. The following practice exercise is designed to help you become aware of your own listening style and how it may influence how clients tell their stories to you. The exercise will work most effectively if you audiorecord the three brief storytelling sessions and listen to them together with the client. Keep your use of the skill of questioning to a minimum.

1. Use the basic listening sequence to draw out the issues related to a volunteer client's story. Summarize the story at the end, feeding back to the client as accurately as you can the main facts and behaviors, thoughts, and feelings related to the story.
2. Use the BLS to draw out the same story once again, but this time, attempt to focus solely on the *eigenwelt*—the client before you. Summarize as before, but make sure this time that your summary focuses almost totally on the individual. What are the client's behaviors, thoughts, and feelings? How does the client "live with" the story?
3. For a third time, use the BLS, but this time focus solely on the *mitwelt* (other people, family) and the *umwelt* (environmental, contextual, and multicultural issues). Again, summarize the client's story from these frames of reference.
4. Discuss this experience with your volunteer client and consider how these issues of "nondirective" counseling relate to you and your work. Can we ever be truly nondirective as we listen to and work with clients?

heard, and we as counselors and therapists need to learn their constructions of the world. Through empathy and by using the listening skills, we provide clients with a chance to learn what they themselves think.

However, a pure listening approach, as represented in the foregoing transcript, is not always appropriate. At times, the nondirective style can bring about difficulties in multicultural counseling. For example, African-American clients working with a European-American therapist sometimes mistrust the Rogerian mirroring response. They might want to know who you are as a person, and they might reject a helping approach that is solely focused on mirroring back what is said. Sue and Sue (1990) found that some traditional Asian-American clients often prefer a more directive approach and will not respect a counselor who cannot and will not give advice and direction.

Thus, although listening is considered a central skill in counseling and therapy, it is one of many techniques that form the total strategy of professional helping. During the client-centered period, Rogers was increasingly willing to interpret and influence clients.

The Client-Centered Period
(1950 to 1961)

Most excerpts from Rogers's work from this period are highly verbal and are most relevant to clients who are deeply interested in introspection. Thus, there may be less of value in this period for multicultural counseling than in his other two periods. The client-centered style of helping is currently used relatively infrequently and thus is of limited historical interest.

Interview Example

The following interview segment illustrates the work of the second period of Rogers (1961). The client, Mrs. Oak, talks about how hard it is for her to accept any help or positive reactions from others. The complexity of the counselor's sentences has greatly increased compared with those in the nondirective period interview. Although the emphasis is still very much on the client and the client's perceptions, there is also an interpretive dimension in that the counselor seems to lead the client at times.

> *Client:*   I have a feeling . . . that you have to do it pretty much yourself, but that somehow you ought to be able to do that with other people. [She mentions that there have been "countless" times when she might have accepted personal warmth and kindliness from others.] I get the feeling that I just was afraid I would be devastated. [She returns to talking about the counseling itself and her feeling toward it.] I mean there's been this tearing through the thing myself. Almost to—I mean, I felt it—I mean I tried to verbalize it on occasion—a kind of—at times almost not wanting you to restate, not wanting you to reflect, the thing is mine. Course all right, I can say it's resistance. But that doesn't mean a damn thing to me now . . . The—I think in—in relationship to this particular thing, I mean, the—probably at times, the strongest feeling was, it's mine, it's mine. I've got to cut it down myself. See?
>
> *Counselor:*   It's an experience that's awfully hard to put down accurately into words, and yet I get a sense of difference here in this relationship, that from the feeling that "this is mine," "I've got to do it," "I am doing it," and so on, to a somewhat different feeling that "I could let you in."
>
> [*The counselor's reflection of meaning catches the main points of Mrs. Oak's statement in brief form, thus feeding back to her what her inner world is truly like. In addition, the basic incongruity between real and ideal self is reflected back to the client. Mrs. Oak's statement has a vagueness that would prompt many other counselors to search for more concreteness and to ask for specifics. A psychodynamic therapist might observe the sexual symbolism in the words "I've got to cut it down myself" and the therapist's response "I could let you in."*]

Client: Yeah. Now I mean, that's—that it's—well, it's sort of, shall we say, volume two. It's—it's a—well, sort of, well, I'm still in the thing alone, but I'm not—see—I'm—

Counselor: M-hm. Yes, that paradox sort of sums it up, doesn't it.

Client: Yeah.

Counselor: In all of this, there is a feeling, it's still—every aspect of my experience is mine and that's kind of inevitable and necessary and so on. And yet that isn't the whole picture either. Somehow it can be shared or another's interest can come in and in some ways it is new.

[*There is an interpretive flavor to the last two therapist statements as new meanings are put on old experience. Yet as they very much come from the client's worldview, these leads are a reflection of meaning but close to a paraphrase. The increased involvement of the therapist since Rogers's first period is apparent. Note also that the therapist goes so far as to use "I" when talking about the client rather than "you"; this could be considered a sign of strong empathy in that the counselor can see the world through the client's eyes.*]

Client: Yeah. And it's—it's as though, that's how it should be. I mean, that's how it—has to be. There's a—there's a feeling, "and this is good." I mean, it expresses, it clarifies it for me. There's a feeling—in this caring, as though—you were sort of standing back—standing off, and if I want to sort of cut through to the thing, it's a—a slashing of—oh, tall weeds, that I can do it, and you can—I mean you're not going to be disturbed by having to walk through it, too. I don't know. And it doesn't make sense. I mean—

Counselor: Except there's a very real sense of rightness about this feeling that you have, hm?

Client: M-hm. (pp. 84–85)

[*It is particularly important to note the emphasis in the paraphrase. The therapist has selectively attended to the positive aspects of the client's message ("this is good") and simultaneously ignored negative aspects ("it doesn't make sense"). Behavioral counselors have often pointed out that Rogerian counseling involves selective attention and that as complete a verbal "shaping" process occurs in this mode of counseling as in more systematic behavioral approaches. Regardless of whether this view is accepted or not, the selective attention to positive, forward-moving aspects of the client is an example of the positive emphasis of this theory.*]

Rogers goes on to comment that this was a turning point for Mrs. Oak, who learned that it was all right to accept others and to discover positive things in herself. This acceptance is, of course, crucial in the development of a positive self-actualizing personality.

Commentary on the Client-Centered Period

The focus in the foregoing interview is still very much on the individual (*eigenwelt*) and her construction of events. Very little attention is paid to how others might view the same events. The goal of the interchange seems to focus on Mrs. Oak finding her own "space." Rogerian theory holds that after Mrs. Oak has found herself, she will be better able to relate with others. A feminist or multicultural critique might be that Mrs. Oak could find herself even more rapidly given a more immediate focus on relationships and the role of women in society, with a secondary focus on her own perceptions.

A critical issue in Rogerian counseling is the discrepancy that often occurs between the real self and the ideal self. Individuals need to see themselves as worthy. Often individuals lose sight of what they really are in an effort to attain an idealized image. This discrepancy between thought and reality, between self-perception and others' perceptions, or between self and experience leads to incongruities. These incongruities in turn result in areas in which individuals are not truly themselves. The father who strikes the child lacks congruence. The objective of therapy with this client is to resolve the discrepancies between ideal and real self, thus eliminating the tension and substituting forward-moving self-actualization.

From a multicultural frame of reference, the emphasis in Rogerian theory on ideal self and real self tends to obscure relational and broader environmental issues. As such, it may be helpful to add a broader focus when working with many clients. For example, it would be within the Rogerian tradition to help clients focus on *real relationships* and *ideal relationships*. Such a focus would help individuals think of themselves as persons-in-relation to significant others. This focus would entail a change in the style of counseling and therapy usually associated with Rogers. But considering Rogers's life development, these concepts likely would fit with the direction he was heading at the end of his life. Clearly, Rogers was focusing on a more *ideal world* as contrasted with the *real world* (*umwelt*).

Furthermore, theorists of a more psychodynamic orientation have argued that Rogers's emphasis on the self as a central construct goes back to his own roots in a strict German family. His self-psychology from this frame of reference represents an unconscious rebellion against and an attempt to cope with family and cultural controls. Rogers, who once studied for the ministry, constantly stressed the importance of a natural relationship among human beings. He rejected the concepts of psychoanalytic transference and countertransference as unnecessary. Research Exhibit 11.2, however, presents data supporting the idea that Rogers was not as free of past developmental history as he stated in his theories.

The emphasis in the first two periods of Rogers's work was on individual counseling and therapy. LaFromboise and Low (1989) comment that a broader approach than just individual problem solving may be necessary with Native Americans:

Traditionally, Indian people live in relational networks that serve to support and nurture strong bonds of mutual assistance and affection. Many tribes still engage in a traditional system of collective interdependence, with family members responsible not only to one another but also the clan and tribe to which they belong. The Lakota Sioux use the term *tiospaye* to describe a traditional community way of life in which an individual's well-being remains the responsibility of the extended family. . . . When problems arise among Indian youth, they become problems of the community as well. The family, kin, and friends join together to observe the youth's behavior,

=== **Research Exhibit 11.2** ===

 ## A Controversy in the Field: Does Transference Exist in Rogerian Therapy?

Rogers emphasized the importance of here-and-now interactions between client and counselor and felt that transferential concepts and discussion of the past were not useful dimensions of the counseling process.

In the film *Three Approaches to Psychotherapy* (Shostrum, 1965), the client, Gloria, is interviewed by Carl Rogers, Fritz Perls, and Albert Ellis. The film has had an immense influence on the acceptance of Rogers's work. In the film, he appears warm and accepting toward Gloria, who indicates that she enjoyed his work with her above the others.

Rogers commented in some detail that the film is evidence that transferential concepts are not needed and used the film to stress the importance of focusing on the person. This film and Rogers's negation of transference have influenced many counseling and therapy training programs, which prefer to ignore psychodynamic concepts.

Weinrach (1990) discovered that a final extra 249 words were deleted from this famous film. Just prior to the deleted words, Gloria comments, "Gee, how nice I can talk to you and I want you to approve of me and I respect you, but I miss that my father couldn't talk to me like that. I mean I'd like to say, 'Gee, I'd like you for my father.'" Rogers comments that Gloria would make a "pretty nice daughter." The film concludes as they discuss Gloria's father's inability to accept her as she is. At this point, Rogers

makes his points against a transferential interpretation.

Weinrach presents the full text that continues the father-daughter issue. The following interpretation missing from the published film is an example of a psychodynamically oriented statement that one would not expect of Rogers: "Rogers: The phrase that comes to my mind—I don't know if it is appropriate or not—you're slapping your father in the face, aren't you?" [*Interpretation; the focus is on Gloria transferring unconscious feelings toward her father to her present behavior.*]

Weinrach points out that transferential relationships can complicate our interventions unless we are aware of them and their implications. He also points out that Rogers himself may be seen as involved in a complex countertransferential relationship with Gloria. Weinrach comments that if the full film had been shown, Rogers might have been seen less as a role model and more as a "mortal therapist who missed or unintentionally ignored an important clinical issue."

Bohart (1991) takes issue with Weinrach, commenting that transferential concepts are highly intellectualized and miss the essence of the Rogerian relational approach. He describes the above missing segment of the interview as more evidence of Rogers's caring and empathy.

Beaver (1991) adds additional comments on the failure of Rogers to consider Gloria as a woman in a society dominated by men. Rogers's focus was on a single person in front of him, and he did not consider any contextual issues except as Gloria constructed them. Clearly, Gloria faced many multicultural issues in terms of male-female relationships, societal expectations, and father-daughter relationships. These matters must be considered in understanding how a woman's *self-in-relation* is established.

This is the type of controversy you as a therapist or counselor will encounter again and again. Given the discussion in this chapter, do you endorse Weinrach's, Beaver's, or Bohart's interpretation of the data? Recall that more than one perspective may be "correct" and that the meaning of "correctness" depends on the constructed worldview of the observer. On this last point, we might expect Rogers to concur.

draw the youth out of isolation, and integrate that person back into the activities of the group. (p. 121)

If Mrs. Oak was a Lakota Sioux, the individual-focused approach of the interview likely would be inappropriate. Although it would be important to listen to her individual constructions (as in the nondirective period), the focus of counseling interventions would probably emphasize the *mitwelt*, the family, extended family, and community. For a Lakota Sioux, an individual issue remains unsolved until it is considered in the broader network of relationships. In addition, it would be important for you as therapist to present yourself in the interview as a real person with real thoughts and feelings. In multicultural settings, the boundaries between therapist and client change, which presents a very real challenge to the practice of traditional counseling and therapy. Rogers was moving toward multicultural emphasis and understanding in his final, person-centered period.

The Person-Centered Period
(1961 to 1987)

The final phases of Rogers's career brought forth a flowering of new ideas and continuous additions to his framework. He became interested in encounter groups and was personally deeply affected by his learnings in group work. During this period, he also developed an interest in couples counseling (1972), personal power (1977), the learning process (1969), and world peace (Gendlin, 1988). Despite these diverse interests, which continued to grow and expand until his death at the age of 85 in 1987, Rogers maintained his consistent respect for the individual, stressed the importance of research, and constantly emphasized the ability of individuals to find their own direction, but always in relationship to other human beings. To the traditional skills of paraphrasing, reflection of feeling, and summarizing, he added new skills of self-disclosure, feedback, and questioning. In this period, he seemed to be less interpretive than he was in the client-centered period.

Interview Example

In the following interview, Rogers (1970) acts as facilitator for an encounter group:

Art: When the shell's on it's, uh . . .

Lois: It's on!

Art: Yeah, it's on tight.

Susan: Are you always so closed in when you're in your shell?

Art: No, I'm so darn used to living with the shell, it doesn't even bother me. I don't even know the real me. I think I've, well, I've pushed the shell away more here. When I'm out of my shell—only twice—once just a few minutes ago—I'm really me, I guess. But then I just sort of pull in a cord after me when I'm in my shell, and that's almost all the time. And I leave the front standing outside when I'm back in the shell.

Facilitator: And nobody's back in there with you?

[*Art is the focus of group interaction at the moment. He describes his feelings of being shut off from people in a vivid metaphor of life in a shell. Art as a group member is using effective self-disclosure skills. Lois and Susan, through completion of Art's sentence and the focused closed questions, show that more people than group leaders and counselors can be helpful. The facilitator's interpretation is critical because it brings past and present experience together in one existential moment. Art is experiencing being alone in the shell at this moment as he has in the past in other situations. Yet, paradoxically, he is alone with a supportive facilitator and group. This integration of past and present experience in "moments of truth" appears in most theories of helping and is particularly important.*]

Art: (crying) Nobody else is in there with me. I just pull everything into the shell and roll the shell up and shove it in my pocket. I take the shell, and the real me, and put it in my pocket where it's safe. I guess that's really the way I do it—I go into my shell and turn off the real world. And here—that's what I want to do here in this group, y'know—come out of my shell and actually throw it away.

Lois: You're making progress already. At least you can talk about it.

Facilitator: Yeah. The thing that's going to be hardest is to stay out of the shell.

Art: (still crying) Well, yeah, if I can keep talking about it I can come out and stay out, but I'm going to have to, y'know, protect me. It hurts. It's actually hurting to talk about it. (p. 26)

[*Lois provides a good example of a feedback statement, and the facilitator expresses his opinion and reaction. Together the two support Art in the immediate moment and help him clarify his own experience.*]

Commentary on the Person-Centered Period

Rogers's best-known book is entitled *On Becoming a Person* (1961), and this title is a reflection of the theory and the man. In the Rogerian view, there seems to be no definable end to counseling work; this emphasis on process toward possible futures is particularly illustrative of the existential-humanistic orientation, which stresses individual choice.

At the same time, there is a potential problem in the term *person-centered* in that counselors and therapists have sometimes limited the scope of what Rogers meant by relating to others and to the world. Although Rogers did not use the language of German existentialism, he was very concerned that persons extend their view beyond themselves to others and to the world at large. Rogers would endorse expanding his and others' humanistic concepts to issues beyond the individual.

In expanding our view beyond self, one of the most powerful things we can do in groups and in complex negotiations is to hear how others construct the world. In an interview with eighty-two-year-old Rogers (Rogers calls peace . . . , 1984), the *APA Monitor* reported:

> His work over one weekend with Irish Protestants and Catholics joined by a representative of the British government achieved what he called "surprising results" and led to a film that the participants hoped to take to schools, churches, and similar neutral settings. The proof of its success, he added, came when paramilitary groups on both sides, who were opposed to his attempt to overcome centuries of hostility, destroyed four copies of the film before it could be shown.
>
> This summer he attended a conference in Hungary in which 300 persons from 27 countries—Western democracies as well as Eastern-bloc communist countries—grappled with the issues that divided their nations. Although participants were often more revealing in private conversations than in public sessions, Rogers said the conference was extremely successful in teaching individuals to *listen to the view of others.* (p. 15) (Emphasis added)

In these workshops, Rogers (1) encouraged participants to explore their hostile attitudes and feelings, which the facilitator had accepted, thus helping remove irrational aspects of their thinking; (2) focused on persons and attitudes, thereby forging an important beginning once the underlying rage was accepted and understood; and (3) fostered "direct confrontation of opponents in a confined area." Rogers found that in a group environment in which members listened and sought to understand, combatants could learn to accept one another and work toward mutual goals.

The theoretical movement of Rogers seems to have begun and ended with careful listening. Rogers fostered the awareness that listening could serve as a foundation for challenging sharing and feedback, interpretations, and even direct hostile confrontation. The first step toward mutual understanding is listening and learning how others construe events. Until we really hear others and understand their modes of being-in-the-world, very little will happen in any relationship.

Clemmont Vontress: Searching for Life's Meaning across Cultures

Clemmont Vontress has long been a proponent of multicultural counseling and therapy (Vontress, 1979, 1986, 1995a, b). He was drawn to the concepts of empathy and positive regard of his colleague Carl Rogers but expanded on his approach by focusing in even more depth on the therapeutic relationship as an expression of intimacy, openness, and real human exchange. Vontress's concern is that therapist reliance on techniques may obscure the possibility of a real relationship with the client. Only in a situation of caring and authenticity, Vontress (1986) believes, can true healing and growth occur. The following interview by Lee (1994) of Vontress indicates why Vontress reconsidered the Rogerian approach.

> *Lee:*   What was your theoretical position, and how would you describe your ideas on multicultural counseling in the early years of your degree?
>
> *Vontress:*   Well, when I left Indiana University with a Ph.D. degree in 1965, the professors and students were excited about the Rogerian approach to counseling. I remember Dr. Rogers came to Indiana University to make a presentation, and I occupied the stage with him to ask questions; that was a big honor. So, when I left graduate school I was, I thought, a Rogerian. But, during my years at Crispus Attucks High School as director of counseling, I learned from counseling the students that the approach wouldn't work with them. I remember once I was asking a Black student, How do you feel about this and that? The student finally exploded with great frustration and said, "What is all this 'how do you feel' stuff? I feel like you feel when something like that happens to you." (p. 68)

Although Rogerian philosophy is a useful and popular approach, the skills and strategies for implementing this philosophy should change with the individual and cultural background. Vontress did not abandon the Rogerian position but rather integrated it with an important new understanding of existentialism. Whereas multicultural counseling and therapy tends to focus on differences, Vontress emphasizes commonalties among people.

Spirituality and Multiculturalism

One of the most vital commonalties emphasized by Vontress is being together with another person in relationship (*mitwelt*). Vontress (1986) illustrates the importance of "being with" another person in ways that respect cultural uniqueness (*umwelt*). Counseling and therapy are usually thought of as highly verbal occupations, but Vontress notes that many Appalachian Whites and Native American Indians spend considerable time together without saying a word. Thus, silence can be a way of respecting the individual (*eigenwelt*), developing a trusting relationship *(mitwelt)*, and working within the client's culture *(umwelt)*. As an existential therapist, Vontress would remind us that all three dimensions of existentialism must exist as a whole for counseling and therapy to be effective.

This point is echoed by work in Japan, where Rogers's approach was originally accepted with great enthusiasm but later fell into some disrepute. Hayashi and others (1992) state that originally Rogers's work was accepted uncritically in Japan, resulting in a dogmatic approach that at times was highly inappropriate for the cultural setting. Although Rogerian and existential philosophies remain important in Japan, newer approaches add a focus on culture and *umwelt* that has been vital.

Vontress believes that spirituality is a vital part of any truly multicultural encounter. He is one of the few theorists to state unequivocally that the spiritual/religious *überwelt* is critical to understanding not only the person but also the culture. Japanese culture is heavily based in Buddhist and Shinto spiritual dimensions. Buddhist holistic concepts and Shinto veneration of human-nature connections are key aspects of the very being of many Japanese people. Any revision of the Rogerian approach in a Japanese context would benefit by considering these particular religious/spiritual influences.

The Japanese example illustrates how important it is to include the spiritual dimension for a more complete understanding of the individual and cultural dimensions of human experience. The individual lives in relationship in a cultural and spiritual frame, according to Vontress (1995a):

> Human beings need the respect, devotion, love, and affection of parents, elders, departed ones, and spiritual figures. In Africa, the spirit world connects the living with people who have been here before and who therefore still reside in the living via genetics, culture, and the collective unconscious. Ancestors are invisible neighbors of the living. Their love sustains them and often directs their lives. (p. 2)

From the perspective of traditional counseling and therapy this statement seems radical and perhaps controversial. Spirituality and the connection with the distant past are seldom associated with here-and-now action-oriented counseling and therapy. Nonetheless, there is a precedent for Vontress's views in the work of Carl Jung (1958). Jung constantly stressed the importance of spirituality, and his idea of the collective unconscious represents a foundation for much of what is considered spiritual.

Whether you find Vontress's views compatible with your own worldview and frame of reference, it is nonetheless true that many cultures in different ways subscribe to the spiritual foundations he suggests. Many Africans and African-Americans, Chinese, Japanese, Jews, Mormons, Native American Indians, Hindus, Roman Catholics, and others would find counseling and therapy incomplete without the inclusion of spiritual and religious traditions.

As an example of the importance of including the spiritual dimension in counseling, consider the anger many African-Americans feel as they experience racism in society. This anger can become internalized, affecting the mind, body, and spirit. Vontress (quoted in Lee, 1994) makes a connection between spiritual and bodily disease in speaking of middle-class African-American men:

> It's terribly fascinating to try to understand why these Black men die in their sleep more than any other men. I maintain it's because they are working in the mainstream culture around White people and have to suppress their hostility during the day. It's only when they're sleeping at night that their system allows that hostility to express itself, and it expresses itself very often in sleep. This helps to explain why there's such an inordinate number of Black middle-class men who die in their sleep at night. (p. 71)

In working with clients suffering emotional distress, existential understanding and spiritual connection can elevate not only clients' thinking but also their bodily functioning. Applying these ideas in counseling practice requires you as therapist or counselor to seek a full Rogerian relationship, but with a balanced focus on *eigenwelt, mitwelt, umwelt,* and *überwelt.* Practice Exercise 11.2 seeks to adapt the Rogerian and existential approaches to allow for cultural difference and new styles of relationship.

Limitations and Practical Implications of the Existential-Humanistic Tradition

The beauty and strength of the existential-humanistic tradition lie in its strong faith in humankind, opportunity for personal growth, and the infinite possibility of experience. However, some naive therapists and counselors have taken only the concept of "infinite possibility" and have led clients into destructive, closed circles of existence.

As with psychodynamic theory, the existential-humanistic approach tends to be highly verbal. Concerned with the meaning of life and individual satisfaction, the therapy can be a way to avoid reality and the need for action. The positive philosophy of Rogers is applauded by many of a multicultural orientation, but the nature of Rogerian methods—slow reflection and a lack of action and immediate problem solving—seems inappropriate for multicultural clients. The tendency for existential-humanistic counseling to ignore person-environment transactions in daily practice also can be a major limitation. The intense preoccupation with the individual and free choice is at times incompatible with a more environmentally oriented and contextually aware approach.

However, the existential-humanistic philosophic tradition does speak to multicultural concerns in that it, perhaps more than any other set of theories, focuses on *human relationship.* If we supplement the basic ideas of Rogers with more focused emphasis on the *mitwelt* and *umwelt,* perhaps we are doing as he would wish.

Clemmont Vontress adds a challenging dimension to Rogerian and existential-humanistic thought in suggesting an increased emphasis on the cultural/environmental context (*umwelt*) and a focus on the holistic and spiritual dimensions of counseling (*überwelt*). Mainstream counseling and therapy have tended to ignore spirituality, and Vontress's ideas, although controversial, add an important dimension.

What does the existential-humanistic movement offer the beginning counselor or therapist that is immediately useful? Perhaps the major contribution of Rogers has been his emphasis on empathic and accurate listening and his willingness to open the interview to inspection and research through audiotape and film. The attending skills (Chapter 3) are basic to Rogers's classifications and discussion in his early work. The qualitative conditions of warmth, respect, and concreteness (Chapter 2) are derived from his seminal thinking. The methodological message that

Practice Exercise 11.2

 # Reviewing the Meaning of One's Being-in-the-World

The exercise is designed to integrate ideas of Carl Rogers with those of existentialism, particularly as suggested by Clemmont Vontress. Vontress emphasizes the importance of the meaning one makes of one's life and the situations one encounters. Through meaning making, we can redefine our world and develop more effective means of making sense of what we are, our relationships with others, and what it is like to be-in-the-world.

This exercise will take a half hour or more and requires a volunteer or real client who is willing to explore the meaning of a significant stressful experience. The five-stage interview approach is used to provide a structure for the suggested activities of this session.

Stage 1. Rapport/Structuring

As you start, outline with your client the purpose and general structure of this practice session. Talk with the client in appropriate language about the idea of making meaning of old situations in new ways through the multiple lenses of *eigenwelt*, *mitwelt*, *umwelt*, and *überwelt*. The goal is to review a stressful incident from the distant or recent past and to see what sense can be made of it. Before you start, spend some time examining the degree of rapport and trust between you. You can do this using words or through nonverbal awareness. Your own and the client's comfort are vital. Vontress often speaks of the importance of finding commonalties

between people. What are your commonalties with this client? Are you co-equal with your client, or have you established a therapist-client hierarchy? *Is your relationship real and authentic?*

Stage 2. Data Gathering

Ask your client to tell you the story of the concern or issue. Use the basic listening sequence to draw out the facts, feelings, and thoughts of the client as the story unfolds. As you listen to the narrative, note how much attention is paid to the individual, the relationship with others, and the environmental/contextual situation. Listen for underlying spiritual dimensions.

As you listen to the story, pay special attention to positive assets and strengths of the client, relationships, and the cultural/environmental context. These positive resources in the *eigenwelt*, *mitwelt*, *umwelt*, and *überwelt* can lead to positive reframing and new meanings for action. You may wish to directly ask where the client stands on each of these dimensions. As in the approaches of Vontress, feminist therapy, and multicultural counseling and therapy, you may wish to share some of your own beliefs briefly and concisely, making sure not to take the lead away from the client.

Stage 3. Determining Outcomes

Your client has very likely indicated or implied a desire for how things should be ideally. The clarification of the "real world," as compared to the "ideal world," is an important part of Rogerian theory. Clarification of the discrepancy between the real and the ideal often impels clients to more serious thought, feeling, and action.

Once there is a clear understanding of the present and possible future, summarize the interview to this point, including the original story, and contrast this summary with the ideal narrative. Of course, a complete resolution may not be possible in one session. Thus, you may want to ask your client which part of the discrepancy should be considered at this time.

Stage 4. Generating Alternative Solutions and Meaning

The word *solutions* may not always be appropriate in a therapeutic setting. Instead, the goal might be rephrased as finding new meanings in old situations and narratives. There are a variety of ways to explore new meanings, including drawing on other theories (cognitive-behavior, multicultural, etc.) at appropriate points. However, within the existential-humanistic tradition, the focus is on finding positive new meanings. Following are two concrete intervention styles that may be useful:

1. *Multiple storytelling.* Most likely the client has focused the narrative on a personal frame of reference. Ask the client to tell the story from the frame of reference of significant others—How would other people tell the same story? Then, ask the client to tell the story from a gender, ethnic/racial, spiritual, or other multicultural perspective. If the

client told the story from an external perspective (significant other [*mitwelt*] or culture [*umwelt*]), it might be necessary to ask the client to tell you a story focusing on I statements in which the *eigenwelt* becomes the focus.

Vontress notes that the body stores these stories and that one's narrative can even affect immune system functioning. You may wish to make bodily experience part of this discussion (see Chapter 4 for a review of skills in this area). At another level, consider retelling the story from the spiritual (*überwelt*) perspective. For many of us, this will be uncomfortable. However, this is a time to test and experience new dimensions in a co-equal relationship with your client.

Then review the multiple stories and ask the client what meanings were found. Useful questions here may include "What sense do you make of the different stories?" "What one idea stands out for you?" "We've looked at your situation from several perspectives now—how would you integrate them into a new story?"

2. *Developing a shared or coconstructed narrative.* This is a more difficult task, as it asks you to share your own struggles with meaning with the client. The focus is on commonalties and differences between you and the client, which emphasizes the relationship (*mitwelt*) between you. This approach also requires a judicious use of self-disclosure and an effort not to force your meaning on the client. Buber might consider this a focus on the I-Thou of counselor and client. This intervention can be supplemented by focusing on cultural, environmental, and contextual issues (*umwelt*) you and the client encounter.

Stage 5. Generalization

"What shall be?" Existential-humanistic philosophy often views therapy as a solely explorative process. Existentialism can be viewed as a search for meaning as an end in itself. Thinking in new ways about old stories can change body functioning and may lead automatically to new actions. If you and the client choose to generalize the ending, seek to follow up with the client in the coming week to check on success and how the client is doing.

An alternative to generalizing about the session is to ask if the client would like to select one specific task for "homework." If so, the task may be behavioral and based on the cognitive-behavioral paradigm. Or the client may set a goal of thinking in new ways about old situations. You may wish to have the homework focus on Beck's automatic thoughts, Ellis's rational-emotive behavior system, or Glasser's more externally focused reality therapy.

Rogers has given us is that we as counselors and therapists must listen to the client and open the interview and ourselves to scrutiny. Only in this way can we grow and learn about our own possibilities to enrich the lives of others.

NOTE

1. Although three main periods have been identified in Rogers's development, his early major work, *Counseling and Psychotherapy* (1942), first presented typescripts of his work and commentary on counseling theory. He talks about nondirective therapy in this book, and gives considerable attention to insight and practical matters of the counseling interview. Further, at that time, Rogers used more questions and interpretations than he did later in his nondirective period.

REFERENCES

ABBAGNANO, N. (1967). Humanism. In P. Edwards (Ed.), *The encyclopedia of philosophy* (Vol. 3, pp. 69–72). New York: Macmillan.

ANTHONY, W., & CARKHUFF, R. (1977). The functional professional therapeutic agent. In A. Gurman & A. Razin (Eds.), *Effective psychotherapy* (pp. 103–19). Elmsford, NY: Pergamon.

AUERBACH, A., & JOHNSON, M. (1977). Research on the therapist's level of experience. In A. Gurman & A. Razin (Eds.), *Effective psychotherapy* (pp. 84–102). Elmsford, NY: Pergamon.

BAKER MILLER, J. (1991). The development of a woman's sense of self. In J. Jordan, A. Kaplan, J. B. Miller, I. Stiver, & J. Surrey (Eds.), *Women's growth in connection.* New York: Guilford.

BARRETT-LENNARD, G. (1962). Dimensions of therapist response as causal factors in therapeutic change. *Psychological Monographs, 76,* 43: (Ms. No. 562)

BEAVER, A. (1991, September). *Some potential issues of unconscious sexist behavior in counseling and therapy.* Paper presented at the University of Massachusetts, Amherst.

BINSWANGER, L. (1958). The existential analysis school of thought. In R. May, E. Angel, & H. Ellenberger (Eds.), *Existence* (pp. 191–213). New York: Basic Books.

BINSWANGER, L. (1963). *Being-in-the-world: Selected papers of Ludwig Binswanger.* New York: Basic Books.

BLOCKSMA, D., & PORTER, E. (1947). A short-term training program in client-centered counseling. *Journal of Consulting Psychology, 11,* 55–60.

BOHART, A. (1991). The missing 249 words: In search of objectivity. *Psychotherapy, 28,* 497–503.

BOSS, M. (1958). *The analysis of dreams.* New York: Philosophical Library.

BOSS, M. (1963). *Psychoanalysis and daseinanalysis.* New York: Basic Books.

BUBER, M. (1970). *I and thou.* New York: Scribner's.

CAMUS, A. (1942). *The stranger.* New York: Random House.

CAMUS, A. (1958). *The myth of Sisyphus.* New York: Knopf.

FIEDLER, F. (1950a). A comparison of therapeutic relationships in psychoanalytic, nondirective, and Adlerian therapy. *Journal of Consulting Psychology, 14,* 435–36.

FIEDLER, F. (1950b). The concept of an ideal therapeutic relationship. *Journal of Consulting Psychology, 14,* 239–45.

FIEDLER, F. (1951). Factor analysis of psychoanalytic, nondirective, and Adlerian therapeutic relationships. *Journal of Consulting Psychology, 15,* 32–38.

GARFIELD, A., & BERGIN, A. (1986). *Handbook of psychotherapy and behavior change.* New York: Wiley.

GENDLIN, E. (1970). A short summary and some long predictions. In J. Hart & T. Tomlinson (Eds.), *New directions in client-centered therapy.* Boston: Houghton-Mifflin.

GENDLIN, E. (1988). Carl Rogers. *American Psychologist, 43,* 127–28.

HAYASHI, S., KUNO, T., OSAWA, M., SHIMIZU, M., & SUETAKE, Y. (1992). The client-centered therapy and person-centered approach in Japan: Historical development, current status, and perspectives. *Journal of Humanistic Psychology, 32,* 115–36.

HEIDEGGER, M. (1962). *Being and time.* New York: HarperCollins.

HUSSERL, E. (1931). *Ideas: General introduction to pure phenomenology.* London: Allen & Unwin.

INBAR, D., AVIRAM, U., SPIRO, S., & KOTLER, M. (1989). Officers' attitude toward combat stress reaction: Responsibility, treatment, return to unit, and personal distance. *Military Medicine, 154,* 480–89.

JUNG, C. (1958). *Psychology and religion.* New York: Pantheon.

LAFROMBOISE, T., & LOW, K. (1989). American Indian adolescents. In J. Gibbs & L. Hwang (Eds.), *Children of color* (pp. 114–47). San Francisco: Jossey-Bass.

LAING, R. (1967). *The politics of experience.* New York: Ballantine.

LAMBERT, M., & BERGIN, A. (1994). The effectiveness of psychotherapy. In A. Bergin & S. Garfield (Eds.), *Handbook of psychotherapy and behavior change* (4th ed.). New York: Wiley.

LAMBERT, M., DEJULIO, S., & STEIN, D. (1978). Therapist interpersonal skills. *Psychological Bulletin, 85,* 467–89.

LEE, C. (1994). Pioneers of multicultural counseling: A conversation with Clemmont E. Vontress. *Journal of Multicultural Counseling and Development, 22,* 66–78.

LERNER, H. (1992). The limits of phenomenology: A feminist critique of the humanistic personality theories. In L. Brown & M. Ballou (Eds.), *Theories of personality and psychopathology* (pp. 8–19). New York: Guilford.

MAY, R. (1958). The origins and significance of the existential movement in psychology. In R. May, E. Angel, & H. Ellenberger (Eds.), *Existence* (pp. 3–36). New York: Basic Books.

MAY, R. (Ed.). (1961). *Existential psychology.* New York: Random House.

MAY, R. (1969). *Love and will.* New York: Norton.

MENCHER, J. (1990). Intimacy in lesbian relationships: A critical reexamination of fusion. *Work in Progress.* Stone Center Series No. 42. Wellesley College, Wellesley, MA.

MITCHELL, K., BOZARTH, J., & KRAUFT, C. (1977). A reappraisal of the therapeutic effectiveness of accurate empathy, nonpossessive warmth and genuineness. In A. Gurman & A. Razin (Eds.), *Effective psychotherapy* (pp. 482–502). Elmsford, NY: Pergamon.

RIGNEY, M. (1981, April). *A critique of Maslow's self-actualization theory: The "highest good" for the aboriginal is relationship* [Videotape]. Adelaide, Australia: Aboriginal Open College.

ROGERS, C. (1942). *Counseling and psychotherapy.* Boston: Houghton-Mifflin.

ROGERS, C. (1961). *On becoming a person.* Boston: Houghton-Mifflin.

ROGERS, C. (1969). *Freedom to learn.* Columbus, OH: Merrill.

ROGERS, C. (1970). *On encounter groups.* New York: HarperCollins.

ROGERS, C. (1972). *Becoming partners.* New York: Delta.

ROGERS, C. (1977). *On personal power.* New York: Delacourt.

ROGERS, C., GENDLIN, G., KIESLER, D., & TRUAX, C. (1967). *The therapeutic relationship and its impact: A study of psychotherapy with schizophrenics.* Madison: University of Wisconsin Press.

ROGERS, C., & WALLEN, J. (1946). *Counseling with returned servicemen.* New York: McGraw-Hill.

Rogers calls peace results "surprising." (1984, November). *APA Monitor,* p. 15.

SARTRE, J. (1946). *No exit.* New York: Knopf.

SARTRE, J. (1956). *Being and nothingness.* London: Methuen.

SHOSTRUM, E. (Prod.). (1965). *Three approaches to psychotherapy* [Film]. Santa Ana, CA: Psychological Films.

SLOANE, R., & STAPLES, F. (1984). Psychotherapy versus behavior therapy: Implications for future psychotherapy research. In J. Williams & R. Spitzer (Eds.), *Psychotherapy research: Where are we and where should we go?* (pp. 203–15). New York: Guilford.

SLOANE, R., STAPLES, F., CRISTOL, A., YORKSTON, N., & WHIPPLE, K. (1975). *Psychotherapy versus behavior therapy.* Cambridge, MA: Harvard University Press.

STRUPP, H. (1977). A reformulation of the dynamics of the therapist's contribution. In A. Gurman & A. Razin (Eds.), *Effective psychotherapy* (pp. 1–22). Elmsford, NY: Pergamon.

STRUPP, H. (1989). Psychotherapy: Can the practitioner learn from the researcher? *American Psychologist, 44,* 717–24.

STRUPP, H., & HADLEY, S. (1976). Contemporary view on negative effects in psychotherapy. *Archives of General Psychiatry, 33,* 1291–1302.

SUE, D. W. & SUE, D. (1990). *Counseling the culturally different.* New York: Wiley.

TILLICH, P. (1961). Existentialism and psychotherapy. *Review of Existential Psychology and Psychiatry, 1,* 8–16.

VONTRESS, C. (1979). Cross-cultural counseling: An existential approach. *Personnel and Guidance Journal, 58,* 117–22.

VONTRESS, C. (1986). Social and cultural foundations. In M. Lewis, R. Hayes, & J. Lewis (Eds.), *An introduction to the counseling profession.* Itasca, IL: Peacock.

VONTRESS, C. (1995a). The breakdown of authority: Implications for counseling young African-American males. In J. Ponterotto, J. Casas, L. Suzuki, & C. Alexander (Eds.), *Handbook of multicultural counseling* (Vol. 1). Thousand Oaks, CA: Sage.

VONTRESS, C. (1995b). The philosophical foundations of the existential-humanistic perspective: A personal statement. Washington, DC: George Washington University.

WALLERSTEIN, R. (1989). The psychotherapy research project of the Menninger Foundation: An overview. *Journal of Consulting and Clinical Psychology, 57,* 195–205.

WEINRACH, S. (1990). Rogers and Gloria: The controversial film and the enduring relationship. *Psychotherapy, 27,* 282–90.

WEINRACH, S. (1991). Rogers' encounter with Gloria: What did Rogers know and when? *Psychotherapy, 28,* 504–6.

Skill Classification of Nondirective Session (pp. 360–61)

Focus	Microskill
2. Client, topic	Closed question
4. Client	Reflection of feeling
6. Client	Paraphrase
8. Client, other	Paraphrase
10. Client	Reflection of feeling/paraphrase. Note check-out, "Is that it?"
12. Mutual	Expression of content and feeling—self-disclosure

The Existential-Humanistic Tradition II: Logotherapy and Experiential Gestalt Therapy

CHAPTER GOALS

This chapter seeks to:

1. Present Frankl's logotherapy—its central constructs, example techniques, and a multicultural examination of the approach.

2. Explore some central techniques of Perl's Gestalt therapy from a multicultural perspective.

3. Enable you, through practice exercises, to conduct or engage in
   - Logotherapy in an interview to help a client find new meanings
   - Gestalt therapy and techniques in an interview

Implementing the Existential-Humanistic Tradition

The existential-humanistic tradition has many variations, but its core emphasis is on lived experience and on client experiencing and interpretation of life events. In the existential-humanistic approach, the client's story is central to the counseling and therapy process.

As a counselor or therapist, you will likely work with individuals who have suffered severe life difficulties and trauma. You may conduct counseling and therapy with survivors of physical, sexual, and emotional child abuse, rape, or extreme racism or discrimination. One of the most difficult situations you may face will be working with individuals who find that they carry the HIV virus or actually have AIDS. Each of these clients has suffered major personal assaults. How can you then make any sense of what has happened?

Two additional existential-humanistic systems are presented in this chapter: the reflective, meaning-oriented logotherapy of Viktor Frankl and the experiential Gestalt therapy of Fritz Perls. Viktor Frankl developed logotherapy as his response to a personal major life crisis. You may find his courageous answer to the most complex issues of life beneficial not only to your clients, but also to you. When concrete actions fail and life seems to have no positive meaning, Frankl's logotherapy can be invaluable.

Fritz Perls takes a very different direction from Rogers and Frankl and also offers an important humanistic view of the individual. His techniques are extremely directive. Whereas Rogers would listen, Perls would be active in directing the change process.

Frankl provides a balancing force between Rogers and Perls. Rogers might be described as an attending or listening therapist and Perls as an influencing therapist. Frankl appears to use both attending and listening skills according to the varied needs of the client. All three individuals offer much of practical value to the practice of counseling and therapy.

Viktor Frankl and Logotherapy

Logotherapy holds that the critical issue for humankind is not what happens but how one views or thinks about what happens. Although Frankl stresses the importance of cognitive change, logotherapy is also concerned with action and with changing behavior in the real world. Frankl was a forerunner to the cognitive-behavioral movement (Mahoney & Freeman, 1985; Frankl, 1985a), and his position provides an important bridge between existential-humanistic and cognitive-behavioral theories.

Frankl is a cognitive theorist with an existential-humanistic message of faith and hope. His logotherapy is concerned with the search for meaning in life. Frankl was able to reframe his life situation while in a Nazi concentration camp and to find positive reasons for living in the midst of negatives. He faced the existential dilemma of the meaning of life under the most extreme conditions. By finding positive meaning in suffering, Frankl gives us new hope, and his philosophy has profound implications for multicultural counseling and therapy and for those who have suffered trauma. Many have benefited from reading Frankl's *Man's Search for Meaning* (1946/1959), and simply reading this book can be therapeutic for many clients. Rather than presenting a clinical case study, quotations from Frankl's writings are offered in the hope that you will be encouraged to read further.

Frankl's Search for Meaning

Frankl's positive view of the human condition reflects a lifetime of struggle to find the positives in humankind. Frankl is best known through his compelling and important book *Man's Search for Meaning* (1946/1959). In this small but highly affecting volume, Frankl relates his experiences in German concentration camps during World War II. Although Frankl describes the horrors of the concentration camp, the book is more a testimony to the power of the human spirit and its capability of survival under the most inhuman of conditions.

Following are some quotations from Frankl's book. Despite the dehumanizing environment, Frankl finds something meaningful that enables him and others to survive. In the following quotes, the positives in the negative situation have been highlighted by using italics. In many cases Frankl focused his attention away from the immediate situation and toward positive relationships with the world—an action that helped him survive.

We stumbled on in the darkness, over big stones and through large puddles, along the one road leading from the camp. The accompany guards kept shouting at us and driving us with the butts of their rifles. Anyone with very sore feet supported himself on his neighbor's arm. Hardly a word was spoken; the icy wind did not encourage talk. Hiding his mouth behind his upturned collar, the man marching next to me whispered suddenly: "If our wives could see us now! I do hope they are better off in their camps and don't know what is happening to us."

That brought thoughts of my own wife to mind. And as we stumbled on for miles, slipping on icy spots, supporting each other time and again, dragging one another up and onward, nothing was said, but we both knew: *each of us was thinking of his wife.* Occasionally I looked at the sky, where the stars were fading and the pink light of the morning was beginning to spread behind a dark bank of clouds. *But my mind clung to my wife's image, imagining it with an uncanny acuteness. I heard her answering me, saw her smile, her frank and encouraging look. Real or not, her look was then more luminous than the sun which was beginning to rise.*

A thought transfixed me: for the first time in my life I saw the truth as it is set into song by so many poets, proclaimed as the final wisdom by so many thinkers. The truth—that love is the ultimate and the highest goal to which man can aspire. Then I grasped the meaning of the greatest secret that human poetry and human thought and belief have to impart: The salvation of man is through love and in love. I understood how a man who has nothing left in this world still may know bliss, be it only for a brief moment, in the contemplation of his beloved. In a position of utter desolation, when man cannot express himself in positive action, when his only achievement may consist in enduring his sufferings in the right way—an honorable way—in such a position man can, through loving contemplation of the image he carries of his beloved, achieve fulfillment. For the first time in my life I was able to understand the meaning of the words, "The angels are lost in perpetual contemplation of an infinite glory."

In front of me a man stumbled and those following him fell on top of him. The guard rushed over and used his whip on them all. Thus my thoughts were interrupted for a few minutes. *But soon my soul found its way back from the prisoner's existence to another world, and I resumed talk with my loved one: I asked her questions and she answered; she questioned me in return, and I answered.* (pp. 48–49)

In the winter and spring of 1945 there was an outbreak of typhus which infected nearly all the prisoners. The mortality was great among the weak, who had to keep on with their hard work as long as they possibly could. The quarters for the sick were most inadequate, there were practically no medicines or attendants. Some of the symptoms of the disease were extremely disagreeable: an irrepressible aversion to even a scrap of food (which was an additional danger to life) and terrible attacks of delirium. The worst case of delirium was suffered by a friend of mine who thought that he was dying and wanted to pray. In his delirium he could not find the words to do so. *To avoid these attacks of delirium, I tried, as did many of the others, to keep awake for most of the night. For hours I composed speeches in my mind. Eventually I began to reconstruct the manuscript which I had lost in the disinfection chamber of Auschwitz, and scribbled the key words in shorthand on tiny scraps of paper.* (p. 46)

These quotes show how Frankl shifted attention from the immediate horror of the here and now to other issues. Particularly, he thought of his wife and his relationship with her. His was a sane response in an insane situation. At a more basic level, Frankl found meaning outside the horror of the immediate situation, which gave him strength to cope with life's difficult reality.

There are times when problems cannot be solved—the rape has occurred, the HIV infection proven by a medical test, an automobile accident prevents the client from returning to previous employment. In such cases, how we think about what happened and the meaning of our lives—our cognitions—are as important as or more important than any concrete behavioral change we can make.

Central Theoretical Constructs and Techniques of Logotherapy

The task for the logotherapist is to help the client find meaning and purpose in life—*and then to act on those meanings.* Logotherapy could be described as a therapy balanced between the listening skills of Rogers and the influencing skills of Perls, with a greater stress on the importance of generalizing change to the real world.

Logotherapists are interested in carefully learning how the client constructs a worldview. Once they have this understanding, they are willing and ready to move actively to promote client change. Logotherapy, like much of the cognitive-behavioral tradition, is also a metatheoretical orientation in that its practitioners will not hesitate to use techniques from other orientations to help clients find meaning and real-life goals.

Cognitive Change and Finding Positive Meanings

Many Vietnam and Persian Gulf veterans will raise issues of the meaning of life in therapy, as will a Latina/o youth who has experienced discrimination and feels hopeless. Almost all clients of any cultural background will bring problems relating to meaning. Since the definition of meaning sometimes depends on the religious, ethnic, and cultural background of your client, you need to be prepared to deal with a variety of meaning and belief systems ranging from Christian and Jewish to

Mormon to Islamic. Being a gay male or lesbian, physically challenged, economically disadvantaged, or from a particular ethnic/racial group will also challenge and change the structure of the meaning system.

The route toward intentionality and meaning is through carefully listening to the client's construction of meaning of the world. Then, if necessary, the logotherapist will intervene directly and actively to facilitate change in the client's construct or meaning system, but always in accord with the cultural tradition of the client. Frankl is keenly aware that meaning is constructed not only in the individual, but also from the cultural tradition of the client.

Cultural and family traditions are often keys to meaning change in clients. This change in meaning may be represented in thought or played out in direct action. It is important that you be aware of many differing types of constructed meaning systems among individuals of varying cultural backgrounds. The listening aspect of Frankl's logotherapy seems close to that of Rogers, and the influencing aspect is almost as powerful and direct as that of Perls. Yet logotherapy extends existential-humanistic thinking and practice in its awareness of cultural traditions as part of meaning making.

To help clients find personal meaning and to make more sense of their lives, Frankl offers a positive philosophy, as exemplified by his life and by his influential writings. Talking with or listening to Frankl personally is an exercise in life itself— a sermon in motion—and in this sense, Frankl is very similar to Rogers. The person you are in the interview is as important as or more important than your therapeutic skills. *In addition, you must find the person in your client and what is meaningful to that child, adolescent, man, or woman before you.*

Many clients suffer from day-to-day problems of meaning. How does one make sense of a meaningless job, learn to cope with a less-than-satisfactory personal relationship, or relate to difficult parents or in-laws? Helping clients find positive meanings obviously is not a technical skill of helping. There is no formula that can be easily applied to any one client or group. The kind and hopeful approach of Rogers to humanity is helpful, that of Perls is demanding, and that of Frankl provides a basic philosophy that helps us to focus on meaning and may enable us to search with our clients as they find their unique meanings—perhaps differently constructed meanings than ours, but nonetheless workable for them.

Taking Meaning into Behavioral Action

Frankl (1946/1959, 1969) has framed a theory and a method of helping that are gaining increasing prominence (see also Mahoney & Freeman, 1985). The techniques he developed—dereflection, paradoxical intention, and change of attitudes—are important popular methodological and research areas (Frankl, 1985b; Lukas, 1984; Fabry, 1984). Frankl's conceptions of change of attitudes and dereflection may be found in varying forms in cognitive-behavioral modification, rational-emotive therapy, and the structural/systemic family theories. Paradoxical intention is one of the key "new" methods that can be used to produce rapid change, yet it was used by Frankl as early as 1929.

Lukas (1984), a major logotherapy theorist and practitioner, has outlined four main logotherapy techniques that therapists can use to facilitate client growth and movement toward meaningful living: modification of attitudes, paradoxical intention, dereflection, and the appealing technique.

Modification of Attitudes

Clients can hold negative attitudes toward themselves despite overtly positive life situations. For example, many attractive and personable clients may see themselves quite negatively. Also, clients may have actual serious problems and be unable to do anything about them. In each case, the logotherapeutic task is to change the way the person thinks about the situation—a goal similar to that of the cognitive approach. Modification of attitudes is most often conducted directly through sharing opinions, arguing (as in Ellis's rational-emotive behavior therapy), or offering positive suggestions for the client. At issue is assisting the client to take a new view of the situation.

Reframing Attitudes. The positive asset search or positive reframe (Chapter 2) is one technique in logotherapy for modification of attitudes. However, it is of crucial importance to first listen carefully to clients' negative meanings and constructions. Clients need first to tell their stories fully and completely and to feel heard. If you use the techniques of positive reframing or the positive asset search too early, the client may likely be put off. An important guideline is: *Do not try to modify attitudes or cognitions until the client feels thoroughly and respectfully heard.*

The following brief example from a videotaped interview by Ivey (1984) illustrates the specifics of finding positive meanings in negative situations:

Counselor: (after listening to the client's deepest fears and hearing how he thought himself close to death in quicksand—the client had talked about feelings of guilt about survival—"Why me?") Is there anything positive? I know it sounds like a totally negative experience. Was there anything you could see that was positive about what happened?

[*This short counselor comment catches the essence of the search for positive meanings. It is a simple point, so direct that its importance is sometimes lost in professional jargon and theorizing.*]

Client: Well, it sure felt good when they saved me. I was scared, I felt guilty, but at least they came and got me.

Counselor: So you felt that help was there even though you were afraid.

Client: And you know what, one of the guys who helped me get out I thought didn't like me before. But he asked me to work for him the following week. I never thought of that before.

This example illustrates the central dimensions of cognitive reframing. The client's story about his near-death experience was listened to carefully and respectfully. The cognitions associated with the experience in the original narrative were all negative, being associated with guilt and shame. Many clients who share stories of trauma focus on the negative. Frankl would call this negative focus "hyperreflection," in that the individual only reflects on one aspect of the experience.

The simple question, "Was there anything you could see that was positive about what happened?" opens the way for positive reframing of attitudes around the basically negative experience. There is sometimes a tendency for counselors and therapists to focus solely on the negative. The search for positives in even the most difficult of situations is basic to Frankl's logotherapy and to cognitive reframing. Obviously, finding positive reframes will not be as easy with many clients as it was in this brief example. Nonetheless, the reshaping of negative events through positive reframing is a basic dimension of all counseling and psychotherapy.

Changing the meaning system toward a more positive direction has been a major theme in this book. The community and family genograms (Chapters 1 and 2) focus on positive images in the belief that the negative can be addressed more effectively if the client has solid information and resources. The positive asset search (Chapter 2) and the microskills of positive reframing (Chapter 3) all stress that clients can best change through the use of positive resources. These ideas have been influenced by Frankl's approach to positive meanings and the therapeutic importance of finding positives in the midst of problems, issues, and concerns.

Deciding for the Future.   Although what is past is past, one can modify and change the way one thinks about it. Thinking of the past negatively is making a "decision for the past." By questioning the client's past interpretations, the therapist can help the client make a decision for the future. Those who suffer trauma often make decisions for the past—and for very good reason, since it is difficult not to focus on the negatives of trauma. The modification of attitudes, as demonstrated in the foregoing interview, undergirds much more complex survivor issues. Combining an understanding of the specific needs of trauma survivors with the basic approaches of Frankl or Lukas will give you a good foundation for helping your clients live and cope with the effects of trauma.

Frankl (1985b) reminds us that some people must live with impossible situations and impossible memories:

> This was the lesson I had to learn in three years spent in Auschwitz and Dachau: those most apt to survive the camps were those oriented toward the future, toward a meaning to be fulfilled by them in the future. . . . But meaning and purpose were only a necessary condition of survival, not a sufficient condition. Millions had to die in spite of their vision of meaning and purpose. Their belief could not save their lives, but it did enable them to meet death with heads held high. (p. 37)

The ultimate existential issue is survival and finding something positive in the simple act of being-in-the-world. Those who have experienced the Vietnam war, child abuse, rape, serious illness, or other trauma have all survived.[1] Mere survival for some will be sufficient to satisfy existential needs, but the issue will be more complex for others.

Modification of attitudes cannot change the past, but it can help people live with the past and the present more intentionally. The point is to find something positive, something to live for out of and beyond the trauma experience. As a therapist or counselor, you will need a good deal of patience, strength, belief, knowledge, and power to help your clients modify their attitudes toward these impossible traumatic situations.

Paradoxical Intention

Frankl was the first therapist to use the concept of paradox. In 1929 Frankl had a phobic client who was suffering from severe agoraphobia. Analysis and other methods were not working. Improvising, Frankl suggested that instead of being afraid of fainting on the street, the patient should deliberately try to collapse. Frankl (1985a) unequivocally defines his paradoxical intention technique as "encouraging the patient to do, or wish to happen, the very things [she or] he fears—albeit with tongue in cheek." The next week the patient was cured. Frankl did not recall what he had advised, so the patient told him, "I just followed your advice, Doctor. I tried hard to faint but the more I tried, the less I could, and consequently—the fear of fainting disappeared!" Thus the technique was born.

Paradoxical intention has become an important therapeutic skill. Ascher and Turner (1979) were the first to experimentally validate the clinical effectiveness of paradoxical intention in comparison with other behavioral strategies. Prior to this work, Solyom et al. (1972) first proved experimentally that paradoxical intention was useful.

However, Frankl (1985a) warns of confusing paradoxical intention with so-called symptom prescription. In symptom prescription, patients are told to exaggerate the symptom, say, a fear. In paradoxical intention, however, patients are encouraged to wish to happen what they fear will happen. In other words, the fear itself is not dealt with, but rather the object of fear.

In Frankl's hospital was a patient suffering from a severe washing compulsion who had been washing her hands several hundred times a day. One of the doctors suggested that instead of being afraid of bacteria, the patient should instead desire to contract an infection. She was advised to tell herself: "I can't get enough bacteria. I want to become as dirty as possible. There is nothing nicer than bacteria." The patient diligently followed this advice. She asked other patients to let her borrow from them as many bacteria as possible and came up with the resolution no longer to wash "the poor creatures" away but instead to keep them alive. None of Frankl's staff would have dreamed of recommending that this patient no longer wash her hands several hundred times a day. However, it would be in accord with "symptom prescription" to advise her to do so several thousand times a day.

As one can see from this case example, "an integral element in paradoxical intention is the deliberate evocation of humor" (Lazarus, 1971). After all, a sense of humor is an aspect that logotherapy regards as a specifically human capacity, namely, to be self-distancing.

Some authorities (for example, Lankton, 1980; Bandler & Grinder, 1982) argue that the client should not know that a paradoxical intervention is being used. Clinical experience and new research data suggest that clients can profit from knowing that a paradoxical technique is being used. It may even be helpful to explain to the client your theory as to why the technique works.

Dereflection

Dereflection, according to Lukas (1984), uses our ability to "forget ourselves" and brings about a therapeutic reordering of attention—turning it from the problem toward other more positive content of our thinking. Many of us "hyperreflect" on our problems and our negative feelings and experiences. The objective of dereflection is systematically to change the focus of our attention. Put in its most simple and direct terms, the task of the therapist is to encourage the client to think about something else other than the problem.

Techniques of dereflection may be as simple as encouraging a person who has lost a limb to start thinking about a new career, helping a cancer patient focus on helping others rather than on self, or encouraging a retired person to find an interesting hobby. It is true that the facts of the situation cannot be changed and that it is difficult to reframe problems of illness, age, and loneliness as having positive components. However, it is possible to find something else on which to focus one's attention.

Instead of being depressed about the loss of a limb, the disabled person, through refocusing of attention, can work toward a new goal, the cancer patient can think about others, and the aging individual may make new friends in the process of enjoying a new hobby. The concept of refocusing has many important variations that are clearly described by Frankl (1946/1952) in a chapter on dereflection, in which he also devotes special attention to issues of sexual functioning. Lukas (1984) is another useful source for ideas about this concept.

Dereflection may be especially useful in therapy with those with sexual dysfunction. For example, impotence can be caused when the man focuses excessive attention on whether or not he will have an erection. He is hyperreflecting on himself and his fear, which in turn causes more impotence. The logotherapist would help this client dereflect and possibly focus attention on the wife or on sexual stimuli. When one focuses attention on another, it is difficult to think about oneself; at such a time, natural autonomic functions start working effectively.

A similar approach may be used with a person suffering from insomnia. Instead of trying to fall asleep, the individual may decide to use this time to study or for an enjoyable activity. After a relatively short period of time, many clients will naturally get tired and fall asleep.

This simple technique is partly born of logic and of common sense. However, it takes considerable creativity and expertise to find what each individual client needs to avoid hyperreflecting on the negative. Furthermore, changing patterns of attention may require you to use modification of attitudes as well as some form of paradoxical intention.

The Appealing Technique

The appealing technique, Lukas (1989) suggests, may be effective for clients experiencing drug or alcohol detoxification or for those clients you cannot reach via other methods. The appealing technique is reminiscent of the concepts used by Alcoholics Anonymous (AA) and some drug therapy groups. In this approach, one simply appeals to the client to do better and to change. The counselor takes the position that the client's situation is not hopeless and directly attempts to bring the client to a similar awareness. For example, the drug-abusing client may be asked to state out loud, "I am not helpless. I can control and direct my fate."

In some situations, with an understanding and supportive counselor or therapist, the appealing technique can work. It is clearly different than the "sophisticated" techniques of psychoanalysis or behavior therapy. Some counselors are embarrassed by this approach. Some feel it does not have sufficient theoretical implications. However, if you believe in what you say, some clients will respond to your exhortative approach, which appeals to the human spirit. Witness the effectiveness of AA and some drug treatment programs that use techniques similar to the appealing process.

Maintaining Flexibility of Approach.   Logotherapy in the application of technique is an intentional approach to change. There are theoretical and practical reasons for trying to help clients change in a certain direction, but if the first technique does not work, logotherapy does not hesitate to "mix and match" and change the approach to meet the unique human needs of the client. Practice Exercise 12.1 offers some dimensions of logotherapy that you may find beneficial in your own work in counseling and psychotherapy.

Logotherapy and Spirituality

Spirituality and Medicine

Van Pelt (1993) has explored the border between medicine and logotherapy. She argues persuasively that the healthy human spirit is important to psychological and physiological well-being. Moreover, she points out that if broad human issues are considered from the philosophic framework of logotherapy, new dimensions for mental and physical health, and even world peace, can be the result. Van Pelt's (1993) emphasis on spirituality was detailed previously in Chapter 1 (see Figure 1.2) and is enlarged on here:

> Many therapists do tend to avoid getting involved with religious thoughts or struggles. They feel ill equipped or see it as inappropriate to deal with religious quests or meaning issues; it does not fit into the therapeutic model.
>   The logotherapist addresses primarily the client's healthy human spirit. . . . By awakening this human spirit, . . . one opens up the road toward meaning and fulfillment in life. For the logotherapist it will be irrelevant whether the client's search for

Practice Exercise 12.1

An Exercise in Logotherapy and Meaning Issues

Viktor Frankl and his colleague, Elisabeth Lukas, give almost as much attention to hearing and understanding the worldview of the client as does Carl Rogers and person-centered therapy. Thus, you can easily adapt Practice Exercise 11.2 of Chapter 11 to logotherapy.

Indicate to your real or role-played client that you are going to be talking about what the problem means and that problem solving will be secondary. Particularly good topics for this exercise include procrastination, a difficulty with a colleague or housemate, boredom, or concern over illness or the loss of someone important.

Stages 1, 2, and 3. Rapport/Structuring, Data Gathering, Determining Outcomes

It is suggested that you use the same structure of the interview in Practice Exercise 11.2 for the first three stages of the interview. Use listening skills and the basic listening sequence to draw out the problem.

However, add one central dimension: Ask yourself and your client, "What does this mean to you?" "What does this say about your deeper values?" "Why is this important?" Ask these meaning-oriented questions after you have heard the problem defined clearly.

As you reach the third stage of the interview and the goal is established, ask what the goal *means* to the client and why the client *values* that goal. In the process of asking questions about meaning, you will find that a new depth is added to the interview and that clients frequently start talking about their lives when before they were talking about problems.

In this process you will want to add the skill of reflection of meaning. A reflection of meaning is similar to the paraphrase but focuses more on deeper issues underlying the surface structure sentence.

Stage 4. Generating Alternative Solutions and Meaning

Once having heard the client and the client's meaning, you have two main alternatives:

1. You may summarize the problem and its meaning to the client and contrast it with a summary of the ideal goal and its meaning. Throughout the summary, you will point out possible discrepancies and mixed messages in the client's meaning system. Then, through listening skills and reflection of meaning, you can encourage further self-exploration. The goal here is to discover the underlying, more deeply felt meanings guiding the client's action.

2. If the client wishes to act on meaning, select one of the four major

techniques of logotherapeutic action (change of attitudes, paradoxical intention, dereflection, or the appealing technique). If the first technique does not work, try another. Logotherapy does not hesitate to try several approaches in an attempt to meet the unique needs of your client.

Out of this portion of the interview, your goal is to facilitate client examination of meaning and through the influencing approach to help your client change and act on the personal meaning system.

Stage 5. Generalization

As with other existential-humanistic orientations, logotherapy does not give extensive attention to generalization and maintenance of behavioral change. It is suggested that you may ask your client to "think about" the interview over the next few days and talk with you personally or by phone. If it seems relevant, ask your client to try one thing differently during the time period before you have a follow-up talk.

meaning will lead to the discovery or rediscovery of religious faith—the emphasis is on meaningful living from moment to moment. Meaning, and certainly higher meaning, however, contains a "faith factor."

. . .

Logotherapy bridges the gap between psychology and religion. Outreach to others, transcendence, is known as loving your neighbor. Higher meaning is known as God's Will, a Higher Power. Logotherapy even acknowledges the redeeming factor of forgiveness. (pp. 106–7)

Van Pelt (1994) provides an example in the form of treatment for chronic headaches and conflict resolution. She presents several case histories in which issues of meaning appear to be central to the documented physiological condition. For example, a fifty-eight-year-old Greek woman at a headache clinic was able to reduce aspirin use from three hundred tablets a month to five. The treatment focused on the client's loneliness and homesickness and the refocusing of internal conflicts over personal loss to a positive approach to the meaning of life and an awareness of possibilities. Critical in this process was an emphasis on the human spirit and the ability to transcend present-day experience. Van Pelt notes that conflicts between personal values *(eigenwelt)* and societal expectations *(umwelt)* are critical issues in logotherapy. The *überwelt*, or spiritual connection as described by Vontress (Chapter 11), was vital in this process.

Spirituality and Psychotherapy as Reconciliation

In a paper entitled "From Self-Actualization to Global Responsibility," Lukas (1989) talks about "education toward responsibility" and maintains that individual self-examination is a most limited way to view therapy and counseling:

We must be concerned about a *future worthy of human beings*. . . . This concern deserves the trouble to look up from our navels and focus our feelings on something beyond our Ego—feelings which in turn could release energies for the spiritual renaissance of our generation. (p. 5)

Lukas argues for three sensitivities: the feeling for the sacred, the feeling for the necessary, and the feeling for Otherliness. The sacred is spiritual being—our relationship with transcendence and Nature. The necessary represents our ability to deal with challenging situations—for example, trauma, oppressive situations, physical disfigurement. Life, as Frankl discovered in the Nazi concentration camp, is not all positive. We must do all we can to cope with the impossible.

The feeling for Otherliness speaks to our relations with friends, family, and strangers. "The Otherliness of the other person is not something just to be tolerated; it is, instead, something to behold, something that in fact enriches the beholder" (p. 15). Lukas stresses that we must learn to accept and appreciate the Other—"The I and the very different You can be integrated in a common We." Lukas describes logotherapy as an *agent of reconciliation*. Logotherapy seeks to reconcile us to God and Nature, to the most difficult of challenges we face, and to each other.

Multicultural Implications of Logotherapy

Logotherapy grew out of cultural oppression—the German treatment of Jews during the Holocaust. Frankl's powerful existential-humanistic approach appeals to the human spirit and thus is particularly adaptable to multicultural counseling and therapy. Many culturally diverse groups may find Frankl's philosophy and specific methods particularly applicable because they represent a response to personal and cultural oppression.

The listening style of Rogers is particularly compatible with Frankl's ideas, and it is easy to integrate the views of humankind put forth by Rogers and Frankl. Each was an admirer of the other's work.

Logotherapy leaves considerable room for you to generate your own culturally relevant integration of theory and practice. Frankl would endorse drawing from traditional and meaningful helping techniques from each culture. Perhaps more than any other single theory of helping, logotherapy is represented throughout the world with commitment and passion from its adherents. Logotherapy appears to be highly adaptable to multicultural and to gender differences.

Fritz Perls and Gestalt Therapy

Frederick (Fritz) Perls devised Gestalt theory to fill the theoretical gaps of psychoanalysis, and he came to be regarded as a "guru" of existentialism in the 1960s. So popular was Perls that his "Gestalt Prayer"[2] was widely available in poster form:

> You do your thing, and
> I'll do my thing, and
> If by chance we meet, it's beautiful.

A relatively large group of admirers waited outside the hospital in Indianapolis when he passed away in 1970. It seemed the end of an era.

"Doing your own thing" in many ways captures the essence of Perls and his approach to therapy and explains the relationship of his movement to existentialism. Perls deeply believed that individuals who became aware of themselves and their experience in the immediacy of the here and now could become more authentic and purposeful human beings. Many of his techniques were directed to helping individual clients and groups become aware of who they were and what they really wanted.

Perls saw human nature as holistic, consisting of many varied parts that make a unique individual. We start life more or less "together," but as we grow and develop, we encounter experiences, feelings, and fears in life that cause us to lose parts of ourselves. These "splits" from the whole, or the gestalt, must be reintegrated if we are to live intentional, self-actualized lives. Thus, Gestalt therapy is centrally concerned with integrating or reintegrating our split-off parts into a whole person.

The Gestalt worldview is that people can be responsible for their actions in the world and, further, that the world is so complex that very little can be understood at any given moment. Thus, Gestalt therapy tends to focus extensively on the present-tense, immediate, here-and-now experience of the client. These two key construct are reflections of the basic existential view.

Case Example: Gestalt Dreamwork

The following excerpt is typical of the work of Perls (1969a). In this case, he was working with a client's dream. In Gestalt dreamwork, each part of the dream is believed to represent a part of the dreamer. The task of the Gestalt therapist is to find how the parts relate together as a unity. Note particularly the consistent present-tense immediacy in the session and the willingness to direct client action. It is astonishing that these techniques, now thirty to forty years old, still catch our interest and astonish us with their power.

1. *Meg:*   In my dream, I'm sitting on a platform, and there's somebody else with me, a man, and maybe another person, and—ah—a couple of rattlesnakes. And one's up on the platform, now, all coiled up, and I'm frightened. And his head's up, but he doesn't seem like he's gonna strike me. He's just sitting there and I'm frightened, and this other person says to me—uh—just, just don't disturb the snake and he won't bother you. And the other snake, the other snake's down below, and there's a dog down there.

2. *Fritz:*   What is there? [*Open question*]

3. *Meg:*   A dog, and the other snake.

4. *Fritz:*   So, up here is one rattlesnake and down below is another rattlesnake and the dog. [*Paraphrase; note how Perls works in the present tense. The emphasis is on immediate sensorimotor and concrete experience rather than formal operational analysis.*]

5. *Meg:*   And the dog is sort of sniffing at the rattlesnake. He's—ah—getting very close to the rattlesnake, sort of playing with it, and I wanna stop—stop him from doing that.

6. *Fritz:*   Tell him. [*Directive*]

7. *Meg:*   Dog, stop! / *Fritz:*   Louder. / *Meg:*   Stop! / *Fritz:*   Louder. / *Meg:* (shouts) STOP! / *Fritz:*   Louder. / *Meg:*   (screams) STOP! [*This example is particularly representative of Gestalt repetition exercises. Repeating words again and again often leads to deeper, more emotional experience.*]

8. *Fritz:*   Does the dog stop? [*Closed question*]

9. *Meg:*   He's looking at me. Now he's gone back to the snake. Now—now, the snake's sort of coiling up around the dog, and the dog's lying down, and—and the snake's coiling around the dog, and the dog looks very happy.

10. *Fritz:*   Ah! Now have an encounter between the dog and the rattlesnake. [*Directive*]

11. *Meg:*   You want me to play them?

12. *Fritz:*   Both. Sure. This is your dream. Every part is a part of yourself. [*Directive, interpretation*]

13. *Meg:*   I'm the dog. (hesitantly) Huh. Hello, rattlesnake. It sort of feels good with you wrapped around me.

14. *Fritz:*   Look at the audience. Say this to somebody in the audience. [*Directive*]

15. *Meg:*   (laughs gently) Hello, snake. It feels good to have you wrapped around me.

16. *Fritz:*   Close your eyes. Enter your body. What do you experience physically? [*Directing. This type of sensorimotor body technique is particularly emblematic of Perls and Gestalt therapy. Emotions are to be experienced immediately rather than reflected on abstractly. As such, Gestalt exercises should be used with care with children and many less-verbal clients.*]

17. *Meg:*   I'm trembling. Tensing.

18. *Fritz:*   Let this develop. Allow yourself to tremble and get your feelings . . . (her whole body begins to move a little) Yah. Let it happen. Can you dance it? Get up and dance it. Let your eyes open, just so that you stay in touch with your body, with what you want to express physically . . . Yah . . . (she walks, trembling and jerkily, almost staggering) Now dance rattlesnake . . . (she moves slowly and sinuously graceful) . . . How does it feel to be a rattlesnake now? . . . [*Directive, open question. The building and magnification of sensorimotor experience are considered basic to Gestalt work.*]

19. *Meg:*   It's—sort of—slowly—quite—quite aware, of anything getting too close.

20. *Fritz:*   Hm? [*Encourager*]

21. *Meg:*   Quite aware of not letting anything get too close, ready to strike.

22. *Fritz:*   Say this to us. "If you come too close, I—" [*Directive*]

23. *Meg:*   If you come too close, I'll strike back!

24. *Fritz:*   I don't hear you. I don't believe you, yet. [*Feedback*]

25. *Meg:*   If you come too close, I will strike back!

26. *Fritz:*   Say this to each one, here. [*Directive*]

27. *Meg:*   If you come too close, I will strike back!

28. *Fritz:*   Say this with your whole body. [*Directive*]

29. *Meg:*   If you come too close, I will strike back!

30. *Fritz:*   How are your legs? I experience you as being somewhat wobbly. [*Open question, feedback. Perls was often concerned about clients' bodies being physically grounded on the earth.*]

31. *Meg:*   Yeah.

32. *Fritz:*   That you don't really take a stand. [*Interpretation*]

33. *Meg:*   Yes, I feel I'm . . . kind of, in between being very strong and—if I let go, they're going to turn to rubber.

34. *Fritz:*   Okeh, let them turn to rubber. (her knees bend and wobble) Again . . . Now try out how strong they are. Try out—hit the floor. Do anything. (she stamps several times with one foot) Yah, now the other. (stamps other foot) Now let them turn to rubber again. (she lets knees bend again) More difficult now, isn't it? [*Directive, closed question*]

35. *Meg:*   Yeah.

36. *Fritz:*   Now say again the sentence, "If you come too close—" . . . (she makes an effort) . . . (laughter) . . . [*Directive*]

37. *Meg:*   If—if you . . .

38. *Fritz:*   Okeh, change. Say "Come close." (laughter) [*Directive*]

39. *Meg:*   Come close.

40. *Fritz:*   How do you feel now? [*Open question*]

41. *Meg:*   Warm.

42. *Fritz:*   You feel somewhat more real? [*Interpretation*]

43. *Meg:*   Yeah.

44. *Fritz:*   Okeh . . . So what we did is we took away some of the fear of being in touch. So, from now on, she'll be a bit more in touch. [*Interpretation and the beginning of formal reflection on the experience*] (pp. 162–64)

It is useful to compare Perls and Rogers on their use of microskills. In Rogerian counseling, attending and listening skills are primary, whereas Perls predominantly used the influencing skills of directives, feedback, and interpretation. Whereas Rogers emphasized empathy and warmth and positive regard, Perls was somewhat personally distant and remote during the session. His respect for others showed only when they became truly themselves. Although both Rogers and Perls sought genuine encounters with others, Rogers tended to wait patiently for them, whereas Perls demanded that authentic relationships develop quickly and strongly.

Central Theoretical Constructs and Techniques

Gestalt can be described as centrally concerned with the totality of the individual's being-in-the-world. The complexity and possibility of the world can be dealt with, according to existential thought, in a wide variety of ways. Perls chose to emphasize here-and-now present-tense experiencing as a way to integrate people in relation to themselves, others, and the world. There is thus a corresponding decrease in emphasis on past or future.

Perls (1969a) writes: "Whenever you leave the sure basis of the now and become preoccupied with the future, you experience anxiety" (p. 30). Perls suggested that the mode of being-in-the-world is to center on oneself and get in touch with one's own existential experience; this makes for a very "I-centered" individualistic view of therapy.

The Role of Relationship and Multicultural Issues

The focus of Perls on individuals making decisions alone—"doing their own thing"—is similar to the emphasis of Rogers on self-actualization, but Perls carries the idea considerably further. In terms of actual practice, Perls did not give much attention to the individual-in-relationship. Yet when his clients truly were able to find themselves, to identify themselves as authentically in real relationship to others, Perls would often embrace them with joy.

Thus, although Perls's system does not focus on relationships, it should be stressed that *real and authentic relationships* were important to him. In the final stages of his life, he established a Gestalt community on Vancouver Island, British Columbia. The idea of the community was to extend Gestalt ideas of the "whole" to group and community interaction. Unfortunately, Perls died before his ideas could be tested. Clearly, in his last works he was moving toward environmental and interpersonal interaction and action.

Lerner's (1992) critique of Perls is more gentle than her commentary on Rogers (Chapter 11). She recognizes that Gestalt therapy is more concerned with environmental reality than with person-centered theory. However, she feels that Perls gave insufficient attention to the role of trauma in therapy and that he uncritically accepted a Maslow (1971) type of need hierarchy. In her view, the emphasis on self-actualization misses the importance of self-in-relation.

Enns (1987) gives special attention to Gestalt therapy's implications for women. She suggests that Gestalt exercises can be helpful for women in three ways: (1) helping women become aware of themselves as distinct individuals having their own power (particularly in that "I" statements are used); (2) facilitating the expression of anger through a variety of Gestalt exercises; and (3) enabling more choice. Gestalt therapy is highly concerned that individuals make their own choices and, as such, can be very helpful to women who have been culturally discouraged from making their own choices.

These three advantages may be less applicable with individuals of different cultural groups. The direct personal affirmations of individual choice suggested by Perls can be in serious conflict with the cultural values of Asian-Americans and Native Americans, who may believe that decision making is made in context rather than as a purely individual matter. Gestalt therapy contains a strong confrontational element and quickly moves clients to direct emotional expression. The emotional expressiveness required in Gestalt may be seen as immature in some Native American Indian and Asian-American communities. Trust between client and therapist is needed before people can reveal themselves fully. Rigney (1981) speaks to the condition of the Australian Aboriginal, making specific comments on how unsuitable much of traditional counseling and therapy is for many cultural groups, particularly the Aboriginal.

The word *gestalt* implies that the individual is a whole in a context of family and community. It seems clear that clients of many cultures can and will respond to Gestalt interventions, if used with cultural sensitivity and an egalitarian, nonhierarchical approach. The culturally sensitive use of Gestalt therapy requires that you be sure that your client is ready and understands why you are using these particular interventions.

Gestalt Techniques

Perls was a charismatic, dynamic therapist who was trained in classical psychoanalysis but profoundly aware of its limitations. He brought his formal knowledge and a formidable clinical talent to the counseling interview. He and his coworkers have been able to document both Gestalt therapy theory and technique in a rather complete form (see Perls, Hefferline, & Goodman, 1951; Fagan & Shepherd, 1970; Perls, 1969a, 1969b). However, the most effective way to understand Gestalt therapy is to experience it.

Although Gestalt theory can be discussed in considerable detail, the primary purpose of this section is to examine some techniques for enhancing awareness of interpersonal experiencing developed by Perls and his coworkers. It can be argued that Perls's major contribution is methodological rather than theoretical. Over the years, he developed a wide range of techniques that vitalize existential experiencing.

The following techniques should always be used in a working relationship and with a full sense of ethics. *Reading about them will be of no value unless you practice them experientially.* These methods are easily integrated into interviews, regardless of theoretical orientation.

1. *Here-and-now experiencing.* Most techniques of Gestalt therapy are centered on helping the client experience the world *now* rather than in the past or future. What is done is done, and what will be will be. Although past experiences, dreams, or future thoughts may be discussed, the constant emphasis is on relating them to immediate present-tense experience. In the transcript, Perls again and again directed the client to awareness of the here and now.

2. *Directives.* Gestalt therapists constantly tell their clients what to do in the interview, although decisions for their own later action are clients' own. For example, Meg (number 5) talks in the past tense about her dream. Perls, through

the simple directive "Tell him," brings the past to the present. Throughout this session, Perls constantly directs the movement of the client. Feedback (number 24), questions relating to feelings (number 30), and interpretations (number 32) give additional strength to the directives.

3. *Language changes.* Gestalt clients are encouraged to change questions to statements in the belief that most questions are simply hidden statements about oneself. For example, "Do you like me?" may actually be the statement "I am not sure that you like me." The therapist suggests that the client change questions to "I" statements. Clients are also often asked or told to change vague statements about some subject to "I" statements, thus increasing the personal identification and concreteness in the interview.

The client is frequently directed to talk in the present tense ("Be in the here and now"), as this also adds power and focus to the problem. Gestalt therapists point out that the counselor can see and understand only what is before him or her. Talking about problems is considered less effective than experiencing them directly. Although questions are generally discouraged, "how" and "what" questions are considered more acceptable than "why" questions, which often lead to intellectualization.

4. *The empty chair technique.* Perhaps the best-known and most powerful of the many Gestalt techniques, the empty chair technique is also one of the easiest to use in counseling practice. When a client expresses a conflict with another person, the client is directed to imagine that the other person is sitting in an empty chair and then to talk to that person. After the client has said a few words, the counselor directs the client to change chairs and answer as the other person might. The counselor directs a dialogue between the client and the imaginary other person by constantly suggesting chair changes at critical points. Through this exercise, clients learn to experience and understand feelings more fully. Clients also often learn that they were projecting many thoughts onto the other person. Research on and practice with the empty chair technique are provided in Research Exhibit 12.1 and Practice Exercise 12.2.

5. *Talking to parts of oneself.* A variation of the empty chair technique is to point out client splits, immobility, or impasses to the client. The two sides of an issue, or conflicting parts within the person, are drawn out. Sometimes the therapist seeks details for clarity; at other times, the counselor moves immediately to the exercise. The two sides of the person then engage in a dialogue, using the empty chair technique. By discussing the conflicted issues reflected by the split, the person often spontaneously generates a new solution or answer.

A variation on the foregoing often occurs when the counselor notes incongruities or mixed messages in client body language or between client body language and words. In such cases, the Gestalt therapist may have the tense right hand talk to the loose left hand or the jiggling right leg talk to the upset stomach. Through such imaginative games of body dialogue, quick and important breakthroughs in understanding often occur.

Research Exhibit 12.1

Studies on the Empty Chair Technique

Research demonstrating the effectiveness of Gestalt techniques is finally beginning to bear some positive fruit. Paivio and Greenberg (1995) examined the empty chair technique as a method to help clients work through "unfinished business." Unfinished business could include the failure to resolve emotional issues around divorce, issues with one's parents, or other interpersonal conflict. The authors note that clients with unfinished business tend to have unresolved anger and sadness, which in turn result in anxiety, depression, and other clinical symptoms. When clients talk about their issues using the empty chair technique, they can release their emotions. Greenberg and Saffran (1987) and Foerster (1990) note that resolution often occurs and clients tend to see themselves as less weak and more empowered after using this technique.

Paivio and Greenberg (1995) provided empty chair therapy for twelve weeks of treatment. In the sessions, the therapists guided clients to express their unresolved feelings to an imaginary person. A comparison group of clients engaged in a lecture and discussion around issues of unresolved business for the same period of time. The empty chair technique was found to be effective in producing clinically meaningful changes with a large effect size. Example changes were less hostility, more self-acceptance, and more understanding of the other person's point of view.

Patients who profited most from this experience were those "able to experience anxiety . . . [and allow] accessing of the emotional memory" (Paivio & Greenberg, 1995, p. 424). In effect, those able to handle stress most effectively were those who gained most from the twelve-week experience. This type of finding is typical of psychotherapy and counseling research, which often reveals that those who are "most well" benefit the most from professional helping.

Despite some methodological difficulties, this study is important, as it demonstrates that areas previously thought to be inaccessible to research are indeed measurable. Clinicians intuitively have known for years that strong emotional discharge often leads to improvement. The type of study done by Paivio and Greenberg needs replication and extension. One possibility would be to include Gestalt empty chair work in the lecture and discussion group sessions. This, of course, is classic Gestalt group work, and it is possible that effectiveness with the empty chair technique could be demonstrated in other than one-on-one interviews.

6. *Top dog and underdog.* Gestalt therapists constantly search for the authoritarian and demanding "top dog," which is full of "shoulds" and "oughts." In contrast, the "underdog" is more passive, apologetic, and guilt ridden. When these two dimensions are observed, the empty chair technique or a dialogue often helps the client to understand and experience them more fully.

═══ Practice Exercise 12.2 ═══

Using the Empty Chair Technique to Resolve Unfinished Business

Gestalt techniques often focus on the here and now. How can one talk about past issues in the present? The empty chair technique is particularly suited to this purpose, as it provides you and the client with a way to bring the past into the present and to work toward a new, more positive future. The techniques and strategies of the empty chair are powerful and should be used with care and a full sense of ethical responsibility.

1. Before you start this practice exercise, fully inform the client (real or role-played) about what to expect. Mention that the client can stop at any point.

2. Use the basic listening sequence to draw out a story of unfinished personal business from the client. As always, listen carefully and be sure to summarize the story's major facts and feelings to the client's satisfaction.

3. Inform the client about the nature of the exercise. For example:

   You seem to have unfinished business with your uncle. We have found that if you imagine that he is sitting in that empty chair over there it may be helpful to you in resolving and understanding some of your issues. I'd like you to talk directly to your uncle as if he were there right now.

4. As the client talks to the uncle, the following prompts and appropriately used directives may be helpful in bringing the conversation more into the here and now:

   Look at your uncle sitting in that chair, not at me.

   Don't say "I would say X to him." Rather, use his name and talk as if he were there right now.

   Use here-and-now language, not there-and-then language.

   To make the situation more powerful, ask the client to tell the other person the same thing again (and again) with increasing feeling. Gestalt repetition often builds emotion quickly, so work *with* the client rather than *on* the client.

5. An even more powerful approach is to ask the client to move to the chair and take the role of the other person. In the above example, the client would physically move to the empty chair, become the uncle, and answer the now-imaginary client in the empty chair. Many Gestalt therapists will continue this dialogue until a resolution to the problem seems to have been reached.

6. The emotional release that often occurs during this exercise is powerful. Spend sufficient time "talking down" your client and encouraging deep breathing in the here and now to help the client readjust to present reality and leave the recently completed work in the there and then.

As you review the above exercise, note that the four techniques of Gestalt are used—here-and-now experiencing, therapist directives, language changes, and the empty chair technique.

7. *Staying with feeling.* When a key emotion is noted in the interview, particularly through a nonverbal movement, the Gestalt therapist will often immediately give attention to the feeling and its meaning. Perls's suggestion (number 18) to Meg to let her trembling develop exemplifies the use of this technique. *This is a simple technique, but it can be invaluable whether you are a Rogerian, a psychodynamic helper, or a feminist therapist.*

8. *Dreamwork.* In dreamwork, the Gestalt approach most closely resembles its psychoanalytic foundation. Yet, unlike psychoanalysis, Gestalt does not use dreams to understand past conflicts, but rather as metaphors to understand present-day, here-and-now living. The parts of a dream are considered as aspects of the client. Any piece (person, object, scene, or thing) of a dream is a projection of the client's experiential work. Through acting out the dream, the client can integrate the split pieces into a whole person.

Each of these techniques can be used in multicultural settings, *providing there is a base of sufficient understanding and trust between client and therapist.* For example, Gestalt dreamwork can be expanded to include the multicultural family and dream concepts mentioned in Chapter 8. When combined with Gestalt interventions, dreamwork can be very powerful and emotional. For other examples, the empty chair technique can be used to increase women's or gay males' understanding of how others may have mistreated them. The top dog/underdog technique is made to order for discussion of oppression.

Through these and other powerful techniques, Perls made an impressive impact on the practice of counseling and psychotherapy. More than any other therapist, he has been able to show that clients can rapidly be moved to deep understanding of themselves and their conditions. Although his theoretical foundations have been criticized and there is little empirical evidence validating his approach, there is no question that his work and life are an important expression of the existential-humanistic tradition.

Perls, Rogers, and Frankl

Like many other orientations to helping, Gestalt therapy has been influenced by the Rogerian tradition. For example, in a discussion of the present state of Gestalt theory, Yontef and Simkin (1989) place a greater emphasis on the relationship of client and therapist and argue for more softness, as compared with the "hard-ball" approach of Perls.

Unfortunately, research studies comparing Rogerian, logotherapy, and Gestalt methods are virtually nonexistent. In fact, there is very little research on Gestalt therapy itself. However, opinion is that Gestalt therapy facilitates change faster than do Rogerian methods, but that it also has the potential for more destructive impact on the client if the therapist moves too fast. The Gestalt therapist is often seen by the client as a "guru," which means that the therapist has even more power. Strupp and Hadley (1976) have documented thoroughly the dangers of the charismatic therapist for fragile clients.

It seems wise, particularly for beginning counselors and therapists, to use these powerful techniques with a real sensitivity to the worldview and experience of the client. Be advised to seek specific training and supervision before implementing these techniques.

Limitations and Practical Implications of the Existential-Humanistic Tradition

Of the existential-humanistic approaches, Frankl's logotherapy sometimes can be overly verbal, reflective, and formal operational in nature, whereas Perls's direct sensorimotor approach may be inappropriate for clients who are uncomfortable with the emotional realm. Also, if Gestalt exercises are used too soon, they may be personally and culturally offensive.

The powerful Gestalt activation exercises described in this chapter have become an important part of the techniques of many effective therapists of varying orientations, from cognitive-behavioral to psychodynamic and even those with a multicultural orientation. There are now relatively few individuals who practice Gestalt as a theory in itself. Transactional analysis (Berne, 1964; James & Jongeward, 1971) has incorporated many Gestalt techniques into its framework.

Current theory and practice indicate that the balanced listening and influencing approach of Frankl may gradually become the most prominent existential-humanistic theory. This approach deals openly and honestly with issues of pain and how to surmount these difficulties through personal action with the support of the therapist or counselor.

However, as stressed throughout this book, manipulative and insensitive therapists are the greatest danger in the field. Theories may not always be personally and culturally sensitive, but if you are aware and growing, you almost always can adapt theory to meet the needs of the client.

NOTES

1. Resources for understanding the worldview and specific needs of trauma victims can be found in the work of Wilson (1989) on veterans, Katz (1984) on survivors of rape, Miller (1990) on child abuse, and Sue and Sue (1990) on racial discrimination.

2. Perls was also criticized for his individualistic approach. For example, the journal *Rough Times* (1972, *3*, p. 7) published "The Getsmart Prayer." The first three lines are the same as above, but *Rough Times* added the following as its conclusion:

> You are you, and I am I,
> And if by chance we find
> Our brothers and sisters enslaved

And the world under fascist rule
Because we're doing our thing—
It can't be helped.

REFERENCES

Ascher, L. M., & Turner, R. M. (1979). Controlled comparison of progressive relaxation, stimulus control, and paradoxical intention therapies for insomnia. *Journal of Consulting and Clinical Psychology, 47* (3), 500–508.

Bandler, R., & Grinder, J. (1982). *Reframing: Neurolinguistic programming and the transformation of meaning.* Moab, UT: Real People Press.

Berne, E. (1964). *Games people play.* New York: Grove Press.

Enns, C. (1987). Gestalt therapy and feminist therapy: A proposed integration. *Journal of Counseling and Development, 66,* 93–95.

Fabry, J. (1984). Personal communication. *International Forum for Logotherapy.*

Fagan, J., & Shepherd, I. (1970). *Gestalt therapy now.* Palo Alto, CA: Science and Behavior Books.

Foerster, F. (1990). *Refinement and verification of a model of the resolution of unfinished business.* Unpublished master's thesis, York University, Toronto, Canada.

Frankl, V. E. (1952). *The doctor and the soul.* New York: Bantam. (Original work published 1946)

Frankl, V. E. (1959). *Man's search for meaning.* New York: Pocket Books. (Original work published 1946)

Frankl, V. E. (1967). *Psychotherapy and existentialism.* New York: Simon & Schuster.

Frankl, V. E. (1969). *The will to meaning.* New York: New American Library.

Frankl, V. E. (1985a). Logos, paradox, and the search for meaning. In M. J. Mahoney & A. Freeman (Eds.), *Cognition and psychotherapy* (pp. 259–75). New York: Plenum.

Frankl, V. E. (1985b). *The unheard cry for meaning: Psychotherapy and humanism.* New York: Simon & Schuster.

Greenberg, L., & Saffran, J. (1987). *Emotion in psychotherapy.* New York: Guilford.

Ivey, M. (1984). Reflection of feeling [Videotape]. In A. Ivey, N. Gluckstern, & M. Ivey, *Basic attending skills.* North Amherst, MA: Microtraining.

James, M., & Jongeward, D. (1971). *Born to win: Transactional analysis with gestalt experiments.* Reading, MA: Addison-Wesley.

Katz, J. (1984). *No fairy godmothers, no magic wands: The healing process after rape.* Saratoga, CA: R & E Publishers.

Lankton, S. (1980). *Practical magic.* Cupertino, CA: Meta.

Lazarus, A. A. (1971). Behavior therapy and beyond. New York: McGraw-Hill.

Lerner, H. (1992). The limits of phenomenology: A feminist critique of the humanistic personality theories. In L. Brown & M. Ballou (Eds.), *Personality and psychopathology* (pp. 8–19). New York: Guilford.

Lukas, E. (1984). *Meaningful living.* Cambridge, MA: Schenkman.

Lukas, E. (1989, June). *From self-actualization to global responsibility.* Paper presented at the seventh World Congress of Logotherapy, Kansas City.

Mahoney, M., & Freeman, A. (Eds.). (1985). *Cognition and psychotherapy.* New York: Plenum.

Maslow, A. (1971). *The farther reaches of human nature.* New York: Viking.

Miller, A. (1990). *The untouched key: Tracing childhood trauma in creativity and destructiveness.* New York: Doubleday.

Paivio, S., & Greenberg, L. (1995). Resolving "unfinished business": Efficacy of experiential therapy using empty-chair dialogue. *Journal of Consulting and Clinical Psychology, 73,* 419–25.

PERLS, F. (1969a). *Gestalt therapy verbatim.* Moab, UT: Real People Press.

PERLS, F. (1969b). *In and out of the garbage pail.* Moab, UT: Real People Press.

PERLS, F., HEFFERLINE, R., & GOODMAN, P. (1951). *Gestalt therapy: Excitement and growth in human personality.* New York: Dell.

RIGNEY, M. (1981, April). *A critique of Maslow's self-actualization theory: The "highest good" for the Aboriginal is relationship* [Videotape]. Aboriginal Open College, Adelaide, Australia.

SOLYOM, L., GARZA-PEREZ, J., LEDWIDGE, B. L., & SOLYOM, C. (1972). Paradoxical intention in the treatment of obsessive thoughts: A pilot study. *Comprehensive Psychiatry, 13* (3), 291–97.

STRUPP, H., & HADLEY, S. (1976). Contemporary view on negative effects in psychotherapy. *Archives of General Psychiatry, 33,* 1291–1302.

SUE, D., & SUE, D. (1990). *Counseling the culturally different* (2nd ed.). New York: Wiley.

TAUB-BYNUM, E. B. (1984). *The family unconscious.* Wheaton, IL: Quest.

TAUB-BYNUM, E. B. (1992). *Family dreams: The intricate web.* Ithaca, NY: Haworth Press.

VAN PELT, I. (1993). Logotherapy—Mission for the future. *International Forum for Logotherapy, 16,* 105–8.

VAN PELT, I. (1994). Logotherapy—Mission for the future. *International Forum for Logotherapy, 17,* 70–75.

WILSON, J. (1989). *Trauma, transformation, and healing.* New York: Brunner/Mazel.

YALOM, I., & LIEBERMAN, M. (1971). A study of encounter group casualties. *Archives of General Psychiatry, 25,* 16–30.

YONTEF, G., & SIMKIN, J. (1989). Gestalt therapy. In R. Corsini & D. Wedding (Eds.), *Current psychotherapies* (4th ed.) (pp. 323–61). Itasca, IL: Peacock.

13

Toward Integrated Counseling and Psychotherapy

CHAPTER GOALS

This chapter seeks to:

1. Review the major concepts of this book.
2. Encourage you to start generating your own personal view and integration of the helping process in a more concrete fashion through
   - Examining and defining your own counseling and therapy worldview
   - Developing your own construction of the counseling and psychotherapeutic process

Becoming a Samurai

The samurai, Japanese champions of sword handling, learn their skills through a complex training program. The special movements and philosophy of sword work are broken down into specific components that are studied carefully, one at a time. In learning the precise handling of the sword, even the naturally gifted sword handler can find that there is a temporary decrease in dexterity and performance. Awareness of the many components involved in learning a skill can interfere with coordination. Nonetheless, skills and concepts are learned thoroughly and practiced again and again.

Once the skills reach close to virtuoso level, the samurai retire to a mountaintop to meditate. There they deliberately forget what they have learned. When they return to the valley, they find that the discrete skills they have learned have been naturally integrated into their style or way of being. They seldom have to think about skills at all; they have become samurai.

Consider the samurai and your own experience. You may be naturally talented as a musician, dancer, writer, or athlete. You likely also have found that practicing the fundamentals of your art or sport made a large difference in your performance. Similarly, you may be a naturally gifted helper. The rehearsal and practice of the skills and concepts contained in this book can help you become even more accomplished as a counselor or therapist. Mastering these basics can build a new understanding that later will be integrated into your personal style and approach.

The Search for the "Best" Theory

The field of therapy and counseling has changed dramatically since its beginning with Freud. As Yogi Berra aptly put it, "If Sigmund Freud was alive today, he'd be turning over in his grave" (cited in Cummings, 1988). In many ways it was simpler during much of Freud's lifetime. Then there was really only one major theory, and all one had to do to train for therapy work was learn the Freudian approach. Next, cognitive-behavioral theory and existential-humanistic theory were added to the picture, but still one only had to decide which was the "best" theory. The task for new counselors and therapists as recently as twenty years ago remained simply deciding on a single theoretical approach.

Historically, the field tends to talk about first-, second-, and third-force theories of helping, and these categories reflect the major theories in the historical order in which they appeared. Psychodynamic is considered the first force, due to Freud's vast original influence. Later, object relations theory, self-theory, and attachment theory brought new life to Freud's at times outdated constructs.

Cognitive-behavioral psychology is considered the second force, being connected to the work of early behavioral theorists such as Watson and Skinner. With the advent of cognitive approaches and the influence of Beck, Ellis, and Meichenbaum, the second force broadened its scope and became metatheoretical and integrative.

Rogers's person-centered therapy brought a more humanistic view to the field—the third force. The work of Rogers and of Maslow focused the attention of a generation of therapists on the importance of the person and relationship in therapy. The ideas of Rogers, Frankl, and Perls are now part of the approach and practice of most counselors and therapists, even if they claim to adhere to another theoretical orientation.

Multicultural counseling and therapy (MCT) has become recognized as a distinct fourth force in the field. Traditional theories gave minimal attention to the cultural base of helping until MCT developed. In a short period of time, this theoretical orientation has begun to reshape the field. MCT is also different than the other three forces in that it does not discount the importance of any theoretical orientation. Rather, MCT recognizes, adapts, and supports all approaches to therapy. However, MCT also requires developing increased awareness and sensitivity to multicultural issues. MCT is perhaps becoming the central metatheory of helping owing to its recognition that all helping stems from a cultural base.

The Foundational Theories

The first four chapters explored concepts that can be useful in understanding the four major theoretical orientations above: cultural intentionality and community, empathy and family understanding, microskills and solution-oriented therapy, and developmental counseling and therapy (DCT). If you are skilled in these concepts, you have a solid foundation for mastering the many complexities of theory and practice in counseling and psychotherapy.

The empathic conditions, particularly as they integrate community and family concepts, are important in all theoretical orientations. Positive regard and the positive asset search of the microskills approach have been stressed throughout this book. Helping clients build on strengths is increasingly recognized as a basic foundation for change and growth in counseling and therapy.

The basic listening sequence of the microskills framework is used by virtually all theories to draw out client stories and narratives. The five-stage structure of the interview not only is useful in decisional counseling, but also is a way to structure your work in existential-humanistic, cognitive-behavioral, and other frames of reference.

The DCT model is an integrative framework that focuses on entering the meaning-making world of the client. DCT argues that helping theory needs to start with the client. Once we make sense of how clients organize the world, we can select theory and strategies systematically and support our actions with a theoretical rationale.

As you move toward your own theory of choice, you may also want to consider what issues you consider most foundational and basic to all other theories. On what substructure will you develop your own construction of the world of helping theory and practice?

Searching for Theoretical Integration

Over time, research and clinical practice have revealed that traditional theories have considerable value. However, a key concern has been how to integrate these concepts in a meaningful fashion.

In 1967 Gordon Paul made the classic statement "What treatment, by whom, is most effective for this individual with that specific problem, and under which set of circumstances?" Thereafter, drawing the best from many theories, as opposed to working within only one approach, became respectable. Nonetheless, eclecticism has still been criticized as lacking a central theoretical rationale for therapeutic action—changing theories or methods with clients other than the intuitive preference and clinical experience of the practitioner.

Lazarus's multimodal therapy (1981, 1995) is an attempt to organize eclecticism into a more coherent and organized way of thinking, primarily from a behavioral frame of reference (see Chapter 10). Lazarus divides treatment into seven parts, the BASIC-ID (*B*ehavior, *A*ffective response, *S*ensations, *I*mages, *C*ognitions, *I*nterpersonal relationships, and *D*rugs). The goal is to draw from each dimension in creating a holistic treatment plan.

Integrative theories are currently becoming more numerous and influential. Meichenbaum's construction of cognitive-behavioral theory (Chapter 9) brings diverse theories together in a coherent fashion and thus offers a broader scope than traditional behavioral frames of reference. Developmental counseling and therapy (DCT) integrates theory and practice in a different format (Chapter 4) and provides an overall rationale for moving from sensory to behavioral to cognitive to systemic approaches. DCT, perhaps more than other theories, emphasizes sensorimotor and systemic/cultural foundations of experience, arguing that a network approach is essential if change is to be maintained over time.

In this book, you have been exposed to many alternatives that have stood the test of time or, if new, show some promise of influencing future change. As a professional, you will be part of the process of moving the field toward new approaches. How can you continually add new dimensions while retaining the best of the past?

Multicultural Counseling and Therapy as the Theoretical Fourth Force

Multicultural counseling and therapy (MCT) recognizes the value of traditional methods of helping *as long as they are employed in a culturally meaningful and culturally sensitive fashion.* Furthermore, MCT starts from a different place than traditional theory, beginning with client assessment of individual, family, and cultural experience. Rather than impose a theory on a client, MCT seeks to find how the client constructs and makes meaning in the world. MCT stresses an egalitarian, nonhierarchical therapist-client relationship. MCT suggests that counselor and client together can draw from and integrate other theories to meet individual, family, and cultural needs.

In seeking a major new direction, the multicultural orientation works to turn the history of counseling and therapy "on its head." The issue is not imposing a theory on a client, but rather working *with* the client in a culturally sensitive fashion to find a technique, strategy, theory, or set of theories that meets the client's needs. *Self-in-relation* becomes the focus rather than individually oriented self-actualization.

MCT stresses the importance of using traditional first-, second-, and third-force theories in practice. Working together, client and therapist first identify the goal and then match the goal with the culturally and individually appropriate approach. For example, if a European-American client seeks self-understanding, perhaps a Rogerian or psychodynamic approach may be appropriate. However, if the goal is to feel less anxious in social situations, the approach may be cognitive-behavioral. If the client is a woman, gender-aware CBT assertiveness training may be undertaken. If the client is a Latina, culturally sensitive assertiveness training that acknowledges the complexities of changing a woman's role and behavior may be an appropriate action.

MCT might expand Gordon Paul's earlier statement by adding the following:

> What set of treatments, by whom, is most effective for this individual or family with what specific problem, with what specific culturally and individually appropriate goal, and under which set of circumstances? Additionally, how can relapse of treatment be prevented, and how can we involve this client (and family) in treatment planning in an egalitarian culturally sensitive fashion?

How might you rephrase the above comments? How will you personally organize this exciting, but extremely complex, field? What sense do you make of the integrative approaches such as those of Meichenbaum, Lazarus, and Ivey and Rigazio-DiGilio's DCT? Would you place multicultural issues at the core of your theory, or will they be more peripheral? These are important questions that will define you as a professional. Not only will you be making these decisions, you will be asked to define the rationale for what you decide. A final exercise in this book (Practice Exercise 13.2) asks you to start the process of generating your own integrated approach.

The following summary of major theories is designed to help you work toward your own integration of counseling and psychotherapy theories.

A Summary of the Four Major Theoretical Forces of Counseling and Psychotherapy

There are many ways to consider the field of counseling and psychotherapy, and no one perspective has all the answers. This book is about multiple perspectives on reality. Clients often can get "stuck" in a single perspective. The theories and practice presented in this book and summarized in this section offer a range of ways of thinking that may be helpful with clients.

The four broad orientations to counseling and therapy stressed in this book are summarized in Table 13.1. As you review these theories, think about how you personally would integrate them. There are many ways to describe the field. What are your own preferences at this moment? What concepts appeal to you personally? And what can you find in your own developmental history, family history, and multicultural background that might help explain your answers?

Qualitative Research—Multicultural Issues

Many might agree that an ethical practice of multicultural counseling and therapy is a practice that, among other things, constantly examines and evaluates effectiveness. Furthermore, the importance of reading and conducting one's own research is

Table 13.1 Overview of Four Major Forces in Counseling and Psychotherapy Theory

Theoretical System and Relationship to Foundational Theories and Family Theory	Worldview	Major Concepts and Techniques
Psychodynamic (First Force)		
Foundational theories not explicitly considered, but post hoc examination shows that these concepts help explain the value of these orientations and makes their implementation more explicit. Family concepts not prominent, although attachment theory and the family unconscious are adding this emphasis. Historically, minimal attention to gender and multicultural issues.	The past is prelude to the present, and much of the past is held in the unconscious. Individuals are deeply influenced by the past, and we must understand this past if we are to facilitate individual growth. Sigmund Freud is major philosopher. The pragmatic and optimistic Bowlby stresses that we can facilitate growth through understanding and action. Taub-Bynum focuses on family and cultural history playing themselves out in the individual.	These are the most complex set of theories available. The development of the person rests on early life experience. The interaction of person and environment is largely played out in the unconscious. Traditional Freudian theory emphasizes the Oedipal complex as central to development, whereas object relations and attachment theories focus on early infant and child experience as more important. Free association, dream analysis, and awareness of transference, countertransference, and projective identification are important.
Cognitive-Behavioral: Behavioral Foundations (Second Force)		
Foundational theories often integrated into understanding and planning treatment. Decisional counseling and social skills portion of microskills a standard part of counseling and therapy. Family concepts historically have not been important.	Deeply rooted in the idea of progress and faith in science to solve human problems. B. F. Skinner often seen as major philosopher. Meichenbaum's more recent construction is more humanistic in orientation and provides a new integration of behaviorism with other theories. Cheek supplies a culturally relevant view.	Through functional analysis, it is possible to understand the antecedents, resultant behavior, and consequences of the behavior. Many highly specific and proven techniques of behavioral change available. Has had profound influence on popular cognitive-behavioral movement, particularly the work of Meichenbaum in social skills training.
Cognitive-Behavioral: Cognitive Foundations (Second Force)		
Foundational theories tend to be implicit rather than explicit. Cognitive aspects of developmental counseling and	Roots lie in stoic philosopher Epictetus—"We are disturbed not by events, but by the views we take of them."	Currently a popular theoretical orientation, as the system allows integration of many ideas from seemingly competitive theories.

(continued)

Table 13.1   (continued)

Theoretical System and Relationship to Foundational Theories and Family Theory	Worldview	Major Concepts and Techniques
therapy may help integrate this framework more closely with MCT, particularly action at the sensorimotor and systemic level, which is often missing in CBT. Family concepts historically have not been important but are compatible.	Attempt to integrate ideas about the world with action in the world. Ellis's rational-emotive therapy. Beck's cognitive therapy. Glasser's reality therapy. Lazarus's technical eclecticism.	Major focus is on thinking patterns and their modification, but maintains a constant emphasis on homework and taking new ideas out into the world and acting on them. Glasser's work is similar, but focuses very effectively on schools and youth in institutions.

Existential-Humanistic (Third Force)

The foundational concepts of empathy and the listening portion of microskills have been derived from this orientation. Family concepts historically have not been important but are compatible. Has not consciously embraced MCT but is compatible. Vontress adds this dimension.	The human task is to find meaning in a sometimes meaningless world. Rogers stresses the ability of the person to direct one's own life; Frankl, the importance of positive meanings; and Perls, that people are wholes, not parts, and can take direction of their own lives. Heidegger, Husserl, Binswanger, and Boss have been most influential at a basic philosophical level.	Each individual constructs the world uniquely. Rogers stresses the importance of self-actualization and careful listening to the client. Frankl emphasizes spirituality and a variety of specific techniques to facilitate the growth of meaning. Perls, with his many powerful techniques, may be described as an action therapist.

Multicultural Counseling and Therapy (Fourth Force)

Foundational theories (empathic dimensions, microskills, developmental counseling and therapy) explicitly and implicitly utilized as part of overall theoretical conception but modified with cultural frames of reference. Family therapy concepts considered essential. Attneave's network therapy often an essential ingredient.	Counseling and therapy have been culturally encapsulated. The individual and family are based in the culture. The counselor or therapist needs to approach counseling with multicultural awareness. Many authors stress issues of development in the family and society. Seeks to integrate first-, second-, and third-force theories as part of worldview and counseling and therapy theory and case conceptualization.	As a newly evolving major theoretical group, the main point of agreement is that issues of culture, gender, and other multicultural issues need to take a central place in the helping process. Collaboration and network treatment planning are essential. Consciousness raising about ethnicity/race and gender issues often critical in the helping process.

often stressed. Research and reading keep us all alive and aware of new developments.

Too often counselors and therapists think about research as something that is "elsewhere"—something found in professional journals and not part of "real life." The busy practitioner sometimes finds journals boring and irrelevant and often cannot find the time to read. However, reading, research, and writing can be important and even vital to avoiding burnout and staying alive in the profession. It is unfortunate that some therapists choose not to read or conduct research and thus often continue to provide therapy that research data and new theory clearly show to be irrelevant, time consuming, expensive, and perhaps even damaging to the client.

How can you surmount this challenge? Research Exhibit 13.1 shows how individual qualitative research can be used in the active practice of counseling and psychotherapy. Qualitative research has been especially popular in the MCT movement, as it has the flexibility required for work with complex multicultural issues.

Integrating Multiple Approaches with a Client or Family

Attneave's network therapy, drawn from her work with Native Americans, reminds us that multiple interventions are often necessary to produce and maintain change (Attneave, 1969, 1982; Speck & Attneave, 1973). Furthermore, action needs to be conducted in the larger community to change systems that continue to adversely affect individuals and families.

Throughout this book, there has been frequent emphasis on the importance of multiple, multilevel interventions to support client change. Developmental counseling and therapy focuses on multiple approaches to clients and families. DCT argues that interventions planned at the sensorimotor, concrete, formal, and dialectic/systemic levels are needed if change is to be initiated and secured. DCT endorses the multicultural counseling and therapy approach as essential in any choice of treatment.

Case Management: Integrating Network Treatment and DCT

It is critical to arrange many interventions for complex client cases and for lasting change. Many clients need only one or two interventions to provide a lever for permanent change. Figure 13.1 visually indicates that any intervention can be conducted at one or more cognitive-developmental levels. Moreover, it is possible to integrate concepts of DCT and relapse prevention as part of the overall treatment plan. The following list summarizes individual, family, group, and community interventions that can be used in a case management/network treatment approach. Developing a network of interventions to provide change is the best way to prevent relapse. Such a network includes the following:

═══ Research Exhibit 13.1 ═══

Using Qualitative Research in Counseling and Clinical Practice

Ponterotto and Casas (1991) define four key characteristics of qualitative research methodology.

1. *Use an inductive approach based on observation of client needs and wishes.* Imagine you are working with a client who presents you with issues of anxiety and tension. Rather than deciding beforehand what to evaluate or measure, focus on your observations of this particular client and generate hypotheses about what issues might be important in therapy. In addition, think about ways in which you might evaluate whether or not therapy is helpful to this client.

2. *Take a holistic stance and set joint client-counselor objectives for evaluation of therapy.* Much of quantitative research focuses on single dimensions of human experience. You are working with a whole client who comes from a family and cultural background. As part of a holistic stance, you may want to consider the whole life of the client, not just single dimensions. Obviously, you cannot measure everything in your client's life, but with your client you can set goals for therapy that can be validated by both you and the client.

At Flinders University in Australia, Kapelis (personal communication, 1991) has built on the concept of joint goals and, with the client, selects concrete thought, feeling, and behavioral changes based on jointly agreed-on criteria for success. In some cases, stan-dardized tests are used, but in these cases, the client is always a participant in the selection. With a client struggling with anxiety, you might jointly decide that feeling relaxed and easy in interpersonal contacts is one objective of therapy. Another objective might be sleeping through the night. These objectives lead to certain specific types of treatment plans (e.g., assertiveness training, relaxation training).

3. *Be flexible and change objectives and evaluation design as therapy progresses.* Establishing joint goals for counseling is important, because therapy does not always proceed as you and the client predict. You and your client may find new objectives as therapy progresses. For example, the client may discover an abusive family history in the process of stress management training. If your qualitative research contract is open ended, with a joint commitment for exploration, you will be better positioned to evolve a new evaluation design as therapy enters new areas. For example, a short-term evaluative research agreement may be client satisfaction with the process. At the same time, you must work to concretize such a goal more precisely at the next stage of counseling or therapy.

4. *Emphasize clinical significance.* This point is vital to the qualitative researcher. The change and evaluation design must be important to the client and to the therapist.

Ponterotto and Casas list a variety of possibilities for qualitative research, including journal entries, case studies, structured interviews, reports by the client's family members or friends, asking the client's permission to audio- or videotape certain types of interactions, and so on. When conducting qualitative research, it is essential that your client be involved in the process throughout.

1. *Individual Interventions*
   Counseling and therapy (drawing from first, second, third, fourth, or other major theoretical orientations)
   Helping clients fill basic needs for money, shelter, clothing
   Advocating and crisis intervention
   Medication

2. *Family Interventions*
   Family therapy and counseling
   Family education in parenting skills

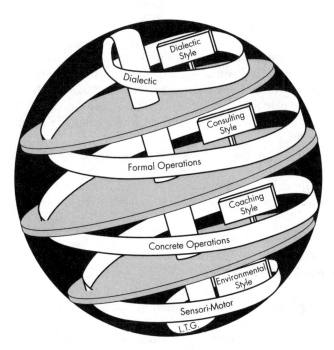

Figure 13.1 The Multilevel Nature of Therapeutic Intervention

SOURCE: This figure was originally conceived and drawn by Lois T. Grady and is used here with her permission.

Marital counseling
Divorce, legal issues
Mediation
Family support groups

3. *Group Interventions*
   Group counseling and encounter groups
   Multicultural consciousness-raising groups (women, African-Americans, Vietnam vets)
   Self-esteem groups
   AA, ACOA, and other self-help groups
   Psychoeducational and skills training groups
   Peer counseling

4. *Community Interventions*
   Network therapy
   Racism/oppression training
   Community action (organizing local government, church, and school groups)
   State and federal action and advocacy

Relapse Prevention

Change gained through therapy often disappears in the complexities of life after therapy unless support for the change is planned. Although we may help clients feel less anxious via Rogerian therapy or by implementing assertiveness training, both techniques may fail if there is no plan for follow-up and treatment generalization. It may be useful to review the sections in Chapter 4 on decisional counseling and Chapter 9 on relapse prevention.

Relapse prevention can be greatly facilitated by the case management/network approach suggested in the foregoing list. Relapse prevention is a multidimensional, multimodal approach to maintaining human change. To avoid relapse and therapeutic failure, we may want to work with families, schools, and other systems as well.

Constructing Your Own View or Theory of Counseling and Therapy

This book has suggested that it is important that you learn multiple theoretical and practical approaches and think through your own view of the helping process. However, because no one individual can "do it all," you likely will benefit from developing a network of cooperating helping professionals. It is important not only that you define your own place in the network of counseling and therapy, but also that you envision how you can collaborate with other professionals for the benefit of clients.

These last two sections ask you to think about yourself and your own reactions to the many ideas of this book. The construction you make of the helping process can be derived from your worldview. Chapter 1 defined worldview as how you think the world works. A worldview is a theory about the nature of things. A theory may be described as a framework in which you organize facts and their relationship one to another. Identifying your own worldview is critical to your role as a professional and your own integration of the helping field.

Ahia (1991) and DeEsch (1991) state that individual counseling that does not include family issues and fails to consider cultural background is incomplete. Family and cultural issues play themselves out in the individual, and thus in both the client and the therapist. These authors also claim that first-, second-, and third-force theories miss this important issue of context. Although Freud, Skinner, and Rogers all generated their theories from a family and cultural context, they did not adapt their approaches to multicultural contexts.

Ahia (1991) challenges the traditional "objective" approach implicit in much of our traditional theory, stating: "Who you are determines your use of theory— counseling and therapy are issues of *being*. We counsel from our *being*." The objective approach means that we "objectively" select a theory, much as Gordon Paul suggests, and then apply it correctly to the client. Ahia argues for *intersubjectivity*, which can be defined as the awareness that we make our choices from often unconscious family and multicultural experience. Intersubjectivity also implies that therapists are sensitive to their own as well as clients' family and multicultural selves.

Figure 13.2 offers a visual representation of intersubjectivity in the counseling and therapy process. The questions in Practice Exercise 13.1 can help you in looking at yourself, your worldview, and your intersubjective thoughts and feelings about clients and yourself.

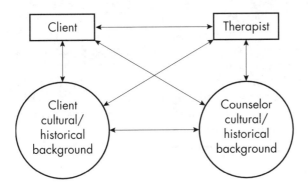

Figure 13.2 Intersubjectivity in the Counseling and Therapy Process

SOURCE: From *Developmental Therapy: Theory into Practice* (p. 321) by A. E. Ivey, 1986, San Francisco: Jossey-Bass. Copyright 1986 by Jossey-Bass, Inc. Used by permission.

Practice Exercise 13.1

 What Is Your Counseling and Therapy Worldview?

The purpose of this exercise is to ask you to consider your own construction of counseling and therapy. What is important to you? Where do you stand? Where are you heading? How does your family and cultural history relate to these issues?

1. How do you view the goals of counseling and therapy?

Client-centered theory focuses on self-actualization; behavioral theory, on behavioral change; psychodynamic theory, on awareness of unconscious forces; family theory, on an adequate family organization; feminist theory, on awareness of one's gender; multicultural theory, on becoming aware of how individual and family have been shaped and affected by the environment and history. These are only a few of the types of goals offered by different theoretical orientations.

Consider these and other personal goals and values of your own. What do you want to have happen for your clients in your work as a counselor and therapist? Write a statement of your values and convictions regarding the key goals and values you have for the helping process.

2. Where do your values and convictions come from? How were they derived? Do they come from reading this book? Or are they influenced by your own life-span developmental process? How does your family, gender, and multicultural background affect your values?

The key constructs in your worldview are generated in a gender, family, and multicultural context. Write a statement in which you discuss how your own life-span development relates to your selection of worldview and goals?

3. Where might your worldview be limited with some of your clients? Given the vast array of multicultural experience you will encounter, what types of groups do you need to learn more about? What types of values and behaviors might give you difficulty?

None of us can relate equally well with all clients. Write a statement describing areas where you need to learn more, and indicate some specific steps you plan to take to reach an expanded awareness.

4. What additional questions would you ask of yourself and others? The questions here are only the beginning of serious questioning on the nature of counseling and psychotherapy practice.

You as an Integrative Theorist
in a Multicultural World

It is the task of the professional counselor and therapist to know as many theories and techniques as possible—their similarities and differences—and to select from each theory that which is most helpful to the client. At the same time, the counselor seeks to enter and understand clients' worlds and to learn how clients construct and make sense of the world—what their meaning-making system is. The suggestion in this book is that rather than impose a theory of your choice on the client, you may want to engage clients as coparticipants in finding a therapeutic approach that fits.

The theories in this book are only "views"—constructions about how the world works. It is helpful to remember that *theories are simply descriptions—ways to examine reality.* If we become wrapped up in the belief that our theory of counseling and therapy is reality, we risk operating under an illusion. Although a particular illusory view of the world may work for you, it will not work for everyone. Just as in the Escher print "Relativity" (Chapter 1), the world really has no "right side up." By turning the Escher print, you can gain a new view, a new way of thinking. Similarly, there are many perspectives on "reality."

In the practice of counseling and therapy, you likely will encounter many who claim to have found the "truth," the "final answer," "the one way" to conduct counseling and therapy. These people are likely false prophets. But, as the authors of this book have learned, even false prophets often speak important truths.

For example, there was a time when meditation was considered irrelevant to the practice of counseling and psychotherapy. Now, meditation is a standard technique in many stress management programs. Similarly, issues of women's development and multicultural understanding, now considered to be increasingly important, were once considered to be outside the field. Thus, it seems important that we all listen, learn, and be willing to accommodate an alternative perspective or a challenging new theory. The advice in the following maxim seems worth considering: Beware of prophets proclaiming a new truth—they just may be right! Practice Exercise 13.2 provides a final exercise in which you are asked to review your own thinking about this book and organize its meaning in your own way.

The general or metatheoretical position requires that each counselor or therapist develop her or his own conception of the counseling process and remain constantly open to change and examination. A student working through the draft of this book commented, "I think I've got the point. I find myself rewriting the book in my own way. I use some of it, but ultimately the book I am rewriting in my head is mine, my own general theory that is similar in some ways to the book, but in other ways very different."

We hope that you will rewrite this book and use it authentically in your own way. At the same time, we hope that you will extend that same privilege to your clients. How might they seek to help you rewrite and reconstrue your constructions of counseling and therapy? Counseling and therapy are very much about listening and learning—for all of us as therapists and for our clients as well.

Practice Exercise 13.2

Ten Questions to Ask Yourself about Your Own Construction of the Counseling and Psychotherapy Process

1. What is your overall worldview, and how does it relate to multicultural issues? Have you carefully elaborated your worldview and its implications for your future practice?

2. What are the central dimensions of your definition of ethical practice? (These dimensions were introduced in Chapter 1. The effective professional is constantly examining ethical and moral issues.)

3. As you think about each of the empathic concepts, what is your personal construction of their meaning? What sense do you make of them?

4. With which microskills and concepts do you feel particularly comfortable? Which have you already mastered, and which need further work so that they can actually be used in the clinical session?

5. How do you make sense of the focusing concept? How might you choose to focus your interventions? Can you focus on individuals, family context, and the multicultural surround?

6. What is to be your position on research and keeping up with new ideas?

7. What is your understanding and integration of the challenge of multicultural counseling and therapy? What place will this fourth force of helping have in your mind and in your practice?

8. At several points in this book, issues of spirituality have been raised. What has been your reaction to these ideas? Would you avoid them or carry them further?

9. What theories of counseling and therapy appeal to you? What type of integration of these diverse theories are you moving toward? (This book has attempted to stress that all theories are potentially valuable to some clients, but you are not expected to be immediately skilled in all. Learning theories in more depth is a lifelong practice.) From what approach do you personally plan to start practice, and what type of professional curriculum for further learning do you see for yourself in the future?

10. Return to Practice Exercise 4.5, Identifying Your Own Personal Style, Present Competencies, and Goals. Repeat this exercise again, noting any changes since your first response. If you have completed several of the practice exercises in this book, you undoubtedly have a better sense of where you stand personally and professionally. Taking theory into practice—and then returning to theory for reflection and possible change in your work—is the route toward competence.

11. Have you examined how your personal developmental history in family and culture affects your answers to the above questions? (It is critical that you constantly be able to reflect on yourself and how your personal history and present life issues affect your performance as a counselor or therapist.)

REFERENCES

AHIA, E. (1991, October). *Enhanced therapeutic skills: Family and ethnic dynamics, part I.* Paper presented at the North Atlantic Association for Counselor Education and Supervision, Albany, NY.

ATTNEAVE, C. (1969). Therapy in tribal settings and urban network interventions. *Family Process, 8,* 192–210.

ATTNEAVE, C. (1982). American Indian and Alaska native families: Emigrants in their own homeland. In M. McGoldrick, J. Pearce, & J. Giordano (Eds.), *Ethnicity and family therapy* (pp. 55–83). New York: Guilford.

CUMMINGS, N. (1988). Emergence of the mental health complex: Adaptive and maladaptive responses. *Professional Psychology, 19,* 308–15.

DeESCH, J. (1991, October). *Enhanced therapeutic skills: Family and ethnic dynamics, part II.* Paper presented at the North Atlantic Association for Counselor Education and Supervision, Albany, NY.

LAZARUS, A. (1981). *The practice of multimodal psychotherapy.* New York: McGraw-Hill.

LAZARUS, A. (1995). Adjusting the carburetor: Pivotal interventions in marital and sex therapy. In R. Rosen & S. Leiblum (Eds.), *Case studies in sex therapy* (pp. 81–95). New York: Guilford.

PAUL, G. (1967). Strategy of outcome research in psychotherapy. *Journal of Consulting Psychology, 31,* 109–18.

PONTEROTTO, T., & CASAS, M. (1991). *Handbook of ethnic minority counseling research.* Springfield, IL: Thomas.

SPECK, R., & ATTNEAVE, C. (1973). *Family process.* New York: Pantheon.

Credits

Practice Exercise 1.1 (the community genogram) and other material presented in Chapter 1 are copyrighted 1995 by Allen E. Ivey and used by permission. Portions of Chapters 5 and 6 are excerpted from *A Theory of Multicultural Counseling and Therapy* by S. W. Sue, A. E. Ivey, and P. B. Pedersen, 1996, Pacific Grove, CA, Brooks/Cole Publishing Company; reprinted by permission. The interview transcript in Chapter 6 is used by permission of Mary Ballou, copyright 1996. The information on the Liberation of Consciousness in Chapter 6 is taken and/or adapted from "Psychotherapy as Liberation: Toward Specific Skills and Strategies in Multicultural Counseling and Therapy" by A. Ivey in J. Ponterotto, J. M. Casas, L. Suzuki, and C. Alexander (Eds.), *Handbook of Multicultural Counseling*, 1995, Beverly Hills, CA, Sage; copyright by Allen E. Ivey and used by permission. Practice Exercise 9.6 is adapted from the relapse prevention worksheet by Robert R. Marx, University of Massachusetts; adapted by permission. Quotes in Chapter 10 are taken from: *Growth Through Reason*, by A. Ellis, 1971, Palo Alto, CA, Science and Behavior Books; reprinted by permission; "Aaron Beck: A Profile" by A. Diffly, 1984, *Brown Alumni Monthly*, 83 (4), 368–75; reprinted by permission. The quotes in Chapter 11 are from: *Counseling with Returned Servicemen* by C. Rogers and J. Wallen, 1946, New York, McGraw-Hill; reprinted by permission; *Carl Rogers on Encounter Groups* by Carl Rogers, 1970, New York, HarperCollins, and London, Penguin Books; reprinted by permission. The quote in Chapter 12 is from *Man's Search for Meaning* by Viktor Frankl, copyright 1959, 1962, 1984, 1992, Boston, Beacon Press; reprinted by permission. The material in Chapter 12 is from *Gestalt Therapy Verbatim* by Fritz Perls, 1969, Moab, UT, Real People Press; reprinted by permission.

Name Index

Subject Index